Data Warehousing on the Internet

Accessing the Corporate Knowledge Base

Copyright ©1998 International Thomson Publishing Company

I(T)P® A division of International Thomson Publishing Inc.
The ITP Logo is a trademark under license.

Printed in the United States of America.

For more information, contact:

International Thomson Publishing GmbH
Königswinterer Strasse 418
53227 Bonn
Germany

International Thomson Publishing Europe
Berkshire House 168-173
High Holborn
London WCIV 7AA
England

International Thomson Publishing Asia
221 Henderson Road #05-10
Henderson Building
Singapore 0315

Thomas Nelson Australia
102 Dodds Street
South Melbourne, 3205
Victoria, Australia

International Thomson Publishing Japan
Hirakawacho Kyowa Building, 3F
2-2-1 Hirakawacho
Chiyoda-ku, 102 Tokyo
Japan

Nelson Canada
1120 Birchmount Road
Scarborough, Ontario
Canada M1K 5G4

International Thomson Editores
Campos Eliseos 385, Piso 7
Col. Polanco
11560 Mexico D.F. Mexico

International Thomson Publishing Southern Africa
Bldg. 19, Constantia Park
239 Old Pretoria Road, P.O. Box 2459
Halfway House, 1685 South Africa

International Thomson Publishing France
1, rue st. Georges
75 009 Paris France

1 2 3 4 5 6 7 8 9 10 01 00 99 98 97
Library of Congress Cataloging-in-Publication Data

ISBN: 1-850-32857-9

Production: Jo-Ann Campbell • mle design • 213 Cider Mill Road, Glastonbury, CT 06033

Data Warehousing on the Internet

Accessing the Corporate Knowledge Base

Tom Hammergren

International Thomson Computer Press

I(T)P® An International Thomson Publishing Company

London • Bonn • Boston • Johannesburg • Madrid • Melbourne • Mexico City • New York • Paris
Singapore • Tokyo • Toronto • Albany, NY • Belmont, CA • Cincinnati, OH • Detroit, MI

This book is dedicated to my two lovely children, Brent and Kristen, who are my primary motivators. They have a zest for life and a thirst for knowledge that provide me with much of my inspiration; yet they have endured great sacrifice as I wrote this book.
I love you both!
Dad

Table of Contents

Acknowledgments

Winston Churchill said, "Personally, I'm always ready to learn, although I do not always like being taught." This quotation matches my attitude toward life-long learning, so I want to recognize those who have helped me with my learning process.

As I observed in my first book, *Data Warehousing: Building the Corporate Knowledge Base*, writing a book is much harder than it sounds and it involves extended support from a multitude of people. These people comprise a team of professionals who brought this book to you, the reader. Though my name is on the cover, I would like to acknowledge those who provided assistance and support through the creation of this, my second book in the data warehousing series.

Probably the most important thank you I can give is to my wife, Kim, and children, Brent and Kristen. As I discuss in the dedication of this book, my children have sacrificed to allow me to fulfill my dream of writing this second book, as my wife. On many weekends and evenings, we put fun on the back burner so that I could deliver this book as timely as possible. And these three encouraged me throughout the process—probably so I would get done and we could get on with the fun.

From a professional standpoint, I am forever grateful to an enormous list of people. This list includes those on the publication side of my book writing experience, including my agent, Carole McClendon, and her wonderful staff at Waterside Productions; Theron

Shreve and Jim DeWolf at International Thomson Publishing; Trudy Neuhaus, who managed the project through its half-way point (Trudy, we missed you); and Jose Cartagena and his associates at Sybase Press. I want to give special thanks to Jerry Olsen, probably the best editor I know. Jerry took my rough words and truly brought the real meaning out so that you, the reader, could better understand the content. Jerry also assisted me with the first book in this series and has done a wonderful job on both. Thanks Jerry, I hope we can continue with number three. In addition to Jerry, Jo-Ann Campbell once again joined my production team for the physical layout of the pages in the book. Jo-Ann has struggled now through the illustrations of two of my books, and for that mammoth effort I am deeply grateful.

I want to thank those who work at the various software companies with which I interacted during the creation of this book. These vendors went out of their way to explain how their software functioned and how it was best utilized. This list includes those from Sybase's Data Warehousing Group: Ellen Salisbury, David Harris, Guy Washburn, Pamela Whitmore, Paul Murphy, Clark French, and all of their supporting staff. It also includes Sybase's Design Tools Group: Marc Chanliau, Matt Dahlman, Sam Coe, Steve Clark, R. Todd Bowes, and all of their supporting staff. The list further includes Cognos' wonderful crew of business intelligence people, including Alan Rottenberg, Robin McNiell, and their supporting staff.

I would be remiss to not recognize one of my technical reviewers. Don Grinstead, who has become more than just a business colleague over the years, spent extra time and energy pouring over early releases of the book to validate the contents and accuracy of the material. Though I am sure he learned a lot from this process, he also sacrificed to perform such a duty. Don, thanks for all the support, assistance, and advice; they are greatly appreciated. Along with Don, several other people at Indiana University attached themselves to my methodology and provided a continuous stream of support and motivation, including Jay Sissom, Barry Walsh, and Art Lindeman.

I would also like to thank my business colleagues and mentors, who have taught me all they know and challenged me to push the envelope of technology and knowledge more than once. This list includes Don Leonardo and Eric Schurr, who convinced me to enter this crazy software industry, then further taught me never to become complacent or quit. This list also includes the customers who have taught me what quality, partnership, and compassion really mean—especially those of you at The Procter & Gamble Company, with whom I worked during the creation of PowerPlay and Impromptu in my days at Cognos. The list also includes those who showed enormous faith in me during those early creative days at Cognos and the birth of their Business Intelligence Division, including

Ron Zambonini, Mike Potter, Alan Rottenberg, Jeff Papows, Jim Sinclair, Joe Smarkala, Graham MacIntosh, Robin McNeill, Rob Rose, Glenn Rassmussen, Colin McAlpin, Rick Soderstrom, Phil Dana, Ron Nordine, Mike Green, Mickey Gill, Sue Hardeman, Stan Hirose, and everyone else from the PowerPlay and Impromptu teams. And this list also includes those involved with my most recent project at Reynolds & Reynolds: Jeffrey Hart, Bob Schaffer, Mic Nealeigh, Kevin Wiley, and my incredible project team, including Chris Howland, Joe Polivick, Tim Wendt, Rincy Issacs, Darrel Spears, Prudence Byas, Harsha Puttaswamy, Prasad Bhamidipati, Ron Olsen, and Kurt Herman.

It would be tough not to thank those who have formed my life personally, including my mother and father, Betty and Gordon Hammergren, who sacrificed many times and supported me through the good, the bad, and the ugly times of my life. Without their life-long commitment of support and teaching, I would never have become who I am. My sisters, Jane and Beth, have also been there throughout my life, to challenge my mind and to relieve my stress. To them, I say a million thanks—and I owe you. I also thank my wife's family, including Kenneth, MaryLou, Cheryl, Dania, Kenny, Stewart, and Kendra. They continued to support and promote my wild ideas even when I was writing the book and shuffling to various cities for presentations during our joint family vacation. When you have so many people who believe in you, it is easy to accomplish what I have.

Finally, I would like to thank you, the reader, for purchasing this book. I hope it will help you to achieve success and continue your education. I look forward to sharing more with you in the future and hope you will share your ideas, compliments, criticisms, and suggestions with me as you experience them. Contact me at *hammergren@objx.com*. Also monitor our World Wide Web site for valuable support information. The URL is *http://www.objx.com*.

Prologue

Delivering Corporate Knowledge

Somewhere in the 21st Century ... Brent, an unseasoned service technician for a copier repair company, receives a dispatch to a customer site. The customer has an older model copier with paper jamming problems. Because Brent is new to the repair business, he dons his virtual reality cap and enters a simulation of the copier as if he were a sheet of paper.

A server-based simulation program provides Brent with visual clues that indicate the parts involved in the highest incidence of paper jamming problems. Brent works through the simulation, playing what-if games and allowing the computer to further educate him on the mechanics of the copier. Queries help to determine the impact of changing one part on other parts. If he changes one part, will two other parts fail within 30 days? A corporate knowledge base manages all of this information, allowing Brent to share the experience of others who have solved the same problem he is about to attack. Brent makes his decisions and the factory carousel system automatically loads his work bag with the requested parts for his customer visit.

Brent proceeds to repair the customer's copy machine, including those parts known to fail within 30 days of each other. The result is fewer customer service calls, which brings back memories of the Maytag repair man and higher customer satisfaction. Both of these results are positive and increase customer loyalty and ability to be referenced, allowing Brent's company to gain significant competitive advantage over the nearest competitor.

The data warehousing craze has reached nearly every enterprise with computerized systems that manage information assets. Everyone is trying to make the process of harvesting business intelligence simpler, allowing the harvested information to support a broader set of users in the company. These changes have evolved with the decision-support industry, which began shortly after companies began to automate the operational aspects of their business processes. The primary difference between the early information centers and the data warehouses of today is the scope and focus of influence.

In the 1980s, decision support systems and information centers focused on providing access only to top management. These systems required high numbers of support personnel and support dollars. Typically, several tiers of management were involved, which grew to include middle management. The systems that supported these people were strategic in scope and content.

During the 1990s, companies have begun to downsize their operations and eliminate several layers of middle management. This trimming of staff has placed more of the decision making process on front-line workers, who previously depended on middle managers to assist them in making decisions. With this reduction in force, companies now have people making decisions who are relatively uninformed. Data warehousing is the first step to correct this flaw in the current business information systems arena. The focus has shifted from strategic decision making to strategic and tactical decision making.

The Future of Data Warehousing: The Corporate Knowledge Base

As we view into the future, we see examples like the one at the beginning of this chapter in which all employees of an enterprise will be able to review information that includes all electronic forms of data stored in an enterprise information asset base. I refer to this trend simply as a corporate knowledge base, while the industry is beginning to coin it as knowledge management systems or knowledge management environments.

Data warehouses are complex. They contain many moving parts, which will change and interchange with each other as technology improves over time. Your focus should be on ensuring that your enterprise can in fact leverage technological advances to better support the users of your knowledge base. This is a far larger problem than many people have faced with current systems; this is a problem that revolves around data and the architecture on which you build. For this reason, I wrote my first book, *Data Warehousing: Building the Corporate Knowledge Base*. In that book, I discussed the information packaging methodology that will assist you and your colleagues in delivering a corporate knowledge base.

A corporate knowledge base focuses on providing users with a uniform source of corporate information. This information has sprouted from more than 20 years of data in corporate computers for the operational aspects of a business. Users are now demanding to learn more from this asset and are asking questions such as:

- Who are my customers?

- What are the behavior patterns of my customers?

- What are purchasing trends and how do the company's marketing campaigns affect these trends?

- Who are my top suppliers?

- How do the suppliers to the company affect the customer satisfaction ratings of the company?

- What does it cost the company to do business with a specific supplier?

- Could areas be optimized to make the supplier relationship work better?

- What is the trend for product sales versus sales margin?

- Do the company's resources match its strategic plan requirements?

- How well does the sales force forecast sales activity?

- How quickly is inventory turned?

- What factors help to increase repeat business with customers?

- With whom does the company do 80 percent of its high-margin, high-repetition business?

As an information system professional, you need to harness the data available in your current systems and allow for easy access to the corporate knowledge base. This job is complicated when the requirements are hazy at best. It is difficult to characterize the types of queries that might be asked of such an information repository and furthermore where those questions may originate.

Information Packaging Methodology

This book is a logical extension to my first book, *Data Warehousing: Building the Corporate Knowledge Base*. The first book's focus was on the details associated with the entire information packaging methodology process: gathering business requirements from users, analyzing and modeling these requirements, creating a data warehouse, and finally administering and maintaining a data warehouse system. The information packaging methodology provides a uniform methodology for capturing the data that is required by a user community and transforming it into a corporate knowledge base. This second book in the series focuses more on the concepts required to provide ubiquitous access to a data warehouse.

The current book begins with a review of the information packaging methodology for those who are unaware of this powerful technique for delivering optimized data warehouses. However, the Internet has introduced a new technology that easily plugs into the overall technology architecture built by the information packaging methodology. As my colleagues at Indiana University state, the Internet and Web browser interface deliver FUI to users. As opposed to *other, more diverse* GUIs (graphical user interfaces) a FUI is a single, *familiar* user interface.

The paradigm supported by the Internet has taken flight in part due to its simplistic delivery of shared information in a widely dispersed environment. Online services such as America Online have gradually taken people with limited computer backgrounds and transformed them into expert Internet surfers. These abilities have provided a new extension to data warehouses, which are emerging from infancy into adolescence.

With users becoming more comfortable with the Web browser interface, we can now begin to deliver production environments such as data warehouses and knowledge management systems with nearly zero administration cost on the client processor. This ease of administration and the ability to share information with virtually everyone in an enterprise and an extended enterprise—partners, suppliers, shareholders, and so on.

Who Should Read This Book?

This book is for Information System professionals who need to deliver or understand how to deliver data warehouse information to their users over the Internet, intranets, and extranets. This includes, among others, project managers, architects, database administrators, data modelers, analysts, developers and subject matter experts.

Information System professionals actively engaged in or contemplating development of an Internet-based data warehouse will benefit most from this book. The techniques disclosed in the chapters that follow provide a fully integrated life cycle development process for delivering data warehouses—the information packaging methodology. Building on this successful method, this book provides the required technologies and real-world examples of how to implement the methodology, allowing you to build your first data mart or data warehouse on the Internet. Those who follow these techniques will find development of data warehouses more effective, more comprehensive, and more accepted by their user community. The goal of these techniques is to deliver an easily maintained set of objects that manage and maintain the proper data for delivering business intelligence. Therefore, the book presents topics of interest for a cross-section of data warehousing teams.

Why This Book?

The futuristic example at the beginning of this chapter will take time to evolve in most enterprises, but the current rapid changes in the market may bring us closer to this future faster than we may imagine. The ultimate information system, a corporate knowledge base, requires Information System professionals to rapidly deliver business intelligence to users. This book discloses techniques that allow you to begin this process and grow your own corporate knowledge base.

We provide these techniques by first investigating the information packaging methodology and then venturing into the technologies required for delivery of information over the Internet. This book has therefore been broken into the following four sections.

- **Section I: Introduction to the Information Packaging Methodology.** This section investigates the proper methodology for building your data warehouse. This methodology has been cultivated over several years in better understanding how to gather user requirements, formally model those requirements, and deliver an architecture that supports the business process supported by data. This section also looks at business factors that drive the need for better organization of your information assets; how to build an adaptable architecture to support the management and delivery of these information assets; proper techniques for modeling the information that is managed; and finally how to transform your data from current systems into a data warehouse.

- **Section II: Technical Essentials.** This section provides in summary form the technical essentials that you need to understand how data warehousing information is delivered and presented to users. These chapters discuss Web architectures and how they relate to your current development architectures; how you develop applications to interact with data warehouses that are stored in a relational format through industry standard SQL syntax; the HTML syntax for presenting information to users via Web browser technology; and how to bring the presentation dialog with your users to life with more interactive presentations utilizing JavaScript.

- **Section III: Product Essentials.** This section discloses how you can use Sybase products to deliver data warehousing across the Internet. As with Section II, this section uncovers the essential knowledge needed to begin your work as a data warehouse delivery resource. The products covered in this section include Sybase's PowerDynamo, which serves user requests by merging templates and database result sets in a highly dynamic application server; Sybase's Adaptive Server IQ, which is a specialized data store that specifically addresses applications that require ad hoc analysis of large amounts of data; and Sybase PowerDesigner, which is a design and architecture tool that assists Information System development personnel in properly delivering a data architecture to support data warehousing efforts.

- **Section IV: The Case Studies**. This section builds several data marts to assist you in better understanding the information in Sections I, II, and III. This section contains four sample data marts that address different views of a business. These views include a financial or shareholder's view of a business; a supplier's view or supply-chain view of a business; an employee's or intellectual capital of a business; and a customer's view of a business. These views and examples disclose greater detail than the previous sections and bring together a complete result. These solutions also are provided on the companion CD-ROM so that you can further master the technology in your own environment.

This book has a goal of developing and cultivating the information packaging methodology in you and your organization, allowing you to deliver your own data warehouse in a highly adaptable architecture that will absorb the information requirements of your users for years to come. With that goal in mind, this book also includes reference materials in the appendix and on the companion CD-ROM to assist you in completely following the information packaging method. The CD-ROM also includes several working products to assist you in evaluating the contents of this book including Sybase SQL Anywhere, PowerDesigner, PowerDynamo, and NetFactory's NetCharts.

It is our hope that with this book, *Data Warehousing on the Internet: Accessing the Corporate Knowledge Base*, and with the first book in this series, *Data Warehousing: Building the Corporate Knowledge Base*, you will begin to understand corporate knowledge bases and how the futuristic examples at the beginning and end of this prologue can be achieved in your environment.

A data warehouse is a complex environment with many moving parts, but the most important aspect of delivery is not the software or hardware platforms you select—it is the proper organization and categorization of an enterprise's informational assets. If you fail to organize data properly, your system will have a huge maintenance burden. Following the information packaging methodology and the technical essentials presented in this book will assist you in avoiding such a fate.

An Adaptable Data Architecture

With technology advances such as the information superhighway (the Internet and World Wide Web), information systems are beginning to become as commonplace as telephones. When a company originates, it tends to purchase the necessities—and computing resources are beginning to appear as a necessity. The productivity that these systems offer us is enormous, and businesses are beginning to leverage the concepts of electronic transfers as legal tender for business deals.

Even our children are becoming highly computer literate. Our sons and daughters are more proficient in automated technologies than we were at their age, and schools have begun to implement sweeping technology plans to train these future business professionals in the proper utilization of technology.

The work facing most Information System departments lies in the area of improving data architecture so that all information assets are held in a highly-optimized information categorization system. As you will find in the information packaging methodology, we hold this principle as a foundation for information delivering. Users want to see their data and information categorically, whether it is text and numbers, or multimedia objects such as audio, video, or images. Great work still must be done to get our information systems in line with this categorization as well as supporting an enterprise's overall mission. Most of the innovations of the future will be more nuts-and-bolts oriented, but the most important innovation is the concept and advancement of a data architecture.

The overall data architecture of our future will provide an all-encompassing definition of the real world data that drives a business. This architecture will bring together operational systems that are fixated on daily transactions, the ability for a company to stay operational, and the historical and external data to analyze important measurements in a business' purview. This allows users to re-create a business event in the future, analyze this event, and make proper decisions based on the analysis. This shared data concept is not far from reality for those who have begun the process of warehousing information.

Factors That Drive a Successful Data Warehouse Project

Data warehouse projects differ from those that most development staff have experienced. Many companies plow into the development effort without placing themselves in a position in which they can be successful. We find amazing how many data warehouse projects have significant cost overruns or are never delivered. In the Information System world, user satisfaction, cost, and time are the measures of success, with management grading far too many data warehouse projects as failures. To assist you in avoiding failure, we list here some key requirements to make a data warehouse project succeed.

Throughout this book, we reinforce these items. While each of the items may seem basic, you would be amazed at the basics that are dropped under pressure to deliver. So if you want a successful data warehouse project, make sure to address the following issues:

- **Obtain management commitment.** The proper sponsor is critical for the success of a data warehouse. Obtain commitment from a senior-level manager in the user organization, such as the vice president of marketing, vice president of sales, or vice president of manufacturing. This person will become the driving force to correctly complete your project and will give the project credibility beyond that of a traditional development project.

- **Begin with a manageable project.** You should not set out to create an enterprise data warehouse; this scope is far too large for any development team—including those who are highly experienced at building data warehouses. We always recommend that the enterprise data warehouse be the architecture and structure for development projects, which are data marts, or subject-oriented data warehouses. Each of the data mart development projects will be integrated into the central data warehouse. With this philosophy, you build an enterprise data warehouse one component at a time.

- **Clearly communicate realistic expectations.** Project management encompasses many things, including estimation, resource management, and budget management. However, the most important aspect of managing a project is communication. Nobody appreciates surprises when those surprises involve cost overruns, but surprises in lack of functionality are an even ruder awakening for those paying the bills. Effective communication with proper project management ensures that you do not commit to unrealistic time lines or system capabilities.

- **Assign a user-oriented project management team.** Select a project manager for a data warehouse project. It is unwise to assume that just any project manager will do. To properly guide and develop a data warehouse, the project manager and other key development personnel require a user-oriented mind set. The project manager is required to interact frequently with users. Assigning someone who cannot communicate or who quickly becomes frustrated with users is a death shot to a data warehousing project.

- **Use proven methods.** Though a data warehouse may be a new type of system, the tasks at hand are no different than in the past—and somehow we forgot the past with the client/server revolution. When you ask individuals with a mainframe background to show you their policies, procedures, and standards for system development, they take you to a room filled with books, much like a library. Ask the same question in the client/server world and you may get a 20-page document. Defining the best common practices for data warehousing promotes consistent use of information and tools that support the process of information delivery. Building standards that are more robust than the ones used for client/server projects establishes an efficient development shop, which allows you to build systems that more effectively support the development decision-making process.

- **Design based on data patterns, not queries.** The design of a data warehouse is far different from an operational database design. New technologies, such as Sybase Adaptive Server IQ (which is discussed in Chapter 10), are optimized for data warehousing and decision support systems. Designing with such technologies allows you to build your data structures based on the characteristics of the data, not on the elusive characteristics of user queries. You want to build data structures that are optimized regardless of user query activities. The only way to do this is to tune your data structures based on the data characteristics rather than on the query characteristics, because you will never know all of the queries that users will ask, so tuning will be continuous. You will, however, understand the characteristics of the data in a data warehouse, so tuning will be done less frequent.

- **Only load data that is needed.** Many data warehouses begin with a data dumping ground—that is, a *data junkyard*. Placing all available data in a database and calling this a data warehouse is a bad practice. You will be forced to manage all of the bad data and associated queries. And guess what? The cost of maintenance far exceeds the cost of development in virtually every system you build. You need to clearly differentiate the data that your users need and the data that the operational systems need. You want to place the data that your users need in the data warehouse. (This could include data that you do not currently have.) Managing data placement from the onset yields a highly optimized data warehouse that is easy to maintain. Placing extraneous data that is outside the scope of the users' business intelligence needs becomes a data junkyard.

- **Define the proper data source, or system of record.** Data is everywhere, and most of it we don't currently control. When scouring the land for data throughout your distributed organization, you will find several payroll systems, several accounting systems, several budgetary systems, and numerous more human resource systems. You need to trace data from its original data capture system through the process to the ultimate data source and store the reference information in a *metadata repository*. Metadata is data that describes raw data and includes information such as source system, transformation rules, and final destination. This metadata is a valuable source of information that assists development staff and the user community in better understanding the contents of a data warehouse. When a proper data source is located, log all relevant information into your metadata repository. This procedure gives you a management tool for versioning and verifying the data managed in a data warehouse.

- **Clearly define unique entities.** Every business has common ways of evaluating information. As you discover in Section I of this book, a data warehouse refers to these methods as measure, dimension, and category detail entities. These entities must have a unique definition that is standardized across the enterprise. Does your company need more than one product entity defined, more than one customer geography entity defined, or more than one customer entity defined? I hope that your answer to all of these questions is no. If you need to define more than one entity in each of these areas, you need to further analyze the definition. If you do not provide common pathways in to your corporate knowledge base, users will be unable to cross-correlate information and unable to navigate the corporate knowledge base. These uniform definitions and implementations should be used across your data marts and in your enterprise data warehouse. Getting unique definitions correct initially dramatically improves your ongoing success rate as you proceed with additional data mart implementations.

- **Force use of, and reference to, a data warehouse.** Information is a deceptive thing. Think for a moment about how many meetings you have attended in which a presenter was full of unsourced information. Finding data that supports your position, your need, or your desire has become a way of selling individual points. How are people getting this information? Many ways exist, but it should be noted that numbers can be bent to support even the weakest of business cases. You should have your executive sponsor and steering committee support a policy early in your data warehousing project to force the use and reference of data in your data warehouse in their reports. An action such as this accomplishes three things.

First, it forces better use of the warehouse for continuous improvement of content quality. Second, it makes employees aware of such a valuable resource. And third, it saves significant time in meetings by avoiding discussions in the style of: "Where did you get this data?"

When Will the Future Arrive?

Some questions are nearly impossible to answer, and when the future goals that observed in this prologue will be achieved is one of them. But our hope is that the information in this book will spark your creativity, allowing you to move closer to the future. Time and enormous amounts of money are required to create the ultimate environment to support a user community. However, with a little fortitude and common sense, you can create a mini-Xanadu for your users, giving them information to better perform their job, while making your company more knowledgeable and competitive.

Meanwhile, you can watch those who wait for the ultimate solution. By the time that solution is available, your company may have acquired those who waited—or they may have disappeared altogether! Either way, our recommendation is to not wait for the technical community to come to you to deliver the future. Create your own future—your own solutions. Don't believe the marketing hype that tends to surround the technology industry. Challenge the technology industry and force it to deliver what you really need. Soon enough the future will be here—maybe your users will include the person in the dialog that began this chapter, or in the one that follows:

Also in the 21st century … Kristen, a brand manager for a growing consumer product's company, is evaluating how best to spend her promotional budget. For years, the company has purchased data about the stores that sell her product. This data includes the inventory bin locations as well as shopping cart data. The inventory bin locations allow Kristen to better understand how the store floor is laid out and where the products are located. The shopping cart data allows Kristen to see what consumers purchase together when they shop at a store. Kristen has determined that it would be beneficial to enter her virtual world and see how the consumers in her product's target market might shop, and more specifically how her product is presented in the shopping experience.

Entering this virtual world, Kristen can see that her target market of shopper's does in fact purchase either her product or a competitor's product on a regular basis. However, Kristen's product is on a shelf that is above the visual scope of most of her target market. Therefore, Kristen determines it would be better to spend her dollars in convincing grocery stores to place her product on a better shelf rather than running a coupon promotion. From this vantage point, she can make these decisions and quickly evaluate the effectiveness of her decision—from her office and from her corporate knowledge base.

Introduction to the Information Packaging Methodology

To deal with the new strategic requirements for success, all the tools to induce and support action taking must be available at the front-line. Therefore we must:

- *Share virtually all information with everyone.*

- *Decentralize control systems, and decentralize the accountants/systems people who oversee them.*

- *Provide very high levels of expenditure authority for division general managers and all other levels as well.*

- *Decentralize strategic planning.*

The ability to take action close to the market—and fast—is the first requirement for competing. Therefore both information availability and the authority to move forward at the front line are musts.

—Tom Peters, *Thriving on Chaos*, Harpers & Row Publishers Inc., 1987, pg. 608.

1

Business Factors Driving Ubiquitous Computing

You need to make yourself and your business more information literate. Information is a tool that improves your ability to execute within your specified job. One of the most challenging tasks you face as the builder of your data warehouse, a corporate knowledge base, is in getting the user community to decide what is to be measured.

The measurement system that you develop in conjunction with your user base will become one of the most important assets of your enterprise. After all, measurements lie at the very heart of a company's vision and strategy. The measures that are contained in a data warehouse shape the attitudes and behavior of the organization. The choice of business measures communicates values, channels employees thinking, and sets the priorities of a company.

The second biggest task is to motivate your users to exploit technology to understand what is happening on the inside and outside of your enterprise. Though internal data will assist the management of any enterprise in streamlining the cost structures of a business, we must realize that the most important information for a company is that which will drive revenue and expand the business. Therefore, the information packages that are contained in a data warehouse system focus on four primary centers, all involving humans who can drive the business to new highs, or new lows. These knowledge centers that surround a business mission and strategic plan include customers, employees, shareholders, and suppliers.

This chapter focuses on defining how to best define the measurement systems you utilize within your data warehouse. From this point of view, the remainder of the book begins to explore how to build your data warehouse and support every employee who requires information from your corporate knowledge base.

The Pressure of Today's Economy

The competitive position and profitability of most companies is under serious and increasing challenges in today's markets. When too many similar businesses migrate to a specific market, profits become scarce or nonexistent for every competitor. Industries such as airlines, long distance telephone providers, and electric utilities have found themselves in markets where their products are viewed as commodities with very small margins. Businesses such as these are impacted by many forces, including:

- A more global economy.
- Aggressive new competitors.
- New technology advances.
- Deregulation.
- Changes in customer behavior.

A company lacking the knowledge or understanding of these forces and other changing events is a company that will have extreme difficulties in growing its business beyond its current size and viability. For businesses to thrive in these changing times, they must understand and manage their business processes and the associated information that describes their market and business as a whole. Those companies that develop an inherent ability to quickly analyze their processes and proactively change their strategy when required will exploit opportunities, allowing them to win in the end. To thrive, companies must go beyond managing their own processes. They must manage the entire process that impacts their businesses, including better linkages with suppliers, customers, shareholders, and employees. These forces have also invaded our personal lives. Just look at the statistics; or better yet, test yourself by asking these questions:

- Is your average work day longer or shorter than it was five years ago?
- Are employees asked to do more for themselves today compared to five years ago?
- Are support services such as secretaries and other administrative support as abundant as they were five years ago?

- Can you imagine what you would do without a microwave?

- After listening to a CD, how does a LP album sound, and do you enjoy changing sides after 20 minutes?

- Is the computing system with which you started your career similar in size and capacity to the one you use today?

- In the late 1960s, who was the leading car manufacturer? 1970s? 1980s? 1990s?

- Are there more manufacturing jobs today than there were in the 1970s? 1980s? 1990s?

- How many labor positions have been eliminated through automation?

- How many times do you call someone and get voice mail? Is it more frequent than it was five years ago? Ten years ago?

The Business Process

Everything in your lives and businesses has a process, typically with a cyclical orientation. The goal is to master the process, maintain high quality deliverables, and perform the process in less time. Doing so allows one to do more for less, while earning more, growing competitive advantage, and achieving market prowess. Sir Isaac Newton's third law of motion states: *for every action there is an equal and opposite reaction.* This statement is more profound than Sir Newton may have ever imagined. Just think for a moment of its meaning in the following areas:

- **Microsoft's domination of the personal computer market:** Microsoft gained rapid dominance within a marketplace where other vendors such as Apple had clearly superior technology. Microsoft realized that if its software was portable to all platforms, it could quickly shift as technology advances occurred within its marketplace. Microsoft also realized that if its software was made available at an economical price, it could sell more than its competitors and gain the much needed leadership in market share. With these plans, Microsoft stayed away from areas such as hardware and stuck with a strategy around operating systems and other software solutions. Apple, on the other hand, went into a tightly integrated and proprietary strategy in which it sold a solution based on hardware and software. These two strategies have driven the actions of the companies and also driven the marketplace. Which has been more successful? Microsoft's action of low entry cost and high portability offered consumers a greater choice. This action also made it easier for developers to deliver solutions to consumers and businesses in a wider market. And through its actions in leveraging business partners Microsoft was able to dominate a highly growing, yet competitive market place.

- **Wal-Mart's growth to the largest discount retailer in the United States:** Wal-Mart has achieved its impressive success by executing a series of actions that allowed it to create, expand, and dominate its niche market. Wal-Mart started by focusing on areas in which competition did not exist, smaller and rural towns. This action allowed Wal-Mart to dominate the smaller towns. In these markets, Wal-Mart was the best-stocked, lowest-priced retailer. This action became a barrier to entry for competitors such as Kmart; the loyalty that Wal-Mart built with its customer base and the size of the market would not allow a competitor to enter the market. Upon growing and capitalizing in these areas, Wal-Mart built up strength to become more aggressive and challenge the market leaders in other areas. Actions that Wal-Mart strategically made in the areas of distributed store management, technology infrastructure, supply chain management, and information analysis lead to a well-run, efficient business—factors that were lacking in its competitors.

- **General Electric's ability to expand its business:** General Electric has established a well-publicized quality program, which was borrowed from Motorola. This plan involves a rigorous training program that schools its employees in the areas of statistical and other quality enhancing measures. These employees then roam the General Electric plants and set up quality improvement projects. General Electric has invested hundreds of millions of dollars in this quality program, which includes investments in training, computer systems, and quality control programs. Why the investment? General Electric can now avoid much of the traditional business fire fighting. It has created a proactive environment—not a reactive one. This has resulted in the company avoiding costly mistakes that will save them $7 billion to $10 billion over the next decade and thus bolster their profits. With these actions, General Electric has shown that it understands the frailty of being ahead and is acting to avoid slippage in profits and market leadership.

- **Procter & Gamble's ability to help its customers grow their business:** For decades, P&G prospered by making life easier for housewives, with breakthrough products such as Tide and Pampers. Shoppers browsed store aisles, clipped coupons, saved box tops, and chased promotions. But the 1980s brought a major consolidation among retailers, and P&G's sales growth slowed. There were fewer revolutionary products, and more knockoffs from competitors. P&G, and its retailers have collected enormous amounts of information that assist them in attacking today's market. For example, today's average consumer more often than not is a woman and takes just 21 minutes to shop. In that time, she buys an average of 18 items among 30,000 to 40,000 choices. She has less time to browse; down 25 percent from five years ago. She isn't even bothering to compare prices. She wants the same product, at the same price, in the same row, week after week.

This information helped P&G restructure its sales force. P&G replaced its sales personnel, who represented specific products, by teams consisting of sales people and experts on market research, logistics, shelf management, and manufacturing. Today, a retailer deals with a focused P&G customer account team that handles all aspects of its account.

This data also helped make the new customer account teams more effective. These teams know the truck schedules and can give retailers delivery times within 30 minutes. In addition, trucks deliver only what is needed, based on data from checkout registers that indicates how much of a particular item has been sold. P&G says retailers have saved about $250 million since 1993, most of which had been locked up in inventory.

Understanding the driving forces within the consumer goods market has allowed P&G to make the right decisions and perform the right actions to win high marks from customers. It has also help P&G to markedly improve its relationship with retailers. Two recent national surveys show P&G outscoring every other consumer goods company by two to one in helping retailers become more efficient. This type of information also assisted P&G in strategically deciding to reduce the overall number of products and pricing schemes, which has saved P&G millions of dollars without impacting customer satisfaction.

These examples show that Sir Newton knew more than physics. When you have an appreciation of how actions can drive reactions, you can control the motion—the ability to propel your company into a leadership position. This law of motion can also help you deal with the actions and reactions that impact the running of your businesses and lives. Every process contains a set of actions that assist in defining the reaction or end results. During the process, you can alter the course, and potentially the outcome, by introducing additional actions and hope that you guide the process to a successful conclusion.

Within any process, information can assist you in determining the proper action, Depending on the process, the action can impact the ultimate reaction or outcome. Through the entire process, data artifacts are produced. Gathering these tidbits of information can assist you in further defining the proper actions in any given process. As shown in Figure 1.1, a depiction of a television set's trouble shooting guide, the ability to evaluate these data artifacts allows you to properly, or at least more intelligently, determine the relevant actions to drive the outcome to a desired result—the reaction.

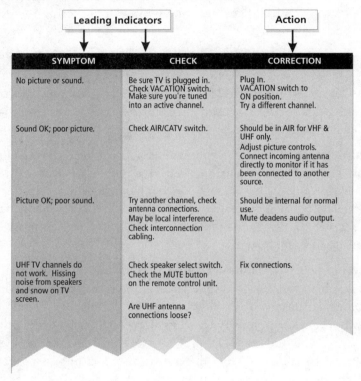

Leading Indicators		Action
SYMPTOM	**CHECK**	**CORRECTION**
No picture or sound.	Be sure TV is plugged in. Check VACATION switch. Make sure you're tuned into an active channel.	Plug In. VACATION switch to ON position. Try a different channel.
Sound OK; poor picture.	Check AIR/CATV switch.	Should be in AIR for VHF & UHF only. Adjust picture controls. Connect incoming antenna directly to monitor if it has been connected to another source.
Picture OK; poor sound.	Try another channel, check antenna connections. May be local interference. Check interconnection cabling.	Should be internal for normal use. Mute deadens audio output.
UHF TV channels do not work. Hissing noise from speakers and snow on TV screen.	Check speaker select switch. Check the MUTE button on the remote control unit. Are UHF antenna connections loose?	Fix connections.

Figure 1.1 *Many products ship with a trouble shooting guide, such as this one for a television set, that provides users with leading indicators and proper actions to be taken to achieve the resultant trailing indicator.*

As you evaluate the ability to control a given process, you quickly find that indicators can assist you in defining the proper action to take. If you hope to have a proper understanding of a given process, you must clearly define the measurement of success, the boundaries of the process, and the value created in the process. Understanding each of these items allows a business to build the proper portfolio of information derived from well-managed processes, which assists the business in performing best in its market. As shown in Figure 1.1, any discrete, or atomic, process has leading indicators, an action taken, and trailing indicators. The following sections take a closer look at each of these items.

Leading Indicators

A *leading indicator* is one that apprises someone of the need for an action. Leading indicators become the drivers and definers of the proper action to take. As you look at the overall processes in an organization, it is important to note that any process can be comprised of several discrete processes. An *atomic process* is one that has a single action and single outcome. A light switch is a prime example of an atomic process. The light switch can be turned off or turned on. When the light switch is in the off position, the room is not illuminated. However, when the switch is in the on position, the room is illuminated. Understanding this process and the meaning of on or off allows one to illuminate a dark room.

Leading indicators are best interpreted when they are associated with atomic processes, such as walking into a dark room would cause one to flip on the light switch to illuminate the room and make it easier to navigate. Unfortunately, most processes in a business are composed of many atomic processes, so we must manage the actions to produce proper reactions to feed further processes down the line. Hence, the results produced from actions taken based on leading indicators will become leading indicators for atomic processes that follow. Figure 1.2 is an illustration of this concept depicting a cooking recipe, which comprises several atomic processes. Failure to follow the recipe results in the fudge becoming too runny or too hard—being inedible. The ability to interpret leading indicators and define the proper action is directly proportionate to the ability to be successful or have a successful outcome.

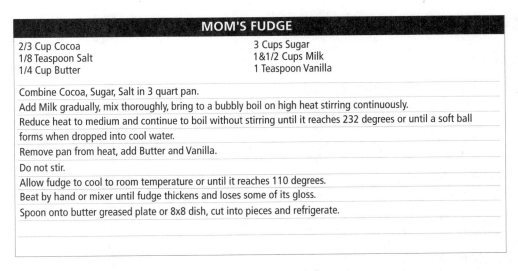

MOM'S FUDGE	
2/3 Cup Cocoa	3 Cups Sugar
1/8 Teaspoon Salt	1&1/2 Cups Milk
1/4 Cup Butter	1 Teaspoon Vanilla

Combine Cocoa, Sugar, Salt in 3 quart pan.
Add Milk gradually, mix thoroughly, bring to a bubbly boil on high heat stirring continuously.
Reduce heat to medium and continue to boil without stirring until it reaches 232 degrees or until a soft ball forms when dropped into cool water.
Remove pan from heat, add Butter and Vanilla.
Do not stir.
Allow fudge to cool to room temperature or until it reaches 110 degrees.
Beat by hand or mixer until fudge thickens and loses some of its gloss.
Spoon onto butter greased plate or 8x8 dish, cut into pieces and refrigerate.

Figure 1.2 *A cooking recipe demonstrating an entire cooking cycle.*

Figure 1.2 highlights the importance of understanding subprocess measures, those that result from more atomic processes in an overall process. You must measure the process in various stages of the cooking process, because each of them will ultimately control the quality of the final deliverable. The atomic process variables that are measured include the use of the appropriate quantities of ingredients, the speed of a mixer, the length of time in which a process is executed, the temperature of a burner or oven, and the amount of time elapsed between atomic processes. Some examples of leading indicators in areas of a business include:

- Dollars invested in research and development as ratio of sales or profit.

- Grievances or complaints filed by employees.

- Requests for transfers by employees into or out of specific departments.

- Training or retraining hours for employees.

- Safety audit reports.

- Dollar volume in proposals that are outstanding.

- Forecast sales.

- Forecast resource requirements.

- Market segmentation.

- Prospect demographics.

Actions

Results that occur from any process are the result of some action being taken. As we sit here writing this book, our minds compose ideas, communicate the proper actions to our hands, which is are positioned on our keyboards, and when pressure is applied to the keys, our thoughts are recorded for posterity's sake so that you may read and learn through our writings.

An *action* tends to describe the state or process of acting or doing. In this sense, the action described typically characterizes a verb—something that is done. Businesses are blessed with an abundance of actions. Consider those that follow.

- The act of hiring someone increases a company's expenses and, we hope, its revenues.

- The act of signing a contract commits both parties to legally binding actions related to a service offering or a product purchase.

- The act of shipping a product to a customer may fulfill the legal action of the seller to the buyer as described in the contract.

- The act of sending payment in response to an invoice fulfills a customer's legal or contracted obligation to a supplier.

- The act of receiving a shipped product confirms acceptance of materials from a supplier.

Actions result in outcomes. Even the act of not making a decision is a valid action that will drive an outcome. In today's competitive environments, it is important to take action in an informed, rapid manner; hence, the need to monitor the data points associated with any given process and its associated actions.

Trailing Indicators

The data artifacts that are the result of actions are what we refer to as *trailing indicators*. These data points allow us to evaluate the success or failure of any action in an atomic process. As stated earlier, the results from any set of atomic processes could be leading indicators for the next atomic process in a cyclical manner, as shown in Figure 1.3. Note that, in this grocery store promotion illustration, trailing indicators formulated in atomic processes become the leading indicators for other atomic processes that comprise the overall buying cycle of a consumer. The ability to monitor process outcomes often has been the primary focus of today's data warehousing systems.

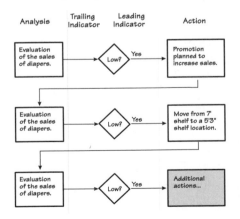

Figure 1.3 *The cyclical nature of indicators is demonstrated in this grocery store promotion.*

Some examples of trailing indicators include:

- Profit.

- Return on investment (ROI).

- Stock price.

- Defect rate.

- Cycle time.

- Scrap/yield.

- Hours of rework.

- Absenteeism.

- Employee turnover.

- Market share.

Today's Imposing Business Factors

In today's highly competitive and imposing business environment, providing top value for a given price is a rapidly moving target. To sustain growth, a company has to refine current products and continually introduce products faster than its competitors. With such odds placed on companies, success is typically bestowed on those who have mastered the management of their business process cycle times—allowing them to be faster than their competitors' cycle times.

A *business cycle* is defined as the period of elapsed time that begins during the initial identification of an input, or stimulus, into the cycle. such as a customer's need, and concludes with the completion of the task, such as receipt of payment for the product shipped or service delivered to the customer, fulfilling the need. Time is a critical measure that affects the cost and customer satisfaction in these cycles. The overall cycle is composed of many sub-cycles, such as new product development, production, sales, and hiring. The overall cycle will repeat itself many times. How many times? The repetition in the overall cycle will be fundamentally based on how well the product or service continues to meet the customer's needs. The logic behind process measurement is that if you can control all of your processes and you have good raw materials, you will be able to deliver the same output every time.

Figure 1.4 depicts two business cycles. One represents a new need defined by a customer. This cycle forces a company to complete a development process that allows it to deliver the required product to a customer. The other cycle is a demand cycle, where the products already exist. This cycle involves delivering an ordered product to the customer in a timely fashion.

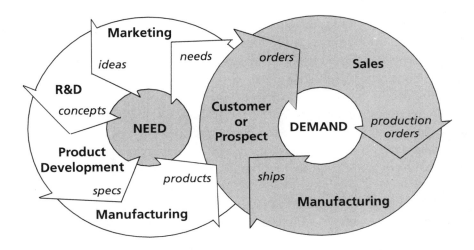

Figure 1.4 *Two complete business cycles are depicted, one representing a newly-defined need, the other a demand cycle for an existing product.*

Every time a business completes a full cycle, it accumulates raw data about the relationship among itself, its customers, and its suppliers. An organization's ability to adapt to change is determine by its ability to take this data and quickly transform it into business intelligence. In this context, a business cycle can also be referred to as a business' learning cycle. Each time a company defines, develops, and introduces a product, a cycle is completed. Evaluating the raw data associated with a full cycle allows a company to uncover opportunities to alter the consequences of the decision making process in future cycles. The more repetitive the cycles is, the greater is the potential for learning and optimizing the overall cycle time.

Cycle time becomes a lightning rod, allowing those in management positions of a company to quickly monitor or recognize defects in business processes. Each process in the cycle produces information that should be the focus of the company's management team. These items include how long the process takes to complete; whether the process delivers the required quality deliverable; and how much the process costs.

Cycle Time Speed Up

A key for increasing the speed of any cycle time is learning faster, not working faster. Compressing the same activities into a shorter time frame increases the error rate, escalates costs, and degrades the quality of any business process. To achieve speed, you cannot afford to repeat any task in the overall business process. The ability to have successful yield the first time through a process is essential for speed. Therefore, when cycle time grows, you can largely guarantee that rework is involved. Cycle time speed up depends on managing the connection points in a business process—the interdependent elements of the overall process. This is in stark contrast to the philosophy of increasing the capability of individual functions. Therefore, sustainable cycle time improvements will come when managers focus on cross-functional process improvements.

The combination of leading indicators that drive actions and in turn produce trailing indicators constitutes a complete process cycle. To be successful at speeding up cycle time, companies need to manage the time that is elapsed during these indicators. The ability to maintain high quality levels while shrinking overall cycle times allows a company to innovate and excel in its core competency—gaining competitive advantage and more than likely market share or margin share. As shown in Figure 1.5, market share is capturing a bigger piece of the overall pie in a given market; margin share is driving larger profits per unit offered.

People-Centered Analysis

Many organizations today evaluate themselves with the same bottom-line oriented measures of performance that they did 30 or more years ago. Measuring the right variables has a lot to do with the likelihood of your company's future success. Companies succeed when people view them as a great organization. Therefore, it is best to analyze indicators, or business metrics, that focus on positive, value-added propositions in people-centric areas, or a company's human assets, as shown in Figure 1.6. The four key areas in which your analysis should be mapped to include are customers, employees, shareholders and suppliers. Even glamorous awards that manufacturing, service, and small business companies seek, such as the Malcolm Baldridge National Quality Award, focus on such criteria. Therefore, when focusing on the information to gather in your company, make sure they align with one of the four critical human asset centers. Your customers drive your revenue; your shareholders drive your capital; your employees drive your efficiencies; and your suppliers drive quality and production through their raw materials.

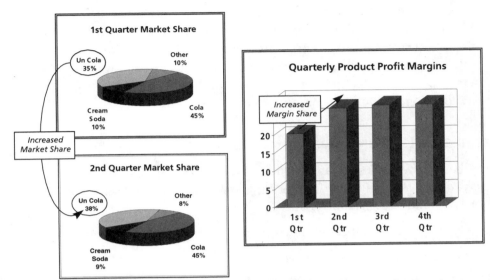

Figure 1.5 *Market share, shown in the left side, is defined by how much of a given market is captured by a given vendor. Margin share, shown to the right, is defined by how much profit is driven through sale of individual units.*

Figure 1.6 *A company should place its measurement base in the human asset centers, or knowledge centers, that deliver value to the overall business mission, goals and objectives: customers, shareholders, employees, and suppliers.*

Data Warehousing: Capturing Process-Related Data Artifacts

The ability to learn from raw business cycle data is why your organization requires a data warehouse. Taking the raw data and transforming it into business intelligence is a fundamental purpose of data warehousing. The data warehouse helps your company learn and become more intelligent—it will become your *corporate knowledge base*. Leveraging and learning from a corporate knowledge base provides the heart and soul of sustained competitive advantage in an enterprise. This learning process assists your customers, employees, shareholders, and suppliers in improving the operation of your business, allowing you to excel beyond your competitors.

What Is a Data Warehouse?

Literally, *data* is defined as facts and information about something, while *warehouse* is defined as a location or facility for storing goods and merchandise. A data warehousing system has the following characteristics:

- It provides a centralization of corporate data or information assets.

- It is contained in a well-managed environment.

- It has consistent and repeatable processes defined for loading operational data.

- It is built on an open and scaleable architecture that will handle future expansion for the collection of data assets.

- It provides tools that allow its users to effectively process the data into information without a high degree of technical support.

As characterized in Figure 1.7, a data warehouse is similar to traditional warehousing of products in the manufacturing industry. In the information systems world, there is a need to accomplish the following steps, which are keyed to Figure 1.7.

1. Produce or purchase the materials required to build finished inventory; that is, capture operational data.

2. Take materials and produce finished inventory; that is, transform the operational transaction data.

3. Store the finished inventory until it is required in the distribution channels; that is, store the transformed data in a data warehouse.

4. Ship the finished inventory to the distribution channel based on demand; that is, deliver business intelligence upon receipt of a user data request or query.

Data warehouse systems have become a rapidly expanding requirement for most information system departments. What is causing this astronomical growth? No one circumstance has launched us into this new paradigm. The concepts behind the data warehouses of today have been around for years. In the past, you had information centers, executive information systems (EIS), and decision support systems (DSS).

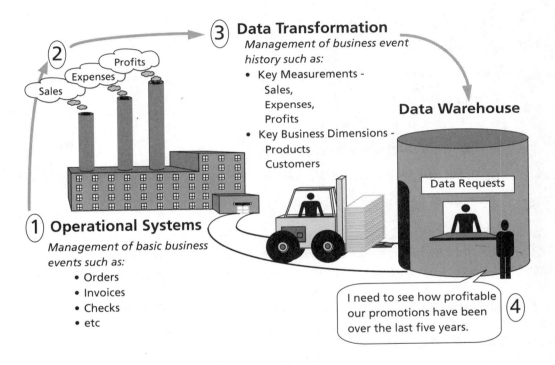

Figure 1.7 *The data warehousing process is similar to the traditional product manufacturing process; raw materials are used to produce finished goods, which are distributed to wanting users.*

The reasons for growth in this area stem from many places. With regard to data, most companies now have access to more than 20 years of data on managing the operational aspects of their business. With regard to user tools, the technology of user computing has reached a point where corporations can now effectively allow the users to navigate corporate databases without a high need for technical support. With regard to corporate management, executives are realizing that the only way to sustain and gain an advantage in today's economy is to better leverage information.

The Information Architecture: Becoming Information Literate

As Peter Drucker, a leading business consultant has stated, today's competitive organizations are rebuilding around information. These organizations are taking the time to train their employees to use information as a tool. Together, the users of today's computer systems and information systems departments must respond to questions such as:

- What information do I need to do my job?

- From whom do I obtain this information?

- In what form do I require this information?

- When must I receive this information?

- What information do I owe to others?

- In what form do others expect my information?

- To whom do I owe this information?

- When do others expect me to deliver my information?

For companies to better manage their processes and their associated cycles, they must become information literate. The moment an organization and its employees examine the questions above, it realizes that the information they need; the really important information. Employees who can proactively respond to these questions are more effective, accountable, responsible, and literate about their business cycle and process drivers. However, the information required by these employees often cannot be obtained from the current information systems.

On becoming information literate, we realize that the data artifacts that are required to assist us in managing our processes include more than just data about internal operations. The information system departments that support any company must realize this and assume the responsibility to find and deliver the required information. Today's information systems give their users information inside the company. But to truly be successful, these users need an abundance of information from the outside—on markets, on customers, and on competitors. The big challenge is not be to get more or better inside information, but to add high quality outside information into their new information systems. This outside information fulfills many of the leading indicators that allow business decision makers to properly determine actions that will drive the proper reactions and results in overall business cycles. Business decisions that are based on a complete set of data, inside and outside data artifacts, will be good decisions.

It is important when building your data warehouse to determine the proper information to store in it. Corporations need a new measurement approach that can be fulfilled with the proper data warehousing strategy. This approach focuses on reporting about the human asset centers much like the balance sheet and income statement report on the accounting system. The data warehouse provides a system of measures that link the human assets, which permits an enterprise to manage the entire value-creation process. Our aim is to build a framework for an integrated repository that links the various components of a business together in relationships that can be quantified. This allows employees to establish goals, spot failures, use standard financial analysis techniques, evaluate tradeoffs, and learn from the results. The goal of this investigation is a complete information architecture that supports a business in achieving its strategic plan by providing the critical data assets at the proper time to its user base.

The Application Architecture: Accessing Business Cycle Data Artifacts

Many of today's business cycle time improvements have been provided through a strong understanding of the data artifacts that are generated by internal business operations, such as accounting, order fulfillment, and manufacturing. The data related to these processes is easier to obtain and decisions associated within internal operations are easier to monitor, because the work performed in these areas is tangible. An order can easily be tracked through an entire system until fulfillment. Even when it gets lost in a bureaucratic quagmire, the order ticket itself provides a tangible target. The same occurs in manufacturing, where parts are tracked from the moment they land on the receiving dock to the time they reach the shipping dock in the form of a final product. Depending on the particular business, these may provide the highest leverage points for process and cycle time improvement.

However, for businesses to gain substantial competitive advantage, it is important for them to understand data external to the currently managed processes. This data is associated with the marketplace and prospective customers who are not currently utilizing products and services provided by the enterprise.

A data warehouse is quickly becoming the only systematic means an executive has for storing this information and allowing those who use it to turn their ideas into actions. Data warehousing systems enable today's organizations to integrate the data artifacts produced by business cycles and processes, including the leading indicators, actions, and trailing indicators. Providing the users of your data warehouse with these data artifacts provides a valuable feedback loop about whether the planned strategy remains viable and successful. Users of your data warehouse will be able to question whether the fundamental assumptions made when they launched a strategy were valid. For example, how long before improvements in product quality and on-time delivery will lead to an increase in the share of a customers' business and higher margins on existing sales? How large will the effect be?

A data warehouse and its associated application architecture enable today's organizations to integrate a wide variety of business cycle and process data, and provide it through easy-to-use interfacing technologies. Providing a well-planned application architecture for a data warehouse enables all operational units along the value chain to realize enormous improvements in cost, quality, and response times. The consolidation of these pieces of information and proper presentation, or accessibility, tools improve a company's ability to learn.

The Technology Architecture: Distributing the Information

Companies traditionally have stored this data in some sort of data structures to allow easier analysis. The models used internally for reporting have undergone dramatic cycle time reduction, from the paper-based, server-centric reporting of the Information Center in the early 1980s to today's data warehouses and data marts. Providing information to users faster has been a priority of information systems and tools providers.

In the olden days, this process included hard copy reports distributed from a server-centric Information Center. These systems were revised to allow for user-based reporting in Executive Information Systems or Decision Support Systems, which were built on client/server technologies. We now are facing a growing need for all employees and partners of a company to better understand their metrics. This form of demand pushes weaknesses in the client/server and distribution technologies of today and is driving a specialty server marketplace that is supported by technologies such as the Internet/intranet, World Wide Web, and Java.

Vendors will increasingly adopt a strategy of integrating tool suites that address a data warehouse developer's or user's diverse needs. These tool sets will continue to evolve and support technologies that are offered by the Internet and the Web. This will improve the developer's ability to keep up with the rapid pace of user demands through the use of well-integrated and consolidated tools for back-end delivery of data warehouse information.

The Internet, and more specifically the Web, provides a technology architecture to support widespread distribution in an expeditious fashion. The Web allows us to have access to huge amounts of information, while simplifying the task of finding, viewing, and making use of this information. The intention when Tim Berners-Lee created the Web was to provide a hypertext system to enable efficient and easy information sharing among geographically separated teams of researchers. The important aspects of the proposed system were:

- A consistent user interface.

- The ability to incorporate a wide range of technologies and document types.

- Universal readership to allow anyone located on the network to read the same document.

The Web provides a robust information and communication system. This technology architecture allows organizations to perform operations associated with both information dissemination and information collection. Thus, the Web is not merely a one-way system for disseminating information, but includes the potential for interactive communication. As an information dissemination system, the Web can reach audiences of an arbitrary size, ranging from an individual to a group to a mass audience.

The Information Packaging Methodology: Architecting a Corporate Knowledge Base

An information packaging methodology comprises a set of best practices for delivering a complete data warehouse to your enterprise. As shown in Figure 1.8, this methodology covers the complete life-cycle from specification gathering through data and process modeling to overall process management techniques, which allows those who are tasked with developing a data warehouse to be successful in delivering one that is quick to assemble, quality focused, easy to maintain, and scaleable. This set of best practices was discussed in detail in our first book, *Data Warehousing: Building the Corporate Knowledge Base.*

A fundamental difficulty that most technical people experience in the process of building a data warehouse is how best to control the scope of the data warehouse and to deliver the users' requirements. The information packaging methodology delivers the required philosophy and set of tools for achieving the lofty goals set forth by data warehousing initiatives. From an ease of communication point of view, the information packaging methodology uses specific tools, shapes, and colors to allow those who use it to quickly and clearly determine meaning and purpose of the overall components and entities that reside in a data warehouse. From a quality of deliverables point of view, the information packaging methodology provides a unique data gathering technique that provides hard hitting, information-literate deliverables driven by a business for better understanding that business. These two points of view offer a final delivery technique that quickly allows those who use the information packaging methodology to see rapid and rampant business intelligence overtake their enterprise.

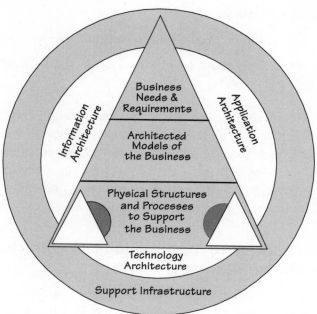

Figure 1.8 *The information packaging methodology provides a set of well-documented best practices, allowing those who use it to deliver proper data warehousing systems to support the business—a corporate knowledge base.*

Data warehousing provides a place to store information and the Internet/intranet provides a distribution channel to deliver the information. What is needed is an overall process to make these technology solutions meet business needs. The information packaging methodology provides the proper techniques to deliver this solution—especially in today's highly diversified environments. When this methodology is incorporated into the philosophy of a data warehousing delivery team, quick pay-back results are delivered, because this methodology focuses on allowing users to make better decisions from organized, easily-accessible information. The information packaging methodology assists in creating general subject areas that can be subdivided to cover all the various facets of your business information. This methodology attacks the most difficult part of this process, which is to define the proper categories and associated structures of information. Whether your data artifacts are derived from ready-made, purchased systems or adapted from your own, in-house system, the information packaging methodology assist you in building, delivering, and maintaining a corporate knowledge base.

A data warehouse is a single source for key performance measurement and historically significant corporate information. All of the entities contained in a data warehouse are interconnected; therefore, the processes that comprise a data warehouse should also be interconnected. Decisions that are required in will rely on these interconnections. These items lead to an iterative development methodology, as shown in Figure 1.9. The process is meant to quickly deliver, in an iterative fashion, the subject-oriented data warehouses required by target audiences. For more details on this development methodology, please refer to Appendix A.

The goal of this methodology is to guide the development staff through a business-oriented process and design, not a technology-driven process and design. The spiral development approach will assist you in more rapid delivery and discovery cycles, which allows your development staff to avoid lengthy cycles that miss the requirement. As you deploy your data warehousing applications, users will provide rapid feedback which in turn assists in educating the development staff on how best to meet data warehouse users' needs. True success involves an architect who can obtain and define user-oriented, atomic processes and their associated leading indicators, actions, and trailing indicators. These items and their associated data artifacts need to be defined, captured, managed, and communicated over time to assist users in better understanding areas or opportunities for improvement in an overall business process.

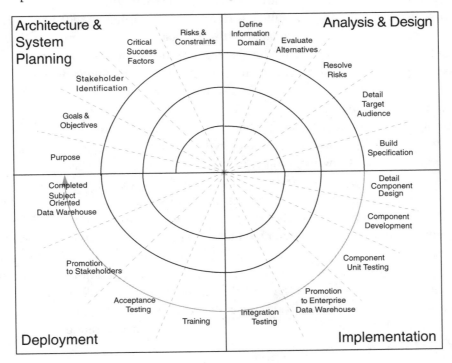

Figure 1.9 *The information packaging methodology follows a spiral development technique that provides rapid feed back and delivery loops, allowing you to progressively build a data warehouse that meets and exceeds your user's expectations.*

Properly Scoping Your Development Effort

You should not set out to create an enterprise data warehouse; this scope is far too large for any development team and will more than likely never be completed. Data warehouses are complex—probably the largest integration effort ever undertaken by those who do so. These projects require the coordination of multiple vendors' components as well as internal organizations in a company. Based on these complexities, you should start with a small and manageable aspect of the business—a subject-oriented, or line-of-business, data warehouse, often referred to as a *data mart*.

A subject-oriented data warehouse is a smaller-scale data warehouse that focuses on the part of a business in need of the most assistance. However, the development team must build an architecture that supports the concept of an enterprise data warehouse, a plug-and-play or building-block approach to data warehouse development. A subject-oriented data warehouse focuses on laying the groundwork for an enterprise data warehouse by slowly automating the areas required by a business in a more manageable fashion—by building decision support databases and associated infrastructures.

The first implementation of a subject-oriented data warehouse will have a relatively high entry cost that is directly associated with the lack of an architecture, a data model, and the tools to properly implement the system. During the initial subject-oriented data warehouse project, the development team faces numerous challenges in these technical areas as well as the large task associated in discovering the users' perception and expectations for the data warehouse.

The architectural work will begin to define how the systems will interconnect. The tool selection work will define how the data will be accessed. And most important, data modeling exercises will allow the project to begin to define the subject areas that will be contained in an enterprise data warehouse, as shown in Figure 1.10.

Over time, subject areas will be reused in different subject-oriented data warehouses, allowing the development team to allocate less time and cost for data modeling and analysis. For example, an initial subject-oriented data warehouse may develop subject areas such as customer, product, and location. Each of these subject areas will be reused in sales management, marketing management, product management, and operation planning subject-oriented data warehouses. Therefore, if the subject areas are developed in a sales management subject-oriented data warehouse, the costs associated with analysis and development of these subject areas will not reoccur in the other data warehouse projects.

Summary

Those who build a complete source for corporate knowledge do so by focusing on all cycles in a business, including those impacted solely by internal data and those impacted by understanding external data. For example, cycle time is the ongoing process that involves the ability to identify, satisfy, and be paid for meeting a customer's need faster than anyone else. Cycle time and the ability to improve cycle time are an ongoing process. Competitors who have the ability to continually improve their cycle times will pass those who pause to relax.

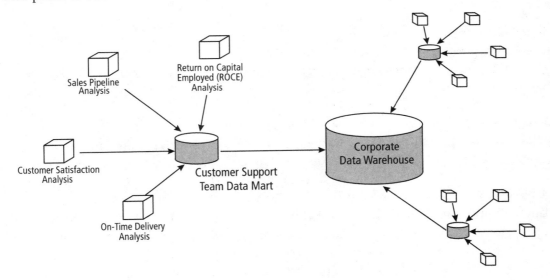

Figure 1.10 *The logical nature and roll up of a data warehouse will see information packages roll into subject-oriented data warehouses (data marts), which roll into a corporate data warehouse. The CDW, or Enterprise Data Warehouse, is a logical entity and should not be viewed as a single, physical database.*

To be successful in your efforts to deliver your data warehouse, be sure to understand the processes that make up all business cycles in your enterprise. From this vantage point, you can determine the important data artifacts that are produced during the processes. This information is the basis for business intelligence, and therefore the data, that you need to gather and manage a data warehouse.

Some companies have become masters at understanding this process and organizing around such factors. Here are some examples:

- Hewlett-Packard's highly successful laser printer business.

- Gateway 2000's creative mail-order personal computer business.

- Intel's its innovative chip manufacturing business.

Upon capturing this valuable information, you must distribute it to a wide population of users. Each job in your company is driven by information points. Therefore, the challenge you face is how to handle this global distribution. The Internet, when combined with a data warehouse, offers an excellent platform for handling this ubiquitous need in businesses.

You have an enormous job ahead of you. You must build systems that give high quality information to those who make decisions. So you must bring together all data processing systems in a highly optimized and maintainable fashion. For your company to be the one passing up the competition, you need a clear strategy of how to lead your company from today's behaviors to tomorrow's behaviors. Your data warehouse provides the foundation for capturing all of the relevant, key information to guide your company in this direction.

No single entity in an enterprise is immune to the need for this key information. Therefore, a corporate knowledge base is quickly becoming a ubiquitous requirement. The Internet and World Wide Web are quickly becoming the best channel to distribute such information in a cost effective structure. These technologies are best served with a comprehensive methodology that ties business needs to delivery realities. The information packaging methodology provides a blueprint to you and your colleagues for delivering a corporate knowledge base and for delivering profound impact to your enterprise.

In the chapters that follow, we will further investigate the major areas of this methodology prior to diving into the technological components of delivery. In all, this book will take you through the complete cycle of delivery, to allow your users to access your corporate knowledge base no matter who they are, no matter where they are.

2

Building an Adaptable Architecture

You've been envious of other companies and their ability to deliver information to their users long enough. You've asked all the questions, listened to all the excuses, and heard all of the complaints. It's now time to deliver your own data warehouse and its associated knowledge to your users. So you go out and buy the hottest products for producing a data warehouse on the market. The companies from whom you purchased these products even help you get a data mart up and running—you're now convinced this is easy, this is fast!

Your first data mart is in place, your small test group is accessing and reporting on the corporate information, and you are as pleased as punch with your product purchases and overall accomplishments. You now begin to take on more responsibility for adding users and information to the data mart—growing your data mart into a desired and much envied data warehouse. You have found a receptive and excited user base just waiting for you to pick their business area for your next project.

But as you begin to expand the scope of your data warehouse, you realize that the products, platforms, and tools that you selected cannot handle the voluminous data and users you need to support. The sales personnel who represented these products over-sold their product's capabilities! The products cannot support the type of data warehouse deployment that is really required for your entire enterprise. No big deal, you'll just work on smaller, more focused implementations of data marts to satisfy the needs of the user community.

However, your users begin to ask questions: Can I bring the data from the sales and marketing data mart together with the product production data mart? Can I take the data mart information on the road? Can I access the data warehouse with this new tool that was purchased at the local computer store? Can the data warehouse support more interactive users? Can the data warehouse bring new users online quicker? Can the enterprise save expenses while bringing new users online? Can the users of the data warehouse work from their home?

The questions get to be too much for you and your staff. On Monday, you call a consulting firm that specializes in data warehouses and beg its staff to come and take this burden off your shoulders. Sometimes, you don't analyze your purchases because of the lack of something—time, money, experience, or motivation. Or you purchase something because a friend, colleague, or competitor has it—or worse yet, because it is a bargain. Therefore, you must ask yourself how you can avoid such a fate, which has attacked many companies.

How to Deliver a Data Warehouse

Data warehousing provides a means to make the information assets of an enterprise available for decision making. Data warehousing enables executives, managers, analysts, and users to query and analyze enterprise data across many facets of their business. And data warehousing allows users to perform complex analysis on these information assets that have been extracted from operational systems, aggregated or summarized to fit their particular criteria, manipulated to derive new data, reformatted or filtered to remove unwanted or unnecessary data, and integrated with other data sources around the enterprise.

An effective data warehousing strategy must deal with the complexities of a modern enterprise. Data is generated everywhere, and controlled by different organizations and operational systems. Users demand access to data, anywhere and anytime, customized to their needs and requirements. Therefore, a data warehouse must fit the business model—not dictate it. And, more importantly, the technology that is utilized to deliver a data warehouse must be flexible enough to evolve with changes in business and user requirements. You need to provide your users with an information framework that represents a comprehensive model of a business. Generally, a business requires its data warehouse to support the following:

- **Rapid response:** Users need to analyze large amounts of data to make business decisions. The users are often faced with a limited window of time in which to perform this analysis to make timely business decisions and to react quickly to changing market conditions.

- **Complex analysis:** Business analysis involves determining the answers to some extremely complex questions, often requiring iterative analysis of data. Business users typically issue queries that invoke multiple conditions, summarizations, and complex subqueries, which places increased demands on a database.

- **Dynamic business environment:** Users need the flexibility to access information in a wide variety of ever-changing ways to resolve specific business problems quickly. As a business environment changes, users need to view and analyze data in complex and ever-changing ways. This often involves the ability to cross-correlate different subject areas and business measures.

The answer to the question of how you can best deliver a data warehouse is easily stated—you need to build an adaptable architecture. We next delve deeper into the meaning of these two words, separately and combined, to describe what is needed to deliver a data warehouse.

What Is an Architecture?

Architecture has many meanings among people who develop and use computer systems. Here is a literal definition of architecture:

ar·chi·tec·ture (är'kĭ-tĕk'cher) *A style and method of design and construction; an orderly arrangement of parts.*

With regard to a data warehouse, an architecture facilitates the creation of a data resource that is accurate, shareable, and easily accessible throughout an enterprise. An architecture provides a blueprint that explains how the enterprise's vision, goals, and objectives of a data warehouse will be delivered. The components of this architecture include shared data, technical infrastructure, and reusable program logic. Such an architecture offers several key benefits to an enterprise, including the following:

- **More consistent data.** As common data standards and models become widely used, data consistency will become the norm in your enterprise. A good information architecture employs consistent data standards and models that are fully inventoried.

- **Simplified application development.** By intelligently designing and implementing a cohesive approach to how an enterprise creates, accesses, and modifies data, the time to implement new applications or change existing ones will be greatly reduced.

- **Better business responsiveness.** The integration of information, applications, and technology architectures will leverage an enterprise's ability to respond to business needs in a high-quality, consistent, and timely manner.

To build a data warehouse, you must establish the proper architecture first, not after development has begun. Your data warehouse architecture should be established and accepted in principle by the enterprise prior to proceeding with development. Without acceptance and support, further development efforts that target an integrated enterprise data warehouse will inevitably fail. A widely accepted architecture, along with its associated components, will explain factors such as what business functions will be supported and which decision-making functions will be enabled by a data warehouse.

What Is an Adaptable Architecture?

For companies to build a sustainable competitive advantage, they must deliver an architecture that changes faster than the business is changing. In Chapter 1, "Business Factors Driving Ubiquitous Computing," we discussed the concept of cycle time, and how the goal of faster cycle time enables a company to be more competitive. The internal information systems development function of companies is not immune to needing faster cycle time, and the way to deliver this goal is an adaptable architecture. Here's a literal definition of adaptable:

adaptable (e-dàp´te-bel) *Capable of being made suitable to, or fit for, a specific use or situation.*

Historically, information systems departments have utilized methodologies that produce rigid and inflexible architectures. These methodologies used the same system development life cycle: Analysts and designers defined a black box; got users of the system to sign off a specification; and in two to three years delivered the system. These development cycles never took into account that in their time period the business might change. Therefore, more times than not, the final system was out of synchronization with the business.

Most information systems departments that still use these methods for system development are failing, because the infrastructure that they built inhibits the ability of the company to address its shrinking business cycles.

One of the most important aspects of a data warehouse is its ability to assist the enterprise in managing shrinking business cycles. Top management is now telling information systems departments to show payback in 18 months or projects won't be approved. What users want is for the business process to drive the application—not for the application to drive the business process. Given this desire—or probably better stated, goal—you must realize you are not data driven, you are process-driven.

Data is the artifact of a process. Any change to the business is in the process and will be reflected and rippled through the data. An adaptive architecture, and adaptive systems, allows you to facilitate changes in your business processes. Taking an adaptive approach to architecture fundamentally changes how a system behaves. Specifically for data warehousing, an adaptive architecture provides users with the ability to take the data that they have always had and adds the ability to dynamically view and navigate through it. This process provides a new, dynamic behavior that is characteristic of interactive data warehousing. Everyone on the development team must understand this concept. Those who understand adaptive architectures succeed, those who do not build systems that are beautiful, but they don't fundamentally allow the type of leverage that is possible. They are simply building old style systems with a face lift.

The Data Warehousing Process

The data warehousing process prepares data from current operational system transactions into information with a historical context required by the users of the a warehouse. This data preparation includes aggregating and time-stamping the data for future analysis. The information that results from the data warehousing process allows users to perform trend analysis in a larger context on the business results that are managed by a data warehouse. The process outlined to deliver a data warehouse assists the information systems staff in the following areas:

- Assembling data for decision making.

- Transforming data into a consistent view that is usable by the business.

- Distributing data where it is needed in the business.

- Furnishing high-speed access to users with tools such as popular PC software and the Internet.

- Capturing descriptive information throughout the process that describes the discrete data elements (valid values), the relationship between data elements, the source of data elements, and the transformations that have occurred and that can be viewed by the developers and users.

Example of the Data Warehousing Process

The following is a high-level example of the data warehousing processing flow in a manufacturing system, as shown in Figure 2.1.

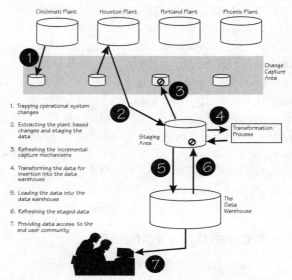

Figure 2.1 *This data warehousing process is representative of a subject-oriented data warehouse targeted at a manufacturing process. The flow of the overall process is demonstrated numerically; and though the single steps are shown to apply only to one plant for clarity, the process applies to all the plants.*

1. Database triggers capture changes within plant-based operational systems. The captured data is stored in tables that assist the data warehouse in identifying what incremental data has changed in plant applications.

2. A centralized warehouse process selects the current data from each of the updated plant tables based on the incremental changes in step 1, and inserts it into a staging area of the data warehouse; that is, into temporary tables. These tables are filled with transactions from all plants and further processed for inclusion into the data warehouse.

3. After the data is successfully inserted into the staging area, the plant update tables are refreshed to reflect the completion of the data movement.

4. Staging area data is converted into the final data warehouse transaction format.

5. The data warehouse is taken offline. The updated data is inserted into the data warehouse production tables.

6. After all of the data is successfully inserted into the data warehouse production tables, the staging area tables are refreshed.

7. The data warehouse is brought back online, making the data available to all users.

Components of a Data Warehousing Process

Many components make up a data warehousing system. This system begins with the current operational systems, part of the back-end process required to support the data warehouse, and ends with the users' tool suite from which the users access and manipulate the data in the data warehouse. In the middle is a distribution process that allows the data warehouse to support its users in a localized rather than a centralized fashion. As with other systems, underlying technologies cover all of these processes, such as security, which controls not only the feeding process for the data warehouse on the back end, but also the user accessibility on the front end of the data warehouse. The components of a data warehouse process, which we will discuss in separately in the following sections, are shown in Figure 2.2.

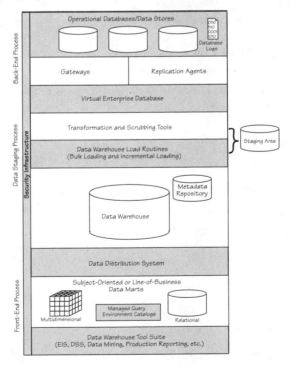

Figure 2.2 *The components of a data warehousing process include the back-end, staging area and front-end processes. Each of these items assists in the overall transformation of data managed by the operational systems to business intelligence derived from the data warehouse.*

Back-End Process

The back-end data warehousing process utilizes operational systems data stores to populate the data warehousing staging area. This process includes the following:

- **Data collection:** The data collection process for a data warehouse starts with current operational systems. This back-end processing for your data warehouse needs to be fragmented into manageable processing chunks. Operational systems generate the transactions that must be processed and entered into the data warehouse. Your data warehousing system architecture must have a way to intercept and collect data that has changed in the operational system to feed the data warehouse input processing.

- **Data gathering:** After you have collected the changes in operational data stores, data warehousing back-end processing must gather all related data to those transactions that have been collected over time. The data collection process typically only captures key information that drives the data gathering processes.

Back-end processing prepares data into a transaction base that updates and feeds the data warehousing system. This process is by far the most complex in the entire data warehousing system, because you are dealing with multiple legacy data sources, some of which may be easy to manipulate, while most may not.

The Data Staging Process

The data warehousing mid-tier process, often referred to as the data staging process, utilizes a staging area to finalize the data that will be made available to users in the data warehouse. This process works on data that is in transition; clearly, the data is neither owned by the operational systems nor the data warehouse. The data structures associated with this process are often referred to as the staging area or operational data store. The data staging process includes the following:

- **Data scrubbing:** After you have gathered all related information from operational data stores, the data must be scrubbed to give it a proper, uniform format and definition prior to its placement in the data warehouse.

- **Data placement and distribution:** After scrubbing, the data must be placed in the data warehouse—in a central location, in a remote location, or in a combination of the two.

- **Standard report compilation and indexing:** After the data has been placed in each of the data warehouse data stores, standard reports that in the data warehousing system must be compiled and indexed. After this process, the reports—much like the raw data in the data warehouse—will be made available online to users, avoiding paper distribution.

The data staging processing updates the data in the staging area of the data warehouse, making it an information base that is more digestible by the ultimate consumer, the users of the data warehouse system. This phase should focus on minimizing the down time of the data warehouse while updating its content.

Front-End Process

The data warehousing front-end process involves granting proper access to users for the information in the data warehouse as well as repopulating any catalog or metadata information required by the users' tool suite. (Metadata is described later in this chapter.) The goal of most data warehouse projects should be to drive this process into the power user's territory and out of the information systems space. However, several critical applications need to be built for the less sophisticated user. This process is similar to a traditional application development process. The tasks contained here include updating the applications that access the data warehouse with new content information as well as improving accessibility through proper view or catalog definitions in the users' tools. For example, the front-end application and overall process may present users with metadata that informs them that the financial data provided by the warehouse is accurate through the end of the latest processing time period.

Defining Individual Architectures

Defining the individual architectures that support the data warehousing process involves extensive research and discussion of the content of the architecture. The foundation of the architecture will be formulated with input from the current architectures utilized throughout the business, as well as the complete set of user requirements that drive new architecture components. Many standard models can assist in developing your own enterprise architecture, including those from technology-oriented organizations such as Sun, Netscape, Microsoft, and Sybase.

These frameworks typically define architectural components, or individual architectures, which will logically segment the overall architectural definition. The architecture components typically include applications, information, and technology. Often, architectures can also be expanded to include the organizations and business functions that support an overall enterprise. Each of these individual architectures should have its own subarchitecture, which describes its individual support of the overall business and overall architecture.

You need to determine for your organization which individual architectural components are most critical. As shown in Figure 2.3, The information packaging methodology focuses on an architecture that includes subdefinitions for applications, information, and technology. This method also ventures into the support organization because, in most companies, data warehousing redefines certain aspects of the overall information support organization.

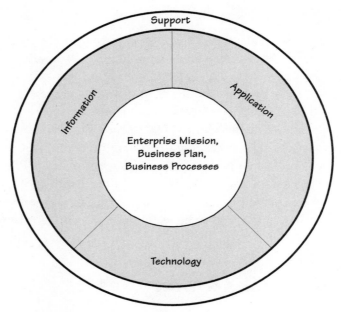

Figure 2.3 *The architecture blueprint for your data warehouse includes complete coverage of the information, application, and technology architectures required to support the business processes and mission of the company. You will also want to include information on how the architecture is supported.*

Prior to the the architecture definition and planning effort, you should obtain the support and commitment from your executive sponsor and other management personnel who are actively monitoring data warehouse activities. Support and commitment imply the allocation of personnel, budget, and time to complete the vision proposed by the architectural development effort. In individual architectures, factors such as those listed in Table 2.1 need to be fleshed out.

Table 2.1 *Individual architecture requirements.*

Architectural Area	Requirement Details
Technology	Geographic support required (dispersed or centralized). Availability. Resiliency, or the ability to recover quickly from failures in the system. Communication and network bandwidth and transmission. Network service. Security and authentication. Disconnected computing. Online and offline data storage. Client and server processing.
Data	Data synchronization. Latency tolerance. Local and other read-only copies of data. Optimization of queries. Static versus dynamic optimization and access. Data size, including number of databases, tables, views, rows, columns, indices, and so forth. Integration of multiple formats. Partitioning. Data quality.
Application	Timing requirements (example: within five days of the close of accounting). Critical interfaces (example: this depends on successful completion of Bill of Materials process). User sophistication, analytical experience, or computer literacy. Design tools. Business function sharing. Software configuration management. Testing tools. Development environment (examples: APIs and GUIs). User tool suite (examples: executive information system, decision support system, data mining, ad hoc reporting, standard reporting, application development, and product reporting).

Information Architecture

The data warehouse target architecture contains a myriad of data components, the most important of which are the operational data stores (input sources) and the data warehouse (target). You will notice that a data warehouse is presented in Figure 2.2 as a network of databases. The subcomponents of a data warehouse include the enterprise data warehouse, the metadata repository, the data staging area, departmental and personal data marts, and multidimensional data stores. These subcomponents are documented separately, because the architecture should present a logical implementation. It is the job of the data warehouse implementation team to determine the proper way to physically implement the recommended architecture. This suggests that the implementation may well be on the same physical database rather than on separate data stores as shown in Figure 2.2.

Your information architecture is critical to the support of businesses requirements in the areas of scalability and connectivity to the business intelligence. The requirements placed on a data warehouse revolve around several characteristics, such as those discussed here:

- **Subject-oriented data:** Data in a data warehouse should be organized by subject. For example, if your data warehouse focuses on sales and marketing processes, you need to generate data about customers, prospects, orders, products, and so on. To completely define a subject area, the back-end processing may require you to draw upon data from multiple operational systems. To derive the data entities that clearly define the sales and marketing process of an enterprise, you might need to draw upon an order entry system, a sales force automation system, and various other applications.

- **Time-based data:** Data in a data warehouse should relate specifically to a time period, allowing users to capture data that is relevant to their analysis period. Consider an example in which a new customer was added to an order entry system with a primary contact of John Doe on 6/17/97. This customer's data was changed on 8/19/97 to reflect a new primary contact of Jane Doe. In this scenario, the data warehouse would contain the two contact records shown in Table 2.2.

Table 2.2 Time variant data.

customer_id	contact_id	last_name	first_name	time_stamp
199706170005	001	Doe	John	08/17/1997
199706170005	001	Doe	Jane	08/19/1997

- **Update processing:** A data warehouse should contain data that represents closed operational items, such as a fulfilled customer order. In this sense, a data warehouse typically contains little or no update processing. Typically, incremental or mass load processes are run to insert data into the data warehouse. Updating individual records that are already in the data warehouse rarely occurs.

- **Transformed and scrubbed data:** Data that is in a data warehouse should be transformed, scrubbed, and integrated into user-friendly subject areas.

- **Aggregation:** Data needs to be aggregated into and out of a data warehouse. Therefore, computational requirements are placed on the entire data warehousing process.

- **Granularity:** A data warehouse typically contains multiple levels of granularity. Data in a data warehouse normally is summarized and contain less detail than original operational data; however, some data warehouses require dual levels of granularity. For example, a sales manager may need to understand how sales representatives in his or her area perform a forecasting task. In this example, monthly summaries that contain the data associated with the sales representatives' forecast and the actual orders received are enough data; there is no requirement to see each individual line item of an order—hence, the summarized data. However, a retailer may need to wade through individual sales transactions to look for correlations that may show that people tend to buy soft drinks and snacks together. This need requires more detail associated with each individual purchase. The data required to fulfill both of these requests may exist, and therefore your data warehouse might be built to manage both the summarized data to fulfill a very rapid query and the more detailed data to fulfill a lengthy analysis process.

- **Metadata management:** Because a data warehouse pulls information from a variety of sources and data warehouse teams perform data gathering on both current data stores and new data stores, you should require that storage and management of metadata can be effectively done throughout the data warehouse process.

The information architecture of a data warehousing system clearly defines the attributes associated with how the data is managed in a corporation. In the following sections, we cover many of the items that comprise the information architecture, including: metadata, volumetrics, data transformation, data synchronization, and data cleansing. (These terms are described in the following sections.) The information architecture also contains the data models, which will be discussed in greater detail in Chapter 3, "Inforamation Modeling" of this book.

Metadata

A crucial area of a data warehouse environment is metadata, data that describes the data and processes managed by the data warehouse. In a data warehouse, metadata describes and locates data components, their origin (which may be either operational systems or the data warehouse), and their movement through the data warehouse process. The data access, data stores, and processing information have associated descriptions about the data and processing—the inputs, calculations, and outputs—documented in the metadata.

This metadata should be captured within the data architecture and managed from the beginning of a data warehouse project. The metadata repository should contain information such as that listed here:

- Description of the data model.

- Description of the layouts used in the database design.

- Definition of the primary system managing the data items.

- A map of the data from the system of record to other locations in the data warehouse, including descriptions of transformations and aggregations.

- Specific database design definitions.

- Data element definitions, including rules for derivations and summaries.

- Data element use history, including standard reports, applications, and user access routines that use the element.

It is through metadata that a data warehouse becomes an effective tool for an overall enterprise. This repository of information tells the story of the data: where it originated, how it has been transformed, where it went, and how often—that is, its genealogy or artifacts. Technically, the metadata repository also improves the maintainability and manageability of a warehouse by making impact analysis information and entity life histories available to support staff.

Volumetrics

The volume of data that will be processed and housed by a data warehouse is probably the biggest factor that determines the technology utilized by the data warehouse to manage and store the information. The volume of data impacts the warehouse in two ways: overall size and ability to load. Too often, people design their warehouse load processes only for mass loading of data from operational systems to the data warehouse. Don't fall into this trap.

When defining your information architecture, you should architect a solution that allows mass loading as well as incremental, or delta, change loading.

Mass loading is typically a high-risk area no matter what database provider you select; database management systems can only load data so fast. Mass loading also forces downtime, and you want your users to have access to a data warehouse in a nearly 24-hour, seven-day environment. Therefore, when attacking this issue you should clearly define what it takes to do the mass load, but focus more of your energy on determining how volatile the data is and what the incremental data loading strategy should be. How will you load the deltas to operational data, and at what frequency?

Gathering information to assist in determining the best responses to these questions should not be difficult. As you begin to define your information architecture, list the major data sources and monitor each of the data source's transaction activity on a daily basis. The most important information is contained in two factors, growth and volatility.

The growth factor assists in defining how quickly the data will grow over time. In a relational, SQL world, this is understanding how many *insert* statements occur—that is, the number of new instances of any data entity in major subject areas.

The volatility factor assists in defining other transaction types that occur on data, allowing you to determine which tables contain relatively static data and which tables are hot spots of activity, containing highly dynamic data. In a relational, SQL world, this is understanding *update* statement patterns. A volumetric data gathering sample is presented in Table 2.3.

Table 2.3 Operational data growth and volatility.

Data Entity	Current Rows	Growth (rows/day)	Volatility (trans/day)	Projected Annual Rows
Orders	797,508	300	100	900,000
Customers	398,754	150	3,500	450,000
Sales representatives	3,543	nil	18	4,000
Products	2,577	2	1	5,160
Suppliers	1,302	20	10	2,604

After gathering the growth and volatility information about major data entities, you can calculate annual projections and begin to determine the size impact that each entity will have on your data warehouse. Notice that, in Table 2.3, orders and customers are the most volatile data sources. The chart indicates that 50,000 new customers are added each year, and that nearly a million orders are processed each year. The sales representative data source is the closest to static data in the table. Each of the columns in the table contains relevant data, allowing you to fully calculate the projected annual rows for the data entities. The Current Rows column allows you to understand the activity up to the point when you are measuring the data. The Growth column indicates how many rows are added (in SQL terms, *inserted*) into the data entity. The Volatility column indicates how many rows are modified (*updated*) in the data entity.

The Projected Annual Rows is a calculated column derived by multiplying the Growth column by the number of business days in a year. This column should be evaluated in relation to the Current Rows column to gauge the reliability of your calculation. Another way to calculate the Projected Annual Rows is to take the Current rows column and divide it by the represented business days for which data has been captured. This number of rows can then be multiplied by the number of business days in a year to determine the Projected Annual Rows.

It is important to obtain this information from raw data sources. However, you should match the raw number against estimates from your business users. Most users can quote major numbers, such as total number of active customers, orders per year, shipments per year, and total number of sales representatives employed. These numbers often are discussed during the business planning process to determine how to establish the infrastructure supporting the business and how to allocate funds to support that infrastructure.

A data warehouse, unlike operational systems, takes these row counts and multiplies them based on a time variable. For example, if an enterprise wants to maintain information about orders for five years, the data warehouse in our example must manage five million orders and their associated entities.

The information that you derive from this exercise assists you in planning load cycles and server configurations. Some data that is highly volatile may require loads as frequently as hourly, while static data may only need to be loaded on a monthly, quarterly, or annual basis. These determinations are made in conjunction with the strategies you implement for capturing individual changes to operational data stores.

Upon completion of this discovery phase, you can assemble a comprehensive loading process schedule to assist in establishing processing requirements and other technology-oriented tasks for managing the data transition process.

Data Transformation

An information architecture needs to provide a clear understanding of transformation requirements that must be supported, including logic and complexity. Transformation tools and standards are currently immature; therefore, your data warehousing team may be required to develop its own transformation strategy without supporting tools.

Operational data stores are vast and varied. Many data stores are unsupported by these transformational tools. The tools support the popular database engines, but do nothing to advance your effort with little-known or unpopular databases. However, with the rapid growth in the data warehousing market, this situation is bound to change soon.

It is often better to evaluate and select a transformational tool or agent that supports a good connectivity tool, such as product families offered by Sybase, Information Builders, Praxis, or Platinum, rather than one that supports a native file access strategy. With an open connectivity product, your development teams can focus on multiplatform, multi-database transformations. Additionally, products such as Sybase Open Server can assist with point solutions for unsupported data structures.

Data Synchronization

In your information architecture, you also need to determine the best way to synchronize data from legacy data stores with a data warehouse. Your synchronization requirements should focus on standardization of the transformation language, staging platform, communication strategy, and support strategy. The synchronization process between a data warehouse and operational data stores can take on various architectures. Each of these synchronization options involves components on the legacy server and the data warehouse server. The primary difference in each of these synchronization techniques is their level of control and sophistication. Also, obtaining greater control and sophistication will increase the cost of your solution. Three of the most popular synchronization options are:

- **Batch file transfer:** Batch file transfer synchronization updates a data warehouse from an operational database on a periodic, batch basis. The legacy operational database continues to be updated on a transaction basis via operational systems, and on a scheduled basis, a flat file containing data changes is created and sent to the data warehouse processing environment. In this architecture, a batch program extracts data from the operational database and transfers it to the data warehouse via file transfer. A batch program in the data warehouse server later applies this data to the data warehouse database.

- **Batch processing through a gateway:** Most initial data warehouse implementations utilize a data warehouse system infrastructure that implements a batch synchronization architecture in conjunction with gateway access. This architecture involves building a batch extraction and update routine on the data warehouse server. This process utilizes a gateway to access the operational data, then transforms that data and places it either in a staging area or the data warehouse. This option allows legacy systems to supply the data warehouse with decision support data, and allows the data warehouse to off-load current operational systems for analytical and historical reporting needs.

- **Data replication:** The final synchronization option, replication, is a distributed architecture in which the data warehouse and legacy databases are treated as current by different applications during the same processing periods. The data is replicated from one of the databases to the other using replication technology. In this architecture, a client application updates data in the transaction database server, and the replication technology queues and "dequeues" the transaction information for updating the data warehouse. This architecture should be viewed as a long-term, strategic implementation plan. This architecture offers enormous flexibility for deployment of applications, which are re-engineered while reducing the cost of the infrastructure through reuse of current hardware and software.

Data Cleansing

Aside from finding tools to automate the transformation process, your team should evaluate the complexity behind data transformations. Most legacy data stores lack standards and have anomalies that can become nightmares for your development staff. Again, tools are evolving to assist you in automating transformations, including complex issues such as buried data, lack of legacy standards, and noncentralized key data. The following is a brief list of common data problems requiring data cleansing.

- **Buried data:** Often, legacy systems utilize composite keys to uniquely define data. Though these fields appear as one in a database, they represent multiple pieces of information. An example of this type of data is a vehicle identification number (VIN). Valuable information about a vehicle is buried in a VIN: the year the vehicle was produced, the manufacturer, the plant where the car was built, the model of the vehicle, and much more. When cleansing data for a data warehouse, each of these buried meanings must be extracted to make the data meaningful for analysis purposes.

- **Lack of legacy standards:** Items such as descriptions, names, labels, and keys have typically been managed on an application-by-application basis. And in many legacy systems, such fields lack clear definition. These problems also exacerbate themselves in application software. The providers of this software often offer user-oriented fields, which can be used and defined as required by a customer. Depending on your company, you will find various levels of quality in these types of fields. These data cleansing issues may cause you to write a cleansing algorithm that applies pattern matching logic to correct and standardize the data in a data warehouse. For example, if two systems are capturing customer name information, do they have clear separation in first name and last name, or is the data in one field? If the data is contained in one field, what is the standard for entry? Is that standard a first name followed by a space, then last name; or last name followed by a comma and a space, then last name; or some combination?

- **Noncentralized key data:** As companies evolved through acquisition or growth, various systems took ownership of data that may not have been in their scope. This is especially true for companies that can be characterized as heavy users of packaged application software and those that have grown through acquisition. In this scenario, the data cleansing effort typically involves a table that cross references the meaning of the decentralized key data. For example, if a company has five divisions, each with its own system to manage customers, and the same customer is managed by each division, do all systems have the same customer key? The answer is typically no. Therefore, a table that centralizes the management of the customer key would be created with columns relating back to the customer key in each of the individual divisional systems. The data cleansing process can, through this cross reference table, resolve who a customer is.

- **Data integrity:** Another critical component is a series of processes that reconcile data warehouse data to its originating source files. This process is essential for audit purposes and general confidence in the data. Through this process, you will discover operational problems with the data that otherwise would be unnoticed.

Concluding Thoughts About Information Architectures

The ultimate goal of an information architecture is to allow your development teams to create a repeatable process by which the data is extracted from current operational systems and is placed in the data warehouse in a highly optimized and correct fashion. Depending on the complexities in your data, you may be unable to find tools to automate this overall process. Tools that are currently available lack the industrial strength required by most diversified enterprises. However, this will change in time, so you should formally review such tools on a regular basis. Therefore, make sure to clearly define your needs for information architecture, including volumetrics, data transformations, data synchronization, and data cleansing. A sense of the requirements in these areas allows you to best define the proper information architecture.

Application Architecture

An application architecture determines how users interact with a data warehouse. The front-end process of data warehouses ranges from a controlled, standard reporting environment to a highly dynamic, ad-hoc, tools-driven environment. To determine the application architecture that is best for your company, evaluate the users and classify their skill set. Technology and budget also have a say in your ultimate deployment. However, for defining the architecture, you should define the what, not the how, of the application architecture. In a standard architecture, the sampling of user categories listed in Table 2.4 can assist you in determining the proper tools to outfit their reporting and analysis needs.

Table 2.4 *User category definitions.*

User Category	Definition
Power users	Technical users who require little to no support to develop complex reports and queries. These users tend to support other users and analyze data throughout an entire enterprise.
Frequent users	Less technical users who primarily interface with power users for support, but sometimes require an information systems department to support them. These users tend to provide management reporting support up to the division level in an enterprise, a narrower scope than for power users.
Casual users	Users who touch the system and computers in general infrequently. They tend to require a higher degree of support, which normally includes building predetermined reports, graphs, and tables for their analysis purposes.
System users	These users are responsible for the management and auditing of systems and data. This management includes overall accountability for the validity and interpretation of data.

Application Framework

A data warehouse is as much an application as it is a database. People often use the terms Executive Information System or Decision Support System to describe how users access a data warehouse. Whatever you call your system, it must surround a set of tools and interfaces that provide the ultimate access points between your users and your data warehouse. EIS, DSS, data mining, Online Analytical Processing (OLAP), ad-hoc reporting, business intelligence—everyone has a term—the fact is that your system will contain a little of each of these concepts. We will simply refer to your deliverable here as an application framework.

The application framework that you build to allow the user to access your data warehouse should follow some specific user interface guidelines, such as those that follow.

- **Consistency:** You should strive for consistency by providing sequences and actions that are similar in comparable situations. This consistency should extend to the standards that you follow for terminology in dialogs, prompts, error messages, menus, and help screens.

- **Error handling:** The system should provide comprehensive error handling. As much as possible, design your system so users cannot make a serious error. If an error is made, try to have the system detect the error and offer simple, concise mechanisms for handling it—including the ability to undo what caused the error.

- **Feedback:** Offer informative feedback for every operation. For frequent and minor actions, the response can be modest, such as a line of text on a message line, or even a delayed message like the ToolTips in Microsoft Windows applications. However, infrequent activities should provide substantial feedback and guiding mechanisms that lead users through the process and make it easy, much like the Wizards in many Microsoft Windows applications.

- **Shortcuts:** You should enable shortcuts for the more technically knowledgeable and frequent users of a system. As users become more aware of the capabilities in the tools to which they have access, they want to reduce the number of interactions with the framework and increase interaction with the live tools. Quicker paths to the tools and the data should be built into a framework, and users should be encouraged to investigate and utilize these shortcuts. These characteristics reduce the amount of application code that a data warehouse project team must write and—better yet—maintain.

- **Direct manipulation:** No single system has all of the admirable attributes or design features desired by a user community. Building a system with all of the desired features may be impossible. However, the concept of direct manipulation is a feature that gains the enthusiastic support of users. People talk of data warehouse access and data manipulation in various ways: wading through data; mining data; and data discovery. Whatever term you use, this access and manipulation basically allow users to focus on the content of a data warehouse, not on how to operate data warehouse applications that provide access to the data warehouse. Remember, we want users to focus on business, not technology. Your framework and the tools that are used to create your framework will guide users' ability to focus on business.

Tools Criteria

Tools must be made available to users to access a data warehouse. These tools should be carefully selected so that they are efficient and compatible with other parts of your architecture and standards. These tools must accommodate all users, though no tools fall into the silver-bullet category. Therefore, realizing that no one tool will fill all users' needs, you must define the criteria for multiple types of tools.

Figure 2.4 suggests the relationship between data warehousing tools and an application architecture. We discuss several of the tools depicted in this figure next.

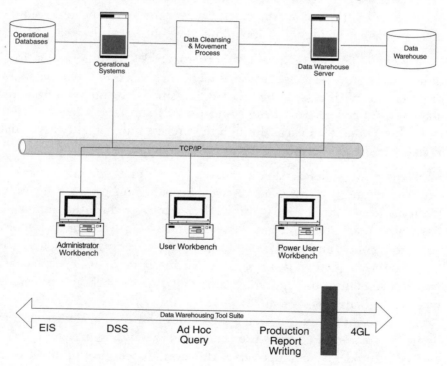

Figure 2.4 *A tools suite should encompass all of the required user tools for a data warehouse application architecture.*

Data warehouses require specialty tools to be successful. Much like the transition that companies made to office automation products, data warehouse tool suites are becoming more and more popular. If you evaluate office automation products, you will quickly realize that you can perform spreadsheet-like functions in a word processor, word processing in a spreadsheet, presentations in a word processor, or databases in a spreadsheet.

However, tools in office automation suites are specifically designed for spreadsheet, word processing, presentation, and database tasks. It makes sense that you buy all of them and use the right tool for the right job. With the boom in the personal computing industry, these tools have become economically priced to allow everyone to purchase a complete suite. Data warehouse tools are beginning to display similar separation; no one-size tool fits all. When selecting your tool suite, you will find unique requirements for the following (and potentially more) tasks.

- **Executive information systems (EISes):** These tools transform data into information and present that information to users in a meaningful and usable manner. These tools support advanced analytical techniques and free-form data exploration, allowing users to easily transform data into information. The "E" in EIS previously stood for Executive. But while these tools still exist in today's market, the "E" now should be characterized more as Everyone's, as in Everyone's Information System. EIS tools tend to give their users a high-level summarization of key performance measures to support decision making. These tools fall into the big-button syndrome, in which an application development team builds a nice standard report with hooks to many other reports, then presents this information behind a big button. When the user clicks the button, magic happens. Maps appear with regions colored, raised, and blinking alerts. Clicking a region drills down and reveals a graphical representation of a summary forecast and actual numbers. Buttons link to relevant news articles, and so on.

- **Decision support systems (DSS):** While EIS tools traditionally targeted executives, DSS tools target a more technical knowledge worker, who requires more flexibility and ad hoc analytical capabilities. DSS tools allow users, as one vendor put it, "to tiptoe through their data." This phrase characterizes the more free flowing, analytical style that knowledge workers utilize to browse their data, transforming it into information. These tools avoid the big-button syndrome and may assist the knowledge workers in creating EIS systems. However, these DSS tools traditionally have worked off a highly summarized data extract, which often is placed in a proprietary, multidimensional database.

- **Ad hoc query and reporting:** The purpose of EIS and DSS applications is to allow business users to analyze, manipulate, and report on corporate data using familiar, easy-to-use interfaces. These tools conform to presentation styles that business people understand and with which they are comfortable. Unfortunately, many of these tools have size restrictions that do not allow them to access large data stores or data in a highly normalized structure, such as a relational database, in a rapid fashion; in other words, they can be slow. Therefore, users need tools that allow for more traditional reporting against relational, or two-dimensional, data structures. These tools offer database access with limited coding and often allow users to create read-only applications. ad-hoc query and reporting tools are an important component in a data warehouse tool suite, because they off-load some types of application development to the user, lowering the cost of information systems operations. However, their greatest advantage is contained in the term ad-hoc. This means that decision makers can access data in an easy and timely fashion.

- **Production report writers:** A production report writer allows your development staff to build and deploy reports that will be widely exploited by the user community in an efficient manner. These tools are often components in fourth generation languages (4GLs), and allow for complex computational logic and advanced formatting capabilities. Data warehouses are not immune to requiring standard reports, which are typically built by information systems departments. A production report writer is utilized by these developers, and the finished product is deployed to users. It is best to find a vendor that provides an ad hoc query tool that can transform itself into a production report writer. However, these vendors are few and far between. SAS from the SAS Institute, SQR from MITI and FOCUS from Information Builders are examples of such tools that scale down and up very well.

- **Application development environments (ADEs):** Application development environments are nothing new, but many people overlook the need for them in a data warehouse tool suite. However, you need to develop some presentation system for your users. The development, though minimal, is still a requirement, and we advise that data warehouse development projects standardize on an ADE. Ease of use and rapid application development (RAD) via iterative prototyping are the hallmarks of this group.

These tools have been popular in targeted environments, such as Microsoft Windows, offering little portability. Examples include Microsoft Visual Basic and Powersoft PowerBuilder. This situation is quickly changing, and many of these tools now support the concept of cross-platform development for environments such as Microsoft Windows, Apple Macintosh, and UNIX. However, the trend appears to be driving the tool set to support, at a minimum, Internet browsing capabilities as well as application partitioning, as demonstrated by Microsoft Visual Basic, Powersoft PowerBuilder, Forte, and Dynasty tools. Web tools such as NetObjects Fusion and, Sybase's PowerSite, and Microsoft's VisualTater Dev are quickly consuming this space. Every data warehouse project team should have a standard ADE in its arsenal.

- **Other tools:** Though the tools just described represent minimum requirements, you may find a need for several other specialty tools. Many new marketplaces are arising to support the concept of tiptoeing through your data. These additional tools include online analytical processing, data mining, statistical processing, and managed query environments.

You should begin to characterize the minimum set of available tools to access the content of your data warehouse and how those tools will be managed. If you characterize your users and investigate their needs, you will find that specific tools are required by user type. Some users require all tools—the entire data warehouse tool suite—while others only require one tool or access to only standard reports.

Data Warehouse Tool Suite Requirements

The tools that you make available to users have specific requirements that will allow you to perform a more focused search based on capabilities or user needs. Samples of these requirements include the following.

- **Quick response time:** Many databases and database tables are quite large. Many tools require the return of an entire result set of a query to a client workstation prior to display of data. These tools typically are slow. Also, some tools work great when they access only one database table; however, when you join two or more tables, performance suffers. Benchmarking tools during your prototype phases allow you to better evaluate if you are buying a tool that will perform properly and consistently in your environment. What is quick response time? You need to define this; different users have different expectations, from a second to a day.

- **Time slicing:** Because some reports take additional time, the ability to submit queries that will be time sliced by the server or that can execute in the background adds great value to the user. Background processing allows the user to continue work in the tool, including the ability to create additional requests against the data warehouse.

These time-sliced reports begin to formulate a strategy that is becoming more popular with the Internet's push and pull strategies. Traditional reporting and analysis work has been performed in a pull strategy—users physically using their reporting tools to pull data from a data warehouse. Solutions that offer a server-based push strategy are now alleviating the concern that reporting tools reduce productivity. Exception reporting and alarm triggering are examples of user reports that a server can managed through the use of agents that do not require user interaction. Tools not currently in the data warehouse space but support this concept include PointCast, Marimba Castanets, BackWeb, TibCo, and Data Channel.

- **File transfer:** Users want the ability to load data into a spreadsheet, presentation, or word processing document—or even into a local database—without assistance from the data warehouse development team. Again, this type of functionality can assist in off-loading processing cycles from the main data warehouse server and can add value to the process.

- **Report scheduling:** Similar to time slicing, the user should be able to submit reports on the server when they realize that the reports will run over long periods of time. If a user has an understanding that he or she is asking for a lot of data, or if a given time period is exceeded during a report, the user should be prompted to place the report in a batch schedule to be run at off peak hours or overnight. Upon completion, the report could be delivered via an e-mail interface, a personal file extract, or another, more optimal method than waiting online for the results.

- **User-designed report formatting:** Users require the capability to easily design and create their own reports. This requirement typically encompasses graphs, forms, multiple query result placements, and presentations. Many reporting tools offer style sheets or templates that allow users to easily prepare these types of reports on their own.

At this point, your application and tools architecture should begin to flesh out. Answers will be developed to questions such as: What classifications of tools are required? How will they correlate to user classifications?

You will be able to map need to class; however, you should remember that these tools are continually upgraded. You should define the *what*, not the *how*. Do not fall into the trap of over-committing too soon to a tool from a given vendor. You need to define the capabilities and some potential technologies—the *what*. Your development project teams should choose the tools that allow them to implement most effectively—the *how*.

Concluding Thoughts About Application Architectures

Your application architecture provides users with a window to view the information assets managed by your data warehouse. Usability should be the number one requirement when selecting, building, and delivering your application architecture.

The following list will help you to gauge how usable your application framework is. These items should be tested with your user community to understand the impact that the overall solution you provide will have on your organization. You should develop a set of benchmark tasks that are associated with the requirements the users define, and have the users solve the problems contained in the benchmark. Such a usability test will greatly assist your team in delivering a proper solution to your user community.

- **Time to learn:** How long does it take typical users in the target community to learn the application, the reports, and their applicability to solving information requirements? How long does it take users to access and use your data warehouse with a relevant set of data to solve a relevant information task or decision problem?

- **Rate of user error:** Error making is a critical component of system usage and therefore deserves extensive study. How many and what kind of errors are made by the users of your data warehouse in some benchmark tasks that are involved in gathering information?

- **Speed of performance:** How long does it take to carry out the benchmark tasks? How long does it take for users to have enough knowledge to make a decision? Does the application framework respond quickly to fulfill user's rapid-fire questioning?

- **Retention over time:** How well do users maintain their knowledge of the system after an hour? A day? A week? Retention may be closely linked to time to learn, and is also based on frequency of use. User testing plays an important role here, so make sure to perform these tests with a cross-section of your user community.

- **Subjective satisfaction:** How much did users like the system? This can be ascertained by interview, written survey, or directly videotaping testing sessions. You want to determine overall satisfaction and allow users to provide free-form comments and feedback on how to improve the system.

- **Usage patterns:** Empirical data should be gathered to assist in understanding the overall usage of the system. This can assist your team in understanding the usability and supportability of the system. Information gathered here will assist you in understanding which applications and data are most and least popular; as well as which are problems in the area of performance and which perform well.

No matter what, the application architecture coordinator for your data warehouse faces an immense job when deploying the system. This individual is required to provide access and customized reports to a large user community with vastly differing reporting needs. These differences include the volume of reporting, the diversity of reporting, and the access strategies involved with both of them. The challenges of providing adequate facilities and resources to support users and giving them timely solutions to their information needs are demanding.

The key to successful deployment is a good architecture that provides flexibility while reducing the requirement for fixed and standard reports. If you can build your data warehouse in an easy-to-understand manner and provide your users with the proper tools to access the data, you will achieve a high user satisfaction rating.

Delivering such solutions also raises internal information systems issues along the lines of performance, security, and ongoing support of the user community. The key to delivering such solutions is insulation. If you insulate the user from being required to understand technology such as data structures, join strategies, networks, and other highly technical things, you will be able to solve their problems. To some database administrators, this means creating a lot of security schemes on top of views in their relational database. To those who have successfully deployed data warehouses, the abstraction is even higher than that.

Technology Architecture

In the technology architectural section of your blueprint, you begin to define the hardware, software, and network topology that will support the implementation of your data warehouse. The goal of a technology architecture is to provide a technical platform that is performance engineered, scaleable, portable, maintainable, supportable, and cost effective. This architecture is composed of three major components—clients, servers, and transports—and the software to manage each of them.

- **Clients:** The client technology component comprises the devices that are utilized by users. These devices can include workstations, personal computers, network computers, personal digital assistants, and even beepers for support personnel. Each of these devices has a purpose in being served by a data warehouse. Conceptually, the client either contains a lot of software to access the data warehouse (the traditional client in the client/server model, which is known as a "fat" client) or it contains little software and accesses a server that contains most of the software required to access a data warehouse (the new model, which is paramount to the network computer and is historically known as the "thin" client). The Internet and Web support the thin client model well.

- **Servers:** The server technology component includes the physical hardware platforms as well as the operating systems that manage the hardware. Other components, typically software, can also be grouped within this component, including: database management software; application server software; Web server software; gateway connectivity software; replication software; and configuration management software.

- **Transport:** The transport component defines the technologies needed to support communications activity between the clients and the servers—often messages. This component includes requirements and decisions for wide area networks (WANs), including the incorporation of the Internet, local area networks (LANs), communication protocols, and other hardware associated with networks, such as bridges, routers, and gateways.

When defining these individual components, it is important to clearly understand the need for the technology architecture. Too often, companies establish the technology architecture without understanding the business requirements that the architecture will support.

It helps to characterize the technical architecture in everyday terms. In plumbing, the technical architecture is the pipes, fittings, and valves. In the area of electric, the technical architecture is the wires, switches, and outlets. Both of these utilities require meeting specifications to select the proper architecture: a gauge of wire to support 110 versus 220 volts; a diameter of pipe to support the water supply for a shower versus a fire hydrant. The same is true for a data warehousing system. A clear understanding of what the business needs from you data warehouse will assist you in defining the proper technical architecture.

Information with which to make the proper decisions includes volume of data, granularity of data, timeliness of data, number of users, distribution of users, distribution of facilities, distribution of administrative staff, and other characteristics germane to the data, users, and uses of your data warehousing system. Understanding these drivers will assist your staff in deriving the proper benchmarking schemes to verify that the technical architecture can and will support your business requirements. Be forewarned that proceeding with technology that is not mapped clearly to business requirements will either yield a higher cost than necessary or a failure due to undersizing. Neither of these outcomes can be viewed as a successful outcome. Therefore, each of the overall phases within the information packaging methodology will provide evidence to define and distinguish the proper technical architecture. These requirements will then be characterized on the overall purpose, including if it is a client, or receiver, process; a server, or responding, process; or a transport, or messaging, process. Upon defining these attributes, you will be able to determine the proper technical architecture.

The Architecture Blueprint

Upon the complete evaluation of the architectural requirements of your data warehousing system, your architecture team will identify the logical architecture and potential technology components that might serve your enterprise's needs. When defining the individual architectures, your team needs to analyze what the data warehouse system is required to do—fleshing out the structures and functions, and beginning to build models for the new architecture. From these models, functional requirements can be specified, and concurrence from the user community can be obtained that the resultant data warehouse will achieve the established goals. It is important to note that this phase defines what the system needs to do rather than how to do it.

The purpose of this phase is to refine the gathered requirements and to transform them into individual architectures. Your focus should be on the requirements to extract relevant data from operational data sources and on how best to provide quick access to this data via a data warehouse. An architecture, such as the one shown in Figure 2.2, should begin to formulate. Requirements should be grouped into more detailed technology areas, such as replication agents, loading processors, data scrubbing, data transformation, and connectivity. The overall architecture that is developed by the team will provide a context for all future systems development activities.

The target architecture shown in Figure 2.2 fits the needs of most enterprises. This target architecture will be valid for large enterprises; for small enterprises; for vertical industries such as banking, insurance, government, manufacturing, or retail; for centralized mainframe shops; and for highly distributed, client/server shops. The architectural planning process deliverable, or data warehouse blueprint, should include clear documentation of the following items.

- **Business requirements:** What does the business want from its data warehouse?

- **Architectural requirements:** How will you deliver what the business wants?

- **Development approach:** What is a clear definition of phased delivery cycles, including architectural review and refinement processes?

The blueprint document essentially translates an enterprise's mission, goals, and objectives for the data warehouse into a logical technology architecture composed of individual subarchitectures for the application, data, and technology components of a data warehouse. Business requirements are mapped to architectural requirements, which in turn are mapped to technology-rich product requirements.

Your blueprint should be developed in a logical sense rather than in a physical sense. For example, in home building, all houses have exterior finishes. It is required; it is logical. The physical implementation can be different for the same architecture—aluminum siding, vinyl siding, brick, wood siding, or stucco. For database components, you will state things like, "The data store for our data warehouse will support an easy-to-use data manipulation language that is standard in the industry, such as SQL." This is a logical architecture-product requirement. When you implement your data warehouse, this could be Sybase Adaptive Server Enterprise, Sybase Adaptive Server IQ, Oracle, or another database product. However, the logical definition allows your implementation to grow as technology evolves. If your business requirements do not change in the next three to five years, neither will your blueprint.

On the other hand, if you had placed a physical implementation component in your blueprint, you might be forced to change it even though business requirements had not changed. An example of this scenario is stating that the data warehouse should be implemented utilizing Digital Equipment Corporation' CMOS VAX Processor running VMS 4.1. Three to five years ago this may have been state of the art. Is it today?

An architectural blueprint is important, because it serves as the road map for all development work, and as a guide for integrating a data warehouse with legacy systems. When the blueprint is understood by your development staff, decisions become much easier. The real worth of an architecture is to give context to all system development activities. In other words, you will define the hows so that they withstand the test of time.

Summary

To deliver what is required in a data warehouse, you must establish a solid foundation infrastructure; that is, an adaptable architecture. This architecture is critical to the overall success of your data warehousing system. The deliverable from your architecture work will be a blueprint document that clearly defines what the data warehouse will contain, for what purposes, at what level of granularity, and with what level of retention. Most enterprise data warehouses start with smaller, subject-oriented data warehouses that inevitably will connect. This means that, over time, you will build an enterprise data warehouse through smaller, iterative phases. Without a proper architecture, the interconnectivity required by your data models, tools, and underlying technologies will not occur.

The adaptable architecture that you define for your data warehouse should allow for an information systems development philosophy that allows systems to be built with components. These components improve the overall quality of a system by offering shared data and reusable program logic in the technical infrastructure. With this type of standardization, support for data warehousing systems will be well defined and efficient: No more square pegs will be built to fill round holes.

An architecture offers the following characteristics:

- **Shorter lead time:** The architecture clearly defines how components plug into, or interface with, other components of a data warehousing system. The only required lead time is for the assembly process. Without an architecture you will be required to re-evaluate the proper foundation technologies as well as assembling the final solution.

- **Flexibility:** Within a data warehousing system, prefabricated parts can and will be added or removed as necessary.

- **Less expensive to produce:** Costs are cut with the shorter lead time, the simplified development process, and the higher reliability of the parts or components of a data warehousing system. The lack of an overall, adaptable architecture will increase lead times and incompatibilities between systems; ultimately forcing you to incur a greater expense.

- **Less expensive to maintain:** With well-defined standards established at the beginning of a process, the ability to add technical components or improve the quality of components is greatly enhanced. The lack of an architecture will force you to build a support organization which is familiar with a wider breadth of technologies, increasing the maintenance burden and exposing your solution to incompatible components.

This adaptable architecture is the foundation that will support user requirements and should be logical in scope. With a logical definition, the architecture will be flexible and support technology swings in the market without requiring massive change. The only time that you will be required to change your logical architecture is when business or user requirements are dramatically modified.

The physical deployment and implementation of an architecture depends on current best-of-breed technologies, allowing you to physically map the technology at any point in time. If requirements have not changed, the architecture should not change even though, at any time, the physical implementations may be different.

When working on your architecture, make sure to attend to the following.

- Focus on strategic use of technology for managing data in your enterprise. This data should be viewed as an asset, and therefore managed like other assets of value to your enterprise.

- Build models of the business that explain the business and assess the impact of changes on it. These models will assist in understanding areas that may benefit from a data warehouse as well as those in which risk may be high.

- Focus on delivering an adaptable architecture that complements the long-range business plan of your enterprise. Scaling up to the enterprise data warehouse should focus on how the business is growing and on what strategic information is required to assist executives.

- Eliminate complex and costly interfaces (typically in house-developed code) among incongruent systems with software or technology solutions that better manage the interfacing between these systems.

After your architecture is completed, you can easily assess the benefits and impact of new subject-oriented data warehouses that are added to your enterprise data warehouse as well as of the addition of new tools to assist in the management and accessibility of the warehouse. From a business point of view, your information systems staff. will also be able to easily analyze the impact of business changes on your data warehouse architecture. These business changes include items such as mergers, acquisitions, new products, and new lines of business. New systems can be developed faster and at a lower cost with a proper architecture in place. This architecture benefits the enterprise through common data, common code, and shortened requirements phases in new development projects.

This process of establishing an adaptable architecture is an integral part of the information packaging methodology. In many ways, this is the glue to bring all of the parts of the system together and to allow them to stick to each other. In the chapters that follow, we will further explore the data and process modeling activities that are integral to the information packaging methodology and to the overall architectural definition in a successful data warehousing system.

3

Information Modeling

A majority of data warehouses today are working with multi-dimensional data; business data by its very nature is multi-dimensional. The information packaging methodology comprises techniques that greatly assist you in understanding how to model and package this multi-dimensional business data for your data warehouse implementations, because it focuses on the dimensional nature of business data. For example, if you were a sales manager for cola products within the Midwest, you might want to understand key measurement data about your area. Figure 3.1 breaks out the information package, often referred to as a data cube, for the following business dimensions:

- The time period dimension, which is isolated on the month of January.

- The product dimension, which is isolated on the cola drink product family.

- The geography dimension, which is isolated on the Cincinnati area.

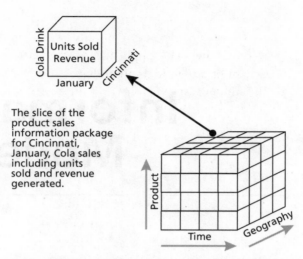

Figure 3.1 *A view of product sales information across three distinct dimensions–time, product, and geography. Based on these slices of the overall data, the user can evaluate the units sold and associate revenue for cola products sold in Cincinnati for the month of January.*

This data cube allows the user to better understand how well cola drinks sold in the Cincinnati territory during the month of January. As you can see, three dimensions are associated with this data—time, product, and geography—hence, the statement that business data tends to be multi-dimensional. The information packaging methodology offers techniques that are open to many technical architecture implementations of data warehouses and decision support databases. As you will see in the sections that follow, the information package methodology offers a uniform and complete method that covers the complete development life cycle, from data gathering techniques through to data delivery.

An information model is typically a representation of the data structure that is used in some segment of a business. Information models become part of the overall information architecture in a company. These models are particularly useful in documenting the data resources in the organization. The models provide a basis for planning and designing new information systems, or in the case of a data warehouse, subject-oriented data warehouses. The ultimate benefits derived from the information packaging methodology include as follows:

- Data consistency and availability. A stable, integrated data structure results in consistent data that can support any user need. Because the data definitions are shared by all users, it can be easily accessed. Though your enterprise may go through organizational changes or experience employee turnover, the data remains stable. The result is data documentation for the entire data warehouse.

- Cost-effective systems development and maintenance. Perhaps the most significant benefit is cost-effective systems development and maintenance. Information models act as a neutral buffer between applications and the databases that are developed. When properly built, the models are independent enough that changes to the design through the model can expedite a revamping of internal interfaces. This process results in better systems design, because the systems are based on a stable data structure.

Level of Refinement

The information packaging methodology focuses on several different levels or cuts of the information models that are derived during the process of building a data warehousing system. As shown in Figure 3.2, each level is essentially a refinement or more detailed version of the previously developed data model.

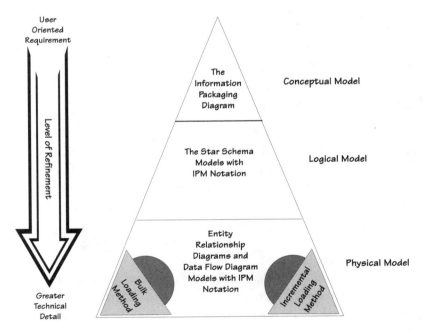

Figure 3.2 *The information packaging methodology (IPM) focuses on several diverse cuts of the overall information model managed in a data warehousing system, including a conceptual layer that is more in line with the users view of information packages, all the way to a detailed technical mapping of this model.*

By working through multiple levels of detail during design of a data warehousing system, your project team builds in quality and delivers subject-oriented data warehouses that more closely align with what the users have requested. Some of the other benefits of the information packaging methodology include the following:

- **A more precise representation of data:** The refinement of data models continually provides a more precise representation of the data that is involved in delivering a data warehouse.

- **Planning for project deliverables:** As the process unfolds, enough analysis will be completed to plan complete implementation and deployment schedules. These models will verify, and in many ways guarantee, that the data models and their associated subject-oriented data warehouses will be successfully integrated and reused.

- **Discovery and validation:** The refinement of data models also is the beginning of work on an overall integration of an enterprise data warehouse. The greater the detail is, the better is the understanding of that which the future environment will consist. This process will also assist in the discovery and validation of previously developed work breakdown structures and activity plans.

The Information Package Diagram

The first and most generalized level of an information model is its information package diagram. This model focuses on the data gathering activities for the users' information packaging requirements. An information package diagram defines the relationships between subject matter and key performance measures. The information package diagram has a highly targeted purpose, providing a focused scope for user requirements. Because information package diagrams target what the users want, they are effective in facilitating communication between the technical staff and the users, indicating any inconsistencies between the requirements and what the data warehouse will deliver. Figure 3.3 presents an information package diagram that captures the relevant information model, allowing users to evaluate and analyze sales performance. We will further investigate this information package diagram later in this chapter in the section "Data Gathering Through Information Package Diagrams."

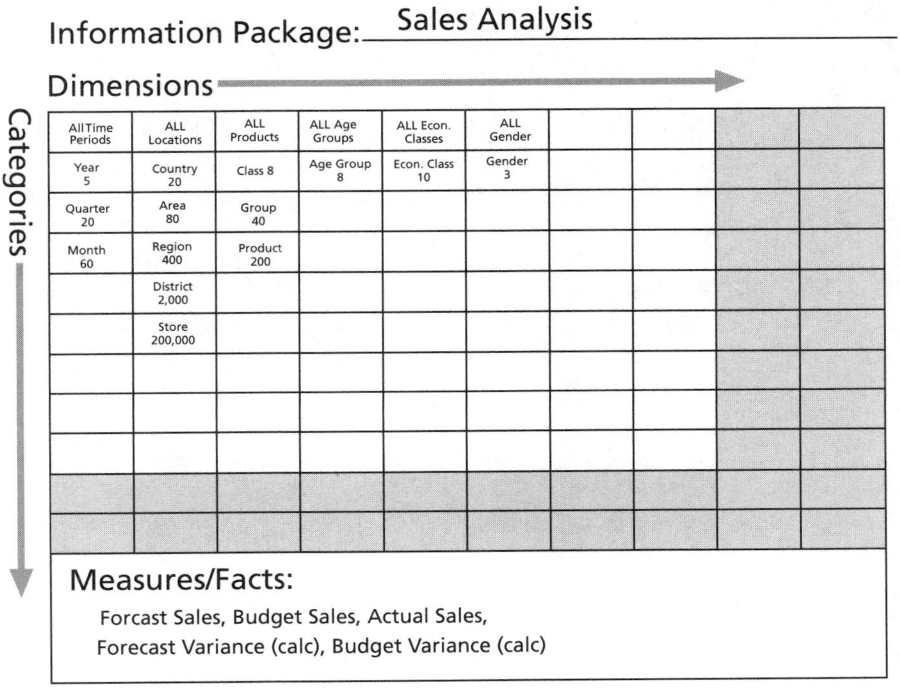

Information Package: Sales Analysis

Dimensions ⟶

Categories ⟶

All Time Periods	ALL Locations	ALL Products	ALL Age Groups	ALL Econ. Classes	ALL Gender			
Year 5	Country 20	Class 8	Age Group 8	Econ. Class 10	Gender 3			
Quarter 20	Area 80	Group 40						
Month 60	Region 400	Product 200						
	District 2,000							
	Store 200,000							

Measures/Facts:

  Forcast Sales, Budget Sales, Actual Sales,
  Forecast Variance (calc), Budget Variance (calc)

Figure 3.3 *This information package diagram depicts user requirements for performing sales analysis. It allows users to evaluate sales metrics by time, product, location, and customer demographics.*

The Star Schema Data Model with IPM Notation

The second level of an information model is a star schema with the information packaging methodology (IPM) notation set, which adds refinement to the structure of the data. Entities are defined and characterized with specific purposes to assist users. These entities are characterized as follows: measure entities with fact-based content, dimension entities with navigational content, and category detail entities with subject-descriptive content. Also, a star schema begins to define attributes, or columns, that are contained in each of the major entities and the relationships among those entities. A star schema data model provides more depth in preparation of fully defining the physical data entities. Again, this design is validated with the user community to clarify the process of decision-oriented data and the requirements for additional supporting data, further detailing the original information package diagram. The star schema representing the information contained in Figure 3.3's information package diagram is presented in Figure 3.4. We will further investigate the star schema data model later in this chapter.

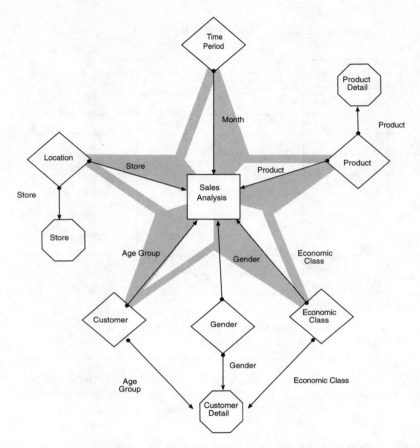

Figure 3.4 *This star schema presented with the information packaging methodology notation set depicts the logical model for the information package diagram in Figure 3.3. The information packaging methodology notation set applies a common set of colors and shapes to entities, allowing the design team to better communicate the purpose of individual entities in the information model.*

The Physical Data Model

The third level of a data model is a fully attributed data model, which becomes part of an enterprise's information architecture. The star schema data model should be used as a foundation for physical database design and implementation, because it specifies what data should be included and the relationships among these entities. This data model represents an information package in the greatest amount of depth and detail. The physical data model representing the information contained in Figure 3.3's information package diagram is presented in Figure 3.5. We will further investigate how to finalize the physical data model later in this chapter in the section titled "Building the Physical Model."

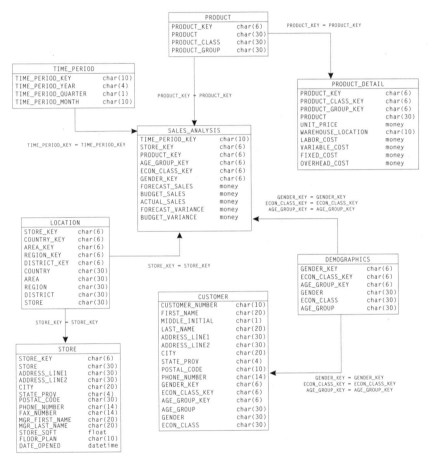

Figure 3.5 *This physical data model depicts the physical model for the information package diagram in Figure 3.3. The transformation that occurs between the logical data model and physical data model follows a fairly traditional normalization process.*

Many of the unique modeling transformations within a data warehouse include the denormalization of entities such as dimensions. My experience has been that de-normalization of the operational tables provides useful data warehouse objects without requiring a lot of manipulation from the client application. While de-normalization can be at times controversial with database purists, the price of disk is quickly becoming an insignificant cost, and the results of de-normilzation include a more useful product for the user. Not to mention the performance savings you will experience by avoiding dynamic or user defined joins! This final model will optimize the data warehousing system's ability to perform queries to fulfill the user requirements.

Data Gathering Through Information Package Diagrams

Data gathering within the information packaging methodology is performed with an information package diagram. This tool assists an analyst in gathering the user requirements for an information package. An information package diagram provides a common, consistent, and coherent design and communication tool. This diagram conveys the right information at the right time to those who understand its purpose. It models a user's required information package. The information package diagramming technique is a productive way to define and communicate user business query requirements, or information package requirements. The information package diagram assists in performing the following tasks:

- Defining the common dimensions utilized in a business, such as time, customer, geography, and product.

- Designing key business measures that can be tracked to determine how a business is performing and operating.

- Deciding how data should be presented to the user of a warehouse.

- Determining how the user aggregates, or rolls up, data along common hierarchies.

- Deciding how much data is involved in a user's analysis or query.

- Defining how data will be accessed, what its entry points are, where the user wants to go, and how the data will be navigated.

- Establishing data granularity.

- Estimating the size of a warehouse.

- Determining the frequency of refreshing the data in a data warehouse.

- Formulating how information should be packaged for distribution to the user.

An information package diagram presents the conceptual definition of the users' required information package. A blank information package diagram is shown in Figure 3.6. Note the line at the top of the information package diagram is used to write a unique information package description. You may choose to augment this description with a summary description, detail description, or both to identify what the information package diagram describes. From there, you work with users to further define and describe the proper packaging of data warehouse information.

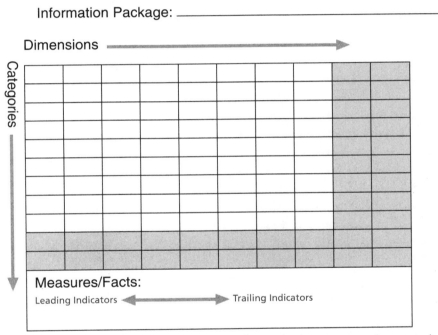

Figure 3.6 *An information package diagram for gathering user requirements in the conceptual data modeling phase of the information packaging methodology.*

In the remaining sections of this chapter, we will analyze, dissect, and formulate an information package for the following user requirement:

Users of a data warehouse need to see product revenues detailed by demographic information about their customers; these demographics include age, gender, and economic class. This information should be presented by the users' store locations and present product sales information for the last five years. The product sales information should include revenues presented in budget, forecast, and actual figures.

Defining Key Performance Measures

A *measure* (also referred to as a key performance measure, a fact, a key business measure, or an indication) is a piece of data that measures business information along dimensions. Measures are typically quantities, capacities, or money that are ascertained by comparison with a standard. These data points are used for the quantitative comparison of business performance. For example, product revenues in dollars, wasted raw materials in pounds, new minority hires as a count, or plant up time in hours are measures.

In the user requirement described above, the measures included:

- Budget revenue from product sales.

- Forecast revenue from product sales.

- Actual revenue from product sales.

A key to building successful information packages is guaranteeing that users can have multiple performance measures from which to report. Combining measures with dimensions provides an extremely useful model that allows users to gain significant insight into their business and its trends. For a measure to be valid, there must be some way of relating it to each dimension in the information package. When we get to the physical implementation, we will further verify this type of relationship. However, you may want to begin your investigation now. If a given measure is only valid or referenced by certain dimensions, you may want to complete multiple models on separate information package diagrams. When information packages are implemented on a relational database, we can perform SQL join logic to bring the information together at a later date, and therefore support the concept of cross-correlating measures.

You write the names of the required and related measures in the box at the bottom of your information package diagram, as shown in Figure 3.7. When considering the measures, it is important to also think about derived or calculated measures. Often, after the initial design users will request that you include precalculated measures. When considering these special forms of data, determine how they might impact key performance measures, and specifically if they will further inform the user. Here are two examples of precalculated measures:

- Forecast Variance = Forecast Revenue - Actual Revenue.

- Budget Variance = Budget Revenue - Actual Revenue.

Defining Dimensions

A *dimension* is a physical property, such as time, location, or product, that is regarded as a fundamental way of accessing and presenting business information. Consider two examples:

- The time dimension comprises all days of the year, the weeks of the year, the months of the year, and possibly multiple years.

- The location dimension comprises all cities in which your company has offices, the districts that contain those cities, the regions that contain those districts, and the countries that contain those regions.

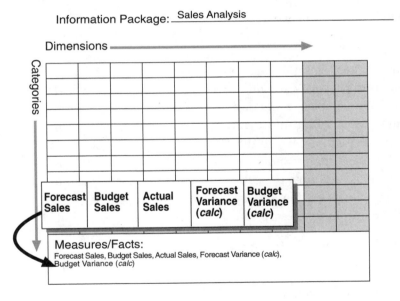

Figure 3.7 *The business measures for an information package are placed in its bottom box labeled "Measures/Facts," labeled measures, on an information package diagram. These measures need to relate to all of the dimensions, or access paths, defined in the user requirements.*

A dimension typically acts as an index for identifying quantitative and qualitative data. We commonly think of standard reports that present rows and columns as two dimensional. A manager who is evaluating a budget may look at a two-dimensional spreadsheet containing accounts in the rows and cost centers in the columns. The intersecting point between the rows and columns, or a cell, contains relevant numeric information about the specific cost center and account, such as product development's salary budget.

It logically follows that multidimensional refers to information that is defined as, or accessed by, more than two dimensions. In a geometric world, the easiest description of a multidimensional entity is a cube. The cube has three dimensions: width, height, and depth. Surprisingly, most business models are actually represented in a multidimensional view. The budgetary example described above contains two dimensions, cost center and accounts. In reality, this example is missing a very important dimension, time.

Most financial analysts evaluate their data with a minimum of these three dimensions. Pick up a publicly traded company's annual report, turn to the pages that give the overview of performance, and you will see information about how the company has performed over time, typically three to five years. You will see graphs and charts representing important business measures, such as sales revenues, expenses, profit, stock performance, and earnings per share, tracked over multiple dimensions, such as time, product, and division.

An information package diagram provides a technique for modeling user information in a multidimensional space. This design provides a visual representation of a business analyst's mental model of an information package. This diagram provides a solid design that is both simple and fast. If you think of a Rubik's Cube, solving the puzzle is similar to the way a business analyst moves through multidimensional data. Each analyst has a different way to twist and turn the cube until the desired result is found, much in the way that different people have different ways to solve the puzzle.

In the user requirement described earlier, the dimensions included:

- Products that are sold.
- Age group of the customer.
- Gender of the customer.
- Economic class of the customer.
- Location of the sale to the customer.
- Time periods for the last five years.

The dimensions can now be placed on an information package diagram, as shown in Figure 3.8. Remember, the dimensions are the high-level paths that the user requires to gain access to the measurement data. Each dimension presents a uniform access path into the information contained in the data warehouse. These dimensions also typically define a complete subject classification, or grouping of data, that will be used as reference material to support the key business measures. When defining dimensions, be careful to cover only the primary paths for the information; do not try to cover all of the possibilities.

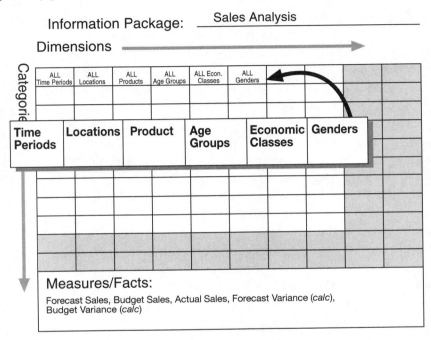

Figure 3.8 *The dimensions are placed in the top row of an information package diagram. The dimensions indicate how users traverse the data to understand the meaning contained in the measures of an information package.*

Each of the dimensions is written in a column of the first row of an information package diagram. To designate that this row contains the high-level dimension definition, utilize the word ALL. Example: ALL Time Periods and ALL Locations.

Tip: When working with an information package diagram, try to minimize your access paths, or dimensions. This helps the user by simplifying the manner in which the data is obtained. Keep the number of dimensions within a reasonable number, such as under 10. This is not a fixed limit, and many information models require a larger number of dimensions. However, usability is hampered when you exceed this number. Usability should be the number one focus of your warehouse project. The shaded columns on an information package diagram remind you of this usability tip.

Defining Categories

Categories provide detail information for a given dimension. Often, these details are referred to as the aggregation levels or the hierarchy of the dimension because the information that comprises a dimension is typically hierarchical data that summarizes, or aggregates, upward. A *category* is a division specifically defined in a dimensional hierarchy that provides a detailed classification system. This discrete member of a dimension is used to identify and isolate specific data. For example, San Francisco and Western Region are categories in a location dimension. Similarly, December and Quarter 4 are categories in a time dimension.

Following the definition of your key dimensions, you need to further define how the user will navigate to the detail information, or how the data will be aggregated. On an information package diagram, categories are contained in the cells of the dimension's column. As shown in Figure 3.9, you should place the category's name and an estimate for the number of data points represented by that category in the cell of your information package diagram. These numbers assist in many areas, including usability and data sizing.

You should keep the ratio of categories between levels reasonable. If the numbers becomes too high, you may want to insert an artificial level in the dimension hierarchy to refine navigation for the user, as shown in Figure 3.10. This action is typically taken to improve the usability of the dimension and information package. An indication that an artificial category is needed typically is in the ratio between levels.

Tip: The relationship between category levels and a dimension should be under a 1:10 ratio. This assists the user in navigating and understanding the data. This is not a fixed limit, and many information models require a larger ratio between dimensions and categories. However, usability is hampered when you exceed this number. Usability should be the top focus of your warehouse project. The shaded rows on an information package diagram remind you of this usability tip.

Figure 3.9 shows reasonable ratios: five years to 20 quarters, or a 1:4 ratio between levels. It also shows 20 quarters to 60 months, or a 1:3 ratio between levels. On the other hand, Figure 3.10 shows an unreasonable ratio between location category levels, 50 states to 150,000 customers, or a 1:3,000 ratio. To correct this situation, an artificial category has been placed in the hierarchy to allow the user to navigate customers via an alphabetizing system. Inserting the alphabetizing category might reduce the ratio to 1:115, a much more reasonable number.

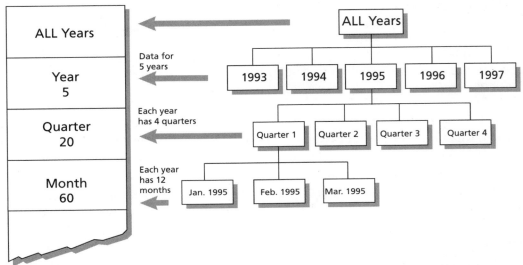

Figure 3.9 *Categories provide the detail required to build a complete dimension. The category levels define a hierarchy that will be important for assisting the user in filtering, aggregating, and visualizing key performance measures. This figure defines the categories for a time dimension.*

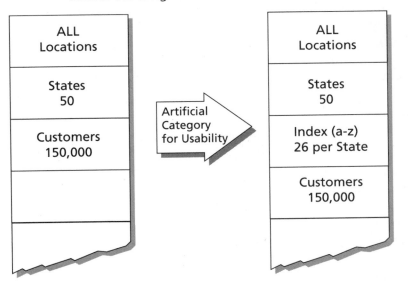

Figure 3.10 *Often, it is necessary to manage the category levels in the dimensional hierarchy through the use of artificial categories. Here, the ratio from States to Customers is far too high, so an alphabetic category has been inserted to assist the user in navigating the customer dimension.*

Tip: If you get in a situation in which you exceed a reasonable ratio between category levels, you can place an artificial category in your information package that logically organizes the category level into a manageable ratio. A ratio between category levels that exceeds 1:150 should be further analyzed for applying this tip. This is not a fixed limit, and many information models require a larger ratio between category levels. But, usability is hampered when you exceed this number.

Category level ratios also play a key role in assisting you with sizing the data contained and managed in an information package. While gathering the information about how many potential values exists for a category, you should obtain information on the density of the rows that the information package defines. Density is a term often used with multidimensional databases to refer to the percentage of possible combinations for data compared to the actual data. If a relatively high percentage of dimension combinations exists, the data is referred to as *dense*. When a relatively low percentage of the dimension combinations exists, the data is referred to as *sparse*.

For example, an antique shop that contains products such as chairs, tables, books, pictures, artwork, and other rare collectibles is unlikely to sell all products in a given month. It follows that the intersection of time and product dimensions will be sparse, because many products in the inventory will not be sold each month. On the other hand, a grocery store with food products such as bread, vegetables, fruits, and snacks is likely to sell all products in a given month, turning over its inventory. The grocery store will therefore have a dense relationship between time and product dimensions, because each product will be sold in a month.

Performance is greatly impacted by the size of an information package, because the size is a direct reflection of the number of data rows that must be read or scanned to obtain a result. Depending on how dense the data is that your information package diagram represents, you may choose to take action to minimize performance implications. These actions occur during the physical implementation of the data warehouse and include either utilizing software (indexing technology) or hardware (parallel processing) to minimize performance impact.

Tip: Try to insert the numbers that represent the unique occurrences of a category value in your category cells. These numbers assist you in understanding the volume of potential data and the relationships on types of data that could greatly impact the size of your warehouse. This data assists you if you need to split an information package in the future.

Figure 3.11 demonstrates an information package diagram through the category definition phase. Each dimension is listed in the column headings. The cells that comprise a column are filled with their associated category title and the number of unique occurrences that will potentially exist in the information package. At the bottom of the information package diagram, the key measures or facts that are important to the user are also listed. This information package, as stated early in this chapter, represents business data in a multidimensional fashion. Someone who desires to analyze the data can now look across six dimensions (time, location, product, age group, economic class, and gender) and evaluate business measures (forecast sales, budget sales, actual sales, and their associated variances).

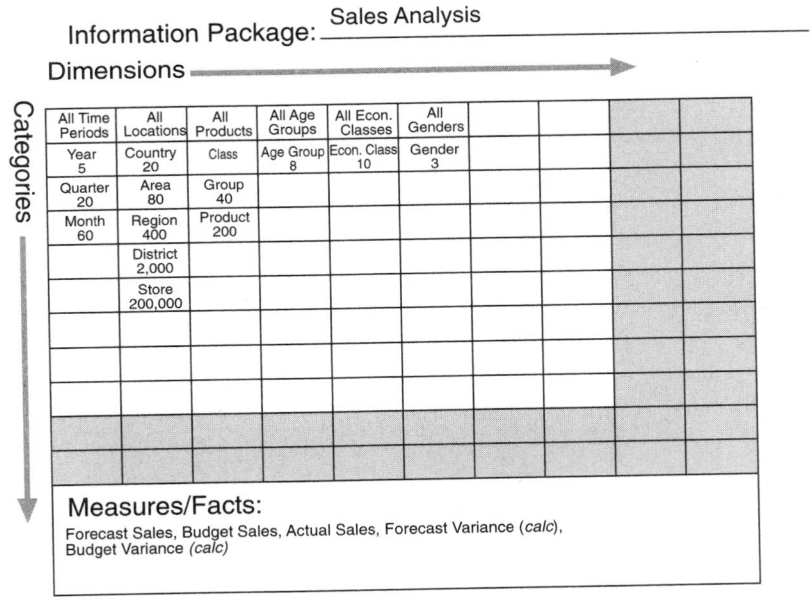

Information Package: Sales Analysis

Dimensions →

	All Time Periods	All Locations	All Products	All Age Groups	All Econ. Classes	All Genders				
	Year 5	Country 20	Class	Age Group 8	Econ. Class 10	Gender 3				
	Quarter 20	Area 80	Group 40							
	Month 60	Region 400	Product 200							
		District 2,000								
		Store 200,000								

Categories ↓

Measures/Facts:
Forecast Sales, Budget Sales, Actual Sales, Forecast Variance *(calc)*, Budget Variance *(calc)*

Figure 3.11 *After you have a clear understanding of the categories and levels of a dimensional hierarchy, you place them in the cells underneath the dimension on an information package diagram.*

The detail required by users for proper analysis and reporting of data determines how many categories you define. It isn't necessary that the levels in each dimension be perfectly balanced. Balanced means that every dimension is represented with even hierarchies that provide the same level of detail. For example, a time period dimension that is represented by a hierarchy made up of year, quarter, and month would be balanced if each measurement was represented down to the month. This is often not the case. In fact, it is quite typical that the data is unbalanced. For example, the business may desire the measurement data to be represented to the month for two trailing years and to the quarter for the prior three years. Make sure to capture the potential levels required and make sure to document any anomalies along the way. They may become more important as you near physical implementation of your data warehouse.

Defining Multiple Hierarchies or Access Paths

Often, users request relative categories. These are categories that change in definition relative to the moment that the information is queried. Again, the best example involves time periods. The definitions that we have shown for time comprise a clean hierarchy of year to quarter to month. Now, let's say that your user desires to see multiple hierarchy definitions pointing to the data, such as day of the week (Monday through Sunday), holiday business (Easter, Christmas, Fourth of July), month to date, quarter to date, year to date, or last 90 days.

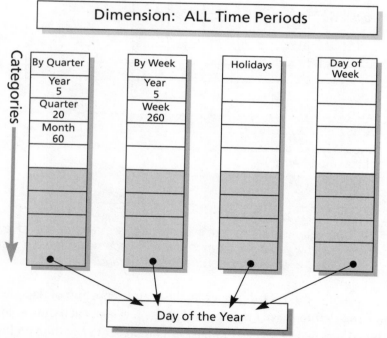

Figure 3.12 *Often, a dimension contains multiple hierarchies, or access paths, allowing the user to slice or aggregate the data in different ways. This dimensional access path diagram demonstrates the multiple access paths supported in the time dimension.*

When you gather the information, you want to document these special definitions in a chart, as shown in Figure 3.12. In your information package diagram, clearly document the primary access path; this is the access path that will be predominately used. However, other access paths should be defined on the dimensional access path diagram, as shown in Figure 3.12. These multiple access paths will be important during physical data definition.

Another multiple access path example, which often occurs in sales analysis, is redefining the location dimension by physical geography as well as by management structures. In this situation, it may not initially be clear whether this will be two separate dimensions or the same dimension with multiple access paths. Document this and move on. Research from other information packages may resolve the issue. If, after you complete all of your information package diagrams, this has not been resolved, experiment with giving the data separate dimensions versus multiple access paths. Let the user be the ultimate judge through the user interface.

Define Category Details

In an information package diagram, each cell in a dimension is a category and represents an isolated level that might require more detail information to fulfill a user's information package requirements. The detail information required by a user typically includes textual matter that supports the measurement data and provides more detail or qualitative information to assist in the decision making process. In an information package diagram, those categories that require more detail data should be indicated by shading the designated cell, highlighting it for further analysis in the information modeling refinement process, as shown in Figure 3.13.

Logical Data Modeling: Star Schema Design with IPM Notation

Data warehouses are best modeled with a technique known as star schema modeling. The star schema is optimized for query-based activities versus traditional database modeling techniques such as normalized schema models. Normalized schema models contain natural entities and their associated relationships. However, they provide an irregular structure for query processing and user comprehension. By contrast, star schema models define data entities in a way that supports the decision makers' view of the business as well as the data entities that reflect the important operational aspects of a business. This is because a star schema contains within the information packaging methodology three logical entities: dimension, measure, and category detail entities. A star schema is optimized to queries, therefore providing a database design that is focused on rapid response to the users of a system. Also, the design that is built from a star schema is not as complicated as traditional database designs. Hence, the model also is more understandable by users of a system. Users can better understand the navigation paths available to them through interpreting a star schema. This logical database design's name hails from a visual representation derived from the data model: It forms a star, as shown in Figure 3.4.

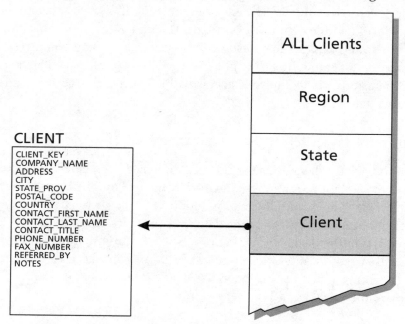

Figure 3.13 *Often, a category points to measurement data, a level in a dimension hierarchy and additional textual, or qualitative data. This type of category should be clearly indicated as a category detail entity. This figure demonstrates such a category a client category detail entity in the ALL Clients dimension.*

In the information packaging methodology, the information package diagrams provide the conceptual basis for a logical star schema and allow for the star schema to be easily generated. The star schema defines the join paths for how users access the facts about their business or the information packages defined in information package diagrams.

Entities in a Star Schema

Within the information packaging methodology, a star schema, like the data warehouse it models, contains three types of logical entities: measures, dimensions, and category details. Each of these entities performs a specialized function. When modeling an information package, it is important to graphically represent each entity in your logical data model. Traditional data models do not utilize the power of a graphical model to depict anything; they simply organize the information into entities (boxes) and relationships (arrows). No significance is placed on how the entities are drawn graphically and what functionality the entity provides to the overall model. When detailing a data model in the information packaging methodology, we utilize the graphical symbols and colors depicted in Figure 3.14 for each mentioned entity.

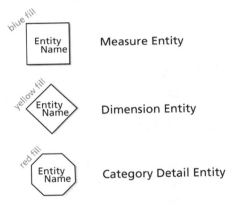

Figure 3.14 Symbols and colors for graphically representing data warehouse logical entities is a unique feature of the information packaging methodology. The star schema with IPM notation allows developers and sophisticated users to clearly understand the purpose and functionality provided by each entity within any information package modeled. A measure entity should be depicted in blue, a dimension entity in yellow, and a category detail entity in red.

These symbols show common characteristics for the entities that they represent. You will find in modeling a star schema that a business has many common dimensions, measures, and category details. As a result, the stars begin to collide and overlap. This problem makes it difficult to present a star schema at the enterprise level. However, with an information package diagram, a conceptual model of user requirements, the star schema model for logically depicting the data models, and common entity characteristics, you can simplify your data models for analysis purposes with the information packaging methodology notation set (IPM notation) shown in Figure 3.14. With these graphical representations, your project team and sophisticated users can visually understand the information package managed by a data warehouse, its associated entities, and the functions of each entity.

Measure Entities

The information package diagram represented in Figure 3.11 is a good starting point for understanding a measure entity. This information package diagram defines a sales analysis information package. In a star schema, the center of the star—and often the focus of users' query activity—is the measure entity, the low-level contents of an information package modeled in an information package diagram. The data contained in a measure entity is factual information from which users derive *business intelligence.* This data is therefore often given synonymous names to measure, such as key business measures, facts, metrics, performance measures, and indicators. The measurement data provides users with quantitative data about a business. As stated earlier, this data is numerical information that the users desire to monitor, such as dollars, pounds, degrees, counts, and quantities. These key indicators allow users to look into their corporate knowledge base and understand the good, the bad, and the ugly of the business processes being measured.

The data contained in measure entities grows large over time and therefore is typically of greatest concern to your technical support personnel, database administrators, and system administrators. As an example of data's potential for growth, imagine the largest retail store's cash register receipts in one of these entities—that is a lot of data! A measure entity is where this type of data will be managed in a data warehouse.

Within IPM notation, a measure entity is represented by a rectangle shaded in blue, and placed in the center of a star schema diagram, as shown in Figure 3.15. The placement in the center of the star is due to this entity's focus; the measurement data will be contained in a majority of the user's query activity. Though the transformation from an information package diagram to a star schema presents a logical data model, these entities will typically become physical entities in a data warehouse as we refine the information model.

A measure entity represents a set of related facts, and often corresponds to a real-world transaction or an event such as a shipment or sale. The measure entity typically represents a summary level of a real-world transaction and is related to just one point in every associated dimension. Characteristics of a measure entity include the following:

- Provides a primary focus for quantitative data, business measure data, or factual data.

- Contains numerous access paths, dimensions, or pointers into measurement data.

- Encompasses relatively normalized data.

- Comprises the lowest categories in each dimension and the measures from an information package diagram.

- Can grow to become very large tables.

- Will be the heart and soul of analytical activity.

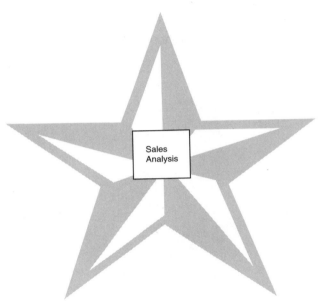

Figure 3.15 *In the information packaging methodology, the measure entity is placed in the center of a star schema and utilizes a blue rectangle in IPM notation.*

Dimension Entities

Dimension entities are much smaller entities than measure entities. The dimensions and their associated categories, or hierarchies, allow users of a data warehouse to browse measurement data with ease and familiarity. These entities assist users in minimizing the rows of data returned during queries from within a measure entity, and the dimension entity also assists users in aggregating key measurement data. Both of these tasks are required to fulfill a user's information request. In that sense, these entities filter data or force the server to aggregate data so that fewer rows are returned from measure entities. In IPM notation, the dimension entities are represented as the points of a star schema.

Dimension entities are utilized by users of a data warehouse as navigational aides to filter and aggregate data in measure entities. In IPM notation, a dimension entity is graphically represented by the traditional flow chart symbol for filtering, shaded in yellow. In Figure 3.16, the time, location, product, age group, gender, and economic class dimensions demonstrate the proper notation. This visual representation of the dimension entity correlates to the entity's major function of restricting the result set rows returned from user query activity. But, as will be demonstrated later, dimension entities also form a common link between entities of a data warehouse, including measure-to-measure relationships and measure-to-category detail relationships.

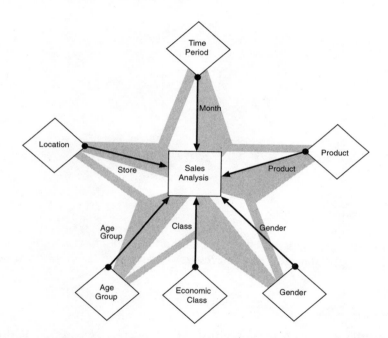

Figure 3.16 *A dimension entity is placed at the points of a star in the information packaging methodology and utilizes a yellow diamond, or filter symbol, in IPM notation.*

Characteristics of a dimension entity include the following:

- Represents the dimensional hierarchy.

- Has primary foci of navigation and filtering measure entities.

- Encompasses relatively denormalized entities.

- Contain codes, or keywords, and their related description for an entire dimensional hierarchy.

- Maps to the columns of an information package diagram.

- Are typically small tables when physically implemented.

- Provides the gateway to a data warehouse.

- Is often used to fill pick lists, such as list combo boxes, in front-end graphical applications.

Category Detail Entities

In an information package diagram, each cell in a dimension is a category and represents an isolated level in a dimension that might require more detail information to fulfill a user's information package requirements. Those categories that require more detail data are managed in category detail entities. These entities have textual matter that supports the measurement data and provides more detail or qualitative information to assist in the decision making process. Category detail entities, such as measure entities, typically translate into a physical database table. These entities map relatively cleanly to transaction database structures and may in fact be mapped that way to a data warehouse in situations where the transaction database can support query loads. (This circumstance is infrequent.)

A category detail entity corresponds to a real-world entity or object, such as a customer, store, or market. These entities contain data that provides more qualitative information to users and assists in supporting the decision making process. The stop sign symbol, shaded in red, graphically depicts these entities, as shown in Figure 3.17. This visualization tool has been chosen because users typically flow through the dimension entities to get the measure entity data, then stop their investigation with supporting category detail data.

Some common attributes of a category detail entity are as follows:

- Contains data for reference and support information to complete the intelligence of measurement data.

- Provides data that is more qualitative.

- Maps closely to transaction structures.

- Typically contains normalized data structures.

- Is represented by an individual cell, or a category, on an information package diagram.

- Typically contains a medium amount of data rows—less than measure entities and more than dimension entities.

- Contains descriptive, or qualitative data—not merely numbers.

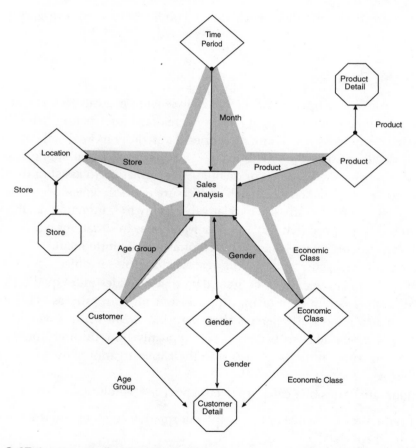

Figure 3.17 *A category detail entity is placed on the perimeter of a star schema, outside the dimension entities. This entity is represented by a red stop sign symbol in IPM notation.*

Defining the Star Schema Logical Attributes

Optimization originates from an information package diagram, or conceptual understanding of a user's requirements. When defining information requirements through an information package diagram, we focus on manageable information packages and usability. The true power of a star schema design is to model a data structure that allows filtering, or reduction in result size, of the massive measure entities during user queries and searches. A star schema also provides a usable and understandable data structure, because the points of the star, or dimension entities, provide a mechanism by which a user can filter, aggregate, drill down, and slice and dice the measurement data in the center of the star.

Now, we will demonstrate how to translate an information package diagram into a star schema. Each star represents an information package diagram and its associated information package. The measure entity is placed in the middle of the star. To define the logical measure entity, you take the lowest category, or cell, in each dimension of an information package diagram, along with each of the measures and make them attributes in a logical data entity, as illustrated by Figure 3.18.

Tip: Measure entities are composed of the keys to the detail, or lowest level, category in each dimension of an information package diagram. Each column must relate to all measures on the information package diagram. At this point, determine whether you will store calculated measurements. It is wise to estimate the overhead of users calculating the measurement data each time they access an information package versus the additional storage space and processing time required to precalculate the measurement data.

To define the logical dimension entities, take each category or level of a dimension on an information package diagram and make it an attribute in the logical dimension entity. These logical data entities will be further transformed into physical database entities, as will be discussed in the "Physical Database Design" section later in this chapter. Dimension entities may span information package diagrams, so at this point make sure that you consolidate on a standard definition per dimension entity. As shown in Figure 3.19, each dimension entity of an information package diagram is placed on the periphery of the star of a star schema, symbolizing the points of the star. Following the placement of the dimension entities, you want to define the relationships that they have to the measure entity. Because dimension entities always require representation in the measure entity, there always is a relationship. The relationship is defined over the lowest-level detail category for the logical model; this is the last cell in each dimension. These relationships typically possess one-to-many cardinality; in other words, one dimension entity row exists for many measure entity rows. For example, you may hope to make many product sales (Sales Analysis) to a female (Gender) in the star illustrated in Figure 3.19.

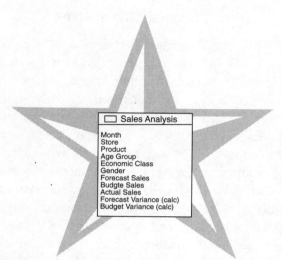

| Sales Analysis |
| Month |
| Store |
| Product |
| Age Group |
| Economic Class |
| Gender |
| Forecast Sales |
| Budgte Sales |
| Actual Sales |
| Forecast Variance (calc) |
| Budget Variance (calc) |

Figure 3.18 The measure entity is logically mapped to each dimension of an information package diagram by its lowest level category. The measure entity also contains references to all measures listed on the information package diagram. The resultant entity is placed in the middle of the star schema.

Tip: Dimension entities are placed on the points of a star schema and have a relationship that projects inward to the center of the star. The relationships between dimension and measure entities is one to many; one dimension row instance relates to many measure entity rows. Dimension entities are logical in nature and are the most denormalized of the three major data warehouse entity structures.

A star schema model simplifies a logical data model by organizing data entities in a more optimal fashion for analytical processing. In a simple star schema, a central entity—the measure entity—is surrounded by dimension entities for navigation. However, it is more likely that you will have additional relationships extending off the points of the star. This extended schema begins to take the appearance of a constellation of stars where common dimension entities allow users to cross-reference measures.

The final step in defining a logical model transforms a star schema into one of these snowflake schemas. Each individual cell of an information package diagram must be evaluated and researched to determine if it qualifies as a category detail entity. If the user has a requirement for additional information about a category, this formulates the requirement for a category detail entity. These entities become extensions of dimension entities, as suggested by Figure 3.20.

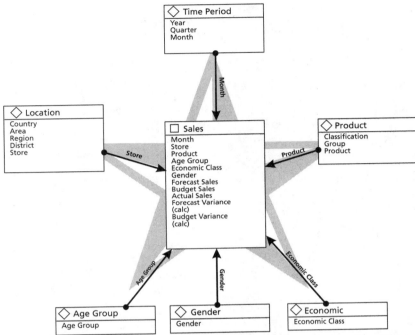

Figure 3.19 *Each dimension column translates into a dimension entity. The categories that make up a dimension become logical attributes of the overall dimension entity. After these entities are formulated, you place them on the points of the star schema diagram. The dimension entities then have relationships defined so that they map the navigation to the measure entity.*

In our information package diagram, we have a requirement to see more detail information about data, such as store, product, and customer categories. These entities, when added into the current star schema, appear as shown in Figure 3.21. Notice how it has acquired a snowflake look. Notice too how easy it is to determine the meaning of each entity and its relationship to the other entities contained in the information package. This unique offering of the information packaging methodology allows you to clearly define and communicate the purpose and role played by each entity in a data warehouse.

Tip: Category detail entity definitions contain information that enhances and adds qualitative data to the measurement, or quantitative data. The category details transform your star schema diagram into a snowflake schema because of the branching effect that the category details deliver to the star schema. (Note: Some industry gurus have different meanings for snowflake schemas. The type we discuss here is controlled and is not a detriment to your implementation.)

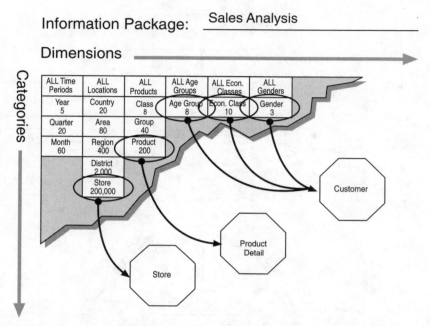

Figure 3.20 *Categories which require additional detail beyond the navigational purposes of a dimension will be translated into Category Detail Entities.*

Tip: Uniquely and clearly define all entities in your data warehouse: What is a Customer? Product? Region? You should realize that it is okay for different measure entities to require the same dimension entity to provide relationships at differing levels of category detail: A Time Period relates to Measure Entity 1 at the month level, while Measure Entity 2 relates at a day level. Remember, a relational database, which you typically utilize to implement a data warehouse, allows you to join tables with various entity columns. Therefore, you can take the Month column and join it from the Time Period dimension entity to the Month column in Measure Entity 1. You can also join the Date column from the Time Period dimension entity to the Date column in Measure Entity 2. Month and Date are both time periods and are contained in the same entity even though they provide different levels of detail.

Building a Physical Model

The following sections describe the translation of a star schema into a physical data model. Though we primarily cover this information in summary fashion, this is the most traditional part of the data development process.

Defining Data Standards

Prior to defining your first physical entity, relationship, or column, you should clearly define naming conventions that provide meaningful and descriptive information about represented components. In general, your standards should adhere to the following guidelines.

- **Complete words:** Because data is accessed by users, you should attempt to use complete words wherever possible. When abbreviations are required, try to utilize standard and well-known abbreviations. Example: OrdNo is better represented as OrderNumber or ORDER_NUMBER.

- **Character case:** Lowercase? Uppercase? Some database management system vendors recommend a specified case standard. But whatever you do, be consistent. If you introduce the concept of mixed case, you may provide a more readable name, but one that is technically difficult to enforce. Example: Which do you find more readable: order_number, ORDER_NUMBER, or OrderNumber?

- **Underscores versus hyphens:** Underscores improve the readability of any component name and should be the standard. If you utilize a data source that does not support underscores as a valid character, a hyphen is the next best thing. However, consistency is again an overriding factor; Use one of these characters to improve the readability of component names, not both. Example: first_name, first-name, or firstname.

- **Domains:** When possible, create a list of common data definitions for components that represent similar data. Examples: Dates, Time, Time Stamps, Elapsed Time, Codes, Names, Descriptions, Pounds, Currency (Cost, Revenues, and so forth).

It is important to publish and enforce these guidelines throughout a data warehouse. The enforcement should be placed in the hands of those who oversee object management, such as the database administrator or object administrator.

Tip: Standards should be defined for each of the components or pieces of a data warehouse, including the following:

columns	constraints	databases	devices
datatypes	defaults	security groups	indexes
logins	rules	segments	servers
stored procedures	tables	triggers	information packages
views	standard reports	users	catalogs
domains	relationships		

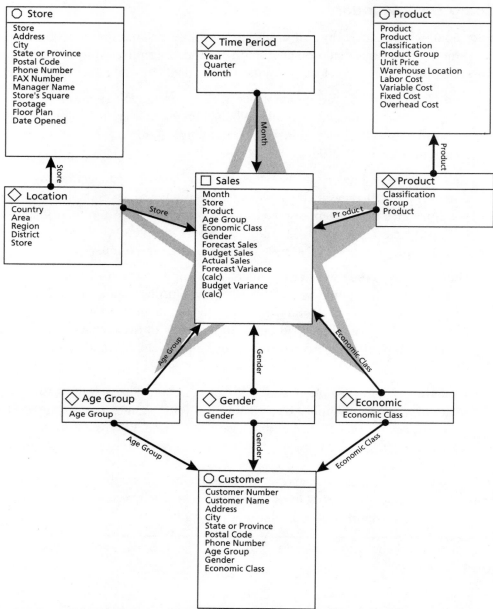

Figure 3.21 *Upon completion, the translation of an information package diagram acquires the appearance of a star schema. This star schema utilizes IPM notation to logically model the user's requested information package.*

Defining Entities

The star schema has us well on the road to defining the common entities for any given subject-oriented data warehouse. When defining the entities, you want to verify them and completely define their properties. This allows you to physically implement the entities in your chosen database management system.

Verifying Entities

When you transfer entities from a star schema to a physical model, you need to ask questions to verify if the entity is part of another entity or one that can stand on its own. Here are some typical questions you need to ask:

- Can the entity be described?

- Does the entity have columns, or attributes, relevant to the user requirements?

- Are there several instances of this entity? (If there is only one instance of an entity, it may need to collapse into another entity or multiple entities.)

- Can one entity instance be separated or identified from another? (If not, they may be the same entity.)

- Does the entity refer to or describe something else, such as another entity? (In this case, it might be a column in that entity versus an entity that can stand on its own.)

Defining Physical Entities

During the physical modeling of your database, you make key decisions about which entities will be transformed from the logical definitions to the physical database. When you physically implement the data structures, you must take reasonable precautions in the area of performance: Don't overly analyze the data, just be reasonable.

An example of such a transformation is contained in the demographic tables shown in the logical model we have used in this chapter. In looking at these tables, there are only approximately three genders (male, female, and unknown), 10 economic classes, and 10 age groups. These tables, though valuable to the overall system, are too costly to maintain as individual tables. The cost is not in maintenance; it is the cost to users, who would be required to perform three additional joins to retrieve the demographic information. The resolution to this issue is to merge the entities and populate all permutations into one demographic table. The number of rows that will be contained can be calculated by figuring the overall permutations for the three entities.

```
3 genders * 10 economic classes * 10 age groups = 300 rows
```

A table with 300 rows, though still small, is much more maintainable as we now incur only one join versus the previous three. This is a frequent example of the denormalization that occurs in the physical implementation of a data warehouse. This denormalization greatly assists the performance of the overall system by reducing the server-based overhead required to obtain all of the relevant detail information that users require. However, when contemplating these denormalizations, be sure to consider the domain of information that will be managed in these entities. Our collapsed entity contains demographic information, and therefore manages related information. Denormalizing unrelated domains into the same entity isn't recommended. This confuses those who must maintain and manage these entities. Another consideration on denormalized entities is the potential need for splitting them in the future. Should these entities not belong to the same domain of information and need to be separated in the future, you may incur numerous problems.

Entity Properties

Now that we have defined the fundamental building blocks of a data model—including the entities, the relationships, and some of the columns—we need to examine refinement of these items more specifically. Let's identify and define the properties of the data by looking at key and nonkey columns, and at data characteristics.

Key and Nonkey Columns

Data columns may provide key information about a row in a given data entity. If the data associated with this column uniquely identifies the row or is a common access path for users, the column may qualify to become a key. In query-oriented systems, keys and indexes assist in retrieval of data. However, they also introduce overhead to most database management systems, so use care when defining such attributes.

- **Primary key:** A primary key is a column or set of columns whose values can be used to uniquely identify instances of an entity. For example, the key to an order is typically an ORDER_NUMBER, which uniquely defines all of the associated data that is managed by that order.

- **Alternate key:** An alternate key is a column or set of columns that is designated as a preferred or common means of accessing the instances of a given entity. For example, the primary key to a customer table might be CUSTOMER_NUMBER, while an alternate key might be CUSTOMER_NAME. CUSTOMER_NAME does not guarantee uniqueness of the instance of a customer; therefore, a number is typically generated by the operational system to uniquely represent the customer. However, users of the system are more likely to remember the name of a customer, so we should provide them with that way to access the data.

- **Foreign key:** A foreign key is any column or group of columns in an entity whose values exist as primary key values in a parent entity. When verifying an entity instance's relationship at the key level, the value of the primary key must be present in the instance of the foreign key and vice versa. Example: In an order entry system, the order is typically represented by ORDER_HEADER and ORDER_LINE entities. ORDER_HEADER is typically referred to as the parent entity and ORDER_LINE as the child entity. ORDER_NUMBER is a primary key within ORDER_HEADER, because it defines a unique occurrence of an order. ORDER_NUMBER is considered a foreign key in the ORDER_LINE entity, because it defines the relationship between ORDER_LINE and ORDER_HEADER. Each ORDER_LINE must contain an ORDER_NUMBER, because without an ORDER_HEADER instance, an ORDER_LINE instance should never exist.

- **Nonkey data:** A column that is not part of a primary or alternate key is referred to as nonkey data. This data is primarily used to further describe an instance of an entity. Example: On an order, you would typically not provide a key for a line item's units sold. However, this data gives further explanation to what a customer ordered.

- **Null values:** If a column of data is contained in either a primary or alternate key, it may not contain a null value. Null refers to a column that has no value and is therefore unknown by the system. A null value allows you to distinguish between a deliberate entry of zero, or blank, and a nonentry.

Data Volumetrics and Update Frequency

Each entity in a data warehouse must be evaluated with regard to its volume of information processed and its frequency of update. This information becomes valuable during the transformation process. You should build a chart, as shown in Table 3.1, that for each entity clearly defines the volumetrics, including the number of expected rows and growth patterns; and the update frequency of the entity. Accurate figures may not always be available for these characteristics, so you should model the figures based on existing systems.

Table 3.1 *Entity volumetric and update frequency chart.*

Entity	Volumetrics	Update Frequency
STORE	Low volume; multiple of COUNTRY, AREA, REGION, and DISTRICT; approximately 200,000 rows.	Monthly, though tied to the other territory information; stores are added periodically, so to avoid missing a store, we will refresh monthly.
LOCATION	Low volume; dimension entity that is impacted any time COUNTRY, AREA, REGION, DISTRICT, or STORE changes.	Monthly; see note on STORE.
TIME_PERIOD	Low volume; contains the calendar of approximately 100 rows.	Annually load the new calendar.
PRODUCT	Low volume; approximately 200 rows; dependent on PRODUCT_DETAIL.	Monthly; see note on PRODUCT_DETAIL.
PRODUCT_DETAIL	Low volume; approximately 200 rows.	Monthly; in this example, we show a potential specialty store that manages only about 200 products; however, because some new items could be added monthly, we load at that frequency.
ECONOMIC_CLASS	Approximately 10 rows: < $20,000 $20,000 to 30,000 $30,000 to 40,000 $40,000 to 50,000 $50,000 to 60,000 $60,000 to 70,000 $70,000 to 80,000 $80,000 to 90,000 $90,000 to 100,000 > $100,000	Static data.
GENDER	3 rows: male; female; unknown	Static data.

Continued

Table 3.1 *Continued*

Entity	Volumetrics	Update Frequency
AGE_GROUP	Approximately 10 rows: < 18 18 to 22 23 to 30 30 to 35 36 to 40 41 to 55 56 to 70 > 70	Static data.
CUSTOMER	Each STORE has approximately 100 regularly monitored customers.	Monthly, because the volume of data is relatively low and changes are periodically made, we load at that frequency.
SALES_ANALYSIS	High volume; will contain all transactions for purchases at the store level; if the database were 100% dense, the potential is for 576 billion total rows with a monthly transaction volume of 9.6 billion. This dense number would assume that, every month, every store sold every product to every age group for every economic class and gender. The odds of this are low, but this upper limit assists in planning.	Daily; though data is rolled up to the monthly level, transactions are stored to the daily level to avoid a large batch job at the end of the month, a time period that is volatile in an operational system environment.

Entity Characteristics

It is important to fully identify the characteristics of each individual entity in a data warehouse. These characteristics are important for final implementation and deployment of the actual data model, including the concepts of fragmentation and data access. Entity characteristics include the following:

- Individual columns of distinct data items.

- Key attributes.

- Valid range of data values.

- Integrity constraints placed on the data.

- Type and size of the data.

These characteristics can be mapped to each entity utilizing a table like the one in Table 3.2, which is associated with the SALES_ANALYSIS entry in Table 3.1.

Table 3.2 *Entity characteristics for the SALES_ANALYSIS entity in Table 3.1.*

Column	Key Attributes	Valid Range of Values	Integrity Vonstraints	Type and Size
TIME_PERIOD_KEY	Primary key; foreign key	Month for last 5 years from TIME_PERIOD entity	A row can't exist char (6); without time period key.	YYYYMM format
STORE_KEY	Primary key; foreign key	Valid store key from STORE entity	A row can't exist without a store key.	char(6)
PRODUCT_KEY	Primary key; foreign key	Valid product key from PRODUCT entity	A row can't exist without a product key.	char (6)
AGE_GROUP_KEY	Primary key; foreign key	Valid age group key key from AGE_GROUP entity	A row can't exist without an age group key.	char(6)
ECON_CLASS_KEY	Primary key; foreign key	Valid economic class key from ECON_CLASS entity	A row can't exist without an economic class key.	char (6)
GENDER_KEY	Primary key; foreign key	Valid gender from GENDER entity	A row can't exist without a gender key.	char (6)

Continued

Table 3.2 *Continued*

Column	Key Attributes	Valid Range of Values	Integrity Vonstraints	Type and Size
FORECAST_SALES		Positive dollar amount		money (float)
BUDGET_SALES		Positive dollar amount		money (float)
ACTUAL_SALES		Positive dollar amount		money (float)
FORECAST_VARIANCE		Positive or negative dollar amount		money (float)
BUDGET_VARIANCE		Positive or negative dollar amount		money (float)

A Closer Look at a Physical Data Warehouse

Now that a physical data model is present, let's take a closer look at what would be populated for the information package example utilized throughout this chapter. As shown in Figure 3.5, the data model includes entities that were derived from the information package diagram. While you may have an information package diagram that is nearly identical to the one in this book, the physical data model may be totally different. (We hope that yours will be more robust and complete.)

- **Dimension Entities:** Dimension entities illustrate the denormalization concepts that in The Physical Model section of this chapter. Each level in the hierarchy has an associated key and description. This allows us to retrieve all of the data for the complete hierarchy without requiring a relational join and its associated overhead. With dimension entities, a data warehouse access tool can navigate and filter the measure entity by presenting users with dimension and category descriptions, while behind the scenes the tool utilizes the dimension and category keys to perform the actual filters and joins. The keys reduce the overhead and therefore offer a physical optimization that is native to a database. The descriptions are also isolated outside the measure and category detail entities, which allows easier maintenance if a description requires modification. If we look closely at the LOCATION dimension entity, we see that it possesses the following physical columns.

```
COUNTRY_KEY
COUNTRY
AREA_KEY
AREA
REGION_KEY
REGION
DISTRICT_KEY
DISTRICT
STORE_KEY
STORE
```

- **Measure Entity:** The columns that we further define in the measure entity include the foreign keys for relationships to the demographic entities. Decisions that are made with regard to the dimension entities will be incorporated in the measure entity. In taking a closer look at the SALES_ANALYSIS measure entity, the following are the foreign keys that were added.

```
TIME_PERIOD_KEY
STORE_KEY
PRODUCT_KEY
GENDER_KEY
ECON_CLASS_KEY
AGE_GROUP_KEY
```

- **Category Detail Entities:** Category detail entities have a similar appearance to their transaction-oriented counterparts in operational systems. Often, people will advise to collapse dimension entities into category detail entities. I advise against this for the following reasons: We want to map as closely as possible to the star schema model; we want the model to be easy to understand and navigate; and we want to provide a facility for optimizing data quality in description or label maintenance. In our sample model, STORE, CUSTOMER, and PRODUCT_DETAILS all exemplify category detail entities.

- **Relationships:** Each of the relationships primarily stems from dimension entities and extends to measure and category detail entities. In category detail and measure entities, you will create foreign keys that relate to associated dimension entities. The following are the relationships that are contained in our sample information package among the measure and dimension entities. We represent them here as SQL *join* logic.

```
WHERE TIME_PERIOD.TIME_PERIOD_KEY = SALES_ANALYSIS.TIME_PERIOD_KEY
WHERE LOCATION.STORE_KEY = SALES_ANALYSIS.STORE_KEY
WHERE PRODUCT.PRODUCT_KEY = SALES_ANALYSIS.PRODUCT_KEY
WHERE DEMOGRAPHICS.GENDER_KEY = SALES ANALYSIS.GENDER_KEY AND
```

```
DEMOGRAPHICS.ECON_CLASS_KEY = SALES_ANALYSIS.ECON_CLASS_KEY AND DEMOGRAPH-
ICS.AGE_GROUP_KEY = SALES_ANALYSIS.AGE_GROUP_KEY
```

Tip: Data warehouse entities should be driven by users' query behavior. To this end, dimension entities assist users in navigating and filtering measure entities, and allow them to focus on data in category detail entities.

Summary

The level of refinement that produces a final data warehouse physical database design has us building three separate models that provide greater detail each step of the way. We start with an information package diagram, which gives us a definition that is highly understood by users, yet is relatively incomplete for a database administrator. Through our research, analysis, and design, we transform this information package into a star schema, and finally produce a database management system's specific physical data model.

You should proceed with your projects utilizing this set of refinements to your data model. You will discover many areas where improvements can be made to the data model along the way, such as the demographic dimension entity merger we discussed in our refinements. These techniques are important and will assist your team in becoming better information packagers—a requirement for the architects and designers of a data warehouse. Too often, designers try to take the short route to the final deliverable and lose much value-added information along the way.

Though entity relationship modeling has played a part in this process, it should not be the first and only part. The concepts of the information packaging methodology build the required data architecture and functionality for your data warehouse. The information packaging diagram technique of data gathering and star schema modeling design technique provide consistency in design as well as a set of standardized communication tools that will make your warehouse more cost effective and easier to develop and maintain. Remember, this is the users' system, not yours. To cut directly to design techniques that have been developed over the years for transaction processing systems rather than data warehousing systems will not benefit anyone—your development team or users.

There is no simple way to transform an entity relationship model into a multidimensional model or design. Decision support systems and traditional business analysis require the multidimensional aspects found in such a model. Therefore, remember the steps of refinement for the information packaging methodology listed here.

1. Build a conceptual model of your information packages with information package diagrams. These diagrams are completed based on your interview sessions with users and the executives overseeing the business area covered by your subject-oriented data warehouse.

2. From the information package diagrams, begin to unify your three major warehouse entities—the measure, dimension, and category detail entities. You should guarantee in this step that you clearly distinguish entities and do not deliver overlapping information. The delivery vehicle for these logical data models is the star schema design. Clearly build each star on a graphical entity map utilizing symbols to define and distinguish the entities and their operational characteristics. A rectangle defines a measure, a filter symbol defines a dimension entity, and a stop sign defines a category detail entity.

3. From your star schema design, transform your multidimensional model into a physical database model. It is wise to pick one of the many standard data modeling tools available in today's marketplace to assist in automating this process. It is key that you work from a data modeling tool that natively supports your data warehouse architecture and delivers productivity for ongoing maintenance of an enterprise data model.

Now that we have a data model in place for your data warehouse, let us proceed with the transformation and movement process. The following chapter discusses the data flow diagramming technique utilizing IPM notation. This component of the information packaging methodology assists you in clearly defining the requirements and specifications for your development teams to implement an efficient back-end transformation process.

4

Transformation & Movement Process Modeling

The data model that we produced in Chapter 3, "Information Modeling," only provides half of the needed back-end development effort. This model just gives us a data store that users can easily navigate; it gives us no firm way to load a data asset. At this point, we basically have a house with no furnishings—and no moving company. We have proceeded to this point in a methodical manner. Too often, development resource staff want to retrieve the operational system data models and begin dumping operational data into the data warehouse. ("Let's see what they use and how they use it.") These data junkyards fail, because the key *user-driven* ingredient is lacking; little to no thought has been given to how users want the data. The information packaging methodology discussed in this book assists your team in avoiding this approach.

The construction of a data warehouse begins with careful attention to an overall architecture and data model, and with their sizing components. It is key that the correct architecture is firmly in place to support the activities of a data warehouse. After the architecture is in place and the information model is developed, the builders of a data warehouse can figure out which data they want to deliver to their users, in what form, and how it will flow through the organization. And as stated earlier, the architecture—specifically the information architecture—is more important than the tools that are used.

The transformation and movement process modeling component of the information packaging methodology will deliver the goods. This is where data is extracted from its current environment and transformed into the user-friendly information model managed by a data warehouse. This is also the part of the methodology that focuses on improving the overall quality of the data. A data warehouse is only as good as the data that it manages, so you need to focus your project team on the overall principles of quality.

Time is not the most important element of data warehousing. A user would readily accept a delay in your project rather than accept bad data. If you are working with systems that are 10 to 15 years old, you may face some unknown data quality problems in redundancy and inconsistency. Be aware of these issues and plan accordingly.

Extraction Processing

Extraction processing is key to the success of a data warehouse. Remember: garbage in, garbage out. In an extraction process, data will be formatted and distributed to sources requiring shareable data from the operational environment. This obviously includes shipping data to the data warehouse.

The Role of Metadata

A metadata repository is instrumental in this process. A metadata repository defines and explains data sources and data standards. Therefore, translation processes that execute on operational data should place the data in standard data formats as defined in the metadata repository. For example, a legacy operational system may store date information in a Julian format; however, the domain standards that have been set for future information systems state that the date domain will be stored in a Gregorian date format. The extraction process should read this domain definition from the metadata repository and transform or fix the legacy data to conform to the new standard prior to passing the data to other systems, such as a data warehouse.

Uniform Extraction Definitions

Instead of creating multiple copies of shareable data, the extract processing should define a uniform, standard, single copy of data that is passed to requesting systems, such as the data warehouse. This avoids additional overhead that may occur in the extraction processing. Too often, you will find great resistance in the information systems community to allowing the data warehouse extraction process without the elimination of something.

This is because batch windows on most operational systems are out of control and near to exceeding the allotted nightly time window. So, be careful to design the most optimal method for your extraction, and if possible determine other processes that will be eliminated after the data warehouse is delivered.

The processing of an extract is driven by an individual situation. The basis of design for any extract is determined by application requirements, data volume, and data volatility. You should have these items well documented by the time you request your data. The data requirements of a data warehouse are clearly defined in the information model; data volume is clearly defined in the information package diagram; and volatility charts provide details of the volatile nature of the data. Therefore, if you follow the procedures in this book, you should be well prepared to go to the glass house and request your data.

In most instances, you will want incremental changes sent to your extraction routines. You will need to clearly define the process of determining the deltas, or changes, in operational data through techniques such as time stamp identification. If a time stamp is accessible and clearly defined, you will simply build load files that utilize transactions as of the last extraction. With this technique, processing is done by comparing the extraction time stamp data in the metadata repository against an operational data store's time stamping data auditing mechanism. When this is not possible, additional methods must be defined, standardized, and developed. Some of these methods include the following:

- Inserting logic into an application that creates a file of changes as those changes occur.

- Developing a file comparison algorithm that produces the differences.

- Creatively accessing and utilizing a database log.

- Placing triggers in the application databases to simulate log activity.

Extract Specifications

The extraction design of a data warehouse is best documented with data flow diagrams and process specifications. The transformation and movement processing presents an obvious data flow, with the inputs being operational systems and the outputs being the data warehouse. However, the key to the extraction process is what happens to cleanse the data and transform it into usable information that the user can access and parlay into business intelligence. Therefore, additional inputs and outputs will exist in the staging area of the data warehouse based on data quality standards and multipart transformation processing.

In the information packaging methodology, we have introduced visual notation methods to clearly define what each process and data store provides–in both content and functionality. Much like the visualization that occurred in the information model, the data flow diagram utilizes the information packaging methodology (IPM) notation set to bring more clarity to overall design. These techniques are beneficial when defining extraction specifications for your development staff.

Tip: An important input to an extraction specification may be the useful reports that you collected during user interviews. Often, you can take a standard report or two and utilize the data access logic in these reports to place the data represented in the report in a data warehouse. Typically, the two largest problems that users have with the report are the following:

- It contained too much data. It was created for everyone to use, but the users only required three pages of data.

- The presentation of the data was incorrect. There was only one presentation style, but the user wanted graphics or subtotals before the detail report items.

If you are so lucky as to land on such a report, you may simply utilize the logic in the report's source module to guide you through the process of data compilation.

To demonstrate the transformation and movement process specification, we will be working with a different information package than the sales analysis example in Chapter 3, "Information Modeling." The examples in this chapter focus on another important and common information package—On-Time Deliveries (OTD).

In the information packaging methodology, the specification will be self-contained, much like the information packages that support the users' requirements. The specification becomes the sole document explaining the data flow, process, and concepts that drive the OTD information package. This packaging technique draws on various resources, including your data models and metadata repository, to drive the developed logic to the optimal solution.

Throughout this example, we refer to items that are documented in the figures and tables. Also, the syntax that we utilize in this example relies on an understanding of Sybase's Transact-SQL and its associated syntax. We assume that you have some preliminary understanding of Transact-SQL or industry-standard SQL. A couple of good sources for those who are not already up to speed on SQL include *Sybase SQL Guide* by Joe Celko

(International Thomson Computer Press, 1997, ISBN: 1-85032-849-8) or your Sybase Adaptive Server Commands Reference Manual.

The standard information packaging method template for the transformation and movement specification contains a table of contents as follows:

```
1. Introduction
 1.a. Purpose
 1.b. Scope
 1.c. Information Package Diagram
 1.d. References
2. Transformation and Movement Process Overview
 2.a. Legacy Entities
 2.b. Data Warehouse Entities (including Star Schema and Physical Data Model)
 2.c. Data Flow Diagram
 2.d. Processing Notes
3. Detail Subprocess Information
 3.a. Individual Process (for each step in the process)
 3.a.1. Source Inputs
 3.a.2. Filter and Join Criteria
 3.a.3. Sorting and Aggregation Criteria
 3.a.4. Target Outputs
 3.b The next process…
```

On-Time Delivery Information Package Diagram

For the OTD example, we will build and information package that monitors data during a five-year period. Obviously, a company's ability to ship finished product on time to its customers determines, to some degree, customer satisfaction. Everyone in the company from sales to production should be made aware of the company's on-time delivery record. Employees have a greater understanding of their impact if presented with this data. Customer satisfaction is a key business measure, because this is the ultimate revenue source for the company. If you consistently ship product on time, it is hard to lose your customer base. However, if you do have a bad delivery track record, the business may be able to take several actions, including the following:

- Change estimation procedures.

- Increase inventory levels, if you are selling standard products.

- Modify how you deliver products to a customer.

The dimensions that will be key in this information package include the following:

- **Time:** The time dimension comprises the data for five years, down to the monthly level. The time period monitors the production calendar so that users can better understand, based on calendar year or business year, if deliveries are impacted. Typically, during the fourth quarter companies become extremely efficient at shipping product.

- **Location:** The location dimension allows us to further define our analysis on a plant-by-plant basis. Some factors could arise from facilities from which products are shipped. One plant may be more efficient than another. From there, you can investigate the reasons for potential problems in deliveries. Is it a more modern facility? Does it have more capacity? Does it have better management procedures? Does it just have better people?

- **Product:** The product dimension allows you to analyze the data for any individual product that you manufacture. Again, are delivery problems isolated to an individual product, or do they involve all products? This clearly is a factor that impacts your overall decision making processes. You would not want to change delivery procedures for all products if you only had problems with one.

- **Customer:** The customer dimension allows you to determine if delivery problems are isolated on regional boundaries (such as someone not doing paperwork properly), or if they are in fact global problems. This also allows for continuous monitoring of delivery performance to a customer who has complained in the past. You will be able to isolate that customer's delivery records and show how you have improved the process of servicing them, hopefully changing the customer's opinion and attitude toward your company.

- **Shipment method:** Monitoring shipment methods assists in determining where a problem lies—in your process or in the shipment process. The shipment method dimension allows you to monitor different shipment methods. Is the rail system better than trucking? This allows you to understand how your outside suppliers of shipping services are performing and, more importantly, how they are impacting your business.

- **Measures:** Measurement data includes how many deliveries are made. This may assist you in understanding why deliveries were late if you saw a dramatic increase in deliveries for a problem month. There are also the metrics of what percentage deliveries were on time or late. These metrics are basically calculated numbers that you determine will always be queried. Therefore, you will preaggregate them for users. The alternative is to incur a calculation for each query. The two percentage items will be important to users. And, based on the simplicity of the percentage equation, you will probably store the data definition rather than the raw data for this information.

An information package diagram and star schema for the OTD example are illustrated in Figures 4.1 and 4.2, respectively.

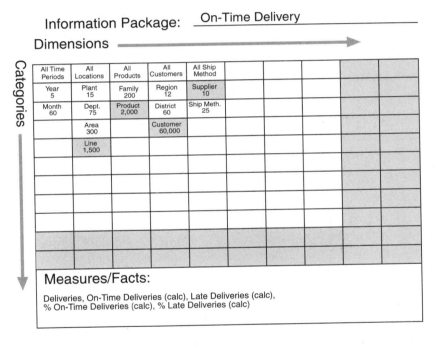

Figure 4.1 *The on-time deliveries information package diagram assists the company in understanding how effective it is at providing customers with promised orders. This information can be cut across the time, product, location, customer, and shipment method dimensions, allowing users to see trends with the number of deliveries and late deliveries.*

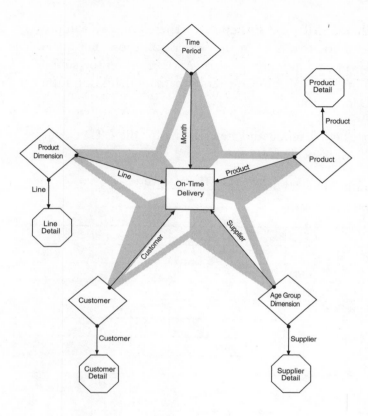

Figure 4.2 *The logical data model for the on-time deliveries information package is presented here. Notice the ease at which you can determine the functionality of the entities presented in this star schema utilizing IPM notation.*

Data Flow Diagram with IPM Notation

The transformation and movement process can be easily documented utilizing data flow diagrams. The purpose of a data flow diagram is to define at a lower level the transformation subtasks and associated data components that make up an extraction process. As with a star schema diagram, the information packaging methodology has added several graphical symbols and colors to depict each component of a data flow diagram to assist those who read it with visual notations. The IPM notation set for data flow diagrams is shown in Figure 4.3.

Entities Within a Data Flow Diagram

Data flow diagrams contain two primary entities—process and data sources—each of which perform a specialized function. These graphical entites will be integrated with the target entities defined within the information model—dimensions, category details, and measures. When modeling the transformation and movement process, it is important to graphically represent each entity with your data flow diagram. Traditionally, data flow diagrams have been far better than data modeling diagrams at using graphics to clearly define the purpose of each component. However, data entity functionality is deficient in these methods—hence the IPM notation. The following is a summary of each component in the data flow diagramming IPM notation.

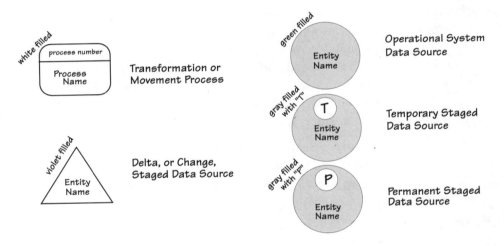

Figure 4.3 *Symbols and colors for graphically representing data flow diagrams is a unique feature of the information packaging methodology. The data flow diagram with IPM notation allows developers to clearly understand the purpose and functionality provided by each entity in the modeled transformation and movement process.*

- **Process components:** A process component portrays a specific query that transforms input data flows into output data flows.

- **Delta entity:** A delta staged entity stores data that originates from an operational, or transactional, system. These entities are permanently staged data entities that drive the incremental load processing with a replication technology.

- **Source entity:** A source entity is a data store that is clearly managed and contained in the operational system. These entities are used to extract information from daily operations and pass it to transformation and movement processes, which will clean and standardize the data for entry into a data warehouse entity.

- **Temporary staged source entity:** A temporary staged source entity is a data store that houses in-flight transformation data. Many transformation or movement processes require multiple passes at data, either due to gathering data from multiple sites or requiring multiple calculations that cannot easily be managed in SQL. This data is purged on completion of the transformation and movement process; however, this purging needs to be clearly documented as part of the process.

- **Permanent staged source entity:** A permanent staged source entity is a data store that assists in data quality processes. Transformations which focus on data quality typically involve consolidation or synonym transforms as discussed in Chapter 2, "Building an Adaptable Architecture." The data which drives the data quality transformations can be stored and managed within the permanent stated source entities. Great care should be taken to manage these entities as permanent entities much like those data stores associated with a data warehouse. The overall management of these data stores include full backup and recover techniques.

- **Data warehouse target entity (measure, dimension, category detail):** These entities were fully detailed in Chapter 3, "Information Modeling." Each of them is the output flow of an overall transformation and movement process.

Building Manageable Transformations

When defining transformation and movement requirements through a data flow diagram, we focus on building manageable and high-performance-oriented methods on data warehouse data entities. Figure 4.4 illustrates a data flow diagram utilizing IPM notation for our on-time delivery example. This data flow diagram is specifically targeted at the measure entity.

The technology architecture drives how these extraction processes and data flow diagrams are designed. The best technology architecture is one that provides a common and consistent repository and syntax across data structures, including legacy systems and a data warehouse. A tool such as Sybase OMNIConnect effectively provides this consistency in a technology architecture. Similar tools are on the market from IBM, Information Builders, Oracle, Platinum, and others. However, Sybase OMNIConnect provides a more robust and open solution for this required connectivity middleware.

When attempting to build extraction components, you want your tool of choice to provide the following functions.

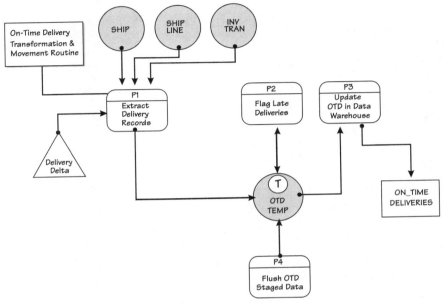

Figure 4.4 *This data flow diagram design represents the transformation and movement of the on-time delivery measurement entity utilizing the information packaging methodology notation set.*

- Transparent read/write access to all of your data stores.

- Location transparency, so that you can process on the operational platform, the warehouse platform, or staging platform without requiring coding modifications.

- Heterogeneous joins across data structures, including across multiple system data structures.

- Standardized coding techniques for all extraction processes, which assists in management and maintenance of extraction sequencing and schedule.

On-Time Delivery Process Definitions

From a data flow diagram, documentation should be developed that details each process component. The detailed process descriptions allow you to provide development staff with a connect-the-dots implementation plan. This should include defining the following points.

Source tables for the input of the extraction process. In your definition, be sure to include the platform, database, and tables that will be utilized for input parameters. Table 4.1 illustrates the documentation of these source tables.

Table 4.1 *Process P1 (from Figure 4.4): source tables for the extraction process.*

Platform	Database	Table Name
VAX/VMS	MCS (Manufacturing Control System)	SHIP
VAX/VMS	MCS (Manufacturing Control System)	SHIP_LINE
VAX/VMS	MCS (Manufacturing Control System)	INV_TRAN

• **Filter and join criteria:** Because our discussion is in the context of a relational connectivity tool like Sybase's OMNIConnect, define how the answer sets will be formulated. In this definition, the specific column and its parent table should be defined, along with the operation or operator that will be utilized in the filtering of the data and the value on which the operation will be performed. This step helps to consolidate data in a consistent format for placement in your data warehouse. Often, legacy systems utilized techniques such as coded record structures in which one file housed multiple definitions of a record. A code determines the record layout that will be used. You will want to make sure you are getting the right data and using the right data layout for the input data. Table 4.2 demonstrates how to document filter and join criteria. A simple table that presents the compound conditions, the table name and column involved, the filter or join operation to be performed, and the comparison values assists developers in building the correct syntax to extract the data for any process.

Table 4.2 *Process P1 (from Figure 4.4): filter and join criteria for the extraction process.*

Compound Conditions	Table Name Column	Filter or Join Operation	Comparison Value
	Join over the primary index for SHIP, SHIP_LINE, and INV_TRAN		
AND (	SHIP.SHIPMENT_STATUS	equal	"50"
OR	SHIP.SHIPMENT_STATUS	equal	"90"
) AND	SHIP.SHPMNT_NBR characters 1 and 2	not equal	"CI"

- **Sorting or aggregating criteria:** Sorting and aggregating criteria are important, because they define the proper level of granularity. With regard to on-time deliveries, we are only interested in seeing monthly shipment numbers for each customer, product, plant, and shipment method. This may include all of the shipments, but on the other hand it might return one row that represents thousands of shipments. Table 4.3 presents the proper sequencing of the result data by defining the column and its associated table name that will be sorted, the ordering of the data, and whether a SQL *group by* clause is needed for aggregations.

Table 4.3 *Process P1 (from Figure 4.4): sorting and aggregating criteria for the extraction process.*

Table Name.Column	Order	Group
SHIP.SHPMNT_NBR	ascending	yes

Target or projected column definitions. In the target or projected column definitions part of the specification, you define all manipulation, calculation, and general cleansing that must take place on data prior to its placement in its target environment. Important information includes the result or target column name, the source column or source calculation, and a brief process description to assist in understanding the calculation or cleansing details. See Table 4.4.

Table 4.4 *Process P1 (from Figure 4.4): target column definitions for the extraction process.*

Result Table Name.Column	Source Table Name.Column	Description/Notes
OTD_TEMP.SHIPMENT_NBR	SHIP.SHPMNT_NBR	Shipment number.
OTD_TEMP.SCHED_SHIP_DATE	Calculated: convert SHIP.SCHED_SHIP_DT from Julian date to Gregorian date	Scheduled ship date.
OTD_TEMP.ACTUAL_SHIP_DATE	Calculated: convert SHIP.DATE_SHIP from Julian date to Gregorian date	Actual shipment date.
OTD_TEMP.ACTUAL_NET_WT_SHIP	SHIP.NET_WT_ACT_SHIP	Net weight of the actual shipment.
OTD_TEMP.SHIPMENT_STATUS	SHIP.SHIPMENT_STATUS	Shipment status.

Continued

Table 4.4 Continued.

Result Table Name.Column	Source Table Name.Column	Description/Notes
OTD_TEMP.QTY_TO_SHIP	Calculated: SUM(SHIP_LINE.QTY_TO_SHIP)	Quantity that was to be shipped.
OTD_TEMP.SHIP_LINE_STATUS	SHIP_LINE.SHIP_LINE_STATUS	Shipment line item status.
OTD_TEMP.CONT_CODE	SHIP_LINE.CONT_CODE	Container code.
OTD_TEMP.DAY_OF_WEEK	Calculated: convert SHIP.SCHED_SHIP to	Day of the week scheduled to ship determine the day of the week.
OTD_TEMP.DAYS_LATE	Calculated: SHIP.DATE_SHIP SHIP.SCHED_SHIP	Number of days the shipment was late.
OTD_TEMP.ITEM_NBR	SHIP_LINE.ITEM_NBR	Item number.
OTD_TEMP.ITEM_SPEC_NBR	SHIP_LINE.ITEM_SPEC_NBR	Item spec number.
OTD_TEMP.LATE_FLAG	NULL	Based on calculations within P2; the shipment may not be late even though there are days late (see adjustment calculations in P2).

Loading Data

The specification discussed in the preceding sections allows development staff to adequately map the logic required in a SQL statement. Remember, this example is utilizing Sybase's standard SQL syntax, Transact-SQL. The resulting module is a stored procedure. The SQL syntax mapping is depicted in Figure 4.5. If you are utilizing tools other than one based on SQL the mapping will be similar, however, the benefits of a set level syntax may be lacking.

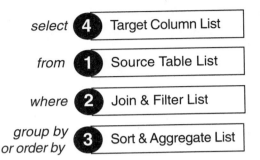

Figure 4.5 The specifications defined in the information packaging methodology cleanly map to a SQL select statement as shown in this mapping.

You may find it interesting to find that the mapping of the specification illustrated by Figure 4.5 is to an SQL *select* statement. We had two reasons for the mapping to a *select* statement as illustrated in Figure 4.6.

- First, if you load into a staging area, you want to utilize bulk copying concepts such as the SQL *select into* statement. This approach allows you to parse the source data and place it into a staging area with one statement.

- Second, you may want to utilize SQL cursor logic, which allows you to perform specific logic on each row of a result set. In this situation, you may be selecting the data as shown, then performing row-at-a-time conversion to the data. The results of this process would then be processed in an *insert* or *update* statement.

Multiple Passes of Data

It is important to realize that productivity tools such as Sybase's OMNIConnect and other set-oriented tools are unable to complete everything in one pass of data. Our on-time delivery example could potentially be done in one pass; however, the operational staff for a production system may have told you to get your data and move on—no calculating, no processing, just get what you need and get off the machine. More complex extractions require you to pull data from multiple systems and merge the resultant data while performing calculations and transformations for placement into a data warehouse.

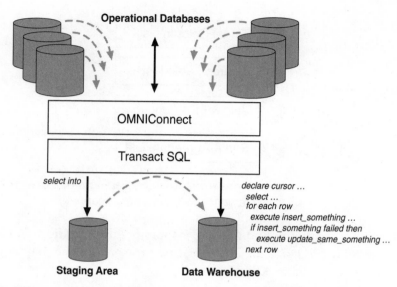

Figure 4.6 *Processing extracted data can be done quite effectively with tools such as Sybase's OMNIConnect. The syntax to load your data will vary based on the technology architecture; however, the bulk loading concepts of insert into and row-at-a-time processing used in cursors will assist in your loading efforts.*

The sales analysis example that we carried through the information modeling phase in the preceding chapter might be such an application. We may be obtaining budget sales information from a budgetary system, which is different from the order entry system from which we get actual sales data, which in turn is different from the forecast management system from which we get forecast sales data. In this scenario, we would need to access three separate systems to fill one row in the sales analysis measure table. So, be aware that the extraction and loading process is easier if you break it into smaller processing units and let the tools in your architecture, such as Sybase's OMNIConnect, work for you rather than against you.

Staging Area

Creating and defining a staging area assists your cleansing process. This is a simple concept that allows you to maximize up-time of a data warehouse while you extract and cleanse the data. You simply utilize a temporary work space—a staging area—to manage transactions that will be further processed to develop data warehouse transactions. You will need to define a permanent staging area to assist in things such as checkpoint restart logic, replication agent management, and data quality loops that may be driven by pattern matching and data tables.

Checkpoint Restart Logic

The concept of checkpoint restart has been around for many years. The concept originated in batch processing on mainframe computers. This type of logic states that if you have a long running process that fails prior to completion, you restart the process at the point of failure rather than at the beginning. You should implement similar concepts in your extraction and cleansing logic. In the staging area, define the necessary structures to monitor the activities of transformation stored procedures. Each of these programming units has an input variable that determines where in the process it should begin. Therefore, if failure occurs in the seventh procedure of an extraction procedure that has 10 steps, assuming the right rollback logic is in place you would only conduct the last four steps (steps 7 through 10).

Data Loading

After data has been extracted, it is ready to be loaded into a data warehouse. In the data loading process, cleansed and transformed data that now complies with your data standards is moved into the appropriate data warehouse entities. Data may be summarized and reformatted as a part of this process, depending on the extraction and cleansing specifications and the performance requirements of your data warehouse. After the data has been loaded, data inventory information is updated in your metadata repository to reflect the activity that has just completed.

Data loading most likely occurs during a batch window period during which utilization and access by users is not required. This period is typically late evening or early morning hours. However, with an architecture defining the staging area and technologies such as replication, there should be an ability to perform real-time updates via asynchronous extraction and loading. This situation is typically not a requirement for data warehouses, though real-time updating of the staging area is a real requirement.

The loading of data should utilize a standard methodology and common utilities. Tools such as these provide the most efficient manner of loading a data warehouse, while minimizing the need for custom-developed utilities. Depending on the nature of an extraction or transformation process, you may have to perform some customized loading. This should not be the norm, but the possibility should be reviewed closely by the architecture team as a case arises for the best solution.

Tip: Just because SQL is a set-oriented language does not mean that everything can be easily and most efficiently done in one pass of data. Remember the policy of keeping things simple; simplicity often, but not always, equates to efficiency. Many cleansing and load processes require more than one pass at data. Design your load modules with your eye on the future and your mind in the past. That is, don't forget things such as checkpoint restart logic, which optimized batch jobs of old. These techniques can bridge to the future and optimize your loading process.

Optimize Extractions with Replication Agents

Replication technology has begun to emerge as a viable solution to many problems that previously hindered the implementation of distributed data sources. Specifically, the concepts of data placement in a distributed data environment are beginning to be mastered by replication technologies. Replication is simply defined as the process of creating and maintaining associated copies of original data at distributed sites.

Typically, a replication architecture involves a publisher of data and a subscriber of data. The publisher is the original, or controlling, source. A highly effective tool for capturing this type of information is a CRUD Matrix. CRUD stands for Create, Reference (or Read), Update, Delete. The matrix maps data entity events to systems, including when an entity is created, read, updated, or deleted. A CRUD Matrix matches the major data entities with business functions and application processing. If we utilize a CRUD diagram to represent the publisher, it would be characterized as the source that creates and deletes data; or more easily stated, it controls the capturing and purging of data from a corporation. A subscriber, on the other hand, is a system that needs access to the data, but only from a reference data perspective. In other words, subscribers are readers in a CRUD diagram of the specified entities.

The concept of replicating data may on the surface appear to be simple. However, upon complete investigation, you will find that these architectures have evolved to solve some complex problems with a simple interface. Replication is more than just copying data from one site to another. A complete replication architecture accomplishes the following:

- Provides reliable replication that is not exposed to problems such as system failures.

- Delivers consistent data that adheres to all data integrity rules.

- Optimizes the delivery process to reduce the latency between the capture or modification of data and the delivery of replicas.

These objectives are high-level items for guiding your selection of a replication agent. Additionally, the replication system that you choose should be easy to administer, provide an architecture that allows for as many of your data sources as possible to be replicated, and be independent of location.

How Does Replication Work?

For purposes of this discussion, we refer to implementations utilizing Sybase's Replication Server. However, each database management system vendor as well as transaction processing monitor vendors and other third parties may provide you with a replication solution.

Sybase's Replication Server provides the capability for individual servers to publish data and for others to subscribe to the replicas. Sybase's replication technology offers an enormous benefit to the overall performance and management of replication, because it allows us to simply monitor the log activity of a given publisher to provide the required replica information. This contrasts with some other replication technologies that work from an actual data record image in a transaction window. The approach provided by Sybase provides a great benefit to our extraction processing. We can now trap data changes without changing the application logic or increasing the transaction window. Both of these characteristics will be greatly resisted in most organizations as too costly or unachievable. The processing flow works as follows, and is illustrated in Figure 4.7.

1. The operational system changes the data.

2. The change is committed to the operational database.

3. Upon completion of the commit, the transaction is logged to the operational database's log.

4. The Log Transfer Manager component of Replication Server recognizes the data change.

5. The Log Transfer Manager obtains the data that has been subscribed (which can be partial data).

6. The Log Transfer Manager sends the transaction to Replication Server.

7. Replication Server distributes the transaction to subscribers.

8. The subscriber receives the Replication Server transaction and processes it as a transaction.

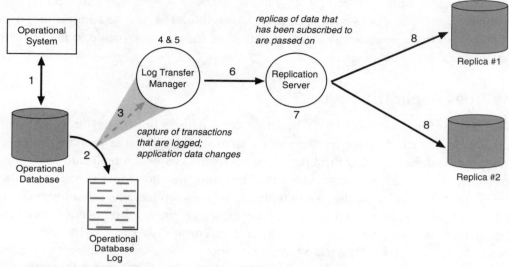

Figure 4.7 *Sybase Replication Server provides the capability for individual servers to publish data and for others to subscribe to replicas. This technology offers an enormous benefit to the overall performance and management of a data warehousing load process.*

Sybase's Replication Server offers many benefits, one of the greatest of which is its overall architecture. This technology can be mapped to heterogeneous sources with relative ease, because it is based on the Sybase Open Client/Open Server architecture. Several off-the-shelf replication agents for heterogeneous data sources allow you to easily integrate this component into your overall data architecture.

How Can the Extraction Process Use Replication?

The extraction process is sensitive to loading volumes, or the number of rows from an operational data store that must be transformed and placed in a data warehouse. When you design your extraction processes, you must cover two situations: mass loading and incremental loading.

Mass loading is relatively easy to handle. The extraction process grabs all of the operational data and refreshes the data warehouse. However, this does not account for many factors, among them:

- **Volume considerations:** The volume of some data sources prohibits a pure mass loading concept; or probably better stated, it forces you to surround the data warehousing problem with expensive software and hardware to handle the processing of large volumes of data.

- **Historical content considerations:** A data warehouse is meant to provide a historical perspective to the data assets of an enterprise. The mass loading concept typically correlates to a refreshing of data, which means that data may be inadvertently purged from a data warehouse if it is purged from an operational data store. This conflicts with the overall goal of a data warehouse system to provide historical context.

- **Optimization of resources:** The resources that surround operational and data warehouse systems, such as a network, processors, and memory, will be thoroughly saturated if the only loading strategy implemented is mass loading.

The solution to this loading dilemma is to develop an extraction and loading process that can perform incremental loads. When possible, each of the Transact-SQL stored procedures that were discussed for loading data warehouse entities will be triggered off a shadow key table.

A shadow key table is a database table, typically stored in a data warehouse's staging area, that contains replicas of the keys and associated modification information for an associated table in an operational database environment. This technique provides a way for a data warehouse to subscribe to the source of the data and capture the information associated with daily transactions that have transpired on that data: What changed? How did it change? And so on. This type of information allows you to apply selective logic in your loading process to reduce the overall volume of data, in essence optimizing a data warehouse's loading process.

Selective logic assists in optimizing the load in several ways, as listed here:

- It utilizes keys from a data source, so you can perform indexed reads versus table scans on the data source, thus minimizing access time and overhead to the source system.

- It permits no transaction window increase. If you implement shadow tables in an operational system, either through code or other database triggering devices, you increase the time to commit transactions. Reading the log for information assures that the transaction is already committed prior to any work being done by a process that in fact has no bearing on the transaction. This nonintrusive way of capturing changes will please your application support staff.

- If an application has not been written with a time stamping algorithm (most legacy systems lack this characteristic), you still can perform incremental processing.

- Because more than just the key can be replicated, you may reduce the need to access the original data source through subscribing to more of the data. This circumstance allows all changes to be sent to a staging area for further processing, again maximizing resources by minimizing the overall query load.

However, like all new technologies, replication won't fit in every environment. Therefore, you will probably incur a mixed environment for your data loading in which you utilize the best available strategy. The ranking of these implementations is as follows:

1. Replication of operational transaction information.

2. Time stamping of operational data.

3. Triggering of operational transaction information into shadow key tables.

If none of these options is available, you should still look to minimize the burden of mass loading, which can have an overall impact on the cost and content of a data warehouse. An inability to implement incremental strategies for data loading forces an enterprise to spend more money on hardware and software to throw at the resource problems; otherwise, the company must suffer having less data in its data warehouse. Neither option is appealing.

Tip: Replication technologies can be extremely useful for a data warehouse loading process. Search for the least intrusive method of trapping data modifications in operational systems. These systems can ill afford an increase in the transaction window or code revisions. A good replication technology that monitors a data store's log file delivers this least intrusive solution.

Data Distribution

The process of data distribution can be similar to the job of a newspaper delivery person. After the newspaper is printed and made available to a central distribution center, the delivery person goes to individual subscribers and provides them with their own copies of the newspaper. The concept is the same in a data warehouse. Systems feed off a centralized data warehouse. The data warehouse subsystems must be provided with properly sourced data from the extraction, cleansing, and loading processes.

A set of standard utilities in the overall architecture should be implemented to support this distribution concept. Again, today's modern replication software can be invaluable in this area. However, you may find that there is no one clear-cut solution for your data distribution problem. Therefore, make sure that your utilities can work in harmony within the allotted time window for performing the distribution of the data and for making it available to all users. These utilities hold the burden of physically moving data from a data warehouse to data consumers, which could include users, standard reports, multi-dimensional analysis systems, or departmental data marts.

Technology and data architectures should guarantee that a data distribution system accomplishes the following:

- Ensures that data distribution occurs in a timely and efficient manner.

- Ensures that only data that has been ordered is delivered.

- Establishes proper and required service level standards.

- Gathers data to provide statistical evidence that the service level standards are being achieved.

Extraction Processing Standards

To achieve consistency in your extraction processing environment, a comprehensive set of standards is required, similar to the data standards discussed in Chapter 3, "Information Modeling." These standards ease coding, facilitate debugging, and simplify maintenance of the back-end processing managed by a data warehouse system. The success of this methodology, as in other methodologies, is the enforcement of and adherence to overall standards. Therefore, proper enforcement personnel must be defined in a data warehouse management structure.

The recommended strategy for implementing your extraction processing is a programmable database management environment that supports server-based logic, stored procedures, and replication technology to reduce the volume of data loads. This strategy requires that the database management system vendor provides adequate facilities for connecting to your operational data stores and a common syntax standard that operates on each of these data stores.

A stored procedure is simply a collection of SQL statements that are precompiled, stored in a database under a given name, and executed as one unit. Stored procedures have evolved over the years with relational database management systems and are now the common technique for implementing a programmable database and optimizing performance. Common processes that are implemented as stored procedures include business rules such as data validations, referential integrity checks, and frequently used queries. Stored procedures offer a modular development technique that is focused on reuse of program logic while providing a layer of abstraction between the database management system and the application development environment, including user data presentation.

Stored procedures typically run faster than the same group of commands executed interactively. Therefore, implementation of store procedures also offers performance benefits. These benefits are derived from the reduction of overall network traffic, because the execution logic merely references the name of the stored procedure and any required input parameters. From there, the server executes multiple requests without further prompting from the client application. Prior to the implementation of stored procedures, a client application was required to call the database server for every SQL statement in a transaction. Therefore, an application executing a transaction that requires an insert of data followed by a select that feeds an update can be executed in one stored procedure versus three separate client requests. Note that stored procedures can call other stored procedures. Therefore, a client request can trigger a series of server-oriented activities in one network packet.

Standards should be established in stored procedures for defining the individual components. Many of these standards will be driven by current data standards, because SQL statements contained in stored procedures will reference those data items. However, you will also be required to define the standards for the following objects:

- **Stored procedure names:** The names of stored procedures are typically only visible to development staff. Therefore, meaningful naming conventions that help to define the purpose of a stored procedures should be developed. For an example, consider pAction_object, whose elements are described in Table 4.5. Therefore, the incremental loading process for on-time deliveries might be named as pn_ON_TIME_DELIVERY.

Table 4.5 *Stored procedure naming standards for pAction_object example.*

Element	Description
p	Defines this object as a stored procedure.
Action	Defines what the stored procedure's primary processing is, such as: d—Delete i—Insert s—Select u—Update n—Incremental load m—Mass load
object	Defines the objects affected by the stored procedure.

- **Parameter names:** Stored procedures can receive input parameters as well as define output parameters. These parameters should be named according to good programming conventions, again focusing on the content, data type, and purpose of the defined entity. You may want to utilize a well-established standard for these values, such as Hungarian notation.

In addition to naming conventions and standards, recognize that stored procedures are code modules. Therefore, explicit standards for the development of code must also be defined for your development team. Examples of these items include the following:

- **Return codes:** Because stored procedures are simply modular code that is managed by a server rather than a client, good communication regarding processing and execution between code modules is needed, including use of return codes. A common set of return codes should be developed to define what has transpired and any further activities that should occur based on the status of execution, such as messages and aborting of a process. All stored procedures should return a status code that indicates completion of the process, with or without errors.

- **Documentation blocks:** Each stored procedure should provide some common documentation to improve its management and maintenance. This documentation block should include items such as the name of the procedure, a brief description, parameters used by the stored procedure, return codes (including result sets and processing status codes), and modification history. Here is an example.

```
/*********************************************************
** PROCEDURE NAME: pn_ON_TIME_DELIVERY
**
** DESCRIPTION: This procedure performs the
** incremental load process for the on-time
** delivery data warehouse information package.
** This procedure accomplishes the following.
** 1 - Extracts data from the
** manufacturing control system on the
** plant-based UNIX machine utilizing
** Sybase OMNIConnect
** 2 - Stores the data in the data warehouse
** staging area
** 3 - Processes the on-time delivery calculations
** that flag deliveries as either late or on time
** 4 - Places the data in the data warehouse
** 5 - Purges the staging area
**
** RETURNS
** ----
** Result Sets - none
**
```

```
** Status Codes
** '4' - Row count of zero
** '8' - Invalid Action code
** '16' - An error occurred
**
** MODIFICATION HISTORY:
** Author Date Comments
** T. Hammergren 12/10/97 Initial Build
**
*********************************************************/
```

- **Code comments:** Develop a standard that requires adequate comments for the source logic. This standard should state that no more than a specified number of lines of code can be written without a comment. This again improves the management and maintenance tasks of stored procedures.

- **Error checking:** Global variables *@@error* and *@@rowcount* should be checked after each SQL statement. The *@@error* variable indicates whether a statement was successfully executed or an error was detected. The *@@rowcount* variable indicates the number of rows affected by the execution of a SQL statement. This may be important for guiding further processing in a stored procedure. Also, if you perform nested stored procedure calls, check the return status code to verify that execution either completed successfully or aborted with an error status.

- **Passing parameters by name:** When passing parameters to a stored procedure, pass them by name rather than by positional reference.

- **Do not use "*" in place of all columns:** Explicitly state all desired column names in a *select* column list. Do not use *"select *. ..."* Following this rule enhances maintainability of a system.

To guarantee that the standards you develop are easily adopted, you may want to purchase a generation tool for stored procedures, or simply define stored procedure templates from which all stored procedures evolve.

Building Data Quality Loops

Data quality is one of the biggest problems in the data warehousing industry. Systems that were and are in control of the data capture have neither traditionally monitored, nor cared about, the overall quality of the data input. Having said this, we should realize that this problem will always be with us. A data capture system cannot think of all of the permutations that users will think of upon entering data.

One humorous story along these lines involves a claims processing arm of a company that was providing data that was being placed in a data warehouse. The data warehousing team began testing its initial systems and noticed that this specific claims processing department had a very high incidence of claims with "hemorrhoid problems." Upon investigation, the data warehouse team discovered that the field that contained this diagnosis was never strictly monitored. If the claims agents had a claimant who was not to their liking, the agents tagged the claimants as a "pain in the backside." The system understood this to mean that the agents entered the code for a hemorrhoid problem! This is just one of numerous examples that indicates that what was good enough for operational systems may in fact skew the results produced by the data warehouse. As a matter of a fact, these types of data quality problems have caused some companies to totally abandon their data warehouse efforts.

The true answer for fixing this problem is to build a data quality process into your data warehouse architecture. This process has the primary goal of capturing data quality problems as they are discovered, either in the loading process or by the users analyzing the data. The principles that many manufacturing companies have adopted are based on the work of Edward Deming and other pioneers in the area of total quality.

Some of the most common data quality solutions include:

- **Format patterns:** Often, legacy systems stored data with multiple pieces of information in one field. Worse, no edits were applied to these fields, and users was left to determine the best way to enter the data. An easy example is a name field. If users are asked to enter a person's name and are prompted with only one field—how should they enter it? Tom Hammergren? Mr. Tom Hammergren? Hammergren, Thomas C.? All three of these entries are correct; however, if others need to extract the first and last name, how do they do it? Building a quality process that evaluates such fields for common patterns and applies the transformations accordingly will help you clean up this data. However, if you build such a routine, you may want to pass the requirements for cleansing the data back to the system developer, the cleansing process should begin within the data capture system from where the data originated.

- **Consolidation and duplicates:** For companies that implemented departmental systems without data standards, or that acquired smaller companies that had their own infrastructure and their own way of doing business, data warehousing has become a challenge. Each of these smaller divisions has its own set of employees, customers, products, and chart of accounts. With each of these major entities came a set of key identifiers. And the divisions actually did business with some of the same customers, using some of the same products, and charting this to similar accounts. However, each of these same entities have different keys! Division A may have Customer A entered in the system with a CUSTOMER_KEY of 123, while Division B has Customer A entered in its system with a *CUSTOMER_KEY* of *abc*. To fix this data quality problem, permanent staging source tables can be created in the staging area that contain all of the CUSTOMER_KEY references in all the systems. The data cleansing effort then can be as trivial as an SQL *join*!

- **Synonyms:** Similar to pattern rules is the concept of synonyms. A synonym is a word having the same or nearly the same meaning as another word. Again, a data capture system cannot force users to spell correctly or stop abbreviating. Therefore, a repository can also map the different meanings of descriptors in the same way keys were mapped. Two examples here are Digital Equipment Corporation and DEC, and International Business Machines and IBM.

A data quality loop can be inserted in any of the data flows that feed a data warehouse. The data quality feed should be able to perform exception-based reporting to your data warehouse administrator or data warehouse quality personnel, who can evaluate the exception and correct the problem for future loads.

Summary

A data warehouse consists of a set of storage facilities containing shareable data for use by reporting and decision support processes. Data is moved to a data warehouse in a structured extraction process that accesses operational data, transforms the data into proper data warehouse format, and distributes the data to sites requiring replicas.

The notion of a single, logical enterprise data environment begs the question of the number of physical operational data stores and physical data warehouses. The architecture that is defined for a data warehouse should accommodate the number of physical data stores and their underlying technology, making them as transparent as possible to the overall data warehouse processes. If this architecture is provided, the process of data extraction and cleansing is greatly simplified. Connectivity tools from vendors such as Sybase offer enormous flexibility in this area. The benefits derived from standardizing on such a connectivity platform include more consistency in the transformation process and the ability to standardize on a process definition.

Data flow diagrams can be used to model the process of transformation and movement. These processes can be complex subsystems, compounded by the data extraction and cleansing processing. Data flow diagrams become useful when the development of transformation processes from operational data stores to a data warehouse are further detailed. The information packaging methodology further enhances these data flow diagrams through the use of visual entity representation, graphics, and color, which assist a designer in capturing transformation and movement requirements. These diagrams and associated specifications form the foundation of the back-end development effort and defines the following tasks:

- Steps in the process.

- Order of the steps.

- Reference to the data used and affected by the process.

- Business rules that govern the process.

- Transformations that can occur in the process.

These models assist development staff in evaluating system requirements, providing a visual communication medium and a basis for the physical design or implementation of a system.

Because the extraction and cleansing process is a development effort, traditional development standards such as data flow diagrams are utilized to successfully implement a data warehouse and its associated processes. It should be the job of your central data warehouse support team, especially your database administrator, to ensure that the extraction and cleansing process that loads a data warehouse conforms to the overall architecture. This conformance includes the following goals.

- All data that is loaded into a data warehouse conforms to corporate data standards. These standards should be published and available through a means such as a metadata repository or an electronic manual.

- Anytime data warehouse data is modified, the inventory information for that data area is updated to reflect the changes and logged in your metadata repository. Remember, the repository gives you the life history of any entity.

The remainder of this book delves into front-end processing in greater detail. For more information on the back-end process and the information packaging methodology, be sure to read the first book in this series, *Data Warehousing: Building the Corporate Knowledge Base* by Tom Hammergren (International Thomson Computer Press, 1996, ISBN 1-85032-856-0).

Section IV of this book, "Case Studies," references many of the concepts covered here in Section I. This foundation will assist those looking to develop front-end applications immensely. A stable and strong back-end is critical to deploying the front-end applications in a data warehousing space.

We now move to Section II, "Technical Essentials," in which we examine the concepts that are critical to building applications on the Internet that will interact with these back-end structures—the corporate knowledge base.

SECTION II

Technical Essentials

To many managers let themselves get weighed down in their decision making, especially those with too much education. I once said to Philip Caldwell, who became the top many at Ford after I left: "The trouble with you, Phil, is that you went to Harvard, where they taught you not to take any action until you've got all the facts. You've gotten ninety-five percent of them, but it's going to take you another six months to get that last five percent. And by the time you do, your facts will be out of date because the market has moved on you. That's what life is all about—timing."

A good business leader can't operate that way. It's perfectly natural to want all the facts and to hold out for the research that guarantees a particular program will work, after all, if you're about to spend $300 million on a new product, you want to be absolutely sure you're on the right track.

That's fine in theory, but real life just doesn't work that way. Obviously, you're responsible for gathering as many relevant facts and projections as you possibly can. But at some point you've got to take that leap of faith. First, because even the right decision is wrong if it's made too late. Second, because in most cases there's no such thing as certainty. There are times when even the best manager is like the little boy with the big dog waiting to see where the dog wants to go so he can take him there.

What constitutes enough information for the decision maker? It's impossible to put a number on it, but clearly when you move ahead with only fifty percent of the facts, the odds are stacked against you. If that's the case, you had better be very lucky—or else come up with some terrific hunches. There are times when that kind of gamble is called for. But it's certainly no way to run a rail road. At the same time you will never know 100 percent of what you need.

—Lee Iacocca with William Novak, *Iacocca An Autobiography*,
Bantam Books, 1984, pp. 50-51.

5

Web Architecture
Essentials

The World Wide Web burst onto the Internet scene in 1993, rapidly changing the way people think about disseminating and distributing information. But the Web actually dates back to 1989, when Tim Berners-Lee of Geneva's European Particle Physics Laboratory (then known as Conseil European pour Récherche Nucleaire, or CERN) circulated a proposal to develop a hypertext system. The proposed system's purpose was to enable efficient and easy information sharing among geographically separated teams of researchers in the high energy physics community. The important aspects of the proposed system included: a consistent user interface; the ability to incorporate a wide range of technology and document types; and the ability to allow anyone with any computing device anywhere on the network to read the same document. CERN announced the Web to the high energy physics community in 1991. And in 1993 browsers began to become available to the general public, including Mosaic, which was developed and released by the National Center for Supercomputing Applications in Champaign, Illinois. The chief developer was Marc Andreessen, now of Netscape fame.

The technologies behind the explosive growth of the Internet are highly leveraged and focused on open standards. This openness permits flexible system designs and architectures. Designs are established based on a rich mix of service components, which are put in place to match the user's requirements in a Web architecture, as shown in Figure 5.1.

Web architectures are built through various service component solutions. When placed together, the open components formulate the basis for an architecture that meets users' requirements.

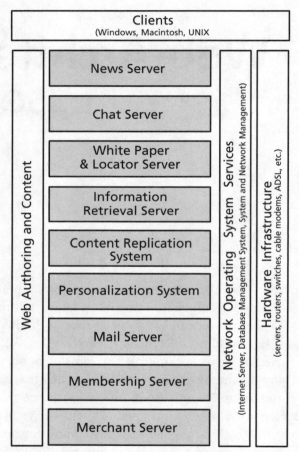

Figure 5.1 This Web architecture demonstrates Microsoft's Commercial Internet System Server Architecture, their Internet server, and services blueprint.

Web software simplifies and standardizes data presentation and the user interface components of an application. And as we will see in Chapter 6, "Database Essentials," the database management system organizes and standardizes data retrieval and storage. This combination of the Web and database provide a very powerful architecture, allowing companies to quickly disseminate information to their users.

The designs and architectures of the Web have a simple and intuitive user interface; a well thought out declarative language for defining content; a robust protocol that permits high volume traffic; cross platform usability; and low deployment costs. Based on these factors, data warehousing is a natural application for the Web. Prior to getting into the details of implementing a Web based data warehouse, let's look at several of the requirements and standards that comprise a complete Web foundation architecture.

Web Requirements and Standards

To be successful in building a data warehouse system utilizing the Web for access, you must be aware of the requirements and standards that will drive your architectural decisions. In Chapter 2, "Building an Adaptable Architecture," we discuss the critical components of an architecture, which include:

- **An Information Architecture:** This component of an overall architecture organizes the sources and stores of business information.

- **An Application Architecture:** This component provides the software framework for building your applications. The resultant framework will guide the overall implementation of the required business functionality.

- **A Technology Architecture:** This component provides the computing infrastructure, including hardware, software, and communication, that enables the data and applications architectures to communicate efficiently and scaleably.

These three architectural components will surround your company's business processes to deliver a proper solution. To best implement this type of solution, you must also look at the support infrastructure that will build and maintain these delivered systems. Each of the architectural components will be surrounded by this support infrastructure, which is typically a people-intensive resource that allows you to truly deliver your finished solution.

Failing to recognize the need to architect a solution for your Web data warehouse is a critical mistake. While you will undoubtedly make mistakes throughout your development, do not let architecture be one of them. The cost of an architectural error far exceeds any other costs associated with a project. Implementation errors, programming errors, and system design errors pale in comparison to the overall cost of an architecture error. Frank Lloyd Wright, a world renowned architect, once stated: "A physician can bury his mistakes, but an architect can only advise his clients to plant vines." This quotation exemplifies the serious posture you and your team should take when delivering your Web based solution: Architecture is at the heart and soul of your deliverable.

Questions to Ask

So, what questions are important to ask when ascertaining the requirements of your Web architecture? The following list includes some of the more important questions:

- What is the purpose and goal of the application?

- What will be published in the application?

- What types of data will be included in the application?

- Can the components of the overall architecture support content or data in different media?

- Who is the target audience for the application?

- How many concurrent users do you expect to access your application?

- How many concurrent users must be supported during peak hours?

- How much bandwidth is required to support the users, the application, and the data distribution or retrieval requirements?

- Will the application be a part of the Internet (publicly accessible) or an intranet (only accessible within your company) solution?

- What availability requirements will be placed on the system?

- What is the current security model of other applications on the Web in your company? How does this model fit your needs?

- What browsers will be supported in the application? Can you dictate which browsers are used?

- Will your application scale as the implementation of the data warehouse becomes more robust? As the business grows?

- Is the server platform open enough to allow for open, customized extensions, which may be required by your application?

The answers to these and many other questions allow you to investigate how versatile, reliable, and open your final architecture will be. Of course, each implementation of a data warehouse is different, but opening up your data warehouse to the Internet could increase your user base to tens of thousands of concurrent users, millions of users each day, and hundreds of gigabytes of content. The openness and interoperability aspects of most Internet components makes it easy to set up and administration of the servers to support these burdens. But "easy" has two dimensions—time and money. Ask technical personnel about a solution and their response typically contains the word "easy." Sometimes that "easy" answer might take a week and cost $10,000; other times, the easy solution could take five years and $20,000,000—but both are "easy!" Therefore, you need to clearly ask the right questions to determine the true requirements, both in time and monetary terms. From there, you can integrate standard and proprietary components to deliver your required architecture.

Internet and Web Services

When looking for the proper solution to deliver access to your data warehouse over the Internet, you will find a large number of services. These services are incorporated in a growing number of standards and de facto standards used by application developers to deliver various solutions and information to their users. The following sections contain a list of services, standards and de facto standards for Web and Internet application development. They are organized by common functionality, including connectivity services, transport protocols, server application programming interfaces (APIs), development languages and syntax standards, file-related services, mail-related services, and security-related services.

Connectivity Services

Most Web and other Internet activity is performed across a network. To perform any network-based activity, you must have a protocol that is supported on both ends of the connection. The most popular and de facto standards for Internet connectivity are:

- **Transmission Control Protocol/Internet Protocol (TCP/IP):** This standard has become the preferred protocol to enable Internet services such as Telnet, FTP, and e-mail. TCP/IP allows computers to communicate, even if they do not belong to the same network.

- **Serial Line Internet Protocol/Point-to-Point Protocol (SLIP/PPP):** This communications protocol is used across telephone lines with modems to allow computers to dial into a network and establish a simulated network connection. The resultant connection appears as if the user is connected directly to the network with a TCP/IP connection.

Transport Protocols

The Internet is similar to the interstate highway system; that is, it is a transport mechanism. To easily direct your information around the world of the Internet, standards have been developed. Here are the most notable of these transport standards:

- **Uniform Resource Locators (URLs)** provide the addressing system of the Internet and Web. URL is a standard for locating and accessing an object on the Internet. URLs can specify servers, Web pages, e-mail addresses, files, newsgroups, or other content addresses in the vast world of the Internet. A URL consists of four separate parts which when combined, completely define the location of a file or service located anywhere on the Internet. The first part of the URL specifies the access method, such as HTTP, FTP, NEWS, and MAILTO. The remainder of the URL specifies the domain location and other specifics of the desired object. For example, the URL http://www.objx.com/assets /images/ book1.gif is broken down into the following parts: the protocol request (http://); the domain name (www.objx.com); the path (/assets/images/); and the filename (book1.gif).

- **HyperText Transport Protocol (HTTP)** is the standard language that is utilized by Web servers to communicate with Web clients (browsers). HTTP sits on top of the backbone network connecting the Web clients and Web servers, serving as the traffic cop—managing the content delivery and redirection services for Uniform Resource Locators. HTTP is a stateless and asynchronous language, so it is much faster than session-oriented protocols for processing large numbers of user requests for information. It does this by opening a connection for only as long as it takes to deliver the requested content, typically a Web page. This connection typically involves four interaction points between the server and the client: a connection, a request, a response, and a disconnect. This short interaction between client and server poses a challenge to successfully implementing a data warehouse on the Internet.

- **Network News Transport Protocol (NNTP)** is the standard protocol for newsgroup distribution (such as Usenet, the most common newsgroup) . Newsgroups are discussion of interested individuals congregate around a specific topic to frequently exchange messages. These special interest groups can form around various topics, so an understanding of newsgroups may be beneficial to your data warehouse implementation. Data warehousing newsgroups include: comp.databases, comp.databases.*, comp.databases.olap, comp.databases.sybase, and comp.infosystems.gis.

- **Wide Area Information Services (WAIS)** is an information retrieval service and protocol. WAIS was designed to create a distributed network publishing system that can help people find information simply by asking questions. This has since evolved into an indexing engine and a query engine that allow users to access textual archives with a simple ad-hoc query mechanism—the search engine.

- **File Transfer Protocol (FTP)** is the Internet protocol for transferring files from one computer to another. Most popular browsers now directly support FTP. Additionally, there are various proprietary FTP interfaces which allow anyone in a networked environment to transfer files. The most primitive interface is a command-line interface, while the more popular are GUI driven. However, the browser interface is similar to most operating system file listing interfaces. You select files from a series of hierarchical folders, which are then transferred to your computer.

- **Gopher** is an information system designed at the University of Minnesota that provides an efficient way to organize information and provide it for other people to browse on the Internet. Many current services of Web browsers have made Gopher obsolete, or at least seldom utilized.

- **Multipurpose Internet Mail Extensions (MIME)** types tell computers what kind of program to use to view a file. Originally MIME was used for electronic mail; however, over the years this has been modified so that MIME informs a Web browser about what component, plug-in, or helper application should be launched. The MIME specification uses a system of message types and sub-types to identify the format of a message. MIME types include image, audio, text, video, and application to name a few. Some MIME examples include: Graphic Interchange Format (GIF) is a standard file format for graphics presented on the Web which was developed by CompuServe; Joint Photographic Experts Group (JPEG) is another very popular format for displaying images on the Web, this image format utilizes a standard algorithm for compressing still images; Portable Document Format (PDF) is a standard developed by Adobe Acrobat to display a richly formatted document on any computer with the proper viewer typically a plug-in for your browsers.

- **Telnet** is a protocol to enable a user to log into a remote host computer. After logged into the remote computer, you can interact with the software running the session similar to using a keyboard directly connected to that computer.

Development Languages and Syntax Standards

A variety of languages must be learned to successfully develop Internet and Web-based applications. These languages allow you to build a full complement of services, including user interface logic, presentation logic, and application processing logic. The most notable languages in these areas include:

- **HyperText Markup Language (HTML)** is the standard language for creating richly formatted documents on the World Wide Web. In essence, HTML is a descriptive language that assists developers in creating hypertext documents. It is an international standard whose specification is maintained by the Internet Engineering Task Force. We further discuss this essential component of Web-based applications in Chapter 7, "HTML Essentials."

- **JavaScript** is a scripting language, originally developed by Netscape, for the creation of simple applications that can be entirely embedded in HTML documents. Like other scripting languages that extend the capabilities of the applications with which they work, JavaScript extends the standard Web page. JavaScript code is embedded in HTML code and allows the resultant Web pages to provide immediate feedback to the user without interacting with the Web server. JavaScript is based on the action-oriented model of the Web and has quickly been adopted as the standard way to script Web applications. We further investigate JavaScript in Chapter 8, "Scripting Essentials."

- **VBScript** is a scripting language created by Microsoft that enables the creation of simple applications that may be entirely embedded in HTML documents, much like JavaScript. VBScript is a subset of Visual Basic for Applications. In turn, VBA is a subset of Visual Basic.

- **Java** is an object-oriented programming language created by Sun Microsystems that enables the creation of network-centric applications. The origins of Java are in the areas of research, where Sun desired to create software for consumer electronics devices such as television sets, VCRs and microwaves. Based on these target platforms, Java was built to be small, fast, efficient, and easily portable to a wide range of hardware devices. Sun later realized that these attributes made Java an ideal language for distributing executable programs on the Web. Java has become a popular, general-purpose language for developing applications that are easily usable and portable across different platforms. We further investigate Java in Chapter 9, "Java Essentials."

- **Virtual Reality Modeling Language (VRML)** is the standard modeling language for creating three-dimensional worlds on the Internet, through which users can interact and navigate. VRML is not a markup language; it is closer to a graphical and geometrical language—hence the "M" for modeling.

Server Application Programming Interfaces (APIs)

Extending the server of an application has become an important aspect of Internet development. These extensions allow developers to better control the activities and responses that occur based on user requests beyond simple file transfer mechanisms. The popular server interfaces include:

- **Common Gateway Interface (CGI)** is the Internet standard interface for invoking server-based scripts or compiled programs at the request of clients. It is currently the most common way of providing dynamic content to client browsers. In the early days of database interaction with the Web, CGI was the primary means of access. An application developer would write server side applications or scripts utilizing popular tools such as Perl or C. For database access, tools such as sybperl and OraPerl provided extensions to Perl5 by supporting a native SQL dialect for Sybase and Oracle respectively. These extensions made the accessibility of databases across the Web and Internet a simple task—as long as you understood UNIX, CGI, Perl, and the native database interface.

- **Netscape API (NSAPI)** is Netscapes's proprietary Web server API. This API, like Microsoft's ISAPI (below), allows third-party developers to write programs that interface with Web servers. These interfaces allow writing third-party solutions in an optimized fashion compared to the traditional CGI interface.

- **Internet Server API (ISAPI)** is Microsoft's proprietary Web Server API. This API, like Netscape's NSAPI, allow third-party developers to write programs that interface with Web servers. These interfaces allow writing third-party solutions in an optimized fashion compared to the traditional CGI interface.

Mail-Related Services

Electronic mail is becoming the vogue communication channel for people in the '90s. Delivery of electronic mail is similar to the United States Postal Service in an electronic form. If someone wants to communicate, all they need to do is purchase a mail package, write a note, and send it to another person's e-mail address. The standards that are important to note in this area include:

- **Simple Mail Transfer Protocol (SMTP)** is the standard for transferring mail to and from various mail servers. The primary objective of SMTP is to transfer mail reliably and efficiently. SMTP is the standard by which various e-mail packages can effectively communicate.

- **Post Office Protocol (POP)** is the standard for managing server-side mailboxes for users as well as passing messages addressed to a particular user to the appropriate POP client.

Security-Related Services

A system on the Internet is vulnerable to an attack from outside hackers. Also, transmitting data and transactions across an open environment such as the Internet poses a risk. Hackers can intercept data transmissions and decode their content. In each of these cases, a security service can lend a hand. Many components and standards are quickly being developed to shore up your line of defense. The most notable of these components and standards include:

- **Firewall** is a combination of hosts, routers, and associated software that partitions your company's internal network (intranet) from the public Internet. The router component of a firewall performs packet filtering to block traffic to and from the internal hosts. The host component performs application level filtering, hiding internal network addresses from the outside and authenticating users desiring to access the internal network.

- **Secure Electronic Transactions (SET)** is an electronic commerce standard originally developed by Visa and MasterCard, among others. SET is part of a collection of electronic standards and protocols that are necessary to make the Internet a viable platform for electronic commerce. SET is a protocol specifically for safeguarding credit card transactions across the Internet.

- **Secure Sockets Layer (SSL)** is an open and widely endorsed channel security protocol standard. It originally was defined by Netscape and is in the process of being signed over to the Internet Engineering Task Force. SSL provides message encryption, client and server authentication, and message integrity services to many application protocols such as HTTP, FTP, and NNTP.

- **Secure HTTP (S-HTTP)** is a security-enhanced variation of HTTP proposed by Enterprise Integration Technologies and commercially implemented by Terisa Systems, which was co-founded by EIT and RSA Data. S-HTTP provides general-purpose transaction security services that are necessary for transaction security in electronic commerce applications. SSL and SHTTP are not mutually exclusive; rather, they can easily complement each other by layering SHTTP on top of SSL

The Standard Application Architecture

Client/server is a computing architecture in which client processes request services, including data, from server processes. Clients and servers, which communicate via messages and data, can coexist within this architecture in the same memory space on the same processor, on diverse, geographically distributed platform, or in a combination of these configurations. When client and server components are distributed, they exchange messages and data across a network.

The client/server architecture grew out of modular programming, in which developers separate their applications into small, coherent functional models. The most common modular partitioning scheme includes the user interface, which is the client typically running on a personal computer, and the database management system, which is the server that typically runs on a multitasking host platform such as UNIX.

Approximately four distinct layers and their associated touch points make up a complete application architecture. These layers are a user interface, presentation logic, processing logic, and data access. This architecture is depicted in Figure 5.2. Well-defined, standard interfaces between the layers of the architecture allow you to delivery an application which is distributed across a wide geographically separated network. The interfaces include:

- **Events** is a well documented application programming interface which notifies a program that the user has performed an operation which requires further actions

- **Remote procedure calls (RPC)** is a formal protocol used within distributed systems for executing a procedure on a remote server

- **Structured query language (SQL)** is a standard interface between application programs and relational database management systems.

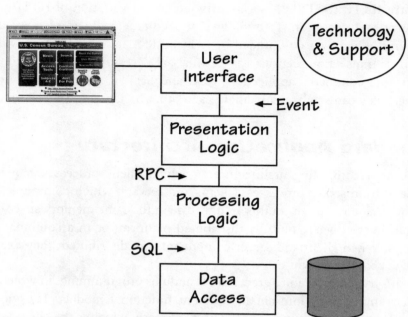

Figure 5.2 *A standard application architecture consists of four distinct layers and the communication between those layers.*

Though the architecture presented in Figure 5.2 is stated as a "standard architecture," most systems in production don't adhere to such clean architectural separation. However, we should begin to formulate plans to implement such an architecture, and your data warehouse is a great place to start. We look closer at each of the distinct layers in the architecture in separate sections that follow.

User Interface Layer

A user interface contains all of the windows and menus that interact with a user. This layer controls the presentation of data with common graphical widgets such as list boxes, combo boxes, text boxes, and labels. These widgets are typically delivered by the operating system vendor, such as Microsoft or Apple. Many tools have been developed that allow developers to construct these interfaces and avoid low-level coding. The user interface is then generated and the developer simply connects the user interface objects with presentation logic.

Presentation Logic Layer

In the presentation logic layer, a developer defines localized management of the events that are generated by a user in the user interface of an application. These events are fired whenever a user interacts with one or more of the presentation objects in the user interface. The processing triggered by these events may include formatting data to output to the user or performing localized edits of data input by a user. Either way, the code is close to the user interface and tends to involve simple tasks that are not associated with transaction management or data integrity. These tasks are placed in server components so they are uniformly managed closer to the data store. This layer also contains logic associated with distributing the workload using remote objects.

Processing Logic Layer

The processing logic layer manages remote objects that are utilized by clients and servers in a central fashion to control and standardize business rules in an application. Client and server applications can access the objects managed by this layer as if they were local objects. This layer provides background services to one or more client applications. However, it may also function as a client to the data access layer. It is the responsibility of the processing logic layer or application server to coordinate and handle the interactions among all clients and servers as well as to provide computationally intense applications with a platform with which processing is optimized.

Data Access Layer

The data access layer is responsible for data integrity and information resource management. This layer guarantees that all client requests for data are fulfilled and that all transactions submitted to the uniform data store are committed or rolled back as complete units of work. This layer has traditionally been the mainstay of database management systems that manage text and numbers.

Systems are beginning to support additional abstract or unstructured data types. We have yet to see whether the current data access layer will take on this responsibility or multiple data access servers will fulfill these requirements. Either way, a layer in your application architecture will manage the various data-oriented components—structured and unstructured—to fulfill client requirements.

Communication Between Layers

Each of the four layers in a standard architecture communicates in a two-way fashion to complete an entire chain, as shown in Figure 5.2. When the user interface is modified by a user, the method of communication is typically an *event*. An event, or notifier, springs the presentation logic components into action to perform their duties. If the presentation logic layer requires assistance from the processing logic layer, a Remote Procedure Call is fired. This RPC is a package of information and instruction that is sent across a network to a remote service. On receipt of an RPC, the processing logic takes the packet of information and applies the instruction on a higher powered processor. This could be the termination point in an overall processing stack. If so, typically a response is sent back through the presentation layer to inform the user of the success or failure of the request. However, if the processing logic layer requires information from the data store, it communicates via SQL and typically the native database vendor API to query the database and return the results to the calling program.

The Web Standard Architecture

We can apply the standard architecture for distributing the workload in a service-oriented design that we have just discussed to the Web—its services and standards discussed earlier in the "Internet and Web Services" section of this chapter. Not much is really so new about the Internet and Web based architecture and interfacing techniques. Those of us who have made the transition from the block mode days of mainframe computing to client/server and distributed solutions have improved our designs to accommodate such an architecture. In many ways, the good designs of the mainframe are more adequate for the Internet than the designs of the client server world.

A typical Web architecture consists of: a user interface (Web browser) with HTML pages and some scripting language; a presentation logic services (scripting language); a logic server (Web Server) with server-oriented extensions to process user requests; and a content server (database management system), which feeds users with dynamic information that fulfills their requests.

Tables of contents, headings, paragraphs, lists, and graphic elements make up the pages of books, magazines, and newspapers; these are the essential elements of a Web system. Through the use of hypertext, the Web can provide access to mountains of information in a very usable way. The primary reason is that the information and its associated links are provided in a manner with which readers are familiar. The Web provides a book-like interface and layer on top of the Internet. Let's investigate each of these components in more detail in the separate sections that follow.

The Web Browser: The User Interface Layer

The universal user interface, a single user interface across all platforms, does not exist yet for the Internet. Web browsers are vying to deliver a universal user interface. The browser provides a tool access the Web and much of the rest of the Internet. As the name implies, you can browse through many different types of documents, files, and services provided by many different types of servers on the Internet. Built into most browsers is the capability to communicate with HTTP (Web) servers, FTP servers, newsgroup servers, and WAIS or gopher servers. Users traverse the Web by reading pages, clicking links, making selections from list boxes, entering queries, and inputting data into fields on forms. Information that is retrieved from the Internet can be displayed as text, images, tables, graphs, and multimedia objects. The browser is in essence the navigator or explorer of the Internet, hence the names chosen by Netscape for Netscape Navigator and Microsoft for Microsoft Internet Explorer.

As applications mature on the Web, the only program a user will require is a Web browser. Browsers are driven by HTML, which is a simplified derivative of the Standard Generalized Markup Language (SGML). HTML operates through a series of tags in an ASCII text document. These tags permit Web designers to include links, lists, headings, titles, images, forms, maps, and so on on their sites. But HTML is severely limited. Compared to robust client/server tools, HTML and browsers have weak input validation and transaction controls. However, client application programming interfaces (APIs) allow developers to extend the capabilities of browsers for more complex applications. These extension objects, or components include:

- Inline plug-in APIs that provide a means of incorporating dynamically loadable modules into the client process itself. Together with Java and JavaScript facilities, plug-ins enable high-performance application delivery of rich content such as sound, graphics, and video.

- Netscape and Microsoft client APIs allow developers to write applications on native operating system platforms such as Windows, MacOS and UNIX that can communicate and remotely control a client application such as Netscape Navigator or Microsoft Internet Explorer. These APIs allow applications to communicate via Apple Events, OLE Automation, Dynamic Data Exchange (DDE) and X Events.

These client-side extensions, including Java Applets, Netscape Plugins, Microsoft ActiveX components, and MIME Helper Applications technologies, have allowed the Web to become a medium for professional developers.

Scripting Languages: The Presentation Logic Layer

Scripting languages react to, control, or drive a series of events that extend the capabilities of an application. For years, PC applications such as spreadsheets, databases, and word processors have supported scripting, though this scripting was often referred to as macros.

Scripting languages such as JavaScript and VBScript extend the capabilities of a standard Web page. These scripting languages bring your Web site to life. With standard Web pages, you obtain new information by clicking a hypertext link, which triggers the Web server to retrieve a new file for you or triggers your browser to move to a different location in the current file. Retrieving new files takes time as you must wait for the server to validate your request, formulate the response, and send that response to you.

Scripting languages allow you to enhance Web pages by embedding code directly into the HTML of the Web pages that interacts with the user. In a scripting language, you can define interactions between user actions and a Web page. Therefore, the scripting language allows you to implement rules such as what to do when a button is clicked, when a mouse is moved over a field, or when data is entered into a field on a form. Scripting languages are typically limited in scope to the environment that they interface or script, in the Internet world, this means the Web page. Other than functions surrounding data manipulation (such as string, math, and date functions), most scripting languages are limited to operating on browser objects and other objects exposed by the browser. These other objects can include plug-ins, Java applets, and ActiveX controls. These objects allow you to do quite a lot, including creating new Web pages, modifying the existing Web pages, and building complete applications. At this point, the most popular scripting language is JavaScript. However, Microsoft has introduced VBScript; and as with any Microsoft product, they will find a way to make it popular. These client side scripting mechanisms have allowed development teams to make Web pages come to life and perform more of the functionality required by applications in today's fast paced world.

The Web Server: The Processing Logic Layer

Traditionally, the Web has used a stateless protocol, the HyperText Transfer Protocol. That is, basically every interaction between a Web client and a Web/HTTP server terminates after each request is satisfied. The browser sends a message to the server, the server delivers a response back to the browser, then they forget they ever met until the next exchange. This stateless protocol allows a lot of simple transactions to take place, but doesn't permit a session in which a sequence of controlled input transactions take place. This poses a problem to many applications, including data warehouses, which require multiple interactions with users prior to actively processing their requests. Different techniques and tools must be used to deal with portions of this problem, such as client extensions, server extensions, and cookies.

Client and server extensions come in various flavors. On the client side, these extensions include Java Applets, ActiveX components, plug-ins, and logic in the form of scripts. The server also provides similar ways of extending itself. The server extensions available include:

- Java servlets, which you can think of as Java Applets that run on the server and have no user interaction.

- Server-side scripting, including JavaScript, VBScript, and other scripting languages such as Perl.

- Server-side applications that are executed through the Common Gateway Interface (CGI) or the HTTP server's native application programming interface (API). The server-side APIs include Netscape's NSAPI, Microsoft's ISAPI, and Quick and Reilly's WSAPI.

These options allow professional development teams to build robust Internet applications. However, fundamental issues still nag every development team in defining how to properly manage the state of a client. Managing the state defines where the user is in an overall process, are they retrieving data, modifying data, or what have they done since they have been connected to the Web site. The statelessness of Web interaction results in complete user interaction for a single page—the user signs on, requests information, and signs off. The inability to manage state within your application poses problems for developing a highly interactive and secure site. Currently, no standard defines how to handle both stateless protocols and session-oriented protocols. But the leading way is through "cookies."

Cookies are tokens that are temporarily stored and managed by the browser or the server to allow information about the Web Client to be exposed to server-based applications. Cookies are in essence the temporary or working storage area that allows developers to store key information that is missing in the Web client, Web server and other components of the standard Web/Internet architecture. Cookies are stored in a browser and can be retrieved by a server-side application. For example attributes about a user, such as user name, and a user's session, such as a session identifier, might be stored inside a cookie for the duration of their interaction with your Web site. Some important facets of cookies include:

- Cookies are set and retrieved for a specific server reference.

- Cookies can be sent securely using the Secure Sockets Layer (SSL) standard described in the "Security-Related Services" section earlier in this chapter.

- Cookies are persistent and stay stored in the browser until they expire or are deleted by an application.

- Cookies are supported by almost all commercial browsers.

Cookies are important to managing the state of your data warehouse application, from the client perspective as well as the server perspective. State management includes monitoring where a user is in the process of building their query selection criteria, remembering previous browser activities of the user such as previous queries of the data warehouse, and maintaining security access through user names or IDs for future interaction with your Web site.

With the current, largely stateless nature of the Web, a user can come and go without a server's knowledge. Each interaction is similar to signing onto a database, performing a query, getting the results, and signing off the database. You will want to manage the client side activity to eliminate forcing the user to sign on for each database request. One of the easiest ways to do this is with Cookies.

The Web server will be the chief controlling mechanism for all interaction between the users and the back end systems managed in your organization. This server is the traffic cop of the overall system. Understanding how to extend this server is a key to succeeding in building applications on the Internet. The magic keys of server-side scripting and server API access allow you to fully develop sophisticated logic into your data warehouse while controlling and securing information assets.

The Database Management System: The Data Access Layer

The final stop in the many layers of the Web standard architecture is the data store. Just like our legacy systems, Web-based applications need a way to store and manage their dynamic content. Though a database is not a requirement for all Web applications, your application—a data warehouse—requires a complete database management system.

Interfacing with the database is done as it has been done with other generations of application development. However, some special considerations need to be made when thinking about placing information assets on the Internet. More than ever, you must manage the concepts of information overload. As you will see in Section IV of this book, "Case Studies," you want to manage the output provided to a user in a more controlled fashion than you did with client/server or host-based applications.

The Internet and Web present documents, typically of fixed length, to a user's browser. Though a database management system allows a user to query and return thousands of rows of data, you will probably want to eliminate this ability—passing the user more manageable chunks of information as they work through the result set. The entire Web architecture is built to support small bursts of information distribution to a large number of users. Meanwhile, the data warehouse community historically has focused on distributing large amounts of data to a small number of users. When you merge these two concepts, you begin to deliver large amounts of data to a large number of users in a controlled and scaleable fashion. The information packaging methodology and other techniques presented in this book will assist you in achieving this objective.

The Web Service Architecture: A Multi-Tier Solution

Typically, we think of Web standard architecture software utilizing TCP/IP to connect and communicate across the Internet. However, this entire architecture can also run on a single processor without a network. For example developers may want to perform all requests and activities in isolation for newer versions of the data warehouse. Therefore, it is important to realize that the communication between layers requires software and hardware components that may not be required in all implementations. Some implementations may place the application services and database services on the same processor, while other implementation may have multiple application servers and multiple database servers.

The best way to approach this architecture is to think in terms of specialized services or appliances. You will quickly find that each component behaves as a client, a server, or a middleman. Whichever role the component plays, you should architect them to provide a unique and required service to the overall system. From that point of view, you can then define the dialogs that will occur among the services and build a common messaging system to allow them to communicate.

This type of an architecture is not too different from modern day communication. Humans interact in many ways, including e-mail, voicemail, facsimile, telephone, postal mail, and video teleconferencing. This communication then drives activities that we schedule and execute based upon agreements among the interested parties. This is the same architecture that you should build for your data warehouse Internet access strategy.

Let's take a closer look at the two architectures that may be used to build and deliver your data warehouse, a two-tiered architecture and a multi-tiered architecture.

The Two-Tiered Architecture

The two-tiered architecture became popular in the early days of client/server systems. Depending on your networking heritage, these systems became known as either "fat client" systems or "fat server" systems.

Fat client systems placed the user interface, presentation logic, and processing logic layers on the client and placed the data access on the server. These systems were grown from a personal computing mentality and utilized product sets such as Microsoft's Visual Basic, Powersoft's PowerBuilder, and Borland's Delphi. These systems worked against a plethora of servers that were evolving from departmental computing platforms such as Digital's VAX, Hewlett Packard's Precision Architecture Servers, and everyone's UNIX boxes. These lower-end servers were typically equipped with a relational database management system from either the hardware manufacturer or popular third-party database developers such as Sybase and Oracle. But the typical implementation had most of the code resident on a personal computer running Microsoft Windows and most of the data on the server in these databases.

The processing logic in these systems might flow as follows:

- Client system manages the user interface.

- Client system validates the data entered by the user.

- Client system dispatches data to the server programs.

- Server system accepts the requests from the client system.

- Server system executes database retrievals and updates.

- Server system executes business logic and business rules.

- Server system manages the data integrity.

- Server system controls the transaction.

- Server system sends the result set or data back to the client system.

Fat server systems typically placed only the user interface and portions of the presentation logic on the client, while a majority of the presentation logic, processing logic, and data access layers were on the server. These systems were grown from a mainframe perspective and were often called "screen scraped" applications. The products utilized for these solutions included tools such as Sterling Software's Flashpoint. The systems would present a pretty version of the 3270 terminal image and process complete transactions on the server or mainframe as if it were a dumb terminal. However, with the onset of the graphical user interface, several widgets were incorporated to assist in the usability of screens. These widgets included drop-down lists, radio buttons and check boxes. For these graphical items, code was required to translate the user's actions back into the proper 3270 buffer streams.

Web base solutions can easily implement both the fat server and fat client models. As shown in Figure 5.3, the components in traditional client/server systems are the database client and the database server. In the Internet application space, these components translate into a Web browser client and Web server, which includes an HTTP server and database server.

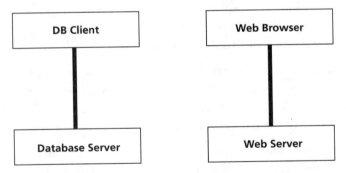

Figure 5.3 *You can easily build a Web service architecture around a two-tiered model. A traditional client/server system (left) parallels the architecture of today's Internet applications (right).*

This scenario maps closest to the traditional fat server model. Tools providers in the client/server world, such as Microsoft and Powersoft, have also promoted a fat client model. In the fat client architecture, the client side is extended with traditional tools such as Visual Basic or PowerBuilder; as well as with components such as plug-ins and ActiveX controls. However, this two-tier architecture has been losing significant ground to the multi-tiered architectures that focus on application services or appliances.

The Multi-Tiered Architecture

The multi-tiered architecture model begins to look at components, or specialty servers, that are loosely coupled with each other. (Each specialty server is unique, however.) This architecture is much the same as the stereo architecture of the late 1970s, in which you bought the best receiver and connected it with the best turntable and best speakers— typically from different manufacturers.

There is a natural migration for these specialty servers to fall in line with the four standard layers described in "The Standard Application Architecture" section earlier in this chapter. A specialty server may focus on presenting data to the user, manipulating the information prior to presenting it to the user, massaging the data for insertion into a data store, or physically storing the data.

Figure 5.4 illustrates the parallel between a traditional multi-tiered client/server and its Web counterpart. The components in a multi-tier architecture of a Web application can be as follows:

- **Client**: The client (browser and its extensions) manages the user interaction, navigation, formatting, and reporting of data retrieved from a data warehouse. In a multi-tiered architecture, the client relegates many calculation tasks and most database interaction tasks to the application server.

- **Application server**: The application server (Web server and its extensions) manages the interaction with the data warehouse, provides a valuable load balancing role for computationally intense workloads, and sends the results to the client, typically in HTML format or in a Java applet data stream.

- **Data warehouse server**: The data warehouse or data mart server manages the information assets contained in a corporate knowledge base. The data warehouse server optimizes query activities and delivers a unified view of the corporation to all users who have access. This service is provided to Internet access tools, traditional client/server tools, and host-centric reporting tools. The data warehouse server is the single interface to information assets.

The multi-tiered architecture allows both the client and server to lose weight. The true benefit to this architecture is that components, or specialized servers, can be built. These devices can then be interconnected to provide the proper services for fulfilling the user requirements behind your solution. Through this specialization, your final architecture and associated systems scale far more easily, because the load on each server is minimized. The scaling benefits include the ability to handle the user explosion that occurs when a data warehouse goes into production without requiring a server migration; enhanced security through authentication servers; simplified maintenance through the isolation of modifications and their impact on all users; and reduction in network traffic through smaller, more distributed work loads.

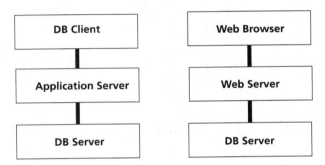

Figure 5.4 *The multi-tiered architecture introduces application servers to manage computationally intensive operations and to minimize data transfer across slow communication lines. These functions assist in the overall scaleability of a data warehousing solution.*

Process Flow in a Web Architecture

The following discussion will assist you in understanding how a Web architecture comes together to service user requests for database access. This discussion is directly mapped to the steps identified in Figure 5.5.

1. An HTML form is built and presented to the user with a Web browser, such as Netscape Navigator or Microsoft Internet Explorer. The user fills in input fields with information for an information request. The user presses a submit button to notify the browser to send the information to an HTTP server. The browser contacts the HTTP server to ask permission to run the associated request.

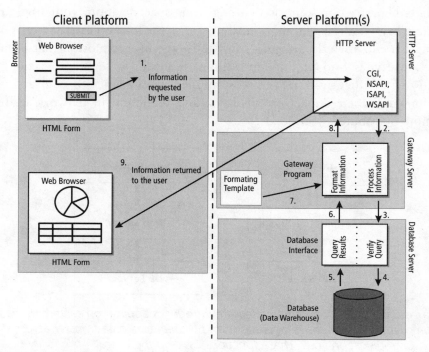

Figure 5.5 *The process flow of a Web-based Internet application which has been constructed to service user's requests for information from a database such as a data warehouse.*

2. In most database access scenarios, the HTTP server notices that the request needs more than just an HTML page. The HTTP server verifies that the specialty server exists and that the user has permission to access the specialty server. The packet of information received by the HTTP server the is transmitted to the specialty server, a program written to one of the major server gateway APIs (CGI, NSAPI, ISAPI, and so on).

3. The gateway program takes control from the HTTP server and processes the information. With regard to database access, this typically involves taking host variables and placing them into SQL syntax to forward to a database. After the database request is formulated, it is passed to the database interface.

4. The database is activated through a sign-on procedure. The request is submitted to the database kernel and optimizer for validation. If a valid SQL statement has been passed, the database begins to formulate a result set.

5. The database management system populates a temporary workspace with the results of the query request. Upon completion of the result set compilation, the database returns control to the database interface.

6. The database interface indicates to the gateway program that the request has completed. Typically, this notification occurs with a status code, or error code. The gateway program interprets this code to understand how to proceed. The two basic alternatives are that the request failed and an appropriate message must be sent back to the user, or that the request succeeded and the results will be passed back to the user.

7. The gateway program typically takes an HTML template that indicates how to format the results and builds an HTML stream to send back to the browser for presentation to the user.

8. The HTTP server takes the output from the gateway program and passes the data stream of HTML back to the client's browser.

9. The browser recognizes that it is receiving HTML and presents the results to the user in the proper format.

Important in this process are the main interaction points between the browser and the associated specialty services. The specialty services which support and fulfill user's application request includes the HTTP server, the gateway program, and the database. The logical browser to specialty services interface has four distinct phases, which constitute a complete communication loop. These phases are:

1. **Connection:** The Web browser attempts to connect to the primary specialty service, typically a Web HTTP Server.

2. **Request:** After connected, the browser sends a request to Web HTTP server, including the transport protocol used, what object is being requested, and which transport protocol should be used for the servers response. For example, the browser may specify a transport protocol of HTTP, NNTP, Gopher, or WAIS. The specialty service will interact with all other application services required to fulfill the user's request.

3. **Response:** Assuming the Web HTTP server can handle the request of the Web browser, it executes the response. If it can't handle the request an HTML response indicating the failure is returned to the client.

4.   **Close:** The connection between the Web browser and Web HTTP server is closed.

After the connection between the Web Client and the Web Server is closed, the browser loads and displays the requested information, saves the information to a file, or launches a graphic viewer, sound player, video viewer, or another player to run program.

The connection between the Web server and the database is similar in that the connection is viewed as a single and complete event. In essence each connection between a Web Client and Web Server is a sign-in, request, request fulfillment, and sign-off process. That is unless you use the concept of cookies and associated server side scripts to hold a connection open longer than one physical Web page interaction.

Sticky Areas in the Implementation of a Web Architecture

As with an application, good application architecture is differentiated from bad application architecture in many areas. The areas that pose the greatest risk to the Web architecture you design for your data warehouse implementations include defining the best session management and user selectors. The following sections discuss these two areas separately in detail.

Session Management

Session management is an important aspect of any application. A session is best defined as a complete interaction between a user and the application. When setting up your Web architecture you will want to be extra sensitive to session management due to the importance of the information assets managed by your data warehouse. Session management has two primary process oriented tasks: the state of each session and the logging of all session activity. Each of these two process tasks is discussed separately in the following two sections.

Managing State of Each Session

Great advances have been made in the state management features of specialty servers, such as Sybase's PowerDynamo. However, due to lack of development experience in building Web applications, developers still misunderstand how to implement session states within their Web applications. The misunderstanding comes from the immaturity and the lack of integration of the various tools and services, often from different vendors, required to build a complete Web application solution.

The leading way to manage state in a Web application is with cookies, which were initially discussed in the "The Web Server: The Processing Logic Layer" section earlier in this chapter. Server-side applications use cookies as a general mechanism to store information in a file on an individual user's computer. These cookies can be managed by a server application through retrieval and modification. The cookie standard is sufficiently open for any type of variable storage to occur. The problem is that most of the key processes for a data warehouse require additional server side code to accommodate the use of cookies. In other words, cookies are just a mechanism utilized to support more server side programming.

Lets walk through an example of how you might use cookies to enhance your security and the management of state in your data warehouse front-end Web access tool.

1. The user requests access to the data warehouse home page through a browser.

2. The Web server presents this user with a sign-on screen, from where the user's universal authentication occurs.

3. The user enters a user name and password, which are transmitted to the Web server via the Secure Sockets Layer standard described in the "Security-Related Services" section earlier in this chapter.

4. After receiving this security information, the Web server passes the information to a server side extension, or gateway program, to be processed against a database.

5. The gateway program passes this information within a stored procedure to the database, which logs the sign-on into a user table and presents a uniquely generated session ID, which in turn is returned to the gateway program.

6. The gateway program formats the session ID information into a cookie variable, which is passed to the client browser for storage.

7. The user, now authenticated for accessing the data warehouse, can begin to work. Each subsequent request from the user utilizes this session ID as the variable to which to log the work.

As you see, this process complicates all work of the overall application. In the client/server world, the concept of signing onto a database or application occurred when users initiated the application. When authenticated, they were passed handles associated with their connections and they used those handles until they completed their work. This was even easier in host-based systems, because users were tightly coupled with the system.

On the Web, a user can disappear at any time without notifying the server. Therefore, you want to ensure in your session management that cookies that you create expire. Management tasks should regularly evaluate whether a user is assumed to have gone away. This is based on a time variable. For example, if a user has had no activity in the last 30 minutes, he or she is officially gone and must be reauthenticated.

Tools such as Java can assist in better managing sessions, because these tools follow a more traditional client/server model. An application written in Java can, within a single HTML form, perform tasks including authentication, query definition, query submission, result set presentation, and disconnection from a central database. However, solutions such as Java are not always optimal in today's COBOL heritage world. Adopting Java as a development language of choice requires yet another paradigm shift. As a result, many IS shops are not choosing this avenue.

Logging User Activity

Logging the activity of users in a data warehouse assists you in better understanding who is there and what they have done. Unlike session management, logging user activity is a problem that isn't unique to the Web space. Logging user activity is generally needed in any data warehouse. Numerous start-up companies are building software to solve this issue.

In the earlier example of session management, a server-based stored procedure defined user sessions, which at any time indicates who is and has been online. Additional information that you should be logging includes what information a user accesses and how frequently these interactions occur. This information allows you to build a data warehousing system with intrinsic intelligence. The log can become a data warehouse for the data or system administration staff.

This information allows you to better understand if tables you have built within the data warehouse are being used as well as which tables are most frequently joined together in user queries. You may also want to better understand user behavior patterns, and this data will help you there as well.

Your user activity logs can become complex. But at a minimum, the data model for your logs might follow that illustrated by Figure 5.6. (The various tables presented in that figure for the activity logs are described in Table 5.1.)

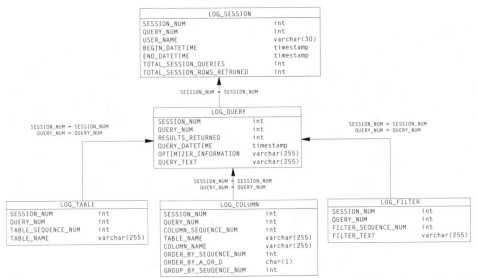

Figure 5.6 *A data model for performing data warehouse activity logging, allowing you to build a knowledge base of user activity.*

Table 5.1 *Data warehouse logging subsystem data structure descriptions.*

Table	Description
log_session	Stores information regarding when users sign onto the data warehouse and when they officially signed off. Additional summary statistics stored in this table allow managers of the data warehouse to quickly gather information about individual sessions or overall activity on the data warehouse. These columns include the number of queries performed and the number of rows returned from the data warehouse to the user.
log_query	Stores information about the queries that are run in individual sessions by users of the data warehouse. This table provides details of the query, such as the actual query text, optimizer information, and the date/time when the query was run. Summary information about the number of results that were returned to users are also stored here.
log_table	Stores information, by query and session, about the tables that were accessed. This table assists data warehouse administrators in querying for tables in the data warehouse experiencing no activity, as well as those experiencing high activity. This data may assist in partitioning schemes based on activity.

Continued

Table 5.1 Continued

Table	Description
log_column	Stores information, by query and session, about columns accessed. This table assists data warehouse administrators in managing columns and derived columns in associated tables of the data warehouse. The administrators will be able to understand which columns and calculated columns are experiencing high user activity, again assisting in potential partitioning or indexing schemes for future revisions of the warehouse based on user activity. Additional information is stored about columns, including data associated with the sorting and grouping of data contained in the columns. This information assist administrators in managing preaggregated data in the warehouse as well as indexing schemes.
log_filter	Stores information about join conditions and other filters performed in where clauses of SQL passed to the data warehouse. This information assists administrators in view management, indexing schemes, and table partitioning schemes for future revisions of the data warehouse.

As these few tables indicate, you can obtain much intelligence as to how a data warehouse is used. This information becomes the technical staff's data warehouse. If filled from the beginnings of the data warehouse project, you will gather enormous amounts of information to assist you in fulfilling your users' desires from the data warehouse in the most optimal fashion.

User Selectors

A selector is a dialog or series of forms presented to users that allow them to build a custom query against a data warehouse. In most ad-hoc query and reporting tools, this process is the starting point to building a report and analytical model. A selector tells a database specifically what is being requested. Properly building selectors for your data warehouse will assist you in managing several problematic areas of your data warehouse implementation, including: avoiding rogue queries, avoiding meaningless queries, and simplifying the presentation of the data warehouse model to users. The next three sections address these issues separately.

Avoiding Rogue Queries

A *rogue query* is a query that requests far more data than is humanly digestible, which I tend to refer to as "meaning of life" queries. You need to build selectors that will, in most cases, avoid this scenario. Many of today's more popular query tools have adopted a query environment that includes a well-managed catalog to assist in avoiding these runaway queries.

The information packaging diagram presented in this book provides a framework that may be best for performing this task. If you present the data in well understood data structures, your users will be guided properly to selecting data from well related database tables. You will also want a server-based process that queries the optimizer prior to running a query. This process introduces some overhead to the processing of a user's data request, but it allows you to assist users in fine-tuning their requests. If a query will take 24 hours to run, the user will more than likely want to place it in a batch queue or resubmit a narrower scope query. Either way, your development efforts and architecture should build in this type of processing from the beginning.

Avoiding Meaningless Queries

As with rogue queries, ad hoc queries can at times lead to totally meaningless query activity. You should do everything in your power to make sure your selectors are built with intelligent processing which will avert such meaningless query generation. The information packaging methodology presented in this book will assist you here.

If a user selects a given dimension for inclusion in a query, you already know which measures and category details are related. This knowledge allows you to present users with intelligent ad-hoc selection, but updating their selection lists with related data and controlling this presentation. If users are permitted to simply join any data warehouse table to any other data warehouse table, they will be permitted to create meaningless query activity. The impact of such a user selector is the ability to seriously impact other users' performance, as well as to provide data to a user that has little to no value. Your selector should guard against this. Most "meaningless queries" in fact are not the users' fault; they typically do not fully understand the data model and feel they are requesting the proper data. They discover their error when the results are returned, then blame the system and you for allowing them to waste their time.

Simplifying the Presentation of Your Data Warehouse Model

The presentation of your selector needs to be simplified, and much of this simplification will come in the form of dynamic inter-field editing. For example, if you had built a selector which assisted users in performing queries against automobiles, you would want dynamic inter-field editing to occur on the fields manufacturer and model. In building the car selector, your code would make sure that only valid models for a manufacturer were displayed. Therefore, when someone selects Chevrolet they would not see Intrepid in the models list since this is a Chrysler model. Dynamic inter-field editing therefore defines the user interface application logic which makes sure that each field is properly representative of valid values in relation to all other fields.

HTML forms are static and have little redeeming qualities for selectors. There is really no event processing other than the *submit* event. In this sense, HTML forms are similar to the block-mode forms of the mainframe era. To bring your forms to life, you need to build in the ability for the selector to change based on events in the form—that is, in events driven by users. You have several alternatives, including scripting, fat-client models such as web.PB (PowerBuilder's application services for the Web), and Java applet development.

Java probably presents the ultimate solution, because within one HTML form it allows you to present a user with one selector that changes based on what the user requests. This capability allows you to build a selector in a simplified fashion that works on an event model. This type of selector can be built to be much closer to the popular client/server reporting tools. However, to code such a tool requires a detailed knowledge of Java and its associated tools, such as Java Database Connectivity (JDBC) the set of class libraries which provide database interaction within Java. Therefore, you may want to opt for an alternative such as JavaScript, which offers multiple HTML forms to cover the entire query definition process.

Putting It All Together: Data Warehousing on the Internet

No single chapter—or book—can cover all of the combinations of services available for Internet-based data warehousing. We have chosen the architecture shown in Figure 5.7 to serve as a basis for describing the components of Internet-based data warehousing. This implementation will give you enough information to successfully implement your own data warehouse using the Web and the Internet (or more than likely, an intranet), and to permit access to the data managed in the data warehouse. We focus on describing the implementation strategies at a sufficiently high level so that if you choose a different architecture (which is highly likely), you will have the basic understanding of what is required to deliver your final solution.

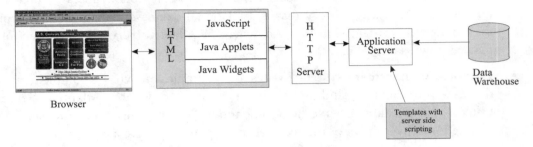

Figure 5.7 *A sample architecture of data warehousing on the Internet.*

The following components make up our architecture which will be utilized within our samples shown in Section IV, "The Case Studies."

- **HTML:** HTML is the basis for framing all presentation components and presenting them to the users of the data warehouse within the Web architecture.

- **JavaScript:** JavaScript has garnered an enormous following as the standard for dynamic HTML development. Use of JavaScript allows us to build a dynamic system of HTML pages, which in turn allows us to assist users through a highly intuitive interface.

- **Java Applets:** We will use several Java Applets, primarily for presenting data and information back to users. These applets, or graphical widgets, are pre-built components that take simple input parameters and bring the resultant data to life for presentation to users. Applets such as spreadsheets and graphs are far more understandable to users than HTML output or standard reporting output.

- **HTTP server:** For our HTTP server we using the personal web server provided with Sybase's PowerDynamo product. This HTTP server is easy to install, administer, and use, and works nicely in local, intranet, and Internet implementations. A majority of our examples will also work with Microsoft or Netscape server technologies.

- **Application server:** The application server we use is Sybase's PowerDynamo product. This server specifically allows us to work flexibly with database management systems that support the ODBC standard. Other products that fill this space perform tasks in a similar fashion, such as Allaire's Cold Fusion. PowerDynamo operates with a series of HTML-like tags to frame and format queries and their results. These descriptive documents are referred to as templates and are stored on our server within a repository that is a relational database management system, such as Sybase's Adaptive Server Anywhere or Adaptive Server Enterprise (formerly known as SQL Server).

- **Database management system:** We test our examples on Sybase's complement of database products, including Adaptive Server Anywhere, Adaptive Server Enterprise and Adaptive Server IQ. These products formulate a powerful back-end service for delivering all of the required horsepower to drive a data warehouse.

Summary

For a data warehouse to be effective, companies must equip all employees with the information that is vital to do their jobs. Companies need to provide their employees with industry information, customer information, internal process information, and market information. To be successful, this information needs to be provided in a constant and effective vehicle for communication. Today, all of this is possible. In fact most growing businesses already have much of what they need to do the job: the technology, computing power, and knowledgeable workers. The only thing left is to put it all together, and this can be accomplished with the Internet.

The Internet, or more specifically an intranet, with a Web interface provides your users with several benefits, including:

- **Ease of Use:** Whether your users are utilizing PCs with a Windows interface, MACs, or UNIX, the Internet and Web provide a layer of independence that is unmatched in other tools. Anyone running almost any platform and network can access information on a corporate Web server with the same browser he or she uses to surf the World Wide Web.

- **Inexpensive:** Intranets are quite easy to install and administer. These systems are inexpensive compared to the proprietary solutions offered in the client/server and host-based worlds. Web browsers are inexpensive when purchased in mass quantity and Web servers are beginning to be bundled on server platforms. Therefore, the cost tends to revolve around development and management, while productivity tools are all competing for market share via low entry prices.

- **Safe:** The intranet variety of Internet access is safe. Corporate information assets are not accessible via the public Internet, so security isn't an issue until you open the doors of your data warehouse to the public.

- **Productive:** Because the Internet is based on open technology standards, it is much easier to find multivendor solutions that work with each other. The Internet is also a technology with which most of your employees already are acquainted, so your training and support costs will be manageable. These types of productivity help your development staff to focus on the business of software development—building what users need, not integrating incompatible product sets.

Currently, data warehousing is a more suitable use than online transaction processing (OLTP) for the Web. The Web is primarily a presentation oriented medium, and user actions against data warehouse applications are primarily query and display oriented. These behaviors allow your developers to focus on the proper retrieval and presentation of information assets rather than on issues such as data integrity. Additional reasons that make access to a data warehouse a natural application for the Web, include:

- There is a high need to deliver information from production databases to managers and business analysts throughout an enterprise and Web based applications can easily be distributed to these users with near zero costs.

- The Web provides high value because its interface, the browser, is simplistic, requiring minimal training and other deployment infrastructure costs.

- Users are only interested in querying a data warehouse. Therefore, no updates occur in data warehouse access applications, and database integrity is not compromised, overcoming additional work required by OLTP applications.

- The Web has great facilities to present information graphically, enhancing the delivery and understanding of the data from a data warehouse.

As we proceed with the remaining chapters in Section II, you will learn the essentials behind the core technologies required to deliver your data warehousing solution on the Internet. This will include database access techniques, HTML coding, and script development.

6

Database Essentials

A data warehouse is all about data—gathering the proper data, managing the data throughout the overall process, and providing access to the data. If you do not get the data right, you might as well not proceed. We now focus on the first area of development—data management services—which comprises the foundation of your data warehousing system.

As we discussed in Section I, "Introduction to the Information Packaging Methodology," you need to clearly define the information architecture and associated supporting technology architecture of your data warehouse, both critical components in a solid foundation. An overall data warehouse architecture contains several physical data stores. Many companies have chosen to only focus on one of these data stores—a centralized data warehouse. Through the evolution of the data warehousing market, this thinking will be modified to include a more robust architecture.

Data Warehouse Data Stores

A data warehouse is by its very nature a distributed physical data store. Distribution of information assets assist in performance and usability, two cornerstones of your data warehouse mission and objective. Distributed solutions enhance performance, because parallelism can be implemented, and usability is enhanced, by placing the data closer to the user in a more useable format.

The important data stores of an architecture incorporate source data feeds, a corporate (or enterprise) data warehouse, an operational data store, and data marts. Figure 6.1 depicts the overall architecture and associated interfaces between the components of the architecture. When considering these data stores, it is important to understand the operations which will be performed on these technologies—this will dictate the proper technology to be implemented. The following sections discuss these items.

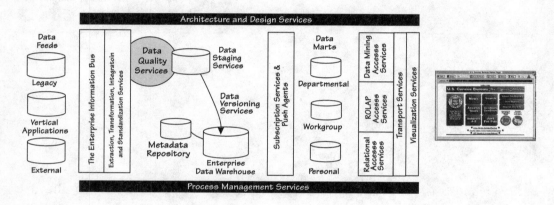

Figure 6.1 *A data warehouse information architecture incorporates distinct and layered data stores, including data feeds, corporate data warehouse, operational data store, and data marts. (All of these stores are not required for successful implementation of your data warehouse.)*

Source Data Feeds

Source data feeds are the inputs that feed the data warehousing process and overall system. These feeds include the traditional data capture systems that are managed by your company as well as outside data feeds, such as demographic information, which are typically purchased from third-party vendors. Though the data and architecture associated with these data stores is not managed by the data warehousing project team, understanding the data feeds is extremely important, the heart and soul of the process.

The most difficult process your data architects will face is clearly defining the proper source for data feeds. Many companies face the challenge of dated systems that co-mingle data and share ownership of data. As discussed in Chapter 2, "Building an Adaptable Architecture," we must realize that the inputs into a data warehouse require various degrees of scrubbing, cleansing, transformation, standardization and integration. These processes are your primary focus in the overall data warehousing system. The management of the data feeds and data stores remains in the current support infrastructure. Therefore, your will be best served by clearly understanding who manages this data and gaining his or her insight into the problems in data quality that you will face in your attempts to unify corporate information assets.

Operational Data Store (ODS)

An ODS is a data store that permits the staging of data prior to placement into a data warehouse. This staging environment provides a data store for near-time data reporting and staging of data that is prepared for the data warehouse. This type of data store typically is used with larger scale implementations that integrate highly disparate and distributed systems, or is used by those companies who have leveraged application software packages from third parties. This is an optional data store, though many current industry beacons are pointing to the inclusion of an ODS as an important step in the overall data warehousing process. Based on the timeliness of the data, this data store can also assist your information systems in off-loading production reporting from critical applications while assuring that you do not migrate production style reports to the data warehouse.

Data Marts

Data marts are highly focused data stores that are aligned to a subset of an overall business. Segmentation of the data in data marts is typically based on an application, line of business, or specific subject area. Examples of these categories might include:

- **A human resources data mart**, with a focused set of data fed from an application such as PeopleSoft.

- **A sales and marketing data mart**, with data sourced across the various areas of a business, which impact sales and marketing activities from an application such as Seibel.

- **A supply chain management data mart**, with a focused set of data fed from an application such as SAP or Baan.

Data marts offer an optimization capability in the overall data warehousing architecture. By filtering the data and focusing the content of a data mart, you can provide a highly optimized and interactive data store. Data marts vary in size and content, to the point where you can develop three target areas: departmental, workgroup, and personal data marts. Each of these data marts can be fed by the corporate data warehouse, other data marts, or directly from data feeds. To manage the delivery of this data, we recommend a subsystem that supports subscription and push technologies.

Corporate (or Enterprise) Data Warehouse

A corporate data warehouse (CDW) is often referred to as an enterprise or consolidated data warehouse. This data store is the central store for all data and data management in a data warehousing system. This structure is not always implemented, especially because, in recent years, companies have begun to implement data marts more frequently as their entree into their data warehousing environments. A CDW is typically recommended for companies that have begun to implement multiple data marts. The CDW is a consolidation and concentration data store for all information that is shared across multiple data marts.

Processing Techniques

As you begin to consider the data stores that will directly support your data warehouse, it helps to understand the processing models and techniques that will typically be required by your users. No matter what data store you focus on, the distinct processing models that are required include: standard relational query processing, online analytical processing (OLAP), statistical processing, and data mining processing. User requirements are comprised of functionality that is fulfilled by each of these processing disciplines. Therefore, to achieve the lofty goals required by the users of your data warehouse system requires components in each of these areas. Other areas of processing, including extraction, transformation, and movement processing, were covered in Chapter 4, "Transformation & Movement Process Modeling." This component, which won't be detailed again here, is a critical element of the processing techniques of data warehousing systems.

Relational Processing

Relational processing involves traditional query activity that plots data in a tabular format. As shown in Figure 6.2, relational processing involves passing data variables from a data store, a data mart, or a data warehouse and presenting this data down the page in a series of rows organized by columns of data. Mapped closely to the relational model, this technique has been the mainstay of reporting for operational systems for years and provides a valuable function for data warehousing systems. Often, this processing is utilized to retrieve summary level data as well as detail level data to be placed in production style reports.

The data is accessed in a relational format, and then processed by a tool such as a fourth generation language or COBOL to present the data in the format required by the user. These reports tend to be produced for distribution to a wider base of users as required information.

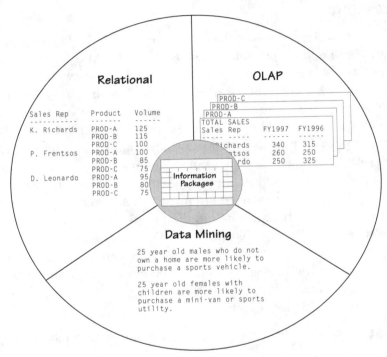

Figure 6.2 *The processing techniques that occur on a data warehouse include traditional relational processing, online analytical processing, and data mining.*

Relational processing tends to be most useful for extracting and formatting data that is more textual or descriptive. Many functions allow users to report on numerical information. However, this tends to be closely tied to textual or descriptive reporting. Ad-hoc reporting tools also are traditionally based on relational processing. In the ad-hoc space, tools have been provided to support gaps as well as production reports.

Sample relational queries include:

- Show me all customers in the Midwest who have purchased office furniture.

- Show me the top 10 sales people in the company, providing a breakdown of their sales in the major product classifications.

- Show me the current accounts receivable listing, including the total amount outstanding in common groupings of time, such as 30 days, 60 days, 90 days, and greater than 90 days.

OLAP Processing

OLAP (online analytical processing) has overtaken much of the traditional Decision Support System (DSS) applications of the 1980s. These OLAP systems work with a processing model that correlates data in a cross-tabular style, as shown in Figure 6.2. Unlike relational processing, which presents data variables in rows that are organized in a columnar fashion, OLAP presents variable data in rows and columns on a page and correlates these two variables' relationship data in the cells as an intersection point. OLAP processing, as the name implies, is most useful for analyzing data. This analysis typically involves mapping numerical trends across dimensions such as time, product, and geography. However, the OLAP model works best on filtered or summarized (aggregated) data and is best performed in a highly interactive environment. OLAP sessions with users tend to be highly interactive and support rapid-fire question-answer-question interactions between the user and system. Each answer that the system provides to a user typically generates several additional questions, which require answers. If significant time delays are interjected into this process, the user is inhibited. Therefore, highly interactive and rapid-response tools have emerged.

Sample OLAP processing requests include:

- Show me the total number of customers by region and purchase category.

- Show me the comparison of product classification sales (trend) over the last five years by sales personnel.

- Compare our accounts receivable of the past three years; organize the data by area and by time groupings such as 30 days, 60 days, 90 days, and greater than 90 days.

Data Mining Processing

Data mining processing offers statistical algorithms that are applied to the data warehouse providing data driven analysis. The results of data mining on a data warehouse are reports that identify and characterize interrelationships within the requested data. Often data mining processes can be executed without requiring a human to ask the questions. This process assists users by extracting previously unknown, actionable information from data warehouses, a process often characterized as knowledge discovery. As information packages become more complicated, with multiple dimensions, the analysis of cause and affect relationships can become time consuming if not impossible for humans to perform. Data mining tools step into this vulnerable area to help users find answers to questions they never even thought to ask.

This processing tends to be more batch oriented and compute intensive than either relational or OLAP processing. The process of data mining involves characterization inherent in the data, development of a hypothesis from these patterns, and using the hypothesis to predict future behaviors. More than the other processing areas, data mining is very dependent on the quality of the data. If you have high quality data, data mining will enable your users to work more intelligently with data. The users will not be required to prepare queries or set out to resolve a particular problem before they mine. Instead, the system works for the users and prepares findings in an agent-oriented fashion.

Sample data mining processing requests include:

- Show me what influences someone to purchase office furniture from us.

- What product features appear to be driving current trends in product sales?

- What type of company is likely to pay its bills on time and therefore is likely to assist us in managing our accounts receivable?

Database Architectures

Developers have architected databases to manage data using differing techniques and for differing management spaces. The major classifications of databases have evolved from the flat-file systems of early computing days to relational databases of modern systems. Growing requirements associated with system have impacted this evolution. Most of us have lived through the maturation of computing systems, and much more is still to come.

Databases previously required developers to retrieve the data by explicitly defining the navigation through the data structures. Though these systems were good for the transaction systems used in operational systems, they posed an incredible burden on those who desired to quickly and easily retrieve data from a database for reporting purposes. The two most prominent database architectures that are used in today's data warehouses are multi-dimensional databases and relational databases. Each of these architectures is described separately in the sections that follow.

Multidimensional Database

Multidimensional databases optimize the storage and retrieval of dimensional data. This storage optimization is typically found in a proprietary database that is closely aligned with a proprietary query and visualization tool. The combination of the database and visualization tool typically outperforms relational implementations. This optimization is provided through highly specialized functionality. In the analytical world supported by multidimensional databases, matrix operations calculate and manipulate dimensional data effectively. These matrix operations include drilling down on dimensions, "slicing and dicing" dimensions, and pivoting display variables.

Drill down operations are performed on dimensions allowing users to gain more insight to details of the underlying data. A user can work with the time period dimension, starting their analysis at the yearly level and proceed to drill down to the quarterly or monthly level of the data.

Slice and dice operations involves multiple dimensions. In working with an information package which contains multiple dimensions (for example time, product and geography) a user may begin their analysis with two of the dimensions such as time and geography. Upon discovery of trends within the data along these two dimensions, the user may isolate on a category level within a dimension, for example the West Region of the geography dimension, and slice in another dimension to continue their analysis. The slice of the product dimension would allow the user to further investigate the product and time dimensions while filtering on the geography dimension which was sliced out and isolated on the West Region.

Pivot operations involve changing the display coordinates of a multidimensional information package. Depending on the type of display in use by the user, they may want to change the coordinates. If the X axis is currently time and the Y axis product; a pivot operation would involve swapping these coordinates—the X axis becoming the product dimension and the Y axis the time dimension.

Multidimensional databases provide the specialty data stores that best support OLAP tools. These structures focus on a core storage structure for multidimensional data, which is typically referred to as a cube. Typically, these data structures are more closely aligned with proprietary, nonrelational data structures. The leading vendor in this area is Arbor Software with its Essbase product. Based on this technology, most multidimensional databases are not as open as relational databases and therefore do not support the same breadth of tools. Two basic approaches can be followed to resolve this lack of support.

The first approach arms users with tools that support cross-tabulation, pivoting, drill-down and other multidimensional analysis features. Cross-tabulation is a form of reporting the data where variables are placed in both the rows and columns of a spreadsheet style display, while the value being investigated is placed in the intersecting cells of the report. This approach is currently supported by tools such as Andyne's Pablo and Brio Technology's BrioQuery. Both of these vendors also have either delivered or soon will deliver Web-based interfaces for their products. These tools provide graphical query building interfaces, send SQL to a relational database, and perform multidimensional analysis through fat client features.

The second strategy places a multidimensional analytical application server between a relational database and front-end query tools. These products adhere to the three-tiered architecture discussed in Chapter 5. The analytical logic is placed on a specialty server, between the relational database and the client tools. This approach is supported by products including DecisionSuite from Information Advantage and WhiteLight Server from WhiteLight Systems Inc. These tools rely on metadata repositories that store the mappings of multidimensional structures in the relational database managing the data. The analytical server receives requests from client tools, translates that request into a series of SQL queries, obtains the data from the relational database, perform the multidimensional processing, and return the results to the client.

These two strategies provide more flexibility to your information architecture. Multidimensional databases require you to initially load and periodically update another OLAP server. The advances in recent years with intermediate multidimensional servers and a supporting relational database is quickly proving to be a more robust architecture for data warehousing.

Relational Databases

Relational databases evolved from the research of Dr. E.F. Codd and others. Dr. Codd started the relational era with his paper, "A Relational Model of Data for Large Shared Data Banks," which was published in *Communications of the ACM* in June, 1970. This was the first documentation of the relational model, a model that was more in alignment with the way data relates and queries are performed than the databases of first generation systems including hierarchical and network oriented databases. Dr. Codd is a mathematician, and therefore his documents focused on the mathematical nature of proving the relational theory.

In additional articles such as "Relational Database: A Practical Foundation for Productivity," in *Communications of the ACM* (February 1982), Codd further described the business need for relational databases and relational products. In this article, he stated that: the growth in user demands for new applications was outstripping the capability of data processing departments to implement corresponding application programs. He further described the inherent problems relating to prerelational database technology as:

- These systems burdened application programmers with numerous concepts that were irrelevant to their data retrieval and manipulation tasks, forcing them to think and code needlessly a low level of structural detail.

- No commands were provided for processing multiple records at a time—in other words, DBMS did not support *set processing* and, as a result, programmers were forced to think and code in terms of iterative loops that were often unnecessary.

- The needs of users for direct interaction with databases, particularly interaction of an unanticipated nature, were inadequately recognized; a query capability was assumed to be something one could add on to a DBMS at some later time.

These articles and many others produced by Dr. Codd have become the foundation of relational database technology that support our current data warehouses. The objectives set forth by Dr. Codd and those who assisted him in his research efforts were as follows:

- The relational model should provide a clear boundary between the logical and physical aspects of database management, including design, retrieval and manipulation.

- The model should be simple, so that programmers and users can have a common understanding of the data and communicate with each other regarding the database.

- A high-level language should be introduced to enable users to express operations on sets of information at one time.

Relational databases have become the core technology that supports the data warehouses in most companies today. Therefore, it is important that you understand the structures and access techniques behind these relational databases. This knowledge will allow you to build an optimal solution that allows your users to retrieve their business intelligence out of the corporate knowledge base.

Relational Structure Essentials

All information in a relational database is represented by values in a table. Addressing data by value rather than by position boosts the productivity of programmers as well as users. To best understand the relational model and relational database management systems (RDBMSes), we begin by defining some of their common terminology.

- **Column:** A discrete attribute, such as First Name or Last Name for an entity such as Employee.

- **Row:** A complete set of one or more columns and their associated data, which is retrieved from a database entity such as Product.

- **Table:** A collection of rows and columns that are physically stored in a database. A table is often referred to as an entity contained in a database such as an Order.

- **Primary Key:** A column, or set of columns, which uniquely identifies a row in a table such as Employee Number.

- **View:** A virtual, or logical, table in a database that is defined by an administrator. A view typically is composed of a portion of one or many related tables. For example, a human resources database may store employee information in an Employee table. However, this table contains information that should not be seen by all who have access to the database, such as Current Salary information. The administrator of the database can create a view of the Employee table that presents all relevant and publicly accessible information about an employee and call it Employee View. This view would contain all columns from the Employee Table except for Current Salary information.

- **Database:** A collection of tables that are logically contained in the same application. An order entry system has tables that relate to the recording of a customer submitting an order to your company. This might include tables such as Order, Order Line Items, Product, Inventory, Employee, Customer, to name a few. Together, all of these tables comprise one database.

- **Data Normalization:** A process that optimizes the way your data is represented in tables. Relational databases work best when the data contained in a given table relates only to that table's primary key in a one-to-one manner. For example, the primary key of Employee Number exists in an Employee table. Each Employee has one first name and one last name, which are placed in the Employee table. However, an employee can have many skill sets that are important to the company; therefore, you would manage these skill sets in a separate table, Employee Skills. The Employee Skills table would have a primary key composed of the Employee Number and Skill, and this table would relate to the Employee table in a one-to-many fashion (one employee has many skills).

Access Essentials

To again paraphrase Dr. Codd, the *manipulative part* of the relational model consists of the algebraic operators (*select, project, join,* and so forth) that transform relations into relations (hence, tables into tables). Relational databases support a relational language known as Structured Query Language.

Structured Query Language (SQL): *A specialized language for set-based data access. This language is used to formulate operations that define and manipulate data in a relational form.*

SQL is typically the only means of accessing data in a relational database. A main advantages of SQL and the relational data model is its independence from navigational data access. In other data structures, a user (or, typically, a programmer) must tell the database two things: what data is needed and how to get it. The *how* is done by providing navigational logic to the database. Therefore, users of these databases are forced to understand the physical implementation of the data model. SQL based databases only require users to request the data that they need, not how to obtain that data. Therefore, relational databases provide a simple interface with the data and associated data structures.

SQL, and databases that support SQL such as relational databases, are based on relational theory. The relational model isolates users from underlying data structures, which makes SQL far easier to use than previous database access techniques. Users familiar with the relational model should be able to access data with fewer problems. SQL is not a procedural language, which also simplifies the usability of this language. This simplicity should result in increased productivity for application development and in many ways explains why relational databases have been so widely accepted as a base technology for data warehousing.

SQL has three primary subsets of commands: *data manipulation language, data definition language, and data control language.*

- **Data Definition Language (DDL):** The subset of SQL that defines the data, its structure, and its physical layout. An example of a DDL statement is the *create table* command. The command *create table sales_analysis (time_period_id int, product_id int, geography_id int, units_sold int, sales_revenue money)* creates a table to house the sales data that is required for analysis.

- **Data Control Language (DCL):** The subset of SQL that defines the parameters within which the server works. An example of a DCL is the set command, which is used to set Sybase Adaptive Server query processing options for the duration of a user's work session. The command *set rowcount 100* processes a user's query request, stopping the processing after the hundredth row.

- **Data Manipulation Language (DML):** The subset of SQL that allows a user to manipulate the data that is managed by a database. An example of a DML is the *select* command, which is used to retrieve data from the database. The command *select * from sales_analysis* retrieves all of the rows and columns from database table sales_analysis, allowing the user to view, analyze and verify this table.

Because this book primarily focuses on accessing the contents of a data warehouse across the Internet, we focus our energies on retrieval operations and their associated commands in the DML and DCL subsets of SQL. The most vital operations in this subset of SQL include: select, project and join operations.

- The *select* operation, also called the *restrict* operation, takes one table and produces a result set consisting of selected rows of the table.

- The *project* operation transforms one table into a results set, consisting of selected columns of the table.

- The *equijoin* operation takes two tables and produces a result set consisting of rows of the first concatenated with rows of the second, but only where specified columns in the first and specified columns in the second have matching values.

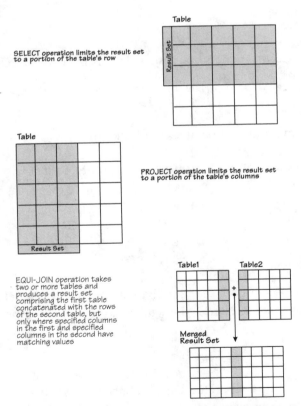

Figure 6.3 *The most vital data manipulation operations of the standard SQL select statement include select, project, and equijoin.*

These operations are presented graphically in Figure 6.3. As we will see in the next section, the SQL *select* statement is the command allows you to realize each of these operations. The *select* statement and its associated clauses provide the database essentials required for retrieval systems such as data warehouses.

Select Statement

In the standard data manipulation language of RDBMSes, the select statement allows you to retrieve data from database tables. The formal syntax for a select statement is:

```
SELECT [ALL | DISTINCT] select_clause
FROM from_clause
WHERE where_clause
GROUP BY [ALL]
 group_by_clause
 [HAVING having_clause]
ORDER BY order_by_clause [ASC | DESC]
```

The most basic *select* statement requests columns from an individual table as follows:

```
select time_period, geography, product, units_sold
from sales_analysis
```

The results of a hypothetical database look like this:

time_period	geography	product	units_sold
1997-10	VT	Diapers	875
1997-11	NH	Paper Towels	1,500
1997-11	VT	Napkins	365
1997-12	NY	Diapers	1,200
1997-12	MA	Napkins	2,200

Now let us look closer at each of the individual clause's for the select statement including the from clause, the select clause, the where clause, the order by clause, the group by clause, and the having clause.

From Clause

The *from* clause is a comma separated list of tables or views from which the *select* statement retrieves data. A *from* clause is always required, except when the select statement contains no columns. Many database management systems restrict the total number of tables or views in a from clause to 16. You should check your database administration handbook to verify how many tables and views you can place in your *from* clause. The order of the tables and views in the from clause should not affect the results. Examples of *from* clauses include:

```
from sales_analysis
from sales_analysis, time_periods, product_details
```

Tables and views can be given aliases, either for convenience or to distinguish the different roles that a table or view might play in a self-join or subquery. You may require a self-join in instances where a recursive relationship exists, such as in the relationship between a manager and a subordinate, where both are employees. To uniquely identify the role that a table plays in a *select* statement, you might choose to label it as shown in the examples below:

```
from employee subordinate, employee manager
from sales_analysis t1, time_period t2
```

Select Clause

The *select* list is a comma-separated list of columns. The *select* list can be replaced by an asterisk, (*), indicating to the relational database engine that it should retrieve all columns from the associated tables in a *from* clause. The *select* list should be entered in the order in which you want to see the resultant data. It is often a good practice to specifically refer to a column by indicating the table from which it came, because multiple tables within your query may have the same column names. This is done by pairing the table name and column name together, separated by a period as illustrated in the next code listing. With this syntax, the result set returns a column heading for each column using the table name and the column name. Therefore, within the column list, you may want to change the heading that is returned in the result set. To change the heading for any column, simply equate the new heading with the column definition. For example, order number will exist in the order header table (order_header.order_number) and order line item table (order_line.order_number), both of these tables will be accessed within many queries and uniquely defining the column to present will assist in optimizing the generation of results and avoid any errors. Valid *select* list clauses for a SQL *select* statement include:

```
*
month, product, geography
subordinate.fname, subordinate.lname, manager.fname, manager.lname
"Product" = t2.product_name, "Units Sold" = t1.units_sold
```

Where Clause

If you plan to include more than one table, or you want to limit the result set, you apply search criteria to the *select* statement. The *where* clause specifies filter conditions to apply to a set of records. These filter conditions include the ability to bring two tables together —a join as well as the ability to restrict the results produced by the *select* statement—a filter. The following code example demonstrates a join between four tables representing an information package. The base tables include a fact table (sales_analysis) and three dimension tables (time_period, product, and geography). As discussed Chapter 3, "Information Modeling," the relationships between these tables is across the lowest-level category of each dimension (month, product, and store).

```
select
 quarter, month, product, region, geography,
 units, revenue
from
 sales_analysis, time_period, product, geography
where
 sales_analysis.month = time_period.month and
 sales_analysis.product = product.product and
 sales_analysis.store = geography.store
```

A hypothetical result set for the above command looks like this:

quarter	month	product	region	geography	units	revenue
Q1	JAN	Soda	East	NY	135	1,250
Q1	JAN	Pretzels	East	NY	425	757.5
Q1	FEB	Chips	West	CA	245.75	325.35
Q2	MAY	Soda	Central	IL	210	1,950

You may also elect to utilize both a join and a filter condition in your *where* clause. The code example below combines the same join as shown above with a filter restricting the product sales for the Eastern region of the country during 1997.

```
select
 quarter, month, product, region, geography,
 units, revenue
from
 sales_analysis, time_period, product, geography
where
 (sales_analysis.month = time_period.month and
 sales_analysis.product = product.product and
```

```
sales_analysis.store = geography.store)
and
geography.region = 'East' and time_period.year = '1997'
```

A hypothetical result set for the above command looks like:

quarter	month	product	region	geography	units	revenue
Q1	JAN	Soda	East	NY	135	1,250
Q1	JAN	Pretzels	East	NY	425	757.5
Q1	APR	Chips	East	MA	145	210
Q2	MAY	Soda	East	NY	210	1,950

Order By Clause

The *order* by clause returns the results of a given *select* statement in a user-specified order. This clause assists in presenting the data from the results in a more readable fashion. An example of ordering, or sorting, is to order the results of a query by department name and then, in the department, to list the employees by last name oand then first name. To accomplish this, you issue the following *order by* clause:

```
order by
  department.name, employee.lname, employee.fname
```

You can sort results in either ascending or descending order. To indicate this, simply add the token *ASC* for ascending order or *DESC* for descending order following the appropriate column. The default order for results is ascending. Here is an example.

```
order by hire_date DESC, job_title ASC
```

The *order by* clause is optional in a *select* statement. However, the ordering of a result set assists in performing control break processing, such as footers and subtotals. Therefore, many tools incorporate *order by* clauses to assist in properly presenting the data with breaks and subtotals.

Group By Clause

To perform aggregate functions, you use the *group by* clause of SQL. This clause consolidates the rows in a result set as rows of summary or aggregate values. Many relational database engines force you to apply an aggregate function to all columns in a *select* clause not represented in the group by clause. You can use aggregate functions such as *MIN*,

MAX, SUM, and *COUNT* to return calculated columns based on result set groups. Not applying an aggregate function to a column not in a *group by* clause but presented in a *select* clause produces erroneous results and therefore is not recommended. The *group by* clause compresses the summary data in the order that it appears in the result set. Therefore, you will typically want to order the result set so that the groups of data returned are in the proper order, as shown in the example below.

```
select
 product_name, year, sum(units), sum(revenue)
from
 sales_analysis, time_period, product
where
 sales_analysis.month = time_period.month and
 sales_analysis.product = product.product
group by
 product_name, year
order by
 product_name, year
```

A hypothetical result set for the above command looks like:

product_name	year	sum(units)	sum(revenue)
Floss	1995	25,000	45,000
Floss	1996	32,000	54,500
Floss	1997	37,000	64,750
Toothbrush	1995	65,000	75,000
Toothbrush	1996	57,000	72,000
Toothbrush	1997	66,400	78,000
Tooth Paste	1995	37,500	72,000
Tooth Paste	1996	33,000	67,000
Tooth Paste	1997	35,250	71,000

Having Clause

After results are grouped together in a summary form, you can further filter the data with the *having* clause. The *where* clause worked specifically on rows as they were retrieved from a database into a result set. The *having* clause restricts the groups you retrieve in a group by clause based on your specified search condition. Below is a code example that only retrieves data associated with customers who have ordered more than five times from a company.

```
select
  company.name, year_month, sum(units), sum(revenue)
from
  company, time_period, order_analysis
where
  order_analysis.company_id = company.company_id and
  order_analysis.time_period_id = time_period.time_period_id
group by
  company_name, year_month
having
  count(order_id) > 5
order by
  company_name, year_month DESC
```

A hypothetical result set for the above command looks like this:

company_name	year_month	sum(units)	sum(revenue)
Beckett & Co.	1997-02	2,575	12,100
Beckett & Co.	1996-11	1,750	8,075
Richards Ent.	1996-12	875	3,250
Richards Ent.	1996-11	1,100	4,250
Richards Ent.	1996-09	950	4,000
Richards Ent.	1996-07	750	2,965
Smith LLP.	1997-06	1,200	6,450
Smith LLP.	1996-12	1,425	8,100
Widgets Inc.	1997-07	3,000	15,000
Widgets Inc.	1997-05	1,575	8,000
Widgets Inc.	1997-02	2,100	10,125

Expressions

You can create expressions in SQL statement, such as *select*. An expression can be thought of as a general term for a constant, a column name, or a variable name used in a clause of a SQL statement. Expressions play a key role in the flexibility of SQL. Each clause that we explored in the previous section leverages expressions to build a more dynamic statement that is driven by data. The following sections describe the components of an overall expression. *However, you should closely review the SQL Commands Reference Manual provided by your database management system vendor for more details on the specific syntax required by your database management system.*

Arithmetic Operator

Arithmetic operators allow you to perform math functions in expressions. These operators allow you to perform addition (+), subtraction (-), division (/) and multiplication (*) on any numeric column. All arithmetic operators can be used in a select clause with column names and numeric constants and in any combination. The following example shows a forecast-oriented query determining the impact of a price increase of 4% on revenues if units slipped by 10%.

```
select
 product_name,
 (sum(quantity)) "96 Actual Unit",
 (sum(quantity) * avg(price)) "96 Actual Revenue",
 (sum(quantity) * .9) "97 Forecast Units",
 (sum(quantity) * avg(price) * 1.04) "97 Forecast Revenue"
from
 order_line
group by
 product_name
order by
 product_name
```

The results look like this:

product_name	96 Acutal Units	96 Acutal Revenue	97 Forecast Units	97 Forecast Revenue
Lawn Mower	300	37,500	270	35,100
Leaf Rakes	175	3,500	158	3,286
Shovels	210	4,200	189	3,931
Weed Wacker	250	18,750	225	17,550

Where an expression has more than one arithmetic operator, the precedence of operators is as follows. Multiplication and division operators are processed before subtraction and addition operators. When arithmetic operators are at the same level of precedence, the operators are executed from left to right. Using parentheses in your statements to control precedence is important, because expressions inside parentheses take precedence over all other arithmetic operations.

Comparison Operators

Comparison operators allow you to compare constants, columns, and expression results to determine an action to take. Table 6.1 lists the available comparison operators in most relational database management system SQL processors.

Table 6.1 *SQL Comparison Operators.*

Operator	Meaning	Example	Description
=	equal to	zip_code = "45140"	Zip code is equal to 45140.
>	greater than	units_sold > 1500	Units sold are greater than 1500.
<	less than	revenue < 1000000	Revenue is less than one million.
>=	greater than or equal to	uptime >= 12	Uptime is greater than or equal to 12.
<=	less than or equal to	downtime <= 2	Downtime is less than or equal to 2.
!=, <>	not equal to	margin <> target_margin	Margin is not equal to target margin.
!>	not greater than	act_rev !> bud_rev	Actual revenue is not greater than budget revenue.
!<	not less than	act_exp !< bud_exp	Actual expense is not less than budget expense.
IN	in list	state in ("CA", "NY", "TX")	States that match one of the values in the list of "CA","NY", and "TX".
BETWEEN	between values	sales between 50000 and 100000	The range of sales between and including 50,000 and 100,000.
LIKE	string like value	paint like "%white%"	All paints containing the word white. (See the "Wild Card Characters" section later in this chapter for more details.)
IS NULL	no value has been set	sales_rep is null	Locate values not containing a value for sales representative.

Continued

Table 6.1 *Continued*

Operator	Meaning	Example	Description
IS NOT NULL	a value has been set	customer_code is not null	Locate all customers. Prospects will not have initialized their customer_code and therefore it will be null. A value in customer_code indicates that a company is a customer.

Comparison operators are typically utilized in a *where* clause or *having* clause of a SQL statement to restrict the result set to be operated on. It is important to validate that the two values being compared are of like type, such as strings or numbers. Also, when comparing values to constants, strings and dates should be placed in quotation marks, while numbers should not be placed in quotation marks. The following code example filters the sales_analysis table for all customers who don't have a sales representative and have purchased more than $1,000,000 of product for year to date.

```
select
 company_name, sum(revenue)
from
 sales_analysis, customer, time_period
where
 (sales_analysis.cust_id = customer.cust_id and
 sales_analysis.time_period_id = time_period.time_period_id)
 and
 time_period.year = '1997' and
 customer.rep_id is null
group by
 company_name
having
 sum(revenue) >= 1000000
```

Wild Card Characters

Wild card characters can be used in *where* clauses to compare variables that contain patterns, partial words, or literal strings. These characters are typically utilized in *like* operations, such as when searching for all paints that contained the word *white*. Placing the % wild card in front of and behind the word *white* accepts any string of zero or more characters. This returns values such as *pearl white* and *white off white*. Besides the % wild card character, you can compare any single character, any single character in a range or set, or any single character not in a specified range. These wild card characters are presented in Table 6.2.

Table 6.2 *Wild Card Characters in SQL.*

Wildcard	Meaning	Example
%	Any string of zero or more characters.	paint *like* "%white%" returns *pearly white* and *white off white*
_	Any single character.	fName *like* "_ob" returns *Bob* and *Rob*
[ ]	Any single character in the specified range.	LName *like* [CK]arson returns *Carson* and *Karson*
[^]	Any single character not in the specified range.	lName *like* "M[^c]%" returns *Meyers* but does not return *McMillian*

Logical Operators

Logical operators (*and*, *or*, and *not*) connect search conditions in *where* clauses of SQL statements. The *and* operator joins two or more conditions and returns results only when all of the conditions are true. The following statement only returns sales data for the first quarter in the state of Florida.

```
select quarter, state, units from sales_analysis
where quarter = 1 and state = 'FL'
```

The results look like:

quarter	state	units
1	F	1250

The *or* operator joins two or more conditions and returns results for which any one or more of the conditions is true. The following statement returns sales data if the sale occurred in either the first quarter or in the state of Florida.

```
select quarter, state, units from sales_analysis
where quarter = 1 or state = 'FL'
```

The results look like:

quarter	state	units
4	F	950
1	KY	540
1	OH	1250

The *not* operator negates the expression that follows it. The following statement would return sales data which did not occur in the first quarter.

```
select quarter, state, units from sales_analysis
where (NOT quarter = 1) and state = 'FL'
```

The results look like:

quarter	state	units
2	FL	750
3	FL	850
4	FL	950

When a statement has more than one logical operator, not is evaluated first, then and, and finally or. Note that arithmetic operators have precedence over logical operators. Therefore, like other operators, it is important to utilize parenthesis to control the interpretation of your desired precedence when working with logical operators.

Functions

Common functions in the SQL language set allow you to build a comprehensive query engine to supports your user's requirements. These functions allow you to manipulate the data stored in a data warehouse for presentation and comparative purposes. These functions include string, math, and aggregate functions, which we discuss separately in the sections that follow. In addition, most database management systems provide date functions. However, we will not be covering those here for two reasons. First, most information packages will contain a time period dimension entity which will eliminate the need for most date functions from within your queries. And secondly, date functions are still very proprietary, developed specifically for a vendor's database management system. To gain more detail information on date functions please review your database management systems date function or syntax documentation.

String Functions

You can use string functions only on character data types, such as *char* and *varchar*, as well as datatypes that implicitly convert to character data types. More information on implicit conversions can be found in your database management system's commands reference guide; Sybase Adaptive Server users will find this information under the *convert* command. String functions are used for various operations such as concatenation, which are commonly needed to better present the data from a query to a user. String functions can be nested and they can be used anywhere an expression is allowed in a SQL statement, including a *select* or *where* clause. The most commonly used string functions are listed in Table 6.3. For more information on the string functions available to you, see the database management systems user guide.

Table 6.3 *Common String Functions in SQL.*

Function	Parameters	Result
+	*character expression +* *character expression*	Two or more character strings are concatenated to form one character string.
LOWER	LOWER(*character expression*)	The character expression is converted to lowercase.
LTRIM	LTRIM(*character expression*)	Leading spaces (those on the left) are removed from the character expression.
RIGHT	RIGHT(*character expression,* *integer*)	The substring of the character expression starting at the integer position is returned.
RTRIM	RTRIM(*character expression*)	Trailing spaces (those on the right) are removed from the character expression.
STR	STR(*float expression* [, length [,decimal]])	The numeric data represented in the float expression is returned as character data.
SUBSTRING	SUBSTRING(*character expression, start, length*)	The portion of the character expression starting at the *start* position for the total number of characters indicated by *length* is returned.
UPPER	UPPER(*character expression*)	The character expression is converted to uppercase.

Mathematical Functions

Mathematical functions manipulate numeric values. These functions allow you to perform a variety of mathematical operations on expressions composed of columns, constants, and combination expressions. Table 6.4 lists the most common mathematical functions. Check your specific database users guide to further understand all of the mathematical functions available to you.

Table 6.4 *Common Mathematical Functions in SQL.*

Function	Parameters	Result
ABS	ABS(*numeric expression*)	The absolute value of the numeric expression is returned. For example, ABS(-1) or ABS(1) returns 1.
CEILING	CEILING(*numeric expression*)	The smallest integer value greater than or equal to the numeric expression is returned. For example, CEILING(12.3) returns 13.
FLOOR	FLOOR(*numeric expression*)	The largest integer less than or equal to the numeric expression is returned. For example, FLOOR(12.3) returns 12.
ROUND	ROUND(*numeric expression, integer expression*)	The numeric expression is rounded to the precision specified in the integer expression. For example, ROUND(123.45,0) returns 123.00.

Aggregate Functions

Aggregate functions allow you to summarize values with a query based on common groups. These functions are important for data warehouse applications since they will enable users to perform trend analysis on summary information, prior to drilling into the detail data. You can apply aggregate functions to all of the rows or to groups of rows in a result set. When applied to a set of rows, an aggregate function produces a single value. Valid aggregate functions include average (AVG), row count (COUNT), value subtotal (SUM), maximum value (MAX), and minimum value (MIN).

To use an aggregate function, give the function name followed by an expression enclosed in parenthesis to which the aggregate function applies. You can use an optional key word, DISTINCT, with SUM, AVG, and COUNT to eliminate duplicate values before an aggregate function is applied.

The expression to which the aggregate function is applied is usually a column name. However, the expression can also be a constant, a function, or any combination of column names, constants, and functions connected by arithmetic operators.

Aggregate functions can be used in a *select* or a *having* clause. A *group by* clause must exist if you use a *having* clause. Whenever an aggregate function is used in a *select* clause that does not contain a *group by* clause, a single value is produced for all rows read into the result set. Such a function is called a *scalar aggregate*.

Joins

Join operations retrieve data from more than one table. Typically, these tables are from the same database. However, some databases such as Sybase Adaptive Server and some middleware products such as Sybase OMNIConnect allow you to perform join operations across different databases. When a join occurs, the database management system compares the data specified in columns designated to be joined and utilizes the comparison results to form a new result set from the rows that qualify.

In a join statement, you specify the columns from each table to join. The database then compares the values in those columns row by row, scanning the entire table until all rows have been compared in each table in the join. Qualifying rows are placed into the result set as new values in new rows.

The join operation is the hallmark of the relational model and relational database management systems. In structured database management systems of the past (hierarchical or network databases) the relationships between data entities was predefined and explicitly stated in the data definition. Defining navigational attributes in these older databases made them difficult to query, especially for unanticipated queries.

The relational model leaves navigational and relationship mapping unstated in the definition phase. Relationships are stated during the query process. These characteristics allow users to ask virtually any question about the data regardless of what was intended when the database was developed. These user questions are translated into various types of joins which we will discuss in the following sections. These joins are defined as Equi Joins, Self Joins, Theta Joins, and Outer Joins.

Equi Join

Requested comparisons typically involve values that match exactly or have a characteristic of equality. This type of a join is known as an *equijoin*. As we will see in the sections of this chapter covering *self joins, theta joins,* and *outer joins*; equality within the join statement is not required and is not always the case; other types of joins may occur. As we discussed in an earlier section of this chapter, "Where Clause," join conditions are placed in the *where* clause of a SQL statement. The following example demonstrates an *equijoin* that produces a result set showing the names of sales representatives and their customers.

```
select sales_rep.fname, sales_rep.lname, customer.name
from sales_rep, customer
where sales_rep.rep_id = customer.rep_id
```

Self Join

To retrieve data more than once from the same table, you use a *self join*. This is a common occurrence in personnel systems. Data about employees is typically stored in a common table. The data about an employee's organizational structure and reporting structure is normally buried in this table, requiring a *self join* to extract employee information and the associated managerial reporting structure from the same table. The following example queries the employee table twice to report each employees manager.

```
select emp.fname, emp.lname, mgr.fname, mgr.lname
from employee emp, employee mgr
where emp.mgr_id = mgr.emp_id
```

Because this query involves a join of the employee table to itself, the employee table is aliased according to its two roles. To distinguish these roles, we temporarily gave the employees table two different aliases (emp and mgr) in the *from* clause. These aliases qualify the column names in the rest of the query as shown in the *where* and *select* clauses.

Theta Joins

Relational operators define the basis for comparing the columns in a join. These operators, discussed earlier in the "Comparison Operators" section of this chapter, include equal to (=), greater than (>), greater than or equal to (>=), less than (<), less than or equal to (<=), not equal to (<> or !=), not greater than (!>), and not less than (!<). Joins that use relational operators are collectively known as *theta joins*. The following example uses a greater than or equal to join and a less than or equal to join to print a commission table for all sales reps.

```
select
 sales_rep.fname, sales_rep.lname, sales.ytd_sales,
 commission.rate
from
 sales_rep, sales, commission
where
 sales_rep.rep_id = sales.rep_id and
 (sales.ytd_sales >= commission.low_range and
 sales.ytd_sales <= commission.high_range)
```

Outer Joins

At times, retaining information that includes nonmatching rows in a result set is desirable. For example, a user requesting information on all customers who have not purchased products within the last three months will involve retrieving data from the customer table which do not have rows in the order table. On such occasions, you use an *outer join*. An outer join includes all of the rows from one table regardless of whether a match is also located in the other participating table. The outer join operators are a left outer join (*=), which includes all rows from the first named table, and a right outer join (=*), which includes all rows from the second named table. The following example lists all customers whether or not they have an associated sales representative. The results of this query will show all customers and list their sales representative's name unless they do not have a sales representative, in that case the name columns will be blank.

```
select customer.name, sales_rep.fname, sales_rep.lname
from customer, sales_rep
where customer.rep_id *= sales_rep.rep_id
order by customer_name
```

The result set is as follows:

customer.name	sales_rep.fname	sales_rep.lname
ABC Inc.	Kirk	Richards
Bay Company	Paul	Frentsos
Cast Away	NULL	NULL
Doyle & Doyle	NULL	NULL
Erognomic Inc.	Don	Leonardo
Frankfurter & Sons	Eric	Schurr
Gordon Beverages	NULL	NULL

Additional Query Processing

Though a majority of query activity involves *select* statements, we need to discuss next several specialized queries. These queries assist in building the proper application services on the Web for accessing your databases. Most data warehousing applications require a standard relational interface supported by the select statement and an OLAP interface that uses a combination of *select* statements and *union* queries. We next investigate the *union* query as well as subqueries, cross-tabular queries, and querying the optimizer in the sections that follow.

Union Queries

The *union* operator manipulates the results of two or more queries as if they were one. This manipulation is a result of combining the results of each query into a single result set, or union. The syntax for a *union* query is as follows:

```
select statement 1
UNION
select statement 2
```

Suppose you have a data mart for your West region and a data mart for your East region. Further imagine that these two data marts have the same data structures and have simply been partitioned based on the region. To establish results that span the entire company, you need to query both data marts and merge the results. This is exactly what the *union* query accomplishes.

```
select
 "West Region" "Region",
 t2.rep_id "Rep ID",
 max(t2.fname) "First Name",
 max(t2.lname) "Last Name",
 sum(t1.revenue) "1997 Revenue"
from
 west_sales_data t1, west_sales_rep t2
where
 t1.rep_id = t2.rep_id
 year = '1997'
group by
 sales_rep.rep_id
UNION
select
 "East Region" "Region",
 t2.rep_id "Rep ID",
 max(t2.fname) "First Name",
 max(t2.lname) "Last Name",
 sum(t1.revenue) "1997 Revenue"
from
 east_sales_data t1, east_sales_rep t2
where
 t1.rep_id = t2.rep_id and
 year = '1997'
group by
 sales_rep.rep_id
```

The result set is as follows:

Region	Rep ID	First Name	Last Name	1997 Revenue
West Region	012	Kirk	Richards	1,200,000
West Region	021	Bruce	Marshall	750,000
West Region	033	Ellen	Fisher	2,300,000
West Region	052	Paul	Frentsos	1,500,000
West Region	051	Tom	Lonzo	1,750,000
West Region	008	Karen	Richards	1,575,000
East Region	011	Eric	Schurr	1,850,000
East Region	060	David	Berg	1,150,000
East Region	065	Benn	Doyle	1,025,000
East Region	073	Jim	Callahan	1,015,000
East Region	005	Ron	Nordin	2,100,000
East Region	003	Ed	Bauer	2,250,000
East Region	002	Don	Leonardo	2,350,000

A SQL statement can contain any number of *union* operators. Most database parsers evaluate the result sets from left to right unless you use parentheses to control the evaluation order. The following is a list of guidelines for utilizing this powerful operator.

- All select clauses in the *union* statement must have the same number of expressions, which include column names, arithmetic expressions, aggregate functions, and so forth).

- The column names in the result set produced by a *union* statement are derived from the first *select* statement in the *union* statement. Therefore, if you want to define a new column heading for the results set, you must do it in the first query.

- Corresponding columns in all tables, or any subset of columns in the individual *select* statements, must be of the same datatype or an implicit data conversion must be possible between the two dissimilar datatypes. If either of these conditions is not met, you must explicitly convert the data into a common datatype. When different datatypes are combined in a *union* statement, numerical data is converted to the datatype with the most precision.

- Corresponding columns in the individual queries of a *union* statement must occur in the same order, because the union compares the columns one to one in the order of the individual queries.

SubQueries

A subquery is a *select* statement that is nested inside another SQL statement. A SQL statement that includes a subquery operates off the values returned in the subquery's *select* statement. *Select* statements that contain one or more subqueries are often referred to as nested queries or nested *select* statements. Many subqueries are equivalent to joins and therefore can be replaced with a join. However, in some complex queries a subquery is required.

A whole culture of SQL purists love subqueries. Unfortunately, many popular tools for querying databases do not natively support subqueries.

Statements that include subqueries usually take on one of the following formats:

```
WHERE where_clause [NOT] IN (subquery)
WHERE where_clause comparison_operator [ANY | ALL] (subquery)
WHERE [NOT] EXISTS (subquery)
```

The following subquery example retrieves all sales greater than the average sale of the year.

```
select
 company_name, revenue, sales_date, sales_rep
from
 sales_data
where
 revenue > (select avg(revenue) from sales_data)
```

A subquery must adhere to the following rules:

- The *select* clause of a subquery with a comparison operator can include only one expression or column name. The exceptions to this rule are comparison operators that support lists of values, such as the *exists* or *in* operators noted in the preceding subquery syntax formats.

- The data returned by the subquery must be compatible with the column or expression with which it is being compared.

- Subqueries generally should not include *order by* clauses.

Cross Tabular Queries

Cross tabular queries are essential for data warehouses, because they allow users to compare multiple variables, or dimensions, based on intersecting values. Cross tabular queries are those which present variable dimensions in rows and columns, and present values, or measures, in the intersecting cells. Most relational queries return data in a row-oriented fashion—the column name is used as a heading and the variable data is filled under the heading row by row. Analytical models require data to exist in both the rows and the column headings, allowing the data to intersect and provide more meaning. ROLAP (relational online analytical processing) servers such as products offered by Information Advantage and Platinum (InfoBeacon) perform these types of queries on your behalf either directly against the database or in their expression engines. If you are to build a serious front-end for your users, you will undoubtedly need to deliver on this requirement, either with a tool or through SQL. The following example demonstrates a cross tabular query that returns the sales revenue for five years for all territories.

```
select
  Territory = territory,
  FY1997 = (select sum(arev) from sales where year = 1997),
  FY1996 = (select sum(arev) from sales where year = 1996),
  FY1995 = (select sum(arev) from sales where year = 1995),
  FY1994 = (select sum(arev) from sales where year = 1994),
  FY1993 = (select sum(arev) from sales where year = 1993)
from
  sales_data
order by
  FY1997, Territory
```

The result set from this query would look like this:

Territory	FY1997	FY1996	FY1995	FY1994	FY1993
Los Angeles	1750	1600	1425	1175	1025
Chicago	1500	1354	1200	1175	900
Boston	1200	1125	900	750	500
Dallas	1100	1075	975	875	600
Detroit	925	746	678	625	490
Seattle	925	850	775	725	600
Cincinnati	735	642	575	400	250
Houston	735	625	615	598	550

Querying the Optimizer

The optimizer of a database processes user queries and determines to its best ability the proper way to access and retrieve data. Most databases provide a mechanism that allows query developers to instruct the database on how to handle the queries. These mechanisms allow developers to tune queries in various ways, overcoming some of the inherent weaknesses in the software and specific optimizer. So it is important for query developers to understand how to query the databases optimizer.

In Sybase Adaptive Server, the *set* command allows you to tell the database to return a description of the processing plan for each query. The *set* statement turns these options on or off for the duration of a user's work session. Table 6.5 lists the most important *set* statement options in Adaptive Server.

Table 6.5 *Set Statements for Gathering Optimizer Information on Sybase Adaptive Server Queries.*

Statement	Description
set noexec on	The *noexec* option of the *set* command instructs Adaptive Server to compile each query but not to execute it. The *noexec* option is often used with the *showplan* option. After *noexec* has been turned on, subsequent statements are not executed until *noexec* is turned off.
set showplan on	The *showplan* option of the *set* command causes Adaptive Server to generate a description of the processing plan for a query. If the *noexec* option is turned on, the query is not processed and the plan results are returned. If *noexec* option is turned off, the query is processed and the plan as well as the results are returned. *Showplan* indicates valuable information about the optimizer, including use of indexes and table scans.
set forceplan on	The *forceplan* option of the *set* command forces Adaptive Server to process table joins in the order that the tables appear in a *from* clause. This option overrides the optimizer and allows you to better control how the data is formulated.
set statistics io	The *statistics io* option of the *set* command displays the number of scans, logical reads (pages accessed), and physical reads (database device accesses) for each table referenced in a SQL statement.
set statistics time	The *statistics time* option of the *set* command displays the time it took to parse and compile each statement and the time it took to execute each step of the statement.

Metadata Essentials

Metadata describes the contents of a data warehouse and overall data warehousing processes. Metadata has evolved over the years from simple catalogs to dictionaries to enormous repositories. A data warehouse is one area that can greatly leverage the contents of a metadata repository. When planning your data warehouse, you want to evaluate your overall needs for metadata. The following sections briefly present the minimal metadata required to assist in building your own query selection engine on the Web. This metadata repository utilize the native database catalog as well as some application-specific tables to store information about your information packages.

A Minimal Repository to Manage Information Packages

The information packaging methodology clearly defines three types of physical database tables that comprise all information packages managed by a data warehouse. These entities include the dimension entity, the measure entity, and the category detail entity. To best manage the metadata about these information packages, you want to create the following three application-specific tables to manage the metadata repository information.

- **Information Package Master (IPM):** This table stores the master list of information packages. At a minimum, this table has an identifier, or key, defining a unique information package; a unique description—both long and short; a physical database table that manages the measure entity and preferably some help text to assist the user in understanding the uses of the information package.

- **Information Package Dimensions (IPD):** This table stores the table names for each of the dimension tables in an information package. This table relates to the IPM table in a detail fashion; one IPM has many IPDs. At a minimum, this table has the IPM identifier, which allows the relationship to be maintained between the master and detail data; the sequence or position of the dimension column in the information package; the physical database table name of the dimension; the logical descriptor of the dimension; the join clause that allows the IPD table to be joined with the IPM measure entity; and preferably some help text to assist the user in understanding the uses of the dimension.

- **Dimension Category Detail (DCD):** This table stores the table names for each category detail table in a dimension of an information package. This table relates to the IPD in a detail fashion; one IPD has many DCDs. At a minimum, this table has the IPM identifier, the IPD identifier (sequence); the DCD identifier (level);

the logical descriptor of the category; the join clause that allows the proper joining the DCD, IPD, and IPM tables; and preferably some help text to assist the user in understanding the uses of the dimension.

Utilize your own metadata repository tables, similar to these, will allow you to build a Web-based query tool for your users. Building such a semantic layer to drive your web based data warehousing tool, you will find a great deal of flexibility, with control and focus on user requirements. While not all encompassing, these tables provide metadata for monitoring query activity and usage, the loading processes, the data quality processes, and other areas of a data warehouse.

Catalog Queries

The structure of every database is described in a number of system tables, known as the catalog. These system tables contain the metadata describing the structures of objects in the database.

You should become intimate with the tables and queries that will assist you in obtaining information on tables, columns, and indexes in your database management system. These queries, when combined with your mini-metadata repository (discussed in the preceding section), allow you to build a relatively sophisticated query selection engine as a front end of your data warehouse. Your database vendor's system administration guide will typically present the system tables as well as any recommended strategies for accessing this information. The tables in a Sybase Adaptive Server that are most useful for querying include:

- **sysobjects:** This table contains one row for each object contained in the database. Objects include tables, views, stored procedures, rules, defaults, triggers, and so on.

- **syscolumns:** This table contains one row for each column in each object, such as a table or a view. This table also provides a well of information regarding the definition of each column.

- **sysindexes:** This table contains one row for each index in each object. This table also provides details of an index's definition, including its physical attributes and definition such as if the index is clustered or nonclustered, unique, repeating, and so on.

When you put these tables together with the metadata repository described in the preceding section, you have the workings of a query selection engine. Figure 6.4 presents the data model for this metadata repository in an entity relationship diagram.

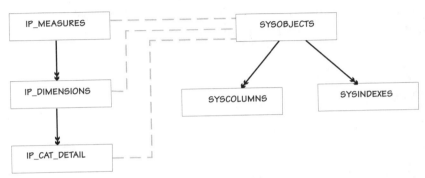

Figure 6.4 *The minimal repository for building your own query selection engine with the information packaging Methodology and Sybase Adaptive Server is depicted here.*

Summary

A data warehouse is all about data gathering the proper data, managing the data throughout the overall process, and providing access to the data. If you do not get the data right, you might as well not proceed. This chapter has given you the essential knowledge about database management systems, including their architecture and the proper way to access the data. Visualization of query results is a key skill that you must learn to be successful in building a data warehouse and in supporting those who utilize the data warehouse.

Make sure to fully understand your database management system, its storage facilities, its loading facilities, its query facilities, its metadata, and its optimizer. All of these components, when combined with an intimate knowledge of your data, allow you to visualize the results that are returned when querying your data warehouse. This skill is of the utmost importance when proceeding to build your user interface.

Users don't understand what a database is and they don't care. What is important to them is retrieving the data from the data warehouse in the proper format and in a timely fashion. As we discussed in Section I, "Introduction to the Information Packaging Methodology," you need to clearly define the information architecture and associated supporting technology architecture of your data warehouse, both of which components are critical in a solid foundation.

Your job from this point forward is to hide these data management essentials from your users. Present them with clear, understandable information packages. Underneath the fancy packaging, you need to clearly manage the technology underpinnings, including the data management essentials. Meanwhile, we now proceed in the remaining chapters of Section II to consider the user interface on the Web and the relevant markup language syntax required to present the data to the user in an easy-to-use fashion.

7

HTML Essentials

Languages using some form of markup syntax have become commonplace on the Internet and in its delivery protocols. The currently prevailing standard for presentation on the Web is called Hypertext Markup Language, or HTML. The first wave of Web development primarily used HTML in a static form to display documents and images to users through a user agent, such as Web browser software. Vendors have begun to build their own markup languages for exploring dynamic database content in Web pages, such as PowerDynamo's data access and formatting tags for dynamic site creation from Sybase.

The additional markup languages have become popular mechanisms for merging text and image information with dynamic database content, driving a second wave of Web development. This second wave has taken static first generation Internet sites and made them far more interactive and dynamic. The new influx of development in markup languages has fueled the emergence of a new standard, Extensible Markup Language (XML), which is in draft form at the time this book is written.

This chapter investigates HTML, giving you the essentials of presentation on the Web. It also briefly discusses the evolution of the new XML standard.

Standards of Document and Report Layouts

Graphical applications have evolved in a dramatic fashion from the early days of Microsoft Windows and Macintosh applications, where few standards existed, to today's highly standardized and integrated applications. The new evolution of graphical applications has been driven by the larger software houses, such as Microsoft. The vendors of these applications have driven the standard look and feel, as well as the integration, of applications.

The most popular graphical environment today, Microsoft Windows, offers a well-integrated platform for vendors to interject their wares. Users can easily maneuver around applications if the vendor who built the software follows the standard user interface guidelines. These guidelines fall into categories such as menu bars, tool bars, message lines, and standard windows interfaces.

The Windows menu bar typically has items such as a File menu, which allows the application to work with new or existing files. Other common menus include a Edit menu for manipulating the contents of a document or a session; a Windows menu for manipulating the layout of an application's workspace; and a Help menu for informing users with how best to use the application. If an application closely ties its design with these standards, it will overcome some obstacles to entry into an ever crowded software marketplace, because integration and training will prove to be less costly.

The ability to bring various functional components from differing vendors into a single, well-integrated application also has evolved in Windows and other environments. The object linking and embedding (OLE) standard clearly defines the component object model, while distributed the component object model (COM/DCOM) standard allows vendors to componentize their applications. The components can be embedded in standard desktop applications such as word processors, spreadsheets, and personal databases. This level of integration allows for a larger number of vendors to participate in the marketplace and has fueled specialty vendors, such as the Visual Components Division of Sybase, which provides Formula One (a spreadsheet component), First Impression (a graphics component), and GeoPoint (a mapping and spatial data component). Each of these components can be used in other Windows applications or Internet applications to extend functionality without the exorbitant cost associated with developing similar components in-house.

A set of standards for documents and reports has evolved along with standards for applications. These document and report standards include the presentation and content of the document that is represented. Just like menus, tool bars, and status lines; documents and reports have common areas whereby standardization can assist users in assimilating the information presented. The three most common of areas of documents and reports include their heading (at the top of each group of data), footing (at the bottom of each group of data), and body (sandwiched between the heading and footing). These areas are illustrated in Figure 7.1. Each of these three common areas within documents and reports are discussed separately in the sections that follow.

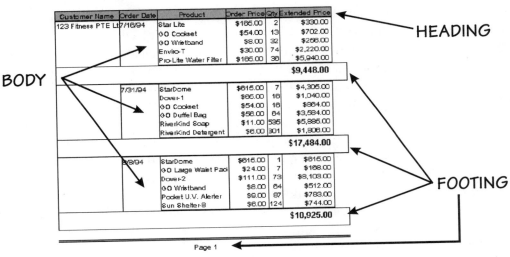

Figure 7.1 *The most common areas of documents and reports include the heading, the footing, and the body.*

Heading

Headings indicate the beginning of an information flow in documents and reports. Headings are typically located in three areas: at the beginning of a document (a title page); at the top of a page (a page header); and the top of control or flow breaks (control break heading). A heading instruct users of a document that a new flow of information is being presented. The heading region of a document gives users time to pause and collect their thoughts from the closing of a preceding region.

To assist users in understanding a header, reports often change the display attributes associated with the text that is presented. At a minimum, this change includes adding different font characteristics (typeface, size, and style). The change may also introduce shading, color, and images to further frame the context of the new data. The heading content is also not as verbose as the detail data that the heading frames. Often, all that headings comprise are key words or short phrases. These visual clues assist users of a document in understanding meaning and framing of the flow of content.

Footing

A footing, like a heading, frames the detailed content of a document. The difference between a footing and a heading is that a footing indicates the ending of an information flow in a document. Footings are typically located in three areas of a document or a report: at the bottom of a control or a flow break (a control break footer); at the bottom of a page (a page footer); or at the end of a document (a final footer). A footer instruct users that the information being presented in a document or topic area has concluded.

Footings are more prevalent in reports than in documents; however, documents have their share of footings too. Much as a new heading, a footing indicates that content is about to end or to change to a new subject or content area. Like a heading, a footing also takes on visual cues to assist the user in quickly understanding the summary. These visual clues include font characteristics, color, shading, and other formatting changes. A footing often summarizes the content of a document, and therefore may include additional text that presents final findings for the area being summarized. Therefore, footings often contain more substantial data than a word or phrase, and may also include summarization of a document's content.

Body

The body of a document houses the document's detail content. In a report, the body contains the detail data that is being presented. The body of a document consists of multiple blocks of information presented in a common visualization set, including font, color, and shading attributes. The blocks of data may consist of items such as text paragraphs, lists of data, definitions, and figures, to name a few. These blocks of detailed information allow users to absorb the details that are presented in summary form in the footings. In reports, the detail housed in the body is primarily a source for managers to defend their findings—backup data to support the footing or summary data. For example, if a sales manager releases a sales representative due to under-performance in key monthly performance metrics, their daily bookings may be used to justify the termination of the sales representative by the sales manager. The listing of daily bookings would be the body of a report that summarized by month for each sales representative's performance against budget and forecast in the footing; inadequate or exceptional performance can easily be addressed from these details.

Hypertext Markup Language (HTML)

Hypertext Markup Language (HTML) allows you to write user interface applications that are accessible from almost any type of computer. HTML is an implementation of the Standard Generalized Markup Language (SGML). SGML was approved as an international standard in 1986 (ISO-8879). SGML is a metalanguage for formally describing document markup systems. HTML utilizes SGML to define a language that describes a document's structure and interconnectivity for World Wide Web (Web) applications.

Metalanguage: *A metalanguage, such as the Standard Generalized Markup Language (SGML) is a formal language used to describe other languages.*

HTML is formally defined by the HTML Working Group of the Internet Engineering Task Force (http://www.ietf.cnri.reston.va.us/html.charters/html-charter.html). Browser manufactures such as Microsoft (http://www.microsoft.com/workshop/author/default.asp) and Netscape (http://developer.netscape.com/library/documentation/index.html) are also building proposed extensions to the standard set of HTML. Based on the current use of HTML, vendors such as Microsoft and Netscape are beginning to push the HTML standards to become more of a layout standard rather than a semantic markup language.

HTML Processing

HTML requires only a text editor and browser to create an operational system to present and interconnect a series of documents. HTML is good for quickly creating graphically based applications that offer simple functionality.

Delivering HTML application does not require a compiler, because HTML is not a programming language. HTML cannot execute instructions in response to user input or perform calculations. These and other functions are relegated to tools that are investigated in this book, such as JavaScript (Chapter 8, "Scripting Essentials").

Users access and visualize HTML applications through a user agent or rendering tool, the most popular of which is a graphical tool called a browser. The browser interprets HTML files, which contain content and associated tags. The browser interprets the content, applies formatting attributes to the content based on the tags, and then presents users with a graphically based application. Currently, many browsers are available on the market, yet Netscape and Microsoft are clearly the industry leaders in this space with the Netscape Navigator or Communicator and Microsoft Internet Explorer products. If you utilize standard HTML, your applications written for one machine utilizing one type of browser can run on another type of machine utilizing another browser.

HTML is used for defining the structural parts of a document, such as its heading, body (paragraphs, lists, forms, and links), and footing components. The data or content contained in an HTML document consists of text, multimedia, and additional information about the content, such as administrative or technical information about the document. Using the markup syntax provided within HTML you can build a series of integrated documents formulating an online information system that can be efficiently distributed, retrieved and searched electronically in a way that is independent of the appearance details of the associated documents. (An example of HTML components is provided in the next section.)

Using a markup language such as HTML, your company can easily delegate various development tasks to organizations based on their expertise. You might focus only on creating document content without having to worry about the details of the document's appearance or presentation. Other people in your company, such as graphic artists, can create a pleasing specification for a document's appearance that is uniform and consistent across all organizational HTML documents. A company can have many reusable components that allow for a common look and feel in a browser. These reusable components, much like code libraries, can be stored and managed in a central repository to assist in the quality and overall capabilities of an organization. Creating these types of development disciplines assists in reuse, allowing expedited writing and production.

When you use HTML, you create files of tagged text, which in turn are interpreted for presentation with a hypertext browser. HTML doesn't use a complicated syntax, but developing Web based applications is enhanced when you understand the specifications and rules associated with the tags in HTML. This base knowledge allows you to properly assemble the documents for your information systems.

After you are satisfied with your understanding of HTML and its inherent rules, you will be ready to investigate some of the productivity tools that can assist you in rapid application development (RAD). Many popular tools support HTML document editing in a what-you-see-is-what-you-get (WYSIWYG) manner, as are a growing number of tools that support the management of HTML document environments. Your overall success in delivering Web based data warehouse solutions, requires that you are familiar with raw

HTML syntax. Most tools focus on standard HTML and do not go outside the bounds of the standard to include extensions for the standard browser environment or scripting syntax. At times, this limits your ability to be creative in implementing a required system that solves your specific business problems.

After an application is developed, all that is required by the user of an application is a user agent, typically a browser. After a browser is installed on a computer, your users are only required to learn a single graphical user interface (GUI). The browser's uniform GUI allows your users to navigate all of their HTML applications. Browsers support direct manipulation, which aid your users in ease of use and navigation. With a few clicks of the mouse, users can navigate and interact with the system. The browser and associated HTML documents hide the user from the program interaction and nuances of presentation logic required by most applications.

By using HTML and a browser, a development staff is relieved of custom written GUI code. No longer are developers required to build and maintain code specifically for multiple GUI platforms such as Windows, Macintosh, and UNIX. The browser is now charted with handling common events such as sizing windows, menu selections, error alerts, and memory management. The distribution of programs and their updates can also be optimized with HTML applications and browsers, delivering a near-zero deployment cost for client workstations. Based on these savings, your development staff gains time and money that can be rechanneled into building more functional components of applications, including business transactions and analytical queries.

HTML Elements

An HTML document consists of text used to convey the data of a document and tags used to mark the structure of a document. For example, here is an HTML document. The resultant HTML page as it appears in a Web browser is presented in Figure 7.2.

```
<HTML>
<HEAD>
<TITLE>The Power of Information</TITLE>
</HEAD>
<BODY>
<P>
Knowledge in the form of an informational commodity indispensable to productive
power is already, and will continue to be, a major -- perhaps the major -- stake in
worldwide competition for power. It is conceivable that the nation-states will one
day fight for control of information, just as they battled in the past for control
over territory, and afterwards for control over access and exploitation of raw
materials and cheap labor.
```

```
</P>
<I>John Francois Lyotard</I>
</BODY>
</HTML>
```

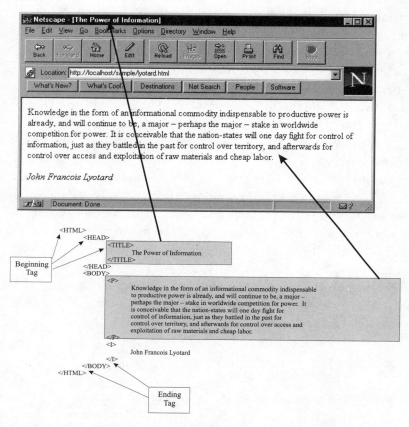

Figure 7.2 *A sample HTML document presented through the Netscape Navigator browser. Notice the beginning tags, text content on which the tags act, and the final presentation within the browser.*

The embedded tags in the content of an HTML document instruct a browser to perform special tasks. In the above code sample, "The Power of Information," is the title element, which is delimited by the start tag of <TITLE> and the end tag of </TITLE>.

All tags in HTML are classified in the heading or body of a document. (To implement a document and report standard footing, of which no equivalent exists within the HTML standard, you simply distinguish body element tags highlighting your footing at the proper location in the content flow of the body.) With an understanding of what tags do, a developer can quickly learn sets of familiar structures, such as titles, headings, lists, forms, and paragraphs. After a developer knows the meaning of the tags, the meaning of the overall document structure becomes clear. However, the overall appearance of a document cannot be derived from this information alone, it is solely realized when the HTML document is presented in a browser. That is, tags alone don't specify such characteristics as precise fonts. The precise characteristics are determined by each browser.

The remaining sections of this chapter further investigate HTML tag syntax. The HTML understanding you gain here is essential for you to successfully deploy the user interface of your web-based data warehouse system.

Markup Basics

Tags are the heart and soul of a markup language such as HTML. The application server that interprets the text stream passed to it by a client application focuses on these tags. The tags initiate different behaviors on the application server. Based on the content of any given tag, different processing will occur. In HTML, a tag consists of the following attributes, in the order presented here:

1. A left angle bracket (<, also known as a "less than" symbol).

2. An optional slash (/, which indicates the termination or ending of a tag's boundary).

3. The tag name, or keyword, which when interpreted by an application server initiates specialized processing and establishes internal structures to manage the overall processing logic required based on the tag.

4. Optionally, if the tag can have attributes, a blank followed by one or more attribute specifications (such as ALIGN=CENTER) can follow the tag name.

5. A right angle bracket (>, also known as a "greater than" symbol), which completes the tag and allows the application server to begin its internal processing. If the tag is proceeded with a termination slash (/) indicated above, this brings closure to the internal interpretation of some structure. Therefore, in this context you can read the slash character as the end of the tag name. For example, </TITLE> indicates the end of the TITLE element, section, or tag.

Examples of valid HTML tags include:

```
<H1>
<P ALIGN=LEFT>
<TITLE>
</BODY>
```

As with any standard, HTML offers many overriding or basic rules that are followed throughout the base-level tags. The following are some of the common rules associated with tags and elements in the HTML standard:

- Tags are case insensitive; that is, a browser interprets <TITLE> the same as <Title>, <title>, or <TiTlE>.

- Most tags are delimited by both a start and end tag, such as <TITLE> and </TITLE>. However, some elements such as the line break element have only one tag—in this case, <BR>. Other tags have an optional end tag, such </P> for the paragraph element, <P>.

- Many elements contain attributes that allow the behavior of the text on which tags act to be further defined or enhanced, such as the ALIGN=LEFT attribute, which indicates the information contained between the tags should be aligned to the left side of the page. Attributes are not positional and can appear in any order in a tag.

- Several HTML tags may contain an attribute that has a Uniform Resource Locator (URL) as a value. URLs are addresses that reference other objects on the Web or in other information systems. (URLs are discussed in more detail in the sidebar, "Uniform Resource Locator.")

- HTML treats contiguous sequences of white space characters as equivalent to a single space character. Therefore, record boundaries that end immediately following a start tag are typically discarded. This rule allows you considerable flexibility when editing an HTML document, because you can interject carriage returns and spacing to improve the readability of your HTML source documents through the use of white space without impacting the presentation of these documents in a browser.

The Anatomy of Uniform Resource Locators

Within the Internet, documents are retrieved utilizing a common addressing scheme known as the Uniform Resource Locator. The general syntax of a Uniform Resource Locator (URL) is:

```
protocol://domain name/path/filename
```

This sidebar briefly introduces URLs. For a more detailed explanation, please visit The World Wide Web Consortium's site at the following address. This address is itself an example of a URL.

```
http://www.w3.org/pub/WWW/Addressing/Addressing.html
```

In a URL, the protocol defines the protocol to use to access the target resource. The major protocols include:

- http: Hypertext Transfer Protocol retrieves a Web document
- ftp: File Transfer Protocol retrieves a file from an FTP server
- gopher: Retrieves a file in a Gopher server
- mailto: Transmits electronic mail
- news: Access a newsgroup
- telnet: Starts an interactive session for a remote user on a host machine via the Telnet protocol, which is part of TCP/IP

In a URL, the domain is the Internet host name in domain notation, such as www.objx.com. Typically, the domain is defined in logical terms. However, sometimes a numerical TCP/IP address is utilized, such as 127.0.0.1. A domain may also contain a port number, which indicates the listening port utilized by the TCP/IP addressing schemes. This is typically omitted, because most HTTP servers have a reasonable default. However, should you require the port number, it will be included in the domain name with a colon separator, for example: www.objx.com:80.

In a URL, the filename is a filename in a directory of the domain previously indicated in the URL. The filename may be proceeded with a path, which relates to the directory structure on the file's hosting machine. Special interpretations are applied for other protocols in URLs. For example, a mailto URL interprets the text following the protocol as an Internet e-mail address in the form of: mailto:address, for example mailto:hammergren@objx.com.

HTML Document Structure

To properly identify the markup language, HTML documents should start with a <!DOC-TYPE> declaration followed by HTML syntax containing a HEAD element and then a BODY element. Each of these items is discussed in the sections that follow.

For your documents to conform to the HTML standard (from 3.2 onward), they must start with the <!DOCTYPE> declaration. This tag distinguishes among the various versions of HTML. Every HTML 3.2 document must also include a descriptive title element, which is contained in the <TITLE> tag. Therefore, after the HTML 3.2 standard was adopted, a minimal HTML document appears as follows:

```
<!DOCTYPE HTML PUBLIC "-//W3C//DTD HTML 3.2 Final//EN">
<TITLE>The Information Packaging Method—Samples Menu</TITLE>
```

The document type declaration tag, <!DOCTYPE> at the start of an HTML document identifies its conformance with a standard body and a level of the HTML standard. The above example identifies the W3C, World Wide Web Consortium (http://www.w3c.org), as the standards body and indicates HTML 3.2 Final standards compliance.

Heading Elements—Contained in the HEAD Element

The heading of an HTML document is typically contained in a HEAD element. This element has a start tag of <HEAD> and an end tag of </HEAD>. Though it is not required, the HEAD element is a major block of a Web page and therefore is typically placed within all HTML documents. In the HEAD element, you also place content associated with the TITLE, STYLE, SCRIPT, ISINDEX, BASE, META, and LINK tags.

TITLE Element

The TITLE element defines the title of a document and is required for conformance to current HTML standards. The TITLE element is the only required tag within an HTML document. Every HTML document must have one TITLE element in the document's HEAD element. This provides information to the browser for display in the window caption area. The TITLE element includes both a start tag, <TITLE>, and an end tag, </TITLE>. The following is an example of a TITLE element:

```
<TITLE>The Information Packaging Method—Samples Menu</TITLE>
```

STYLE Element

The STYLE element allows you to include information describing how to render information in the presentation device. The STYLE element can include how to present the information on the presentation device, such as on the screen or in print. One or more style elements may be included in your document's HEAD element. The STYLE element requires a start tag, <STYLE>, and an end tag, </STYLE> An example follows.

```
<STYLE>
 H1 {color : navy}
 P { font-size: 12pt;}
</STYLE>
```

Style Sheets and their associated tags are not supported in HTML versions 2.0 and below. By attaching style sheets to HTML documents, you can influence the presentation of documents without sacrificing device independence or adding new HTML tags. Style Sheets are also supported in three other ways:

- Using the "LINK" element to incorporate an external style sheet.

- Using an imported style sheet through the cascading style sheets (CSS) "@import"notation.

- Using a STYLE attribute on an element inside the BODY element of an HTML document. This option does not offer the benefits of the previous options, because it mixes style with content and loses the corresponding advantages of style sheets.

The example that follows shows these four ways to include style notations in an HTML document:

```
<!DOCTYPE HTML PUBLIC "-//W3C//DTD HTML 3.2 Final//EN">
<HTML>
 <HEAD>
 <TITLE>Sample Style Implementations</TITLE>
 <LINK REL=STYLESHEET TYPE="text/css"
  HREF="http://www.objx.com/style"TITLE="site_style">
 <STYLE TYPE="text/css">
  @import url(http://www.objx.com/style/basic);
  H1 { color: blue }
 </STYLE>
 </HEAD>
 <BODY>
```

```
<H1>All H1 (Heading Level 1) headings are blue</H1>
<P STYLE="color: red">This paragraph is read.
</BODY>
</HTML>
```

SCRIPT Element

The SCRIPT element allows you to place in-line scripting information in your HTML documents. The commands you place in the SCRIPT element are client-side scripts that permit better user interaction in a specified Web page. The most common scripting language, which is placed between a start tag, <SCRIPT>, and end tag, </SCRIPT>, is JavaScript. Details on scripting are covered in Chapter 8, "Scripting Essentials."

ISINDEX Element

The ISINDEX element indicates that the document is searchable. Including the ISINDEX element in your HTML document indicates that the browser should present the user with a field for entering in information for which they want to search. The server on which the document is located must have a search engine defined that supports this searching. You can use the PROMPT attribute to specify a string that proceeds the search field on an HTML page. When a user enters a search phrase and presses the Enter key, the query string is sent to the server identified by the base URL for this document. For example, if the query string entered is *base tables* and the base URL is http://www.objx.com, then the query generated is http://www.objx.com/?base+tables. An example ISINDEX element follows:

```
<ISINDEX PROMPT="Search phrase: ">
```

BASE Element

The BASE element provides the ability for relative referencing of file and document locations in an HTML document. In the BASE element, you define the base URL using the HREF attribute. An example follows.

```
<BASE href="http://www.objx.com/home.html">
...
<IMG SRC="images/objxlogo.gif">
```

In the above IMG element, the image is interpreted to be located at http://www.objx.com/images/objxlogo.gif.

The BASE element is not required in a document. Should you choose not to include the BASE element in your HTML documents, the base URL of your document is used as a default.

META Element

The META element provides information about a document itself. This tag has several additional attributes that identify information useful in the HTML parsing by the browser or the server. Attributes that are used by the META element include: NAME, CONTENT, and HTTP-EQUIV.

- **NAME:** This attribute specifies the property that you are defining by name.

- **CONTENT:** This attribute specifies the property value that you are defining.

The following META element example utilizes NAME and CONTENT attributes:

```
<META NAME="Author"CONTENT="T. Hammergren">
```

- **HTTP-EQUIV:** This attribute has a special significance when documents are retrieved via the Hypertext Transfer Protocol. HTTP servers may use the property name specified by the HTTP-EQUIV attribute to perform specialized processing. For more information on this attribute, see the HTTP specification (http://www. ics.uci. edu/pub/ietf/http/).

For example, the following META element can be used by caches to determine when to fetch a fresh copy of the associated document.

```
<META HTTP-EQUIV="Expires"CONTENT="21 Jul 1997 12:00:00 GMT">
```

LINK Element

The LINK element provides site structure information. This element defines relationships between an HTML document and other documents or resources. Though the link element has been part of the HTML standard since early specifications, most browsers still ignore it. The HTML 3.2 specification states uses of the link element in principle: to define for document specific navigation toolbars or menus; to control how collections of HTML files are rendered into printed documents; for linking associated resources such as style sheets and scripts; and to provide alternate forms of the current document. The attributes for the LINK tag include HREF, REL, REV, and TITLE.

- **HREF:** This attribute specifies a URL that identifies the document or part of a document to which the link refers.

- **REL:** This attribute defines the relationship defined by the LINK element, in other words the relationship from this link to the destination.

- **REV:** This attribute defines a reverse relationship for the LINK element, in other words the relationship of the destination to this link.

- **TITLE:** This attribute defines a logical title for the LINK element.

Examples of LINK elements include:

```
<LINK REL=QueryBuilder HREF=qrybld.html>
<LINK REL=Previous HREF=home.html>
<LINK REL=Next HREF=results.html>
```

Body Elements—Contained in the BODY Tag

The body of a document is contained in its BODY element. The start tag for the BODY element is <BODY> and the end tag is </BODY>. Many attributes can be identified in the body element's start tag, including BGCOLOR, TEXT, LINK, VLINK, ALINK, and BACKGROUND.

- **BGCOLOR:** This background color attribute specifies the background color for a document's BODY element. Table 7.1 lists the standard colors for this and other color-oriented attributes.

- **TEXT:** This attribute specifies the color of the document's text. You generally want to assure that your text color is compatible with the background color or the background image that you specify. For example, a light background is incompatible with a light text color.

- **LINK:** This attribute specifies the color for the text of unvisited hypertext links—that is, of the path to another document that the user has not yet taken. Unvisited hypertext links are covered in greater detail in the "Linking Documents" section later in this chapter.

- **VLINK:** This visited link attribute specifies the color for the text of visited hypertext links—that is, the path to another document that the user has previously taken. Visited hypertext links are covered in greater detail in the "Linking Documents" section later in this chapter.

- **ALINK:** This activated link attribute specifies the highlight color for the text of hypertext links at the moment the user clicks on the link. This color is activated when the user presses the mouse button down on the link until the link is activated.

- **BACKGROUND:** This attribute specifies a URL for an image to display on a document's background in lieu of a color.

These BODY element attributes control the colors that are used to present a document to users. Colors in HTML are coded as RGB hexadecimal numbers, or as one of 16 predefined HTML standard color names. These colors relate closely to the 16 original Windows VGA palette colors. A list of these colors is presented in Table 7.1

Table 7.1 *The 16 predefined colors in the HTML standard.*

Logical Color Name	RGB Hexadecimal Representation
Black	#000000
Green	#008000
Silver	#C0C0C0
Lime	#00FF00
Gray	#808080
Olive	#808000
White	#FFFFFF
Yellow	#FFFF00
Maroon	#800000
Navy	#000080
Red	#FF0000
Blue	#0000FF
Purple	#800080
Teal	#008080
Fuchsia	#FF00FF
Aqua	#00FFFF

You should take care in selecting colors in the BODY element. Compatibility between the foreground colors (TEXT, LINK, VLINK, ALINK) and the background color (BGCOLOR) or background image (BACKGROUND) is important. For example, a yellow TEXT color would not be a good selection for a white BGCOLOR—black or navy would be a better TEXT color. Also, the use of colors to distinguish whether or not a link has been visited should be monitored. If the colors do not distinguish themselves from each other or are not readable by a user, they will not serve their purpose. For example, consider the following BODY element start tag:

```
<body bgcolor=white text=black link=red vlink=maroon alink=fuschia>
```

This body tag utilizes a combinations of colors which will work well with each other. A white background with black text is easily readable by the user. Any links will be marked with red text, once again standing out from the standard black text. And any visited links will be presented with a maroon color, or darker red, indicating the link has been previously viewed. The activated link is only highlighted while the user is pressing the mouse on the link, however, fuschia coloring will demonstrate that the mouse click was accepted.

Body-level elements are those tags that are contained in the BODY tags. Most body-level elements in a document fall into one of two groups: *block-level elements,* which logically group text into paragraph with breaks, and *text-level elements,* which logically group text into paragraphs without breaks. These two groups are discussed in the following sections.

Block-Level Elements

Block-level elements logically group text into paragraph with breaks. Common block-level elements include headings, paragraphs, list items, and horizontal rules. Block level elements generally act as containers for text-level elements and other block-level elements (excluding headings and address elements). When using block level elements as text containers, you can apply common formats to various blocks of text in the body of your HTML document.

Heading Elements

Standard HTML provides for six levels of predefined heading element formats. These heading elements are designated with a <H*level_number*> start tag and a </H*level_number*> end tag. These start and end tags are always required by the heading elements. The level number indicates the importance weighting of the heading in the document, <H1> is more important than <H2>, which is more important than <H3> and so on. More important headings are generally rendered in a larger font so they stand out more to the user than less important ones. The heading element also has an optional ALIGN attribute, which is used to indicate how the text should be aligned in the heading element. The default alignment is LEFT; however, you can define this alignment to be LEFT, CENTER, or RIGHT. An example of a heading element follows.

```
<H1 ALIGN=CENTER>IPM Query Tool</H1>
<H2 ALIGN=LEFT>Dimension Selection Page</H2>
```

Address Element

The ADDRESS element specifies information such as contact details for the publisher of a document. The ADDRESS element requires a start tag of <ADDRESS> and end tag of </ADDRESS>. Upon interpreting this tag, a browser renders the content with paragraph breaks before and after the associated text. Here is an example address element:

```
<ADDRESS>
The Coriolis Group<BR>
14455 N Hayden Road, Suite 220<BR>
Scottsdale, AZ 85260<BR>
</ADDRESS>
```

Paragraph Element

The PARAGRAPH element specifies the information contained in a block or paragraph. The PARAGRAPH element requires a start tag of <P>. An the end tag of </P> is optional. As with headers, you can use an ALIGN attribute to set the text alignment of a paragraph. The default alignment for a PARAGRAPH element is LEFT, however, you can override this with the values of LEFT, CENTER, or RIGHT. Here is a sample paragraph element:

```
<P ALIGN=RIGHT>

    This paragraph is aligned on the right. You can use the align attribute to posi-
tion your text on a horizontal axis of left, center, or right. Left alignment posi-
tions the text on the left margin of the page. Right alignment positions the text on
the right margin of the page. Center alignment centers the text horizontally on the
page.</P>
```

Preformatted Text Element

The preformatted text element specifies that the contained text be rendered with a mono-space font while preserving the layout defined by the embedded white space and line break characters. The preformatted text element requires a start tag of <PRE> and an end tag of </PRE>. Here is an example of preformatted text:

```
<PRE>
The following is a comparison of the last three years forecast variances:

Region    FY97    FY96    FY95
------    ----    ----    ----
Western   106%     98%    101%
Eastern   103%    102%     94%
Central    91%     98%     97%
</PRE>
```

Block Quote Element

The block-quote element specifies that contained text be rendered with indented margins and is used to enclose extended quotations. A block quote element requires a start tag of <BLOCKQUOTE> and an end tag of </BLOCKQUOTE>. The block quote element is used to indicate more than a few lines from a document are being quoted.

Lists

Lists are useful for itemizing information that logically consists of separate items. List items can contain block-level and text-level items, excluding headings and address elements. Lists can also include nested lists—lists within lists.

Type of List

You should be primarily concerned with two types of lists: unordered lists and ordered lists. Both types of lists logically block the items of the list, allowing the user to notice the relationship among them.

- **Unordered List (UL Element):** For a list when the order of items is not significant (such as an ordinary grocery list), you should use the UL element. An unordered list presents information in a list form without numbering the items. Instead of numbering the items in the list, a browser renders the items with leading offset bullets. The presentation is often indented in a manner that causes nested lists to be indented according to their nesting level structure. The UL element has a start tag of <UL> and an end tag of </UL>. The unordered list element has two attributes TYPE and COMPACT. The TYPE attribute sets the default bullet style for the list items. Valid TYPE attribute values include DISC, SQUARE, and CIRCLE. The COMPACT attribute is used to reduce the interim spacing between list items.

- **Ordered List (OL Element):** For list of items where the order is significant needs to be explicit (such as a sequence of instructions to be followed in a particular order), you use the OL element. An ordered list presents information in the form of a numbered list. The list items are presented separately. The presentation is often indented in a manner that causes nested lists to be indented according to their structure. The items in an ordered list are numbered consecutively by default. The ordered list element has a start tag of <OL> and an end tag of </UL>. The ordered list element also has three attributes: TYPE, START, and COMPACT. The TYPE attribute defines the numbering style that will be used for displaying the list items. (The acceptable values for the TYPE attribute are presented in Table 7.2.) The START attribute is equated to the starting sequence number for the list; by default this is set to 1. The COMPACT attribute is used to reduce the interim spacing between list items.

Table 7.2 *Valid TYPE Attribute Values for an Ordered List Element.*

Type	Numbering Style	Sample Series
1	Arabic numbers	1, 2, 3, …
a	Latin letters in lower case	a, b, c, …
A	Latin letters in upper case	A, B, C, …
i	Roman numbers in lowercase	i, ii, iii, …
I	Roman numbers in uppercase	I, II, III, …

List Item (LI Element)

To present an item in a list, you use the list item element, which has a start tag of <LI> and an end tag of </LI>. The presentation of a list item is dependent on the type of enclosing list (UL or OL). For example, the following list presents the individual list items with bullets.

```
<H1>Block Elements</H1>
<UL>
```

```
<LI>Paragraphs</LI>
<LI>Unordered Lists</LI>
<LI>Ordered Lists</LI>
<LI>Definition Lists</LI>
<LI>Preformatted Text</LI>
<LI>Document Divisions</LI>
<LI>Center Text Alignment</LI>
<LI>Block Quoted Text</LI>
<LI>Forms</LI>
<LI>Horizontal Rules</LI>
<LI>Tables</LI>
</UL>
```

By contrast, the following list precedes each list item with a number. This type of list should be used to indicate the importance of the sequencing between list items.

```
<H1>Information Packaging Diagram Steps</H1>
<OL>
 <LI>Define the key measures</LI>
 <LI>Define the common dimensions for accessing the
  measures</LI>
 <LI>For each dimension, define the access paths or
  hierarchy details</LI>
 <LI>For each dimension level, determine if additional
  details are required to support the category</LI>
</OL>
```

Definition List

A definition list is a specialized list tag for presenting items with short titles or tags, such as a list of definitions, terms, or abbreviations. These lists use the definition list element, which has a start tag of <DL> and an end tag of </DL>. In this type of list are:

- Definition terms that are distinguished by means of layout, font usage, or both layout and font usage. Definition terms only have a start tag, <DT>.

- Detail definitions that correspond to the terms. Detail definitions only have a start tag, <DD>.

- Typically, a definition list presents users with the term left justified on the page, while the definition is somewhat indented underneath the term without bullets. A sample of a definition list is shown here:

```
<H1>Glossary</H1>
<DL>
```

```
<DT>Information Package <DD>a logical representation of
  data that will fulfill a user's requirements for data
  warehouse-based reporting.
<DT>Information Package Diagram <DD>a data gathering tool
  that is part of the information packaging methodology
  for gathering user requirements to fulfill data
  warehouse-based reporting requirements.
<DT>Information Packaging Methodology <DD>a technique for
  properly defining, architecting and delivering data
  warehouses first documented in <I>Data Warehousing:
  Building the Corporate Knowledge Base</I> by Tom
  Hammergren, International Thomson Computer Press, 1997.
</DL>
```

Input Forms

Just as data is the heart and soul of a data warehouse, forms are critical to any information system that interacts with users. A form allows a user to enter data that will be captured and transmitted to an application server for processing. This application server is typically an extension of the HTTP server such as a CGI, NSAPI, ISAPI, or WSAPI oriented application. With a form, your users can perform such functions as:

- Provide feedback about the Web site supporting the data warehouse.

- Request technical support on a data warehouse application or capabilities of the data warehouse.

- Inquire about the content of the data warehouse.

- Request information from the data warehouse by issuing a query to a database.

- Register for information packages or submit requests for new information packages.

- Place orders for materials supporting the data warehouse, such as training courses or manuals.

HTML forms are created using the FORM element, which has a start tag of <FORM> and an end tag of </FORM>. A form requires both start and end tags. FORM elements cannot be nested, but several FORM elements can exist on one HTML page. The FORM element indicates that processing for an input form will occur in the HTTP server. The FORM element has three primary attributes: ACTION, METHOD, and ENCTYPE.

- **ACTION:** This attribute specifies the name of the script or program that the Web server executes when the form is submitted. This script or program is presented to the server as a URL. If the ACTION attribute is missing, the base URL of the form (the URL where the form is located on the server) is used as the default.

- **METHOD:** This attribute indicates how the data is transferred to the Web server. The transferred data is often referred to as the input data. Two methods are valid for input data: POST and GET.

  The GET method is the default value and is typically used for forms with a limited parameter list that requires minimal data to be transferred to the server. This includes forms that perform searches or simple queries to a database. When a form is submitted to the server using the GET method, a command string is passed that includes the URL defined in the ACTION attribute and a set of arguments that are added by the browser for the application server program. The HTTP server places these arguments in a QUERY_STRING host variable, which typically has a 255 character limit. The arguments are placed in the host variable as variable and value pairs. Variable-value pairs are separated by an ampersand (&). Based on the host variable's length limitation, the GET method is typically not recommended.

  The POST method passes data from an input form to a Web Server as individual variable-value pairs. The POST method is therefore preferred by most application server programmers for processing logic that requires serious data transfers. The POST method is not subject to the limitation that restrict the GET method. Each variable is passed with its associated value without limit.

- **ENCTYPE:** This attribute identifies the media type used for encoding variable-value pairs of a form's data. The default ENCTYPE value for all forms is *application/x-www-form-urlencoded*. This type of encoding translates to the following rules: When variable-value pairs are sent to the server, they are passed in order of appearance on the form; the variable-value pairs are separated from each other by an ampersand (&); the variables are separated from values within the pairs with an equal sign (=); all space characters in the variable names or values are replaced by a plus sign (+); nonalphanumeric characters are replaced by a percent sign (%) followed by two hexadecimal digits representing the character's ASCII code.

Forms can include a complete set of body-level elements. As well, additional elements can provide special functionality in the FORM element. These elements—INPUT, SELECT (OPTION), and TEXTAREA—are discussed in the following sections.

INPUT Element

You use the INPUT element to collect information from users. The INPUT element defines many types of graphical user interface (GUI) objects that obtain user input, including pulldown menus, text input boxes, radio buttons, text fields, checkboxes, and buttons. Each of these GUI objects is an INPUT element with a different TYPE attribute. Additional attributes you can use with the INPUT element include TYPE, NAME, VALUE, CHECKED, SIZE, MAXLENGTH, SRC, and ALIGN.

The TYPE attribute defines what kind of graphical user interface object is presented to users. Valid types are presented in Table 7.3.

Table 7.3 *Input field types that control presentation of graphical user interface objects in an HTML form.*

Type	Description
TEXT	TEXT is the default type for an input element and presents a single line text field. You can set visible size of the text field with the SIZE attribute. Example: A field that presents 40 characters would be set using SIZE=40. You can also enforce an upper limit on the number of characters that can be entered with the MAXLENGTH attribute. Example: To limit a field to 80 characters, you set MAXLENGTH=80. With these two parameters set, users can type no more than the limit of 80 characters. The browser will allow users to keep the input cursor in view as they enter characters beyond the original 40 characters by scrolling the text.
PASSWORD	The PASSWORD type is similar to the TEXT type, but as a user types characters, the browser echoes back to the display a character such as an asterisk, thus hiding the text from prying eyes when entering passwords. You can use the SIZE and MAXLENGTH attributes to control visible and maximum length exactly like other text fields.
CHECKBOX	A CHECKBOX type is used in two situations: for simple Boolean attributes when one input variable is presented; and for attributes that possess multiple values simultaneously when several check box fields with the same NAME attribute and a different VALUE attribute are presented to the user for selection. Each checkbox that is selected generates a separate variable-value pair in the submitted data utilizing the NAME and VALUE attributes, even if this results in duplicate names. The CHECKED attribute initializes the checkbox in a checked state. By default the checkbox is presented in an unchecked state.

Continued

Table 7.3 *Continued*

Type	Description
RADIO	A RADIO type is used for attributes that can have a single value from a set of alternatives. The RADIO type creates a radio button object. Each radio button object in a group is given the same NAME attribute. Radio buttons require an explicit VALUE attribute. Only the checked radio button in a group generates a variable-value pair in the submitted data, utilizing the NAME and VALUE attributes. You should initially check one radio button in each group with the CHECKED attribute.
SUBMIT	The SUBMIT type defines a button that users can click to submit the form's contents to the server. The button's label is set from the VALUE attribute. If the NAME attribute is given, the submit button's variable-value pair is included in the submitted data. You can include several submit buttons on a form.
IMAGE	The IMAGE type creates a graphical submit button rather than a button with a text string created with the SUBMIT type. The URL for the image is specified with the SRC attribute. You can modify the image's alignment by specifying the ALIGN attribute. In this respect, graphical submit buttons are treated identically to IMG elements, so you can set the ALIGN attribute to LEFT, RIGHT, TOP, MIDDLE, or BOTTOM. In the data submitted by the form, image fields are included as two variable-value pairs that correspond to the x and y values of the location clicked. The variable names are derived by taking the NAME attribute of the field and appending ".x" for the x value, and ".y" for the y value.
RESET	The RESET type defines a button that users can click to reset the fields on a form to the state when the document was first loaded. The label of a reset button is set with the VALUE attribute. Reset buttons are never sent as part of the data transmitted from a form to the server.

Continued

Table 7.3 Continued

Type	Description
FILE	The FILE type provides a means for users to attach a file to a form's content. A FILE type input element is generally rendered as a text field. When clicked, an associated button invokes a file selection dialog that allows a user to select a file by name. The filename can also be entered directly by the user in the text field. Like the TEXT type input element, you can use the SIZE attribute to set the visible width of the field. You can also set the upper limit to the length of filenames using the MAXLENTH attribute. Additionally, some browsers support the ability to restrict the kinds of files that are presented in the file selection dialog to those matching a comma-separated list of MIME content types. (MIME content types are discussed in more detail in the sidebar, "Multipurpose Internet Mail Extensions.") To provide a restricted list of file types, you utilize the ACCEPT attribute. Example ACCEPT="image/*".
HIDDEN	Fields defined with the HIDDEN type are not rendered. Hidden fields have various uses, including allowing servers to store state information with a form and providing the ability to process localized edits with a scripting language. Data contained in a hidden field are returned to the server when a form is submitted using the variable-value pair using the NAME and VALUE attributes.

Multipurpose Internet Mail Extensions

Multipurpose Internet Mail Extensions (MIME) supply vital technology for extending the capabilities and functionality of standard Internet e-mail. MIME overcomes many of the obstacles for integrating nontext messages into the Web. The extensions provided by MIME to Internet messaging, including e-mail, include the ability to handle images and other objects in an ordinary Internet message body.

MIME is the basic specification for how computer systems can exchange multimedia information using Internet standards. In addition to supporting many predefined multimedia file types, MIME allows users to define a format type and exchange information using it.

The native MIME types include image, audio, video, application, multipart, message, and extension token. MIME subtypes provide more clarity on the content in the message. For example, *video/quicktime* defines the type (video) and sub-type (quicktime) for an Apple QuickTime Standard video stream. A Web browser uses the MIME content-type to interpret a file sent from the server. The browser can then invoke a helper application to present the message more effectively to the user.

MIME provides numerous mechanisms for describing and specifying format of an Internet message body. These mechanisms are specified in header fields that provide the following information:

MIME Version: Identifies the version of MIME to which the message conforms.

Content-Type: Specifies the general type and subtype of data in the body message. The MIME content type declaration states what the enclosed MIME body type is (example: *application*); it then describes the sub-type (example *excel*). To see a complete list of MIME types supported by your browser, look at your browser's helper applications dialog box. Here you will find the type, subtype, action, and extension that triggers the MIME type.

Content-Transfer-Encoding: Specifies ancillary encoding applied to the data.

Content-ID: A unique message ID (optional).

Content-Description: A text description of the body content (optional).

You use the NAME attribute to logically define the name of an input field. The NAME attribute becomes the variable name of the variable-value pair that is passed to the server when the form is submitted. The NAME attribute also plays an important role in scripting your Web pages. Scripting is discussed in Chapter 8, "Scripting Essentials."

The VALUE attribute initializes the value of an input element. The data contained in the value of an input element is passed in the variable-value pair when a form is submitted to the server. As with the NAME attribute, the VALUE attribute is important for scripting Web pages. Values that are present at form load time behave as an initial value for the represented field. For button type input elements, the value attribute provides a text label.

You use the CHECKED attribute for RADIO and CHECKBOX input elements. The presence of the checked attribute initializes checkboxes and radio buttons to their checked state.

The SIZE attribute sets the visible size of text fields to a given number characters, while you use the MAXLENGTH attribute to set the maximum number of characters a user can enter in an input field.

The SRC attribute specifies a URL of an image that is presented as a graphical submit button. The ALIGN attribute specifies the alignment of an image for a graphical submit button. The align attribute takes one of the following values: TOP, MIDDLE, BOTTOM, LEFT, RIGHT, or BOTTOM. The default alignment is BOTTOM. These values are further discussed in Table 7.4.

Table 7.4 *Align attributes used for IMAGE type input element image IMG elements.*

Value	Description
TOP	Aligns the top of the image at the top of the current text line.
MIDDLE	Aligns the middle of the image with the baseline of the curent text line.
BOTTOM	Aligns the bottom of the image with the baseline of the current text line. This is the default alignment.
LEFT	Aligns the image to the left margin of the browser's window. Text content from the HTML page wraps on the image's right side, though the right side of the image were the left margin. At the end of the image, the text resumes wrapping at the left margin of the browser's window.
RIGHT	Aligns the image to the right margin of the browser's window. Text content from the HTML page wraps on the image's left side, as though the left side of the image were the window's right margin. At the end of the image, the text resumes wrapping at the right margin of the browser's window.

Here are some examples of valid INPUT elements. The one that follows next prompts the user for their username and password. The username input field is presented as a freeform text field and has a default value of *guest*. The password field uses the type password in a freeform text field. The indication to the browser that this is a password field will force asterisks to be displayed for each character input by the user, protecting the secrecy of the password.

```
<input type=text size=40 name=username value="guest">
<input type=password size=12 name=pwd>
```

The following input element presents a check box that allows the user to indicate whether the value is on or off, or in this instance whether or not the entered information is for an employee. The default value is set to yes.

```
<input type=checkbox checked name=employee value=yes>
```

The following input element example presents a series of radio buttons indicating the age band demographic information. The user will select one of these values or use the default of "31 to 40" which is set through the checked option.

```
<input type=radio name=age_band value="0-18">
<input type=radio name=age_band value="19-22">
```

```
<input type=radio name=age_band value="23-30">
<input type=radio name=age_band value="31-40"checked>
<input type=radio name=age_band value="41-50">
<input type=radio name=age_band value="51-60">
<input type=radio name=age_band value="61-70">
<input type=radio name=age_band value="70-over">
```

The following example presents a button with the label of *Register*. Upon clicking this button, the form's input would be presented to the HTTP server. In addition, the second example input element presents a reset button that allows the user to reset all input values to their initial settings.

```
<input type=submit value="Register ...">
<input type=reset value="Clear Form...">
```

The following input element example presents an image, *map.gif*, to the user.

```
<input type=image name=location src="map.gif">
```

The following input element example of attaching a file to a form's content. Pressing the associated button will present the file open dialog and load all image mime types for the user's selection.

```
<input type=file name=photo size=20 accept="image/*">
```

The following input element example presents a hidden field. Hidden fields allow you to easily interact with a scripting environment to manage items which you do not want displayed to the user, such as their session identifier as shown below.

```
<input type=hidden name=sessionid>
```

SELECT (OPTION)

The SELECT element defines a list of valid selections from which a user can choose. Like the INPUT element, the SELECT element queries a user for information that will be passed to the server. However, the SELECT element presents the options which the user can select within a list. The SELECT element can create drop-down or scrollable lists of data from which a user selects data values. The SELECT element has a start tag of <SELECT> and an end tag of </SELECT>.

```
The OPTION element is a partner to the SELECT element. An OPTION element is used to
delimit the choices from which the user selects, in essence creating a selection
list. The OPTION element has a start tag of <OPTION>, but has no end tag.
```

The SELECT element can have three attributes: NAME, SIZE, and MULTIPLE.

- **NAME:** This attribute specifies a name that identifies a user's choice when a form is submitted to the server. Each selected option causes a variable-value pair to be included as part of the form's contents. The variable is set based on the NAME attribute and the value is based on the selection made by the user.

- **SIZE:** This attribute sets the number of choices that are visible to a user in the SELECT element's list.

- **MULTIPLE:** This attribute signifies that the user can make multiple selections. (By default, only one selection is allowed.) Users select multiple options by holding down the CTRL while selecting values with the mouse.

The OPTION element can have two attributes: SELECTED and VALUE.

- **SELECTED:** When present, this attribute makes an option the default option when the document is initially displayed to users.

- **VALUE:** This attribute specifies the value to be used when submitting the form's content. This is combined with the NAME attribute of the parent SELECT element to formulate the variable-value pair.

The basic structure of a selection list and associated options is as follows:

```
<SELECT name="Income Level">
<OPTION>$20,000 or less
<OPTION>$20,001 to $35,000
<OPTION>$35,001 to $50,000
<OPTION>$50,001 to $75,000
<OPTION>$75,001 to $100,000
<OPTION>$100,001 and more
</SELECT>
```

TEXTAREA

The TEXTAREA element provides a text field for users to input data comprising several lines. This is in contrast to the TEXT type INPUT element, which allows the user to enter only one line of text. TEXTAREA elements require a start tag of <TEXTAREA> and an end tag of </TEXTAREA>. The content of the element is restricted to text and character entities that are contained in the start and end tags. This content initializes the text that is shown when the document is first displayed. The TEXTAREA element has three attributes: NAME, ROWS, and COLS.

- **NAME:** This attribute specifies the name that identifies the TEXTAREA element when the form is submitted to the server.

- **ROWS:** This attribute specifies the number of visible text lines for the TEXTAREA element, though users may enter more lines than are visible. Browsers provide a means (typically a vertical scrollbar) to scroll the contents of a TEXTAREA element when the content extends beyond the visible area.

- **COLS:** This attribute specifies the visible width in characters for the TEXTAREA element, though users may enter longer lines than the visible area. Browsers provide a means (typically a horizontal scrollbar) to scroll the contents of the TEXTAREA element when the content extends beyond the visible area.

The following example allows users to enter several lines of text. Though they can see only four rows of forty columns of text while entering it, they may enter an arbitrary number of rows and columns.

```
<TEXTAREA NAME="Feedback"ROWS=4 COLS=40>
Please enter your feedback here...
</TEXTAREA>
```

The following example demonstrates how to define a form. The results of this HTML code are presented in Figure 7.3.

```
<!DOCTYPE HTML PUBLIC "-//W3C//DTD HTML 3.2 Final//EN">
<HTML>
 <HEAD>
 <TITLE>Sales Analysis Query Prompter</TITLE>
 </HEAD>
 <BODY>
 <H1>SALES ANALYSIS</H1>
 <H2>Information Package Selector</H2>
 <P>Please select the time, geography, and product set that
  you desire. Upon selecting these variables, press the
  "Submit Query" button and the sales data will be
  returned to you.
</P><BR><HR>
 <FORM METHOD=POST ACTION=1st_sales.stm>
 <B>Year:</B>
 <SELECT NAME="time_period">
 <OPTION>1997
 <OPTION>1996
 <OPTION>1995
```

```
</SELECT><BR><HR>
<B>Geography:</B><BR>
<SELECT NAME="eography" SIZE=3>
<OPTION>Central Region
<OPTION>Eastern Region
<OPTION>Northern Region
<OPTION>Southern Region
<OPTION>Western Region
</SELECT><BR><HR>
<B>Product:</B>
<INPUT TYPE=RADIO NAME="product" CHECKED>Paper
<INPUT TYPE=RADIO NAME="product">Beverages
<INPUT TYPE=RADIO NAME="product">Food<HR>
<INPUT TYPE=SUBMIT>
</FORM>
</BODY>
</HTML>
```

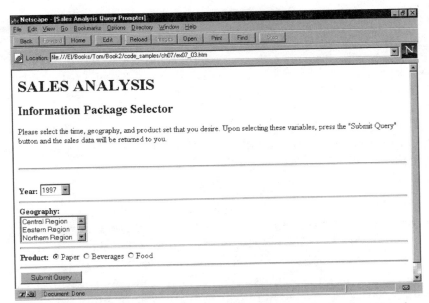

Figure 7.3 HTML form elements are useful for requesting information. This form, which represents HTML code shown in tthe TEXTAREA section, prompts users for information package filtering information.

Table Element

A TABLE element marks up tabular data or material for visual design purposes. A table presents data in a two-dimensional grid of rows and columns. Not only are tables important for formatting tabular data, they can also assist in formatting and presenting lists of information or content in a columnar fashion. In HTML, the TABLE element is a highly robust element. You can create simple displays that are the result of a database query as well as more complex displays such as multidimensional results with cells that span multiple rows or columns. The TABLE element and its associated tags allow you to easily format your tables to include table headings, borders, colored borders, background images, background colors, and much more.

The TABLE element has a starting tag of <TABLE> and an ending tag of </TABLE>. The starting tag for the TABLE element also has several attributes, including: ALIGN, WIDTH, BORDER, CELLSPACING, and CELLPADDING.

- **ALIGN:** This attribute controls the alignment of a table itself, not the individual cells, which are defined by row and column intersections. The valid alignments include LEFT, CENTER, and RIGHT.

- **WIDTH:** This attribute indicates the suggested width of the table. The reason I state "suggests" is that a browser can ignore the value you give it if it is not possible to present the table with your definition. The WIDTH attribute is either a pixel width or a percentage value. A width of *100%* forces the table to span the entire browser window.

- **BORDER:** This attribute indicates whether you desire a border around the table. You can optionally set the width of the border by specifying a number in pixels with the BORDER attribute. A BORDER attribute without a value defaults to a width of one.

- **CELLSPACING:** This attribute controls the white space (the space that is unused by the page's content) inside a table. To define the amount of white space, you equate the CELLSPACING attribute to a number that indicates how many pixels should be between a cell's contents and its border. The CELLPADDING attribute controls the white space between individual cells. As with the CELLSPACING attribute, you equate the CELLPADDING attribute to a number that indicates the pixels of white space between individual cells.

In a TABLE element, additional elements define the layout of a table that is presented to users. These elements define captions, rows, heading cells, and data cells.

- **CAPTION:** This element defines an optional table caption. The CAPTION element has a start tag of <CAPTION> and an end tag of </CAPTION>. The CAPTION element can either appear above or below the table. The position of the

CAPTION element is defined with the ALIGN attribute, which can have one of two values: TOP or BOTTOM. The CAPTION element is then centered to the tablet. The CAPTION element should appear directly below the TABLE start tag and before the first table row. The CAPTION element can also contain text-level markup, such as the type face to be used, to modify the visualization of the table's caption.

- **TR:** Tables are constructed as a sequence of rows, and the rows are made up of a series of data cells. Each row of a table is preceded by a start tag of <TR> and has an optional end tag of </TR>. The TR element has two attributes: ALIGN and VALIGN. The ALIGN attribute controls the horizontal alignment of the entire row. The ALIGN attribute can be set to LEFT, CENTER, or RIGHT. The VALIGN attribute controls the vertical alignment of the entire row. The VALIGN attribute can be set to TOP, MIDDLE, or BOTTOM. Both of these alignment attributes control the cell content appearance for the entire row.

- **TD:** The table data cell element defines individual cells inside a table row. A table data cell can include virtually all HTML elements, including additional tables, which are known as nested tables. If the cell is a label for either a row or a column, you should use the TH element discussed next. A TD element has a start tag of <TD> and an optional end tag of </TD>. To modify the presentation of a table data cell, you can use several attributes, including: ROWSPAN, COLSPAN, NOWRAP, ALIGN, VALIGN, WIDTH, and HEIGHT. The ROWSPAN and COLSPAN attributes indicate how many rows or columns this cell overlaps. The NOWRAP attribute indicates that the table data cell's content should not be wrapped. (If you use the NOWRAP attribute, you must explicitly define where to wrap the cell's content with the BR element; otherwise, the entire content of the cell will appear as one line.) The ALIGN and VALIGN attributes control the horizontal and vertical alignment of the individual table data cell. The ALIGN attribute can be set to LEFT, CENTER, or RIGHT. The VALIGN attribute can be set to TOP, MIDDLE, or BOTTOM. The WIDTH and HEIGHT attributes can be used to suggest the width and height for the individual cell in pixels.

- **TH:** The table header cell element defines a table cell that contains heading information. The TH element has a start tag of <TH> and an optional end tag of </TH>. The attributes for the TH element are identical to those for the TD element. Therefore, the TH element is primarily used for documenting the content of a table cell as a heading, while the TD element defines a table cell as data.

The following example demonstrates how a table is defined. The results of this HTML code are presented in Figure 7.4.

```
<!DOCTYPE HTML PUBLIC "-//W3C//DTD HTML 3.2 Final//EN">
<HTML>
 <HEAD>
 <TITLE>Sample Table</TITLE>
 </HEAD>
 <BODY>
 <TABLE BORDER>
  <CAPTION>Sales Analysis Data</CAPTION>
  <TR>
  <TH>Time Period</TH>
  <TH>Geography</TH>
  <TH>Product</TH>
  <TH>Units Sold</TH>
  </TR>
  <TR>
  <TD>1997-05</TD>
  <TD>VT</TD>
  <TD>Diapers</TD>
  <TD ALIGN=RIGHT>$875</TD>
  </TR>
  <TR>
  <TD>1997-06</TD>
  <TD>NH</TD>
  <TD>Paper Towels</TD>
  <TD ALIGN=RIGHT>$1,500</TD>
  </TR>
  <TR>
  <TD>1997-06</TD>
  <TD>VT</TD>
  <TD>Napkins</TD>
  <TD ALIGN=RIGHT>$365</TD>
  </TR>
  <TR>
  <TD>1997-07</TD>
  <TD>NY</TD>
  <TD>Diapers</TD>
  <TD ALIGN=RIGHT>$1,200</TD>
  </TR>
  <TR>
   <TD>1997-07</TD>
   <TD>MA</TD>
   <TD>Napkins</TD>
   <TD ALIGN=RIGHT>$2,200</TD>
  </TR>
 </TABLE>
 </BODY>
</HTML>
```

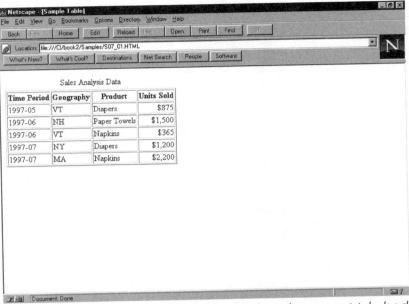

Figure 7.4 *HTML Table elements are useful for applications that present tabular data, such as a data warehouse. This figure illustrates the code listing in the Table Element section.*

Division Elements

Division elements allow you to build visible breaks and section formats into your Web pages. These elements guide users through a series of visible blocks in the information flow, grouping like information together and applying common formats to those blocks. Division elements include the logical division, the centered division, the horizontal rule, and the line break. Each of these elements is discussed in the sections that follow.

Logical Division (DIV Tag)

The division element structures HTML documents and the rendering of all elements in a specified division. The division element has a start tag of (<DIV>) and end tag of (</DIV>). The division tag has only one available attribute, which is ALIGN. The align attribute can set the default horizontal alignment for elements in the content of a division element. Valid values for the ALIGN attribute are LEFT, RIGHT, and CENTER. Because a division is a block element, it terminates an open paragraph (<P>) element. The following code demonstrates the use of a division element.

```
<DIV ALIGN=CENTER>
 <H1>The Information Packaging Methodology Help Guide</H1>
 <H2>Introduction</H2>
</DIV>
<DIV ALIGN=LEFT>
 Welcome to the Information Packaging Methodology Help
 Guide. This online tutorial will assist you and your
 colleagues to properly build and maintain a data warehouse.
 The information contained within this tutorial is further
 described in books titled:
<UL>
<LI>Data Warehousing: Building the Corporate Knowledge
 Base (ISBN 1-85032-856-0)</LI>
<LI>Data Warehousing on the Internet: Accessing the
 Corporate Knowledge Base (ISBN 1-85032-857-9)</LI>
</UL>
 You should verify that you have access to one of these
 books to further explain and augment the information
 contained in this tutorial.
</DIV>
```

Centered Division (CENTER Tag)

The center tag was introduced by Netscape prior to HTML 3.0. The center tag is functionally equivalent to the DIV tag with an ALIGN=CENTER attribute applied. Due to the wide use of the center tag, this tag has been retained through HTML 3.2, but we recommend that you standardize your syntax using the DIV Tag.

Horizontal Rule (HR Tag)

Horizontal rules indicate a change in topic. They provide a visual indicator to the reader of an HTML page of a pause or change in content and flow. A horizontal rule is not a container and therefore only utilize a start tag (<HR>). You may use several attributes with the horizontal rule element, including ALIGN, NOSHADE, SIZE, and WIDTH.

- **ALIGN:** This attribute determines whether the rule is placed at the left, center, or right of the space between the current left and right margins of the page. By default, the horizontal rule is centered.

- **NOSHADE:** This attribute requests the browser to render the horizontal rule without shading. The standard horizontal rule is rendered as a two-colored "groove," or shaded line, which appears indented. Applying this attribute to the horizontal rule renders a solid color line rather than the two-color default.

- **SIZE:** This attribute sets the pixel height of the horizontal rule.

- **WIDTH:** This attribute sets the pixel width of the horizontal rule. The width can be stated in one of two ways: either as explicit pixels (width=100); or as a percentage between the current left and right margins (width="75%"). By default, the horizontal rule is rendered as 100% of the display width.

Link Break

A line break element forces line breaks in text. Browsers ignore spaces and other control characters unless they are inserted in a PRE element. Therefore, if you want to interject line breaks in text that is not in a PRE element, you must insert a line break element. The line break element has a start tag of <BR> and no end tag. The line break tag can also have an optional CLEAR attribute, which can be used when an IMG element is present in text. The CLEAR attribute has four possible values: LEFT, RIGHT, ALL, or NONE. If you want to display text below an image, the CLEAR option forces the browser to scroll down past any floating image to a clear left margin, a clear right margin, or both margins prior to placing any text.

Text Formatting Elements

Text formatting elements (such as bold, subscript, and font size) logically group text into paragraphs without breaks. The primary purpose of these elements is to format the presentation of the text. Each of the text formatting elements requires a start tag and an end tag. The formats are both logical and physical in scope. Logical formats include items such as emphasize, variable, code, and keyboard. Physical format include items such as bold, italic, and underline. Table 7.5 provides a complete listing of the text formatting elements.

You need to verify that text formatting elements are properly nested, or errors may occur. For example, the following tags are placed incorrectly, because the start tag for italics is placed prior to the end tag for the bold tag:

```
Your query returned<B>50 results. <I></B>The first 20</I> are shown here.
```

This HTML code is corrected by properly placing the start and end tags, as follows:

```
Your query returned<B>50 results. </B><I>The first 20</I> are shown here.
```

Most browsers respect nested formatting, but try to keep the proper start tags in order with their respective end tags. Therefore, the following code example is also valid:

```
Your query returned <B>50 results <I>the first 20</I> are shown here.</B>.
```

Table 7.5 *Text formatting elements.*

Element	Start Tag	End Tag	Description
Italic text style	<I>	</I>	Format text using italic.
Bold text style	<B>	</B>	Format text using bold.
Underlined text style	<U>	</U>	Format text using underline.
Strike out text style	<STRIKE>	</STRIKE>	Format text using strike-through. Strike-through normally is rendered as a line through the middle of the text.
Larger text	<BIG>	</BIG>	Format text using a larger font.
Smaller text	<SMALL>	</SMALL>	Format text using a smaller font.
Subscript	_		Format text as a subscript, placing the text slightly lower than the base text position.
Superscript	[	]	Format text as a superscript, placing the text slightly higher than the base text position.
Emphasized text	<EM>	</EM>	Emphasize the text; typically the text is rendered in italic. However, this is a logical format; so when a browser can distinguish that the text is emphasized, it renders it so, even if an italic format is unavailable.
Strongly emphasized	<STRONG>	</STRONG>	Strongly emphasize the text; the text typically is presented in bold. However, this is a logical format, so when a browser can distinguish that the text is strongly emphasized, it renders it so, even if a bold format is unavailable.
Definition of a term	<DFN>	</DFN>	Highlight a definition of a term; the text typically is presented in italic. However, this is a logical format, so when a browser can distinguish that the text is a new term or definition, it renders it so, even if italic is unavailable.

Continued

Table 7.5 *Continued*

Element	Start Tag	End Tag	Description
Code fragment	<CODE>	</CODE>	Highlight sample code. This is a logical font meant for small samples of code embedded in paragraphs. The text typically is presented in a monospaced font.
Sample text	<SAMP>	</SAMP>	Highlight a sample of text intended to be used literally. The sample text format differs from the keyboard text format in that it generally refers to input or output text, while keyboard text tends to refer to input text.
Keyboard input	<KBD>	</KBD>	Highlight text that should be typed by your user exactly as it appears. The keyboard text is typically rendered in a monospace font. The keyboard text format differs from the sample text format in that it generally refers to input text only, while the sample text format tends to refer to input or output text.
Variable	<VAR>	</VAR>	Highlight variables or arguments to commands.
Short citation	<CITE>	</CITE>	Highlight text that has been cited from other sources.
Font modification	<FONT>	</FONT>	Change the appearance of the current block of text in terms of SIZE and COLOR. The SIZE attribute can be either an absolute value, ranging from 1 (smallest) to 7 (largest), or a relative value, such as +1 or -2. The COLOR attribute uses the hex color values shown in Table 7.1.
Teletype	<TT>	</TT>	Format text using teletype or monospace.

Embedded Object Elements

This chapter thus far has primarily discussed text-oriented elements and tags. However, HTML documents can contain much more than text. You can embedded additional objects in documents to add style, flair, and functionality to your final application. The following sections introduce the primary embedded objects among the many kinds of objects from which you may choose. The objects we cover here include images, image maps, and Java applets, the minimum set of embedded objects to professionally job create a Web-based data warehouse.

Images

To insert images in an HTML document, you use the IMG, or image, element. The image element has a start tag of <IMG> and no end tag. An image is not a block element and therefore must be located in a block element. The image element has several attributes, including: SRC, ALT, ALIGN, HEIGHT, WIDTH, BORDER, HSPACE, VSPACE, USEMAP, and ISMAP.

- **SRC:** This attribute indicates the location of an image in the text of a page. The SRC attribute is set to a URL that points to a valid image file, typically a .JPG (JPEG) or .GIF.

- **ALT:** This attribute provides a text alternative to present to a user if a browser is unable to present the image defined in the SRC attribute.

- **ALIGN:** This attribute controls the alignment of the image with respect to text. The ALIGN attribute can be set to one of the following values: LEFT, RIGHT, TOP, MIDDLE, or BOTTOM. See Table 7.4 for a more detailed description of these alignment values.

- **HEIGHT** and **WIDTH:** These attributes contain the image's dimensions. Providing the HEIGHT and WIDTH allows the browser to lay out the page in advance, allowing it to know where the text should be drawn in proximity to the image.

- **BORDER:** This attribute is used when the image is defined as a hyperlink. The browser draws a border around the image, indicating to the user that the image is a link to an area in the same or another document.

- **HSPACE** and **VSPACE:** These attributes indicate the pixel space surrounding an image. The HSPACE attribute defines the horizontal space, while the VSPACE attribute covers vertical spacing.

- **USEMAP** and **ISMAP:** These attributes are used for image maps, which are discussed in the following section. An image map is a single image with multiple hyperlinks. These hyperlinks are based on coordinates in the image, which are defined using either a MAP element or a separate file. The ISMAP attribute specifies that a server file defines the coordinates of the images links. The USEMAP attribute indicates that the image contains a client side image map. The USEMAP attribute is equated to a URL containing the image map coordinates.

Image Maps

An image map is a single image that contains "hot spots," or clickable areas, that allow users to jump to another area in the current document or to a different document. With a client-side image map, the information about the image's hot spots are defined in the MAP element. The MAP element has a start tag of <MAP> and an end tag of </MAP>. The MAP element has one attribute, NAME. The NAME attribute on the MAP start tag assigns a name to the imagemap; the USEMAP attribute of the IMG element discussed in the preceding section should point to this name. For example:

```
<IMG SRC="TOOLBAR.GIF" USEMAP="#toolbar">
<MAP NAME="toolbar">
```

The AREA element defines each of the hot spots in an image map and must be inside the start and end tags of the MAP element. The AREA element has only a start tag, <AREA>. The AREA element has several attributes, including: SHAPE, COORDS, NOHREF, HREF, and ALT.

- **SHAPE** and **COORDS:** These attributes define the actual region that comprises the hot spots on an image. The SHAPE attribute can be a rectangle, circle, or polygon. The COORDS attribute contains a set of coordinates that describe the defined shape and is equated to a comma-separated list of numbers enclosed in quotes. These comma-separated numbers define the detail coordinates for the shape. A rectangle (RECT) has four coordinates: the first specifies the top left corner, the second specifies the bottom right corner, the third and forth provide the height and width of the rectangle in pixels. A circle (CIRCLE) is defined by its center and radius. A circle has three coordinates: the first and second define the center, while the third defines the radius. A polygon (POLY) is built up by a list of coordinates, which are all connected in the order presented and with the last coordinate pair connected to the first. The polygon shape allows the building of abstract figures.

- **NOHREF** and **HREF:** These attributes specify the action to take when a user selects a hot spot defined in the image map. The HREF attribute specifies the URL of the destination when an area is selected. If NOHREF is specified, no action is taken.

- **ALT:** This attribute specifies text that is presented to a user if the browser is unable to present the image map.

The following is the sample source code for a toolbar image map. The resultant Web page is shown in Figure 7.5.

```
<!DOCTYPE HTML PUBLIC "-//W3C//DTD HTML 3.2//EN">
<HTML>
 <HEAD>
 <TITLE>Sample Image Map</TITLE>
 </HEAD>
 <BODY>
 <H1>Sample Image Map Toolbar</H1>
 <IMG HEIGHT=45 WIDTH=248 SRC="icons.gif" BORDER=0
   USEMAP="#map0">
 <MAP NAME="map0">
  <AREA SHAPE="circle" ALT="circle" COORDS="20,20,14"
   HREF="home.html">
  <AREA SHAPE="circle" ALT="circle" COORDS="74,21,15"
   HREF="about.html">
  <AREA SHAPE="circle" ALT="circle" COORDS="120,21,13"
   HREF="save.html">
  <AREA SHAPE="circle" ALT="circle" COORDS="172,20,14"
   HREF="phone.html">
  <AREA SHAPE="circle" ALT="circle" COORDS="223,20,15"
   HREF="emplist.html">
 </MAP>
 </BODY>
</HTML>
```

Java Applets

You use the APPLET element to include Java applets. A Java applet is an application that is written in the Java language specifically to run in a browser or in a similar environment that directly supports Java. Java applets cannot run on their own, which is the primary differentiation between a Java applet and a Java application. Java Applets can add graphics and other special effects to your Web pages and improve the display from your databases. The APPLET element uses a start tag of <APPLET> and an end tag of </APPLET>. In the start tag, the APPLET element can posses many attributes, including: CODEBASE, CODE, NAME, ALT, ALIGN, HEIGHT, WIDTH, HSPACE, and VSPACE.

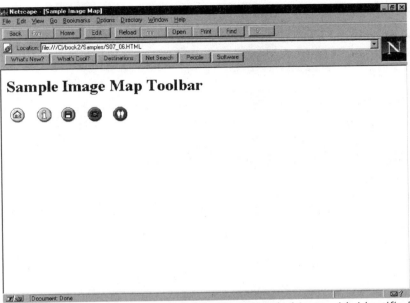

Figure 7.5 *Image maps let you present graphical icons and objects with identified hot spots, allowing users to more easily interact with your system.*

- **CODEBASE:** This attribute specifies an absolute URL for the applet. In this sense, the CODEBASE attribute is similar to the BASE attribute used with HTML documents. (See the "BASE Element" section earlier in this chapter.) This attribute is also searched when other classes are requested for the applet. Java applications rely heavily on classes to fulfill application requests. Classes are the components which are reused within various Java applications and applets, optimizing in an object oriented framework. If the CODEBASE attribute is not specified, the current URL is used for the location.

- **CODE:** This attribute indicates the location of the class of the applet.

- **NAME:** This attribute specifies the name of the applet.

- **ALT:** This attribute defines text to display if the applet cannot be run. Not all browsers support Java applets; and those browsers that do, allow the users to disable the execution of the applet. Therefore, it is highly recommended that you provide alternate text.

- **ALIGN:** This attribute sets the vertical and horizontal alignment of the applet. For valid alignment settings, see Table 7.4.

- **HEIGHT and WIDTH:** These attributes specify the dimensions of the applet's window in pixels.

- **HSPACE and VSPACE:** These attributes control the horizontal and vertical white space around the applet in pixels.

To pass variables from your Web page to a Java applet, use the PARAM element in the APPLET element's start and end tags. The PARAM element in essence provides command-line arguments to a Java applet embedded in a Web page. The PARAM element has two attributes: NAME, which specifies the name of the argument for which you are passing a value; and VALUE, which specifies the value for this argument. Java applets are case sensitive, so use caution when providing a list of arguments to an applet. Ensure that you have the proper parameter names or you will certainly experience errors. The following example uses a graphical Java applet to present tabular sales analysis data. The resultant page is shown in Figure 7.6.

```
<title>Sample Java Applet</title>
<body>
<center>
<applet codebase=file:///C|/widgets/NetCharts/classes
  code=NFPiechartApp.class width=400 height=250>
 <param name=NFParamScript value='
   Background = (lightGray, RAISED, 8);
   LabelPos = 0.6;

   Header = ("North East Region Paper Product Sales",
     yellow, "TimesRoman", 16);
   HeaderBox = (darkBlue, RAISED, 4);

   Legend  = ("Legend", black, "TimesRoman", 14);
   LegendBox = (white, RECESS, 6);

   Slices  = (1240, null, "VT", black,
     "TimesRoman", 14),
     (1500,,"NH"),
     (1200,,"NY"),
     (2200,,"MA"); '>
</applet>
</center>
```

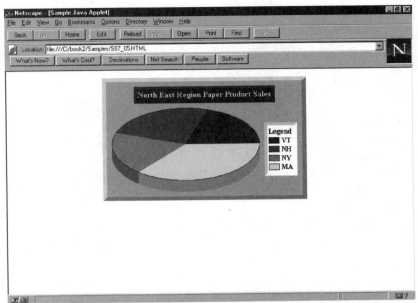

Figure 7.6 *A Java applet embedded in an HTML page demonstrates how applets can enhance the presentation of data in a Web document.*

Putting It All Together

Now that we have discussed the major components of an HTML document, you may be asking how this all fits together. The answer lies in the concepts behind hypertext. Many ways exist to take individual documents and bring them together as a uniform set of linked documents. Creating linkages and associations among documents is what hypertext is all about.

As you create individual pages, you want to bring an organization to the navigation of these pages. You also want to control how the pages are presented. Some pages may be menu oriented, similar to an index or table of contents in a book; other pages may be destinations, such as individuals pages in a book. These physical representations of hypertext pages are possible with HTML links and frames.

Hyperlinks within Documents Anchors

One of the most powerful concepts of HTML is links. An HTML document can contain a link to any other HTML document on any Web server in the world. When users select a link, they jump from page to page without worry about where the pages are located. I remember the first time when I sat down with my wife and "surfed" the Web. We were amazed at how quickly we could change our destination to virtually any country, state, or city in the world—all through a personal computer in our living room. We were searching for medial information and started at a government site in Washington, DC. From there, we went to Cambridge, Massachusetts, England, Los Angeles, and so on. Links allow a user to traverse in a fashion similar to the strands of a spider web.

A link in an HTML document is contained in an anchor element, as shown in Figure 7.7. The link can refer to a different Web page on the same server or to a Web page on a physically different server potentially in a different physical location or a location within the current HTML file. The anchor element is the linkage mechanism for hypertext documents. An anchor element has a start tag of <A> and an end tag of </A>. Any text or image enclosed by the anchor element's start and end tags is selectable by users. When users select an anchor element, they are taken to the location specified by the anchor element. An anchor element has several attributes, including: HREF, NAME, REL, REV, and TITLE.

- **HREF:** This attribute provides a URL or "jump-to" name for the destination of a hyperlink. If that destination is in the same file as the hyperlink, a # symbol is combined with a reference name to create a phrase that names the destination.

- **NAME:** This attribute identifies a place in the text of a Web page. These "named anchors" or "jump-to" names allow users to jump directly to a spot in the text of a Web page. For example, the following definition creates a table of contents. This table of contents can then be referenced in the document via the URL, *#toc*.

```
<A NAME="toc">Table of Contents</A>
```

- **REL** and **REV:** These attributes are not widely used, but have been included in the HTML standard since the HTML 2.0 specification. These attributes mark relationships between the current document and the resource in a link. Because these attributes are not widely used, there is no standard list of values for them.

- **TITLE:** This attribute provides a description of a referenced link or anchor. This title is presented to users by most browsers when the mouse moves over the link or anchor.

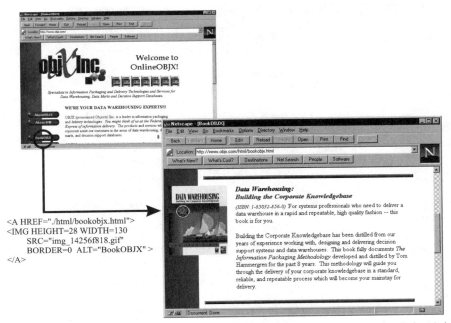

```
<A HREF="./html/bookobjx.html">
<IMG HEIGHT=28 WIDTH=130
     SRC="img_14256f818.gif"
     BORDER=0  ALT="BookOBJX" >
</A>
```

Figure 7.7 *One of the most powerful features of HTML is the concept of a link. Linkage to multiple Web pages allows you to build a complete system.*

As you formulate hyperlinks among documents, you create a series of document hierarchies. Managing this process is tricky and requires a high degree of organization. Many tools have recently hit the market that can assist you in this process. Probably the most significant for comprehensive site management is NetObjects Fusion from NetObjects. However, the product is still weak in integration with other tools, such as database interfaces. Future revisions will surely improve functionality in this area. Figure 7.8 illustrates a complete site in the NetObjects Fusion product set.

Within Section IV, Case Studies, we investigate a tool from Sybase that greatly assists in managing an overall Web site. This tool, originally named NetImpact Dynamo, is evolving to provide complete Web site management for database driven applications over the Web. We will cover this product and its server component, PowerDynamo, in more detail in Chapter 9, "PowerDynamo Essentials."

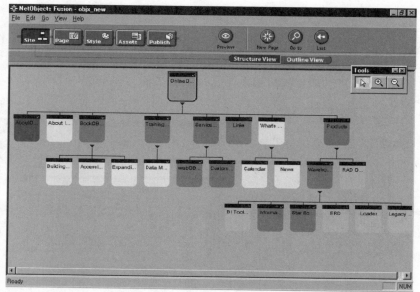

Figure 7.8 *NetObjects Fusion is one of many recently introduced tools that assist in managing a complete set of hyperlinked documents.*

Frames

Frames allow you to create multiple, independent regions in the window of a user's browser. These regions have their own controls and can be quite useful when implementing complex decision-support applications.

The most common use of frames is to display toolbars or menus to guide and control a user's interaction with a Web site. As discussed earlier in this chapter, reports have three common regions: heading, body, and footing. Frames assist you in delivering these areas to users of your interactive Web site.

A framed document has a basic structure that is quite similar to a normal HTML document, except that the body element is replaced by a frameset element. The frameset element, or container, describes HTML documents that act subordinately to the master page. These subdocuments, or frames, make up the actual Web page. Each frame has its own set of navigational and user interaction capabilities. Because of this flexibility, you should use caution when implementing frames so your users don't become flustered by a user interface without a clear structure.

Frame syntax is similar in scope and complexity to the syntax we discussed for tables earlier in the "Table Element" section of this chapter. Frames were designed to be an optimizing component in the display and layout processing that must occur for Internet client engines, such as browsers. Some parts of the page may not be required to be repainted as new information is presented to users. In a graphically intense application, this can greatly speed the process of rendering output. Three elements allow you to define and implement frames. These elements are FRAMESET, FRAME, and NOFRAME, which are discussed in the sections that follow.

FRAMESET Element

Frames are organized into sets of documents, known as *framesets*, which are physically grouped in a common interface. The FRAMESET element is the main container for your frames. A FRAMESET element has a start tag of <FRAMESET> and an end tag of </FRAMESET>. The FRAMESET element and its attributes specify many of the physical properties associated with the layout of the user interface. However, this interface layout information refers specifically to the entire group of frames represented by the FRAME-SET element; each individual FRAME element control its own appearance in the set. A FRAMESET element has two attributes, ROWS and COLS, which define the height and width, respectively, of individual frames in the frameset. The number of individual frames is implicitly specified by the number of FRAME element or nested FRAMESET element entries.

The ROWS and COLS attributes define the dimensions for individual frames. Setting these values can be done in one of three ways:

- **VALUE:** A simple numeric value represents the dimension in pixels. This method normally is not recommended, because you cannot always know the size of a viewer's window. If you do use a fixed pixel value, you typically will want to combine it with relative sizes as described shortly. This mixed strategy assists in defining a proportional frameset that doesn't exceed 100 percent of a display window. You could define a frameset with three fixed-value rows—one for the heading, one for the body, and one for the footing—as follows:

```
<FRAMESET ROWS="100, 400, 100">
  <FRAME SRC="heading.html" NAME="heading">
  <FRAME SRC="body.html" NAME="body">
  <FRAME SRC="footing.html" NAME="footing">
</FRAMESET>
```

- **PERCENTAGE:** You can use a percentage value between 1 and 100 to define the relative size for frames. If the total percentage allocated for the frames exceeds 100 percent, all percentages are automatically scaled down by the browser. On the other hand, if the total percentage is less than 100 percent, the extra space is equally distributed to the frames. You could define a frameset with two percentage-based columns—one on the left to house a menu and one on the right to house data—as follows:

```
<FRAMESET COLS="20%, 80%">
 <FRAME SRC="menu.html" NAME="menu">
 <FRAME SRC="data.html" NAME="data">
</FRAMESET>
```

- ***:** A single asterisk designates a relative-sized frame and gives that frame the remaining space. If multiple relative sized frames exist, the remaining space is divided equally among them. If a value precedes the asterisk, that frame gets that much more relative space. For example, "2*,*" would give two-thirds of the space to the first frame, and one-third of the space to the second. The following example combines the this method and the previous VALUE method: the heading is fixed at 50, the footing is fixed at 100, and the body gets the rest.

```
<FRAMESET ROWS="50, *, 100">
 <FRAME SRC="heading.html" NAME="heading">
 <FRAME SRC="body.html" NAME="body">
 <FRAME SRC="footing.html" NAME="footing">
</FRAMESET>
```

FRAMESET elements can be nested inside other FRAMESET elements. If you nest FRAMESET elements, those framesets are allocated space in an identical manner to the space allocated for individual frames. Note that the nested frameset has a reduced display window compared to the whole screen managed by the parent frameset. The following syntax provides a menu column on the left of the display and divides the right side of the display into three regions of a report.

```
<FRAMESET COLS="20%, 80%">
 <FRAME SRC="menu.html" NAME="menu">
 <FRAMESET ROWS="15%, *, 20%">
        <FRAME SRC="heading.html" NAME="heading">
 <FRAME SRC="body.html" NAME="body">
        <FRAME SRC="footing.html" NAME="footing">
 </FRAMESET>
</FRAMESET>
```

FRAME Element

The FRAME element defines the attributes of each frame in a frameset. For example, the following syntax defines a frame into which *menu.html* will be loaded. This frame is named *menu*.

```
<FRAME SRC="menu.html" NAME="menu">
```

The FRAME element has a start tag of <FRAME> and several attributes, including: SRC, NAME, MARGINWIDTH, MARGINHEIGHT, SCROLLING, and NORESIZE. The FRAME element is not a container and therefore has no end tag.

- **SRC:** This attribute defines the URL of the HTML document to display in a particular frame. If you do not define a SRC attribute, the frame displays as a blank space.

- **NAME:** This attribute assigns a logical name to a frame. This logical name allows other documents to target this frame space. As users interact with your application and select links, a browser can place documents deep in your document hierarchy in this named frame space.

- **MARGINWIDTH** and **MARGINHEIGHT:** These attributes, designated in pixels, provide some control over the margins of a frame. Margins cannot be less than a value of one and cannot be defined so that no space is available for the content of documents. By default, the browser determines the appropriate margins, so these attributes are optional and often unused.

- **SCROLLING:** This attribute indicates whether you want the frame to have scrollbars. The valid values to which you can equate the SCROLLING attribute are YES, NO, and AUTO. A YES value state that you want scrollbars to always be visible. A NO value states that you never want scrollbars to be visible. An AUTO value allows the browser to decide whether to display scrollbars. The SCROLLING attribute is optional and defaults to AUTO.

- **NORESIZE:** This attribute indicates that the frame is not resizable by users. Without this attribute, a user can resize a frame by dragging the frame edge to a new position. The ability to resize a frame is the default behavior.

NOFRAME Element

The NOFRAME element allows you to provides alternate content for older browsers that do not support frames. A frame-capable browser ignores this element and all the data (elements and tags) between the start tag of <NOFRAME> and end tag of </NOFRAME>. This element allows you to define both a framed and nonframed interface in one HTML document.

The Future of Markup Languages: Extensible Markup Language

Many developers, at the direction of their companies, have adopted the Web as their new development paradigm. However, on submersing themselves into this environment, they have discovered that deploying a large Web site is as complex as developing a large client/server or standalone application. More specifically, they have discovered that HTML is not up to the task of developing large and complex systems.

To address the limitations of HTML, the World Wide Web Consortium has formulated the Extensible Markup Language (XML) specification. This specification is becoming widely endorsed by the leaders in Web development strategies. The purpose of XML is to address the glaring limitations of HTML by creating a more flexible language that allows organizations to deploy more sophisticated applications composed of documents and complex data.

It is important to note that XML is simply another markup language based on SGML. The fundamental process of defining a markup language such as HTML or XML within SGML is done by defining a Document Type Description (DTD). The DTD in essence defines the constructs used to interpret the markup language in SGML terms. However, through the years developers have found that creating SGML DTDs is not that easy. If it were, all browsers and development on the Web would be done through SGML, not HTML.

XML is a compromise between the simplicity of HTML and the flexibility of SGML. Like SGML, XML is a metalanguage; but it is easier to use and XML DTDs are much easier to create. The biggest benefit of XML is that it is extensible. Authors can create their own elements and tags. Fortunately, only minor changes will be required to make an HTML document compatible with XML. So the value of simple transformation between HTML and XML and the ability to extend the language make XML a logical progression for developing applications for the Web.

Developers can create clients that are more intelligent. Companies can more easily exchange data. And advanced technologies such as agents can integrate into an application at a base, interpretation layer. Today, agents are far outside the boundaries of the base HTML syntax.

Like HTML, XML is neutral with respect to vendor, application, and platform. Unlike HTML, under XML content providers can easily create tags tailored to their own requirements without loss of compatibility, interoperability, or longevity. These benefits allow content providers to deliver better functionality in indexing, search and retrieval, links, and complex structures. We will see organizations building standards such as Architectural Markup Language, Manufacturing Markup Language, and Financial Markup Language.

XML itself does not replace HTML. HTML is expected to remain in common use for some time to come. XML is designed to make the writing of document type definitions (DTD) much simpler than is the case with full SGML, therefore, you could use XML to redefine all or part of HTML itself for your own use, as you could with any Document Type Definition.

XML defines two levels of conformance, valid and well-formed. If your file already conforms to one of the HTML Document Type Definitions (DTDs), then it may be close to being valid. Three things need changing to make your HTML document valid. First, you need to include the Document Type Declaration in a standard statement as follows:

```
<!DOCTYPE HTML SYSTEM "http://www.foo.com/myfiles/html3x.dtd">
```

Second, there is an optional XML Declaration with a Required Markup Declaration which may preceded the Document Type Declaration. And third, any DTD you reference must be an XML version, as must any other entities the DTD refers to such as files of character entities like ISO Latin-1. All DTDs must all be accessible either through the network or from the user's local disk by supplying a URL or filename for each in their SYSTEM identifiers. Each DTD must also follow the rules for well-formed XML files. Once the DTD has been verified as well formed, you will place an XML Declaration containing a Required Markup Declaration at the top of your document:

```
<?XML VERSION="1.0" RMD="NONE"?>
  <HTML>
    <HEAD>
    <TITLE>Test file</TITLE></HEAD>
    <BODY>
      <BLINK>Test text
        <IMG SRC="foo.gif" alt="A foo"/>
      </BLINK>
```

```
    </BODY>
  </HTML>
```

The specific deliverables of the XML working group are being developed in three phases, as follows:

- **Phase I:** A specification for the syntax of XML (Extensible Markup Language), a simplified version of SGML (ISO 8879) suitable for Internet applications. The latest working draft was released in March 1997. The next XML working draft revision is scheduled to be released June 30, 1997.

- **Phase II:** A specification of standard hypertext mechanisms for XML applications was presented at the WWW6 Conference (Santa Clara, April 1997). The next draft revision of the hypertext mechanisms for XML is scheduled to be released June 30, 1997.

- **Phase III:** The specification of a standard stylesheet language for XML publishing applications is targeted for delivery in draft form at the SGML/XML 97 Conference in Washington, DC, December 1997.

To follow the progress of this exciting new advancement in the area of Web applications see http://www.w3.org/XML.

Vendors such as Microsoft have already begun building extensions in the area of its Channel Definition Language for push services and its Open Financial Exchange for banking and brokerage services. Database vendors are not far behind. As we will see in Chapter 9, "PowerDynamo Essentials," Sybase has also begun to develop its own set of standard markups for creating database-specific applications. All of this will greatly enhance your capabilities to extend the Web in decision-support and database-driven data warehouse applications development.

Summary

HTML provides a syntax for presenting information from a data warehouse to a user. Using HTML is beneficial because it's an international standard that is neutral with respect to vendor, application, and platform. Because the information in HTML documents are marked in a standard way, this information can be shared by other document publishing systems that can interpret HTML.

The tags in an HTML document provide for reuse; sections can be reused in many documents. Because the tags in an HTML document assist in marking the meaning of the associated content, the tags also assist in advanced areas such as electronic searching and system documentation. The benefit of HTML is that it is created in plain ASCII text with no control characters or embedded binary codes, so developers can easily look at or edit an HTML file in a simple text editor. These advances also allow for near-zero dollar, client-side deployment of applications. All that users' workstations require are a browser and a way to connect to your network for them to access the latest version of your application.

Using HTML, you carefully define the structure of a document so that any present or future browser can read it and display it in a way that is best for the user. This makes it possible to develop information in HTML without having to create one version for Microsoft Internet Explorer, another for Netscape Navigator, and yet another for Mosaic. This flexibility on the user interface is one advance that the Internet has delivered. As we will see in Chapter 8, "Scripting Essentials," JavaScript now offers us a standardized way to make these user interface components come to life—again, in a standardized way.

8

Scripting Essentials

In building Web pages for Internet data warehouse, you present information to your users with Hypertext Markup Language (HTML). The design and layout of the HTML pages entice users to explore your site. The hyperlinks that you embed provide predefined paths to valuable information in the data warehouse. (The basics of HTML are covered in Chapter 7, "HTML Essentials.")

But scripting brings your pages to life. In this chapter, you learn how to make your pages respond to requests from your audience beyond a simple click that displays a new HTML page. Scripting provides the ability to deliver interactive elements, making your Web pages more responsive to user needs. Like other scripting languages that extend the capabilities of an application, JavaScript extends a standard Web page beyond its normal functionality. This chapter shows you how JavaScript works in HTML pages.

JavaScript: Breathing Life into HTML Pages

Standard Web sites created solely with HTML provide their users with more information by allowing the user to click on a hypertext link and having the server send another file to the user. The information returned by the server in such a system usually is another Web page, though it may also be a multimedia file like a video clip or audio clip.

JavaScript-enhanced pages embed code in the HTML, which can modify the Web page without interacting with the server. JavaScript can instantly provide a user with information. The information that is contained in the response to the user can come from user input, code that is hidden in a form, or other documents in frames. JavaScript-enhanced pages present users with new information by updating the contents of a current form or by generating an entirely new document, as shown in Figure 8.1.

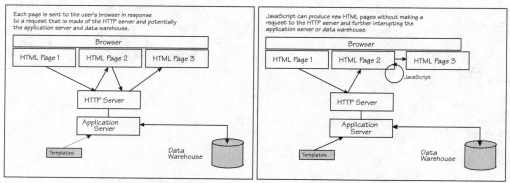

Figure 8.1 *Standard HTML pages interact with the server when requests are made by a user, as shown on the left. JavaScript-enhanced pages can respond to users without interacting with the server. This response can include updating the contents of the current document or creating a new document, as shown on the right.*

JavaScript Is an Object Based Language

JavaScript is object based like many of the newer programming and scripting languages. JavaScript manipulates data through methods and functions that act on the data contained in objects. JavaScript also provides an event-oriented processing model. Elements in a Web page, such as a button or a text input field, may trigger actions based on events, such as clicking the button. When one of these events occurs, a JavaScript function may execute. In JavaScript, your scripts are built with several language elements, including:

- Variables and literal values.
- Expressions.
- Objects.
- Statements.
- Functions.

Each of these language elements is discussed in the sections that follow.

Variables and Values

When performing calculations or other logic in scripts, you often need to temporarily store values. JavaScript, like most programming languages, uses *variables* to store values. But unlike most programming languages, JavaScript variables do not need to be declared and do not have a fixed datatype.

One of the main differences between most other languages and JavaScript is that JavaScript does not have explicit data types. You can't specify that a particular variable represents an integer, string, or floating-point number. A JavaScript *variable* can be any of these; in fact, the same variable can be interpreted as any of these in different contexts.

Each JavaScript variable is identified by a name using the keyword, var. The variable name is case sensitive and limited to lowercase letters, uppercase letters, or underscore characters (_). No other characters are allowed in variable names. You can declare multiple variables on the same line by listing them as a comma-separated list.

A variable name may be given a value when it is declared, which is often referred to as *initializing* the variable. As in other programming languages, you assign a value to a variable using the = operator. In scripts, assigning a value to a variable also sets the initial data type of the variable. For example, the following statements are valid variable declarations:

```
var uname = "Guest" ;
var loop_count = 0 ;
var records_returned ;
var x, y, z ;
```

Though JavaScript does not require you to declare variables, you should declare all of them. Always declaring your variables provides good programming style while assisting you in avoiding problems such as variable scope and variable conflict.

Implicit Data Types

JavaScript does not have explicit data types—those that you instruct the scripting language to use. Instead, JavaScript provides four major implicit data types. Your scripts may use the following implicit data types:

- A number, such as -7, 123.456, or 0, which can be one of two types, integer or floating point.

- A Boolean (logical) value of *true* or *false*.

- A string, such as "Enter your selection here:"

- A special value of null, which means nothing is contained in the field.

Literal Values

It is important to understand the difference between variables and their values. The statement *year = 1997* contains a variable of *year* and a literal value of *1997*. A literal value is anything that is directly referenced by its actual value. A variable is an abstraction that provides a way of giving names to values. Thus, the above statement, *year = 1997*, can be read as: "When I refer to the variable name of *year*, I am referring to the concrete, literal value of *1997*."

A *literal* refers to anything that is referred to directly by its actual value. Literals are fixed values contained in scripts. Literals can include numeric literals (integers, floating point numbers, and Booleans) and string literals.

Integers can be expressed in one of the following three forms:

- A decimal, or base 10, literal sequence of digits from zero to nine (0 to 9) *without* a leading zero. Example: 6418.

- An octal, or base 8, literal sequence of digits from zero to seven (0 to 7) *with* a leading zero. Example: 043.

- A hexadecimal, or base 16, literal sequence of digits from zero to nine (0 to 9) and the letters A through F (which represent the equivalents of decimal numbers 10 through 15). Hexadecimal literals are proceeded by 0x. Example: 0x4F.

Floating point numbers can be specified in either the common decimal point format or the engineering E-notation format. Therefore, a floating point number can have a decimal integer, a decimal point, a decimal fraction, or an exponent ("E" followed by a signed or unsigned integer). The following are valid examples of floating point numbers:

```
123.456
-123E456
12.34E-56
```

A Boolean literal is a logical type of data that is set to one of two values: *true* or *false*. Booleans are typically used to test a condition to determine how best to proceed in a script. It is possible to think of *true* as 1 and *false* as 0. In fact, JavaScript converts these logical values into 1 and 0. JavaScript interprets any nonzero numeric value to be true. Therefore, numbers such as 7 and -2 are interpreted as *true*. Though this is the case in JavaScript and many other languages, it is not recommended to use this practice, because it may lead to confusion in your code.

A string literal is zero or more characters enclosed in either a single quotation marks ("string") or double quotation marks ("string"). When enclosing string literals, you must use the same type of quotation mark (single or double) to start and end a given string. Examples of string variables include:

```
'Tom'
"Press this button for additional help."
```

JavaScript string literals may possess embedded control characters, often known in other languages as *escape sequences*. These control characters denote special characters such as tabs and carriage returns. If you are familiar with the C programming language, it is probably safe to say that all of the escape sequences in C are currently, or will be in the near future, supported by JavaScript. At the moment, the following control characters are supported:

- Linefeed   \r.
- Return   \n.
- Tab   \t.
- Formfeed or vertical tab   \f.
- Backspace   \b.

In addition to the above control characters, you may place quotes and backslashes inside literal strings by preceding them with a backslash (an escape character). For example:

```
"The proper DOS directory is C:\\ROOT\\BIN. Once you arrive there, type \"RUN PROGRAM\"."
```

The preceding example results in the following display:

```
The proper DOS directory is C:\ROOT\BIN. Once you arrive there, type "RUN PROGRAM".
```

Expressions

Expressions are a combination of variables, literal values, operators, and other calculated values. An expression has a value and a datatype. The data type of an expression is numeric, string, Boolean (logical), or null. The following statements illustrate expressions:

```
row_count >= 25 ;
quantity * unit_price ;
counter++ ;
```

Operators

The set of operators in JavaScript are similar to those in C, C++, and Java. These operators provide common capabilities for combining values (both variables and literal values) into expressions. JavaScript's primary operators can be grouped into the following classifications:

- Arithmetic operators.

- Comparison operators.

- Logical operators.

- Bitwise operators.

- Assignment and aggregate operators.

These classifications are based on the functionality of the operators. We further examine the major classifications of these operators in the sections that follow.

Arithmetic Operators

JavaScript arithmetic operators include addition (+), subtraction (-), division (/), multiplication (*), modulus (%), increment (++), and decrement (--). You frequently use these operators to perform arithmetic computations, so these operators are also referred to as *computational operators*. However, the functionality managed by this group of operators is not limited to numerical calculations, for example the + operator is overloaded and allows you to perform string concatenation—the combining of two or more string variables. Here is an example of string concatenation:

```
var last_name = 'Hammergren';
var first_name = 'Tom';
full_name = last_name + ', ' + first_name
```

The result of the above operation follows:

```
full_name = 'Hammergren, Tom'
```

The addition (+), subtraction (-), division (/), and multiplication (*) operators perform standard mathematical functions of add, subtract, divide, and multiply. The modulus (%) operator determines the remainder from a division. Example *100 % 6* evaluates to 4, because 100 divided by 6 results in a value of 16, leaving a remainder of 4.

The increment (++) and decrement (--) operators simplify the common operations of adding or subtracting one from a numeric value. The increment and decrement operators can be used either before or after the operand, for example loop_count++ and ++loop_count are both valid expressions. When the operator precedes loop_count, the value is incremented or decremented before the expression is evaluated. When the operator follows loop_count, its value is incremented or decremented after the expression is evaluated. It is important to understand this functionality to avoid errors. Consider the following example:

```
x = 45 ;
y = x-- ; //Sets y to 45 and then decrements x to 44
y = --x ; //Decrements x to 44 and then set y to 44
```

The preceding example also illustrates how to add remarks in JavaScript code that are ignored when the script runs. Everything on a line after two consecutive slashes is ignored. Alternately, remarks that are longer than one line can be set off as follows; with the begin comment mark (/*), followed by your comment, and terminating with the end comment mark (*/).

```
x = 45 ;   /* This remark extends-
        beyond a single line */
```

Comparison Operators

Comparison operators in JavaScript perform a test or comparison between numbers or strings. A comparison operator returns a Boolean value of true or false. These operators are also often referred to as logical operators. The JavaScript comparison operators include equal to (==), not equal to (!= or <>), greater than (>), less than (<), greater than or equal to (>=), and less than or equal to (<=).

The equality operators include tests for equality (==) or inequality (!= or <>). These operators are tested whether two variables, values, or combination of variables and values are the same or different. For integers, the equality operators strictly test for equality or inequality. For floating point numbers, the equality operators test to see if the two quantities are equivalent to the precision of the underlying floating point data type. For strings, the equality operators test for exact equality. Remember, JavaScript is case-sensitive, therefore testing validates based on case of the characters in the strings. Each of these equality operators returns a Boolean value of true or false.

The other comparison operators include tests for less than (<), less than or equal (<=), greater than (>), or greater than or equal (>=). These operators work on numbers and strings. For numbers, the comparison operators perform based on standard arithmetic comparisons. Example: 6 and 7 are greater than or equal to 6, but 5 is not. For strings, the comparison operators perform based on dictionary order. Example: "This short string" is greater than "a much longer string such as this one," because the initial "a" in the second string is "less than" the initial "T" in the first string. Whether comparing strings or numbers, comparison operators return Boolean values of true or false to indicate the overall results of the comparison.

Logical Operators

Logical operators allow you to build compound operations through the logical AND (&&), logical OR (||), and NOT (!) operators. As with other operators, the logical operators return a Boolean value of true or false. With the logical AND operator, a true value is returned if all of the component comparisons return true values. With the logical OR operator, a true value is returned if any one of the component comparisons returns a true value. The logical NOT operator reverses the value returned by a comparison. Therefore, if the natural comparison between two values returns a true—negating this comparison returns a false.

Bitwise Operators

Bitwise operators treat their operands as a set of binary numbers, comprised of zeros and ones, rather than as decimal, hexadecimal, or octal numbers. Bitwise operators perform their operations on the operand's binary representations and return standard numerical values. A bitwise operator examines each bit position in each of its operands and returns the number that matches the evaluation's criterion. Such operators are required in applications that are immersed in mathematics, such as computations on colors, CAD/CAM (Computer Aided Design/Computer Aided Manufacturing), or VRML (Virtual Reality Modeling Language).

Table 8.1 presents each of the bitwise operators.

Table 8.1 *JavaScript bitwise operators.*

Operator Name	Symbol	Description
Bitwise AND	&	Bitwise AND examines each bit position in each of its operands. If both operands have a 1 bit in a given position, a 1 is returned; otherwise, the output bit position is 0.
Bitwise OR	|	Bitwise OR examines each bit position in each of its operands. If either operand has a 1 in a given position, a 1 is returned; if both operands have a 0 in a given position, a 0 is returned in the output bit position.
Bitwise XOR	^	Bitwise XOR (exclusive OR), a variation of bitwise OR, examines each bit position in each of its operands. If either of the operands has a 1 in a given position, a 1 is returned; however, if both operands possess a 1 or if both operands possess a 0, a 0 is returned in the output bit position.
Bitwise left shift	<<	Bitwise left shift moves a set of bits in an operand left by a specified number of positions. When the move is performed, zero bits are added on the right, while the bits that are shifted out at the left are lost when they exceed an overall 32-bit length.
Bitwise signed Right shift	>>	Bitwise signed right shift moves a set of bits in an operand by a specified number of positionsto the right. When the move is performed, bits on the right are lost as they are shifted out; however, the sign is preserved on the move.
Bitwise unsigned Right shift	>>>	Bitwise unsigned right shift moves a set of bits in an operand by a specified number of positions to the right. When the move is performed, bits on the right are lost as they are shifted out and zero bits are placed on the left. This operation does not preserve the sign of its operand.
Bitwise NOT	-	Bitwise NOT negates the value returned by other bitwise operators.

You should perform bitwise operations only on integer numbers. Floating point numbers do not provide a consistent bit pattern and will make your code unportable, typically resulting in floating-point exception errors.

Assignment and Aggregate Operators

The assignment operator (=) assigns a value to a variable, just as in many other programming languages. In scripts, however, assigning a value to a variable also sets the data type of the variable. For example, the following statement assigns the value 100 to the variable x and assigns it a numeric data type:

```
x = 100 ;
```

If in a given script a variable named x has not been declared, the variable declaration occurs automatically allowing further manipulation within the script. You can later assign a different data type to variable x through an assignment statement like the one that follows. This statement reestablishes x with a string data type.

```
x = "End of query processing." ;
```

In JavaScript, you can combine the assignment operator with any of the computational and logical operators that utilize two operands, also known as binary operators. The binary operators include +, -, /, *, %, &, |, ^, <<, >>, and >>>. Combining binary operators with the assignment operator lets you perform aggregate operations. These compact expressions replace their more verbose expressions, as shown in Table 8.2.

Table 8.2 *Aggregate operators combine the assignment operator with binary operators.*

Aggregate Operator Equivalent	Verbose Expression
`row_count += 10 ;`	`row_count = row_count + 10 ;`
`rows_left -= 25 ;`	`rows_left = rows_left - 25 ;`
`width /= 2 ;`	`width = width / 2 ;`

Operator Evaluation and Precedence

In grade school, my teachers taught me a easily recalled phrase that helped me to understand the precedence of arithmetic operators in simple mathematical equations. This phrase "My Dear Aunt Sally," explained that multiplication took precedence over division, which took precedence over addition, which took precedence over subtraction.

It would be nice if defining the precedence table in JavaScript were this easy. Unfortunately, far too many operators exist to define a memorable acronym or phrase. Therefore, Figure 8.2 presents the operator precedence to assist you in understanding the order of evaluation in JavaScript.

Parentheses allow you to explicitly control the order of precedence. The exceptions are increment (++) and decrement (--) operators, which are operations that always are performed first.

You should use parentheses to explicitly specify the order of evaluation in your JavaScript expressions. This practice makes your code more maintainable and assists you in avoiding logic errors.

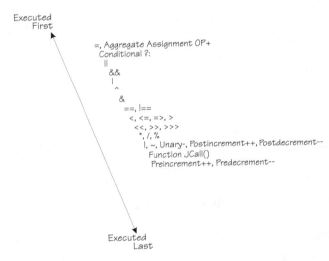

Figure 8.2 *Operator precedence in JavaScript determines final computed value.*

Data Type Conversion

In many expressions, the data type is clear. For example, 4*3 result in a numeric data type with the value of 12. However, at times the resultant data type is not so obvious, such as the expression 10 + " Downing Street." JavaScript uses a set of conversion rules to decide how to treat a value in an expression. These conversion rules are based on the context in which variables and literal values are used in the expression. In the previous example, the 10 is converted to a string and concatenated with the other string to give the final value of "10 Downing Street."

JavaScript attempts to treat all variables in an expression as if they all have the same data type as the first variable in the statement. This interpretation of data types can pose problems for your scripts. The context of a variable in an expression is established by reading the expression from left to right.

JavaScript attempts to treat all variables in a statement as if they had the same type as the first variable in the statement. Therefore, validate that the data type and conversion of variables is proper in your script statements.

Data type conversions pose a complex issue when programming scripts. Basically two approaches can be used in handling this issue: implicit or explicit conversion. You should use explicit conversions wherever possible, while implicit conversions should be used with great care.

Conversion from a numeric value to a string value is always safe and in many ways assists in simplifying your code, because you will avoid the tedious formatting logic that is required in many programming languages, such as C. For example, the following statement is valid for JavaScript:

```
"The following list presents " + fetch_count + " of the " + row_count + " total
rows represented by your query."
```

But highly defensive programming should be used when converting among numeric data type variables. The best approach in this situation is to never allow implicit conversions with numbers.

JavaScript provides many built-in functions that allow you to control the data types of your variables and which will simplify the process of debugging and maintaining your scripts. We further discuss explicit data type conversions in the "Functions" section later in this chapter.

Statements

As in other programming languages, a statement is the basic unit of work in a script (or program). A statement causes the JavaScript interpreter to: evaluate a function; declare and initialize a variable; provide a value for a variable; perform a calculation; or any combination of these actions. Scripts created in JavaScript are collections of statements that are organized into functions. These statements manipulate variables and the HTML environment in which the scripts exists.

JavaScript programs are written in a line-oriented approach. This means that JavaScript interprets each statement in whole at the end of every line. You can explicitly terminate a statement with a semicolon character (;). By explicitly terminating your statements, your script can have more than one statement per line.

You should terminate all JavaScript statements with a semicolon. This practice assists you in avoiding errors and improve the maintainability of your scripts. Placing only one statement per line of your script is recommended for the same reasons.

Up to this point, we have discussed quite simple statements: the declaration of variables and the definition of expressions. Control structures along with the statements we have already discussed allow you to write meaningful JavaScript and control the flow of your script's execution. The true power and flexibility of any programming language, including JavaScript, comes from the ability to change statement order in structures and loops.

JavaScript provides three types of control structures:

- if-else statement.

- while statement.

- for statement.

These control structures are similar and manipulate blocks of JavaScript statements. A block is simply a set of JavaScript statements that will be executed together. In this sense, a block is like one large statement. A JavaScript block is introduced by a left brace ({) and terminated by a right brace (}).

if-else Statement

The if-else statement tests a conditional expression and executes a JavaScript block if the condition is true. The if-else statement can optionally execute another JavaScript block if the conditional expression is false. An example of an if-else statement follows:

```
if (rows_returned = true)
{
   /* IFBLOCK: for example, statements to display the results */
}
else
{
   /* ELSEBLOCK: for example, statements to explain to the user
   that no results were returned */
}
```

while Statement

The while statement executes a block of code while a condition is true. In a while statement, the block of code continues to execute until the test condition no longer returns a true value. The condition is tested before the first iteration of the loop and then prior to the execution of any other iterations. This operation is different than the if-else statement, because it loops through the block of code, while the if-else statement executes its code block only once. Here is an example of a while loop.

```
while (rows_fetched <= total_rows)
{
  /* WHILEBLOCK: for example, statements executed for each fetched
    row */
}
```

Two flow control statements can determine the outcome and processing of a while statement: the break statement and the continue statement. If a break statement is encountered in a while block, the loop is terminated immediately without executing any further statements. The continue statement forces the flow of control back to the top of the while loop without executing any statements between the continue statement and the terminating brace.

for Statement

A for statement continuously loops through statements contained within the for block until a condition is true. The for statement's conditional expression has three parts, which are separated by semicolons: an initialization statement; a conditional test statement; and an update statement. The initialization statement is executed only once—as a script enters the for statement. The conditional test statement is tested at the top of each loop. If the conditional statement remains true, the for loop executes; otherwise, the for loop is ignored and the script moves to the code following the loop. The update statement is executed at the bottom of each loop to update the variable that was initialized in the initialization statement.

The following example shows an initialization statement (row_count = 1); a conditional test statement (row_count <= max_rows); and an update statement (row_count++). The for loop will execute five times, because row_count is initialized to 1, row_count increments by one at the end of each loop, and after the fifth iteration row_count will no longer be less than or equal to max_rows, which was initialized to 5 prior to the for loop.

```
max_rows = 5;
for (row_count = 1; row_count <= max_rows; row_count++)
{
  /* FORBLOCK: for example, statements to process rows */
}
```

As with while statements, you can use a break or continue statement to control the flow of for block statements. One advantage that a for statement provides over a while statement is that the update statement is executed for each loop through the for block, even if the for block is cut short because of execution of a continue statement.

Functions

A *function* is a block of code that has a name. Functions provide a uniform method for organizing code in scripts. A function can be called from anywhere in your script. Because a Web application server processes an HTML document from top to bottom, it is good practice to define functions in the header part of the HTML document. You must define a function prior to its use in other parts of your scripts. The syntax for a function statement in JavaScript is as follows:

```
function function_name ( list_of_parameters )
{
  /* FUNCTION_BODY: block of code represented by the
    function_name */
}
```

Function Statement

A function's name is placed immediately after the function keyword. When naming your functions, be sure the names are unique and do not conflict with any of the JavaScript reserved words.

A comma-separated list of parameters follows the function name. The function parameters, or arguments, are passed to the function by the statement that calls the function. A function can accept string, number, or object parameters. The list of function parameters can also be empty, indicating that the function does not use any arguments. A function without parameters is often called a void function.

Simple parameters, such as strings and numbers, are passed to functions by value. Any change made to the argument inside the function is not passed back to the calling statement or calling environment. Objects can be passed to functions by reference so that any change made to an object property inside a function is passed back to the calling environment. You can also pass values back to the calling statement through the use of a return statement, described later in this section.

Function Body

A function's body is a block of JavaScript statements that provides specific functionality. After a block of code is placed in a function, you will never need to repeat it again. For example:

```
function show_time ( alert_or_return )
{
```

```
var now = new Date() ;
var hours = now.getHours() ;
var minutes = now.getMinutes() ;
var seconds = now.getSeconds() ;
var current_time = "" + hours ;
current_time += ":" + minutes ;
current_time += ":" + seconds ;
if (alert_or_return = "alert")
{
 alert (current_time) ;
}
else
{
 return (current_time) ;
}
}
```

When the show_time function is called, the date object is evaluated. Based on the parameter passed to the function, either the user is alerted with the value of the current time or the value of the current time is returned.

Variable Scope

Variables can exist for part or all of a script; this is referred to as the variable's scope. Two scopes are commonly used with variables: local and global.

In the preceding example, hours, minutes, and seconds are local variables. Local variables are only known within the body of the function in which they are defined. They are completely unknown elsewhere in the script.

Typically, scripts contain many functions. Each of these functions may have its own set of local variables. However, at times you will want a set of variables that can be referenced anywhere in a script. These variables are known as global variables. Global variables can be used anywhere in your script, or more specifically anywhere in the HTML template in which they are referenced.

Objects

Objects provide a uniform method for organizing data in scripts. Objects can hold multiple values so that a group of related data elements can be associated with each another. JavaScript objects are similar to data structures or classes in many other languages.

JavaScript is object-based, which means it supports objects and many of the fundamental object-oriented concepts of encapsulation, polymorphism, and inheritance.

- **Encapsulation:** A JavaScript object is made up of a set of component parts, which are called its properties or members, together with the actions or methods that manipulate the properties.

- **Polymorphism:** Multiple JavaScript objects can respond to the same message in their own ways using their own methods. This action occurs through an object's method, which contains the same name as another object. For example, suppose that you define two object classes called salariedEmployee and hourlyEmployee. Each type has its own PrintAllInfo method that prints employee information in a certain way. To print information for an employee, you simply call the PrintAllInfo method for the object. Depending whether the employee is salaried or hourly, the corresponding PrintAllInfo method is called automatically. If you add more classes of employees, they can redefine their own PrintAllInfo methods. The actual code that calls PrintAllInfo does not need to be changed to accommodate the new object types. Polymorphism is particularly powerful when used in conjunction with inheritance.

- **Inheritance:** You can define new JavaScript objects that extend the capabilities of existing JavaScript objects. This is done by inheriting existing properties and methods from a previously defined JavaScript object and then adding new properties and methods to your new JavaScript object. JavaScript supports the simplest form of inheritance, which is single inheritance. Single inheritance refers to defining a new class, which inherits properties and methods from a single parent class. You can derive a new class from an existing class, adding new properties and methods—or overriding existing properties and methods—as you require. Inheriting objects also means that you can take better advantage of polymorphism, because derived classes can override or redefine existing methods defined by their parent class without needing to change other code that calls these methods.

Properties

A property is a variable in an object that describes some part or attribute of the object. A property can be any data type. Objects can contain other objects as properties. Property names must be unique within the scope of the class and its ancestor classes (if any). You can access an object property using standard dot notation:

```
objectName.propertyName
```

For example, suppose you have an object named query_definition, which you are using to define a SQL select statement. The query definition object might have properties that specify the major clauses of the select statement, including: the select clause, the from clause, the where clause, the order by clause, and the group by clause. To define this object, you write a function as follows:

```
function query_definition (sel, frm, whr, ord, grp)
{
  this.select_clause = sel ;
  this.from_clause = frm ;
  this.where_clause = whr ;
  this.order_clause = ord ;
  this.group_clause = grp ;
}
```

Let's take a closer look at this object definition. First, the name of the function is the name of the object (query_definition). Second, the function does not return anything; using a function to create an object works by modifying the current instance of an object, referred to here as this. Our example shows how an object is defined; however, it does not create a specific instance of the object. Instances are created using the new statement combined with a function call. For example:

```
var user_query = new query_definition( "product, promotion_units", "sales", "region
= 'WEST'", "product", "") ;
```

Now that user_query has been created, you can refer to its properties using the dot operator (.), as follows:

- *user_query.select_clause* contains product, promotion_units.

- *user_query.from_clause* contains sales.

- *user_query.where_clause* contains region="WEST."

- *user_query.order_clause* contains product.

- *user_query.group_clause* contains nothing.

Every object is an array of its property values. Therefore, we can write a function to display the proper SQL select statement as follows.

```
function show_select ( query_stmt )
{
  var SQLstmt = "select " + query_stmt.select_clause ;
  SQLstmt += " from " + query_stmt.from_clause ;
```

```
 if (query_stmt.where_clause != "")
 {
  SQLstmt += " where " + query_stmt.where_clause ;
 }
 if (query_stmt.order_clause != "")
 {
  SQLstmt += " order by " + query_stmt.order_clause ;
 }
 if (query_stmt.group_clause != "")
 {
  SQLstmt += " group by " + query_stmt.group_clause ;
 }
 alert (SQLstmt);
}
```

Methods

A method is a function in an object that acts on one or more properties of the object. The scope of the method depends on how the method is defined.

- If a method is defined inline (within the class definition), its name must be unique within the scope of the class. If it has the same name as a method in one of its ancestor classes, it overrides (redefines) that method for instances of its own class.

- If a method is defined as a global function (outside the class definition), its name must be unique within the scope of the current script.

For example, suppose you extended an object named query_definition to include the method to "show" the content of the object. To include this method in the query_definition object, we write a function as follows:

```
function query_definition (sel, frm, whr, ord, grp)
{
  this.select_clause = sel ;
  this.from_clause = frm ;
  this.where_clause = whr ;
  this.order_clause = ord ;
  this.group_clause = grp ;
  this.show = show_select () ;
}

function show_select ( ){
  document.write("<BR>select_clause = " + this.select_clause);
  document.write("<BR>from_clause = " + this.from_clause);
  document.write("<BR>where_clause = " + this.where_clause);
  document.write("<BR>order_clause = " + this.order_clause);
  document.write ("<BR>group_clause = " + this.group_clause);
```

```
document.write("<BR>") ;
}
```

Upon properly defining the methods for an object, you can call an object method using standard dot notation:

```
function new_query ()
{
  var user_query = new query_definition( "product,
  promotion_units", "sales", "region = 'WEST'",
  "product", "") ;
  user_query.show()
}
```

Functions Built Into JavaScript

JavaScript has several built-in functions, which are not associated to any object. These functions work against strings to assist in the proper interpretation of the data in variables. These functions are equivalent in usage to user-defined functions that you create with the function statement. At present, JavaScript provides five built-in functions, which are explained in Table 8.3.

Table 8.3 *Built-in JavaScript functions.*

Function	Description
escape(str)	Returns a string containing the ISO Latin-1 representation of each character in string. This function is typically used to encode special characters so they can be used in URLs.
eval(str)	If string represents an expression, this function evaluates the expression. If the argument is one or more JavaScript statements, this function performs the statements.
parseFloat(str)	Parses the string and tries to return a floating-point number.
parseInt(str, base)	Parses the string and tries to return an integer of the specified base. Valid bases are: 10 for decimal conversion, 8 for octal conversion, and 16 for hexadecimal conversion.
unEscape(str)	Returns a string containing the ASCII characters for the encoded string. This function is typically used to decode special characters from URLs.

JavaScript Objects

Now that we have covered the essentials of JavaScript, let's look at the actual objects that JavaScript provides. These objects are grouped into the following three classifications:

- **Built-in objects:** String object, date object, and math object are in a built-in class that has nothing to do with Web pages, HTML, URLs, the browser environment, or anything else visual.

- **HTML objects:** These objects are directly associated with elements of a Web page and include elements such as links, anchors, forms, and every element in a form.

- **Browser objects:** This set of objects represent elements of the current browser environment and includes elements such as the current window, list of previously visited pages, and the URL of the current page.

The following sections discuss objects that fall into these various categories.

String Object

The string object is a predefined object that provides properties and methods for working with strings. The string object is an implicit class. You can use its properties and methods on any string directly, without having to explicitly create an instance of a string object. String objects have one property (length) and many methods. The length property indicates how many characters are included in the string data. The methods for a string object are grouped into three categories, as shown in Table 8.4. These categories include:

- **Content methods** access, control, or modify the content of a string object.

- **Appearance methods** control how a string object appears when displayed on a Web page. If you are creating a page with standard HTML, these methods are achieved using standard tags. For example, to make the words Number of Results appear in bold, you use <B>Number of Results</B>. The string appearance methods allow you to achieve the same results in JavaScript without using corresponding HTML elements.

- **Conversion methods** convert a string object into an HTML element.

Table 8.4 *String object methods.*

Method	Category	Description
charAt(idx)	Content	Returns the character at the position identified by idx. This method returns a single character substring from the string object.
indexOf(chr)	Content	Returns the first position of the character chr in the string object. The search for chr begins from the left side of the string object.
lastIndexOf(chr)	Content	Returns the last position of the character chr in the string object. The search for chr begins from the right side of the string object.
substring(fromidx, toidx)	Content	Returns the characters from the position identified by fromidx through the character identified by toidx. This method returns a multiple-character substring from the string object.
toLowerCase()	Content	Converts and returns all of the characters in the string object in their lowercase rendition.
toUpperCase() string	Content	Converts and returns all of the characters in the object in their uppercase rendition.
big()	Appearance	Renders the string object as big text, in the same fashion as the <BIG> string_object </BIG> HTML elements.
blink()	Appearance	Renders the string object as blinking text, in the same fashion as the <BLINK> string_object </BLINK> HTML elements.
bold()	Appearance	Renders the string object as bold, in the same fashion as the <B> string_object </B> HTML elements.
fixed()	Appearance	Renders the string object in the fixed font, in the same fashion as the <TT> string_object </TT> HTML elements.
fontcolor(color)	Appearance	Renders the string object using the font color specified, in the same fashion as the <FONT COLOR=color> string_object </FONT> HTML elements.

Continued

Table 8.4 *Continued*

Method	Category	Description
fontsize(size)	Appearance	Renders the string object using the font size specified, in the same fashion as the <FONT SIZE=size> string_object </FONT>.
italics()	Appearance	Renders the string object as italic text, in the same fashion as the <I> string_object </I> HTML elements.
small()	Appearance	Renders the string object as small text, in the same fashion as the <SMALL> string_object </SMALL> HTML elements.
strike()	Appearance	Renders the string object in the strikethrough font, in the same fashion as <STRIKE> string_object </STRIKE> HTML elements.
sub()	Appearance	Renders the string object in the subscript font, in the same fashion as _{string_object} HTML elements.
sup()	Appearance	Renders the string object in the superscript font, in the same fashion as the ^{string_object} HTML elements.
anchor(namestr) get.	HTML	Creates an anchor location on a page that is a tar- This JavaScript command is equivalent to the <A NAME="anchortext"> string_object </A> HTML elements.
link(hrefstr)	HTML	Creates a link to another page that is a target. This JavaScript command is equivalent to the <A HREF="URL"> string_object </A> HTML elements.

Tip: JavaScript is a zero-based indexing language. All arrays and character methods refer to the first instance of an item as zero. The maximum index is equivalent to the total instance number minus one.

Date Object

The date object provides various date and time conversions, calculations, and general manipulations. JavaScript's date object follows the UNIX standard for storing date and time information internally as the number of milliseconds since January 1, 1970. The date object has no properties, but many methods. To use the date object, you first must understand how to construct new instances of a date, as follows:

```
var myBirthdate = new Date ( 60, 11, 19) ;
```

This code creates a new instance of the date object named myBirthdate. Additionally, this instance of the date object is initialized to November 19, 1960. To create an instance of the current date and time, you leave the parameters blank, as follows:

```
var current_date = new Date() ;
```

You can also create a new instance of the date object by using a string to represent the date. This string is placed in the parameter list. Therefore, the following list represents a few of the ways to create new date instances:

```
// the following sets the date to the current date
var current_date = new Date() ;

// the following sets the date to Nov. 19, 1960 11:45:00 PM,
// my birth date and time
var my_birth_date = new Date(1960, 11, 19, 23, 45, 0);

// the following sets the date to Feb. 17, 1960 my wife's
// birth date
var my_wifes_birth_date = new Date("February 17, 1960") ;
```

The date object has a large set of methods for getting and setting the components of a date instance. These methods are shown in Table 8.5.

Table 8.5 Date object methods.

Method	Description
getDate()	Returns the day of the month as a number from 1 to 31.
getDay()	Returns the day of the week as a number from 0 to 6 (0=Sunday).
getHours()	Returns the hour component of time from 0 to 23.
getMinutes()	Returns the minutes component of time from 0 to 59.
getMonth()	Returns the month in numerical format from 0 to 11 (0=January).
getSeconds()	Returns the seconds component of time from 0 to 59.
getTime()	Returns the number of milliseconds since January 1, 1970.

Continued

Table 8.5 *Continued*

Method	Description
getTimeZoneOffSet()	Provides the difference between the local time and Greenwich Mean Time (GMT).
getYear()	Returns a number representing the year, the precision of the year varies by platform between 2 digits representing the year minus 1900 and 4 digit.
setDate()	Sets the day of the month for a date object.
setHours()	Sets the hours for a date object.
setMinutes()	Sets the minutes for a date object.
setMonth()	Sets the month for a date object.
setSeconds()	Sets the seconds for a date object.
setTime()	Sets the time for a date object. The time is set using the number of seconds since January 1, 1970.
setYear()	Sets the year for a date object.
toGMTString()	Converts the date to a string using the GMT (Greenwich Mean Time) convention. For example, 11/19/60 11:45 PM converts to "Sat, 19 Nov 1960 23:45:00 GMT."
toLocaleString()	Converts the date to a string using the local conventions, such as USA or European conventions.
toString()	Converts the date to a plain, ordinary string.
parse(datestr)	Converts a date string into the number of milliseconds since January 1, 1970 00:00:00.
UTC(datestr)	UTC stands for Universal Coordinated Time and is equivalent to Greenwich Mean Time. This method is static and is always called via Date.parse (year, month, day, hours, minutes, seconds). The time components (hours, minutes, and seconds) are optional.

Date and time methods may result in inconsistent results in different JavaScript plat-forms. These methods are heavily dependent on the execution platform, so you may receive inconsistent results for dates prior to the date considered to be zero, which on UNIX is (1/1/70).

Math Object

The math object is used for various mathematical calculations and is a static object whose properties do not change. All of the properties of the math object already contain values that are similar to those found on some calculators. These properties include:

- **E:** The base of a natural logarithm, approximately 2.71828.

- **LN10:** The natural logarithm of 10, approximately 2.30259.

- **LN2:** The natural logarithm of 2, approximately 0.69315.

- **P:** Approximately 3.141592653589793.

- **SQRT1_2:** The square root of .5, approximately 0.7071.

- **SQRT2:** The square root of 2, approximately 1.4142.

The methods for the math object are shown in Table 8.6.

Table 8.6 *Math object methods.*

Method	Description
abs(num)	The absolute method returns the absolute (unsigned) value of its argument.
acos(num)	Arccosine, the inverse of cosine, is a trigonometric function that takes a floating point number and produces an angle in radians.
asin(num)	Arcsine, the inverse of sine, is a trigonometric function that takes a floating point number and produces an angle in radians.
atan(num)	Arctangent, the inverse of tangent, is a trigonometric function that takes a floating point number and produces an angle in radians.
ceil(num)	This method makes a floating point number as input and produces the largest integer that is greater than or equal to its argument as output.
cos(ang)	Cosine is a trigonometric function that takes an angle in radians and produces a floating point number.
exp(num)	Returns E to the power given by the argument—the inverse of the log method.
floor(num)	Takes a floating point number as input and produces the smallest integer that is less than or equal to its argument as output.

Continued

Table 8.6 *Continued*

Method	Description
log(num)	Returns the natural logarithm of its argument, which should be positive.
max(num1, num2)	Returns the maximum value of its two arguments.
min(num1, num2)	Returns the minimum value of its two arguments.
pow(num1, num2)	Raises the first argument to the power of the second argument.
round(num)	Produces the nearest integer to its argument as output.
sin(ang)	Sine trigonometric function, which takes an angle in radians and produces a floating point number.
sqrt(num)	Returns the square root of the argument.
tan(ang)	Tangent trigonometric function, which takes an angle in radians and produces a floating point number.

User Interface Objects

Because JavaScript has been developed to assist with Web application development, it provides a rich set of objects for interaction among scripts, browsers and interpreted HTML pages. Figure 8.3 depicts these objects. We will further investigate the higher-level objects, including the window, document, form, and element objects.

Window Object

The window object is the top level in the JavaScript user interface object hierarchy. An individual window object corresponds to any browser window that is currently open. The other user interface objects in JavaScript are children, or descendants, of the window object. Figure 8.4 highlights the child objects of the window object.

The child objects of the window object include: the document object, which represents the HTML structure of the Web page; the location object, which represents the URL of the Web page; and the history object, which represents the Web pages that have previously been displayed in the window object in their call order. Another notable child of the window object is the frame object. Frames can be thought of as subwindows, which are created with the FRAME tag in a FRAMESET document. (Frames are discussed in the "Frames" section of Chapter 7, "HTML Essentials.")

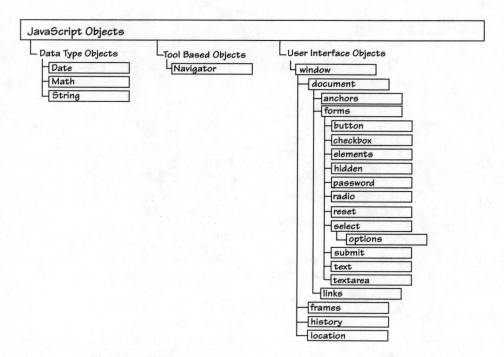

Figure 8.3 *The JavaScript object hierarchy provides various objects that interact with a final Web application.*

A window object is automatically created when you launch your browser. Additional window objects are created each time you choose the New Web Browser option from Netscape Navigator File menu or New Window from the same menu in Microsoft Internet Explorer. As a programmer, you can also create, manipulate, and close window objects in JavaScript. The following statement creates a new window object called wMenu that displays the contents of a file called menu.html:

```
wMenu = window.open("menu.html", "MainMenu", "toolbar = yes, status = yes")
```

The options passed into the open method include: the source URL for loading (menu.html), the logical name that you will use to refer to the window in submit and link methods (MainMenu), and the feature settings for the window (toolbar = yes, status = yes). A window can be closed in JavaScript using the close method for the window object. The following statement closes the wMenu window:

```
wMenu.close()
```

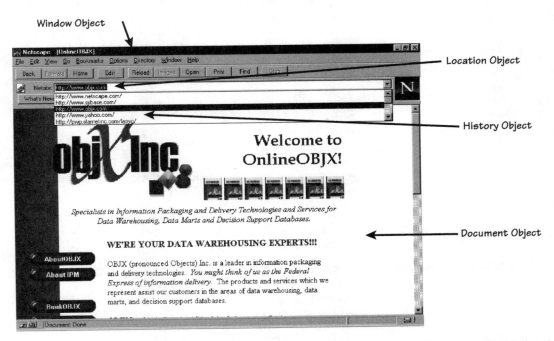

Figure 8.4 *The window object represents a Web page. Here, the child objects are highlighted.*

The window object's methods manipulate the state of a browser's window and its associated properties. Table 8.7 lists the methods available in the window object and their associated properties.

Table 8.7 *Window object methods and associated properties.*

Method Syntax	Description
open("URL", "window name", "window features")	The open method creates a new window. The URL property defines what is loaded into the window. Window name provides a logical reference name for the window object. Window features are a comma-delimited list of options and values that control how the window object is presented. This list includes the following options, which are equated to yes or no values: toolbar, location, directories, status, menubar, scrollbars, and resizable. Additional windows features include the ability to set height and width. These options equate to the desired size in pixels.
window.close()	Closes the referenced window only if it was opened by JavaScript with the open method. If you attempt to close any other window, a confirmation dialog is generated to let the user choose whether the window closes. This security feature assists in controls transmission of devious code that contains self.close() syntax, closing a user window without user control.
window.alert("message string")	Displays an alert dialog with the message string and an OK button. The user must press the OK button to proceed.
window.confirm("message string")	Displays a confirm dialog with the message string, an OK button and a CANCEL button. The user must select one of the buttons to proceed. OK returns a TRUE value; CANCEL returns a FASE value.
window.prompt("message an string", default value)	Displays a prompt dialog box with the message string and optional default value. This dialog solicits input from the user in the form of a text string, which is returned to the script.
window.setTimeout (expression milliseconds)	Evaluates an expression after a specified number of milliseconds elapses. This method returns an identifier that can be used to further reference the timeout in the script.
window.clearTimeout(timeout id)	Cancels a timeout that was set with the setTimeout method.
window.blur	Removes focus from the specified window object.
window.focus	Gives focus to the specified window object.

Document Object

Every window is associated with a document object. The document object contains and manages the information on the current document and provides methods for displaying HTML output to the user. A document object is the parent to other user interface objects, including anchor, form, history, image, link, and location objects. Figure 8.5 highlights these child objects and other common properties associated with the document object.

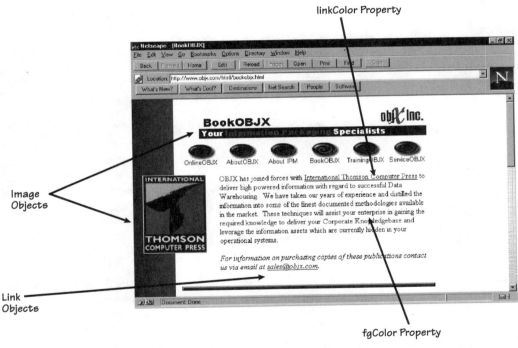

Figure 8.5 *The document object manages the properties associated with HTML documents. Properties include various other objects and properties.*

The document object has four methods: open, close, write, and writeln. The open method of the document object opens a stream to collect the output of various write and writeln methods. The open method is dependent on the MIME type used to present the information, which is in contrast to the open method for the window object. Streams send information to present to users. Based on this description, streams are best thought of as buffered output. A stream could include an HTML presentation of data as well as a plug-in application such as a QuickTime video viewer, which present users with a live, running video. If a document exists in the current window object, it is cleared when you issue the open method for a new document.

A stream is stopped using the close method of the document object. The close method stops the flow of output to a user workstation and allows write operations to be laid out on the targeted page. The heart and soul of the document object methods are the write and writeln methods. Both of these methods write any string expression to a Web page, including HTML statements. Table 8.8 lists the methods available in the document object along with their properties.

Table 8.8 *Document object methods and associated properties.*

Method Syntax	Description
document.open("MIME type")	Opens a stream to collect output of write or writeln methods. The MIME type property is an optional argument that specifies the type of document you are writing. Valid MIME types include: text.html (the default) for ASCII text of HTML formatting statements; text/plain for ASCII plain text with end-of-line characters to delimit displayed lines; image/gif for a .GIF document; image/jpeg for a JPEG document; image/x-bitmap for a bitmap document; MIME plug-in for passing the stream to a helper application or other plug-in, which are only valid if the user has installed and identified the required plug-in software.
document.close()	Closes an output stream and forces data set to the display.
document.write(expressions)	Writes one or more HTML expressions to a document in the specified window in a comma delimited string. The write method displays any number of expressions in a document window. You can specify any JavaScript expressions with the write method, including numeric, string, and logical expressions.
document.writeln(expressions)	Writes one or more HTML expressions to a document in the specified window in a comma delimited string. The writeln method displays any number of expressions in a document window. You can specify any JavaScript expressions with the writeln method, including numeric, string, and logical expressions. The writeln method is the same as the write method, except it places a newline character at the end of the output.

Forms Object

The forms object is a array of objects that correspond to HTML forms created with the <FORM> element. The individual members of the form object are placed in document source order. As you will recall from Chapter 7, "Markup Language Essentials," an HTML form allows users to input text and make choices from form elements such as checkboxes, radio buttons, and selection lists. After completing the process of gathering user input, the form can post its data to a server with the submit method. A form can also be set to its original state with each element containing its default value by using the reset method.

Each HTML form is a distinct object in a document. Therefore, the document object is the parent of a form object. You can reference a form in one of two ways, through a forms array or by referencing the form name. If a document contains four forms, you refer to them in the array as document.forms[0], document.forms[1], document.forms[2], and document.forms[3]. To determine the number if items in a forms array. you use the length object. The value returned from the statement document.forms.length is the total number of members in the forms array. Each form object has two methods, submit and reset.

The submit method is the JavaScript equivalent of the user clicking the submit button on an HTML form. After executed, a form's submit method sends all of the associated data on the form to the target HTTP server. This data is returned using either the get or post method, which is defined either in an HTML <FORM> tag or through the method property of the form object.

The reset method is the JavaScript equivalent of a user clicking the reset button on an HTML form. When executed, a form's reset method restores all elements on the form to their default values.

The form object contains various properties, which are described in Table 8.9. The primary properties are those that are defined on an HTML <FORM> tag. In addition, the form object is a parent to many objects that are elements in the beginning HTML <FORM> tag and the ending HTML </FORM> tag.

Table 8.9 *Form object properties.*

Property	Description
name="form name"	Specifies the logical name of the form object, which can be used to reference the form in scripts.
target="window name"	Specifies the window that the form to which responses go. When you submit the form with a target attribute, server responses are displayed in the target window instead of the window that contains the form. The window name attribute can be an existing window, a frame name specified in a <FRAMESET> tag, or one of the literal frame names (_top, _parent, _self, _blank).
action="server URL"	Specifies the URL of the server to receive the form field input information when the form is submitted.
method="get or post"	Specifies how information is sent to the server. The get method (the default) appends the input information to the URL. Most systems receiving get method information place the data in the host variable, QUERY_STRING. The post method sends the input information to the host variable stdin, with the data length set in the CONTENT_LENTGH host variable.
encoding="encoding type"	The encoding property specifies the MIME encoding of the data sent to the HTTP server.
elements	The elements object is a property of the form. This property is an array of all of the elements on the form. The elements array is the logical way to access items on a form. Elements can also be accessed using their native or physical object type; each of these is optionally a property of a form, including: Button, Checkbox, Hidden, Password, Radio, Reset, Select, Submit, Text, and Textarea.

Elements Object

The elements of a form are managed in the elements object. These objects include form items such as checkboxes, radio buttons, selection lists, and text fields. The form object is the parent of the elements object. You can reference a form's elements in your code using the elements array. This array contains an entry for each object in a form in source order. For example, if your form has three select lists and a set of two radio buttons, these elements are reflected as: form.elements[0], form.elements[1], form.elements[2], form.elements[3], and form.elements[4].

The elements array provides a logical way to reference your form's input items without using their names. So if the first selection list in the above example were created with the name selTimePeriod for the form named frmSelector, you could reference this element in either of two ways:

```
frmSelector.selTimePeriod.value
frmSelector.elements[0].value
```

As with other objects, you can obtain the number of elements on a form using the length property of the elements array. The elements of the elements array are only available to read in your scripts. If you want to update the information, you must directly reference these items as a physical object. Table 8.10 lists the common elements and their properties. Each of these elements corresponds to the HTML tag that creates the object.

Table 8.10 *Elements objects and their properties.*

Object	Property	Description
Text	form	An object reference to the parent form of the text element.
	name	A string specifying the name of the text element.
	type	A string specifying the type of object returns "text."
	value	A string that is related to the value attribute of the object.
	defaultValue	A string containing the default value of the object.
Textarea	form	An object reference to the parent form of the textarea element.
	name	A string specifying the name of the textarea element.
	type	A string specifying the type of object returns "textarea."
	value	A string that is related to the value attribute of the object.
	defaultValue	A string containing the default value of the object.
Password	form	An object reference to the parent form of the password element.
	name	A string specifying the name of the passwordelement.
	type	A string specifying the type of object returns "password."
	value	A string that is related to the value attribute of the object.
	defaultValue	A string containing the default value of the object.
Hidden	name	A string specifying the name of the hidden element.
	type	A string specifying the type of object returns "hidden."
	value	A string that is related to the value attribute of the object.

Continued

Table 8.10 Continued

Object	Property	Description
Checkbox	form	An object reference to the parent form of the checkbox element.
	name	A string specifying the name of the checkbox element.
	type	A string specifying the type of object returns "checkbox."
	value	A string that is related to the value attribute of the object.
	checked	A Boolean value specifying the selection state of the object.
	defaultChecked	A Boolean value indicating the default selection state of the object.
Radio	form	An object reference to the parent form of the radio element.
	name	A string specifying the name of the radio element.
	type	A string specifying the type of object returns "radio."
	value	A string that is related to the value attribute of the object.
	checked	A Boolean value specifying the selection state of the object.
	defaultChecked	A Boolean value indicating the default selection state of the object.
	length	Reflects the number of radio buttons in the Radio object.
Select	form	An object reference to the parent form of the select element.
	name	A string specifying the name of the select element.
	type	A string specifying the type of object returns "select-one" or "select-multiple."
	length	Reflects the number of options in the Select object.
	options	The options array that contains all the option objects available in the select list.
	selectedIndex	Reflects the index of the selected option in the options array.
Options Array	defaultSelected	A Boolean value indicating the default selection state of an option in a select list object.
	index	An integer representing the index of an option in a select object.
	length	An integer representing the number of items in the options array.
	selected	A Boolean value indicating whether an option is selected in a select object.
	selectedIndex	An integer specifying the index of the selected option in a select object.
	text	A string specifying the text that follows an <OPTION> tag in the select object.
	value	A string that is related to the value attribute of the object.

Continued

Table 8.10 *Continued*

Object	Property	Description
Button	form name type value	An object reference to the parent form of the button element. A string specifying the name of the button element. A string specifying the type of object returns "button." A string that is related to the value attribute of the object.
Reset	form name type value	An object reference to the parent form of the reset element. A string specifying the name of the reset element. A string specifying the type of object returns "reset." A string that is related to the value attribute of the object.
Submit	form name type value	An object reference to the parent form of the submit element. A string specifying the name of the submit element. A string specifying the type of object returns "submit." A string that is related to the value attribute of the object.

JavaScript Event Handling

JavaScript applications are event driven. Events are processes that occur as a result of user action. Examples: an event might occur when a user clicks a button, when the mouse is moved over a field, or when the user selects a hyperlink. JavaScript events occur at three levels: for the Web document, for an individual form in a document, or in an element of a form in a document. Each of these levels is discussed in the sections that follow.

Document Events

A document object is the container that holds descriptive content about a Web page. A document object is defined by the HTML body element. You primarily define the events that will occur on a document in the body element's start tag, <BODY>. The two primary events for a document include loading and unloading the document. To define the actions that will occur during these events, you use HTML syntax, as follows:

```
<BODY onLoad="formLoad()" onUnload="formUnload()">
```

The onLoad and onUnload attributes of the BODY tag declare a JavaScript function that handle the associated event. The load event is generated after the entire contents of the Web page have been loaded. This includes the information between the body element's start tag, <BODY>, and its end tag, </BODY>.

The unload event is generated after the page is unloaded. Therefore, the unload event occurs prior to the processing of a new form HTML.

Form Events

A form object is a container for all elements that are used to gather input from a user when interacting with a Web page. An HTML form is defined with the form element. The contents of a form are those input items that are contained between the form element's start tag, <FORM>, and its end tag, </FORM>. The major events that occur at the form level include when a form is submitted to the HTTP server and when a form is reset to its original content state. To define the actions that occur during these events, you use HTML syntax, as follows:

```
<FORM NAME="frmSelector" METHOD="post" ACTION="doQuery.pl"
  onSubmit="checkQuery()" onReset="initQuery()">
```

The onSubmit and onReset attributes of the FORM tag declare the JavaScript function that handles the associated event. The submit event occurs when a form is submitted. The natural use of the submit event is to validate the contents of a form prior to sending it to the HTTP server. The submission may be terminated if the contents appear to be invalid. The reset event occurs when a form is reset either through a JavaScript call or the pressing of a form's reset button. This event allows you to add custom code to the reset function aside from the standard form logic of setting all input elements to their default values.

Element Events

Each element on a form provides an opportunity for event handling. This is the primary area of focus for user interaction and therefore where you will address a majority of your scripting. The type of event handlers varies depending on the input element type. Valid input elements include checkboxes, radio buttons, text fields, text areas, buttons, and select lists. The events for elements include blur, click, change, focus, and select. Table 8.11 provides a cross referencing of the events to the elements. (These events are discussed later in this section.)

Table 8.11 *Element-to-event cross reference.*

Element	blur	click	change	focus	select
checkbox		*			
radio		*			
text	*			*	*
textarea	*			*	*
password	*			*	*
button		*			
submit		*			
reset		*			
select	*			*	

Each event is defined by the associated element's definition. The following HTML code demonstrates the definition of an elements event handler using the syntax: <TAG eventHandler="JavaScript Code">.

```
<INPUT TYPE="radio" onClick="buildQueryWindow()">
```

When the user clicks the radio button in the preceding example, the buildQueryWindow JavaScript function is executed. Table 8.12 provides an explanation of each of the events available to build JavaScript event handlers.

Table 8.12 *JavaScript events.*

Event	Event Handler	Description
blur	onBlur	Occurs when a user removes focus from the input element, frame, or window. This event applies to all windows, frames, and form elements.
click	onClick	Occurs when a user clicks a form element or link. This event applies to buttons, radio buttons, checkboxes, submit buttons, reset buttons, and links.
change	onChange	Occurs when a user changes the value of an element. This event applies to text fields, text areas, and select lists.

Continued

Table 8.12 Continued

Event	Event Handler	Description
focus	onFocus	Occurs when a user gives input focus to an input element, frame, or window. This event applies to all form elements, frames, and windows.
select	onSelect	Occurs when a user selects a form element's input field. This event applies to text fields and text areas.

Summary

JavaScript lets you bring your HTML pages to life by interacting more with your users. JavaScript can be summarized as follows:

- JavaScript is an interpreted language.

- JavaScript is object based and uses built-in, extensible objects, but it lacks true classes or inheritance.

- JavaScript is integrated with, and embedded in, HTML.

- JavaScript provides loose data typing in which data types are not declared.

- JavaScript provides dynamic binding in which object references are not checked until runtime.

- JavaScript cannot directly write to your hard disk.

With traditional HTML Web sites, users get information by clicking a hypertext link and having the server send them another file. With JavaScript-enhanced pages, functional code embedded in the HTML code allows these pages to be more interactive. Users can complete a form and have the client validate its content prior to submitting the form to the server. Better yet, the appearance and selection criteria of an interactive form can change based on user actions. A prime example of this feature is represented by a form for a user to select a car. If the user selects the manufacturer, Ford, from a selection list, JavaScript can modify the model selection list to show only Ford models.

This ability to dynamically change selection forms helps you to deliver an application that is user friendly and performance friendly. The ability to control the input of queries assures that the user won't pass queries to the server that won't return any data or that perform poorly, such as requesting a "Ford Corvette" (which is actually a Chevrolet car) in our automotive example. Along with the HTML you learned in Chapter 7, "HTML Essentials," JavaScript lets you build powerful front-end processing for your application servers.

We now turn our attention, in Section III, "Product Essentials," to products that are complementary to the Web architecture discussed in Chapter 5, "Web Architecture Essentials," and to the information packaging methodology. These products allow you to define the databases and application server components that bring your data warehouse to life for users.

SECTION III

Product Essentials

Why is that some organizations work with such precision that they measure defects per million products or opportunities? How is it that airlines fly thousands of flights per day from airports all over the world and have less than one serious accident for every million flights? Yet, if you take your car in to be repaired or have someone fix your copy machine, the technician fixes it right the first time about 60 percent of the time. Flying a 747 is certainly more difficult than doing a tune-up on a Chevrolet. Some of the reasons for these discrepancies in quality level have to do with training, workload, and quality control techniques. A lot of it has to do with data though. Airline pilots spend the majority of their time monitoring key measures and controlling the plane so that it safely arrives at the right destination almost every single time. Pilots have good data. They understand the relationships between different measures and they know how to adjust various aspects of the plane's controls based upon the data. Managers and professionals in many organizations today are like a pilot trying to fly a plane with only half the instruments needed and a bunch of additional instruments that measure irrelevant data. With the confusing array of data that most managers have, it's no wonder that so many problems occur in so many of the places where we work.

—Mark Graham Brown, *Keeping Score*, AMACOM Books, 1996, pg. 15.

9

PowerDynamo Essentials

Sybase's PowerDynamo product set brings the world of dynamic content and database application services to the Web. PowerDynamo is a Web-based application server that supports client/server and information delivery applications. With PowerDynamo, you store, manage, and access a data warehouse application while using the Web as your transport infrastructure. PowerDynamo is the gateway between a HTTP server and a database. The gateway component of PowerDynamo communicates with the HTTP server via CGI, NSAPI, ISAPI, or WSAPI protocols. The data access component of PowerDynamo communicates with your database via the ODBC protocol.

With PowerDynamo, you use a database as a repository to store HTML pages, DynaScript scripts, and database information; in other words, you manage a data warehouse application and data from a central repository. Additionally, the PowerDynamo architecture enables you to utilize Sybase's Replication Services, allowing replication of data and application anywhere on the network—another server or a remote laptop. This replication allows PowerDynamo to uniquely deliver applications to its user base. Users can work with a data warehouse or other PowerDynamo application, even when they are disconnected from the Web.

PowerDynamo is built on several components, as shown in Figure 9.1, including:

- An application server, which links a database to a Web server.

- A personal Web server, which allows users to work offline with dynamic Web content.

- A site management tool, which manages a database-hosted Web site.

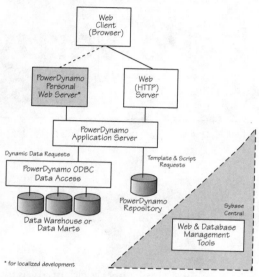

Figure 9.1 *The PowerDynamo architecture lets you implement widely distributed applications that are managed from a central site.*

Delivering Dynamic Content

HTML pages are static documents consisting of text, images, and markup tags. Each of these items defines the meaning and structure of a document. PowerDynamo works with static and dynamic Web pages. The heart and soul of PowerDynamo's dynamic content Web page capability lies in templates.

PowerDynamo templates are generalized HTML documents that support a multitude of user requests that can be fulfilled in a dynamic environment. A template, like a static Web page, contains various HTML tags to drive the formatting of the Web page. Additionally, a template contains other instructions that are processed by a PowerDynamo application server. These instructions are interpreted by PowerDynamo when the document is requested by a Web client, just as HTML instructions are interpreted by an HTTP server.

Upon recognizing a request for a PowerDynamo template, a HTTP server forwards the request to a PowerDynamo application server. The application server interprets the instructions in the template document and returns the resultant dynamic content to the HTTP server in HTML format. The HTTP server in turn passes the HTML back to the Web client. With PowerDynamo, you can embed instructions in any Web page. The following embedded instructions are currently supported in PowerDynamo:

- SQL statements to place database query results into Web pages.

- Scripts to include programmatic control in Web pages that generates HTML.

- Text replacement and host variables to respond to HTML forms and other variables supplied by a Web client.

Embedding SQL Statements in PowerDynamo Templates

One way to increase the flexibility and supported users of a data warehouse is to deliver controlled intranet or Internet access to an organization's databases. In PowerDynamo, you provide database access by embedding SQL statements in HTML templates. When a Web client requests a PowerDynamo template page, the client is provided up-to-the-minute information generated from a data warehouse.

The valueof PowerDynamo comes from its support for dynamic statements in its SQL syntax. You are not limited to static SQL statements. This flexibility allows you to build SQL statements in response to user-driven input, such as entries in an HTML form, from Web clients. For example, you could provide a PowerDynamo template with a list box that contains the categories of a product dimension. When the user selects one of the product categories in the list box and clicks the form's submit button, the Web client sends a request to the Web server. Recognizing the request as a PowerDynamo request, the Web server passes it along to the PowerDynamo application server. The PowerDynamo application server requests the data associated with the selected product category from a database. When receiving the data from the database, PowerDynamo application server constructs a dynamic HTML page with the data from the data warehouse, sending back the information, such as sales figures, to the HTTP server, which redirects the output to the requesting Web client in HTML format.

Scripts in PowerDynamo Templates

The scripting language used by PowerDynamo is DynaScript. As discussed in Chapter 8, "Scripting Essentials," JavaScript is a compact, object-based scripting language for developing interactive Web pages and dynamic Internet applications. DynaScript is a JavaScript-compatible scripting language that creates programs that dynamically generate

HTML from within an application server. DynaScript supports a superset of the Netscape JavaScript syntax as well as several extensions that have been added to DynaScript to allow it to support a more robust, dynamic set of database-driven application services.

DynaScripts are embedded in the body of a PowerDynamo template through the HTML comment element. An HTML comment is marked by a comment tag (<!--comment-->), as demonstrated by the following:

```
<!-- this is a comment in HTML -->
```

When marked with correct tags, DynaScripts are recognized and interpreted by the PowerDynamo interpreter. Be careful not to confuse HTML SCRIPT tags with PowerDynamo SCRIPT tags. The PowerDynamo script tag is one of the subtle differences between Native JavaScript and DynaScript.

Tip: Don't confuse HTML SCRIPT tags with PowerDynamo SCRIPT tags. DynaScripts are defined in HTML comment tags "<!--SCRIPT *script commands* -->, while JavaScript scripts are defined in HTML script tags "<SCRIPT> *script commands* </SCRIPT>.

Originally, JavaScript was developed by Netscape primarily for interpretation at the Web client, not at the Web server. This led a majority of the objects and methods in JavaScript to be tied directly to Netscape Navigator or a compatible browser. Because DynaScripts are embedded in standard HTML comments, no restrictions are imposed on your application or Web client. In PowerDynamo, appropriately tagged scripts are interpreted by the server and generate HTML syntax. Applications have a place for both JavaScript and DynaScript.

In Chapter 8, "Scripting Essentials," we saw how JavaScript client-side scripts can assist in the flexibility of a Web application. DynaScript server-side scripts provide even higher value to your Web applications. With DynaScript server-side scripts, application logic and proprietary code are protected; only the resultant HTML is sent to the Web client, providing a layer of security in your application.

Tip: You can use both JavaScript and DynaScript in HTML templates. However, you cannot embed these scripting languages within each other.

Host Variables and Text Substitution in PowerDynamo Templates

Interaction between a Web client and a Web server is enabled when the client requests an action. This request is initiated at the client through an activity such as the user clicking a form's button or entering a new URL in the browser's location field. The Web client interprets this event and realizes that, to fulfill the request, it must send the information to the Web server. When receiving the request from the Web client, the Web server uses the information to formulate a response for the client. PowerDynamo supports this interactive functionality through host variables.

When the form is sent to a Web server, the user's dynamic request for information is appended to the URL. In the following example, everything after http://www.objx.com represents the user's dynamic request.

```
http://www.objx.com/getSales?region=Central&year=1997
```

Host variables can be placed anywhere in HTML templates. When PowerDynamo interprets templates, the host variables are expanded, replacing the host variables with the proper, interpreted value. In the preceding PowerDynamo template, the variable *$region* is replaced by the value of *Central*, and the variable *$year* is replaced by *1997* wherever they appear. The results of this request are shown in Figure 9.2.

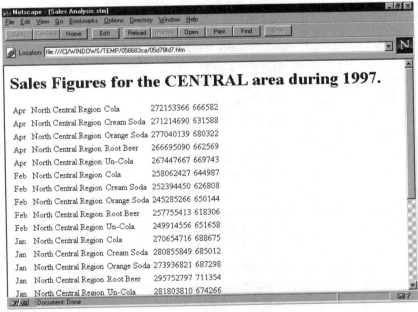

Figure 9.2 *Host variables in scripts and database queries provide a dynamic interface that supports data warehousing efforts. PowerDynamo interprets the variables by inserting proper values during execution.*

The PowerDynamo Architecture

The architecture of PowerDynamo, as shown in Figure 9.1, is similar to the architecture that we described in Chapter 5, "Web Architecture Essentials." PowerDynamo's architecture includes data stores, including application databases and template repository; an application server; and a site manager. These three components are discussed in the sections that follow.

Data Stores

Databases are the heart of all applications, and Web applications are no different. PowerDynamo requires two logical data stores, an application data store and a template repository data store. Physically, these two data stores may be placed in the same database. However, you may also choose to use two distinctly separate databases—one for the application database and another for the template repository.

The Application Data Store

Queries embedded in your PowerDynamo templates are executed against a database that is referred to as the application data store. Your data warehouse or data mart are examples of an application data store. An application data store can be any Open Database Connectivity (ODBC) data source. Communication between PowerDynamo and a database is accomplished through the ODBC interface.

ODBC is a standard application programming interface that provides insulation to applications from back-end database management systems and storage formats. ODBC provides an insulation layer, an abstraction, between your client application and the underlying database. The ODBC architecture, shown in Figure 9.3, includes an client application, ODBC manager, database-specific ODBC driver, and data store.

ODBC is not a language, it is a translation protocol that interprets a base-level dialect of SQL. SQL is the language. The value of ODBC is its ability to understand standard SQL, converting client requests into the appropriate SQL for the target database. With this functionality, you can prototype an application in one data store, such as Excel, dBase, Adaptive Server Anywhere, or Adaptive Server Enterprise, and then deploy the application in another data store, such as Sybase IQ, without requiring a change in application syntax.

For an application data store, PowerDynamo is an ODBC client application. Therefore, any supported ODBC database can be accessed. PowerDynamo speaks SQL to the ODBC drivers that natively speak to application data stores. The SQL statements embedded in PowerDynamo templates must conform to the SQL dialect that is supported by the application data store and its associated ODBC driver.

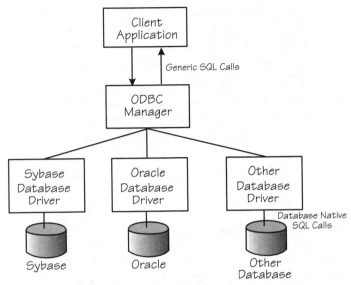

Figure 9.3 *The ODBC architecture provides a layer of abstraction between client application and underlying data stores.*

The Template Repository Data Store

PowerDynamo offers a database-hosted Web site approach. A PowerDynamo Web site is stored and managed in a relational database, and includes any templates and associated files used to deliver a complete application. The template repository may be the same or a different database than the application data store that templates query. However, PowerDynamo requires that a template repository be held in an ODBC data source that can process Sybase's dialect of SQL, Transact-SQL. Sybase Adaptive Server Anywhere or Sybase Adaptive Server (formerly known as Adaptive Server Enterprise) are two databases that frequently act as PowerDynamo template repositories. Additionally, the PowerDynamo Application Server requires that a single template repository manage all templates that are processed as part of a specific application.

A template repository is organized according to a folder-based motif, which easily maps to today's file management systems. This structure allows you to easily import and export Web sites between a template repository database and a file system, such as Windows. This functionality allows you to use other Web tools that are geared toward file-based Web sites, such as rapid application development tools or static site management facilities, which focus on Web-page or Web-site formatting.

The relationship of the PowerDynamo storage motif extends beyond simply importing Web documents from a file system. Web documents that are part of a PowerDynamo Web site can be physically stored in a template repository database or as files in a native file system's directory tree. While storing information in a database has many advantages (such as backup, recovery, and replication), you may want to hold some of your Web site components as files external to PowerDynamo. You can often optimize the retrieval of some files, such as graphics, by storing them as external files. This is accomplished through PowerDynamo's linked folders. A linked folder is a Web site component that provides access to files stored in a directory in a file management system, such as Windows NT. Linking a folder to a directory leaves Web documents physically stored in a file system.

Application Server

At the core of PowerDynamo is an application server that interprets and processes specially tagged instructions embedded in PowerDynamo templates. The role of the application server is to parse instructions and deliver resulting HTML output to the Web server. Queries to a data warehouse are embedded in HTML templates that are stored in a template repository. These queries are interpreted by the application server and executed against a database. In the application server, templates merge static HTML syntax with dynamic data from a data warehouse database. The resulting HTML output is a combination of static HTML and dynamic content served by a database or PowerDynamo.

As shown in Figure 9.4, the interaction between a client or requesting component of an application and a PowerDynamo application server occurs as follows:

1. The Web client submits a request to the Web server.

2. The Web server recognizes the request as a PowerDynamo request and forwards it to the PowerDynamo application server.

3. The PowerDynamo application server receives a request from the Web server in the form of a template-based URL call.

4. The PowerDynamo application server retrieves the template from the PowerDynamo repository.

5. The PowerDynamo application server processes any embedded script instructions.

6. The PowerDynamo application server fetches required data from a referenced database.

7. The PowerDynamo application server passes an HTML document to the Web server.

8. The Web server communicates back to the Web client.

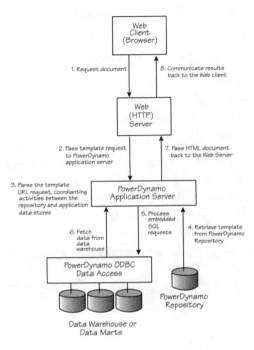

Figure 9.4 *A PowerDynamo application server interacts between templates and a database to provide users with dynamic HTML results.*

Web Site Management Tool

Because PowerDynamo focuses on combining HTML documents and scripting with dynamic content from databases, the product set includes its own Web-site management tool. This tool allows you to administer PowerDynamo templates, DynaScripts, database attributes, and connections. The tool is a plug-in utility to Sybase Central, which has evolved over the years to provide centralized management of data assets. The combination of managing both data and application technologies in a single framework with a consistent interface is a benefit of PowerDynamo.

PowerDynamo's Web site management tool provides the following administrative features.

- A folder-based organization of site components, including PowerDynamo templates, DynaScripts, associated support files such as graphics, and linked folders.

- Wizards to create PowerDynamo components.

- Syntax-aware editors that highlights embedded syntax such as markup tags, SQL, and DynaScripts.

- Browser hooks for quick prototype checking.

- Scheduled processing of scripts and templates, which is particularly useful for pages that require a long time to generate. The execution of a timed based event, such as a scheduled script or template, will allow you to build in a push strategy in your data warehousing system.

The PowerDynamo Web site management facility depends on the Sybase Central framework to properly execute. As Figure 9.5 shows, the Web site management utility is a plug-in to the Sybase Central database management tool and allows you to manage data along with your Web site from the same interface.

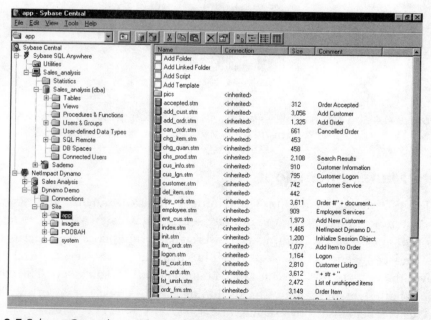

Figure 9.5 *Sybase Central provides a plug-in framework for both database and Web site management from one common interface.*

Folder-Based Site Organization

Sybase Central presents the information managed by its plug-ins in a folder-based motif, similar to the Windows Explorer interface. The folder organization of Sybase Central is associated with the entities managed by the plug-in. For databases, folders organize and manage items such as tables, views, procedures and functions, users and groups, user-defined data types, database spaces, and replication subscriptions. For Web sites, folders organize and manage items such as connections and applications. A Web site application is built with a series of linked folders, templates, and scripts. Additionally, a Web site may contain folders containing supporting components, such as .GIF or JPG images. The hierarchy of folders provides a clean interface from which management tasks associated with implementing and administering the many components comprising an entire Web site can be performed.

The Wizard Interface

The PowerDynamo plug-in for Sybase Central provides a Wizard-based interface to assist you in the initial development of HTML templates. The PowerDynamo Wizard walks you through the various steps of creating a fully-functional, dynamic HTML template. The Wizard prompts include:

1. A unique name of the template for a folder.
2. A description of the template, which can assist others in understanding the contents of the template.
3. The connection that will be used to access the data in the template.
4. The SQL query that interfaces with the database.
5. The format for presenting the dynamic data in HTML.

The SQL Query Builder in the PowerDynamo Wizard provides an additional set of prompters to assist in building *select* statements for query-based templates. This tabbed dialog assists with construction of the major components of a *select* statement, including tabs for defining:

- The tables included in the *select* statement.
- How the tables are joined to retrieve the results from the database.
- The columns projected in the result set.

- How the results should be sorted.

- Filter conditions that are executed in the *where* clause of the *select* statement.

- How the result set are grouped.

- Filter conditions that are executed in the *having* clause of the *select* statement.

- Computed columns.

Several tabs in the PowerDynamo Query Builder dialog include hooks into an expression builder. The PowerDynamo Expression Builder dialog assists in creating expressions that will be included in the *select* statement's projected columns or filters. The PowerDynamo Query Builder dialog also provides a tab that functionally tests the query that you have built. The test tab produces a set of rows that allow you to validate that the query is properly defined and returns the desired results.

Aside from the PowerDynamo Query Builder panel, the remaining PowerDynamo Wizard panels provide a comprehensive, rapid prototyping tool to formulate your required dynamic templates—from a query to a variety of layout formats. After the template is created, you can further enhance the template with either the syntax-aware editors provided by PowerDynamo or with third-party Web page authoring and formatting tools.

Syntax-Aware Editors

The PowerDynamo syntax-aware editors provide an intelligent interface from which to develop and edit your code. The intelligence built into these editors highlights each of the HTML and DynaScript specialty tags and associated attributes. The highlighting in these editors provides a visual interface that allows you to properly place the logic that delivers your dynamic Web site while avoiding errant code. The highlights are presented through color schemes and fonts that distinguish the syntax that enhances the presentation of the dynamic content in your Web site from text blocks.

Besides to the syntax-aware editors provided by PowerDynamo, you may choose to enhance your development environment with third-party interface-aware editors. These editors understand the proper presentation of HTML results. These interface-aware editors give you a development tool for designing HTML pages. The ability to import and export template source files allows you to easily incorporate these types of tools, which enhances your development environment.

Rapid Viewing and Browsing of Site Objects

As you develop a visual application such as a Web site, it is important to periodically see the results of your development efforts. PowerDynamo allows you to hot-link into your browser or the PowerDynamo editors to see the current results of your Web site. In PowerDynamo, you can navigate the folders of your Web site by opening and closing the folders that organize the site's content. After locating a template that you want to visualize, you simply press your right mouse button. This act displays a menu of options, including viewing or browsing the output of the selected template.

This process is more sophisticated than simply visualizing HTML. It is the same as running the application, querying your database, merging the results with the HTML template, and producing the final HTML file. When you select the browsing option, these tasks are executed in your browser, which presents the final results as seen by your users. When you select the viewing option, the tasks are executed and the results are produced and presented in the PowerDynamo editor in their final HTML format.

Scheduling Long-Running Site Objects

Most Web sites support a large number of users. If your data warehouse requires support for a large user base, you may choose to pre-execute some common and frequently requested reports or queries. Pre-execution of common reports and queries which are distributed to most or all of the data warehouse users, such as monthly statements, can be highly beneficial and assist in controlling performance of report execution and delivery. Also individual, long-running data warehouse reports and queries may require scheduling to guarantee a sustained level of required performance and delivery. These scheduled executions of reports will guarantee that during peak periods of activity no one user or report will monopolize the data warehouse, robbing other users of on line reporting time and consistent response time.

In PowerDynamo, you can set predefined frequency intervals for scheduling this type of work. These schedules are site specific and include the ability to run scripts or templates in frequencies such as hourly, daily, weekly, and monthly. This forces the execution of the dynamic task (a script or a template), which results in the production of a static HTML page that others can read.

Scheduling long-running tasks can be defined within the Sybase Central management and development environment or scheduling definition can be performed with DynaScript. You will define long running task schedules which are well defined and known as required components of the data warehouse in advance within Sybase Central. You will want to build thresholds within your code to handle long running tasks which are ad hoc and unknown at development time. If these ad hoc, long running tasks arise during normal operations of the data warehouse, you can force Dynascript to schedule the operation for later execution.

Building a PowerDynamo Template

Within this section, we will build a PowerDynamo template based on the Sales Analysis Information Package which we have discussed throughout this book. In building this template, we will take a step-by-step look at how to create a new PowerDynamo template with the PowerDynamo Wizards so that you can better appreciate what we have discussed to this point. Following this example, we will have created a PowerDynamo template which queries the data warehouse and produces an HTML result set presenting the data from our Sales Analysis Information Package in an HTML table.

1. The tables for the required information package are created in the database. Figure 9.6 shows the tables for the sales analysis information package. These tables include D_TIME_PERIOD, D_PRODUCT, and D_LOCATION dimension tables, along with a M_SALES_ANALYSIS measure table.

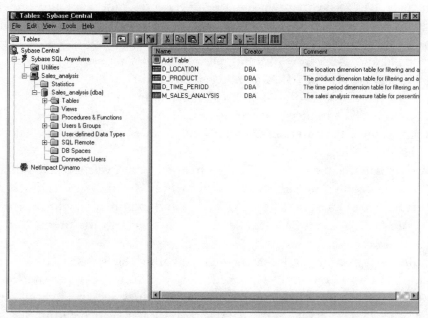

Figure 9.6 *Sybase Central defines your information package tables.*

2. You are ready to attach the database with PowerDynamo. Figure 9.7 shows the connection dialog for PowerDynamo. This dialog prompts for the connection name, ODBC data source, user name, and password for the connection.

3. Because this is the first time PowerDynamo has been connected with this database, you are prompted whether to populate the PowerDynamo repository tables. These tables must be created to store the PowerDynamo templates and scripts.

4. When you indicate that PowerDynamo should populate its repository tables, you need to provide additional information regarding the overall folder scheme used to physically implement this request. As shown in Figure 9.8, PowerDynamo prompts you for the root folder to house the site information and about whether you want to generate PowerDynamo support information in the site.

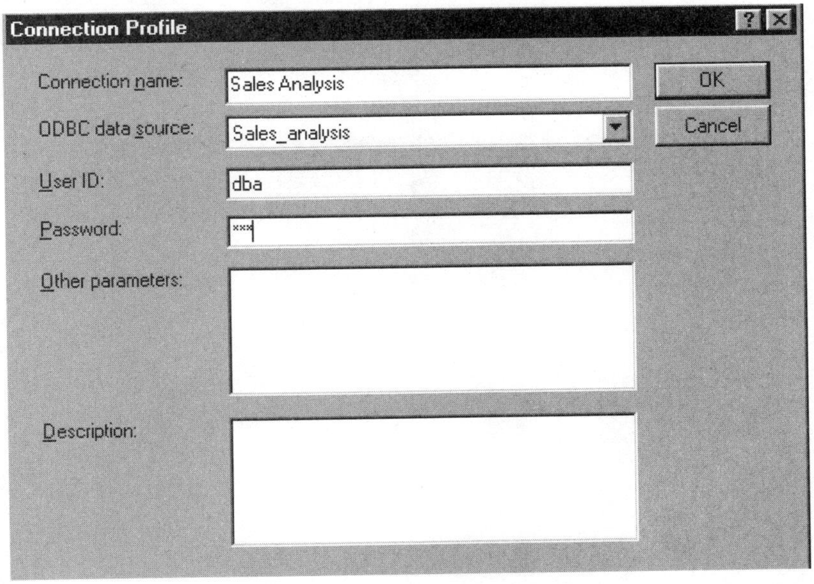

Figure 9.7 *From Sybase Central, you use the PowerDynamo connection facility to attach PowerDynamo to the data warehouse.*

5. The PowerDynamo plug-in to Sybase Central presents your Web site in a folder format. Each folder that you open in PowerDynamo offers content as well as methods for creating and managing the content, as shown in Figure 9.9.

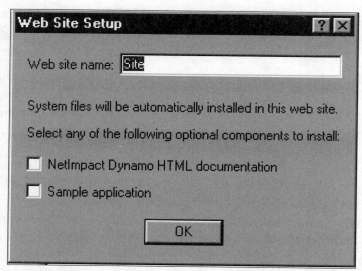

Figure 9.8 *While establishing the PowerDynamo template repository, you are prompted for the site location and related options.*

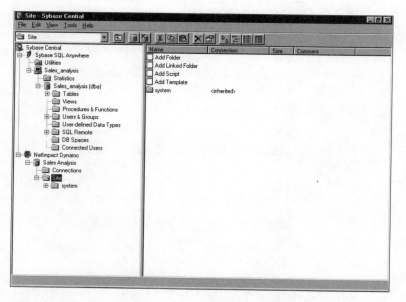

Figure 9.9 *As with other Sybase Central plug-ins, PowerDynamo presents your Web site in a folder motif.*

6. Selecting the Add Template method in your site folder initiates a
    PowerDynamo Wizard to create a template. The Template Name dialog
    prompts you for a unique name for the new template, as shown in Figure
    9.10.

7. Pressing the "Next" button on the Template Name dialog leads to the
    Template Description dialog shown in Figure 9.11. This dialog provides a
    high-level, free-form description of the template's functionally. This text
    assists other developers who might need to work with this template.

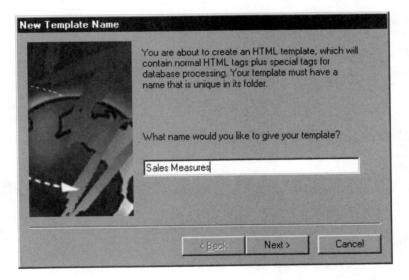

Figure 9.10 *The first dialog for PowerDynamo's Template Wizard prompts for a unique
template name.*

8. You are prompted for the connection that you want to use for this new tem-
    plate. Connections, which are discussed in the "The connection Object" sec-
    tion later in this chapter, can be shared or specific. For this demonstration,
    we choose to inherit the connection from the parent folder—or our current
    sign-on, as shown in Figure 9.12.

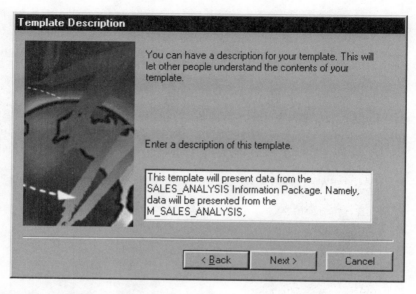

Figure 9.11 *The second dialog in the Template Wizard prompts for a description of the PowerDynamo template.*

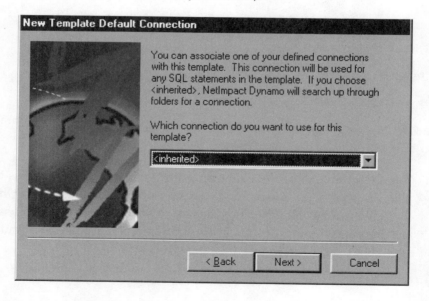

Figure 9.12 *You can select the specific connection to use for any template or inherit the security from the application folder.*

9. The Template Wizard prompts for the SQL select statement used by the new template, as shown in Figure 9.13. You can either enter a free-form SQL statement or press the elect button to bring up the Edit SQL Query dialog discussed in Step 10.

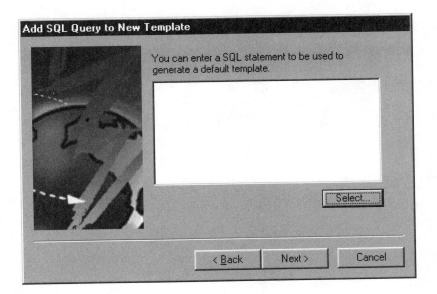

Figure 9.13 *The select statement can be directly entered in the Edit SQL Query dialog of the Template Wizard.*

10. The Edit SQL Query dialog shown in Figure 9.14 assists in building properly formatted SQL select statements. This dialog has several tabs that relate to the clauses in a select statement. These include the Tables Tab, which formulates the from clause, the Joins and Where Tabs, which formulate the where clause, the Columns Tab, which formulates the select clause, the Group Tab, which formulates the group by clause, the Having Tab, which formulates the having clause, the Compute Tab, which formulates the compute clause, and a tab that allows you to test your query.

11. The New Template Initial HTML dialog shown in Figure 9.15 prompts for the initial HTML format for the results. This combo box provides the valid PowerDynamo formats, including tables, lists, and links.

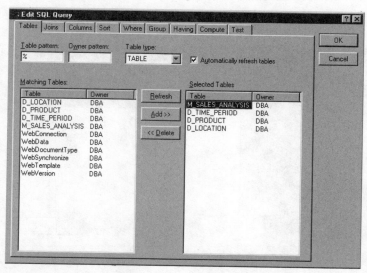

Figure 9.14 *An Edit SQL Query dialog assists entering proper syntax in PowerDynamo templates.*

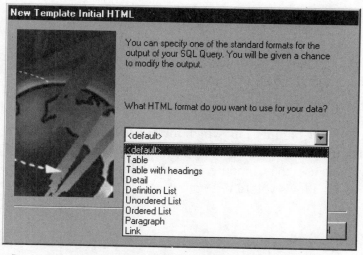

Figure 9.15 *The PowerDynamo New Template Initial HTML dialog allows you to select various HTML formats to present your dynamic data results.*

12. After PowerDynamo has created a new template, you can use the syntax-aware editors to modify the generated syntax.13. You can examine the output of your template in your Web browser. The template we have generated is shown in Figure 9.16 using a browser called directly from the Power-Dynamo environment.

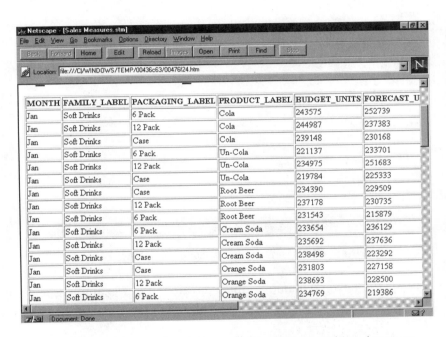

Figure 9.16 *The results of the template is displayed in a browser.*

13. You can view the raw HTML results with PowerDynamo's View option. These results for our example are shown in Figure 9.17.

Figure 9.17 *PowerDynamo displays raw HTML output.*

The syntax for the PowerDynamo template created in our example is as follows.

```
<HTML>
<TITLE>Sales Analysis.stm</TITLE>
<BODY>
<H1> Sales Analysis Information Package by Month, Region, and Product.</H1>
<!--SQL
    SELECT
      DTIMEPERIOD.MONTH,
      DLOCATION.REGION_LABEL,
      DPRODUCT.PRODUCT_LABEL,
      SUM(MSALESANALYSIS.ACTUAL_REVENUE),
      SUM(MSALESANALYSIS.ACTUAL_UNITS)
    FROM
      D_TIME_PERIOD DTIMEPERIOD,
      D_LOCATION DLOCATION,
      D_PRODUCT DPRODUCT,
      M_SALES_ANALYSIS MSALESANALYSIS
    WHERE
      DTIMEPERIOD.TIME_PERIOD_KEY  =
        MSALESANALYSIS.TIME_PERIOD_KEY
      AND MSALESANALYSIS.LOCATION_KEY  =
```

```
          DLOCATION.LOCATION_KEY
      AND DPRODUCT.PRODUCT_KEY   = MSALESANALYSIS.PRODUCT_KEY
      AND DPRODUCT.PACKAGING_KEY =
         MSALESANALYSIS.PACKAGING_KEY
      AND DTIMEPERIOD.YEAR = '1997'
    GROUP BY
      DTIMEPERIOD.MONTH,
      DLOCATION.REGION_LABEL,
      DPRODUCT.PRODUCT_LABEL
    ORDER BY
      DTIMEPERIOD.MONTH,
      DLOCATION.REGION_LABEL,
      DPRODUCT.PRODUCT_LABEL
 -->
<TABLE BORDER>
  <TR></TR><!--formatting-->
  <TR></TR><!--/formatting-->
</TABLE>
</BODY>
</HTML>
```

After the preceding template is processed by the PowerDynamo application server, the following HTML is sent back to the browser for presentation to users.

```
<HTML>
<TITLE>Sales Analysis.stm</TITLE>
<BODY>
<H1> Sales Analysis Information Package by Month, Region, and Product.</H1><TABLE
BORDER>
<TR></TR>
<TABLE>
<TR><TD>Apr</TD>
  <TD>North Central Region</TD>
  <TD>Cola</TD>
  <TD>272153366</TD>
  <TD>666582</TD></TR>
<TR><TD>Apr</TD>
  <TD>North Central Region</TD>
  <TD>Cream Soda</TD>
  <TD>271214690</TD>
  <TD>631588</TD></TR>
<TR><TD>Apr</TD>
  <TD>North Central Region</TD>
  <TD>Orange Soda</TD>
  <TD>277040139</TD>
  <TD>680322</TD></TR>
<TR><TD>Apr</TD>
  <TD>North Central Region</TD>
  <TD>Root Beer</TD>
  <TD>266695090</TD>
```

```
    <TD>662569</TD></TR>
<TR><TD>Apr</TD>
   <TD>North Central Region</TD>
   <TD>Un-Cola</TD>
   <TD>267447667</TD>
   <TD>669743</TD></TR>
<TR><TD>Feb</TD>
   <TD>North Central Region</TD>
   <TD>Cola</TD>
   <TD>258062427</TD>
   <TD>644987</TD></TR>
<!--Table rows are sent back for all matching rows.-->
</TABLE>
</TABLE>
</BODY>
</HTML>
```

PowerDynamo Syntax Extensions

The PowerDynamo markup and scripting languages are compatible with HTML and Netscape's JavaScript. As with standard HTML, PowerDynamo templates use markup syntax to define the layout of Web pages. As with standard JavaScript, DynaScripts are built from language elements that include literals, variables, expressions, operators, statements, functions, and objects. However, with PowerDynamo focused on dynamic Web applications, Sybase has extended the standards by including the following syntax:

- A *script* markup tag for embedding DynaScripts.

- A *sql statement* markup tag for embedding database calls.

- A *formatting* markup tag for defining output formatting of dynamic content.

- A *class* statement, which allows DynaScript to improve on JavaScript's object-based implementation by providing better inheritance and polymorphism.

- An *import* statement, which improves DynaScript's ability to share logic among components of an overall system.

DynaScript has also gone beyond the JavaScript standard in object orientation. DynaScript supports objects and methods, which are operations performed on objects that are provided by most object-oriented languages. PowerDynamo support for the object-oriented paradigm includes:

- **Encapsulation:** Encapsulation refers to the storage of properties and the methods that manipulate those properties in an object.

- **Polymorphism:** Polymorphism is a concept whereby different objects can respond to the same message in their own, unique ways. The translation of the message occurs when an object uses its own methods of the same method name; however, the method may contain different operations.

- **Inheritance:** Inheritance refers to the ability to define new objects that extend the capabilities of existing objects by inheriting existing properties and methods. The newly formed object can be extended to include new properties and methods aside from those contained in the inherited object.

With the addition of the *class* statement, PowerDynamo allows you to define custom classes and then create as many instances of each class as you require. PowerDynamo also includes a number of predefined objects that simplify the task of developing database-driven content and manipulating Web site content. These extended objects include:

- A *connection* object, which defines the method of connecting to a data source, improving your ability to manage security and database connections.

- An enhanced *document* object, which defines a file or a folder on the Web site, improving your ability to work with the interaction between documents and a database.

- A *query* object, which defines a SQL query or other database instruction, improving your ability to integrate a database and a Web site.

- A *session* object, which defines persistent client connection information, improving your ability to manage the application state; this is a major weakness in current standards. This extension allows PowerDynamo to provide state to a stateless environment.

- A *site* object, which defines the Web site, improving control of the application-wide attributes of a Web site.

Each of these objects has its own, predefined properties and methods, which are documented in the following sections. Your scripts can create one or more instances of these objects. The only exception is the *site* object, for which only one instance is permitted.

Tip: Property names and method names are case sensitive. Parentheses must be used when calling a method, even if the method takes no arguments.

The *script* Markup Tag

DynaScripts are embedded in templates as HTML comments. An HTML comment is marked as indicated in the following example. The <!-- characters denote the beginning of a comment. From there, you may enter free-form text and terminate the comment with -->.

```
<!-- The following template will retrieve sales analysis information. -->
```

PowerDynamo interprets comments in templates to locate its specialized tags. Because comments are not interpreted by most browsers, script syntax and other PowerDynamo extensions support most browsers. PowerDynamo interprets the comments and looks for its own markup syntax. When finding a keyword, PowerDynamo interprets the content of the comment.

A DynaScript is marked by a special tag inside the comment, as follows:

```
<!--SCRIPT
     script statements
-->
```

This *script* tag instructs a PowerDynamo application server to parse and interpret the enclosed script. Embedding PowerDynamo scripts in comments also ensures that the proprietary syntax is hidden from other tools that are incapable of interpreting DynaScript syntax. As discussed in Chapter 7, "HTML Essentials," this syntax migrates nicely to the newer XML standard; but for now, the PowerDynamo implementation is an elegant way to extend the HTML standard while still supporting popular browser technologies. While most Web formatting tools throw out proprietary syntax, they retain comments and therefore can assist you in developing your PowerDynamo Web site.

The *sql* Markup Tag

The true value of PowerDynamo is its ability to extend standard Web applications to include dynamic database content. This is accomplished by embedding SQL statements in PowerDynamo HTML templates. As with embedded DynaScripts, you place embedded SQL statements inside a standard HTML comment with the proper PowerDynamo tag, as follows:

```
<!--SQL NAME=db_statement_name
     SQL statement
-->
```

The *sql* statement tag allows the PowerDynamo application server to interact with your database or data warehouse. Because this PowerDynamo tag is enclosed in a standard HTML comment, other interpreters and editing tools ignore it. Doing so allows you to mix and match the components you use to design, develop, and deliver you Web-based warehouse.

A SQL statement can also be named with the NAME attribute of the *sql* statement tag. However if this optional attribute is used, you must start your SQL statement on a separate line. The default name for a SQL statement is *SQL*.

The *formatting* Markup Tag

If your SQL statement is a query, the application server must insert the result set rows into the output of the template's resultant document. PowerDynamo allows you to describe how the results should be presented with the *formatting* tag. This tag, unlike the *script* and *sql* tags, has both a start tag (<!--FORMATTING-->) and an end tag (<!--/FORMATTING-->). This distinction in the markup language allows you to easily embed the resultant data in an HTML document utilizing standard HTML as the formatting syntax. If all of the formatting were contained in the format tags, which are HTML comments, they would not be interpreted properly by tools other than PowerDynamo. The formatting tags allow you to easily format your database query output without writing scripts, though writing scripts provides an additional option for formatting dynamic data.

Data Placeholders

PowerDynamo uses data placeholders to describe the formatting of each row of a query result set. As with other PowerDynamo tags, data placeholders are marked in HTML comments, as follows:

```
<!--data-->
```

Data placeholders reference each item that is returned by a query, or the columns in the select list, as follows:

```
<!--SQL
select year, sum(units_sold) from sales_analysis order by year
-->
<!--FORMATTING-->
  <PRE>
Year: <!--data-->    Units Sold: <!--data-->
  </PRE>
<!--/FORMATTING-->
```

The above example produces results similar to the following:

```
Year: 1993    Units Sold: 1,500
Year: 1994    Units Sold: 1,750
Year: 1995    Units Sold: 1,680
Year: 1996    Units Sold: 2,500
Year: 1997    Units Sold: 3,000
```

Tip: There is no restriction on the HTML that can be included between PowerDynamo tags, so your output can take full advantage of HTML standards.

The MAXROWS Attribute

Because data warehouse queries can return enormous numbers of rows to users, you may want to limit result set rows. This is done in the format tags using the MAXROWS attribute. Normally, the formatting tag causes the contents between the beginning and ending format tags to be repeated for each row in the query result. The MAXROWS attribute causes the contents between the start and end tags to be repeated, at most, MAXROWS times. The following example ranks and returns only the top 25 vendors based on dollar purchases:

```
<HTML>
  <TITLE>Top 25 Vendor Listing</TITLE>
  <BODY>
    <CENTER>
      <H1>Top 25 Vendor Listing</H1>
      <H2>(based on purchase volume)</H2>
    </CENTER>
    <!--SQL
      select vendor_name, sum(purchase_amount)
       from purchase_analysis, vendor
       where purchase_analysis.vendor_id = vendor.vendor_id
       group by vendor.vendor_id
       order by sum(purchase_amount) DESC
    -->
    <TABLE BORDER>
      <TR>
        <TH>Vendor</TH><TH>Total Purchases</TH>
      </TR>
      <!--FORMATTING MAXROWS=25-->
      <TR>
        <TD><!--data--></TD><TD><!--data--></TD>
      </TR>
      <!--/FORMATTING-->
    </TABLE>
  </BODY>
</HTML>
```

Referencing a Named Query

If a PowerDynamo template has more than one query, you will want to name your queries. This is done through the NAME attribute of the *sql* statement tag discussed in the previous "The *sql* Markup Tag" section. To ensure that the format statements are applied to proper query results, you use the NAME attribute of the format tag. The NAME attribute allows you to explicitly define the output formats for a query, as in the following example.

```
<!--SQL NAME=VendorListing
      select vendor_name, sum(purchase_amount)
        from purchase_analysis, vendor
        where purchase_analysis.vendor_id = vendor.vendor_id
        group by vendor.vendor_id
        order by sum(purchase_amount) DESC
   -->
<!--FORMATTING NAME=VendorListing MAXROWS=25-->
```

The *class* Statement: Creating Your Own Objects

The PowerDynamo *class* statement extension provides an explicit method to declare an object type or a class. Classes define whole sets of objects and are easily recognized by their name. Examples include products, locations, customers, and books. Rather than defining individual objects, classes provide a mechanism for centrally managing common objects. The DynaScript *class* statement defines classes of objects; it also derives a new class from an existing class. This DynaScript extension allows PowerDynamo to better support inheritance, outdistancing the JavaScript implementation of classes. A simple class definition follows:

```
class BOOK(isbn, title, author, publisher, publication_date,
            number_of_pages) {
  this.isbn = isbn ;
  this.title = title ;
  this.author = author ;
  this.publisher = publisher ;
  this.publication_date = publication_date ;
  this.number_of_pages = number_of_pages;
}
```

This class describes the structure of a set of objects, known as BOOK. All objects are an instance of this class and all instances of class BOOK have exactly six properties, or fields.

In PowerDynamo, the *class* statement syntax is as follows:

```
class newClassName ( [ paramList ] )
  [ extends parentClassName ( [ parentParamList ] ) ]
{
    statements
} ;
```

The properties of the *class* statement are detailed in Table 9.1.

Table 9.1 *Class statement properties.*

Property	Description
newClassName	A name to define the new class.
paramList	A comma-separated set of parameters contained in the new class. These parameters assigning values to the class properties (or fields). If you are extending an existing class, this parameter list may include the inherited parameters from the parent class in addition to new parameters.
parentClassName	The name of an existing class from which the new class is derived. In defining a base class, the parent class name is not provided.
parentParamList	A comma-separated set of parameters that typically is a subset of the paramList list of the parent class. The parent constructor uses these parameters while executing its constructor method before the constructor of the new class is executed.
statements	Constructor statements for the new class. These statements typically do the following: 1. Assigns the new parameters to the properties you added to the new class, using the `this` keyword to reference the new class. For example: *this.title = title*. The keyword refers to the current object and typically is the qualifier for an object's properties and methods. 2. Defines methods for the new class. If you define a method with the same name as a method in the parent class, the new method overrides the parent method.

Defining a Base Class

A base class is the lowest-level definition of a class. That is, a base class does not inherit anything from an existing class. A base class can be defined in one of two ways.

- **The JavaScript way:** Defines a function that represents the base class. This technique closely aligns with the JavaScript standard. To define a base class, you declare a function using the class name and the property names, assign the property values, and define any methods that are associated with the function.

- **The DynaScript way:** Defines a class statement that represents the base class. This technique uses the PowerDynamo *class* statement extension. The PowerDynamo *class* statement provides more flexibility than the JavaScript standard, because you can use the *class* statement to create derived classes. To define a base object using the *class* statement, you declare the class name and the property names, assign the property values, and define the methods that reference the function.

The only difference in the two approaches is the *class* keyword. The main reason for using the *class* statement is the additional ability to define derived objects.

Tip: If JavaScript compatibility is important, use the JavaScript function-declaration technique instead of the PowerDynamo *class* statement extension to define base classes.

In JavaScript, a base class is defined as follows:

```
function query_definition(sel, frm, whr, grp, ord)
{
   this.select_clause = sel ;
   this.from_clause = frm ;
   this.where_clause = whr ;
   this.group_clause = grp ;
   this.order_clause = ord ;
}
```

In PowerDynamo, the *class* statement syntax is as follows:

```
class query_definition(sel, frm, whr, grp, ord)
{
this.select_clause = sel ;
   this.from_clause = frm ;
   this.where_clause = whr ;
   this.group_clause = grp ;
   this.order_clause = ord ;
   function displaySQLSelect ()
   {
     var SQLselect ;
     SQLselect = 'select ' + this.select_clause ;
     SQLselect = SQLselect + ' from ' + this.from_clause ;
```

```
    SQLselect = SQLselect + ' where ' + this.where_clause ;
    SQLselect = SQLselect + ' group by ' + this.group_clause ;
    SQLselect = SQLselect + ' order by ' + this.order_clause ;
    document.WriteLn('SQL Select Statement: ' + SQLselect) ;
    }
   this.displaySQLSelect = displaySQLSelect ;
}
```

As you can see, with the DynaScript method of definition we defined a function inline and referenced it in a class definition. Each query definition object defined has access to the method that displays the SQL *select* statement. On the other hand, the JavaScript definition merely defines the properties of the object and not the methods, restricting its implementation of object-oriented principles as well as making the code more complex to manage.

Objects: Creating Instances of Classes

An object is an instance of a class. This book, *Data Warehousing on the Internet: Accessing the Corporate Knowledge Base*, is an instance of a BOOK class. After a class has been defined, you can create specific instances of that class. These new instances of the class are referred to as objects.

You create a new class instance through variable assignment. In the *var* statement, the name of the new instance of the class is placed and equated with the *new* operator and the associated name of the class. Besides to the name association, you provide any property values for the new instance of the class. For example, the following creates a query for a sales analysis information package that evaluates monthly sales figures for the current year by location and product.

```
var qrySalesAnalysis =
  new query_definition(
   ' * ",
   ' d_time_period, d_location, d_product, m_sales_analysis ",
   ' d_time_period.time_period_key =
       m_sales_analysis.time_period_key
     and
     d_location.location_key = m_sales_analysis.location_key
     and
     d_product.product_key = m_sales_analysis.product_key
     and
     d_time_period.year = 1997 ",
   ' d_time_period.month, d_location.location,
       d_product.product ",
   ' d_time_period.month, d_location.location,
       d_product.product ") ;
```

Declaring a new instance of a class is identical no matter which technique you use to define a class, JavaScript or DynaScript. The variable definition shown above works with both types of definition.

Inheritance

In object-oriented languages, inheritance is the ability to create new classes of objects that are extensions of existing classes. Current versions of JavaScript do not support this capability, though future releases may. JavaScript lets you define new classes from scratch, but it does not support inheritance. This is one limitation that makes JavaScript an object-based language rather than an object-oriented language.

The simplest form of inheritance is single inheritance, in which a new class can inherit properties and methods from a single parent class. Through its *class* statement, DynaScript adds single inheritance. This PowerDynamo extension allows you to derive a new class from an existing class. When deriving a new, inherited class you can add new properties and methods.

Inheriting objects also means that you can take better advantage of polymorphism. Polymorphism is the ability of object-oriented languages to override or redefine existing properties and methods of inherited, parent classes without changing the code that calls these methods. A derived class, or subclass, is a class that extends the definition of an existing class. The subclass inherits the properties and methods of the parent class, or superclass, and then adds its own, additional properties and methods. To define a derived class, you use the *class* statement as follows:

1. Declare the class name and the property names. The property names typically include the parent properties and any new properties required by the derived class.

2. Identify the parent class and pass the parameters required by the parent class.

3. Assign the property values of the derived class.

4. Define the methods of the derived class as functions. As with base class definition, you can define methods inline or assign methods that are existing global functions.

Class methods can be defined inside the class definition, referred to as inline; or outside the class definition by assigning method names to existing functions. The inline method of declaration is preferable, because it encapsulates the method in the class and allows methods in different classes to have the same name, which makes polymorphism possible. For example, consider a class that described a sales analysis information page named SalesAnalysis. To extend this by adding a class that restricts the presentation of data to the current year, you could use the following:

```
class ytdSalesAnalysis (product, location, sales, current_year)
  extends SalesAnalysis (product, location, sales)
{
  this.year = current_year;
  function GetAllInfo()
  {
    document.WriteLn("Product: " + this.product);
    document.WriteLn("Location: " + this.location);
    document.WriteLn("Sales: " + this.sales);
  }
  this.GetAllInfo = GetAllInfo;
}
```

The Import Statement

DynaScript has extended scripting beyond JavaScript to assist in the central management of common code blocks. The *import* statement is a PowerDynamo language extension that, when executed, imports the text of another script at the statement's position in the current script. This permits centrally-stored, common functions and uses them in other scripts that require the functionality. With this extension, you can dramatically improve the quality and maintainability of a Web application. The syntax of the *import* statement is:

```
import document_name;
```

The *document_name* parameter of the *import* statement is a string variable or literal that defines the script file to be included. If you use a variable or expression to define the document name, you can build file names programmatically, providing yet another way to dynamically deliver a Web site. The following example demonstrates how to import a script called MarketShare.ssc that resides in a *sales* folder at the root of your Web site:

```
rootDoc = site.GetRootDocument();
import (rootDoc.location + "/sales/MarketShare.ssc");
```

When code associated with an imported script runs, it occupies its own execution context. This is important, because the imported script will not share the same variable space as the document that imports it. Therefore, because the two scripts don't exist in the same execution context, imported code cannot normally reference the calling document's objects or site's objects. To reference variables and objects from the document in imported code, you must pass the required variables or objects as arguments to imported functions. After passed, the imported scripts can view and manipulate the variables

The *connection* Object

The connection object describes a connection to a database. As discussed earlier in the "The PowerDynamo Architecture" section of this chapter, PowerDynamo's architecture provides for two distinct types of data stores, a template repository and application data stores. The connection object provides access to the two possible connections to these data stores.

- **Site connection:** A site connection refers to a connection to an ODBC data source capable of hosting a PowerDynamo Web site, such as Sybase Adaptive Server Anywhere or Sybase Adaptive Server.

- **Content connection:** A content connection refers to a connection to an ODBC data source that provides the application content for a Web site, such as your data warehouse or data mart in Adaptive Server IQ.

You define a connection in the PowerDynamo Web site management facility. Each Web site can contain multiple connections to allow you to better manage security and multiple database access from one central point. As shown in Figure 9.18, the connection information stored in PowerDynamo includes the connection name, the ODBC data source, the user identifier, the password, other parameters, and a description.

When defining the content of a Web site, you can apply connections to components. Connections can be defined either explicitly or inherited. depending where you are in the site. When you connect to a PowerDynamo Web site, this initial connection becomes the default for your content connection as well. This connection information is encapsulated in the default connection object.

If your database content is stored in one or more other data sources, you can create more connection objects to manage those sources. Additional connections can be defined in the folder storage of your Web site or explicitly in a template or script, the lowest-level entities of a site. This nesting of connections allows you to apply a flexible security scheme on top of your Web site. It also provides the ability to integrate data from multiple dynamic data stores. Table 9.2 describes connection object properties.

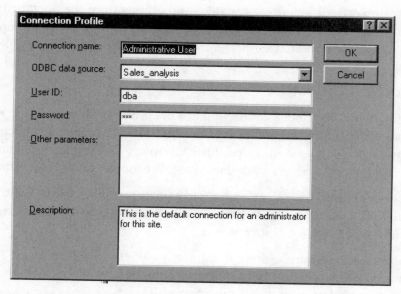

Figure 9.18 *A PowerDynamo connection lets you manage how users access the underlying dynamic data stores of a Web site.*

Table 9.2 *Connection object properties.*

Property	Description
connectParameters	String that contains the connection parameters for an ODBC data source.
dataSource	String that contains the name of an ODBC data source.
dataSourceList	Array of strings that contains the names of all available ODBC data sources.
description	String that contains descriptive comments about the connection to assist in the documentation and maintainability of a Web site, especially in a multideveloper project.
name	String that contains the name of the connection object (default connection name: <default>).
password	String that contains the user password for the ODBC data source (returns null value if requested for security).
userId	String that contains the user name for the ODBC data source.

The following script uses a *connection* object to produce the output shown in Figure 9.21.

```
<!--SCRIPT ListODBCSources.ssc created on 07/13/97 11:39:22
  document.writeln( '<H1>Connection Details</H1>" ) ;
  document.writeln( '<B>Data Source</B> ' +
      connection.datasource + '<P>" ) ;
  document.writeln( '<B>Name</B> ' + connection.name + '<P>" ) ;
  document.writeln( '<B>User ID</B> ' + conneciton.userId +
      '<P>" ) ;
  document.writeln( '<B>Password</B>" + connection.password +
      '<P>" ) :
  document.writeln( '<B>Description</B> ' +
      connection.description + '<P>" ) ;
  document.writeln( '<B>Params</B> ' +
      connection.connectParameters + '<P>" ) ;
  document.writeln( '<H2>Available Data Sources</H2>" ) ;
  sourceList = connection.dataSourceList ;
  nList = 0 ;
  while ( exists ( list[nList] ) ) {
    document.writeln( list[nList] + '<P>" ) ;
    nList++ ;
  }
 -->
```

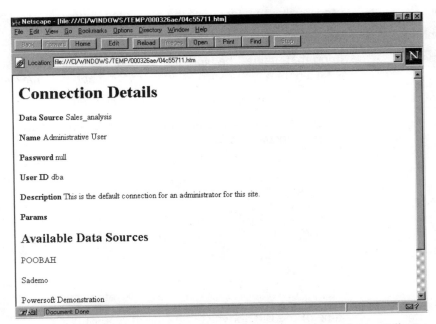

Figure 9.19 *The connection object allows you to access various attributes of database 4connections from your application.*

The Enhanced *document* Object

DynaScript has enhanced the standard JavaScript document object to focus more on working with databases. In standard JavaScript, a document object is associated with every window. The JavaScript implementation allows you to manage and manipulate the content of the information presented to the user in the HTML output.

In DynaScript, the document object represents a document in your Web site, which can be a file or folder. As in the JavaScript implementation, you typically only work with one "current" document object in DynaScripts. The DynaScript implementation offers many of the standard JavaScript properties and methods; however, the focus is on dynamic documents, so extensions have been implemented to assist with connectivity and dynamic content. The *document* object properties are detailed in Table 9.3.

The PowerDynamo *document* object differs from the JavaScript document object. The PowerDynamo *document* object supports a different set of properties and methods that are customized for working with databases.

Table 9.3 *Document object properties.*

Property	Description
connectionId	Integer value that identifies the associated *connection* object.
connectionName	String that contains the name of the associated connection object.
contentType	String that defines the type of document being displayed (standard MIME content types, such as *image/gif* and *application/excel*).
description	Comment string that describe the document object.
id	PowerDynamo internal object identifier for the document object, which is represented as an integer.
lastModified	Returns a string with a timestamp that indicates changes to the document. (Example: document.lastModified = "1997-06-01 12:25:15")
location	Returns a string with the document's full path and filename (example: /Site/Sales_Analysis/Top25Vendors.stm).
name	Returns a string with the document's name (example: TOP_25_SALES.STM).
parent	Returns the folder object that owns the referenced document object.
redirect	Name of the URL to which the current request is directed.

Continued

Table 9.3 *Document object properties.*

Property	Description
size	Returns the length in bytes of the document object.
source allows	Returns the contents of the document in an uninterpreted form, meaning the browser will not interpret the HTML syntax, which you to render the source code of any document.
type	The type of PowerDynamo document. One of: **directory:** indicates a PowerDynamo folder **directoryLink:** indicates a PowerDynamo linked folder **image:** indicates a binary file **script:** indicates a PowerDynamo script file **text:** indicates a PowerDynamo HTML template
value [variable] [array]	Values arguments that have been passed to the document. These arguments are typically URL arguments from an HTML form, where the variable is typically a string of the argument name (Example: document.value["region"] or document.value.quantity).

The methods that you use to manipulate documents are shared between the document object and the site object, Table 9.4 describes these methods.

Table 9.4 *Document object methods.*

Property	Description
ExportTo(pathName)	When executed for a file, ExportTo saves the file as an external file in the designated *pathName* directory. When executed for a folder, the ExportTo method saves a replica of the document tree, including any subfolders, as an external directory tree of files and folders in the *pathName* directory. This method returns a true or a false that indicates whether the export was successful.
GetDirectory( )	For folder documents, GetDirectory returns an array of documents contained in the folder, similar to a directory listing.
GetGenerated( )	Returns the interpreted output from the document as a string. This method cannot be run from within itself.
GetServerVariable()	Returns a value from a server. The server variable is dependent on which server interface is used.

Continued

Table 9.4 *Continued*

Property	Description
ImportFrom(fileName [, replaceOption])	Imports an external file or folder and its content for the named *filename*. If conflicts occur with files and folders, the optional *replaceOption* attribute can assist in determining how to resolve the conflicts. The replace options include:*newer* (default)**:** Replaces existing file if incoming one is newer. *all:* Replaces existing file regardless of modification dates.
Write(outputString)	Appends one or more strings to the document.
WriteLn(outputString)	The same as the Write method, but with a line break. Line breaks produced with WriteLn only work when viewing an HTML document as plain ASCII source in a viewer such as a text editor. When the HTML is processed by a Web client, the resultant layout ignores these line breaks, so WriteLn ultimately produces the same output as Write. To force line breaks in final output, place the HTML paragraph tag <P> in the output. Example: document.WriteLn ("<P>This starts on a new line"). In general, WriteLn makes HTML source easier to read, but does not reflect how the text is ultimately formatted by a Web client.

The *query* Object

The *query* object provides a way to work with SQL query statements that are embedded in PowerDynamo templates. The *query* object corresponds to a cursored view into a database query. A cursored view stores the rows of data in a buffer and points to one row at a time, called the current row. The cursor, or current row, may be repositioned to any row of data with *move* methods (MoveFirst, MoveLast, MovePrevious, MoveNext, MoveRelative).

Some databases do not fully support cursor views. If this occurs with the database with which you are implementing PowerDynamo, you can simulate cursors. You will need to research the PowerDynamo documentation for your specific database.

As discussed in the "PowerDynamo Syntax Extensions" section of this chapter, each embedded query is declared with the PowerDynamo *sql* tag. In the *sql* tag, you can define the name of the query that assists in referencing the queries in your scripts. If you do not provide a name, PowerDynamo provides a default name of *SQL* for the query object. In DynaScripts that follow the embedded query, you can obtain and change information about the query by referencing the query object with the supplied name utilizing the predefined *query* object methods, which are detailed in Table 9.5.

For example, the following query prints the total number of vendors in a result set:

```
<!--SQL
  SELECT vendor_name from vendors where region = 'WEST'
-->
<!--SCRIPT
  document.WriteLn( "We currently have " + SQL.GetRowCount()
    + " different vendors supporting the WEST region".);
-->
```

Because we did not provide a name for the query in the preceding example, the default name of SQL is used with the GetRowCount method to present how many vendors exist in the West region. In the example that follows, the query name is explicitly specified as listVendor:

```
<!--SQL NAME = listVendor
  SELECT vendor_name from vendors
-->
<!--SCRIPT
  document.WriteLn('There are ' + listVendor.GetRowCount()
    + ' total vendors in the vendor master file.");
-->
```

After we provide a name for the query in the preceding example, we can reference all query object methods for that object using its name, such as *listVendor.GetRowCount*. Table 9.5 further explains the methods available for the query object.

Table 9.5 *Query object methods.*

Method	Description
Close( )	Closes the query object.
Execute( )	Executes the query object's SQL statement.
GetColumnCount( )	Returns the number of columns in the query object.
GetColumnIndex(colName) query	Returns the index of the column named *colName* in the object, where the first column's index is 1. If there are no columns, this method returns a 0 (zero).
GetColumnLabel(colNum)	Returns the label of the column referenced by the column number (*colNum*). The label is either the column name or column alias as specified in the SQL statement of the query object.
GetEmpty( )	Returns true if the query object's result set is empty.

Continued

Table 9.5 *Continued*

Property	Description
GetErrorCode( )	Returns the current error code. Returns 0 (zero) if a SQL instruction is carried out correctly or other error codes, to which your script can respond if the SQL instruction fails.
GetErrorInfo( )	Returns a description of the error information.
GetRowCount( )	Returns the number of rows in the result set of the query object.
GetState( )	Returns the ODBC state of the query. Values returned by GetState depend on your ODBC driver. For more information, see your database's ODBC documentation.
GetValue(colNum)	Returns the value in the column referenced by the column number (*colNum*) for the current row of the query object's result set.
Move(rowNum)	Moves to the row in the query object's result set indicated by the row number (*rowNum*) passed into the method.
MoveFirst( )	Moves to the first row of a query object's result set.
MoveLast( )	Moves to the last row of a query object's result set.
MoveNext( )	Changes the current row to the next row of a query object's result set.
MovePrevious( )	Changes the current row to the previous row of a query object's result set.
MoveRelative(relativeRowNum)	Moves to a row that is *relativeRowNum* rows before or after the current row of a query result set. Examples: MoveRelative(-2) moves two rows before the current row while MoveRelative(10) moves 10 rows after the current row.
Opened( )	Returns true if a result set is available for the query object.
Refresh( ) new	Reexecutes the query object's SQL statement to obtains a result set. You should reposition your cursor following this method, because PowerDynamo may be unable to automatically position the cursor due to row deletions. To move the cursor to the first row of the result set, call the MoveFirst method or Move(0) method.
SetSQL(sqlStatement)	Sets the SQL statement in the current query object to the *sqlStatement* string.

The following template shows how you can use a query object in a script to access the results of an embedded query. This template executes a query on a vendor table and formats the result in a table. This functionality can be performed without scripts by simply using the PowerDynamo formatting tag. However, scripts offer more flexibility in what you can do with data prior to presenting it to users.

```
<HTML>
<TITLE>Top 25 Vendors</TITLE>
<!--SQL NAME=listVendors
    select
      vendor_name, sum(order_amount)
    from
      d_vendor, m_order
    where
      d_vendor.vendor_id = m_order.vendor_id
    group by
      vendor_id
    order by sum(order_amount), vendor_name
-->
<!--SCRIPT
    //Get number of columns
    nColCount = listVendors.GetColumnCount() ;
    //Start output results table
    document.Write( '<TABLE BORDER><TR>" ) ;
    //Write table column headers
    for ( nCol=1 ; nCol<=nColCount ; nCol++ ) {
      document.Write( '<TH> + listVendors.GetColumnLabel( nCol ) + </TH>" ) ;
    } ;
    document.WriteLn( '</TR>" ) ;
    //Write top 25 values from the result set
    while ( listVendors.MoveNext() ) {
      document.Write( '<TR>" ) ;
      for (nCol = 1 ; nCol<=nColCount ; nCol++ ) {
        document.Write( '<TD>" + lstVendors.GetValue( nCol ) + '</TD> " ) ;
      } ;
      document.WriteLn( '</TR>" ) ;
    }
    //Write the end of table tag
    document.Write( '</TABLE>" ) ;
-->
</BODY>
</HTML>
```

The *session* Object

Web connections are typically sessionless. Unlike conventional desktop applications, where users sign on and sign off to define a complete session, a Web site never know exactly when a user has ended a session. From any Web client, a user can jump from one Web site to another and back at any time. The Web server is typically ignorant of when a user comes or goes. Each session is a closed loop—a user requests a document and the server fulfills the request, at which time the communication is concluded.

When users leave a Web site, they may return in two minutes, in two days, or never. Some of this navigational activity is controlled by the directional buttons of browsers. Browsers promote such behavior through easily accessible directional buttons and history lists.

When developing a Web site, it is desirable to maintain some concept of a session between a Web client and the Web site, similar to the activities of traditional client-server applications. This can be accomplished through a welcome page that asks the user to log in with a name and password. From this starting point in a Web site, each available page can be required to "know" that the user has already logged in, typically through a session ID. If a page is requested when users aren't logged in with a session ID, the site needs a way to detect this and force them to log in. The PowerDynamo *session* object overcomes this problem by allowing the Web site to store information about a session with a Web client.

The PowerDynamo *session* object provides a way to store session information so that it persists for the duration of a particular client-to-site connection. Because there is no explicit end to a session, though, the duration of the connection must be decided arbitrarily through a timeout facility in PowerDynamo. By default, PowerDynamo considers a session to last five minutes from the time of the user's last action at the Web site. This default can be changed globally (as shown in Figure 9.20 on the following page) for an entire site or for a specific session object. You must restart the PowerDynamo application server for changes to take effect.

For the duration of a session, the site can maintain information about users' connections—login names, their last action, or whatever other information the site requests from the client. This assists in the overall robustness of a Web site. Chapter 5, "Web Architecture Essentials," discusses the concept of the state of a Web site or Web page. The capability in PowerDynamo to store state information based on a session lets you develop applications that recognize the state of any object in your site.

PowerDynamo stores session information in a *session* object. Each client of your Web site possesses one session object. A session object is accessible to all Web pages in the site, so they can check its status as they require. The duration of a session is defined in the *session* object's only predefined property, timeOut. After the specified duration elapses, the session object associated with the client is reset to null. A session object of null tells other Web pages that the session has ended and the user is no longer active.

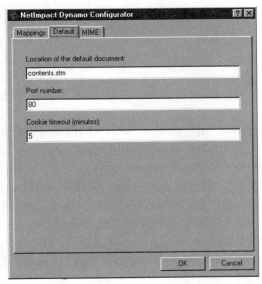

Figure 9.20 *You establish session timeout in the Cookie timeout (minutes) field of PowerDynamo Configurator.*

You can extend the *session* object by defining additional properties that are required to track other application-specific attributes of a client's session, such as state. The information that you associate with the *session* object typically comes from client input, such as an HTML form. A login page might prompt each user for a name and password. The client sends the requested information as a URL with arguments. For example:

```
http://www.objx.com/start_session.stm?uname=dba&pwd=sql
```

The receiving document, **start_session.stm**, reads the incoming values, performs the task of logging the user onto the system by comparing the values to a password list or database table, and sets a property in the session object accordingly. For example, the following statement sets a user-defined property called loginCorrect if the user's login is correct:

```
session.loginCorrect = true ;
```

Until the session times out, other pages can then check the *session.loginCorrect* property when they load to validate the user. For example:

```
<!--SCRIPT
    if ( session.loginCorrect == false ) {
      document.WriteLn( "Permission denied." );
    }
    else {
      // show authorized content here
    }
-->
```

Internally, PowerDynamo implements the *session* object through cookies. A cookie, as explained in Chapter 5, "Web Architecture Essentials," is a small chunk of information that is passed between a Web client and Web server. Cookies are a general-purpose mechanism that server-side connections can use to store and retrieve information on the client-side connection. Cookies provide a way for a site to remember information about an individual client and the client's sessions.

The *site* Object

DynaScript's *site* object extension allows you to interact directly with your Web site. Using the *site* object, you can manage documents and database connections, and customize the management interface of your Web site to suit your needs. Only one instance of a *site* object can exist, so you cannot create additional *site* objects in your scripts.

In a PowerDynamo Web site, you can manage documents and database connections via Sybase Central or by writing your own scripts. Either way, the *site* object is responsible for basic management tasks. The *site* object also provides methods that allow you to perform common management tasks, such as:

- Creation and management of templates and scripts in your Web site.

- Creation and management of the connections to databases, providing the live content for your Web site.

- Creation and modification of wizards to suit your work style and content needs.

- Addition of menu items and icons to the SQL Central interface to use the wizards that you create.

As you work with PowerDynamo, you will quickly realize that the management tasks provided with the Sybase Central plug-in are performed in scripts. With PowerDynamo management driven by scripts based on DynaScript, you can alter these scripts or create new ones to tailor the interface to your development and management needs. You can, for example, extend the PowerDynamo interface to include your own wizard dialog and controls or integrate third party add-ons, such as Java applets, in your PowerDynamo templates and scripts. Table 9.6 highlights the methods that are available with the *site* object.

Table 9.6 *Site object methods.*

Method	Description
CreateConnection (connName, description, dataSource [, userName, password])	Creates and returns a new connection object. *connName* is a string that contains the name of the connection *description* is a string that contains a comment for documenting the pupose and use of the connection object *dataSource* is a string that contains the name of the ODBC data source used by the connection object *userName* is an optional string defining the database user for the connection.*password* is an optional string defining the database password for the database user.
CreateDocument(docName, documentType, description, content [, connectionName connectionId])	Creates and returns a document object. *docName* is a string defining the name of the document, which should include the absolute path for the document. (Example: "/Site/Sales/demographics.stm") *documentType* is a string defining the type of document, which can be one of the following: **directory:** a PowerDynamo folder **directoryLink:** a PowerDynamo linked folder **image:** a binary file **script:** a DynaScript file **text:** a PowerDynamo HTML template*description* is a string that describes the purpose and use of the document. However, if *documentType* is *directoryLink,* the description is the path of the disk-based folder. *content* is a string that contains the document's content *connectionName* and *connectionId* are optional parameters to define the connection used for the document. You provide either the connection name or the connection ID, not both.

Continued

Table 9.6 *Continued*

Method	Description
CreateWizard(wizardObject)	Starts the wizard defined by the parameter *wizardObject*, which is an indexed object. Each array element in the object represents a separate wizard page with the following properties: *type* is the kind of input required for the page, which can be one of the following: **text:** single-line text box **password:** single-line text box with typed characters shown as asterisks for security **textArea:** multiline text box **choice:** combo box of values (uses choices) **sql:** SQL-query textArea with button to open query editor. **fileBrowse:** single-line text box with Browse button to open standard file-selection dialog *explanation* is explanatory text for the page (ignored if type is *sql*) *question* is text that prompts for the value (ignored if type is *sql*) *choices* is an array of the enumerated values for the combo box (if type is *choice*) *selected* is the number of the element of the choices array that is the default when the wizard page is displayed (if type is *choice*) *value* is the value entered by a user when the wizard is created.
DeleteConnection(connName)	Deletes the connection object defined by the string variable *connName*.
DeleteDocument(docName)	Deletes the document object defined by the string variable, *docName*. *docName should* contain an absolute path.
GetConnection(connName | objectId)	Returns the *connection* object defined by either the *connName* string or *objectId* integer. You provide only one of these variables.
GetConnectionIdList( )	Returns an array of IDs of *connection* objects.
GetConnectionNameList( )	Returns an array of names of *connection* objects.

Continued

Table 9.6 Continued

Method	Description
GetDocument(docName | objectId)	Returns the document object defined by the variable string. *docName,* or the integer variable, *objectId.* If you use *docName,* you should include the absolute path. Either*docName* or *objectId* is supplied to this method, not both.
GetEventList([controlType])	Returns an array of all *controlType* event handlers currently installed by the OnEvent method. If *controlType* is not specified, all installed event handlers are returned.
GetRootDocument( )	Returns the *document* object representing the root document of the Web site; in most cases, this the *Site* folder.
Include(scriptName)	Returns a string with the generated output from the script named *scriptName*, which should include either the absolute or relative path for the desired script.
OnEvent(itemType, controlType, , controlLabel description, handlerScript)	Adds an event handler to the management interface, typically for creating an icon or menu item in Sybase Central, for which: *itemType* is the type of item that the control applies to, which may be one of the following: **connection:** any *connection.* **connectionFolder:** the *connection*'s folder. **directory:** any document folder. **image:** binary data; not a script or a template. **script:** any script. **site:** the Web site database; not the Web site folder. **text:** any template *controlType* a variable string that contains one of the following: **Get:** contains the command from the Web server when a document is requested. This applies to *directory, image, script, site, and text* types. **NewMenu:** displays a new menu option with a menu.

Continued

Table 9.6 *Continued*

Method	Description
OnEvent(itemType, controlType, , controlLabel description, handlerScript) *(continued)*	**ContextMenu:** menu that appear when users right click. **Icon:** displays the system routines of a site, directory, or ConnectionFolder. *controlLabel* is the visible name of the control. *description* is descriptive text that documents the control, which is displayed on the Sybase Central status bar *handlerScript* is the script to trigger when the control is used; its path is relative to the script from which the OnEvent method is called.
Schedule(docName, frequency, time)	Adds a template or script to PowerDynamo's list of scheduled documents. *docName* is a string with the absolute path of the scheduled template or script, typically with an *.sts* or *.sss* extension. This scheduled document runs at the defined frequency and writes its output to a document with an *.stm* or *.ssc* extension, respectively. *frequency* is a string that defines the frequency at which the docName is executed, which can be one of the following: **Hourly:** time is the number of minutes into the hour. Example: schedule("/site/bigjob.sts", "Hourly", "45"). **Daily:** time [HH:MM] is the time of day. Example: schedule("/site/bigjob.sts", "Daily", "20:30"). **Weekly:** time [day HH:MM] is the day and time. Example: schedule("/site/bigjob.sts", "Weekly", "Monday 23:45"). **Monthly:** time [DD HH:MM] is the date and time. Example: schedule("/site/bigjob.sts", "Monthly", "1 20:00"). **Yearly:** time [month DD HH:MM] is the date and time. Example: schedule("/site/foo.sts", "Yearly", "December 31 23:45").

The *site* object offers several benefits to improve development and run-time system enhancements in a data warehouse environment. The development enhancements primarily center around generating wizards that incorporate standards when generating prototypes. The run-time enhancements lie in the area of push technologies.

The *schedule* method of the *site* object allows you to take common or long-running reports and execute them at planned intervals. This allows you to define a subscription-based interface to information packages. When a data warehouse is loaded and information package data changes, you can trigger these schedules to be reexecuted. The results of the scheduled templates or scheduled scripts can include static HTML forms or other MIME type documents, such as e-mail. This flexibility allows you to build an interface to your application that queries users for their planned reporting periods—the result being a push oriented data warehouse server.

Summary

PowerDynamo offers the missing link that brings the HTML and JavaScript standards together, allowing you to deliver truly dynamic Web sites to your data warehouse. Sybase extends these standards with syntax and objects that focus on dynamic content. Sybase also delivers a system management framework that merges the tasks of database administration and Web site administration, which allows you to centrally manage your data warehouse.

Sybase's PowerDynamo product set brings the world of dynamic content and database application services to the Web. PowerDynamo has been built on three distinct components, which provide this flexible implementation:

- An application server that links your database to your Web server.

- A personal Web server, which allows your users to work offline with dynamic Web content.

- A site management tool, which manages your database-hosted Web site.

The Powerdynamo architecture allows you to overcome many of the inherent problems of other Web site architectures. For instance, some file-based Web site tools create a separate file for each resource or component of the complete application. For large Web sites, this leads to management problems including the ability to:

- Maintain current copies of hundreds or thousands of components.

- Maintain links among the various components.

- Build common code libraries to support the various aspects of an overall system.

- Have a comprehensive operational architecture for backup, recovery, and replication.

Powerdynamo solves these and many more problems to provide a robust back plane on which a Web-based data warehouse can be built. Section IV, "Case Studies," further investigates Powerdynamo from a physical implementation point of view. The case studies presented in that section provide you with an understanding of the code behind the implementation when you write your Web-based data warehouse. But prior to the case studies, Chapter 10, "Adaptive Server IQ Essentials," investigates Adaptive Server IQ in an optimized data warehousing data store, while Chapter 11, "PowerDesigner Essentials," investigates PowerDesigner, a design and architecture tool for data warehousing.

10

Sybase Adaptive Server IQ Essentials

It is no secret that, to fully succeed in data warehousing efforts, you must team up your information systems personnel with the business users. A data warehouse implementation goes much further than simply focusing on getting data into a traditional database that users can access. Data warehousing is both a technical and a business project; in fact, a majority of today's data warehouse projects are funded by lines of business.

A properly built data warehouse takes operational data that is used to run the business and makes that data available to knowledge workers. The users want to ask questions concerning how the business is running. The answers to the users' questions assist business personnel in growing the business.

One area of great confusion in data warehousing is what database management system to use. Early data warehouses were built with a centralized architecture—a single physical database managing all information. These systems became known as enterprise data warehouses. The process of building this type of centralized warehouse proved to be extremely costly, often resulting in massive project failures. The lesson learned by these initiatives is: *Nothing is simple about building an enterprise data warehouse in a single physical database.* Issues arose, such as:

- It is difficult to get buy-in from all parties who must be involve in such mammoth efforts.

- The various source systems offer too many inconsistent forms of data on incompatible systems.

- The investment requirement for the hardware and software to implement such a system is immense.

- The amount of time and effort to get a satisfactory return on investment is far greater than expected.

These large scale enterprise data warehouse implementations often left those involved with huge disappointments. The finished system typically only functioned for a small number of users, who analyzed a few reports that executed highly predictable, preplanned queries. These user and access restrictions kept the information away from those who desperately needed it.

Data Marts to the Rescue

Subject-oriented data warehouses, or data marts, have proven to be a successful alternative to enterprise data warehouses. Many companies have found data marts that provide a successful strategy for deploying information-centric solutions. A data mart typically:

- Focuses on a single business-problem domain, such as sales or customer management.

- Allows for a high number of user interactions.

- Supplies rapid response to user queries.

- Is highly scaleable to grow as the business grows.

- Costs less to implement due to proper scoping of business requirements.

- Is more distributed with the data being closer to users.

- Provides quicker return on investment than enterprise data warehouses.

Strategies surrounding data marts have become popular because they reduce the cost of implementation and increase the speed of delivery for decision support applications. Many studies have shown that implementing a full-scale enterprise data warehouse is costly and that data marts provide a higher return on investment while reducing the overall cost of development. The reasons for these results stem from the factors shown in Table 10.1.

Table 10.1 *Factors driving strategies behind data marts and data warehouses.*

Factor	Data Mart	Data Warehouse
User community support	Single organization	All organizations in enterprise
Subject areas	Limited number	All enterprise subject areas
Operational sources	Limited applications	All applications
Problem domain	Single functional area	Wide problem scope

Enterprise data warehouses tend to be driven by information systems professionals. These individuals know and understand how to centrally manage, administer, and deliver systems, but they often lack a true understanding of how the business operates. Data marts, on the other hand, are highly distributed, closer to the user, and are driven by the user.

These two belief systems—central versus distributed—are in conflict. A data mart strategy tends to be more successful, because the focus and scope of the problem are on a given user organization. The user will therefore buy into the concepts and process of developing a data mart. This acceptance translates into active involvement in the process of defining the business requirements and problem domain. This clear understanding of the requirements makes data marts and user-driven development the chosen strategy for success in data warehousing. This strategy parlays into success, as follows:

- Data mart projects are completed in a more rapid fashion than enterprise data warehouses—measured in months, not years.

- Data mart projects cost less than enterprise data warehouses—measured in hundreds of thousands of dollars, not millions of dollars.

- Users requirements are met on a more rapid basis through the delivery of data marts.

- User involvement is more focused, based on the problem domain defined by data marts.

- User commitment and participation are much higher with data marts.

Based on these factors, a data mart strategy is a subcomponent of an overall data warehouse for any enterprise. The data warehouse should be view as the consolidation of all of the subsystems that fulfill an enterprise's decision support requirements. In the instance of data marts, the enterprise data warehouse includes all data marts, such as a sales and marketing data mart, a finance data mart, and a manufacturing data mart. In addition to the data marts, the enterprise data warehouse may consist of consolidation data stores, which include operational data stores and staging areas used in the process of transforming data from operational, feeder systems to the ultimate target data mart.

This chapter uncovers the key issues and challenges for selecting a proper data store for your data mart, or subject-oriented data warehouse. This information assists in simplifying your architectural search for a decision support database.

Sybase Adaptive Server IQ: Interactive Decision Support Server

Sybase Adaptive Server IQ is a software tool that is designed to assist and optimize decision support system queries to allow organizations to more readily develop interactive data warehouses. Specifically, Adaptive Server IQ's design goal is to increase the speed of decision support queries performed against large amounts of data. With this understanding, it can be stated that Adaptive Server IQ has been designed to fulfill the large demand for a relational database management system technology that is focused on decision support queries.

In talks around the country, I often ask database administrators in the audience if they would ever place an index on a column that contains a person's area code, a student's grade point average, or a customer's total transactions. The response is a resounding *no!* The reasons for this adamant response is typically technology based, such as:

- We only index based on standard, well known paths, such as name, due to the overhead of indexes.

- The cardinality, or unique occurrence of the data, would force the database to perform a table scan anyway.

Yet, when you ask users what information they need to fulfill their job responsibilities, they respond with requirements such as:

- To see the number of people by area code in my territory to more effectively manage my promotions.

- To understand who the top ranked students are in the graduating class so the proper interviews can be arranged.

- To see which customers do business with our company and spend between $100,000 and $500,000 annually.

Each of these three requirements characterizes a different user request, yet they all perform similar functions: They are decision support oriented queries. User information requirements are driven by a need to access data, but the users' access patterns are not compatible with the traditional relational databases indexing strategies. In short, the technology of traditional relational databases gets in the way of the applications' success. The primary difference is how each technology handles the indexing of data—traditional relational databases build indexes based on query demands; Adaptive Server IQ builds indexes based on data characteristics.

Adaptive Server IQ is one of the only open relational products that have chosen to solve these requirements in the technology. Adaptive Server IQ is a high-performance, decision support server designed specifically for information-centric applications such as data marts. Specifically, Adaptive Server IQ offers a unique solution centered around the following innovative features:

- Vertical data storage management.

- Index-centric storage.

- Data compression.

- No contention parallelism.

- Ad hoc query optimizer.

We investigate these items further in the following sections.

Vertical Data Storage Management

Most relational database managers have been built on a horizontal storage manager, which places all data in a database by row, or record, as a transaction occurs. A database table is represented as a chain of database pages that contain one or more data rows. A horizontal storage manager provides fast online transaction processing (OLTP) support, because most transactions occur in a record format. However, when a user requests a record, the database page that contains the data is moved into memor, which for decision support applications, this technique is highly inefficient.

When a database performs a read to bring in the associated data page, more data than is required to fulfill the user's request is retrieved, including additional, unrequested rows and columns. This type of disk I/O works well for OLTP style applications, which typically have smaller volumes of data and explicit record requests, such as account_number 17. However, reading entire records from disk poses a problem in decision support queries. User queries in a data mart typically involve data from thousands or millions of rows in a table. Further, most user queries focus on a subset of the total columns of the overall row in one of these stored records.

Adaptive Server IQ's vertical storage manager reduces I/Os for queries, which assists those who must manage the decision support database in delivering query performance. Instead of storing data by row, Adaptive Server IQ stores data by column—hence the name, vertical storage manager. The Adaptive Server IQ method of storage is a revolutionary approach to storing data, and is a highly effective way to solve the problem of user queries, because users typically request only certain columns of information.

In Adaptive Server IQ, data is stored as a series of page chains, with each page containing column data for a table, not row data. To process a query, Adaptive Server IQ only reads the required column values from disk. This technique dramatically reduces the disk I/O required to process a query by a factor that can easily reach as high as 500 to 1.

Traditional relational database products often solved this I/O problem by placing parallel scanning techniques into the database. This technology reduced the execution time required to perform these complex queries. However, the same number of I/Os occurred and the cost of implementing such a solution exceeded many companies' budgets. Because Adaptive Server IQ reduces the I/Os required to resolve these decision support queries, the parallel scanning techniques employed by other databases aren't needed. Therefore, Adaptive Server IQ can support more concurrent users with much less hardware than these traditional database products.

Index-Centric Storage

When investigating traditional relational databases, it helps to look at their heritage. Relational databases were developed after years of research that tried to simplify the ability to query data. These databases offered a new and different interface, SQL, which allows users to query a database and deliver reports to reduce the backlog of user's requests for more information and more reports. These databases tried to attack the installed databases, which were focused on transactions. Therefore, vendors of relational databases such as Sybase and Oracle were forced to prove that along with their ease of use they could handle the transaction volume required by in-place production systems. The architecture behind these databases involved physically storing transaction data in rows and building indexes on top of these rows to simplify and accelerate retrieval of the data on common paths, as shown in Figure 10.1.

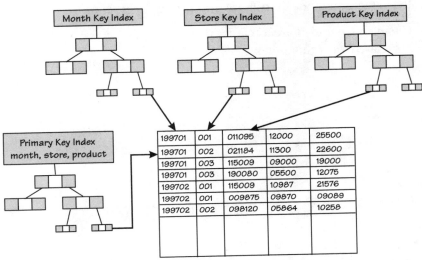

Figure 10.1 *Traditional relational databases store data as transactional rows and overlay these rows with indexes to simplify retrieval of the data.*

Indexes are a set of data structures used by a database management system to reduce the amount of work required to answer a user query or update request. Workload reduction was achieved through the database's capability to avoid searching all or large parts of a database's underlying tables to fulfill user requests.

Traditionally, relational database management systems such as Sybase Adaptive Server Enterprise, Oracle, Informix, and Microsoft SQL Server used a variation of a B-Tree, or balanced tree, index architecture for their indexes, as shown in Figure 10.2. These index technique assists a database management system in locating and identifying the data pages that physically contain the values requested in a query. The B-Tree approach to indexing minimizes the amount of index data that a database management system must browse to retrieve data requested by a user or an application. As shown in Figure 10.2, to select a customer with the name of *Hammergren*, the database management system performs the following steps:

1. Start with the top index and determine that *Hammergren* is less than *I*.

2. Based on the determination of step 1, navigate the index structure to the left.

3. Compare *Hammergren* against the index pointers at the level *E* and *I*.

4. *Hammergren* is greater than *E* and less than *I*; therefore, follow the appropriate index path.

5. Reevaluate the index structure at this new level, *F* and *H*.

6. *Hammergren* and *H* are a match; therefore, retrieve the data page associated with this index.

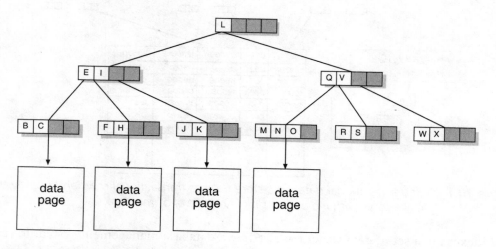

Figure 10.2 *Traditional relational databases use B-Tree Indexing to improve access speeds during query processing.*

B-Tree indexing allows a database management system to traverse the tree that comprises the pointers into the raw data. Upon each descent into a node of the B-Tree, the data pages are cut in half. The root, or top, of the tree has a left or right direction, each representing half of the data. From the second level node, you see a left or right direction, each representing a quarter of the data, and so on. This allows you to quickly traverse the index tree to reach your destination data. The B-Tree index therefore allows user to quickly find and retrieve a small number of rows with well-defined access parameters, such as a name. Without indexes, a traditional relational database must perform a table scan. With indexes, a traditional relational databases can provide faster access to the requested data. Traditional B-Tree index techniques offer two primary benefits: They allow the database to find a particular row quickly and they allow the quick update of individual rows.

Unfortunately, users of decision support applications do not frequently perform either of these tasks, so a decision support system sees less benefits from B-Tree indexes than OLTP applications. OLTP applications benefit from B-Tree indexes due to their frequent need to find and update individual rows within database tables. B-Tree indexes in fact may decrease the performance of some decision support applications; at best, B-Tree indexes minimally help decision support applications.

Part of the reason for such low benefit offered by B-Tree indexes stems from the fact that the index data structures are the same and the performance characteristics are the same regardless of the data type or number of unique values contained by an indexed column. B-Tree indexes excel in highly selective queries. Highly selective queries are those that find a few rows with high-cardinality data, data which has a high number of unique values. These types of queries are common for OLTP systems. B-Tree indexes do not offer performance improvements for low cardinality data, data which has only a few unique values, such as sex with only two values. An index on such a field is costly to implement and does not enhance query performance proportional to this cost.

In decision support applications, highly selective queries are not the norm. In fact, most decision support queries are highly *un*selective. For a decision support database to support typical user queries, other indexing techniques are required. Adaptive Server IQ offers five indexing techniques, each of which is targeted at a different query problem. Sybase built the IQ indexing schemes on a theory that a relationship exists between a column's cardinality, or the number of distinct values in a column, and the column's usage in SQL. (These schemes are detailed in the "Adaptive Server IQ Index Types" section later in this chapter.) Some of Sybase's findings included:

- A column with less than 1,000 unique values (low cardinality) tends to be used most frequently in the SQL *where* and *group by* clauses. These columns are usually used in comparison expressions such as equal or not equal filtering. It is rare to see these columns used in range comparisons. Columns that fit these characteristics include customer demographics, such as sex, income band, and age band or location dimensions, such as country, region, state, and district.

- A column that contains high cardinality data, for example over 100,000 unique values, tends to be used in SQL *where* clauses and in aggregation functions. Columns that fit these characteristics include measures, such as revenue, expenses, units, yield, and waste pounds.

In addition to these usage findings, Sybase noted that the dynamic nature of the data was also closely related to the cardinality. If, for instance, a column started with a cardinality of 50, it rarely grew larger than 100 over time and would certainly not grow to include 100,000 values. Therefore, low cardinality columns tended to be more static than dynamic. On the other hand, columns with high cardinality were frequently dynamic and could continue to grow large over time. The static or dynamic nature of the data managed by Adaptive Server IQ is another area where knowledge of data patterns and data usage can yield additional query performance. This performance is generated by a database better understanding the predictability of query behavior on a given column.

Adaptive Server IQ introduced this patent pending indexing technology, referred as *Bit-Wise* indexing. This technique for indexing data has proven to be quite effective for decision support applications in the range of 100 gigabytes to nearly 1 terabyte. Unlike B-Tree structures, Adaptive Server IQ indexes provide fast access for larger result set retrieval and allow all data to effectively participate as an index. Adaptive Server IQ has also created an environment in which index searches can be evaluated in parallel with each other. This base of technology and architecture make Adaptive Server IQ ideal for applications with the following characteristics:

- Heavy use of ad hoc query.

- Tables that require a large number of indexes.

- Tables that are both wide (large number of columns) and high (large number of rows).

- Queries that involve aggregations (*count, sum, min, max, avg*) contained in data groupings (*group by*).

- Queries that involve range searching (*between, <, <=, >, >=*).

- Applications that do not require real-time updates.

Data Compression

Tools such as Stacker and PKZIP have revolutionized the personal computer industry. The ability for these tools to squeeze more information into a restricted space have offered great benefits to many of their users. It is rare to find someone who has not used PKZIP. PKZIP is often used to fit large documents or presentations onto floppy disks, which is then sent to another user or placed on another personal computer using "sneaker net." Stacker provided similar compression for the entire operating environment or hard disk versus PKZIP's focus on file-by-file compression. Each of these technologies has contributed to better techniques for storing data in the personal computer market. So why have database vendors not delivered similar compression technology?

Traditional relational database products leverage B-Tree indexes to access raw transaction data. A VLDB study conducted by Winter Corporation (http://www. wintercorp. com) in 1996 cited data explosion rates from raw data to realized data warehouse in the 3-to-8 times range due in large part to B-Tree indexes. Table 10.2 presents some of the Winter Corporate findings.

Table 10.2 *Data explosion of raw data to realized data warehouse.*

Hardware	Database	Raw Data	Total Disk	Ratio
Tandem K10000	Non-stop SQL	100GB	286GB	2.86
Digital 8400	Oracle	100GB	361GB	3.61
IBM SP2	DB2/6000 PE	100GB	377GB	3.77
Sun UE	Oracle	100GB	594GB	5.94
HP 9000	Oracle	100GB	643GB	6.43
NCR 5100	Teradata	100GB	880GB	8.80
NCR 5100	Teradata	300GB	880GB	2.93
Pyramid RM1000	Oracle	300GB	1,535GB	5.12
IBM SP2	Oracle	300GB	1,977GB	6.59
HP 9000	Adaptive Server IQ	450GB	235GB	0.52
NCR 5100	Teradata	1,000GB	3,280GB	3.28

The ratio of data explosion shown in Table 10.2 demonstrates the inefficiencies in the B-Tree structures used by traditional relational database management systems. The reason for these inefficiencies are due to issues including:

- Data in traditional databases is stored by row with a horizontal storage manager. This type of storage does not compress well, because the data patterns, such as repeat values, do not highlight themselves when stored horizontally. Compression of 5–10 percent is typically the best case in a horizontal storage management scheme.

- The overhead of compressing and decompressing the small 2–4KB page sizes of these traditional relational databases is high. An OLTP environment has a large mixture of reads and updates. Each update requires a compression operation. A read requires a decompression operation. These costs impose a significant slow down in a traditional relational database's transaction rate. For this reason, many database vendors have avoided such technologies.

Adaptive Server IQ utilizes compression to offer greater cost savings for decision support applications. Because Adaptive Server IQ has a vertical data storage manager, greater compression occurs. Because the data is stored by column, not by row, the patterns of data repetition are more obvious, allowing Adaptive Server IQ to better compress the data. Adaptive Server IQ generally compresses raw data with a ratio of 0.25 to 0.50. This data compression allows queries to gain significant speed compared with traditional database structures due to a large reduction in disk I/O and the ability to represent the data in a smaller space.

No Contention Parallelism

B-Tree indexes are designed for well-defined index paths. This design characteristic supports transaction oriented systems as well as relatively simple query processing. In a decision support environment, we can make several observations about this architecture, including:

- Though originally developed to support better query processing, the relational databases of today are more focused on data that is stored in a transactional format.

- To read the data in a relational database, you typically must make multiple jumps. The first jump reads the index information and finds where the desired data is stored. Then, you move to the physical location in the database to retrieve the raw data. This architecture forces you to design databases that are not query friendly.

- Directing all query activity to use the indexes is preferable if not required. But the concept of an index in a traditional relational database is added after the data and only used sparingly throughout the data.

In addition to these observations, it should be noted that modifications by database vendors allow their databases to store vast amounts of transactional data. This scalability has improved dramatically over the years, making these databases a tempting technology for a data warehouse. However, the more data you have, the greater the need to provide efficient, indexed access to it. So database vendors have developed additional technology to compensate for index architecture flaws. This technology, known as parallelism, has been the rage of the database industry for the past few years.

Every vendor uses the term parallel to describe something about their product, yet there no standard definition exists. The vendors have us all confused. But one thing is for sure: *We all know it will make something happen faster*.

Parallel processing solves performance problems, often I/O based, through the use of additional processing power offered in hardware. Database management system software is modified to leverage additional hardware resources, which optimizes inefficient processes. The easiest way to describe parallel database and query technology is that the database is split into segments and queries are performed against each segment independently to build a consolidated result, as shown in Figure 10.3.

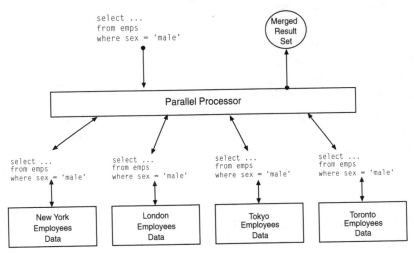

Figure 10.3 *A parallel processing engine can take a query and simultaneously use resources to build a composite result set from multiple working queries. Here, the search is for all employees throughout a human resources databases stored in physically separate locations.*

The parallel processing techniques of traditional relational database vendors produces fast response time to queries, but does so with approximately the same level of I/O as conventional relational technology at a much higher cost. This cost stems from the increased need of hardware to support an overall environment. This additional cost and associated support make these products only financially viable for only the largest database applications.

The ability for traditional relational databases to perform these parallel table scans is an approach that targets symmetrical multiprocessor (SMP) hardware and preplanned queries. This type of processing is similar to mainframe batch processing. However, this approach has many shortcomings, including that these queries can become slow and degrade overall performance of a data warehouse when several complex queries run simultaneously.

Adaptive Server IQ takes a different approach to parallelism, which is focused on decision support usage models. In a multiprocessor SMP environment, Adaptive Server IQ distributes CPUs across users. Adaptive Server IQ uses the parallelism model around users. That is, it is designed for an ad-hoc, multiuser decision support environment. Adaptive Server IQ maximizes total query throughput for multiple, simultaneous queries rather than maximizes throughput for one query at a time.

Adaptive Server IQ optimizes data manipulation operations to maximize query throughput. This processing takes full advantage of modern hardware platforms, which incorporate fast processors, large memory caches, and parallel, or symmetric-multiprocessing, architectures. Adaptive Server IQ breaks low-level operations, such as sorts, bitmap manipulations, and I/O, into nonblock operations, which the operating system can schedule independently. With this type of processing, Adaptive Server IQ ensures scalability and consistency of performance as data or users are added to the decision support application. What is important about all of this is that the Adaptive Server IQ architecture enables multiple processors to share query tasks while permitting the system to execute many simultaneous queries with little or no performance degradation. For specialty tasks such as database loading, Adaptive Server IQ uses parallelism to harness the full resources of the system and provides excellent performance in processing-intensive tasks, typically loading 2–4GB per hour with bursts up to 8GB per hour.

Adaptive Server IQ Indexing

A data warehouse manages and organizes a large volume of operational data for informational and analytical processing. The heart and soul of a data warehouse is a relational database management system in which the data for a data warehouse is stored and managed. When users place their demands on a data warehouse for information to better understand the answers to critical business questions, technological factors often can cause dissatisfaction.

Data warehouse systems issue queries that span a performance range of interactive, ad-hoc queries requiring near-real-time response to complex analysis queries that are submitted for processing and expected to incur long response times. Decision support activities such as drilling down and drilling up force a database engine to perform various aggregation calculations and can force queries to scan and entire or large part of a fact table. Computational aspects of these queries include joins, group bys, sorts, and aggregation functions. Taking all of this activity into account, it is not hard to see why the number one problem for data warehouses and their management is performance.

Typically, a tuning problem is associated with a bad join or *where* condition in a *select* statement of a query. For proper performance, database administrators find themselves forced to constantly tune a database and its associated user queries. This needn't be the case.

Adaptive Server IQ is a revolutionary product that provides a specialty server for interactive data warehousing. Adaptive Server IQ's unique functionality hinges on its ability to manage a data store from a pure index base versus traditional databases, which manage raw data with indexes pointing to that data. The benefits from the indexing approach of Adaptive Server IQ include:

- Elimination of the data explosion forced by traditional data storage techniques, where indexes are added to data managed by relational databases.

- Significant speed up in decision support queries due to processing enhancements offered by indexes, such as the elimination of table scans.

- The ability to work against lower-level detail data, avoiding the denormalization and preaggregation on which developers of data warehouses have come to depend.

Adaptive Server IQ easily integrates into most client/server or host-centric environments due to its architecture, which is based on the standard Sybase Open Client and Open Server connectivity infrastructure. As shown in Figure 10.4, these interfacing techniques allow you to index a variety of data sources via loading from Sybase Adaptive Enterprise Server, Sybase Enterprise Connect(OMNIConnect and DirectConnect) products, or flat files. The product can be accessed from client-side applications through a variety of interfaces, including Sybase's DB-Library, Sybase's CT-Library, or ODBC Open Client APIs using ANSI-standard SQL.

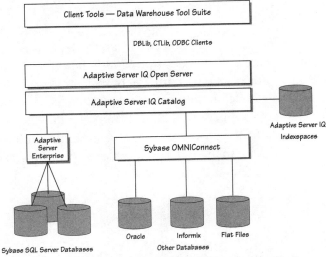

Figure 10.4 *The Adaptive Server IQ architecture relies on the interfacing mechanisms provided by Sybase's Open Client and Open Server connectivity infrastructures.*

Relational Architectural Comparison

To best understand the physical structures behind Adaptive Server IQ, it may help to compare traditional relational structures with Adaptive Server IQ's structures. Adaptive Server IQ is an indexing service that transforms data into a highly interactive environment for query activity, in essence Adaptive Server IQ tunes its internal data structures, or indexes, based on the attributes of the data. Therefore, the place where Adaptive Server IQ content is stored is referred to as an *indexspace* (see Figure 10.4).

Standard relational databases store data in a database. Therefore, an analogy can be drawn between a database and an indexspace. The core storage mechanism in a relational database is a set of columns organized in a table. All relational algebra works against a table with discrete work performed against the columns. Because Adaptive Server IQ works on an indexing paradigm, the core storage mechanism is a set of indexes that are stored in sets much like a table. The equivalent term for a set of indexes is an *indexset*. Table 10.4 illustrates these architectural mappings between a traditional, general purpose, relational structure and the highly specialized, query-centric structures of Adaptive Server IQ.

Table 10.4 *Traditional relational structure compared to Adaptive Server IQ structure.*

Relational Structure	IQ Structure
Database	Index Space
Table	Index Set
Column	Index

Indexes improve performance for data retrieval in databases. Adaptive Server IQ indexes directly represent data and therefore provide much greater performance characteristics than traditional indexes, which utilize B-Tree strategies. Adaptive Server IQ indexes are based on a firm understanding of user query behaviors. Sybase quickly realized that, in decision support applications, all data must be indexed and that data represents either a low number of values (low cardinality), or a high number of values (high cardinality). Understanding how many unique values can occur for a given column allows Adaptive Server IQ to optimize its indexing strategy.

Data Cardinality

An important factor with a technology such as Adaptive Server IQ is the cardinality of data values. Cardinality describes the relationship between two items. In an entity relationship diagram, cardinality defines the relationship between tables, such as a one-to-many relationship. An example of this is ORDERS relates in a one-to-many fashion to ORDER_LINE_ITEMS; or in English, each order has many line items. Cardinality in Adaptive Server IQ refers to the relationship between an index, or data column, and the unique values contained in that index. Understanding the cardinality of data in an index plays an important role in selecting which Adaptive Server IQ index should be used for a column of data. Figure 10.5 presents the cardinality for many of the dimension entities discussed in this book.

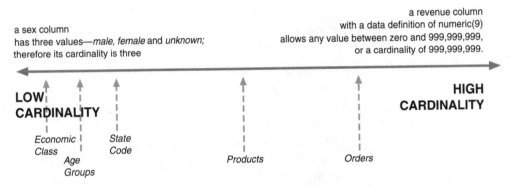

Figure 10.5 *Cardinality of data can span from low cardinality data with few unique values to high cardinality data with a large number of unique values.*

Low Cardinality Indexing

Low cardinality indexing has been around since the 1960s and has been used by a variety of database products, such as Model 204 and Paradox. This indexing technique delivers faster query performance on unselective data than traditional B-Tree Index techniques. Many of the columns in decision support applications contain low cardinality data—potentially up to 75 percent of the columns. Therefore, the ability to handle low cardinality data well is important to data warehouse applications.

Adaptive Server IQ has applied a unique low cardinality indexing technique to relational SQL query processing. In Adaptive Server IQ, a bitmap data structure is created, with each value in the column indexed. The bitmap structure is simply an array of binary data bits, each possessing a value of 1 or 0. Each bitmap structure is a chain of data pages in a database. Each offset in the bitmap represents a row in the database. Adaptive Server IQ's implementation of this indexing scheme makes operations such as obtaining all rows with a specific value quite rapid and the counting of rows with specific values are lightning fast.

Adaptive Server IQ's implementation of low cardinality indexing is vastly different from other implementations. Most of these other implementations are only useful at the low end of cardinality, such as less than 50 unique values contained with a column of data. This strategy allows databases to optimize on columns that contain data such as state codes. As the number of unique values increases, the cost also increases and the usefulness decreases in these non-Sybase implementations. The reason for this decrease in viability in other implementations stems from index size explosion. Adaptive Server IQ solved this problem by adding data compression. Sybase's patented technology in this area allows a Adaptive Server IQ database to optimally store low cardinality indexes with anywhere from 500 to 1,000 unique values.

High Cardinality Indexing

Probably the most radical improvement in data storage technology offered by Adaptive Server IQ rests with high cardinality data. Though 75 percent of stored data may involve low cardinality data, nearly 90 percent of all queries may involve high cardinality data. Think of how many user queries in decision support involve monetary data, units of measure, and other high cardinality data. Adaptive Server IQ's ability to optimally manage this data is what differentiates this product. While other databases resort to table scans of data, Adaptive Server IQ indexes this data and eliminates the concept of a table scan.

High cardinality data typically is used in aggregation functions and *where* clause range selection expressions. If a data warehouse indexes every dimension column in a sales measure table and you do not index the facts, such as revenue, what happens when a user requests all sales between $100,000 and $500,000? Traditional relational databases read each row in the sales measure table, asking itself if the revenue figure is between $100,000 and $500,000. If the data meets the criterion, the row is kept; if the data does not meet the criteria, the row is ignored. What if your sales measure table has a billion rows? Traditional databases are forced to read all billion rows. Adaptive Server IQ will only read those rows which match the criterion, and if this is only 100,00 rows think of the query time savings.

Processing is quite different in Adaptive Server IQ than in these traditional relational database implementations. The primary difference is that Adaptive Server IQ indexes the fact column, such as revenue, providing all of the benefits of indexing to these high cardinality columns. Any decision support query that focuses on this type of data reaps the rewards of such an index, which doesn't include reading the billion rows of the preceding example.

In the Adaptive Server IQ architecture, high cardinality column definitions instruct the product to create a bitmap for each bit of precision in the data that is indexed.

Organizing the data in this fashion reduces the size of the data while naturally clustering the data values. This organization combined with Adaptive Server IQ's data compression allows a high cardinality index to be stored in 20 percent or less of the raw data size.

The optimal storage techniques of Adaptive Server IQ combined along with the indexing of high cardinality values is a potent solution when combined with the operational aspects of a relational database. Adaptive Server IQ's computational capabilities are extremely quick, including the abilities to determine which rows are in a range of values and to compute aggregations such as summaries and averages. Due in part to a unique storage of the data, it is not uncommon to see Adaptive Server IQ perform 10 to 100 times faster than traditional relational databases that use B-Tree scanning.

Adaptive Server IQ Index Types

With traditional relational databases, indexes tune a database for specific queries. Adaptive Server IQ uses indexes based on column data characteristics and usage. This process of defining data structures requires a different mindset than the traditional thinking of preplanning expected queries that occur with traditional database indexes. The basic index types used by Adaptive Server IQ include:

- **Low Fast:** A Low Fast index is composed of columns containing data with a relatively small number of unique values, such as state codes, sex, income band, and age band. The data in such a column can be represented as a bitmap efficiently and effectively. Adaptive Server IQ lets you take advantage of bitmap indexes for columns with up to 500 or more unique values. The Low Fast index can be used for all functions, such as group by, range, or equality searches.

- **Low Disk:** A Low Disk index is an alternate value-based bitmap structure for low- to medium-cardinality data. The data in such a column can be represented as a bitmap efficiently and effectively. Adaptive Server IQ lets you take advantage of bitmap indexes for handling columns with up to 1,000 or more unique values. The Low Disk index can be used for all functions, such as group by, range, or equality searches.

- **High Nongroup:** A High Nongroup index is composed of columns that have many unique values or continuous data. Examples of this pattern of data include monetary values such as revenue and date values such as date of birth. User query behavior on this type of data frequently involves aggregating or range searches. The High Nongroup index uniquely applies bitmap technology to columns with more than 1,000 unique values. The result is an index that provides excellent performance and highly compact storage.

- **High Group:** A High Group index type shares the attributes of the High Nongroup index, but adds the usage pattern of grouping of distinct and ad-hoc join processing. To address these usage patterns by users, Adaptive Server IQ provides the High Group index, which shares the basic configuration of the High Nongroup, but adds B-tree style structures in a database to optimize for group processing. Examples of columns that can use this index type include zipcodes and customer IDs. The High Group index does everything well, but has higher storage requirements than the High Nongroup index due to the addition of the B-Tree style data structures.

- **Fast Projection:** A Fast Projection index covers all data that is directly manipulated in a database's columns. The Adaptive Server IQ Fast Projection index, which stores data in compressed form by column, is optimized for operations that directly use the data. The SQL *like* operator, columns projected in a *select* list, and complex arithmetic operations are some for a Fast Projection index.

Choosing Adaptive Server IQ Index Types

The indexing capabilities of Adaptive Server IQ revolve around the specific index types: Fast Projection, Low Fast, Low Disk, High Nongroup, and High Group. Adaptive Server IQ indexes are extremely small, so you can define multiple indexes for each column. When defining indexes for columns, each column will typically have one Fast Projection index and one of Low Fast, Low Disk, High Non Group, or High Group index types. This strategy allows users to query any attribute of their data with consistently excellent performance. The appropriate index is selected based on three important criteria: data cardinality, as shown in Table 10.5; user query patterns, as shown in Table 10.6; and disk space usage, as shown in Table 10.7.

Table 10.5 Index selection based on data cardinality—the number of unique column values.

Number of Unique Column Values	Recommended Index Type
All columns no matter how many unique values	Fast Projection
Below 500	Low Fast
less than 1,000 (very large values)	Low Disk
Above 1,000	High Group or High Nongroup

Here are some examples of columns with different data cardinality, or numbers of unique values:

- A marital status dimension, which has few unique values (single, married, NULL), making it a candidate for a Low Fast index.

- A gender dimension, which has few unique values (male, female, unknown, NULL), making it a candidate for a Low Fast index.

- A state or province dimension, which has fewer than 100 unique values, making it a candidate for a Low Fast index.

- An account number or social security number dimension, which may have thousands or millions of unique numbers, making it a candidate for a High Group or High Nongroup index.

The information packaging methodology, specifically its information packaging diagram, can assist you in understanding how data in the columns of your data warehouse generally will be queried. For example, answers should come easily for your data requirements in areas such as:

- Will the column be part of a join predicate?

- Will the column be in the projected columns returned by a *select* command of queries that return a large number of rows?

- If the column has a high number of unique values, will the column be used in a *group by* clause, will it be the argument of a *count distinct*, or it be in a *select distinct* projection?

Areas of a information package diagram will assist you in answering these and many other questions. Dimensions and their categories will typically be used to filter or group data, while measures will be used in aggregate functions such as SUM, AVG, and so on. In addition, specific types of data will be used to fulfill user requests, such as: a date column will probably be used for range searches in *where* clauses and a column that contains prices or sales amounts will probably be used in a projection as an argument for aggregate functions (SUM, AVG, and so on). Adaptive Server IQ can still resolve queries involving a column indexed with the wrong index type, although it may not be as efficient.

Table 10.6 shows recommended Adaptive Server IQ index types based on query usage. This recommendation should be combined with the recommendations in Table 10.5 to derive the optimal index type for your data.

Table 10.6 *Index selection based on user query patterns—the type of query activity performed on a column.*

Type of Query Usage	Index Type Recommended	Index Type *Not* Recommended
In a SELECT projection list Nongroup	Fast Projection	High Group, High
In calculations in a *where* clause	Fast Projection	Low Disk
AVG or SUM argument	Fast Projection, High Nongroup, Low Fast, High Group	Low Disk
MIN or MAX argument	Fast Projection, Low Fast, High Nongroup	Low Disk
COUNT argument	Fast Projection, High Nongroup, Low Fast, High Group	Low Disk
LIKE argument in *where* clause	Fast Projection	
Column in ad hoc join	Fast Projection, High Group	High Nongroup
COUNT DISTINCT, SELECT DISTINCT, or GROUP BY arguments	Fast Projection, High Group High Group, Low Fast	High Nongroup
If field does not allow duplicates	Fast Projection, High Group, Low Fast	High Nongroup
Columns in joined indexset	Fast Projection, High Group, Low Fast	High Nongroup
Column in range queries	Fast Projection, High Group High Nongroup	Low Fast

Depending on the type of index you select, Adaptive Server IQ uses different amounts of disk space to manage the index structures. Disk space usage can be estimated based on the index type in conjunction with a direct comparison to the amount of column data in the raw source data, such as underlying database or flat file. See Figure 10.7.

Table 10.7 *Index selection based on disk space usage.*

Type of Index	Estimated Spaced Versus Raw Data
Fast Projection	Smaller than or equal to raw data
High Group	Two to three times larger than raw data
High Nongroup	Less than Fast Projection size
Low Fast	Ranges from very small to 1.5 times to very large
Low Disk	One third to one half the size of the raw data

Implementing Adaptive Server IQ

Adaptive Server IQ uses a data definition language (DDL) that is similar to the standard SQL database DDL. This language allows you to define the proper structures for IQ to store indexed data and populate those data structures. Adaptive Server IQ's catalog information is stored in a physical Sybase Adaptive Server Enterprise database. This catalog database is referred to as the *catalog server*. When you define your DDL, you have two sets of definitions:

- Database definitions that define the traditional database structures, such as tables and columns.

- Index definitions that define the indexes that overlay the database structures, such as indexsets and indexes.

These two definitions are similar to the DDL generated for traditional relational databases. In all databases, you define the tables and columns followed by the indexes for optimizing data access. With Adaptive Server IQ, you typically index all of the raw data. However, you can use Adaptive Server IQ in a mixed environment in which you only index a portion of you data warehouse and leave the remaining data in a more traditional relational database.

Adaptive Server IQ can access many different types of data, including Sybase Adaptive Server Enterprise, Oracle, and flat files. Therefore, this product can enhance any data warehouse environment, regardless of the vendor of choice for your database management. If a request is submitted to Adaptive Server IQ and it cannot be fulfilled in its indexspace, it will simply pass the request along to an attached database for fulfillment.

Using the Information Package Diagram to Assist in Index Selection

Indexing for an information package diagram and its associated measure entities is demonstrated in Figure 10.6. As discussed in Section I, "Introduction to the Information Packaging Methodology," a measure entity is derived from the lowest-level category in each dimension (items 1 through 6 in Figure 10.6) and from each of the measures (items 7 through 11). Each of these columns can be indexed. Figure 10.6 presents a chart describing the potential index types to be used based on the cardinality and use of the associated data.

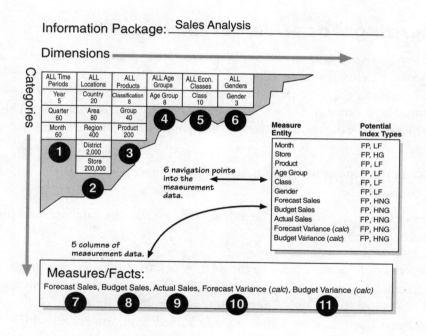

Figure 10.6 *Adaptive Server IQ index selection and translation is easy from an information package diagram, which tells you the cardinality and usage patterns of the key criteria in selecting Adaptive Server IQ index types.*

The DDL for the information package shown in Figure 10.6 is as follows.

```
/* ============================ */
/* Database name: SalesIQmodel */
/* ============================ */
IQ create indexspace for SalesIQmodel,
go
/* ======================= */
/* Table: m_sales_analysis */
/* ======================= */
create table m_sales_analysis
(
 month_key int not null,
 store_key int not null,
 product_key int not null,
 age_group_key int not null,
 economic_class_key int not null,
 gender_key int not null,
 sales_forecast money not null,
 sales_budget money not null,
 sales_actual money not null,
 variance_forecast money not null,
 variance_budget money not null
)
go

/* ========================== */
/* Indexset: m_sales_analysis */
/* ========================== */
IQ create indexset for m_sales_analysis
(
 month_key int not null,
 store_key int not null,
 product_key int not null,
 age_group_key int not null,
 economic_class_key int not null,
 gender_key int not null,
 sales_forecast int(0,2) not null,
 sales_budget int(0,2) not null,
 sales_actual int(0,2) not null,
 variance_forecast int(0,2) not null,
 variance_budget int(0,2) not null
)
go

/* ============================== */
/* Indexes for: m_sales_analysis */
/* ============================== */
IQ create index msa_month_key_fp on m_sales_analysis
 (month_key) FP
go
IQ create index msa_month_key_lf on m_sales_analysis
 (month_key) LF
go
```

```
IQ create index msa_store_key_fp on m_sales_analysis
 (store_key) FP
go
IQ create index msa_store_key_hg on m_sales_analysis
 (store_key) HG
go
IQ create index msa_product_key_fp on m_sales_analysis
 (product_key) FP
go
IQ create index msa_product_key_lf on m_sales_analysis
 (product_key) LF
go
IQ create index msa_age_group_key_fp on m_sales_analysis
 (age_group_key) FP
go
IQ create index msa_age_group_key_lf on m_sales_analysis
 (age_group_key) LF
go
IQ create index msa_economic_class_key_fp on m_sales_analysis
 (economic_class_key) FP
go
IQ create index msa_economic_class_key_lf on m_sales_analysis
 (economic_class_key) LF
go
IQ create index msa_gender_key_fp on m_sales_analysis
 (gender_key) FP
go
IQ create index msa_gender_key_lf on m_sales_analysis
 (gender_key) LF
go
IQ create index msa_sales_forecast_fp on m_sales_analysis
 (sales_forecast) FP
go
IQ create index msa_sales_forecast_hng on m_sales_analysis
 (sales_forecast) HNG
go
IQ create index msa_sales_budget_fp on m_sales_analysis
 (sales_budget) FP
go
IQ create index msa_sales_budget_hng on m_sales_analysis
 (sales_budget) HNG
go
IQ create index msa_sales_actual_fp on m_sales_analysis
 (sales_actual) FP
go
IQ create index msa_sales_actual_hng on m_sales_analysis
 (sales_actual) HNG
go
IQ create index msa_variance_forecast_fp on m_sales_analysis
 (variance_forecast) FP
go
```

```
IQ create index msa_variance_forecast_hng on m_sales_analysis
 (variance_forecast) HNG
go
IQ create index msa_variance_budget_fp on m_sales_analysis
 (variance_budget) FP
go
IQ create index msa_variance_budget_hng on m_sales_analysis
 (variance_budget) HNG
go
```

Using the Star Schema Diagram with IPM Notation to Assist in Tuning

Adaptive Server IQ offers few data oriented tuning options. Aside from index types, the other data oriented tuning option is a structure known as *joined indexsets*. Joined indexsets let you prejoin tables ahead of time when you know that they will be necessary for complex queries. This type of structure may improve performance significantly for queries that involve joins. As with any tuning operation, you should wait until you experience a problem before you solve it. Nevertheless, the information packaging methodology can assist in this tuning of Adaptive Server IQ.

An information package clearly defines all entities that are likely to participate in a relational join. As shown in Figure 10.7, the star schema model of your information package illustrates the dimensions, category details, and measure entities that could be placed in one joined indexset. Creating a Adaptive Server IQ joined indexset structure optimizes searches through fact tables to provide the much needed descriptive information that is contained in the dimension entities.

The DDL required to create a join indexset as illustrated in Figure 10.7 is as follows:

```
/* ======================= */
/* Joined Index: ji_sales_analysis */
/* ======================= */
IQ create joined indexset ji_sales_analysis for
d_time_period(month_key) = m_sales_analysis(month_key) ONE>>MANY,
d_location(store_key) = m_sales_analysis(store_key) ONE>>MANY,
d_product(product_key) = m_sales_analysis(product_key) ONE>>MANY
d_demographics(age_group_key, economic_class_key, gender_key) =
m_sales_analysis(age_group_key, economic_class_key, gender_key) ONE>>MANY
go
```

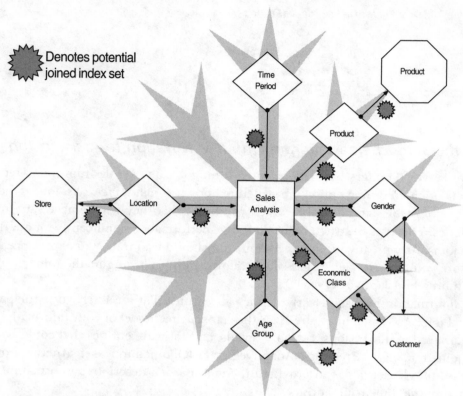

Figure 10.7 *Adaptive Server IQ join indexset definitions can easily be derived from a star schema diagram.*

Adaptive Server IQ Compared to Other Specialty Servers

Adaptive Server IQ is one of the only technologies designed from the ground up to address the complexities of ad hoc decision support query processing for many users. Other database products that target decision support solutions often focus on data storage at the expense of fast, cost-effective data access. The major categories of these database solutions fall into the categories of traditional relational databases, multidimensional databases, and proprietary solutions.

Traditional Relational Database Products

Traditional relational database product are those built on the relational model. These products include Oracle, Informix, Microsoft SQL Server, and Sybase Adaptive Server Enterprise. The products in this category support fast execution of structured queries in an OLTP environment. Based on this design, the indexing technology is optimized for access to individual records, requiring these fixed access paths to be preplanned by database administrators (DBAs) prior to releasing access to users. In other words, traditional relational databases place indexes within the data structures based on the requirements to tune known queries.

Traditional relational database architectures rely on B-Tree, balanced-tree indexes, which typically cause a data explosion rate of two to six times the size of the raw data. These products have begun to introduce additional indexing capabilities to better support decision support applications. These new indexes include bitmap indexes that reduce the amount of data that must be scanned to complete the query. However, for many queries these techniques do not reduce the result set sufficiently to avoid extensive scans of the underlying database tables.

Other techniques used by these products include creating preplanned aggregate tables as part of the overall physical implementation of a star schema. Prestoring aggregate data and hardware-intensive parallel processing techniques add significantly to the cost of the systems.

The approaches used by traditional relational database products tend to limit either query flexibility or the number of users whom the system can support. It should go without saying that all of these tuning approaches require extensive DBA involvement, delaying user requests and limiting flexibility. With this in mind, it is safe to say that traditional relational database products compromise between the needs of OLTP and decision support system (DSS) applications.

Based on their design, traditional relational database products will never be as good at pure DSS as a database optimized exclusively for this purpose. The foundation of Adaptive Server IQ is that all data is indexed and the indexes are based on the characteristics of the data, not the characteristics of user queries. Performance of Adaptive Server IQ is driven by accessing only the information relevant to each query from the Adaptive Server IQ data set. Adaptive Server IQ internally optimizes performance for all types of queries and data types and consumes less system resources. The end result is fast answers to most questions for many users. Though it may be hard to believe, Adaptive Server IQ can be 100 times or more faster than a traditional relational database, especially in processing ad hoc queries.

The limitations of traditional relational databases include:

- Optimized for structured, instead of unstructured (ad hoc), queries.

- Uses space-consuming B-tree indexes, preplanned aggregates (star schema), or costly, hardware-intensive processing techniques.

- Has limited techniques for handling high-cardinality data analysis.

- Degrades ad hoc query performance significantly as users are added.

Parallel Relational Database Products

Parallel relational database products solve many of the tuning problems discussed in this chapter through the use of hardware-enhanced software. These products include offerings from Oracle, Informix, and Teradata. The parallel processing activities performed by the products alone do not reduce the actual amount of work in resolving a query. In fact, it only spreads the work across more hardware. These products spread brute force analysis across many CPUs and disk drives. With the level of resources brought forth by these products, they are very good at processing large amounts of data, specifically preplanned batch jobs. Parallel processing can reduce times for large bulk processing operations that scan all data in terabyte-sized databases.

The downside to parallel relational database products is that these products require a lot of expensive hardware. And as more users try to execute their queries at the same time, the resources allocated to each user quickly diminish and performance degrades. From a support point of view, these products are not for the faint of heart. Parallel relational databases are complex to keep operational and lack the flexibility to respond to changing query requirements.

In contrast to parallel databases, Adaptive Server IQ actually performs less processing work while providing the same query speeds as parallel technologies. Adaptive Server IQ effective solves many of the same problems that have been the mainstay of parallel databases on data in the 100 gigabyte to a terabyte data range. But, because Adaptive Server IQ solves a majority of the problems with its architecture and through software means, a Adaptive Server IQ solution is deployed on far less hardware and at much less expense. Adaptive Server IQ makes extensive use of the most advanced parallel processing techniques to get the most productivity out of any hardware investments.

Multidimensional Databases

Multidimensional database grew from the need for rapid response to users' predefined queries. This makes multidimensional databases ideal for repetitive analysis environments, such as financial analysis and executive information systems (EIS) applications. Products that fit into this classification include Arbor's EssBase and Oracle's Express databases. Multidimensional databases require database administrators to preplan all anticipated queries along specific dimensions and require complete rebuilding of a database if these structures change. Typically, the total number of dimensions that a user may have to navigate a multiple dimension database is restricted.

This type of restriction make multidimensional databases a poor alternative for customer intelligence applications. In an environment in which you are evaluating information about people and their behavior patterns, such as customer intelligence or database marketing, dimensions can easily fall in the 50 to 100 range. This large number of dimensions allows a user to access the data in ways that far exceed the ability of multidimensional database technologies. The database structures supported by multidimensional databases are simply unable to house and deliver this type of information.

With this type of restriction, applications are directly affected. As the number of dimensions or the number of values for a dimension increases, data must usually be constrained into ranges or specific buckets. Multiple databases are created with the same data at different levels of aggregation to circumvent this problem. Such problems restrict users' ability to access or cross-correlate their detail data.

Multidimensional databases deliver smaller data sets while offering limited scalability. Typically, a multidimensional database will not handle more than several hundred megabytes of raw data, and even this may force load times to exceed 24 hours. Many of the problems of data capacity stem from a multidimensional databases data explosion factor, which is often 100 to 1,000 times the size of raw data.

Therefore, multidimensional databases limitations include:

- A requirement of preaggregation of data.

- A loss of ad hoc flexibility due to the lack of detail data.

- A large size explosion from raw data to realized database.

- A need to rebuild if data or queries change.

- Nonstandard access tools; because interfaces to multidimensional products are proprietary, the number of off-the-shelf end user tools is restricted.

Like multidimensional databases, Adaptive Server IQ provides rapid responses to user queries. Unlike multidimensional databases, Adaptive Server IQ keeps the data at the detailed level, providing the full flexibility of the relational model and allowing any relationships between data elements to be explored immediately.

Multidimensional database products support a limited number of proprietary applications, so users have few tools from which to choose. With Adaptive Server IQ, users can look at data in a multidimensional way without incurring the cost of a DBA to set up a customized database each time query requirements change. Adaptive Server IQ is compatible with a wide-range of popular off-the-shelf tools.

OLAP Servers

To overcome many of the weaknesses of traditional relational databases discussed in this chapter, hybrid technologies are beginning to emerge. These products combine the good features of all of the classifications discussed in this chapter into an open solution. These products include ROLAP (relational online analytical processing) tools, such as Information Advantages Decision Suite; DOLAP (desktop online analytical processing) tools, such as Cognos PowerPlay; and HOLAP (hybrid online analytical processing) tools, such as Gentia.

ROLAP tools build a semantic layer, which maps the multidimensional nature of data onto a relational database structure. These products work in various ways, the most common of which is to create "in-memory" data cubes. These data cubes are refreshed directly from a database server such as Adaptive Server IQ. With some ROLAP tools, the in-memory data cubes persist beyond a user's session, although this is rare. Typically, users pay a high price for their initial query, and as they begin to restrict the data in their analysis, the in-memory data speeds their access.

DOLAP tools work by prebuilding a data cube and placing it near users, either on their desktop or a LAN disk device. These tools provide rapid response time to user queries, including drill-down and slice-and-dice operations. This rapid response is on a fixed set of data, which provides insight at an aggregation level. If users want to access more detailed information than is available in a cube, they can perform a drill-through operation to obtain data from the data warehouse. In Cognos PowerPlay, these drill-through operations occur by linking a PowerPlay cube with an Impromptu query. PowerPlay understands when the drill-through design is available and offers to retrieve the detail data for the user only at those points in the data cube.

HOLAP is a hybrid of these approaches. A HOLAP server typically creates a multiuser data cache, or data cube, on a server. Users make their request through a proprietary tool set to this data cube, and like with DOLAP tools, users can drill through to the detail. The benefit that HOLAP offers is that the cubes are more centrally maintained, but you are still restricted to a proprietary tool set.

Summary

Adaptive Server IQ is a database management product that you can place in your architecture as middleware in conjunction with another database or as the actual database server. The engineers at Sybase designed Adaptive Server IQ to provide a software tool that assists and optimizes decision support queries to enable organizations to more readily develop interactive data warehouses. Specifically, Adaptive Server IQ increases the speed of decision support queries performed against large amounts of data. Adaptive Server IQ indexes all the data within the decision support database and the indexes are created based on characteristics of the data not characteristics of user queries.

Adaptive Server IQ fulfills the demand for relational database management system technology that focuses on decision support queries. This database thinks like users think in an ad hoc inquisitive style. Database administrators need not think twice about indexing all of the data required by users. If a user desires to query based on a person's area code, a student's grade point average, or a customer's total transactions—no problem. The initial implementations of Adaptive Server IQ have reduced the technology barriers of traditional relational databases.

Sybase could advertise Adaptive Server IQ similarly to the old Miller Lite television commercials that featured retired football players screaming at each other: "Tastes Great." "Less Filling." With Adaptive Server IQ, if you want your users to truly drink from the information cup, you know that they will want to drink a lot. With the speed and compression of Adaptive Server IQ technology, users can do so fast and at a low cost.

If your users' information requests involve queries, they typically force a traditional database to perform table scans, such as:

- To see the number of people by area code in a territory to more effectively manage promotions.

- To identify the top ranked students in a graduating class to arrange proper interviews.

- To see which customers do business with a company and spend between $100,000 and $500,000 annually to target them for a sales campaign.

Adaptive Server IQ is a high-performance, decision support server specifically for information-centric applications, such as data marts, that can help you deliver on your user requirements. It is one of the only open relational products that solves these requirements. Adaptive Server IQ offers a unique solution centered around the following innovative features: vertical data storage management, index-centric storage, data compression, no-contention parallelism, and an ad hoc query optimizer. The case studies in Section IV further discuss the physical aspects of Adaptive Server IQ. But for now, we move to Chapter 11, "PowerDesigner Product Essentials" to investigate how to automate the design process behind a data warehouse.

11

PowerDesigner Essentials

Sybase has reintroduced its highly successful design tool, SDesignor, under then new name of PowerDesigner. This product is one of the first tools that has placed the focus on designing and architecting data warehouses. The WarehouseArchitect component of PowerDesigner builds models for a data warehouse or decision support system based on multidimensional methodologies, such as the information packaging methodology. WarehouseArchitect defines functionality of entities in a data model through icons and allows designers to use color schemes to enhance the meaning and grouping of entities in a model. These features make PowerDesigner an excellent fit when implementing a data warehouse using the information packaging methodology. Prior to delving deeper into the WarehouseArchitect component, we take a closer look at the overall PowerDesigner product family.

The PowerDesigner Family

Plenty of software are in today's marketplace assist with maintaining data models. However, few focus on the quality required to provide a complete architectural tool for data warehousing. PowerDesigner provides a majority of the functionality needed to automate the complete design and architecture of a data warehouse.

When selecting a tool to manage this process, make sure that it contains items such as:

- Logical data modeling.

- Domain management.

- Physical data modeling.

- Data definition language generation.

- Reverse engineering of legacy data models.

- Native database support.

- Complete model reporting and documenting.

- OLAP semantic layer interfacing and generation.

- Multidimensional modeling.

PowerDesigner supports the various disciplines required to design and architect data-centric applications such as a data warehouse. PowerDesigner has a strong heritage in database modeling. The major components of the PowerDesigner family, shown in Figure 11.1, include:

- **MetaWorks** is a metadata repository.

- **DataArchitect** is to model and architect relational models.

- **WarehouseArchitect** is to model and architect multidimensional models.

- **AppModeler** is to model and architect "data model centric" application objects in data-aware environments.

- **ProcessAnalyst** is to support the data discovery and documentation of processes in an overall system architecture.

This chapter focuses on the functionality of PowerDesigner that will assist you in your data warehousing endeavors. It should be noted that PowerDesigner also provides comprehensive design and architecture functionality for more traditional, OLTP and client-server system development. This means that you can standardize on one tool for your entire enterprise data modeling and architecture needs.

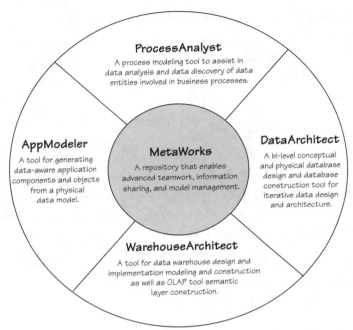

Figure 11.1 *The PowerDesigner Product Family offers a comprehensive modeling solution that business and systems analysts, designers, DBAs, and developers can tailor to meet specific needs.*

PowerDesigner's DataArchitect

PowerDesigner's DataArchitect component allows you to take information package diagrams created with the information packaging methodology and translate them into your targeted relational database environment. Models managed by DataArchitect include a conceptual data model and a physical data model. The interfacing between the conceptual and physical models of information packages is bidirectional, reflecting changes made in one model to the other.

The conceptual, or logical, modeling process is not closely aligned to any given database management system. The separation of a logical definition from a native database management system allows you to begin compiling a model of enterprise data sources without being concerned with physical attributes. The physical attributes are further developed after a conceptual model is ready to be transformed and implemented into a physical model. To demonstrate the conceptual modeling activities in DataArchitect, we use the information package depicted in Figure 11.2.

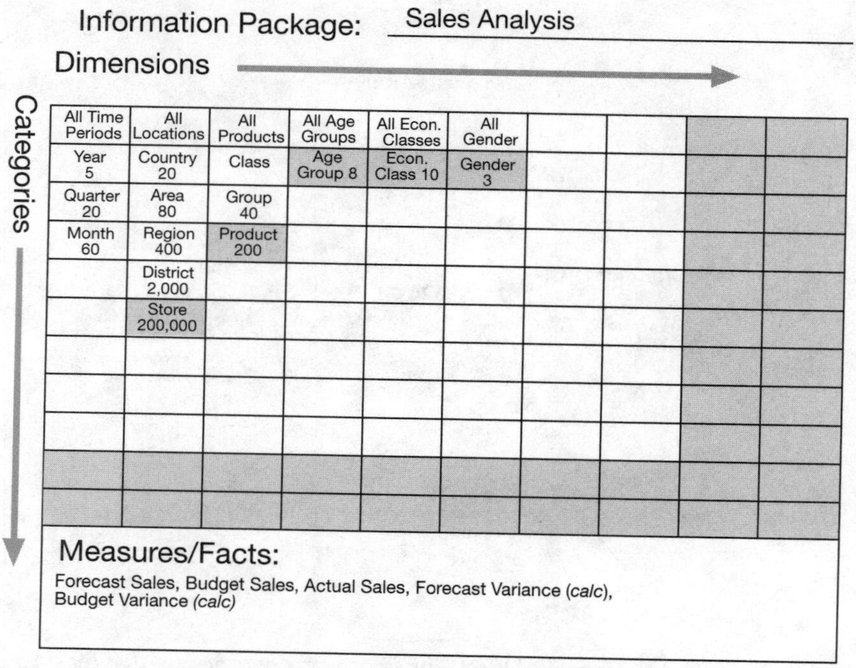

Information Package: <u>Sales Analysis</u>

Dimensions →

	All Time Periods	All Locations	All Products	All Age Groups	All Econ. Classes	All Gender				
	Year 5	Country 20	Class	Age Group 8	Econ. Class 10	Gender 3				
	Quarter 20	Area 80	Group 40							
	Month 60	Region 400	Product 200							
		District 2,000								
		Store 200,000								

Categories ↓

Measures/Facts:
Forecast Sales, Budget Sales, Actual Sales, Forecast Variance (*calc*), Budget Variance (*calc*)

Figure 11.2 *This Sales Analysis information package diagram presents a users' conceptual model of the requirements to analyze sales data.*

Conceptual Modeling

In DataArchitect, the design process is initiated with a conceptual data model (CDM). This model is physically stored in a CDM file. A CDM represents the overall logical structure of a database, which is independent of any software or data storage structure. This conceptual data model provides formal representation to the data required to deliver your information packages, or data warehouse. The CDM therefore:

- Represents the organization of data in a graphic model format.

- Verifies and validates the data design.

- Generates a physical data model, which specifies the physical implementation of the database.

As with any design and architecture component, DataArchitect stresses the importance of documentation. When you begin to define your CDM, it is important to clearly document the contents of the overall model. This is done through the DataArchitect Model Properties dialog box shown in Figure 11.3.

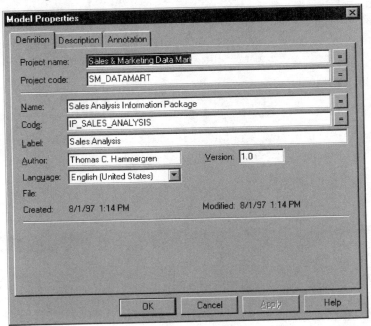

Figure 11.3 *The DataArchitect Model Properties dialog box lets you define the purpose behind a conceptual model. This dialog box accepts specific descriptions from its Definition tab as well as areas for free text input from its Description and Annotation tabs.*

You define many objects in your model. The following sections investigate some of the most important objects: including domains, entities, attributes, and relationships.

Defining Domains

Domains help you identify the types of information in your data warehouse models. A domain is a global and uniform definition for column properties. A domain definition contains a domain name, data type, length of the data, and decimal precision. Domain definition and management assist you in enforcing standards. By characterizing a set of common data types for a data warehouse, you standardize how the data is defined and implemented. As changes are required, you can simply modify the domain. All associated items using the domain will be adjusted to reflect the global change. In our first information package, we define several domains, including:

- **KEY** contains a character key that uniquely identifies a row in the specified table.

- **IDENTIFIER** contains a numeric key that uniquely identifies a row in the specified table.

- **LABEL** is a short description closely related to a key or an identifier. This type of data is primarily used to present data to the user in a friendly fashion.

- **DESCRIPTION** is a long text field that is verbose in its labeling of data.

- **PHONE** includes all the relevant defining characteristics of phone numbers.

- **DATESTAMP** is a data type meant to mark when data has change in some form; includes both the date and time of the change.

These domain definitions can be listed in PowerDesigner DataArchitect, as shown in Figure 11.4.

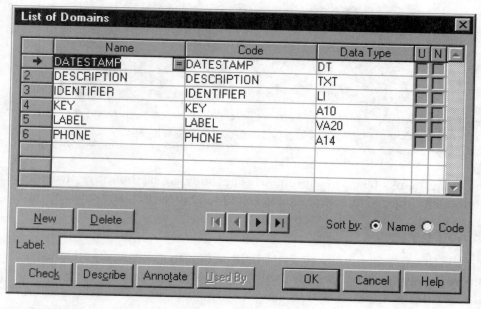

Figure 11.4 *PowerDesigner provides strong domain management facilities for defining and managing common global data definitions.*

Defining Entities and Their Attributes

An entity represents an object defined in an information package about which you want to store data. To derive the entities, we follow the process of transforming an information package diagram into a star schema, as discussed in Chapter 3, "Information Modeling." For our sales analysis information package this includes the entities shown in Table 11.1.

Table 11.1 *Sales Analysis information package entities.*

Entity Name	Entity Type	Comments
Sales Analysis	Measure entity	Manages all key measures regarding sales activities.
Time Period	Dimension entity	Manages all aspects of the company calendar, allowing us to perform time series analysis.
Location	Dimension entity	Manages the data that allows us to analyze the key business measures by location, or geographical territory.
Store	Category detail entity	A detail category in the location dimension, this entity provides more textual information about any store.
Product	Dimension entity	Manage the data that allows us to analyze the key business measures by product classification.
Product Details	Category detail entity	A detailed category in the product dimension, this entity provides us with more textual information about any product.
Age Group	Dimension entity	Contains the age band information that allows us to evaluate data based on the age demographic.
Gender	Dimension entity	Contains gender information that allows us to evaluate data based on the gender demographic.
Economic Class	Dimension entity	Contains the economic band information that allows us to evaluate data based on the economic classification demographic.
Customer	Category detail	A detailed category that provides textual information about customers. This entity can be navigated through each of the demographic entities (Age Group, Gender, Economic Class).

Each entity contains a set of attributes, or columns, that fully define the data that is managed by the entity, or table. These attributes relate closely to the physical model generated in Chapter 3, "Information Modeling."

Figure 11.5 presents the entity attributes definition dialog with the details of the m_sales_analysis entity.

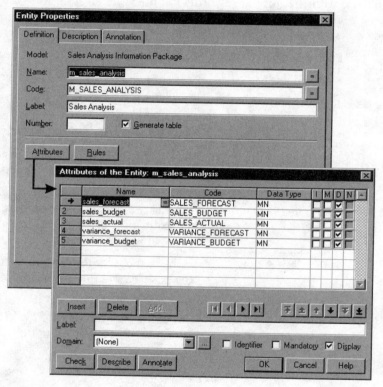

Figure 11.5 *Attributes are elementary pieces of information, or data items, attached to an entity. PowerDesigner DataArchitect lets you begin defining entity details in its Attribute of the Entity dialog box.*

Along with defining the attributes and their associated properties (type, size, and precision) you may also attach the entity attribute to a domain. If you do, the domain supplies the data type filed and related data characteristics. Each domain dictates a standard data type and length; it may also indicate decimal precision parameters.

Defining Relationships

A relationship is an association between entities. The association between entities defines several characteristics of the relationship, including:

- Reason for the relationship.

- Cardinality of the relationship.

- Dependencies between the entities in the relationship.

Relationships in a star schema model are well defined in the information packaging methodology. These relationships include dimension-to-measure and dimension-to-category-detail relationships. Understanding these relationships is critical to overall success in delivering a highly functional data warehouse. And as you will note in both of the above types of relationships, the dimension entities is the driving force in defining the relationship's characteristics.

The dimension-to-measure entity relationship has a cardinality of one to many. Each dimension entity row has at least one—but more than likely many—measure entity rows. In our sales analysis model, this statement can also be read as:

- For each time period, many sales occur.

- For each product, many sales occur.

- For each demographic (gender, age group, and economic classification), many sales occur.

- For each location, many sales occur.

The measure entity is typically depicted in the center of a star schema design. The measure entity is surrounded by dimension entities, which are placed at the points of the star. The dimension entity provides navigational capabilities into the measure entity. In addition, the dimension entity provides aggregation and filtering capabilities for the measure entity.

Various OLAP functions can be performed with this one-dimension-to-many-measure entity relationship. These functions include drilling down or up in a dimension. You also can navigate with one dimension, such as time period, and slice in a new dimension, such as product, to analyze the sales data along multiple dimensions and perspectives. These concepts of slice and dice and drilling down and up are supported through a one-dimension-to many-measure relationship. In PowerDesigner DataArchitect, you define all aspects of your relationships through the Relationship Properties dialog shown in Figure 11.6.

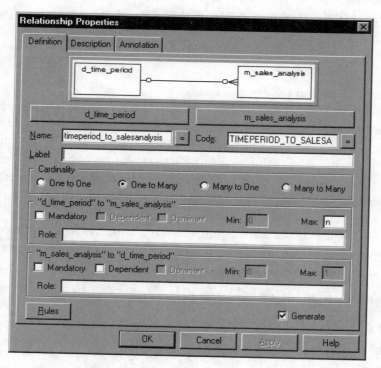

Figure 11.6 *The PowerDesigner DataArchitect Relationship Properties dialog box allows you to define the characteristics of an entity-to-entity relationship, including cardinality, dependencies, and reasons for the relationship.*

The dimension-to-category-detail relationship also has a one-to-many cardinality. Each dimension entity row has at least one—but more than likely many—category detail entity rows. In our sales analysis model, this statement translates into the following:

- Each demographic characterizes many customers.

- Each location locates many stores.

- Each product characteristic describes many products in detail.

The category detail entity is an extension of the dimension entity, which are the points of the star in a star schema model. Some design methods describe the category detail entities as *factless* measures. This definition stems from the ability to use dimensions to perform analysis on category detail entities that utilize counting as the primary metric, such as understanding the demographics of your most profitable customers. Such analysis is performed by counting the occurrences of common attributes in the category detail table. This functionality is heavily used in data mining and other statistically-based decision support applications.

After you have completed the definition of your domains, data items, entities and relationships, your logical model is complete. Figure 11.7 demonstrates the logical model as it appears in the PowerDesigner DataArchitect conceptual data model.

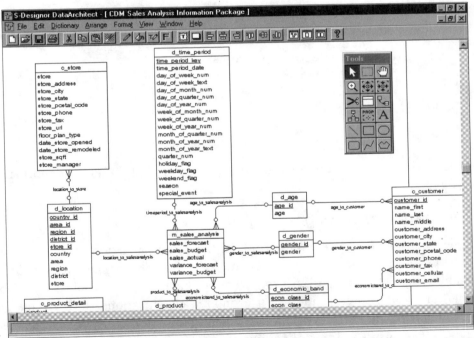

Figure 11.7 *The PowerDesigner DataArchitect conceptual data model allows you to maintain the logical definitions for your information package entities.*

Physical Modeling

Each database management system vendor has nuances, so it is good to build a physical model that shows how you have accommodated physical implementations of your data model. These activities are supported in DataArchitect's physical data model (PDM) and WarehouseArchitect's physical data model (WAM). We take a closer look at the WAM in the "PowerDesigner WarehouseArchitect" section later in this chapter; for now, we investigate the DataArchitect PDM.

DataArchitect automatically generates a PDM from a CDM. After the PDM is generated, you have several options to assist you in preserving the consistency between the conceptual model (CDM) and the physical model (PDM) managed by the DataArchitect. Your modifications which are made to the conceptual model (CDM) when building the physical model (PDM) can involve items such as:

- Defining primary keys.

- Defining referential integrity constraints.

- Denormalizing tables.

- Building aggregate tables.

- Partitioning data.

Let's look closer at a common requirement for modifying the PDM; denormalization of dimension entities.

Denormalization of Demographic Data

In our sales analysis model, we must work on the denormalization of the demographic tables. The tables that describe a customer through common demographics include gender, economic classification, and age group. The volumetrics of these tables (see Table 3.1 for details) are small: three genders, ten economic classifications, and ten age groups. Though valuable to the overall system, these tables are far too costly to maintain as individual tables. The cost is not in maintaining the tables; it is the cost to users, who would have to perform three additional database joins to retrieve demographic information. In reality, typically more than these three demographic tables are required, and implementing each demographic attribute as a separate table would increase the user cost by yet another database join. Additional demographics include items such as: home ownership, number of children, educational level, and other behavioral items related to purchasing trends.

The resolution to this issue is to merge the entities, or denormalize the demographic data structure. To perform this operation, we build and populate a central entity with all permutations of the demographic data. The number of rows can be calculated by figuring the overall permutations for the three entities, as indicated here:

```
3 genders * 10 economic classes * 10 age groups = 300 total demographic rows
```

A 300-row table is still small in terms of data warehousing applications, but offers far better usage for the desired user queries. Now, when a user requests data based on demographics only, one additional table will be joined to the measure entity versus the previous three. This denormalization greatly assists the performance of the overall system by reducing the server-based overhead required to obtain all of the relevant detailed information that users require. With the addition of this table, you should also note that the other tables have gone away, as shown in Figure 11.8.

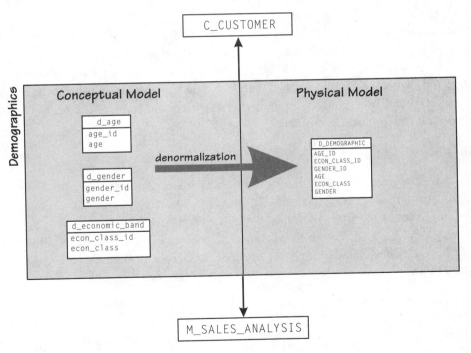

Figure 11.8 *Denormalization occurs frequently in the logical-to-physical database modeling phase of a data warehouse. Here, the demographic information is merged into one demographic table from three original entities.*

The newly merged demographic dimension entity now bridges the data contained in the sales measure entity and the customer category detail entity. In addition to this merger of data, you may also desire to place a single, uniform, system-generated primary key, also known as a synthetic key, to represent the demographic data. The decision on how best to handle the demographic table's primary key hinges on the volume of data involved with the merger and the type of front-end application. For our purposes, we only have three keys and we have kept them as the primary key to the demographic table. This primary key implementation is completed by defining the separate demographic keys and a primary key, which is comprised of a segmented index into the demographic data. This assists in our front-end tool by eliminating additional joins if the keys are easily mapped to user understandable values, such as "M" for male and "F" for female in the gender demographic dimension. In this gender demographic dimension example, *sex = m* or *f* doesn't require a join to the demographic table to retrieve data from the measure table. Such elimination of joins through the use of intuitive data values can easily enhance the performance of user based queries.

In situations that have 10 to 20 demographic items, I highly recommend that you build a synthetic key, potentially an integer field, that represents the intersections for each of the demographics. For example 0110 might be the key pointing to the male, 25–30 year old age band, $75,000–80,000 income band. Synthetic keys often simplify the processing logic and overhead in a database management system and may be the best alternative for an ad hoc query front-end application.

Other Physical Model Changes

Besides the denormalization of demographic dimension entities, we must validate all of the table's primary keys and indexes. These physical attributes of the data optimize the storage and access properties of a data warehouse.

In transforming a CDM to a PDM, both the measure and category detail entities need primary keys defined. The dimension entities primary key includes a segmented index over the identifiers for each level in the hierarchy. Here's an example:

```
d_location (country_id, area_id, region_id, district_id, store_id)
```

The measure entity primary key include the unique identifiers from the lowest-level category in each dimension. Here's an example:

```
m_sales_analysis(time_period_key, store_id, product_id, age_id, econ_class_id, gen-
der_id)
```

The category detail entity primary key is the identifier, or level key, in the dimension that uniquely identifies each row in the table. Here is an example:

```
c_store (store_id)
```

The primary keys are presented in the PDM with an underscored font in the attribute list of each entity.

Generating Native Data Definition Language

Most database management system vendors still require a scripting language, typically SQL, to generate a physical database. You want a tool that understands your database management system and that can generate and manage the DDL required to build you database. PowerDesigner DataArchitect provides an elegant facility, as shown in Figure 11.9. Upon selecting your desired options, DataArchitect generates your script file.

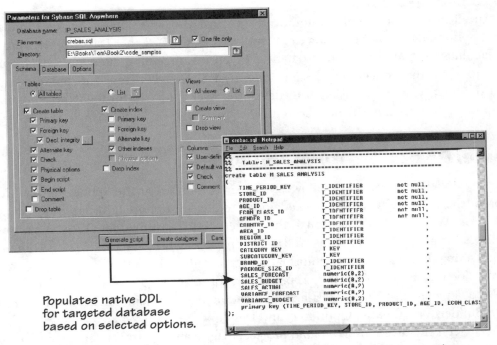

Populates native DDL
for targeted database
based on selected options.

Figure 11.9 *PowerDesigner DataArchitect generates a complete creation script following your native database's DDL syntax.*

PowerDesigner DataArchitect Features

PowerDesigner's DataArchitect component provides database designers and data architects with a robust tool for designing and maintaining relational databases and relational models. DataArchitect supports bilevel-level database designs that separate conceptual and physical models. The conceptual model reflects a database-independent view of a data model. The entities in the conceptual data model may be derived in DataArchitect or from data flow diagrams that are built in the ProcessAnalyst component of PowerDesigner. From the conceptual data model, DataArchitect generates a physical data model targeted at a wide variety of database management systems.

The DataArchitect physical model implements detail characteristics of a chosen database management system. The design of the data model is modified to reflect these changes. Changes that are made at the physical model level typically involve performance and usability improvements. From this physical model, you can generate databases for more than thirty database management systems, including Sybase, Oracle, Informix, DB2, and Microsoft SQL Server.

An effective data model communicates a consistent, adaptable, and understandable structure for a data warehouse development team. PowerDesigner DataArchitect provides the facilitates required to build a database blueprint, including allowing a development team to view the conceptual design and physical design. From the models built in DataArchitect, you can also begin to develop a user interface through the AppModeler component described in the next section.

PowerDesigner AppModeler

The AppModeler component of PowerDesigner is targeted at the application developer. AppModeler is typically used as a standalone product to support application development staff. For Web-based applications, the target audience includes Web development resources for a data warehouse as well as Webmasters who have been assigned the tasks of publishing data warehousing information on an enterprise intranet or the Internet.

We focus on WebGen, the AppModeler for the Web. However, PowerDesigner AppModeler can also work in other application development environments, such as PowerBuilder, Visual Basic, Optima++, and Delphi.

WebGen generates PowerDynamo projects, pages, and controls using predefined templates and information from objects and attributes that you define in your physical database model. Figure 11.10 demonstrates WebGen's generation capabilities.

WebGen ships with several templates and resource files that are the basis for the generation of prototyping algorithms. The projects that you develop with WebGen are based on existing databases. You must ensure that the database on which you are working has been created by DataArchitect, WarehouseArchitect, or even the AppModeler prior to working on your application project. In addition to the database, WebGen needs PowerDynamo to be properly configured prior to commencing your application projects. (PowerDynamo is the subject of Chapter 9, "PowerDynamo Essentials.")

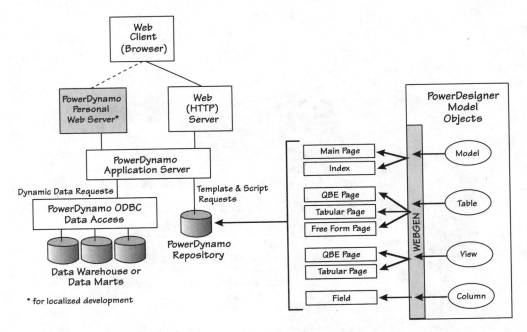

Figure 11.10 *AppModeler allows application developers to rapidly generate prototypes for a data warehouse that is accessible through the Web.*

Model Level Attributes

As with the other components of PowerDesigner, AppModeler has model level attributes that apply to the entire model and that assist with uniform prototype implementation. The model level attributes are set at three levels: the general model, the database, and the Web server, as shown in Figure 11.11.

The general model attributes define which set of templates you will use for creating a new application and what the name and title of your application will be. As your development staff becomes more familiar with the functionality of AppModeler, you may decide to extend beyond the default templates by creating customized templates that perhaps use popular Web plug-ins or Java applets.

The database attributes, shown in Figure 11.12, define which data store will hold your application data. This refers to the data warehouse, or in PowerDynamo terms, the application data store. This information is defined in the fields of the model attributes managed by the Database tab. When you select the Database tab, you are prompted for data source name, user name, and password for the application data store. The data source name refers to the ODBC source name. PowerDesigner connects to your data sources through the standard ODBC connectivity method.

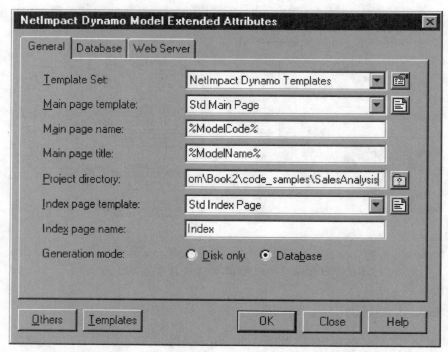

Figure 11.11 *AppModeler model level attributes provide uniform definitions that are the basis for application prototype generation. These attributes are applied in three categories: the general model, the database, and the Web server.*

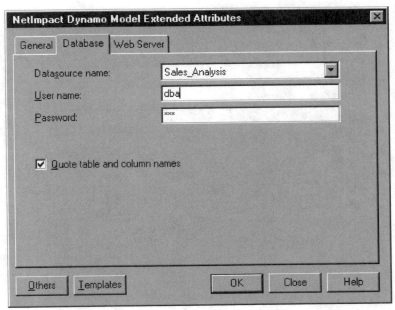

Figure 11.12 *The database attributes for the AppModeler model refer specifically to the ODBC connection defined for an application data store.*

The Web server attributes, shown in Figure 11.13, define the data store that manages your PowerDynamo templates, the template repository data store. WebGen generates PowerDynamo forms and scripts to facilitate you dynamic database system. As discussed in Chapter 9, "PowerDynamo Essentials," the template repository and application data store may physically be the same or two separate databases. As with the database attributes, the Web server attributes define the ODBC connection to the template repository. The information required for WebGen to access and insert objects into the template repository include the ODBC data source name, database user name, and database password.

Following the definition of these three model level attributes—general, database, and Web server—you have done everything necessary to generate a fully functional Web site from your physical database model. The generated application includes three pages for each table: a query by example (QBE) page; a tabular list page; and a free-form page. The generated PowerDynamo site contains a menu-oriented frame, which links to each of the table's QBE pages. The QBE pages, in turn, are linked to the tabular list pages, which are used to display the results from the query generated by user input on the QBE page. Finally, the primary keys on the tabular page link to the free-form page, so users can drill into a detail record to further analyze the data. The site is presented to users through a home page, as shown in Figure 11.14.

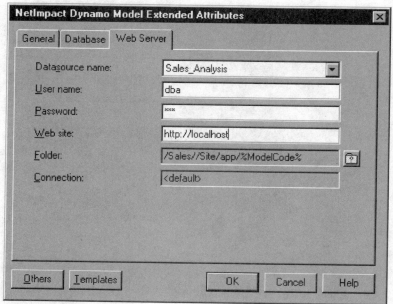

Figure 11.13 *The Web server attributes for the AppModeler model allow WebGen to insert and alter any objects needed for the Web application that is generated.*

Other Modifiable Attributes

In addition to globally defining the attributes for the model drives your Web site generation, you can set individual object attributes. Examples of individual objects include tables and columns. For each of these attributes, you may want to define more specifics to customize how the prototype is generated from WebGen. In the templates for PowerDynamo, WebGen generates three specific Web pages for each PDM table. These include a QBE page, a tabular page, and a free-form page. Along with attributes associated with these three pages, you can modify several of the general attributes associated with the table.

The Query By Example page is the entry point for retrieving information from database tables and views. The QBE templates that ship with WebGen generate pages that allow users to define their own database queries. Attributes that you can modify for each table's QBE page include page name, page title, and the template that is used for the generator. Also, a flag that indicates whether you want the page generated at all allows you to selectively build your prototype.

The left frame provides the user with a navigational menu, which is always active within the generated site.

The main panel, or right frame, presents the primary data to the user.

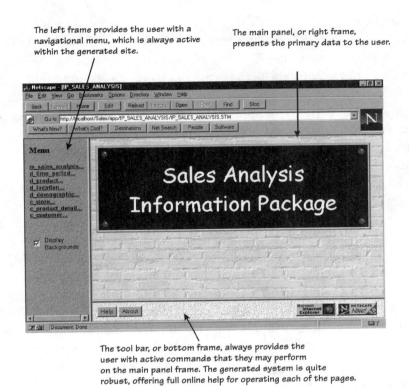

The tool bar, or bottom frame, always provides the user with active commands that they may perform on the main panel frame. The generated system is quite robust, offering full online help for operating each of the pages.

Figure 11.14 *This generated Web site is full functional and includes many unexpected features, such as drill-down from QBE to detail data and a generated help system.*

The Tabular page lists information from the data source in list form. The data is presented in standard HTML table format. After you submit a query from the QBE page, the server processes the query and returns data on the tabular page. As with the QBE page, you can utilize the default global settings for generation of the Tabular page or modify the page template, page name, and page title field. The Tabular page also has a flag to indicate whether you want the page generated.

The Free Form page lists information one row at a time, or record by record. The Tabular pages that list the summary information are linked to free-form pages in one of two ways: directly through a primary key or through a primary-to-foreign key relationship. When users are presented with a list of results that matched their QBE request, they simply select the key item to drill down into the free-form page. Like the QBE and Tabular forms, you can alter the page template, page name, and page title on the Free Form page. The flags that you can alter on the Free Form page include a generation flag and an update flag. The generation flag indicates whether you want to generate the page, while the update flag indicates whether you want update processing to occur in the generated page. For most decision support applications, the update flag is turned off, because users of such applications are only interested in retrieving the associated data not updating the data.

In addition to the table-level attributes, WebGen uses a series of extended column attributes to determine how to properly format data. By default, your Web site is generated with standard edit fields. However, the entire range of HTML field styles are available, including check boxes, radio buttons, drop down lists, and images. You can set these attributes for each column in your physical data model. Based on the field style you select, various additional attributes can be tweaked to improve the generation of a first-cut prototype application. As with table pages, field templates can be developed to fit custom needs, allowing you to extend AppModeler to include third-party widgets or in-house technologies for presenting data to users. Overall, AppModeler for the Web allows you to modify templates or attributes to apply at generation time for the entire model, individual tables, individual views, individual columns, or domains (column groups).

Generating a Web Site

To create a list of objects to generate, you can select the objects directly from the physical data model (PDM) or you can deselect all objects in the PDM and use the Generate PowerDynamo Web Site dialog box to select the list. The Generate dialog presents all of the objects that you consider for generation. This list is presented in a hierarchical format similar to the presentation methods in Microsoft Windows Explorer. Each item in the list contains a check box indicating whether the object will be include in the generation. Figure 11.15 presents our sample Sales Analysis information package generation list.

PowerDesigner AppModeler Features

The Web generation capabilities of PowerDesigner's AppModeler component offer a quick and easy way to build dynamic, data-driven Web sites. The infrastructure of this product allows you to easily customize the templates that control Web page generation to fit you enterprise's needs. In AppModeler, you can design physical database models or instantly create a physical model by reverse engineering an existing database. From this physical model, developers can generate, document, and maintain databases and application objects. The rapid generation of application objects and data aware components in those objects allows you to increase the pace of delivery of your data warehouse development efforts.

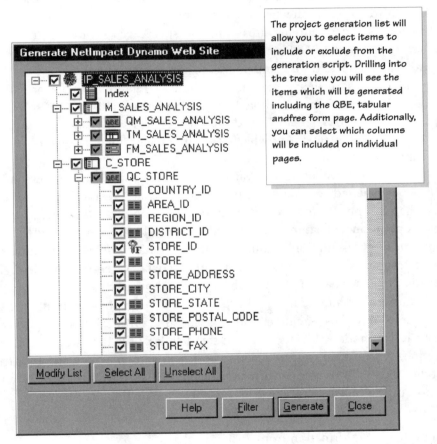

Figure 11.15 *AppModeler's PowerDynamo Web Site dialog box displays an object list in a tree view that indicates the complete contents of what will be generated.*

PowerDesigner WarehouseArchitect

The WarehouseArchitect component of PowerDesigner takes the concepts that emerge from DataArchitect and specifically targets them at the requirements of decisions support data modeling. Data marts and data warehouses tend to focus more on the multidimensional aspects of data rather than OLTP systems, which focus on the relational aspects. So, DataArchitect provides a complete tool for relational modeling but falls short in multidimensional modeling, which is the reason for WarehouseArchitect.

Few if any tools in the design and architecture marketplace go to the lengths of PowerDesigner WarehouseArchitect to focus on the needs and requirements of decision support applications. These unique areas include specialized entities (dimensions and measures), semantic layers (OLAP and managed query catalogs), data oriented optimizations (partitions and aggregations), and source-to-target mappings.

Most methodologies for delivering data warehouses, including the information packaging methodology, focus their data models on star schemas. This type of schema clearly defines specialized entities, including dimensions, measures, and category details. WarehouseArchitect has intrinsic knowledge and understanding of these entities and their associated relationships.

Icons are used to assist users of WarehouseArchitect in better understanding the functionality encapsulated in a data entity. These icons are symbols that present more information than simply the name and columns that comprise the overall entity. The icons convey operational meaning, as defined in the information packaging methodology. The graphical representation of functionality in a data model is highly advanced and makes PowerDesigner a leader in the evolution of data warehouse modeling. Figure 11.16, presents dimension and measure tables in WarehouseArchitect.

The true purpose of WarehouseArchitect is to specify the physical implementation of a data warehouse. WarehouseArchitect and its associated physical model, referred to as a WarehouseArchitect model (WAM,) focus on the details of the data warehouse's physical implementation. A WAM takes into account both software and data storage structures. You can modify the WAM to suit performance or physical constraints. A WAM represents the interaction of the objects described in Table 11.2. Functionally, WarehouseArchitect allows you to:

- Import source information from OLTP databases.

- Design data warehouse and data mart models that support informational and analytical systems using dimensional modeling techniques.

- Optimize data structures using tuning methods often found in decision support databases, such as aggregations and partitioning.

- Generate and maintain data warehouse and data mart specialty databases, such as Adaptive Server IQ and Red Brick.

- Export and import multidimensional semantic layer information to and from OLAP engines and other managed query environments.

- Enable extraction command scripts to automate data transfer from OLTP databases to a data warehouse.

- Generate reports on design activities.

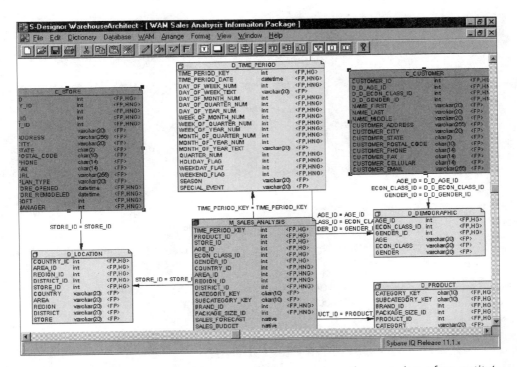

Figure 11.16 *WarehouseArchitect uses icons to convey the meaning of an entity's operational attributes. This allows PowerDesigner to closely align with the information packaging methodology.*

Table 11.2 A WAM represents the interaction of the following objects.

Object	Description
Table	Collection of rows (records) that have associated columns (fields).
Column	Data structure that contains an individual data item in a row (record); model equivalent of a database field.
Primary key	Column or columns whose values uniquely identify a row.
Foreign key key	Column or columns whose values depend on and migrate from a primary in another table.
Index	Data structure that is based on a key, that speeds access to data, and that controls unique values.
Reference	Link between the primary key and a foreign key of different tables.
View	Data structure that results from a SQL query and that is built from data in one or more tables.
Fact	Focus of a decision support investigation; connected to a fact table.
Dimension	Axis of investigation of a fact; connected to a dimension table.
Fact hierarchy	A fact that is split into other facts; results from aggregation or partitioning of a fact table.
Dimension hierarchy	A dimension that is split into other dimensions; each descending level in a dimension hierarchy corresponds to a finer level of detail.
Attribute	Object that qualifies a dimension; is connected to a column in a dimension table.
Metric	Variable or measure that corresponds to the focus of a decision support investigation; is connected to a column in a fact table.

Modeling Adaptive Server IQ Databases

Adaptive Server IQ is a specialty DataStore product that indexes data in a data source for optimized analytical processing. Adaptive Server IQ uses its indexes to rapidly resolve decision support queries without referring to the original data source. An Adaptive Server IQ database schema is called an *indexspace*. An Adaptive Server IQ indexspace contains the data definitions and data for Adaptive Server IQ *indexes*. An Adaptive Server IQ indexspace contains indexsets. An *Indexset* is similar to a table in that it has columns, however, columns in a Adaptive Server IQ indexset do not contain data; only indexes contain data.

Adaptive Server IQ indexsets are linked by join relationships. A *join relationship* represents a link between columns in different indexsets.

The catalog information for Adaptive Server IQ is stored in a Sybase Adaptive Server, known as the Catalog Server. A Adaptive Server IQ indexset must have a corresponding database table with the same name in the catalog server. When you create a WAM for Adaptive Server IQ, you have two workspaces: a Adaptive Server IQ workspace, which contains Adaptive Server IQ indexsets, and a Sybase Adaptive Server workspace, which contains the corresponding database tables. You display and modify Adaptive Server IQ objects in the Adaptive Server IQ workspace, while you display and modify Sybase SQL Server objects in the Sybase SQL Server workspace. Table 11.3 shows the correspondence between objects in Adaptive Server IQ and Sybase Adaptive Server.

Table 11.3 *Adaptive Server IQ and Sybase Adaptive Server corresponding objects in a WAM.*

Adaptive Server IQ	Sybase Adaptive Server
Indexspace	Model
Indexset	Table
Join relationship	Reference

Adaptive Server IQ offers two initial challenges to those unfamiliar with its design. The first challenge is that Adaptive Server IQ's catalog is stored in an underlying Sybase Adaptive Server, known as the Catalog Server, while user data is stored in Adaptive Server IQ's indexsets. The second challenge lies in the indexing alternatives available in Adaptive Server IQ. These index definitions are different than most standard database structure indexes and require a designer to understand the volume of data and use of the data to make proper design decisions.

To overcome the first challenge, WarehouseArchitect supports two levels of representation of a Adaptive Server IQ physical model: the Catalog Server, or Sybase Adaptive Server, view and the Adaptive Server IQ Indexspace view. Figure 11.17, demonstrates the relationship between these views and an overall data model.

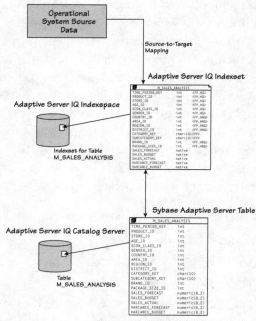

Figure 11.17 *WarehouseArchitect lets a designer see all views of the data warehouse model for Adaptive Server IQ, including the catalog server, IQ indexspace, and operational source.*

Creating an indexset in a WAM is virtually identical to the process of defining an entity in DataArchitect. If you are working in the Adaptive Server IQ view of the WAM, simply placing a indexset (indicated by the dog-eared entity icon on the PowerDesigner tools palette) creates an indexset for IQ and the shadow Catalog Server table entity. Figure 11.18 presents the indexset and column definition dialog boxes. Note that these dialogs are similar to those in DataArchitect for defining relational entities. However, the indexset dialog has an additional field for defining the type of entity (fact or dimension), while the column dialog has additional index options for Adaptive Server IQ.

Defining Multidimensional Objects

Section I of this book, "Introduction to the Information Packaging Methodology," discusses many attributes of multidimensional objects. In the information packaging methodology, these include dimension, measure, and category detail entities. Warehouse-Architect has its own multidimensional objects, which are used in the definition of a multidimensional schema. These objects are listed in Table 11.4.

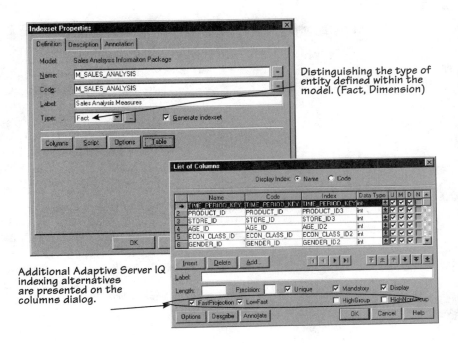

Distinguishing the type of entity defined within the model. (Fact, Dimension)

Additional Adaptive Server IQ indexing alternatives are presented on the columns dialog.

Figure 11.18 *WarehouseArchitect lets you define entities (indexsets and tables) in a similar manner to DataArchitect. Subtle differences exist for multidimensional definition of entities and Adaptive Server IQ index creation.*

Table 11.4 *WarehouseArchitect and information packaging methodology multidimensional objects comparison.*

Object Name	IPM Equivalent	Description
Fact	Measure entity	A fact corresponds to the focus of a decision support investigation. Examples: Sales, Revenue, and Budget are facts.
Dimension	Dimension entity	A dimension defines the axis of the investigation of a fact. Example: Product, Region, and Time are the axes of investigation of a Sales fact.

Continued

Table 11.4 *Continued*

Object Name	IPM Equivalent	Description
Metric	Measure variable	A metric is a variable or measure that corresponds (non-path column) to the focus of an investigation. Metrics are typically numeric. Examples: Total and Price are metrics. A metric can be the result of an operation or calculation involving several columns of a fact table. Metrics are attached to columns in a fact table. Example: a Sales Total metric is attached to the Sales Total column in a Sales fact table.
Attributes	Dimension level (key and label)	An attribute is an object that qualifies a dimension. Example: Year is an attribute of a Date dimension. Attributes are usually attached to columns in a dimension table. Example: a Month attribute is attached to the Month column in a Time dimension table. Attributes can also be attached to facts.
Fact hierarchy	*[no equivalent]*	A fact hierarchy is a fact that is split into other facts. You automatically create a fact hierarchy when you aggregate or partition a fact table. A WAM usually only has one fact hierarchy.
Dimension	Dimension entity	A dimension hierarchy is a hierarchy dimension that is split into other, more detailed dimesions. Each descending level in a dimension hierarchy corresponds to a finer level of detail. The number of levels in a dimension hierarchy corresponds to the available levels of granularity in a query. A WAM can have any number of dimension hierarchies.

WarehouseArchitect provides a central Multidimensional Hierarchy dialog box for completely managing objects. From this dialog, all entities listed in Table 11.4 can be access, modified, or deleted from a WAM. This view of the WAM also is concise, which provides another way to visualize a warehouse model, as shown in Figure 11.19.

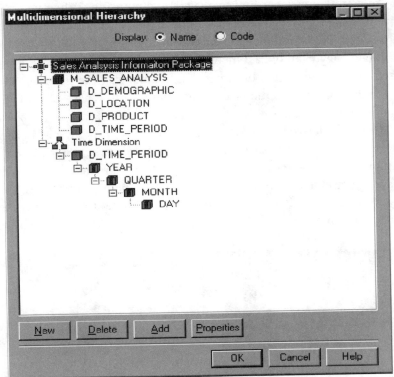

Figure 11.19 *The WarehouseArchitect Multidimensional Hierarchy dialog box provides a concise interface for accessing, modifying, or deleting objects in a model.*

Using WarehouseArchitect Wizards

The designers of WarehouseArchitect went to great extents to understand the problems that are typically involved in delivering a decision support system. This understanding led to a set of wizards to assist in data-oriented tuning for performance. WarehouseArchitect offers two wizards that automate the processes of creating aggregates and partitioning data. These processes are addressed separately in the next two sections.

Creating Aggregates

Operational systems typically load data into a data warehouse at an atomic level of detail. However, most decision support systems require consolidated, or aggregated information, rather than atomic detail. Aggregation is a technique that optimizes data retrieval by summarizing rows of a fact table according to a specific dimension. When you aggregate data, you summarize it along frequently-accessed lines of query. This summarized data is stored in a single aggregated fact table that can be easily accessed by the decision support system.

This technique of aggregating data increases query performance by using prestored summary data based on the aggregation of dimension hierarchies. The purpose is to ensure that the most frequently used aggregations is searched first during a query. The Warehouse-Architect Wizard for Fact Table Aggregation creates additional fact tables based on desired aggregations. The newly derived aggregation fact table along with other associated fact tables, such as the original fact table, are placed in a fact hierarchy. For example, in Figure 11.20 we show the creation of a new aggregate fact table that will contain only annual sales figures. We could also create aggregate tables for each level in the time period dimension, including quarterly, monthly, or even weekly summary tables. In WarehouseArchitect, the fact tables (m_sales_analysis and m_sales_analysis_yr) are placed in a new fact hierarchy.

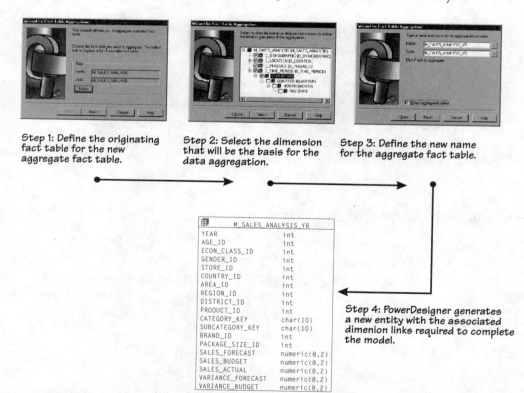

Step 1: Define the originating fact table for the new aggregate fact table.

Step 2: Select the dimension that will be the basis for the data aggregation.

Step 3: Define the new name for the aggregate fact table.

Step 4: PowerDesigner generates a new entity with the associated dimenion links required to complete the model.

Figure 11.20 *WarehouseArchitect's Wizard for Fact Table Aggregation automates the process of creating denormalized tables to contain data derived from an original fact table but aggregated along a specified dimension level.*

Creating Partitions

Information in a data warehouse can be partitioned. This technique is similar to aggregation for providing performance improvements based on data storage. An aggregate reduces the number of rows in a table by summarizing data at a predetermined level in the dimensional hierarchy, while a partition reduces the rows by filtering atomic-level data by value. So, a partitioned fact table contains atomic-level data for specific values of one or more dimension attributes.

For example, Figure 11.21 illustrates a new partitioned fact table to store only sales figures for the USA. This partitioning can become far more sophisticated. For example we could partition a sales fact table to obtain three separate fact tables containing data on the sales of red telephones for years 1995, 1996, and 1997. The number of partitioned tables you create depends on the number of values you specify for each dimension attribute.

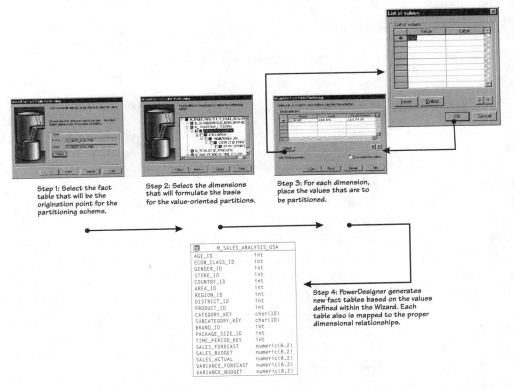

Step 1: Select the fact table that will be the origination point for the partitioning scheme.

Step 2: Select the dimensions that will formulate the basis for the value-oriented partitions.

Step 3: For each dimension, place the values that are to be partitioned.

Step 4: PowerDesigner generates new fact tables based on the values defined within the Wizard. Each table also is mapped to the proper dimensional relationships.

M_SALES_ANALYSIS_USA	
AGE_ID	int
ECON_CLASS_ID	int
GENDER_ID	int
STORE_ID	int
COUNTRY_ID	int
AREA_ID	int
REGION_ID	int
DISTRICT_ID	int
PRODUCT_ID	int
CATEGORY_KEY	char(10)
SUBCATEGORY_KEY	char(10)
BRAND_ID	int
PACKAGE_SIZE_ID	int
TIME_PERIOD_KEY	int
SALES_FORECAST	numeric(8,2)
SALES_BUDGET	numeric(8,2)
SALES_ACTUAL	numeric(8,2)
VARIANCE_FORECAST	numeric(8,2)
VARIANCE_BUDGET	numeric(8,2)

Figure 11.21 *The WarehouseArchitect Wizard for Fact Table Partitioning lets you optimize a model by building new fact tables partitioned by value of specified dimensions at the atomic level of detail.*

Mapping Sources to Targets

You can import OLTP source metadata in WarehouseArchitect with its reverse engineering facilities. PowerDesigner's rich reverse engineering functionality lets you place the metadata from these source systems into your WAM through SQL script files, existing PowerDesigner PDMs, or live connections using ODBC.

WarehouseArchitect's import feature allows you to select one or several operational source systems to provide data feeds into a data warehouse. After imported into the WAM, the external source database tables are presented as entities with dotted lines. These external source tables are not generated when you populate the DDL for your warehouse, they are simply used to marshal source metadata.

Metadata defines the content of a data warehouse system. Typically, data warehouse metadata includes items that define and monitor all data-oriented activities of the data warehouse. These items include:

- Source system (operational systems) data structures.

- Target system (data warehouse or data marts) data structures.

- Source-to-target transformation algorithms.

- Model and algorithm version information.

- User-oriented definitions for OLAP and managed query environments.

WarehouseArchitect brings all of this information together in one model. To bring in source information, follow the process shown in Figure 11.22. During this process, you define the external source databases, select a method for extracting source data, and select the objects to import into your model.

After source tables have been imported into the WAM, you can begin to document various transformations. WarehouseArchitect is primarily a design and architecture tool for data warehouses; however, simple transformations can also be defined with this tool. The interface allows you to perform SQL-based transformations on source data to derive a target data definition. Figure 11.23 presents the External Sources source-to-target mapping dialog box. As with the multidimensional hierarchy dialog, the target mappings in the External Sources dialog box are presented in a hierarchical list structure that allows you to drill into the detail to define simple transformations.

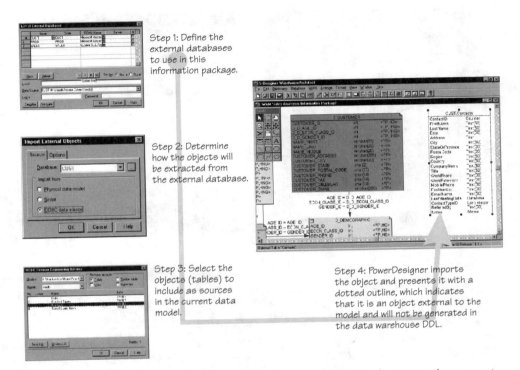

Step 1: Define the external databases to use in this information package.

Step 2: Determine how the objects will be extracted from the external database.

Step 3: Select the objects (tables) to include as sources in the current data model.

Step 4: PowerDesigner imports the object and presents it with a dotted outline, which indicates that it is an object external to the model and will not be generated in the data warehouse DDL.

Figure 11.22 *WarehouseArchitect consolidates your metadata for a warehouse system, including source metadata and the target data warehouse model.*

WarehouseArchitect keeps information on how to move data from an operational environment into a data warehouse. Data may be extracted from OLTP databases into the data warehouse by an extraction tool or through an extraction script. WarehouseArchitect interfaces with industry leading transformation tools such as Platinum Technology's InfoPump. Sybase works closely with transformation tool partners to allow this interface to ease the set up and centralize the design of transformation logic. However, if you don't plan to use a transformation tool in your architecture, the SQL generated by Warehouse-Architect provides an adequate starting point to build your own transformation programs.

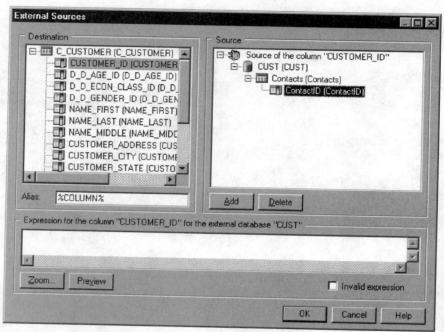

Figure 11.23 WarehouseArchitect's External Sources dialog box lets you begin to integrate transformation logic into designs while centralizing the associated metadata.

Interfacing with OLAP and Managed Query Environments

Query and report-oriented tools in the OLAP marketplace have introduced semantic layers. A semantic layer provides additional performance and security features outside a database. A semantic layer also lets you control what users see in a database and how data is retrieved from the database.

You control what users sees in a data warehouse by properly defining the information packages that those user require. This view of a data warehouse can be set up for relational access for tools such as Cognos Impromptu or Business Objects; or you can build semantic layers that are multidimensional or data-relationship-oriented, such as Cognos PowerPlay or Arbor's Essbase.

In WarehouseArchitect, you can design semantic layers simultaneously with data models. This approach assists in avoiding the complexities of using multiple tools and multiple interfaces.

Semantic layers are required for proper deployment of a data warehouse. If you think about what information systems have done to user information over the years, the reason becomes clear. When you look at an order form, the standard user interface for years was a piece of paper. Information systems professionals ripped this form into many separate pieces—order header, order line items, product master, customer master, shipment header, shipment line items, and so on. Now, for users to analyze sales trends, ordering trends, or shipment trends, they need a way to bring all of the data back together. Some scotch tape would help, but we have provided them with a technological marvel, the database join. I have yet to meet a user who understands what a database join is, much less cares. Users simply want their data.

Most query and reporting tools today still present users with join logic, which is a highly unfriendly interface. Exposing joins to users also introduces some danger into the management of a data warehouse. If not well understood by the user, this data model poses a maze with potential for many wrong turns. Worse yet, the join concept in a relational database is not just table to table, but also includes view-to-view joining. This allows users to easily create "meaning of life" queries that consume major resources and foster fears with IS departments of providing users with ad-hoc access to their data.

Semantic layers offered by tools such as Cognos Impromptu or Business Objects ease this burden by providing users with a logical view of their data, such as an order form, while controlling access plans behind the scenes. In the past, some resistance has emerged to building these semantic layers due to their proprietary interfaces. Now, with WarehouseArchitect, the semantic layers can automatically be generated within the same tool you use to design the data model.

PowerDesigner WarehouseArchitect Features

WarehouseArchitect is based on PowerDesigner's DataArchitect physical data model, which is proven technology. This new component of PowerDesigner is specifically targeted to support dimensional modeling and high-performance indexing schemes. With WarehouseArchitect, you can import heterogeneous databases to form the basis for your data warehouse model. This ability to integrate your target models with the originating source data feeds provides a valuable set of tractability links. Additional WarehouseArchitect features include:

- Complete, four-layer data warehouse architecture support (source data feeds, transformation algorithms and tools, target data stores, and OLAP-managed query environments).

- Support for various dimensional modeling methods, including star and snowflake schemas, which make heavy use of partitioned and aggregated tables.

- Generation of extraction command scripts to automate data transfers from OLTP systems.

- Generation of multidimensional information to popular OLAP engines and other query design tools.

- Robust report generation facilities to document design activities and models.

With these features, you can easily design and architect your data warehouse solution with various databases such as Adaptive Server IQ to interface with popular OLAP and managed query tools. WarehouseArchitect provides value as a seamless, dynamic meta-data broker.

PowerDesigner MetaWorks

The PowerDesigner repository, MetaWorks, provides organizations using PowerDesigner with a facility to share and store the various models generated by the PowerDesigner family of products. This repository provides a single point of control to a enterprise or work-group development team that is building a data warehouse.

MetaWorks runs on a developer's workstation and stores its information—primarily models—on a database server. MetaWorks can use most market leading databases to store its data, including Sybase SQL Anywhere, Sybase Adaptive Server Enterprise, Oracle, Informix, DB2, and Microsoft SQL Server. MetaWorks provides three essential functions: data model and submodel extraction and consolidation; project or dictionary management; and environment administration.

Data warehouses are typically very large projects. When developing applications for these projects, you must divide and organize your labor resources. MetaWorks assists in this task and makes maintaining large applications manageable, while satisfying project time constraints.

Team design presents myriad problems. One of the largest problems stems from the ability to share application development among teams of designers. Designers may have domains of responsibility that overlap and may access the same data simultaneously, thus jeopardizing data integrity of the overall system and architecture. The MetaWorks dictionary, combined with proper communication channels, makes sharing of designs possible while ensuring data integrity and permitting large numbers of users to access the same information.

Equally important to team application design is data centralization. By making it possible to reuse parts of models, you can build additional applications while maintaining model consistency. The overall development process becomes more efficient. As shown in Figure 11.24, the MetaWorks repository centralizes design data for all information system applications and thus ensures consistency and compatibility among different components and disciplines in a data warehouse system.

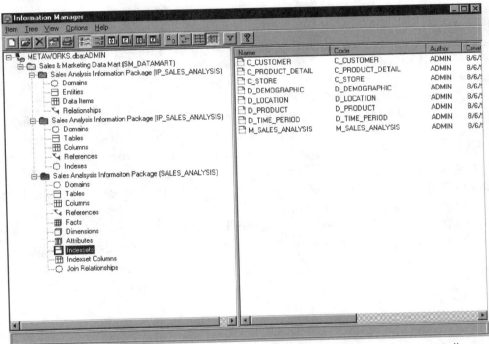

Figure 11.24 *MetaWorks provides a multiuser repository to integrate all components of the PowerDesigner family.*

Summary

The PowerDesigner family offers a comprehensive modeling solution that closely aligns to a data warehouse project team. Business and systems analysts, designers, DBAs, and developers can benefit from the components that PowerDesigner comprises. An organization can apply the tools it needs according to the size and scope of its projects with this product family.

Combining the information packaging methodology with a tool such as PowerDesigner allows you to follow a structured approach to efficiently create and deliver a data warehouse. PowerDesigner adds automation and intuitive interfacing technology to the information packaging methodology, which makes the two a well-designed fit.

PowerDesigner not only assists in accelerating the development process, it also provides an efficient architecture for managing and accessing information related to an overall data warehousing system. Such a product greatly assists in reducing the cost of maintaining systems after they are deployed—typically the largest cost of any system.

PowerDesigner components offer a complete life cycle orientation to a development process. ProcessAnalysis assists in uncovering business processes and in defining data flows, including transformations for a warehouse. DataArchitect assists database administration staff and data architects in building robust relational models and generating the associated relational databases.

WarehouseArchitect assists database administrators, data architects, and OLAP designers in building business-oriented, multidimensional models and in generating the appropriate supporting scripts, including database, transformation, and semantic layer information. AppModeler assists application development staff in rapidly prototyping application objects with data-aware components. This generation capability allows rapidly placement of systems for accessing a data warehouse in users' hands.

As we proceed into the case studies section of this book, you will begin to see the power of each of these components and how they can assist you in more rapidly delivering a data warehouse.

The Case Studies

By any objective measure, the amount of significant, often traumatic, change in organizations has grown tremendously over the past two decades. Although some people predict that most of the reengineering, restrategizing, mergers, downsizing, quality efforts, and cultural renewal projects will soon disappear, I think that is highly unlikely. Powerful macroeconomic forces are at work here, and these forces may grow even stronger over the next few decades. As a result, more and more organizations will be pushed to reduce costs, improve the quality of products and services, locate new opportunities for growth, and increase productivity.

—John P. Kotter, *Leading Change*, Harvard Business School Press, 1996, p.1.

12

The Shareholder
Data Mart

As defined in the information packaging methodology, four human knowledge centers can impact a business' success or its failure—employees, customers, suppliers, and shareholders. In this chapter, we review shareholder metrics, which have been the focus of traditional analysis in the finance department.

Due to consolidation of numeric dollar values from all operations, financial systems historically have provided the best view of a company's health and success. The metrics that are defined to support financial analysis are of primary importance to the shareholder human center. Have you ever wondered why so many investors place their hard earned money with companies like Coca-Cola, General Electric, and Procter & Gamble? It may be due to these companies' ability to properly educate the investment community on the important aspects of the business. This type of education leads to trust, which results in loyalty.

Shareholder education involves explaining a business' strategy and how the four human knowledge centers interact to bring success to the enterprise and therefore defining how long-term value will be created for the shareholders. The education must be clearly backed up with facts and analysis that demonstrate higher profit and earnings over time.

After investors are educated and believe in the various aspects of your business, they want to see measures that gauge your progress. For your company to be successful, you need to find relevant measures that prove your company is worthy of shareholder trust. This is often done with familiar financial based metrics such as profit, return on investment, income, expenses, cash flow, stock price, accounts receivable, accounts payable, and so on. Shareholders are often interested in profit, cash flow, and balance sheet strength.

The analysis of financial metrics is relatively straight forward, because financial systems capture all costs, revenues, and budgets. Financial measure analysis also supports the decision making process of management personnel. By analyzing the cause-and-effect relationships in a data mart, the financial metrics can assist and direct management on corrective actions required to realign departments or the entire enterprise for desired outcomes.

Management activities and financial analysis are closely watched by those with significant interests in a company; namely the shareholders and the banks. This information determines how the investment community will view the enterprise and subsequently value the enterprise.

Improving Financial Analysis

The continual reporting and analysis required to inform shareholders and others with financial interests in your company can be dramatically improved by a data warehouse. Table 12.1 provides a list of benefits derived from data warehousing in the financial area.

Table 12.1 *Traditional versus data warehousing financial analysis.*

Traditional Financial Analysis	Data Warehouse-Based Financial Analysis
Few analysts perform the analysis and aren't held accountable for the data they analyze.	All budget owners who are accountable gain quicker access to their data, allowing more proactive decisions.
Dimensional nature of data is often limited to a chart of accounts and time.	Financial dimensions are combined with additional dimensions, such as organization, customer, and product, allowing better isolation of successes and problems at a detail level.
Analysis is focused on fiscal reporting periods and only on a few financial metrics.	Managers are empowered to analyze the impact of their decisions on a greater frequency, allowing them to better manage to budget.

Continued

Table 12.1 *Continued*

Traditional Financial Analysis	Data Warehouse-Based Financial Analysis
Analysis involves report- and paper-intensive operations with high distribution costs and low efficiency cycles.	Analysis involves ad hoc-, analytical-, online-intensive operations, which decrease distribution costs and increase efficiency cycles.
Peak work periods occur at month, quarter, and year end.	Information dissemination is speeded and analytical resources are freed. There is a leveling effect on work loads. Peaks still exist, but are less focused on correction and more on the required reporting.

Traditional financial measures focus analysis on too many things, so the results often aren't useful in managing or understanding organizational performance. In other words, most financial report metrics do not contain the right amount of data required by shareholders or managers to make sound business decisions.

If executives are good at one thing, it is manipulating an organization's expenses to improve short-term profitability. New executives hired to turn-around a failing enterprise immediately work on removing costs from the business. These cost reductions can come in many forms, including staff reductions, decreases in purchased goods and services, and squeezing suppliers or finding new suppliers. These cost reductions are manipulated to directly impact short term-income and improve the bottom line. However this is often at the cost of long-term success.

Because financial standards have evolved and been improved by companies for the last quarter of a century; executives have become masters at playing with the numbers to make their organizations look good. Creative accounting may stem from large incentive bonuses or the power game of bureaucratic empire building. With short-term cost reductions or other creative accounting, managers become executives with bigger and better jobs and higher salaries. They leave long-term issues for some new and potentially unsuspecting manager. While some of this cost cutting is required to prepare a company for market shifts or business transitions, cost cutting alone will not secure an organization's future success.

Three Views of Financial Metrics

To better meet a shareholder's desire to understand an enterprise's finances, you must provide three perspectives of the data, including historic data, current data, and future data.

- Historic data allows shareholders and others who are interested in a company's financial results to answer questions such as: How did the company do last week? Month? Quarter? Year?

- Current data allows the interested parties to answer questions relating to how the company is doing right now.

- Future data allows the parties to answer questions about what is planned and how the company will do in the next few weeks, months, quarters, and years.

The time dimension of your financial data provides the historic, current, and future perspectives of that data. From a financial stand point, the metrics presented to the shareholders and other interested parties help define how well the company is creating wealth. The past-focused historic data allows an interested party to evaluate the current or future data in the time series provided by the time dimension. Performing time series analysis on the financial data indicates problems that must be further identified and treated.

Typical vital signs for current performance include items such as:

- Cash flow.

- Orders in the pipeline.

- Total dollars in accounts receivable.

- Daily sales figures.

- Amount of cash on hand.

- Unencumbered budget money (for nonprofit organizations).

You can provide future-oriented metrics that can help gauge the future health of an organization through information such as:

- Percentage of total sales from new products.

- Dollar volume value of outstanding proposals.

- Statistics on previous closure percentages.

- Percent of research and development investments as a ratio to sales.

- Growth of sales from a specific geographic region or particular industry.

A Financial Information Package

To best communicate the information required in a shareholder human center, we will build a comprehensive, multidimensional financial information package. The basis of this financial information package will be the accounting systems. This information package will contain facts associated with the budgeted and actual amounts for each account in the chart of accounts. A powerful time dimension will be built to assist in the analysis required to provide the three views of the financial metrics outlined in the preceding section. As a side benefit, standard reports required by the business, such as income, balance sheet, and cash flow statements will be enhanced to include multidimensional analysis capabilities. Users of this information package will be able to see historic information for the financial statements as well as filter information by division or department.

This financial information package will therefore expand on the current, narrow view of the health of the business that is based on the standard financial reports. Traditionally, the financial reports only provided a summary of the income and expense accounts, or asset and liability accounts, or cash positions in the accounting system. This view typically was static and didn't permit managers to specifically manipulate the data to best understand how their actions affected the company's health. Through a multidimensional view of the financial metrics in a data warehouse, you can provide greater flexibility and more detail in a dynamic environment. The information package diagram for our multidimensional financial analysis system is shown in Figure 12.1 on the following page.

The multidimensional financial information package shown in Figure 12.1 includes the following data to meet user requirements:

- **Time periods:** Information is available to users for the last five years. This information includes a fully configured time dimension, which allows analysis by day, week, month, quarter, or year, to name a few periods.

- **Chart of Accounts:** The chart of accounts includes all accounts in the enterprise's financial systems and categorizes these accounts along common accounting principles, including income, expense, asset, liability, and so on.

- **Organization:** The organizational hierarchy is provided so that analysis can be filtered, aggregated, or performed on specific divisions and departments in the enterprise.

- **Measures:** The measures are the key performance indicators to assist users in better analyzing the data. These measures include budget, actual, and variance amounts.

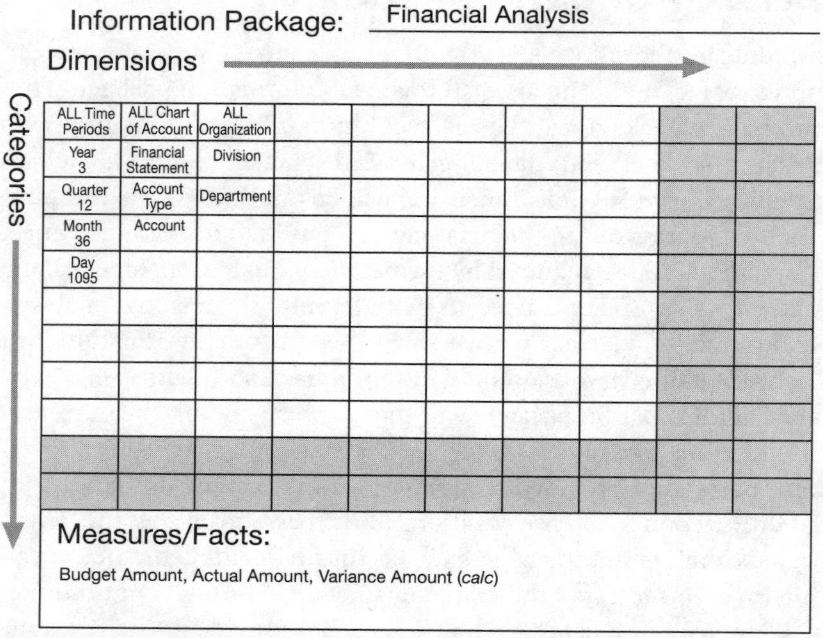

Information Package: Financial Analysis

Dimensions →

Categories ↓

ALL Time Periods	ALL Chart of Account	ALL Organization							
Year 3	Financial Statement	Division							
Quarter 12	Account Type	Department							
Month 36	Account								
Day 1095									

Measures/Facts:

Budget Amount, Actual Amount, Variance Amount (*calc*)

Figure 12.1 *A multidimensional financial information package enhances the analysis and decision making process associated with a company's financial systems.*

Let's take a closer look at each of these data warehouse components to gain a better understanding of their purpose and content.

Financial Measures

In any accounting system, a comprehensive process of budgeting assists a company in conveying future plans. The ability to build a proper business plan and achieve, or exceed, the desired results is a significant way to gain shareholder confidence. Typically, surprises are not welcomed in the financial community. (One exception is the unexpected growth in revenue an profits. Everyone gladly accepts such a surprise!) But the most undesirable surprise in financial systems are out-of-control expenditures. Business planning can assist in controlling such undesirable financial results and therefore gain significant trust in a shareholder community. This trust can then be parleyed into continuous growth in capital and support.

The financial measures that will be managed in our information package relate to the budgeting and actual execution of the company's plan. This information package allows shareholders and others who are interested in the financial health and stability of the enterprise to easily see historic, current, and future metrics, which formulate a scorecard on the management of an enterprise. Such an information package assists in answering questions such as: Does management know how to run the business when times are good? Does the company demonstrate wild peaks and valleys in their operations, or gradual growth?

Time Dimension

Any information package that focuses on an evolving process requires a time dimension. This dimension will be important in nearly all of your information packages and will become the foundation for all time series style reports. This dimension enables the view of the information to be framed by historic, current, or future timing. Any process occurs over time; therefore, this dimension presents the concept of time in the proper context of a business.

Often database administrators and data architects alike may ask why they would want a separate time dimension entity; after all, most database management systems offer a complex set of date functions that permit time series analysis. What these technicians do not take into account is that nearly every user question issues a query requiring the database to perform a date function. Additionally, the functions of a standard database do not parlay into the business calendar maintained in a business.

The unique handling of a time dimension becomes obvious when users begin to ask questions that force the data to be sliced, filtered, and compared over different views of time. For example, how have sales been on the weekend versus weekdays? Over the past five years, how have sales been by week? By day? By holiday? Also, if a business maintains different calendars for operations in Europe versus operations in North America, a time dimension can accommodate such information.

Different information packages may require you to present the time dimension at differing grains. For example, cash flow data may follow a daily grain, while metrics associated with an income statement are better measured with a monthly grain. Because all data warehouse entities are universal to an overall enterprise data warehouse, we will only build one time period dimension. This dimension provides various views of a date, including those views listed in Table 12.2.

Table 12.2 *Alternate views of a date managed by a time dimension.*

View	Description
Date	The unique calendar date for all time, such as 12/25/1997.
Quarter of Year	For businesses tracking, quarterly information is an important milestone in measuring the progress of an enterprise. Each date falls into one of the four quarters in a year. If the enterprise is on a fiscal year calendar, 12/25/1997 occurs in the fourth quarter.
Month of Year	The month represented by the date, such as January, February, and so on. This information can be presented in two ways: as a number corresponding to the month or as the textual month name. For 12/25/1997, the month is numerically 12 (the twelfth month) or textually December.
Month of Quarter	Each quarter is made up of three months. To analyze trends in a quarter, the date can be framed in a specified quarter. For example, if the enterprise is on a calendar year, 12/25/1997 represents a time period in the third month of the fourth quarter.
Week of Year	A year is made up of fifty-two weeks. Providing the option to track metrics based on week provides powerful analytical capabilities. For example, 12/25/1997 falls into the fifty-second week of the year.
Week of Quarter	A quarter is made up of thirteen weeks. Registering which week of a quarter to which a specific date belongs allows determining if trends are seasonal.
Week of Month	A month is made up of four to five weeks. As with the weeks of a quarter, framing a date in the week of a month allows determining if trends that occur during a given week in the months of a year, such as the last week.
Day of Year	A year contains 365 days (except for leap year, which has 366). As with other slices of a date, the ability to view information by day of the year in a year to year comparison assists in viewing the metrics. For example, 12/25/1997 is the 359th day of the year.
Day of Quarter	A quarter contains approximately 90 days. As with other slices of a date, determining the day of the quarter allows comparisons of daily performance in a quarter-to-quarter framework.
Day of Month	The Day of the Month is simply extracted from the date. For example, for 11/19/1960, the day of the month is 19. As with other slices of a date, determining the day of the month allows comparative analysis in a month to month framework.

Continued

Table 12.2 *Continued*

View	Description
Day of Week	The Day of the Week on which a date occurs, such as Monday. This information can be presented in two ways: as a number representing the day of the week or as textual the weekday name.
Season	The Season field is an optional slice of the data that allows you to place seasonal information in the date. Seasons can apply to spring, summer, fall, and winter; or to seasons defined in the business. Either definition allows performing seasonal analysis on the data.
Holiday	A Holiday flag marks a specified date as a holiday. You may also desire to have a Holiday label field that clearly defines what type of holiday occurred, especially for international firms, because holidays may not align worldwide. This flag allows determining if holidays impact the overall business.
Weekend	A Weekend flag allows users to specifically view weekend data. For example, retail sales analysts may want to view weekend sales transactions versus weekday sales transactions, potentially to determine proper hours or days to stay open.
Weekday	Much like the Weekend flag, the Weekday flag allows slicing date information and visualize only weekday information.
Last Day of Year	The Last Day of the Year flag allows framing financial activity specifically for the last day of each year and performing this comparison year to year.
Last Day of Quarter	The Last Day of the Quarter flag allows visualizing activity in a quarter-to-quarter reference for the last day of the quarter.
Last Day of Month	The Last Day of the Month flag allows visualizing activity in the month-to-month reference for the last day of the month.
Event	You may also want to record special events in your time dimension. These events can significantly affect trends in data. However, without understanding what event occurred, future decisions could be swayed incorrectly. For example, the sudden affect that Diana, Princess of Wales' death brought to the flower business in the United Kingdom might be considered an event. In the future, will this trend of purchasing activity continue, or was it a one-time phenomenon? Only time will tell; but with out marking this event, analysts may make poor judgments in the future on items such as inventory levels.

Chart of Accounts Dimension

The foundation of any accounting system is its elaborate chart of accounts structure. The basis of all financial accounting involves accounts that are grouped under the classification of income, expense, asset, liability, and equity. These classifications are important for all shareholders in analyzing the health of a company. As a simple review of accounting terms, we look at each of the accounting classifications.

Balance Sheet Accounts

The properties owned by an enterprise are referred to as assets, and the rights or claims to the properties are referred to as equities. Equities are subdivided into two principal types: the rights of creditors and the rights of owners. The equities of creditors represent the debts of the business and are called liabilities. The equity of owners is called capital, or owner's equity. These three classifications yield the following accounting equation:

```
Assets = Liabilities + Capital
```

The balance sheet is a traditional financial report that lists the assets, liabilities, and capital of a business as of a specific date, usually the close of the last day of a month or year. Asset accounts that are listed on a balance sheet typically include cash accounts, investments, land, buildings, equipment, accounts receivable, and so on. Liabilities are also listed on the balance sheet and include accounts payable, taxes payable, notes, loans, and so on. Finally, equity (or capital) is on the balance sheet and includes common stock, preferred stock, retained earnings, dividends, and so on.

Income Statement Accounts

The principal objective of most enterprises is to increase capital through earnings. Capital is increased when income derived from the sales of products and services exceeds the cost of expenditures of the business. Expenditures of a business can include wages of employees, costs of supplies, rent, and other costs of operating the business. A company shows a profit if income is greater than expenses. This profit, in turn, allows the business to increase cash and other assets, and in the process increase the equity of the owners and shareholders.

An income statement is the traditional financial statement that is used to summarize the income and expenses of a business for a specific period of time, such as a month or a year. Income earned and expenses incurred during the time period are recorded in an equation that increases and decreases capital, respectively. This data can provide the basics for matching the income earned during the time period and the expenses incurred in earning this income to determine the amount of net income or net loss.

Formulating a Chart of Accounts Dimension

Based on fundamental accounting principles, a chart of accounts dimension is built as a hierarchy of accounts. The hierarchy relates the financial statement groupings (balance sheet and income statement), primary account types (asset, liability, equity, income, and expense), a subcategory (for assets: cash, accounts receivable, and so on), and the account. This dimension permits users to apply multidimensional analysis techniques against the core business accounts. The ability to drill into the detail of a financial statement or slice into accounts based on classification provides power not found in the current static financial reporting systems.

Organization Dimension

An organization dimension adds significant analysis capabilities to current financial data. The organization of any enterprise tends to be hierarchical. Even in matrix-managed organizations, some degree of an organizational hierarchy exists between the senior executives and front-line workers. For purposes of our example, we define an organization containing several divisions with departments in each division.

An example of a division is the operations division. In the operations organization are departments that assist in the daily operating of the company. Examples of such departments include sales, marketing, legal, and administration. Each of these departments works on short-term ventures that bring revenue into the enterprise. For analysis purposes, it helps to be able to compare divisions as well as departments within divisions for their overall contribution to the financial health of a company.

Building a Conceptual Star Schema Model

Now that we have investigated the dimensions and measures required for our information package, it is time to build the logical model. As discussed in Chapter 3, "Information Modeling," an information package and associated details are translated into a star schema as follows:

- The columns of the information package diagram are each translated into dimensions.

- The dimensions are formulated with fields from each category, or level, in the column. In this step, you validate that multiple access paths are accounted for, as we discussed in the "Time Dimension" section earlier in this chapter.

- Each of the lowest-level categories is placed in the measure entity.

- Each of the measures is placed in the measure entity.

- If any category is highlighted to include more detail information, a category detail entity is created.

The translation of our information package into a star schema is shown in Figure 12.2.

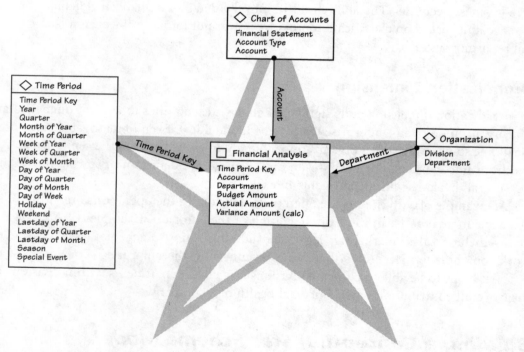

Figure 12.2 *This star schema diagram, using information packaging method notation, assists designers and developers in better translating user requirements into a logical and physical data model for a multidimensional financial information package.*

335

Implementing Information Packages

After user requirements have been gathered in the information packaging diagrams and conceptual data models have been generated utilizing the star schema with information packaging method notation, we are ready to proceed with the actual implementation of these specifications. PowerDesigner assists us in building and maintaining our overall data architecture. In this powerful tool, we refine our current specifications for shareholder data mart and store those specifications in the MetaWorks repository for the enterprise data warehouse.

This process begins with the PowerDesigner Conceptual Data Modeling (CDM) facilities. We use PowerDesigner CDM's domain management capabilities to standardize the model prior to generating the physical data model (PDM). The domains that are used in this model include:

- **Date stamp:** Stores information that contain only date information (example: the time period key).

- **Descriptions:** Stores information that is unknown at the time the data model is built, but that will require input of some length of text (example: the event or season in the time period dimension).

- **Identifiers:** Stores information stored as numeric keys to relate entities with each other (example: the account identifier).

- **Labels:** Stores information to present to users. This data includes text descriptors that are closely associated with identifiers (example: the account field that is the text representation of the account identifier).

- **Monetary_value:** Stores information in the data mart that specifically represents money (example: budget amount or actual amount stored in the fact table).

- **yes-no flag:** Stores information that is used to flag data as *YES* or *NO* (example: the Holiday flag in the time dimension).

The final refinement of a data architecture is its physical data structures—the entities and their relationships that will be implemented in the database management system. We build our model so that it is physically implemented in Adaptive Server IQ. (The demonstration databases on the CD are in Sybase SQL Anywhere; however, code samples for the Adaptive Server IQ databases are also on the CD.) In Adaptive Server IQ, we need to translate the volumetrics gathered in the information package diagram into index types. Upon clearly defining all attributes of the physical model, we will be ready to generate our data mart and begin populating it with data.

The resultant physical model in the PowerDesigner WarehouseArchitect component is presented in Figure 12.3. This model includes icons that indicate the dimensions and facts in the overall model. Because PowerDesigner also supports colors, you can extend its native method to include the additional concept of a category detail entity—an integral part of a model created in the information packaging methodology. The view presented in Figure 12.3 is the Adaptive Server IQ schema. PowerDesigner WarehouseArchitect allows you to view both the Adaptive Server IQ schematic and the underlying catalog manager schema, which is stored in a Sybase Adaptive Server Enterprise database.

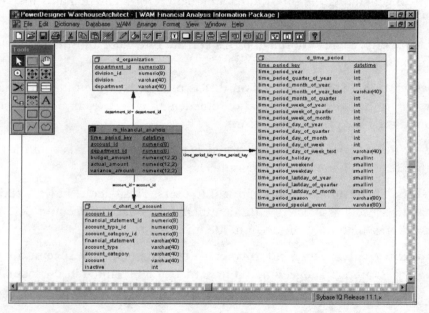

Figure 12.3 *The Warehouse Architect Model (WAM) of PowerDesigner presents the physical multidimensional model for our shareholder data mart.*

After our model has been implemented in PowerDesigner, we generate the data definition language (DDL) syntax for the targeted database environment. This targeted database environment is applied to the physical model, from which the DDL can be easily generated. From PowerDesigner you can apply various different physical database environments. The product will verify that proper syntax is generated so that you can generate the database schema. For Adaptive Server IQ, all required syntax is published, including the DDL for populating the catalog server's Sybase Adaptive Server Enterprise database and the attached Adaptive Server IQ indexspace.

Accessing Information Packages

After a database platform is in place, the database schema is defined, and data is translated and placed in a data mart, it is time to build the front-end system. An application architecture provides the visualization capabilities to users of the data mart. In the client/server world, the application architecture often involved a suite of tools provided by software vendors to address specific access techniques. The most common methods for users to access data include:

- **Relational access:** confirmation-style queries such as "Do I have any customers in New York City?"

- **Online analytical processing:** hypothesis-oriented queries such as "Over time, how many customers have we gained and lost in the Northeast of the USA?"

- **Data mining:** significant pattern understanding from a sound statistical analysis basis such as "What causes a company to become a customer?"

You should investigate the use of tools to enhance your ability to be productive when delivering a data warehouse. The diversity and quick evolution of the Internet marketplace has caught many popular tool suite vendors without available products. Other, new vendors have seized the opportunity in this market while the established players play catch up.

Depending on your situation, you may choose to implement specialized visualization services to implement your Web site. Until the marketplace settles into an established market with clear leaders in reporting categories, early adopters will typically want to build their own visualization service.

With your data model already in the PowerDesigner MetaWorks repository, you can use the PowerDesigner AppModeler to begin the process of building your own visualization tool for the Web. AppModeler will generate a set of NetImpact Dynamo templates to access the dynamic content required to fulfill user requests for data. The generated Web site is a hierarchy of Web templates, as shown in Figure 12.4.

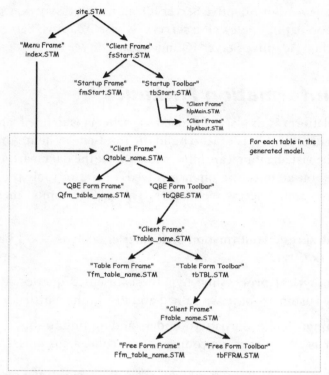

Figure 12.4 *The PowerDesigner AppModeler for the Internet allows you to begin building a data-driven Web site.*

Navigating a New Web Site

As discussed in Chapter 11, "PowerDesigner Essentials," the PowerDesigner AppModeler generates a fully functional prototype Web site. This application is based on PowerDynamo from Sybase, which offers a robust architecture for data driven Web site delivery and management and thus is a good fit for you data warehouse application.

The PowerDynamo template sets that ship with AppModeler define pages and fields. Pages are the primary interface elements of Web projects, while fields are page elements that correspond to database columns. Each page in PowerDynamo is a document stored in the template repository in a file with an .STM extension. A PowerDynamo STM document contains an HTML script. AppModeler generates STM documents from individual tables and views in a data model. In AppModeler, field templates define a control or set of controls that can display data from database rows. Controls are page or field elements that you can use in an application to obtain user input or to display data output. For example, text boxes and command buttons are standard controls.

When generating a Web site from AppModeler PowerDynamo templates, you have a Web application that includes:

- **Main page:** The main page is the home page for the generated application.

- **Index page:** The index page provides functionality similar to a main menu for the generated application.

- **Help subsystem:** The help subsystem assists in navigating the generated application, including detailed help on how to issue complex queries in Query By Example pages.

- **Query By Example (QBE) page:** For each selected table and view, a QBE page is generated, which allows users to perform complex queries against the data mart's database.

- **Tabular page:** For each selected table and view, a tabular page presents results driven by queries generated in the QBE pages against the data mart's database.

- **Free form page:** For each selected table, a free form page presents the details for a row selected from a tabular page in the generated application. Free form pages are not generated for views.

AppModeler templates can be modified to suit your needs. These modifications can include better integration with third-party tools or optimization for targeted applications in your enterprise's application architecture. For now, we look at the standard application that is generated from the default templates.

Home Page

You primarily use the home page generated by PowerDesigner AppModeler to manage your Web application. The home page is generated with the default templates for PowerDynamo that come with PowerDesigner AppModeler for the Web. As shown in Figure 12.5, these templates generate a framed site. The generated site includes two primary presentation frames:

- **Menu Frame:** A left frame contains a menu, or index, of all topics available to the project. This frame contains links to all the Query By Example pages. The menu contains one entry per table and view selected in the generator. The menu frame on the left hand side of the screen extends from the top to the bottom of the screen. The menu frame remains visible during an entire work session for the generated site.

- **Client Frame:** A much-larger right frame contains the working area of the Web site. Pages such as the site's home page, the QBE page, the tabular page, the free form page and the help page display in the client frame. The client frame is loaded on demand with pages that correspond to the topic requested by users when they select items from the menu frame. The client frame is typically split between a working area page and a toolbar page, which spans the bottom of the working area page.

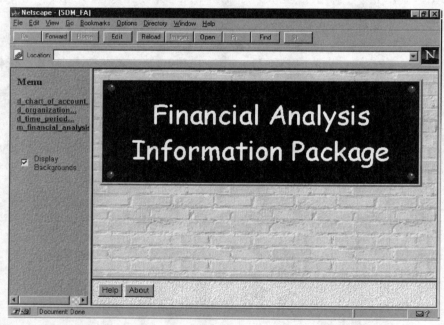

Figure 12.5 *PowerDesigner AppModeler for the Web generates a framed site, which includes a home page and master index for navigating the site.*

These two frames are managed by the individual template pages and scripts that are generated. The individual management of each frame allows the site to be dynamically built within the desired context. Therefore, toolbars are rebuilt in the client frame based on the type of working page displayed in the client frame. A different toolbar is generated for each of the three types of pages (QBE, tabular, and free form) presented to users.

Query By Example Page

The Query By Example (QBE) page is hyperlinked to the menu frame. The menu frame presents one hyperlink per selected QBE page in PowerDesigner AppModeler. When the user selects the table's hyperlink menu option, the QBE page set is activated. This page set splits the client frame into two separate frames, which is a user's working area to perform and execute queries. The two frames include:

- **QBE page frame:** The QBE page presents each field in a table or a view that the designer selected in the PowerDesigner AppModeler generation hierarchy. While these fields can take on various HTML input field attributes, the default is to present all fields as an HTML edit field. (More on customizing this default is provided in the "Altering Field Templates" section later in this chapter.) In addition to the fields in which users can enter selection criteria, a field is presented for determining the rows to be returned for a query. This is important, because you do not want your users to execute queries that return large numbers of rows to the Web. The time to format the result sets into a valid HTML file requires a low number of results for a query—typically between ten and one hundred rows.

- **QBE toolbar frame:** The toolbar associated with the QBE page frame presents users with buttons that execute actions on the QBE page itself. These buttons include: submit query (which takes the user entries, formulates a query, and passes it to the PowerDynamo Application Server for execution); new (which calls the free form page to allow users to enter a new row into a table); home (which returns users to the home page for the Web site); and help (which presents users with detailed data on how to enter query criteria on the QBE page).

The page set templates that ship with AppModeler define the Query By Example page as the entry point for retrieving information based on tables and views in your information package data model. The QBE templates generate Web pages with fields for user-defined database queries. The QBE page contains a set of input fields that corresponds to a database field. A user can enter record retrieval criteria in these fields. The QBE page also has an input field labeled, Number of Records, which lets users specify how many rows will be shown from the result set at a time.

The QBE tool bar includes a Submit Query button. Users click this button to submit an SQL query with a set of entered criteria. When the criteria for a user query is passed to a PowerDynamo Application Server, a query is forwarded to a database. Only the rows that match all specified criteria are returned to the user. If the user enters no criteria, all rows are returned. The QBE tool bar also has a New button. When users click this button, the free form page is opened so they can insert a new row into the database table. If you turn off the update capabilities in the AppModeler generation specifications, this button isn't available. In addition to Submit Query and New buttons, the QBE tool bar has Home and Help buttons. The Home button returns the user to the home page for the Web site. The help button displays the QBE help page in help subsystem, which is further discussed in the "Help Subsystem" later in this chapter.

The valid operators that can be used as criteria in the QBE page are shown in Table 12.3. The criteria are formatted with the following syntax:

```
[operator] Expression
```

EXPRESSION is any set of characters entered by the user that are intended to be interpreted and utilized as comparison criteria. This expression is compared to the database column in which the criteria were entered using an *OPERATOR*.

The operator is optional. If the user doesn't specify an operator, the equal operator is the default. The only exception to this rule is for a character string field. If a character string contains a "%" or a "_" in the string, the default operator is LIKE, for example *INCOME%* is equivalent to *LIKE INCOME%*.

Table 12.3 *Valid QBE operators.*

Operator	Matches Values
=	Equal to the *Expression.*
<	Lower than the *Expression.*
>	Higher than the *Expression.*
<=	Lower or equal to the *Expression.*
>=	Higher or equal to the *Expression.*
<>	Different than the *Expression.*
!=	Not equal to the *Expression* (equivalent to !=).
BETWEEN	In the range specified by the *Expression*, the range expression syntax is BETWEEN low value AND high value.
LIKE	Containing the same pattern as the *Expression.*
NOT LIKE	Not containing the same pattern as the *Expression.*

Continued

Table 12.3 *Continued*

Operator	Matches Values
IN	In the set of values specified by the *Expression*, the *in* expression syntax is (Value[, Value]).
IS NOT NULL	Any specified value.
IS NULL	Not specified (no value).

Expressions can include values as well as pattern matching characters. Two special characters are recognized as pattern matching characters: %, which matches any string of zero or more characters, and "_" which matches any single character. Table 12.4 demonstrates examples of expressions that are valid in a QBE page's fields.

Table 12.4 *Examples of valid QBE expressions.*

Example	Explanation
> 100	Any number higher than 100.
> "100"	Any number or string greater than "100" (examples: 2, 99, and ":12AB").
> "D"	Any string that starts with a letter higher than "D."
BETWEEN 50 AND 100	Any number equal to or higher than 50 and lower than or equal to 100.
BETWEEN "ALPHA" AND "DELTA"	Any string equal or greater than to "ALPHA."
	that is also less than or equal to "DELTA."
"NOT LIKE SALES"	The string "NOT LIKE SALES."
NOT LIKE "SALES"	Matches any string different than SALES.
= "NOT LIKE SALES"	Matches the string NOT LIKE SALES.
LIKE "foo%"	Matches "foo," "food," "foot," "foo bar," and so on.
LIKE "foo_"	Matches "food," "foot," "fool," and so on.
LIKE "f%c_"	Matches any string that starts with the letter "f" and has the letter "c" as its next to last character (examples: "fire truck" and "freight truck").
IN (1, 10, 100, 0)	Matches any of the four values in the set.
IN ("income", "Revenue", "Sales")	Matches any of the three strings in the set.

Figure 21.6 Demonstrates the power of the QBE page. This figure demonstrates a user request to find all sales accounts with negative variances. Such a query involves accounts_ids between 40000 and 49999, and variances less than 0.

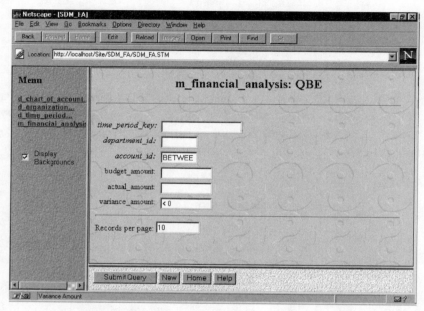

Figure 12.6 *Sample QBE form to retrieve all rows that match specified criteria.*

Tabular Results Page

The tabular results page is invoked from the Query By Example page. When users select the Submit Query button on the QBE tool bar frame, the results from queries are returned by the PowerDynamo Application Server in the tabular results frames. These frames split the client frame into two frames that are the users' working area to evaluate query results. The two frames include the tabular page frame and the tabular toolbar frame.

The tabular page frame displays the query results in a standard HTML table. This page also presents the criteria that produced the results and the total number of rows that match the criteria. The tabular page contains:

- A header line containing a list of the query criteria entered on the QBE page.

- A table displaying a limited number of rows from the database query. For each row, a link is available to open the free form page for the associated database table.

- A text description of the result set that was created by the database for the query. This description states the current position of the rows displayed and the total rows returned by the query.

The toolbar that is associated with the tabular page frame presents users with buttons to execute actions on the tabular page itself. These buttons include:

- A Change Query button, which leads back to the QBE page, allowing the user to modify the current query.

- A New button, which opens the free form page so the user can insert a new row. If the tabular result page is based on a view or a table that was set as not updatable, this button isn't displayed.

- A Home button, which returns to the Web site's home page.

- A |< button, which shows the first rows returned by the query.

- A << button, which moves to previous set of rows.

- A >> button, which moves to next set of rows.

- A >| button, which moves to the last set of rows.

Figure 12.7, on the following page, shows the tabular results page that was produced by the QBE page shown in Figure 12.6.

Free Form Detail Page

As with the Query By Example and tabular results pages, the free form page splits the client frame into two subframes. These subframes include a free form page and a free form toolbar.

The free form page lists information, record by record, from a database table. The free form page is the only place where users can update data (which is highly unusual for a decision support application such as a data mart or data warehouse). Free form pages aren't created for views. The free form page contains a set of input controls, each corresponding to a database field.

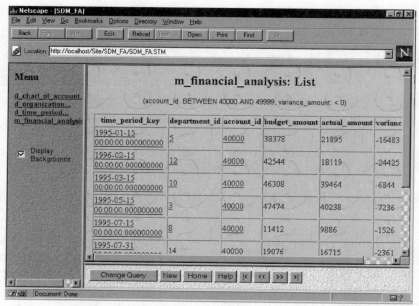

Figure 12.7 *This tabular result page presents users with the database rows that match criteria in the QBE page.*

The user can get to a free form page through hyperlinks from various parts of a generated Web site. These hyperlinks include:

- The New button on the QBE page.

- The New button on the tabular results page.

- The hyperlink that is placed on the key fields in the tabular page.

The free form tool bar frame presents a series of buttons that allow users to manipulate the data presented on the free form page. These buttons include:

- An Insert button, which adds user input from the page into a database table.

- An Update button, which updates the current record in the data source based on changes from users on the free form page.

- A Delete button, which deletes the current record from the database.

- A Back button, which returns to the previous page.

- A Home button, which returns to the home page for the generated Web site.

The Insert button is only available when the free form page is opened by clicking the New button from the QBE or tabular results page. The Update and Delete buttons are available when the free form page is opened by clicking a data row link from the tabular results page. If the database management system does not permit the rows to be updated or inserted, these buttons aren't displayed. Figure 12.8 presents a sample of the free form page for the d_organization entity in our example financial analysis information package.

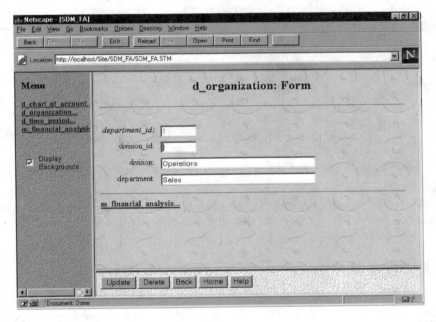

Figure 12.8 *The free form page allows users to evaluate details behind a specific row in a database. Besides query capability, users may also insert, update, or delete rows in the database.*

When a data model contains master-to-detail relationships, the free form page places a hyperlink from the master data to the detail data. In a star schema implementation such as created when you use the information packaging methodology, the fact tables contains data with a detail relationship to the dimension entities. Therefore, the d_organization free form page shown in Figure 12.8 has a hyperlink to the m_financial_analysis entity. This hyperlink allows users to drill down into the measure entity's tabular results page from the associated dimension, as shown in Figure 12.9. Following this hyperlink performs an operation similar to a QBE criteria-setting operation. However, the hyperlink drill-down operation reads the related data based on the dimensions key data.

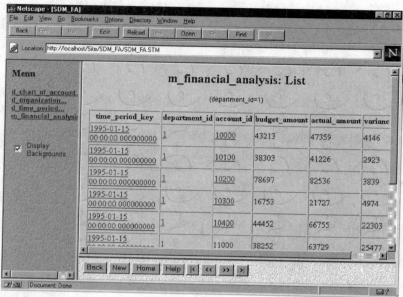

Figure 12.9 *AppModeler places hyperlinks from a free form page to related detail data. Following this hyperlink presents users with the tabular results page. This figure presents the results of following the hyperlink from Figure 12.8.*

Modifying Standard Site Generation

You have various ways to modify the standard site generated by AppModeler. To this point, the samples of our Web site were generated with the standard templates without modification. But you can fine-tune an application either prior to the first generation or during a reiterative generation of the Web site. You can focus your tuning on three areas, which are discussed in the sections that follow.

- Modifying the model properties by using views.
- Modifying the extended attributes by altering the field templates.
- Selective column generation.

Using Views to Enhance a Web Site

A view is a predefined query that is stored in a database and accessed like a standard database table. The primary difference between a table and a view is that views are simply queries stored in the database, not a physical table. Depending on the complexity of the view's definition, it may also be restricted as to the types of SQL statements that may be executed against the view. In general, you use views for predefined queries against database tables. The view definition comprises a subset of columns from one or more tables. Views thus can be presented through a Web site generated by AppModeler to simplify the selection process and drill-down operations for the data.

Views allow you to partition and aggregate data without creating separate physical tables. These views can become the basis of all access to a data mart or data warehouse. Properly defining views lets you easily filter data based on user organization to ensure that users see no more information than they are entitled. Of course, actual performance tuning may be required, which has you building physical partitions and aggregations. (We cover related issues further in Chapter 14, "The Employee Data Mart.")

You could create a view for a financial analysis information package that presents only the annual measures for income accounts. This view could have the SQL definition that follows:

```
create view v_1997_sales_analysis as
select m_financial_analysis.account_id, d_time_period.time_period_month_of_year,
sum(m_financial_analysis.budget_amount), sum(m_financial_analysis.actual_amount),
sum(m_financial_analysis.variance_amount)
from m_financial_analysis, d_time_period
where m_financial_analysis.time_period_key = d_time_period.time_period_key
and d_time_period.time_period_year = 1997
and m_financial_analysis.account_id between 40000
and 49999
group by m_financial_analysis.account_id, d_time_period.time_period_month_of_year;
```

AppModeler generates a QBE page and tabular results page for each view in a model. These views can be used to provide security or summary information to your application, thus refining its functionality.

Altering Field Templates

AppModeler applies field styles and templates to database columns and domains to build the pages that present the information from a data mart or data warehouse. The default field style is a standard HTML edit input control. Field styles describe the types of controls you generate in your application. Any control that is supported by a Web browser can be utilized as a field template.

Each field template has a list of attributes. You can modify the values of these attributes in AppModeler. Table 12.5 presents the available field template styles to modify your Web site.

Table 12.5 *Field template styles and associated modifiable attributes.*

Field Style	Description
Advanced	This field style allows you to build templates for managing ActiveX and Java applet controls. These controls only are generated on free form pages.
Checkbox	This field style is the recommended presentation style for boolean data. Checkboxes present data as either *on* or *off*. You can modify the values that are returned to the database as well as the labels that are presented to users when they activate or deactivate the check box.
Drop down	This presents information with a combination of an edit field and a list box. The style allows an application to present users with valid options for the associated field. Drop downs can include either a fixed list input by the designer or a dynamic list retrieved from another table in a database.
Edit	This field style is the recommended presentation style for text data. The style presents an open box, which may be either a single line or multiple lines. This style allows users to enter text information.
Image	This field style is applied to a database table column that contains the address of a graphic file (example: http://localhost/objx.gif).
Radio Buttons	This field style provides a clear style is for database columns containing only a few values (example: payment type). A radio button presents a multicolumn selection list with a circular selector and an associated label. Users highlight the circular selector to indicate the value to place in the database column.

Selective Column Generation

When you generate your application from AppModeler, you may decide not to present all database columns. From AppModeler's tree view, you can select which columns to generate on a particular page. AppModeler presents what will be generated in a list similar to the Microsoft Windows Explorer interface. When you expand page items in tree view, AppModeler lists the columns that it will generate. You expand a tree view item by clicking on plus sign to its left. Figure 12.10 presents the generation hierarchy for our financial analysis information package. Each column is presented with a checkbox that allows you to select or deselect a column for generation on each page.

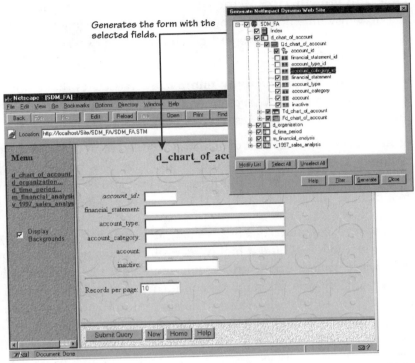

Figure 12.10 *The AppModeler generator allows you to select which columns to place on each page.*

Summary

Today's accounting systems are probably best at measuring the value we provide shareholders or investors. These systems provide information that relates to their primary focus of profit accounting. For a shareholder data mart, you should select measures based on data that focus on the key areas of a business that drive the mission established by the enterprise. Examples of these measures include:

- **Financial:** Metrics relating to growth, profitability, and cash flow that emphasize the improvement in returns from investment.

- **Risk management:** Metrics that present the diversification of revenue sources away from a narrow set of customers, one or two lines of business, or a particular geographic region.

- **Revenue and growth mix:** Metrics that demonstrate the expansion of products and services, reaching new customers and markets, changing the product and service mix toward higher-value offerings, and repricing of products and services to be more competitive.

- **Cost reduction and productivity improvement:** Metrics that emphasize efforts to reduce the direct costs of products and services, reduce the indirect costs of the business, and share common resources among business units.

- **Asset utilization:** Metrics that demonstrate reduction in the working capital levels required to support a given volume and mix of a business, redirection of resources for new business to unutilized capacity, and increase of returns earned on financial and physical assets.

With these measures contained in a flexible data architecture, as provided by the information packaging methodology, and a highly accessible application architecture, as provided by the Internet, shareholders can become more educated on how a business is operating and can quickly gain the required confidence in the overall enterprise—in its mission, goals, and plan to achieve success. The ability to provide this information in a timely and flexible manner is the real purpose of a shareholder data mart.

PowerDesigner, PowerDynamo, and Adaptive Server IQ play integral roles in delivering this information. PowerDesigner assists in designing and architecting the solution, while PowerDynamo helps to provide secure and distributed application services to the Web. These applications provide highly dynamic data from a data mart storage platform, Adaptive Server IQ. From a database point of view, Adaptive Server IQ is crafted to support the various ad-hoc requests that will come from your users—including shareholders, who can ask some rather off the wall questions. The next chapter further investigates the power of PowerDynamo and its scripting language to provide more meaningful presentation of a data mart's content.

13

The Supplier Data Mart

Suppliers are one of the four human knowledge centers defined by the information packaging methodology that can impact the success or failure of your business. The other three human knowledge centers, as discussed in Chapter 12, "The Shareholder Data Mart;" Chapter 14, "The Employee Data Mart;" and Chapter 15, "The Customer Data Mart." Monitoring suppliers is important, because it allows you to integrate supply, production, and delivery process metrics into an integrated supplier data mart. The information in such a data mart enables all organizational units along the value chain to realize enormous improvements in cost, quality, and response time. In this chapter we will review some common supplier metrics which have been the focus of analysis within the vendor management departments of major enterprises.

When building data marts or data warehouses, development teams often forget to look outside their own operations, yet the supply chain can make or break a company. If your suppliers are providing poor quality, late, or high-priced products compared to their competition, it impacts your bottom line. Your supplier data mart should become a system that allows suppliers to be easily compared and scored against benchmarks that are established in your business goals or contracts. Such a data mart should integrate all relevant information from upstream customer orders to raw material suppliers through delivery to the customer.

You also should consider allowing suppliers access to your supplier data mart in addition to sharing this valuable information with your internal employees. This allows suppliers to understand what is expected of them and how they are performing. The last thing any strategic partner, or supplier, needs is a surprise; and too frequently judgment calls are made on such companies without knowing where they went wrong. Strong companies with large supplier communities have done this over the years in one-on-one sessions. For example, The Procter and Gamble Company, which adopted Deming's Total Quality principles early in the 1980s typically assigned a vendor manager and scheduled periodic reviews of the partner's quality.

In my own dealings with The Procter and Gamble Company, I was called into many meetings that made everyone's stress level increase dramatically. However, before the meetings ended, a representative from Procter would detail a plan of how the vendor would regain the desired relationship. This was almost a Marine tear-down and build-back scenario. Being brutally honest with a strategic partner was required, explaining where it was doing things right and where it was doing things wrong. However, Procter also showed pure interest in making this a success by assisting the vendor in understanding how to improve its process of interacting with Procter. Additionally, Procter also expected vendors to have a similar relationship with them—if Procter was wrong, it wanted to know it and how to figure out how to fix the problems.

Why is this so important? Because if you really evaluate the results of working closely with vendors in building a strategic relationship, you see that quality, cost, and response time improve. If a vendor feels like an outsider to your company, more than likely it will not be as committed as you might like them to be. Forming a strategic relationship with a vendor allows you to disclose future plans, including slow down and speed up periods of your business so that the vendor can better support your business mission and ensure that your business is successful. After all, to a supplier you are the customer, and without customers they are out of business.

Building your data warehouse on the Internet allows you to open some of this information to suppliers in a more accessible format. This accessibility translates into more of the supplier's management to evaluate your relationship and determine proper measures to ensure success on both sides—the creation of a true partnership. This exercise expands your data warehouse outside the four walls of your company. If you want your data warehouse to be successful, you must go outside your walls and include any knowledge center that touches and has the potential of impacting your business, and suppliers certainly fit that description.

Improving Supplier Analysis

Suppliers are critical to most organizations, but many organizations do a poor job of measuring supplier performance. How does your organization monitor supplier performance? Think about how much money your company expends with suppliers and then relate this to your answer on how you monitor their performance. Some industries are less dependent than others on suppliers, but without high-quality raw materials at the right time and at the right cost, most manufacturers are out of business.

Your organization's values and beliefs regarding suppliers should be reflected in your data warehouse. The metrics that are established based on your values and beliefs allow you to monitor supplier performance. These metrics should not be viewed as a system to control suppliers, it should be a system that shares plans, objectives, and expectations with suppliers.

Your monitoring system should go beyond checking materials purchased from suppliers and, if the material is damaged or not right, sending it back. Your monitoring system should have a memory, a way to determine if a supplier is good—all of the time, some of the time, or none of the time. Larger companies have an enormous amount of data on suppliers. Most large companies inspect incoming shipments from suppliers and collect detailed data on the extent that supplier products meet required standards.

To improve your ability to analyze supplier performance, you need to define the measures that are critical to a partnership's success. These measures might include items such as:

- Responsiveness.
- Flexibility.
- Attention to detail.
- Ease of doing business.
- Courteousness of staff.
- Follow-through.

These measures can be combined to build a report card of satisfaction with the supplier at planned intervals, such as monthly, quarterly, and annually. The definition of these metrics should be obtained from your user community and will require benchmark data as well as supplier performance data. Your executive sponsor, or user steering committee, should be glad to assist you in collecting this information. Assigning these users such a task gains their commitment and buy-in to your success in building a supplier data mart.

To deliver your final supplier data mart, the desired supplier metrics should be mapped to business drivers. These drivers include areas such as:

- Product or service quality.

- Customer satisfaction.

- Price to value.

- Process performance.

Of course, depending on your business these drivers could change, and each driver should not be given the same weighting. But the steering committee should be instrumental in defining the proper weight and follow on presentation of these metrics by supplier.

Supply Chain Management

A supplier data mart directly supports the supply chain management function of a company. As with a financial data mart, a supplier data mart contains three views of the data along its time dimension: past, present, and future. Applying the same principles as we learned in Chapter 12, "The Shareholder Data Mart," these three views of the data allow us to understanding if performance is improving or degrading as well as communicate this information back to the supplier as an indicator of what is expected in the future.

When discussing supply chain management, it is important that we realize the true view manufacturers should have of the supply chain. This view is a continuum that begins with suppliers providing raw materials to the manufacturer who produces finished product, the carriers who ship the product, and the customer who purchase the product. Your supplier data mart needs to capture all of the relevant data artifacts that are produced throughout these processes. If the customer is not satisfied when receiving the product, can you answer why? It could be many things, including:

- The raw materials provided by the suppliers were of poor quality, which caused the product to fail.

- The production process was improper and forced rework, which delayed the shipment.

- The carrier lost the package, which caused a delay in shipment.

- The delivery person working for the carrier was not courteous to the customer.

Some people would claim that not all of these factors are in your control. However, if you want your business to be successful, they must all be in your control. This means that you must collect data on every aspect of the supply chain to ensure proper results throughout the delivery experience.

A Supplier Information Package

Information on the entire process involving suppliers and production include data sources such as:

- **Orders** are purchase orders for raw materials, customer orders for finished goods.

- **Production process** are recipe management, product campaigns, manufacturing plans.

- **Inventory** are raw materials, finished goods, distribution center, retail outlets or stores.

- **Shipments** are plant to distribution center, distribution center to retail outlet, retail outlet to customer.

Similar to Chapter 12, "The Shareholders Data Mart," we will build a sample information package that would be contained in an overall supplier data mart. This information package will communicate performance metrics for carriers, allowing users to perform carrier score card analysis. As we have discussed up to this point in this chapter, it is vitally important to maintain information that is outside our company's four walls, and carriers are typically outside suppliers of services that can dramatically affect customer satisfaction. Our carrier score card information package is show in Figure 13.1.

Our carrier score card information package contains the following information package conceptual entities.

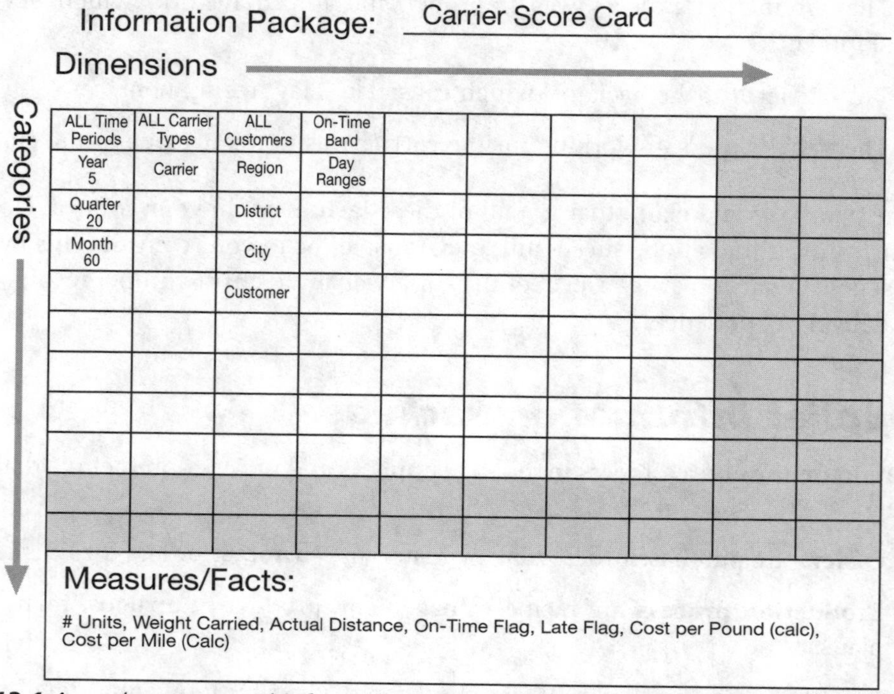

Information Package: Carrier Score Card

Dimensions →

Categories ↓

ALL Time Periods	ALL Carrier Types	ALL Customers	On-Time Band						
Year 5	Carrier	Region	Day Ranges						
Quarter 20		District							
Month 60		City							
		Customer							

Measures/Facts:

Units, Weight Carried, Actual Distance, On-Time Flag, Late Flag, Cost per Pound (calc), Cost per Mile (Calc)

Figure 13.1 *A carrier score card information package allows common communication of key performance metrics that affect customer satisfaction.*

- **Time periods:** Information will be made available to users for the last two years. This information will include a fully configured time dimension that allows analysis by day, week, month, quarter, or year, among other periods. For more details on the time period dimension, see "The Time Dimension" section of Chapter 12, "The Shareholder Data Mart."

- **Carriers:** The carrier dimension contains the information that groups carriers into common classifications, which allows better analysis while allowing users to drill down to any specific carrier.

- **Customers:** The customer dimension allows users to evaluate carrier performance by customer. A customer-specific slice into the supplier data mart allows users to monitor activities down to the most important aspect of the production cycle, the customer. A customer can be viewed in multiple ways, including the geographical aggregation path, destination, or an alternate path known as the *distance band*.

- **Destinations:** The destinations dimension allows better analysis of the data based on regional or destination locations. This dimension is similar to other location dimensions, but specifically focuses on areas of the geographical territory that are a carrier's destinations.

- **Distance band:** The distance band allows analysis of the information in this information package based on distance, in miles, of any specific delivery.

- **On-time band:** The on-time band groups deliveries with days of arrival, including late deliveries and on-time deliveries.

- **Measures:** The measures tracked in this information package are data artifacts that are key to understanding the performance of any carrier. These measures include: number of units carried, weight carried, actual distance, cost per mile, and cost per pound.

Let's take a closer look at each of these data warehouse components and gain better understanding of their purpose and content.

The Supplier Measures

The measures provided in the carrier score card information package include data that assists users in better characterizing the effectiveness of any supplier that performs delivery services for the enterprise. These measures describe the shipment data in real terms of number of packages, weight of the delivery, the distance traveled, and the cost of the delivery. From these raw numbers, calculations can include the cost per weight (pounds) and the cost per mile. Because these two calculated metrics are often requested by users, the design physically stores this data.

However, in training the users we must highlight that these measures are calculated. This training assists users in understanding how to interpret the data in aggregations; for instance, the cost per mile is not additive. By describing a measure as not additive, we mean that it does not make sense to add the detail rows together in a summary calculation. For example, if one delivery of a supplier costs $15 per mile and another delivery costs $21 per mile, it is not true that all the deliveries for the supplier cost $15 plus $21 ($36) per mile. To properly calculate the cost per mile metric, an average aggregation function should be applied. So the overall cost in this example would be (($15 + $21)/2), or $18 per mile on average.

The Carrier Dimension

The carrier dimension categorizes suppliers along a common drill-down structure. As with the customer dimension, the carrier dimension may contain multiple access paths, including geographical location, specialty service, transportation mechanism, or purchasing agent. Each of these alternate paths assists users in analyzing the delivery data and better formulating a carrier score card.

A geographic access path allows you to segment carriers by territory. Therefore, you could analyze the carriers supporting your operations in the East or West. The specialty service access path allows users to analyze the carriers based on the supplier's business focus, such as overnight deliveries versus standard ground services, which may be categorized as small package delivery carriers. The transportation access path might characterize the delivery data base on the type of vehicle used to deliver the packages, for example truck, train, or airplane.

Each of these access paths assists in answering the various ad hoc requests you will receive from users accessing the carrier score card data. Users can segment and slice the multidimensional information to levels of granularity that assist them in viewing the data correctly.

The Customer Dimension and Its Alternate Paths

The customer dimension allows users to cut the data in various ways. Depending on your implementation, these paths can accommodate viewing customers based on your sales organization, the customers' geographic location, the distance from a distribution facility, or primary carrier support. In general, the customer dimension and other alternate paths in the customer dimension refer to similar items, alternate paths viewing where a delivery is being received, or the packages' destination. These items therefore are documented as alternate paths for the same dimension, as shown in Figure 13.2.

The geographical access path takes users to a specified city through a hierarchy of country, region of the country, district of the region, state of the district, zip code of the state, and city of the zip code. This dimension allow users to analyze all destinations based on a charted territory. This might become important if you have purchasing agents assigned to each of these territories. This information assists them in understanding cities that are experiencing problems for quality services so that they can begin to establish new supplier relations in those cities as well as working with current service suppliers to improve their performance in these areas.

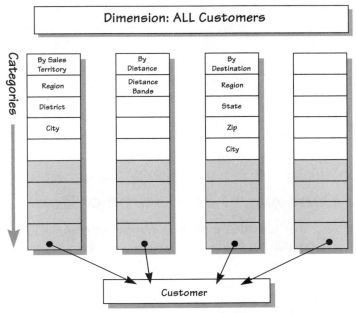

Figure 13.2 *The destination of any shipment can be monitored via separate access paths. Here, the requirements for the customer dimension, including distance band and geographical drill-down paths, are presented.*

The distance band dimension lets users segment carrier shipment information regionally. This granularity of the shipment data allows evaluation of specific carriers to determine which are good at short distances versus long distances. After all, you would hate to severe a relationship with a good supplier if you used them incorrectly. Some carriers may focus purely on short distance deliveries; however, you may have requested that they make a long distance delivery. If they failed to do so with adequate performance, should you cease to use them or should you optimize their core strength business of short distance delivery? The bands are broken into mileage bands. Depending on your business and your customer concentration by geography, you may end up with a similar band. The key groupings for the distance band dimension include: 1 to 50 miles; 51 to 200 miles; 201 to 500 miles; 501 to 1,000 miles; 1,001 to 2,500 miles; and 2,501 to 5,000 miles.

The On-Time Band Dimension

Rather than provide the details of a complete delivery timeline, this information package presents a time band, in days, for gauging on-time delivery. You could implement this with the specific dates of expectation. However, users or tools would then have to repeatedly calculate the elapsed days between when a customer expected to receive a shipment and when the carrier actually completed the delivery. An on-time band dimension is created to avoid this overhead and because this is a common request. The on-time band allows you to measure the effectiveness of any carrier's delivery services. This dimension bands together common periods for expected deliveries. Each of these bands communicates how well a carrier holds to scheduled commitments. The specific bands that characterize our delivery schedule include: 14 or more days early; 7 to 13 days early; 1 to 6 days early; on time; 1 to 6 days late; 7 to 13 days late; and 14 or more days late.

Building a Conceptual Star Schema Model

The conceptual model that is built based on the requirements we have seen include all three of the major information packaging methodology entities. In the example in Chapter 12, "The Shareholder Data Mart," we only utilized dimension and measure entities. The example in the current chapter also has category detail entities. These category detail entities are often highlighted by alternate access paths, such as those that have developed around carrier and customer.

To translate the user's information package requirements into a conceptual star schema model you perform the following activities:

- The columns of the information package diagram and alternate access path diagrams translate into dimension entities.

- The dimension entities are formulated with fields from each category, or level, in the columns of the information package diagram and alternate access path diagrams.

- Each of the lowest level categories are placed in the measure entity.

- Each of the measures are placed in the measure entity.

- Because the customer and carrier dimensions are highlighted on the information packaging diagram, they are translated into category detail entities.

The translation of our information package is shown in Figure 13.3.

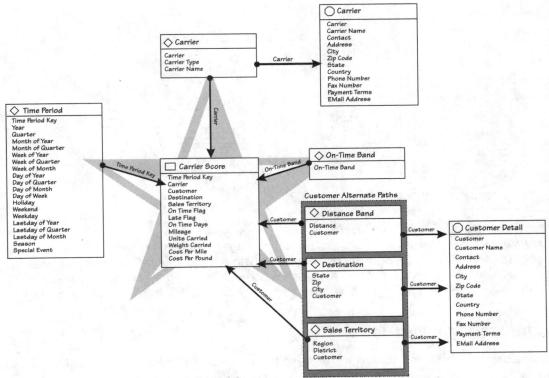

Figure 13.3 *A star schema diagram, using information packaging method notation, assists designers and developers to better translate user requirements into a logical and physical data model for our carrier score card information package.*

Implementing the Information Package

After user requirements have been gathered in an information packaging diagram and conceptual data models have been generated using a star schema with information packaging method notation; we can proceed with the actual implementation of specifications. As demonstrated in Chapter 12, "The Shareholder Data Mart," PowerDesigner allows us to build and manage our data architecture. In this chapter, we further investigate some of the features in the WarehouseArchitect component of PowerDesigner as they relate to a supplier data mart. The data model which we generate needs some additional tables to control security. These tables include aggregates and partitions, which will be generated from the physical database model shown in Figure 13.4.

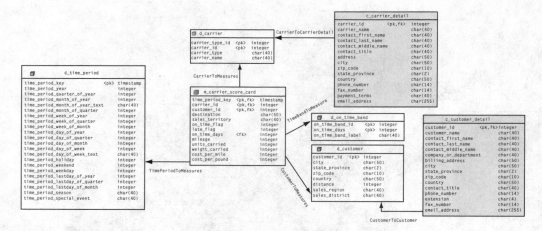

Figure 13.4 Our carrier score card information package generates a physical schema like this one. The fact tables, or measure entities, marked with m_, will be filtered and aggregated by the surrounding dimension entities, which are marked with d_. Further detail on categories in the dimensions can be derived from the category detail tables, which are marked with c_ .

Aggregating a Fact Table

An aggregate table can be used to improve performance or reduce the amount of detail users can view by summarizing rows of a measure entity, or fact table, by a specific dimension. In the carrier score card example, we may want to create an aggregate that only presents monthly, quarterly, and annual shipment information for a carrier. The aggregations that is applied to the measure entity is applied from the time period dimension. This information could be made public, while the data that goes down to daily time periods could be reserved for internal use—in essence securing the data based on the content of the measure entity. In performing such an operation, derived measure entities are created from the daily measures to include monthly, quarterly, and annual measures. If performance is a concern, these measure entities can also be used to formulate a drill-down path on the time dimension. Users can navigate first through the annual measures, selecting quarterly figures into which to drill. After this selection is made, the query would be directed at the quarterly measure entity, and so on.

To build an aggregate in WarehouseArchitect, you perform the following operations, which are depicted in Figure 13.5.

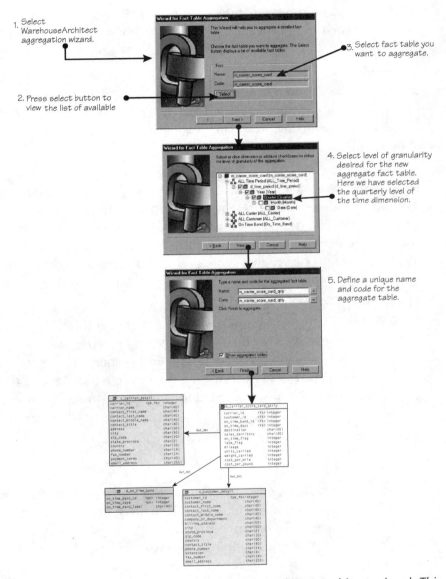

Figure 13.5 *Aggregate tables can be built with the WarehouseArchitect wizard. This operation creates all of the required data definition language syntax required by your physical database management system to build such tables.*

1. Select the WarehouseArchitect module aggregation wizard from the WAM menu of PowerDesigner. Upon selecting this option, PowerDesigner presents the Wizard for Fact Table Aggregation dialog box.

2. Click the Select button to list the current fact tables in the WarehouseArchitect Model. The tables are listed in the List of Fact Tables dialog box.

3. Select the fact table that you want to aggregate and then press the *OK* button to continue with your definition. The name and PowerDesigner code for the selected table appear in the Wizard for Fact Table Aggregation dialog box fields. From this dialog press, click the Next button to proceed with your definition.

4. The subsequent dialog in the Wizard for Fact Table Aggregation presents the multidimensional hierarchy for the fact table you selected. You expand the dimension nodes of the hierarchy and set the checkboxes either on or off to define the level of granularity for the aggregation. By default, all of the checkboxes are selected. When you clear a checkbox for a dimension in the hierarchy, all lower level checkboxes for that dimension are cleared. Pressing the Next button proceeds to the final dialog in the aggregation wizard.

5. The final step in the Wizard for Fact Table Aggregation is to define a unique name and code for the aggregate fact table. These names are logged in your MetaWorks repository with the associated detail you provide during the definition of the entity, allowing other design or development resources to use this entity in other data marts. Pressing the Finish button creates the aggregated table along with any associated foreign key relationships to dimension tables.

Partitioning a Fact Table

Partitioning is a technique that optimizes or secures data retrieval by dividing rows of a measure entity, or fact table, according to one or more dimensions for particular values of a dimension column. You might use partitions when a large quantity of atomic level data is stored in a single table. Applying partitioning to such a table can dramatically improve query response time by partitioning the data into multiple atomic level tables. Additionally, you can use a partition to secure information, for example creating an individual supplier's score card measure entity. This type of security in a database allows you to more readily share data with people outside your four walls. Preparing such a partition, you can use Internet services to push this data to the vendor on scheduled intervals and allow them to perform their own analysis of how they are performing their duties in your enterprises plan.

When you partition a fact table, you group the content of the originating fact table by different dimensions for different values in each selected dimension. The grouped data is stored in separate, derived fact tables that can then be sliced and diced on the information package cube or as secured data partitions.

To build a partition in WarehouseArchitect, you perform the following operations, which are depicted in Figure 13.6.

1. Select the Warehouse Architect module partitioning wizard from the WAM menu of PowerDesigner. Upon selecting this option, PowerDesigner presents the Wizard for Fact Table Partitioning dialog box.

2. Click the Select button to tell PowerDesigner to present a list of fact tables in the current multidimensional model of the WarehouseArchitect Model. Then select the fact table you want to partition and press *OK* to return to the Wizard for Fact Table Partitioning dialog box, where you enter the name and code fields. Then select the Next button to provide the details of the partition definition.

3. The next panel in the Wizard for Fact Table Partitioning wizard displays the multidimensional hierarchy for the selected fact table. You can expand the dimension nodes and select attribute checkboxes to define the partitioning criteria. By default, all of the checkboxes are cleared. After you have selected the partitioning definition, click Next to proceed with your definition.

4. The next panel in the Wizard for Fact Table Partitioning wizard lists the selected attributes and their attached fact or dimension entities. From this panel, you may select an attribute and click Values to define a list of partitioning values to apply to the originating fact table.

5. In the List of Values dialog, type values and labels for each partitioning scheme that you desire to be applied to the originating fact table. Repeat steps 4 and 5 until you have placed all appropriate values for each selected attribute into the definition of the partition. You must type at least one value for each attribute.

6. Upon completing the partitioning values definition step of Wizard for Fact Table Partitioning, click Finish. The PowerDesigner Wizard proceeds to defining all of the associated tables that match your partitioning values. PowerDesigner uniquely names these derived entities so that they may be logged into your MetaWorks repository with their associated detail definition, which allows other design or development resources to use this entity in other data marts.

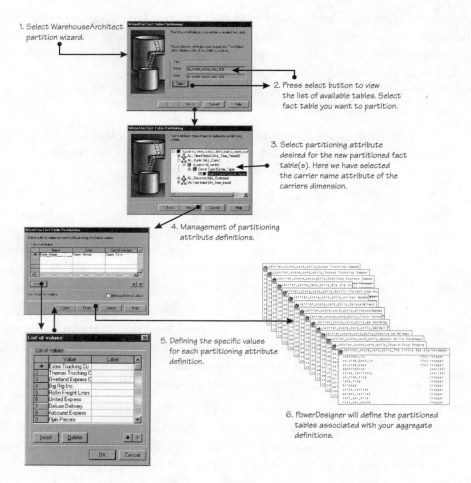

1. Select WarehouseArchitect partition wizard.

2. Press select button to view the list of available tables. Select fact table you want to partition.

3. Select partitioning attribute desired for the new partitioned fact table(s). Here we have selected the carrier name attribute of the carriers dimension.

4. Management of partitioning attribute definitions.

5. Defining the specific values for each partitioning attribute definition.

6. PowerDesigner will define the partitioned tables associated with your aggregate definitions.

Figure 13.6 *You can build partitioned tables with the WarehouseArchitect wizard. This operation creates all of the required data definition language syntax required by your physical database management system to build such tables.*

Developing PowerDynamo Templates with Sybase Central

For the examples in this case study, we use the Sybase Central PowerDynamo plug-in to build templates for presenting information in our data mart via a Web browser utilizing PowerDynamo's ability to generate dynamic HTML syntax. The scenarios we build include the following:

- **Example 1:** Show a summary of vendors who produce late shipments. In this summary, show the total number of late shipments so users can compare or rank the vendors.

- **Example 2:** Allow users to drill into a specific vendor from Example 1 and see the monthly breakdown of their shipments, including on-time and late shipments.

- **Example 3:** For any month in Example 2, allow users to drill into the details and see the regional data for on-time versus late shipments for a selected vendor and time period.

These three examples demonstrate how easily you can build your own application to perform informative drill down and the ability to slice the data cube stored in the data mart via alternate dimensions. These two operations, drill down and slice and dice, are critical operations to allow users to visualize their information, properly analyze trends, and make relevant business decisions following their analysis.

Example 1: Annual Carrier Type Shipment Score Card

The annual carrier type shipments score card template returns the total number of on-time and late shipments by carrier type for the year. The PowerDynamo template is built around the following SQL *select* statement:

```
SELECT
  d_time_period.time_period_year,
  d_carrier.carrier_type,
  sum(m_carrier_score_card.on_time_flag) as "ON TIME",
  sum(m_carrier_score_card.late_flag) as "LATE"
FROM
  m_carrier_score_card,
  d_time_period,
  d_carrier
WHERE
  m_carrier_score_card.time_period_key = d_time_period.time_period_key
  AND m_carrier_score_card.carrier_id = d_carrier.carrier_id
  AND d_time_period.time_period_year = 1997
GROUP BY
  d_time_period.time_period_year,
  d_carrier.carrier_type
```

This select statement retrieves data from the measure entity (m_carrier_score_card) and two dimension entities (d_time_period and d_carrier). The join operations performed in the SQL select statement are shown in the where clause and occur over the foreign keys (m_carrier_score_card.time_period_key and m_carrier_score_card.carrier_id). The data that is presented in the result set includes the year (d_time_period.time_period_year), the carrier type (d_carrier.carrier_type) and the two measure values that are aggregated using the SQL sum function (m_carrier_score_card.on_time_flag and m_carrier_score_card.late_flag). This SQL select statement also instructs the database to group the data by year and by carrier type so that the aggregation function performs properly. The final operation that we use to drive the query is the filter function, which is performed on the year column in the where clause of the SQL select statement. When you combine these attributes in the SQL select statement, you provide users with results as follows.

time_period_year	carrier_type	ON TIME	LATE
1997	Air	89	34
1997	Rail	89	33
1997	Truck	96	24

We use the PowerDynamo Template Creation Wizard explained in Chapter 9, "PowerDynamo Essentials," to build the first prototype of our HTML template. Table 13.1 lists the responses provided to the PowerDynamo Wizard.

Table 13.1 PowerDynamo Wizard responses for Example 1.

Prompt	Response
Template Name	example1
Template Description	Annual Carrier Type Score Card for a specific Year
Template Connection	<inherited>
Template Initial HTML	Table with headings

The PowerDynamo Template Creation Wizard generates the following code for our request:

```
<HTML>
<TITLE>example1.stm</TITLE>
<BODY>
<H1>Annual Carrier Type Score Card for a Specific Year</H1>
<!--SQL
SELECT
  d_time_period.time_period_year,
```

```
   d_carrier.carrier_type,
   sum(m_carrier_score_card.on_time_flag) as "ON TIME",
   sum(m_carrier_score_card.late_flag) as "LATE"
FROM
   m_carrier_score_card,
   d_time_period, d_carrier
WHERE
   m_carrier_score_card.time_period_key =
      d_time_period.time_period_key
 AND m_carrier_score_card.carrier_id = d_carrier.carrier_id
 AND d_time_period.time_period_year = 1997
GROUP BY
   d_time_period.time_period_year,
   d_carrier.carrier_type
 -->
<TABLE BORDER>
<TR>
<TH>time_period_year</TH>
<TH>carrier_type</TH>
<TH>ON TIME</TH>
<TH>LATE</TH>
</TR>
<!--formatting--><TR>
<TD><!--data--></TD>
<TD><!--data--></TD>
<TD><!--data--></TD>
<TD><!--data--></TD>
</TR><!--/formatting-->
</TABLE>
</BODY>
</HTML>
```

Using host variables, the template can be modified to allow users a choice of what year to see in the carrier score card. The following code (*$YEAR*) is added to the template, creating a dynamic *where* condition in the template:

```
<!--SQL
SELECT
   d_time_period.time_period_year,
   d_carrier.carrier_type,
   sum(m_carrier_score_card.on_time_flag) as "ON TIME",
   sum(m_carrier_score_card.late_flag) as "LATE"
FROM
   m_carrier_score_card,
   d_time_period, d_carrier
WHERE
   m_carrier_score_card.time_period_key =
      d_time_period.time_period_key
 AND m_carrier_score_card.carrier_id = d_carrier.carrier_id
```

```
 AND d_time_period.time_period_year = $YEAR
GROUP BY
  d_time_period.time_period_year,
  d_carrier.carrier_type
 -->
```

To execute the template, the calling HTML page or user-entered URL must contain an equated value for the host variable. For example, executing the template for 1997 is done with the following URL.

```
http://localhost/Site/VDM/example1.stm?YEAR=1997
```

Example 2: Carrier Type Shipment Score Card

Our carrier type shipment score card provides statistics for each vendor in a carrier type classification. This query of the information package returns each carrier that fits the selected classification type and the breakdown of all of their late and on-time shipments for a specific year. This query represents a drill-down operation on the results for the query in Example 1. Users select a specific carrier type for which they want to see additional details. This selection alters the grouping of the results and the filtering of the records that have been read to return the results in the SQL *select* statement. The PowerDynamo template is built around the following SQL *select* statement:

```
SELECT
  d_time_period.time_period_year,
  d_carrier.carrier_id,
  max(d_carrier.carrier_name),
  sum(m_carrier_score_card.on_time_flag) AS "ON TIME",
  sum(m_carrier_score_card.late_flag) AS "LATE"
FROM
  m_carrier_score_card,
  d_time_period,
  d_carrier
WHERE
  m_carrier_score_card.time_period_key = d_time_period.time_period_key
  AND m_carrier_score_card.carrier_id = d_carrier.carrier_id
  AND d_time_period.time_period_year = 1997
  AND d_carrier.carrier_type = "Truck"
GROUP BY
  d_time_period.time_period_year,
  d_carrier.carrier_id
```

The major modifications in this query and the one presented in Example 1 include:

- The *select* clause now returns the year, the carrier's name, and the aggregated measures for on-time and late shipments.

- The *where* clause has been altered to simply retrieve all rows that represent trucking shipments for 1997.

- The returned data is grouped by year and carrier name.

When you combine these attributes into the SQL *select* statement, you provide users with results as follows:

year	carrier_id	Supplier Name	ON TIME	LATE
1997	1	Big Rig Inc.	17	3
1997	2	Estes Trucking Company	28	6
1997	3	Overland Express Company	16	8
1997	4	Rollin Freight Lines Inc.	18	6
1997	5	Thomas Trucking Company	17	1

The PowerDynamo Template Creation Wizard is once again utilized to build this second, drill-down HTML template. Table 13.2 lists the responses provided to the Power-Dynamo Wizard.

Table 13.2 *PowerDynamo Wizard responses for Example 2.*

Prompt	Response
Template Name	example2
Template Description	Annual Carrier Score Card for a Specific Year and Carrier Type
Template Connection	<inherited>
Template Initial HTML	Table with headings

The PowerDynamo Template Creation Wizard generates the following code for our request:

```
<HTML>
<TITLE>example2.stm</TITLE>
<BODY>
<H1>Annual Carrier Score Card for a Specific Year and Carrier Type</H1>
<!--SQL
```

```
SELECT
  d_time_period.time_period_year,
  d_carrier.carrier_id,
  max(d_carrier.carrier_name),
  sum(m_carrier_score_card.on_time_flag) AS "ON TIME",
  sum(m_carrier_score_card.late_flag) AS "LATE"
FROM
  m_carrier_score_card,
  d_time_period,
  d_carrier
WHERE
  m_carrier_score_card.time_period_key = d_time_period.time_period_key
  AND m_carrier_score_card.carrier_id = d_carrier.carrier_id
  AND d_time_period.time_period_year = 1997
  AND d_carrier.carrier_type = 'Truck'
GROUP BY
  d_time_period.time_period_year,
  d_carrier.carrier_id
 -->
<TABLE BORDER>
<TR>
<TH>time_period_year</TH>
<TH>carrier_id</TH>
<TH>carrier_name</TH>
<TH>ON TIME</TH>
<TH>LATE</TH>
</TR>
<!--formatting--><TR>
<TD><!--data--></TD>
<TD><!--data--></TD>
<TD><!--data--></TD>
<TD><!--data--></TD>
<TD><!--data--></TD>
</TR><!--/formatting-->
</TABLE>
</BODY>
</HTML>
```

Using host variables, we can modify the template to give users a choice of what year and carrier type to see in the carrier score card. We add the following codes ($YEAR and $CARRIER_TYPE) to the template to create a dynamic *where* condition:

```
<!--SQL
SELECT
  d_time_period.time_period_year,
  d_carrier.carrier_id,
  max(d_carrier.carrier_name),
  sum(m_carrier_score_card.on_time_flag) AS "ON TIME",
  sum(m_carrier_score_card.late_flag) AS "LATE"
FROM
```

```
    m_carrier_score_card,
    d_time_period,
    d_carrier
WHERE
    m_carrier_score_card.time_period_key = d_time_period.time_period_key
    AND m_carrier_score_card.carrier_id = d_carrier.carrier_id
    AND d_time_period.time_period_year = $YEAR
    AND d_carrier.carrier_type = $CARRIER_TYPE
GROUP BY
    d_time_period.time_period_year,
    d_carrier.carrier_id
  -->
```

To execute the template, the calling HTML page or user-entered URL must contain an equated value for the host variables. For example, to call the *example2* template from a browser's location line, you enter the following URL.

```
http://localhost/Site/VDM/example2.stm?YEAR=1997&CARRIER_TYPE='Truck'
```

With DynaScript, you can add a dynamic link between the *example1* and the *example2* template. Doing so provides a dynamic interface that allow users to perform a dynamic drill-down operation.

Example 3: Monthly Carrier Shipment Score Card

The monthly carrier shipment score card provides monthly statistics for a specific vendor in a carrier type classification for a specified year. The statistics returned by this query provides a breakdown of all of the vendor's late and on-time shipments. This query represents multiple drill-down operations on the results for the query in Example 2.

The drill-down operation is represented by successive selections of the carrier dimension. In our *example1* template, users select the carrier type to produce the results in *example2*. In *example2*, users select a specific carrier to produce the results that are presented in *example3*. These operations are classic decision-support drill-down operations.

The multiple drill-down operations occur when the granularity of the results are changed to reflect user activity. In *example3*, we not only provide details for a specific vendor, but also detail of annual statistics at a new, monthly level.

As explained in Example 2, these types of operations alter the grouping of results and the filtering of read records to return the results in the SQL *select* statement. We build the PowerDynamo template around the following SQL *select* statement:

```
SELECT
 max(d_time_period.time_period_month_of_year_text) AS "MONTH",
 sum(m_carrier_score_card.on_time_flag) AS "ON TIME",
 sum(m_carrier_score_card.late_flag) AS "LATE"
FROM
 m_carrier_score_card,
 d_time_period,
 d_carrier
WHERE
 m_carrier_score_card.time_period_key = d_time_period.time_period_key
 AND m_carrier_score_card.carrier_id = d_carrier.carrier_id
 AND d_time_period.time_period_year = 1997
 AND d_carrier.carrier_type = "Truck"
 AND d_carrier.carrier_id = 3
GROUP BY
 d_time_period.time_period_month_of_year
ORDER BY
 d_time_period.time_period_month_of_year;
```

The major modifications in this query and the one presented in Example 2 include:

- The *select* clause now only returns the month and aggregated measures for on-time and late shipments. Notice that we were forced to use an aggregate function (max) on the month that is displayed. The reason that this aggregate function is required is that the field that represents the text month was not used in the *group by* statement. Because the month is best ordered using the numeric representation, but best presented using the text representation, we use both attributes here. All columns in the *select* clause not represented in the *group by* clause must have an aggregate function applied to them. For text fields such as the month text field you will typically use the min or max function to validate the query in the database engine's parser. In reality, all of the month text values in the numeric month group are the same.

- The *where* clause has been altered to simply retrieve all rows that represent the trucking shipments for 1997 specifically for the Overland Express Company.

- The returned data is grouped by the month of the year.

When you combine these attributes into the SQL *select* statement, users receive results as follows:

MONTH	ON TIME	LATE
January	3	2
March	3	0

MONTH	ON TIME	LATE
April	1	0
May	3	0
June	1	0
July	1	1
September	1	1
October	2	2
November	1	1
December	0	1

The PowerDynamo Template Creation Wizard is again used to build the third, multiple drill-down HTML template. Table 13.3 lists the responses that the PowerDynamo Wizard provided.

Table 13.3 PowerDynamo Wizard responses for Example 3.

Prompt	Response
Template Name	example3
Template Description	Monthly Carrier Score Card for a Specific Year and Carrier
Template Connection	<inherited>
Template Initial HTML	Table with headings

The PowerDynamo Template Creation Wizard generates the following code for our request.

```
<HTML>
<TITLE>example3.stm</TITLE>
<BODY>
<H1>Monthly Carrier Score Card for a Specific Year and Carrier</H1>
<!--SQL
SELECT
  max(d_time_period.time_period_month_of_year_text) AS "MONTH",
  sum(m_carrier_score_card.on_time_flag) AS "ON TIME",
  sum(m_carrier_score_card.late_flag) AS "LATE"
FROM
  m_carrier_score_card,
  d_time_period,
  d_carrier
WHERE
  m_carrier_score_card.time_period_key = d_time_period.time_period_key
```

```
    AND m_carrier_score_card.carrier_id = d_carrier.carrier_id
    AND d_time_period.time_period_year = 1997
    AND d_carrier.carrier_type = 'Truck'
    AND d_carrier.carrier_id = 3
  GROUP BY
    d_time_period.time_period_month_of_year
  ORDER BY
    d_time_period.time_period_month_of_year;
  -->
<TABLE BORDER>
<TR>
<TH>MONTH</TH>
<TH>ON TIME</TH>
<TH>LATE</TH>
</TR>
<!--formatting--><TR>
<TD><!--data--></TD>
<TD><!--data--></TD>
<TD><!--data--></TD>
</TR><!--/formatting-->
</TABLE>
</BODY>
</HTML>
```

Using host variables, we can modify the template to give users a choice of what year, carrier type, and carrier to see in the carrier score card. Adding the following code to the template creates a dynamic *where* condition:

```
<!--SQL
SELECT
  max(d_time_period.time_period_month_of_year_text) AS "MONTH",
  sum(m_carrier_score_card.on_time_flag) AS "ON TIME",
  sum(m_carrier_score_card.late_flag) AS "LATE"
FROM
  m_carrier_score_card,
  d_time_period,
  d_carrier
WHERE
  m_carrier_score_card.time_period_key = d_time_period.time_period_key
  AND m_carrier_score_card.carrier_id = d_carrier.carrier_id
  AND d_time_period.time_period_year = $YEAR
  AND d_carrier.carrier_type = $CARRIER_TYPE
  AND d_carrier.carrier_id = $CARRIER_ID
GROUP BY
  d_time_period.time_period_month_of_year
ORDER BY
  d_time_period.time_period_month_of_year;
  -->
```

To execute the template, the calling HTML page or user-entered URL contains an equated value for the host variables. For example, the following URL properly executes the template:

```
http://localhost/Site/VDM/example2.stm?YEAR=1997&CARRIER_TYPE='Truck'&CARRIER_ID=3
```

With DynaScript, you can add a dynamic link between the *example2* and *example3* templates. This provides a dynamic interface that allows users to perform a dynamic drill-down operation. This operation, when sequenced properly, provides users with an interface to view:

- Annual results of all carrier types (*example1*).
- Annual results for a specific carrier type (*example2*).
- Monthly breakdown for a specific carrier in a carrier type and year (*example3*).

This dynamic linkage between data presentations provides a highly useful operation that allows users to easily navigate the carrier score card information package. However, the presentation of the data could be done more effectively with graphics. In the next section, we delve into making this drill-down navigation fully graphical with NetFactory's NetCharts' Java applets (http://www.NetCharts.com).

Integrating NetFactory's NetCharts Java Applets

NetFactory's NetCharts provides a suite of Java applets that offers both Web authors and Java developers a method to include powerful business graphics in their applications. The NetCharts suite is easy to use and requires minimal to no programming for you to integrate it into a Internet data warehouse. The NetCharts suite provides the most commonly used business charts, including pie charts, bar charts, X-Y charts, combination charts, and stock charts.

NetCharts also includes useful applets and utilities for printing HTML documents that contain charts and for generating snapshots of HTML documents containing charts without a browser. You can download the latest version of the NetCharts suite from http://www.NetCharts.com or access the product from the companion CD. As with many Internet software providers, you can try before you buy the NetCharts files. NetCharts can be installed and operational in less than 30 minutes.

You can quickly include NetCharts graphics in your HTML pages by adding an applet tag with a few parameter definitions. The product ships with more than 50 example files that allow you to see the range of possible displays with NetCharts. From these examples, you can determine how to integrate proper parameter definitions in your own templates to generate the desired graphical interface for your information packages. The following HTML code generates a bar chart.

```
<applet name=barchart
        codebase=../classes
        code=NFBarchartApp.class
        width=450 height=250>
<param  name=NFParamScript  value = '
  Background = (lightGray, RAISED, 8);
  Footer = ("Weekday Network Load", black, "TimesRoman", 20);
  FooterBox = (white, SHADOW, 5);
  BottomTics = ("ON", black, "Courier", 12);
  LeftTics = ("ON", black, "Courier", 12);
  LeftScale = (0, 300);
  LeftFormat = (INTEGER);
  BarLabels = "Mon", "Tue", "Wed", "Thu", "Fri";
  LeftTitle = ("Bytes\nPer\nSec", black, "TimesRoman", 20);
  LeftTitleBox = (white, SHADOW, 5);
  Legend = ("", black, "TimesRoman", 14);
  LegendBox = (lightgray, RECESS, 5);
  GraphType = GROUP;
  DataSets = ("Server #1"), ("Server #2"), ("Server #3");
  DataSet1 = 100, 125, 245.78, 147, 67;
  DataSet2 = 85, 156, 179.5, 211, 123;
  DataSet3 = 97, 87, 56, 267, 157;
'>
</applet>
```

This chapter shows you how to integrate NetCharts into your PowerDynamo applications, but is not meant as a detailed discussion of NetCharts. You may want to download the related documentation for further details on the overall product and its parameters from the URL provided earlier in this section.

When you author your HTML or DynaScript logic to integrate NetCharts, you begin by simply presenting a graphic to your users. However, NetCharts provides for sophisticated user interaction in application. All NetCharts charts allow developers to specify one or more parameters to ease users' interaction with the graphic. Examples of these parameters include:

- **Active Labels:** An active label automatically displays information to users when their mouse cursor dwells over a region of data on the graph for a set period of time. This feature is similar to Windows ToolTips. Such labels present additional information to the user, such as an exact data value, or explain something about that data region. The developer has complete control over the look and feel of Active Labels through parameter definitions.

- **Associated URL:** In addition to displaying a label, you can associate an optional URL with each label. If users click the mouse on an Active Label, NetCharts automatically retrieves the associated document in the window specified by the developer. For example, users may click a bar to display its associated tabular data, or they may click a pie chart slice to see the breakdown for that slice displayed in another bar chart or pie chart. By chaining one chart with another, the developer can create a web of charts that allows users to freely browse any information package.

- **Image Maps:** All NetCharts charts allow .gif files as background images. This feature allows you to create an image map using an XY chart to display data points on the map. As users select a point, an associated Active Label could automatically display information about that location. The same techniques can process .gif files representing geographic locations, building layouts, or network topologies.

Modifying Templates

We now will upgrade the templates that we generated in Sybase Central in the "Developing PowerDynamo Templates with Sybase Central" section earlier in this chapter to include NetCharts' Java applets. We will present the data in standard bar code format. In NetCharts, this is done using the bar chart class, which is called *NFBarchartApp.class*.

The NetCharts Applet Attributes

The HTML applet tag includes the following:

```
<applet name=barchart codebase=../classes code=NFBarchartApp.class width=450
height=250>
   //applet parameter list
</applet>
```

The HTML applet tag, which was discussed in Chapter 7, "HTML Essentials," provides information for locating the Java class file to use and other presentation attributes for a browser. The preceding applet tag tells the browser to look for the Java applet classes in the directory *../classes*. This location typically is a URL; but because we are running most of our examples locally; we use a local disk directory. The specific class we want executed is listed in the code attribute. The applet tag also specifies desired display characteristics, including a width of 450 pixels by a height of 250 pixels.

The NetCharts Parameter List

Each individual NetCharts Java applet has a series of parameters that can alter the behavior of the graphic representation of the data. Several of these parameters define the raw data to graph, which we will closely integrate with our template code to ensure that they populate the raw data in the form desired by the NetCharts Java applet. The parameters are feed to the NetCharts Java applet through an HTML param tag as follows:

```
<param  name=NFParamScript  value = '
        //parameter list
'>
```

The *param* tag accepts the attributes of *name* (the variable name for the parameters) and *value* (a long, quoted list of the specific parameters required to drive the NetCharts Java applet). We use region parameters, label parameters, and grid parameters.

A *region parameter* defines how to display a rectangular box in the graphic's background with a given color and border type. The region is defined as follows: (*Color, BorderType, BorderWidth, "Image URL", ImageScale*). The large list of valid NetCharts colors is listed in Table 13.4.

The BorderType can include: NONE, BOX, SHADOW, RAISED, or RECESS. The BorderWidth defines the width of the border in pixels. The image URL specifies an image file to fill the region. ImageScale specifies how the image is displayed and supports the following types: TILE (the default), which tiles or clips the image if it is not the same size as the region, and SIZE, which scales the image to the size of the region. The ImageURL and ImageScale parameters are optional. Region parameters include Background, HeaderBox, FooterBox, LeftTitleBox, RightTitleBox, LegendBox, DwellBox, and NoteBox.

Some examples of region parameters include:

- Background = (lightGray, RAISED, 8).

- HeaderBox = (darkgreen, NONE).

- FooterBox = (white, SHADOW, 4).

- LeftTitleBox = (yellow, RAISED, 10).

- RightTitleBox = (white, BOX, 2, "flock.gif").

NetCharts applets use label definitions extensively to display titles, legends, axis tics, and data labels. Label parameters are defined as follows: (*"Label," Color, "FontName," FontSize, Angle*). The Label is simply the text you want to display.

Color is a valid NetCharts color as listed in Table 13.4. FontName defines the family name of the font style you want to use. Font styles are platform dependent, so be sure to check your specific Java implementation for valid values. FontSize defines the point size of the font. The available values depend on the font style defined and the platform. The Angle attribute defines the angle of rotation (in degrees) for the entire label, with only the following values supported: 0, 90, 180, 270. If a nonzero value is specified, the label is rotated counterclockwise by that many degrees before rendering. Label parameters include: DwellLabel, Header, Footer, LeftTitle, RightTitle, and Legend.

The following are examples of label parameters (\n indicates a newline):

- Header = ("This Is A Default Label").

- Footer = ("This Is A\nMulti-Line\nFooter," darkred).

- LeftTitle = ("Rotated Label", black, "TimesRoman," 16, 90).

- RightTitle = ("Large\nLabel", blue, "Courier," 30).

All NetCharts applets except NFDiagramApp and NFPiechartApp support the display of one or more grids behind data. The grid layouts and styles can be independently specified, and can be associated with any of the axes being displayed.

Examples of grid parameters include:

- BottomTics = ("ON", black, "Courier," 12).

- LeftTics = ("ON", black, "Courier," 12).

- LeftScale = (0, 300).

- LeftFormat = (INTEGER).

Specific parameters are required as we begin to formulate the required parameters to display data for our users. For a bar chart, these parameters include:

- **DataSets** defines a list of datasets with a given name color and type. The names are used as items in the Legend, while the color is used for each bar in the dataset. The following bar types are supported: BAR, TRIANGLEBAR, DIAMONDBAR, CYLINDER, PIEVERTICAL, and PIEHORIZONTAL. At most, 50 datasets may be displayed. If a color is not specified, the previously specified color is used. If the color is specified as *null*, a default color is chosen from the color table.

- **DataSet[1-50]** defines a list of numeric values for each dataset defined by the DataSets parameter. Each dataset may contain a different number of values. If the value of *null* is substituted for a number, no bar will be drawn in that position.

- **GraphType** determines the proper presentation style for the bar chart. The valid values include: GROUP, which is the default value and groups all datasets together; ROWS, which displays all datasets in separate rows; and STACK, which stacks datasets.

- **BarLabels** defines a list of labels to display below each group of bars. This parameter overrides the BottomLabels parameter (for VERTICAL bars) or the LeftLabels parameter (for HORIZONTAL bars).

Table 13.4 *Valid NetCharts colors.*

aliceblue	antiquewhite	aqua
aquamarine	azure	beige
bisque	black	blanchedalmond
blue	blueviolet	brown
burlywood	cadetblue	chartreuse
chocolate	coral	cornflowerblue
cornsilk	crimson	cyan
darkblue	darkcyan	darkgoldenrod
darkgray	darkgreen	darkkhaki
darkmagenta	darkolivegreen	darkorange
darkorchid	darkred	darksalmon
darkseagreen	darkslateblue	darkslategray
darkturquoise	darkviolet	deeppink
deepskyblue	dimgray	dodgerblue
firebrick	floralwhite	forestgreen
fuchsia	gainsboro	ghostwhite
gold	goldenrod	gray
green	greenyellow	honeydew
hotpink	indianred	indigo

Continued

Table 13.4 *Continued*

ivory	khaki	lavender
lavenderblush	lawngreen	lemonchiffon
lightblue	lightcoral	lightcyan
lightgoldenrodyellow	lightgreen	lightgrey
lightpink	lightsalmon	lightseagreen
lightskyblue	lightslategray	lightsteelblue
lightyellow	lime	limegreen
linen	magenta	maroon
mediumaquamarine	mediumblue	mediumorchid
mediumpurple	mediumseagreen	mediumslateblue
mediumspringgreen	mediumturquoise	mediumvioletred
midnightblue	mintcream	mistyrose
moccasin	navajowhite	navy
oldlace	olive	olivedrab
orange	orangered	orchid
palegoldenrod	palegreen	paleturquoise
palevioletred	papayawhip	peachpuff
peru	pink	plum
powderblue	purple	red
rosybrown	royalblue	saddlebrown
salmon	sandybrown	seagreen
seashell	sienna	silver
skyblue	slateblue	slategray
snow	springgreen	steelblue
tan	teal	thistle
tomato	turquoise	violet
wheat	white	whitesmoke
yellow	yellowgreen	

DynaScript Generation of NetCharts Syntax

DynaScript allows you to dynamically generate HTML pages. PowerDynamo templates can easily merge database information with HTML and JavaScript tags to add additional value to your final application. NetCharts is a third-party Java applet that you also can interface into the PowerDynamo environment. To improve this chapter's three-level drill-down example, we interface NetCharts with the PowerDynamo templates through the steps described in the following sections.

Step 1: Building the Applet Tag

The first step in producing a graphical interface to our carrier score card information is to generate the HTML applet tag for the NetCharts Java applet. The code to generate is the following:

```
<applet name=barchart codebase=../classes code=NFBarchartApp.class width=450
height=250>
```

To generate this code in a DynaScript template, you use the *writeln* method of the *document* object as documented in Chapter 9, "PowerDynamo Product Essentials." The DynaScript syntax appears as follows:

```
document.writeln("<applet name=barchart
codebase==../../../widgets/NetCharts2.02/classes code=NFBarchartApp.class width=450
height=250>");
```

Step 2: Building the HTML Parameters Tag

The second step in interfacing NetCharts in the PowerDynamo templates is to build the HTML parameters tag. The HTML *param* tag is where you place all parameters for the Java applet. Therefore, as we build the DynaScript, we populate each of the values associated with individual parameters required for our specific chart type. The required HTML syntax is as follows:

```
<param name=NFParamScript value = '
```

Note that the value attribute of the *param* tag is opened here with a single quotation mark. We will close this attribute after we place all of the required values for the NetCharts applet in the template later in Step 5. To generate this code in a DynaScript template, you use the *writeln* method of the *document object*, as follows:

```
document.writeln("<param name=NFParamScript value = '");
```

Step 3: Building the NetCharts Nondata-Driven Parameters

Several NetCharts parameters are not driven by dynamic data. In fact, all NetCharts parameters are dynamic, but for the purpose of our examples we will only create dynamic data-driven parameters. You can take these examples and easily build your own fully dynamic interface. The specific parameters we generate include: the background of the graph, the presentation style for the heading, how the tic marks should appear on the graph's grid, the presentation style for the left axis title, the presentation style for dwell labels (similar to Window's ToolTips), and the presentation style for the graph's legend.

The nondata-driven parameters are placed in the HTML *param* tag using the *writeln* method of the *document* object, as shown below.

```
document.writeln('Background = (white, NONE, 0);');
document.writeln('HeaderBox = (maroon, NONE, 0);');
document.writeln('BottomTics = ("ON", black, "TimesRoman", 16);');
document.writeln('LeftTics = ("ON", black, "TimesRoman", 16);');
document.writeln('LeftFormat = (INTEGER);');
document.writeln('LeftTitleBox = (white, NONE, 0);');
document.writeln('DwellLabel = ("", black, "Courier", 20);');
document.writeln('DwellBox = (yellow, RAISED, 3);');
document.writeln('GraphType = GROUP;');
document.writeln('Legend = ("", black, "TimesRoman", 14);');
document.writeln('LegendBox = (lightgray, RECESS, 5);');
document.writeln('LeftTitle = ("Shipments", maroon, 0);');
```

Step 4: Building the Data-Driven Parameters

In the fourth step, we build all of the data-driven parameters. For our examples, this is the most detailed section of DynaScript coding. The process of cycling through the result set in a single process to gather all of the required dynamic data is a bit tricky. So we break this section into several smaller discussion areas.

The first task in the DynaScript is to define variables to hold values that are later written to the document or to define variables that control looping statements in DynaScript. The variables that we use for DynaScript control include row and column counters. The variables that we define for NetCharts parameter building include the heading, bar labels, data sets, and maximum axis value. The following DynaScript syntax declares these variables:

```
var nRow = 1; //determines the current row
var nRowCount = SQL.GetRowCount(); //defines maximum rows
var nCol = 1; //determines the current column
var nColCount = SQL.GetColumnCount(); //defines maximum columns
var sHeader = ' Annual Carrier Type Score Card'; //graph heading
var sBarLabels = 'BarLabels = '; //bar group labels
var sDataSets = 'DataSets = '; //data set labels
var sData = new createArray((nColCount - 2), ' '); //raw data array
var nMaxValue = 0; //maximum axis value
```

In the next task for the data-driven section of our DynaScript, we the actual data set labels. NetCharts uses data sets to define the individual bars that will be grouped together in a column of a report. Other graphical tools refer to these specifically as bars and are presented in a legend in a color-coded fashion. In our example, the first two columns of the query are primary drivers of the groups and filters (*time_period_year* and *carrier_type*). The remaining columns are the measures that are the focal point of the graph, including the on-time and late shipments. Therefore, we cycle through the columns and build data sets to hold all of the values in the database result set with the following DynaScript syntax:

```
for (nCol = 1; nCol <= nColCount; nCol++) {
  sData[nCol] = 'DataSet' + nCol + ' = ';
}
```

We now are ready to begin retrieving the results returned by our query and loading the NetCharts parameters. This process is done through a *while* loop DynaScript statement, which continues until no more results are available in the SQL cursor. As we traverse the result set, we must be aware of certain operations that are sensitive to labels versus those that are sensitive to the raw data on the graph. The functionality of this block of code is as follows:

- For the first row in the result set, place the information about the year being viewed in the header; place the column names (labels) in the data sets so they can be displayed properly in the legend.

- For all rows in the result set, place the raw data in individual data arrays; place the data from the second column (carrier_type) into bar labels and test to see if the maximum value for the axis is properly set.

This functionality is reflected in the following DynaScript syntax:

```
//Step through each row of database query result set
nCol = 1;
while( SQL.MoveNext() ) {
  //If on first row, set up label parameters, including
  //header (Header) and data label sets (DataSets)
  if nRow == 1 {
    sHeader = 'Header = ("' + SQL.GetValue(1) + sHeader + '", white, "TimesRoman", 20);';
    nCurCol++;
    for (nCol =3; nCol<=nColCount; nCol++) {
      sDataSets = sDataSets + '("' + SQL.GetColumnLabel(nCol) + '")';
      if nCol < nColCount {
        sDataSets = sDataSets + ', ';
      }
    }
  }
  //Set up bar labels based on values in second column
  sBarLabels = sBarLabels + '"' + SQL.GetValue(2) + '"' ;
  if nRow < nRowCount {
    sBarLabels = sBarLabels + ', ';
  }
  //Set up data value sets (DataSet[1-50]) with values
  //from all columns after title columns of 1&2
  for (nCol = 3; nCol<=nColCount; nCol++) {
    if SQL.GetValue(nCol) > nMaxValue {
      nMaxValue = SQL.GetValue(nCol);
    }
    sData[nCol-2] = sData[nCol-2] + SQL.GetValue(nCol);
    if nRow < nRowCount {
      sData[nCol-2] = sData[nCol-2] + ', ';
    }
  }
  nRow++;
}
```

We are finally through the result set and prepared to write the parameters to the HTML file. The following DynaScript code uses the *writeln* method of the *document* object to write all data-driven variables in their appropriate parameter syntax:

```
nMaxValue = nMaxValue * 1.1;
document.writeln('LeftScale = (0, ' + nMaxValue + ');');
document.writeln(sHeader);
document.writeln(sBarLabels + ';');
```

```
document.writeln(sDataSets + ';');
for (nCol = 3; nCol <= nColCount; nCol++) {
   document.writeln(sData[nCol-2] + ';');
}
```

Step 5: Terminating All Tags

Following the writing of all parameters, we must terminate the HTML *param* tag, which is done with the following statement:

```
document.writeln("'>");
```

The last statement we need to conclude our DynaScript syntax is to close the NetCharts Java Applet. This is done with the HTML applet end tag, as shown below:

```
document.writeln('</applet>');
```

The PowerDynamo Template

The PowerDynamo template to present the results for Example 1 is shown in Figure 13.7. The code that produces these results is as follows:

```
<HTML>
<TITLE>example1_chart.stm (Carrier Score Card/Panel 1)</TITLE>
<BODY>
<H1><CENTER>Carrier Score Card</CENTER></H1>
<!--SQL
SELECT
   d_time_period.time_period_year,
   d_carrier.carrier_type,
   sum(m_carrier_score_card.on_time_flag) as "ON TIME",
   sum(m_carrier_score_card.late_flag) as "LATE"
FROM
   m_carrier_score_card,
   d_time_period, d_carrier
WHERE
   m_carrier_score_card.time_period_key =      d_time_period.time_period_key
  AND m_carrier_score_card.carrier_id = d_carrier.carrier_id
  AND d_time_period.time_period_year = $YEAR
GROUP BY
   d_time_period.time_period_year,
   d_carrier.carrier_type
  -->
<!--SCRIPT
//General purpose array initialization function
function createArray(n, init) {
   var i=1;
```

```
  this.size = n ;
  for (i = 1; i <= n; i++) {
    this[i] = init;
  }
  return this;
}
//Step 1: Write applet HTML starting tab
document.writeln('<CENTER><applet name=barchart
  codebase=../../../widgets/NetCharts2.02/classes
  code=NFBarchartApp.class  width=600 height=250>');
//Step 2: Write HTML param tag
document.writeln("<param name=NFParamScript value = '");
//Step 3: Write nondata-driven parameter values
document.writeln('DebugSet = LICENSE;');
document.writeln('Background = (white, NONE, 0);');
document.writeln('HeaderBox = (maroon, NONE, 0);');
document.writeln('BottomTics = ("ON", black, "TimesRoman", 16);');
document.writeln('LeftTics = ("ON", black, "TimesRoman", 16);');
document.writeln('LeftFormat = (INTEGER);');
document.writeln('LeftTitleBox = (white, NONE, 0);');
document.writeln('DwellLabel = ("", black, "Courier", 20);');
document.writeln('DwellBox = (yellow, RAISED, 3);');
document.writeln('GraphType = GROUP;');
document.writeln('Legend = ("", black, "TimesRoman", 14);');
document.writeln('LegendBox = (lightgray, RECESS, 5);');
document.writeln('LeftTitle = ("Shipments", maroon, 0);');
//Step 4: Write data-driven parameter values
//Step 4a: Local variables to hold values or guide loops
var nRow = 1;
var nRowCount = SQL.GetRowCount() ;
var nCol = 1;
var nColCount = SQL.GetColumnCount() ;
var sBarLabels = 'BarLabels = ';
var sHeader = ' Annual Carrier Type Score Card';
var sDataSets = 'DataSets = ';
var sData = new createArray((nColCount - 2), ' ');
var nMaxValue = 0;
//Step 4b: Set up proper number of DataSets based on columns
for (nCol = 1; nCol <= nColCount; nCol++) {
  sData[nCol] = 'DataSet' + nCol + ' = ';
}
//Step 4c: Step through each row of database query result set
nCol = 1;
while( SQL.MoveNext() ) {
  //Step 4d: If first row, set up label parameters:
  //header (Header) and data label sets (DataSets)
  if nRow == 1 {
    sHeader = 'Header = ("' + SQL.GetValue(1) + sHeader + '", white, "TimesRoman", 20);';
    nCurCol++;
    for (nCol =3; nCol<=nColCount; nCol++) {
      sDataSets = sDataSets + '("' + SQL.GetColumnLabel(nCol) + '")';
```

```
      if nCol < nColCount {
        sDataSets = sDataSets + ', ';
      }
    }
  }
//Step 4e: Set up Bar Labels based on values in second column
sBarLabels = sBarLabels + '"' + SQL.GetValue(2) + '"' ;
if nRow < nRowCount {
  sBarLabels = sBarLabels + ', ';
}
//Step 4f: Set up data value sets (DataSet[1-50])
//with values from all columns after title columns of 1&2
for (nCol = 3; nCol<=nColCount; nCol++) {
  if SQL.GetValue(nCol) > nMaxValue {
    nMaxValue = SQL.GetValue(nCol);
  }
  sData[nCol-2] = sData[nCol-2] + SQL.GetValue(nCol);
  if nRow < nRowCount {
    sData[nCol-2] = sData[nCol-2] + ', ';
  }
}
nRow++;
}
//Step 4g: Display all data driven parameters
nMaxValue = nMaxValue * 1.1;
document.writeln('LeftScale = (0, ' + nMaxValue + ');');
document.writeln(sHeader);
document.writeln(sBarLabels + ';');
document.writeln(sDataSets + ';');
for (nCol = 3; nCol <= nColCount; nCol++) {
  document.writeln(sData[nCol-2] + ';');
}
//Step 5: Close HTML param tag and HTML applet tag
document.writeln("'>");
document.writeln('</applet></CENTER>');
-->
</BODY>
</HTML>
```

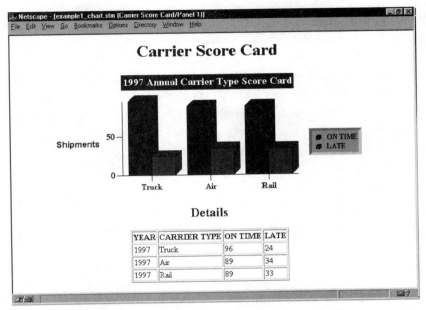

Figure 13.7 *Integrating special purpose Java applets such as NetCharts can improve the usability of your Web data warehouse. Here, annual shipment information is displayed in a easy-to-read bar chart.*

Building a Drill-Down Interface

The PowerDynamo template that we built in the preceding sections delivers easy-to-read graphics for the query examples in this chapter. The templates used by PowerDynamo merge database information with HTML to deliver a final application. Our last improvement to this site is to integrate drill down among three levels: annual carrier type results, annual results for carriers, and monthly carrier statistics.

Inserting Proper Parameters

All NetCharts applets support the display of informational labels, called *dwell* or *active labels*. Operationally, these labels perform an action whenever a mouse "dwells" over a specified data value or label. For example, when a user's mouse hovers over a bar for a short period of time on the bar charts in our example, the value of an individual bar is displayed. Aside from simply displaying of information, which is similar to Microsoft

Window's ToolTips, you can define activities to be performed when users click the label. Here is where our drill-down functionality is performed.

The drill-down operation allows users to click an active label, which executes a defined URL. In NetCharts, this URL can replace the current HTML document with any other HTML document, to alter the display of any named frame or window in the browser or to load new chart parameters from a parameter file. This drill-down capability is extremely flexible and allows a NetCharts chart to serve as a highly intuitive graphical interface to your data warehouse; guiding novice and professional users consistently to the data they desire, whether that data is graphical or textual.

Modifying our existing bar chart is relatively straightforward. The following modifications achieve a drill-down operation:

1. We define another variable to use to build the active labels. This DynaScript statement would be placed in Step 4a of the previous sample code:

```
var sBarActiveLabels = 'BarActiveLabels = ';
```

2. We interject the DynaScript code with the current bar label code to link the bar label with the second query's HTML template. This code would be added in Step 4e of the sample code:

```
sBarActiveLabels = sBarActiveLabels + '("OUTLINE", "http://local-
host/Site/VDM/example2_chart.stm?YEAR=' + document.value.YEAR +
'&CARRIER_TYPE=' + SQL.GetValue(2) + '")';
if nRow < nRowCount {
    sBarActiveLabels = sBarActiveLabels + ', ';
}
```

3. Code to display the active labels is added to Step 4g of the sample code. This DynaScript code would add the active bar labels parameter to the overall list of values passed to NetCharts:

```
document.writeln(sBarActiveLabels + ';');
```

Navigating the Final Application

In the final user interface of our carrier score card application, three PowerDynamo templates are connected to drill down into greater detail. The results of executing these templates are shown in Figure 13.8 and include on-time and late shipment data for:

- Carrier types annually.

- Specific carriers in a carrier type annually.

- A specific carrier's monthly statistics.

The beauty of this interface for spotting alarming trends is quite apparent when you view the graphics versus the predecessor tables.

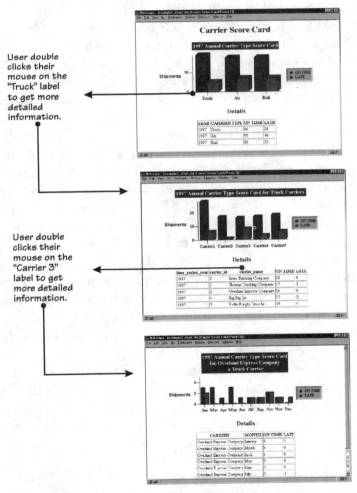

Figure 13.8 *Our carrier score card application integrates NetCharts' Java applets into PowerDynamo templates to build a robust, user-friendly interface to a data warehouse.*

Summary

For years, the service industry has formed major companies without corporate offices, a large number of employees, or much equipment. Is it possible in the future to form manufacturing companies in a similar fashion? A growing number of manufacturers are contracting everything from product engineering, marketing, and assembly. For example, previously at The Procter & Gamble Company, engineers were often tasked with figuring out how to make conveyor belts to run the product assemblies faster until one day when they figured out that they could ship the finished product to a vendor that could provide the packaging and shipping services for them. Arrangements like this are becoming more frequent among manufacturers to optimize operations and manage the enormous costs associated with facilities management.

Therefore, virtual manufacturing companies will be created in the future, allowing start-ups to grow faster with fewer assets and employees, and in less space than the smoke stack ancestors with which we are familiar. Success will depend on greater discipline, communication, and planning. Much of this structure and stability will come from data marts that are filled with information packages that track all aspects of vendor and supplier metrics.

Business intelligence enables the concept of virtual manufacturing. A virtual manufacturing company will do what it does best and farm out the remaining work to others who can perform the job better than the parent company. The business intelligence required to make such decisions as the proper vendor or supplier to take on jobs outside the enterprise's four walls will be provided by placing well-organized supplier data into a data warehouse and permitting the decisions makers to have ready access to this information. Additionally, providing information on an enterprise's plans and objectives to suppliers will allow them to better understand how you want to be served. A data warehouse provides the infrastructure for storing such valuable information assets and the Internet provides the ubiquitous access required to deliver the data inside your company and outside to your extended company.

The corporations that succeed in the future will be those that can utilize both emerging technologies and existing partnerships to support and extend the goals of their businesses to include the extended company. The extended company is outside of your current four walls; it encompasses your suppliers and customers—both current and prospective.

Some observers call this extended enterprise the supply chain, others refer to it as the value chain, and still others look at the demand chain. Automating, storing, and continually analyzing the data artifacts along this process line offers significant value. Any way you look at this information, you will see huge payoffs that include items such as: reduced costs; increased revenues; reduced cycle times; lower inventory; higher availability; more stable supplier and customer relationships; and improved loyalty among the human centers identified in the information packaging method.

In the next chapter, we proceed to the third important human knowledge center that drives metrics that should be managed by a data warehouse: employees.

14

The Employee Data Mart

The intellectual assets of any corporation lie in its employees and the overall success of any enterprise relies heavily on those employees. Employees are the driving force behind the management of the four human knowledge centers in the information packaging methodology—shareholders, suppliers, customers, and employees. However, most automated systems in an enterprise track few key metrics that drive employee satisfaction and loyalty. Therefore, when you build your employee data mart, you may be required to build additional data capture systems in parallel.

The Human Resources department more than likely is the place to originate your employee data mart. Human Resource's role is to drive the enterprise's skills matrix to match the requirements by the enterprise's business plans, including the strategic planning aspects of the company. Gaps in any enterprise skills significant impact the profit potential of a business. Based on this impact, Human Resources has a close linkage to the enterprise's financial statements.

Improving Employee Metric Analysis

When building your employee data mart, you will find significant desire by users to cross-correlate data in the employee information packages with and the other centers of management—shareholder (financial), supplier, and customer. Questions will be asked to resolve items such as:

- Does upgrading employees skills directly impact the cost of sales?

- Do defined core competencies have a material impact on the company?

- What factors influence revenue per employee?

- What are labor costs per employee?

- Based on skills requirements, how are employees organized by job function, organizational departments, and salary grades?

- How many employees are in the enterprise by department? What are the employees' job functions? What kind of growth is occurring in these job functions?

- How quickly are salaries growing in the company? How does this compare with industry benchmarks?

- What is happening to key human resource ratios such as manager to employee? Support services to employee? And so on.

Data stored in an employee data mart assists managers evaluate these questions and derive proper answers to guide the business in the business plan's defined framework. Providing human resources information on the Internet allows you to make these types of analysis "dashboard-like" for managers. Such an interface assists managers in a similar fashion to the gauges and warning lights on a vehicle's dashboard. When the oil light or low-fuel light illuminates, you know it is time to act.

An Employee-Centric Information Package

To assist you in better understanding how to deliver employee information to your management staff, we will build an employee data mart that contains metrics on the review and promotion process in an enterprise. This information should be available from your current human resources system and include data about the organization, job classifications, salary grades, job status, service length, salaries, incentive compensation, and benefits costs.

Figure 14.1 presents the information package for our human resources administration analysis data that is stored in an employee data mart. The sample information package we will build delivers the human resource analysis data to various managers in the organization. In this case study, we also delve into a simple security umbrella for the information package. Security plays an important part in any data marts, but information about employees requires stringent security.

Information Package: <u>Human Resource Administration</u>

Dimensions ⟶

Categories	ALL Time Periods	ALL Organization	ALL Positions						
	Year 3	Division	Job Group						
	Quarter 12	Department	Job Family						
	Month 36		Position						

Measures/Facts:

Number of Employees, Number of Available Positions, Number of Employee Reviews, Number of Promotions, Average Base Salary, Average Incentive Pay, Average Benefits Costs

Figure 14.1 *Our human resources administration information package assists managers in tracking key metrics for their organization.*

Our human resources administration information package contains the following information:

- **Time Periods:** Users are given information for the last three years. This information includes a fully configured time dimension, which allows analysis by month, quarter, year, and otherwise.

- **Organizations:** The organizational hierarchy permits analysis that filters, aggregates, or performs specifically on the divisions and departments in the enterprise.

- **Positions:** The positions dimension categorizes all of the jobs in the organization. This dimension has various alternate paths, including: Job Groups, Salary Grades, Job Status, and Length of Service Band.

- **Measures:** The measures stored in this information package are data artifacts that monitor the management process. These measures include: number of employees, number of available positions, number of reviews conducted, number of promotions, average base salary, average incentive pay, and average benefits costs.

Let's take a closer look at our new data warehouse components to better understand their purpose. To refresh your knowledge of the time period dimension, you may want to review the material in "The Time Dimension" section in Chapter 12, "The Shareholder Data Mart." Additionally, the organization dimension is detailed in "The Organization Dimension" section of Chapter 12. You should also begin to see that even in these simple case studies we are re-using entities within the data warehouse.

Human Resource Administration Measures

The measures provided in the human resource administration information package include data that assists users of the data mart to better characterize the review, compensation, and promotion practices in the enterprise. These measures describe the employee management process in a way to analyze the overall process and quickly find deficient areas, avoiding costly management gaffs. The metrics include:

- **Number of employees:** This measure provides a snapshot of the current employee head count in the organization by month and position attributes, such as job groupings, salary grades, and job status. Additionally, managers can evaluate the number of employees by length of service. Further analysis could also determine cross-correlation of number of managers versus number of employees per department, maintaining proper ratios for these key positions, which often are defined as goals in an enterprise's business plan.

- **Available number of positions:** The number of positions provides a snapshot of job openings in the organization. As with the number of employees metrics, this information can be viewed across the organization, over the time dimension, and by the position attributes. This data shows departments that are not keeping up with the demand in their hiring practices as well as those with the largest skills gap. Many additional evaluations can be made in this metric, including: management support requirements, growing employment gaps between number of employees and number of openings, and rapidly growing departments.

- **Number of employees reviewed:** After employees are hired, it is important that management reviews their progress versus desired plans. This occurs through the formal or informal review, an area often neglected by managers of rapidly growing departments. The number of employees reviewed metric allows managers and those overseeing the management process to validate that proper procedures are implemented to ensure that employee loyalty and satisfaction metrics are met through meaningful communication between manager and subordinate.

- **Number of promoted employees:** One true gauge of a manager's effectiveness is how many employees are promoted from within their organization. All good managers desire to retain their employees, yet they balance this with the desire of all employees to grow their careers in the enterprise. The number of promoted employees metric allows managers and those who oversee the management process to determine how well the objectives of career growth and management effectiveness occur.

- **Average base salary:** The average base salary metric allows management to better understand how employees are compensated in contrast to industry and internal benchmarks. This information can then be corrected over time to improve the cost of doing business, while properly aligning with the benchmarks and continuing to focus on employee satisfaction.

- **Average incentive pay:** Incentive pay is typically given to employees based on mutual success criteria—a company-to-employee win-win situation. Monitoring incentive pay allows managers to determine the overall compensation of individual employees and groups of employees. This information, combined with the average base salary metrics, demonstrates the effectiveness of employees and allows efficient comparison against industry benchmarks for total compensation. This metric certainly is one that management will combine with metrics from the shareholder (financial) data mart, validating that incentive pay is directly correlated with the company's achievement of its objectives.

- **Average benefit costs:** Benefit costs have skyrocketed in the 1990s and have become one of the major foci of management in most enterprises as well as in government bodies. It should be obvious—but typically is not—that employees should be apprised of the benefit cost as well. These costs are indirect compensation, whether the employee wants to believe it or not. The costs are incurred by the employer on behalf of the employee and are part of the overall compensation package of each employee. Therefore, the human resource administration information package presents this metric. Presenting the average cost of benefits metric allows management to better understand the total compensation for each employee and to monitor trends in overall employee costs.

Each of these metrics can be analyzed individually or as part of a comparison for key ratios in human resources. As cited in many of the metrics above, managers will want to cross-correlate metrics either via dimensions, such as departmental comparisons to the overall company; or via other measures, such as the level of compensation increase versus indirect compensation (benefits) increase. The dimensions and overall structure of the database objects in the human resource administration information package enable these types of comparisons.

The Position Dimension

The position dimension provides detail categorizations of each employee working for an enterprise based on standard human resources definitions. The attributes that define the overall position are often placed in a salary schedule used to determine the compensation of all employees. Such salary schedules tend to include job classification or title, educational background, level of service, and job status. Each of these subclassifications of a position comprise alternate access paths into position data, as shown in Figure 14.2.

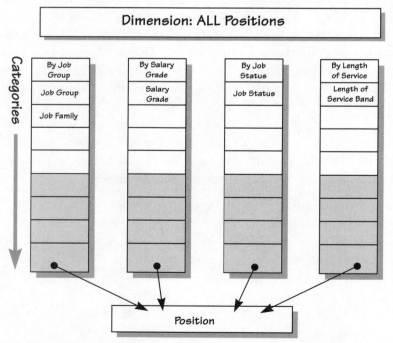

Figure 14.2 *Alternate paths for the position dimension include job group, salary grade, job status, and length of service.*

The alternate paths for position are defined as follows:

- **Job group:** The job group presents classes and families of job titles held by individual employees. A job group might include the middle managers of an entire enterprise, with the job family incorporating staff and line management groupings. In a sales organization, a job group might include field support organizations, with job families including technical support, administrative support, and marketing support.

- **Salary grades:** A salary grade, also known as a step in many salary schedules, defines where an employee fits in the overall salary plan. This is typically a numeric step on the ladder to the top of the compensation chart, which contains defined intervals. However, some enterprises integrate the concept of salary grade with a quadrant system, which means that you have two levels of your hierarchy. For our example, we use the single-depth hierarchy, which includes the step or grade of an employee.

- **Job status:** The job status path into the position dimension determines whether the position filled by an employee is full time, part time or temporary. This classification is important for management to understand the growth in a department. Often fast moving divisions grow through contracted employees.

- **Length of service:** The length of service path is another compensation-related classification. Typically, the longer people are on the job in a specific position, the higher their compensation is, due in part to the intellectual capital and knowledge developed over the years. Additionally, managers will find that some positions, typically those at the entry level, in which tenure is almost invisible; versus other positions in the management ranks which employees spend longer periods of their careers perfecting and honing their skills. This length of service path allows management and human resources personnel to monitor such activities.

Each of these alternate position paths assists users of the human resources administration information package in answering ad-hoc requests for data. Users can segment the data in the data mart in a large number of ways that refine the level of granularity of the returned data. This granularity also assists you in supporting a wide variety of management personnel throughout the company from one specific information package. The differing views, facilitated by one common information package, is advantageous to those who are conscious of the long-term maintenance costs associated with building data marts to support a ubiquitous user base.

Building a Conceptual Star Schema Model

The conceptual model built based on the requirements of our information package includes only two information packaging methodology entities—the measure and dimension entities. To translate our requirements into a conceptual star schema model, you perform the following activities:

• Translate the columns of the information package diagram and alternate access path diagrams into dimension entities.

• Formulate the dimension entities with fields from each category, or level, in the columns of the information package diagram and alternate path diagrams.

• Place each of the lowest-level categories in the measure entity.

• Place each of the measures in the measure entity.

The translation of the information package diagram is shown in Figure 14.3.

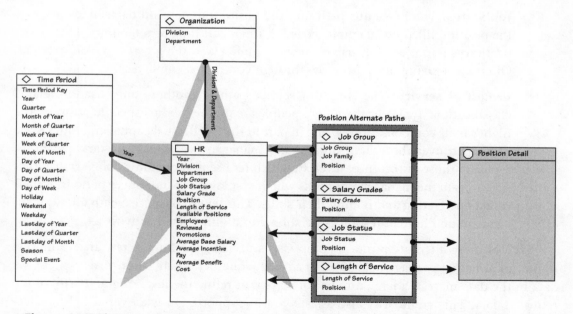

Figure 14.3 *The star schema diagram, using information packaging methodology notation, assists designers and developers in better translating user requirements into a logical and physical data model for our human resources administration information package.*

Implementing the Information Package

After user requirements have been gathered in the information package diagram and conceptual data models have been generated in a star schema with information packaging method notation, we can proceed with physical implementation. As in previous case studies, we use PowerDesigner to implement physical database models. However, before displaying the data model that support the employee data mart case study, we investigate some supporting tables for security purposes.

Embedding Security in a Data Model

Based on the sensitivity of the data maintained by a human resources database and associated employee data mart, you want to develop a security scheme beyond the simple database security of user name and password. A proper security scheme more than likely will incorporate data sensitive security into your overall data model. The best place to interject such information is in your organizational hierarchy.

Typically, users see information about those people whom they manage and below. So, if you are a divisional manager, you see all employees of your division. This scope of security includes all department managers and their employees, but doesn't include other divisions and their employees. Likewise if you are a departmental manager in a division, you would see the managers below you in the organizational hierarchy, including group managers and their subordinates, but you would not see employees in other departments.

To secure the data in our human resources administration information package, we include an additional category detail table. The purpose of this table is to define the security parameters for each user who accesses to the information package. The user's security parameters are defined in terms of the organizational hierarchy—specifically, which division and department they may see when requesting data. Ideally, your front-end application will not present more data than is provided in a user's scope. One exception to this rule might be benchmark data, such as the aggregated data for the entire company or a related division. Such a security table is created to include the following information:

```
create table c_organization_security

(
    security_id     integer not null,
    user_name       char(50)        ,
    welcome_name    char(50)        ,
    division_id     integer         ,
    department_id   integer
);
```

The columns in the *c_organization_security* table are defined as shown in Table 14.1.

Table 14.1 *A data-driven security table.*

Column	Description
security_id	The security_id is a unique id that may be used to further validate users and their privileges. This identifier ensures that the definition is unique to the overall database table.
user_name	The user name may be either the user name that was entered for database security or an application-centric user name. In this design, a specific user could have multiple security rows in the table and therefore view multiple departments and divisions. Searching the table for all instances of a user name returns all of these security definitions.
welcome_name	The welcome name column houses any information that we want to present to users after they have been accepted by the system. An example of a welcome name might be the user's formal name, such as *Thomas C. Hammergren*.
division_id	The division id defines the scope of a user's security privileges in terms of division. The value stored in this field is used in subsequent queries to restrict data to a specified division.
department_id	The department id defines the scope of a user's security privileges in terms of department. The value stored in this field is used in subsequent queries to restrict the resultant data to a specific department.

The Physical Model

After making our security level refinements, we are ready to implement the physical data model, including the entities and their relationships. From PowerDesigner, these data architecture structures are created and then the database management system's specific data definition language is generated from the model, allowing us to automate the creation of the database. The physical model within the PowerDesigner Warehouse Architect component is presented in Figure 14.4.

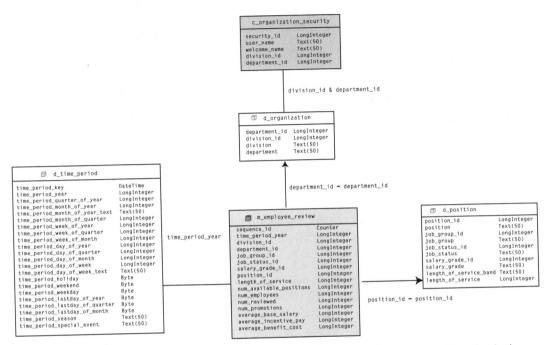

Figure 14.4 *The PowerDesigner Warehouse Architect Model presents the physical, multidimensional model for the human resource administration information package of our employee data mart.*

The model in Figure 14.4 includes the PowerDesigner icons that indicate the type of table implemented in the physical database; these types include fact and dimension tables. The figure also uses the color scheme of the information packaging methodology to indicate entity type. The color schemes include blue for measure entities, yellow for dimension entities, and red for category detail entities. The icons and color schemes add an additional layer of documentation to assist development staff in understanding the purpose and actions performed in each entity of the model.

Implementing A Manager's Dashboard

After the database platform is in place, the database schema are defined, and the data is translated and placed in the data mart, it is time to build the front-end system. Because the data is gathered on a less frequent basis than in our financial and supplier data mart examples, users need a simpler metaphor to interface with the data. Because most of us have cars, we will use the metaphor of a dashboard to provide managers with access to the employee data mart.

The manager's dashboard for this case study includes five primary displays:

- **Dashboard:** The dashboard has a basic menu structure that includes icons and labels to indicate the options available to users. This dashboard could be enhanced with color schemes to indicate the current rating of the manager's organization. Green could indicate smooth sailing. Yellow could indicate that cautionary measures should be taken, because the organization is on the verge of bad things. Red could indicate the department is failing to achieved desired performance. (While we have not gone to these measures for our example dashboard, after investigating the content of this chapter, you may want to try to make such modifications to our code.)

- **Overall management scorecard:** The overall management scorecard provides users with an overview of the key metrics that they monitor. The metrics include filling open positions, completing employee reviews, and subordinate growth through promotions. Each of these metrics is benchmarked against company averages. This scorecard provides a high-level dashboard that indicates above-average scores with a check mark and below-average scores with an *x*.

- **Job filling scorecard:** The job filling scorecard benchmarks the company's average percentage of jobs being filled versus the user's management domain and associated job fulfillment. This scorecard provides a high-level dashboard that indicates above average scoring with a check mark and below average scoring with an *x*.

- **Review scorecard:** The review scorecard benchmarks the company's average percentage of employees receiving reviews versus the user's management domain and associated reviews executed. This scorecard provides a high-level dashboard that indicates above-average scoring with a check mark and below-average scoring with an *x*.

- **Promotions scorecard:** The promotions scorecard benchmarks the company's average percentage of employees receiving a promotion versus the user's management domain and associated number of promotions. This scorecard provides a high-level dashboard that indicates above-average scoring with a check mark and below-average scoring with an *x*.

In addition to these primary displays, we implement several security routines that add secondary displays. These secondary displays are discussed later in this chapter in the "Implementing the Application Security" section.

Separating Template Repository and Data Mart

Our example also demonstrates the separation of the template repository and the data mart database. The data is contained in a small Microsoft Access database, while the template repository resides in a Adaptive Server Anywhere database. This separation occurs through the definition of multiple connections in the template repository.

Any requested database access in a PowerDynamo Web page requires a connection to a physical database. By default, all SQL statements in the Web site execute using the default connection specified when you created the Web site. However, if your data is stored in a different database from your template repository, also referred to as the Web site content, you may want to execute SQL statements using another connection.

In PowerDynamo, each folder, template, and script object has an associated connection, and all database requests in the associated object execute using that object's connection. You assign the connection information when the object is created, and this data is stored in the PowerDynamo repository. Here are the four types of connections:

- **<default>:** The default connection is associated to the connection specified when the PowerDynamo Web site was created.

- **<inherited>:** The first specified connection as you go up the hierarchy of the Sybase Central tree for the NetImpact PowerDynamo templates.

- **<no connection>:** For documents that do not contain database requests, you can define that no connection is required for that script or template.

- **User defined:** A connection created by the user either during the definition or the execution of the application using DynaScript.

Figure 14.5 demonstrates how to create the connection for our Microsoft Access database that separates the data mart from our template repository. To define a new connection called *data* from Sybase Central, you execute the following steps:

1. From Sybase Central, connect to your NetImpact PowerDynamo template repository.

2. Expand the NetImpact PowerDynamo repository hierarchy in the Sybase Central left panel to reveal all available connections in the Connections folder.

3. In the Sybase Central right panel, double-click NetImpact PowerDynamo Add Connection Wizard.

4. Follow the instructions in the NetImpact Add Connection Wizard to create a new connection. The wizard will prompt you for: connection name; connection description; ODBC data source; ODBC data source user name; and ODBC data source password.

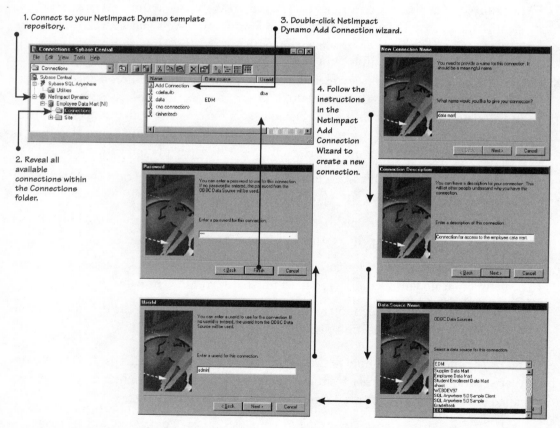

Figure 14.5 *Creating multiple connections with PowerDynamo allows you to split a template repository from data as well as build a secure Web site.*

When you develop your PowerDynamo Web site, you are prompted for a connection name whenever you create a new template, script, or folder. Connections can be changed through these steps:

1. From Sybase Central, connect to your template repository.

2. Open the folder for your Web site.

3. From the Sybase Central right panel, select the script or template for which you want to change the connection and press the right mouse button.

4. Sybase Central presents a menu of options; select Properties.

5. In the properties dialog, from the Connections pull-down menu select a new connection name.

6. Click *OK* on the properties dialog to register your changes to the Web site.

Building PowerDynamo Templates

Each scorecard presented to users of our employee data mart executes a company benchmark query and a departmental detail query. You build your code through the PowerDynamo template wizard by providing one of the queries required by the prototype application. Once the PowerDynamo template has been generated, you can edit the syntax using the Sybase Central PowerDynamo editors. Within the PowerDynamo editors, or third party HTML editor, you will complete the required logic as explained in each of the sections that follow.

Implementing Application Security

We implement only simple application security in this case study. You will want to investigate many other security techniques, including those provided by your database management systems, network management systems, and HTTP servers, for more complete security. However, our example provides a brief glimpse into placing data in your data mart or repository database to control access to data content.

Many security implementations do not provide application-specific security like in this example. Database security focuses on allowing users to access data from a table level. Network access focuses on allowing users access to segments of the network. HTTP security focuses on HTML page-oriented security. This case study demonstrates, in conjunction with all these security options, how you can have further security based on the content of a data mart. We have already discussed the database structures for this securing of the data in our information package within the "Embedding Security in the Data Model" section of this chapter. We now further investigate the coding side of application security.

The PowerDynamo Session Object

The PowerDynamo session object is used in our case study to manage all security information from the application. In PowerDynamo, the session object is a special object that your Web site uses to store information for a Web client session.

Web connections are typically sessionless, or stateless. *Sessionless* and *stateless* refer to the fact that users can jump from one Web Site to another (and back) at any time without the server knowing you've gone away—or in fact even been there. If you jump away from a Web site, you may jump back in two minutes, two days—or never. Unlike conventional desktop applications, the Web site never knows exactly when the Web client ended its session.

To create a more desirable interface and maintain some concept of a session between Web client and Web site, PowerDynamo implements a *session object*. To implement a session object in your Web site, a welcome page asks users to log in with unique attributes, such as name and password. Each of the pages that you then make available to users needs to know that the users have already logged in. If, however, they haven't logged in or their session has been terminated for some reason, the PowerDynamo Web site needs a way to detect this fact and in turn force them to log in again.

The PowerDynamo session object provides a way to store session information so that the information persists for the duration of this particular client connection. Because a traditional Web environment has no explicit end to a session, PowerDynamo allows you to define the duration of a connection. This duration can either be based on factual research or an arbitrary decision.

By default, PowerDynamo considers a session to last five minutes from a user's last action at a Web site. This default duration can be changed globally or for specific session objects. You may desire to store the duration for each individual and therefore control by usage patterns who times out at what interval.

Associating Application Data and Attributes to a Session

For the duration of a session, the PowerDynamo site can maintain information about users' connections, including data such as login name, last action, or whatever other information the site requests from the client. Our example stores information about users' security parameters, including name, welcome name, restricted division, and restricted department. The site stores this session information in a session object. PowerDynamo stores one session object for each client. The following HTML code defines a virtual page that initializes a session object for users of our employee data mart.

```
<HTML>
<TITLE>Initialize Session Object</TITLE>
<HEAD>
<!--script
// id contains id of current user
// It is null when nobody is logged on
session.id = null;
session.user = null;
session.dept_restrict = null;
session.div_restrict = null;
session.welcome = null;
// If timeout is "NO", the session variables are still
// valid. (They haven't been reinitialized by a cookie
// timeout.)  If it isn't "NO," no session variable
// is valid.
session.timeout = "NO";
-->
<!-- Jump to home page of demo -->
<META HTTP-EQUIV="Refresh" CONTENT="0;URL=index.stm">
</HEAD>
</HTML>
```

Page Validation of a Session Object

A session object is accessible to all Web pages on a site, allowing each page to check the status of a user's session as needed. After the specified duration elapses, the session object times out and the associated data stored on behalf of the client is reset. After a session is reset, the Web pages accessing the object can determine that the session has ended. The page initialization script we use in our application processes contains the following logic:

1. We include in the DynaScript some supporting routines for string comparisons. The following code is the beginning of the page initialization script (*page_init.ssc*). The code begins with a PowerDynamo script tag. We then follow with a supporting function to remove spaces from a string.

    ```
    <!--SCRIPT
    function rtrim( instr ) {
      var last_space;
      var ret;
    ```

```
  last_space = instr.length;
  while( instr.charAt( last_space - 1 ) == " " ) {
    last_space --;
  }
  ret = instr.substring( 0, last_space );
  return( ret );
}
```

2. Then next function in the page initialization script file displays information
    to users after a session times out. This function merely writes several HTML
    statements to the document to indicate that the user must log into the appli-
    cation again.

```
function show_timeout() {
  document.writeln( "<TITLE>Session Timedout</TITLE>" );
  document.writeln( "<BODY>" );
  document.writeln( "<H1>Session Timedout</H1><BR>" );
  document.writeln( "<H4>Your session in the Employee Data Mart of
the Human Resources "
    + "Data Warehouse has timed out. If there is no user activity
for a certain"
    + " length of time, the system assumes that your session is
over and resets "
    + " your session.<P>" );
  document.writeln( "For security reasons, you will have to logon
again to the Employee Data Mart"
    + "to continue.</H4><BR><BR>" );
  document.writeln( "<CENTER><A HREF=\"initialize.stm\"><H3>Click
here to logon to the Employee Data Mart</H3></A><CENTER>" );
  document.writeln(
"<BR><BR><BR><BR><BR><BR><BR><BR><BR><BR></BODY> </HTML> " );
}
```

3. Additionally, each page requires a display heading to indicate the current
    session information. This function displays the data mart banner and the
    welcome name we stored in the data mart's security table. The function con-
    tains some conditional logic to display if a user is logged in or if the system
    is waiting for the user to log in.

```
function display_header() {
  str = "<PRE><H4><CENTER>The Human Resources Data Warehouse
";
  if( session.id == null ) {
    str += "No user is logged on";
```

```
    } else {
      str += rtrim( session.welcome + " is logged in. " );
    }
    str += "</CENTER></H4></PRE>";
    document.writeln( str );
}
```

4. The page initialization script also contain a function to check the timeout status of a session. It scans the associated data attributes of the session object, looking for one that indicates a timeout. If such a data attribute is found, the function call the show_timeout() function. The check_timeout() function is here to procedurally check timeout status. You may choose to merge this function with the *page_init* function to have one timeout check. We separate them to distinguish which routine forced the timeout.

```
function check_timeout() {
  timedout = true;
  session.reactivate = true;
  for( i in session ) {
    if( i == "timeout" ) {
      timedout = false;
    }
  }
  if( timedout == true ) {
    show_timeout();
  }
}
```

5. The page init function is executed by each page when it loads. This function is identical to the check_timeout() function described in step 4, but as explained there, we use the page_init() function for Web pages and check_timeout() for scripts. Because this is the last function for the script file, we add the PowerDynamo script termination tag at the end.

```
function page_init() {
  timedout = true;
  session.reactivate = true;
  for( i in session ) {
    if( i == "timeout" ) {
      timedout = false;
    }
  }
  if( timedout == true ) {
    show_timeout();
  } else {
```

```
        display_header();
    }
  }
  -->
```

Each page is initialized with scripts in this script file (page_init.ssc). PowerDynamo allows you to segment your code and include it in multiple templates with the import script command. Therefore, each page contains the following code to initialize and implement the security settings of the session object.

```
<!-- Initialize the page -->
<!--SCRIPT
  import page_init.ssc;
  page_init();
-->
```

Application Logon

Figure 14.6 presents the process flow of a user logging onto our employee data mart. The login process flows as follows:

1. Users enter their application name (the user name of the security table in the data mart).

2. The application retrieves user security information from the database.

3. The application initializes the PowerDynamo session object with the user security filters and general information.

4. The application confirms that the sign-on procedure was successful or unsuccessful.

5. Users are presented with the main application menu.

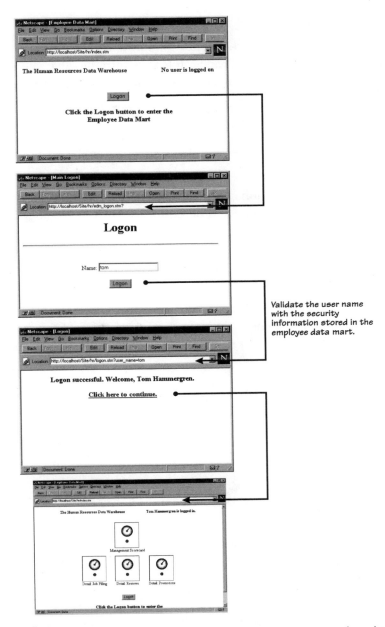

Figure 14.6 *The process of logging onto our employee data mart ensures that the information in our information packages is only exposed to those with the right to know.*

The Main Web Page

The logon process is driven from the application's primary Web page template (*index.stm*). This template processes a series of DynaScripts to determine what should be presented to users of the employee data mart. The code in this template is as follows:

1. Open the form with standard HTML heading information.

    ```
    <HTML>
    <TITLE>Employee Data Mart</TITLE>
    <BODY>
    ```

2. The page initialization scripts are included in the page, and the page initialization function executes to determine if the user has logged on.

    ```
    <!-- Initialize the page -->
    <!--SCRIPT
      import page_init.ssc;
      page_init();
    -->
    ```

3. A script to determine if the user is valid executes. If the session id has been initialized, the user is presented with the options of data mart's main menu.

    ```
    <CENTER>
    <TABLE>
    <TR><TD>
    <!--SCRIPT
    // If someone is logged in, display these options.
    if( session.id != null ) {
      document.writeln( "<TABLE WIDTH=100% CELLSPACING=10 >" );

      document.writeln( '<TR><TD></TD><TD ALIGN=CENTER><A HREF="score
    card.stm?DIV=' + session.div_restrict + '&DEPT=' +
    session.dept_restrict + '"><IMG
    SRC="guage.gif"></A><BR>Management Scorecard</TD></TR>' );

      document.writeln( '<TR><TD ALIGN=CENTER><A
    HREF="job_fill.stm?DIV=' + session.div_restrict + '&DEPT=' + ses
    sion.dept_restrict + '"><IMG SRC="guage.gif"></A><BR>Detail: Job
    Filling</TD>' );

      document.writeln( '<TD ALIGN=CENTER><A HREF="reviews.stm?DIV=' +
    session.div_restrict + '&DEPT=' + session.dept_restrict + '"><IMG
    SRC="guage.gif"></A><BR>Detail: Reviews</TD>' );
      document.writeln( '<TD ALIGN=CENTER><A HREF="promotions.stm?DIV='
    + session.div_restrict + '&DEPT=' + session.dept_restrict +
    ```

```
'"><IMG SRC="guage.gif"></A><BR>Detail: Promotions</TD>' );
   document.writeln( "</TR></TABLE>" );


}
-->
</TD></TR></TABLE>
```

4. A script to determine if the user is not logged onto the system executes. If
    the session id has not been initialized, the user is presented with a logon
    button that requests them to sign onto the system. If the session id has been
    initialized, the user is presented with a logoff button. The logoff button
    allows the user to manually terminate the session.

```
<!--SCRIPT
// If nobody is logged in, display Logon button.
// Otherwise, display a logoff button.
if( session.id == null ) {
   document.writeln( "<FORM ACTION=\"edm_logon.stm\"
      METHOD=\"GET\">&<INPUT TYPE=\"submit\" VALUE=\"Logon\">&
      </FORM></CENTER>" );
} else {
   document.writeln( "<FORM ACTION=\"initialize.stm\"
      METHOD=\"GET\">&<INPUT TYPE=\"submit\" VALUE=\"Logoff\">&
      </FORM></CENTER>" );
}
-->
</BODY>
</HTML>
```

Application Logon Pages

The actual login process incorporates two Web pages. The first page (*edm_logon.stm*) simply requests the user name as known to the data mart in the security table. This form presents users with an input field for their name and a button to submit the form to the Web
server for further processing. The code for this page is as follows:

```
<HTML>
<TITLE>Main Logon</TITLE>
<!-- Initialize the page -->
<!--SCRIPT
   import page_init.ssc;
   check_timeout();
-->
<CENTER><H1>Logon</H1><HR>
<BR><BR>
<FORM ACTION="logon.stm" NAME="log" METHOD="GET">
Name: <INPUT TYPE=TEXT SELECT NAME="user_name">
```

```
<BR><BR>
<INPUT TYPE="submit" VALUE="Logon">
</FORM>
</CENTER>
</BODY>
</HTML>
```

After users enter their name and submit the preceding form to the server, PowerDynamo receives the information for further processing. The logon confirmation template (*logon.stm*) looks up the user name on the security table in the data mart. If the name is found, the user is presented with a successful completion message and the session data attributes initialize to the values stored in the data mart table. If the logon fails, users are presented with an access denied message and must try logging on again. The code for the logon confirmation template is as follows:

```
<HTML>
<TITLE>Logon</TITLE>
<!-- Initialize the page -->
<!--SCRIPT
  import page_init.ssc;
  check_timeout();
-->
<!--SQL
  SELECT
    s.security_id,
    s.user_name,
    department_id,
    division_id,
    s.welcome_name
  FROM
    c_organization_security as s
  WHERE
    s.user_name = '$user_name'
-->
<!--SCRIPT
  if SQL.GetEmpty() {
    document.writeln('<META HTTP-EQUIV=REFRESH CONTENT="0;
    URL=access_denied.stm">');
  }
  else {
    session.id = SQL.GetValue(1);
    session.user = SQL.GetValue(2);
    session.dept_restrict = SQL.GetValue(3);
    session.div_restrict = SQL.GetValue(4);
    session.welcome = SQL.GetValue(5);
    document.writeln( "<CENTER><H3>Logon successful.  Welcome, " + session.welcome
+ ".<P>");
    document.writeln( '<A HREF="index.stm">Click here to continue.</A></H3></CEN-
```

```
TER>' );
 }
-->
</BODY>
</HTML>
```

Application Implementation of the Session Object Timeout Feature

The periodic timing out of a session protects the information in our employee data mart from snooping eyes and from those who obtain cached information through illegal methods. Either way, if you do not have security associated with your application, you run the risk of important data getting into the wrong hands. If users have been away from the application for some time and their session has timed out, their next request of the system is fulfilled with an access denied message indicating the timeout.

The Job Filling Scorecard

The job filling scorecard focuses on the measurement entry columns, *num_available_positions* and *num_employees*. We want to execute the aggregate queries for the company and the users' management area. The query that retrieves the company benchmark information is as follows:

```
<!--SQL NAME=COMPANY
   SELECT DISTINCT
      c.time_period_year,
      Sum(c.num_available_positions) AS 'Company Positions',
      Sum(c.num_employees) AS 'Company Employees',
      (Sum(c.num_employees)/Sum(c.num_available_positions)) As 'Company Job Fill %'

   FROM m_employee_review c
   GROUP BY c.time_period_year;
-->
```

As you can see in the preceding code, the SQL statement has been named *COMPANY*. This naming of a PowerDynamo query tag allows us to reference the specifics of the query results later in our code. Because we execute multiple queries within one template, we want to ensure that each query is suitably named. Other notes about the *select* statement that retrieves the company data: First, we use the *sum* aggregate function of SQL to obtain the total number of positions and employees in the company; second, we define a SQL calculated column as the third column, which shows the percentage of jobs filled to employees; and third, we group the data based on the annual time period.

To provide the equivalent data for users' specific department, we execute the following query:

```
<!--SQL NAME=DEPARTMENT
  SELECT DISTINCT
    d.time_period_year,
    Sum(d.num_available_positions) AS 'Department Positions',
    Sum(d.num_employees) AS 'Department Employees',
    (Sum(d.num_employees)/Sum(d.num_available_positions)) As 'Department Job Fill %'
  FROM m_employee_review d
  WHERE d.department_id = $DEPT and d.division_id = $DIV
  GROUP BY d.time_period_year
-->
```

The PowerDynamo query named *DEPARTMENT* indicated in the SQL tag returns the identical columns as the PowerDynamo query named *COMPANY*, except that a *where* clause has filtered the data to include only the users' department and division. The key to this template is to compare the results of the two queries and score the individual department in relation to the company benchmark. To perform this activity, we follow this five-step process:

1. We write the document's heading information.

    ```
    <!--SCRIPT
    //Step 1: Write out the new document's heading information
    document.writeln("<CENTER>");
    document.writeln("<H2>Your Department Review</H2>");
    ```

2. We write the HTML code to initialize the table and fill column headings.

    ```
    //Step 2: Write out the HTML to initialize the table and fill
    //the column headings
    document.writeln("<TABLE BORDER=2>");
    document.writeln("<TR><TH>Year</TH><TH>Job Fill%</TH></TR>") ;
    ```

3   We loop through each row in the department and company results sets to measure the department against the company benchmark and write a row in the table to indicate the result of the comparison. The result includes a graphical image that indicates a favorable rating with a check mark or an unfavorable rating with an *x*.

    ```
    //Step 3: Loop through each row in result sets from the
    //department and company queries.
    while( DEPARTMENT.MoveNext() ) {
      COMPANY.MoveNext();
      //Step 3a: Begin a new row in the table
    ```

```
document.writeln("<TR>") ;

//Step 3b: Fill in Year column of table
document.writeln("<TD><B>" + DEPARTMENT.GetValue(1) +
"</B></TD>");
//Step 3c: Fill in Job Fill % column of table and indicate
//graphically how the department relates to the company
//benchmark
if COMPANY.GetValue(4) <= DEPARTMENT.GetValue(4) {
   document.writeln("<TD ALIGN=CENTER><IMG
   SRC='HEAVYCHECK.GIF'></TD>");
}
else {
   document.writeln("<TD ALIGN=CENTER><IMG
SRC='HEAVYX.GIF'></TD>");
}
//Step 3d: Terminate the table row
document.writeln("</TR>");
}
```

4. We terminate the open HTML tags.

```
//Step 4: Terminate the table
document.writeln("</TABLE>");
document.writeln("</CENTER>");
```

5. We move the database cursors back to the first row, allowing nonprocedural
    HTML to also execute against the department and company queries, and add
    a terminator for our SQL script.

```
//Step 5: Move cursor position to top of result sets for nonproce-
dural displays
DEPARTMENT.Move(0);
COMPANY.Move(0);
-->
```

After we have built the graphical scorecard, we may also want to provide detailed
numbers to give users a little more information on how the scorecard was derived, especially for those scores for which an unfavorable score was given versus the company
benchmark. Such a display can be done nonprocedurally using HTML and embedded
PowerDynamo tags. The most appropriate display is probably an HTML table. The following code displays the company query results. A similar code segment produce departmental results.

1. We build suitable heading information so users understand what is presented.

   ```
   <CENTER><H2>Company Results</H2></CENTER>
   ```

2. We define the attributes for the HTML table, including presentation formats.

   ```
   <CENTER><TABLE BORDER=2>
   ```

3. Next, we define table headings by issuing an HTML table row starting tab and then place each column heading in suitable HTML table heading tags.

   ```
   <TR>
   <TH>Year</TH>
   <TH>Available Jobs</TH>
   <TH>Employees</TH>
   <TH>Job Fill %</TH>
   </TR>
   ```

4. We now begin to format the results of the *COMPANY* query by issuing the PowerDynamo formatting tag with the proper query name.

   ```
   <!--formatting NAME = COMPANY-->
   ```

5. In the PowerDynamo formatting tag, we execute the code to write a new row in the HTML table. The data markers tell PowerDynamo to insert a column of the result set into the proper column. An HTML column is defined by table data tags. Notice that the numeric data uses the attributes to align the data to the right.

   ```
   <TR>
   <TD><!--data--></TD>
   <TD ALIGN=RIGHT><!--data--></TD>
   <TD ALIGN=RIGHT><!--data--></TD>
   <TD ALIGN=RIGHT><!--data--></TD>
   </TR>
   ```

6. Our last step in the nonprocedural formatting of the results is to terminate open HTML and PowerDynamo tags.

   ```
   <!--/formatting-->
   </TABLE></CENTER>
   ```

The Review Scorecard and The Promotions Scorecard follow similar logic to the Job Filling Scorecard. Depending on your application security, you may present individual managers with differing scorecards. Often, such a practice is associated with the incentive compensation for an individual manager. If this is your practice, the security data would also be extended to include the application flow information for each user.

The Management Scorecard

The complete management scorecard presents one large table with all metrics evaluated simultaneously. This scorecard Web page is based on two queries, much like the Job Filling Score Card—one for the company and one for the department. The company query is as follows:

```
<!--SQL NAME=COMPANY
  SELECT DISTINCT
    c.time_period_year,
    Sum(c.num_available_positions) AS 'Company Positions',
    Sum(c.num_employees) AS 'Company Employees',
    (Sum(c.num_employees)/Sum(c.num_available_positions)) As 'Company Job Fill %',
    Sum(c.num_reviewed) AS 'Company Reviews',
    (Sum(c.num_reviewed)/Sum(c.num_employees)) As 'Company Employee Review %',
    Sum(c.num_promotions) AS 'Company Promotions',
    (Sum(c.num_promotions)/Sum(c.num_employees)) As 'Company Promotion %',
    Avg(c.average_base_salary) AS 'Company Average Salary',
    Avg(c.average_incentive_pay) AS 'Company Average Incentive Pay',
    Avg(c.average_benefit_cost) AS 'Company Average Benefit Costs'
  FROM m_employee_review c
  GROUP BY c.time_period_year;
-->
```

The company query contains all metrics for the entire human resource administration information package as well as several predefined calculations. These calculations include percentages that are used as benchmark figures for each individual department. The specific calculations include the percentage of job openings filled, the percentage of employees reviewed, and the percentage of employees promoted.

The department query retrieves the equivalent data for an individual department based on a user's restriction filters. These restrictions are fulfilled from the session object and its associated data attributes. The department query is as follows:

```
<!--SQL NAME=DEPARTMENT
  SELECT DISTINCT
```

```
 d.time_period_year,
 Sum(d.num_available_positions) AS 'Department Positions',
 Sum(d.num_employees) AS 'Department Employees',
 (Sum(d.num_employees)/Sum(d.num_available_positions)) As 'Department Job Fill %',
 Sum(d.num_reviewed) AS 'Department Reviews','
 (Sum(d.num_reviewed)/Sum(d.num_employees)) As 'Department Review %',
 Sum(d.num_promotions) AS 'Department Promotion',
 (Sum(d.num_promotions)/Sum(d.num_employees)) As 'Department Promotion %'
 Avg(d.average_base_salary) AS 'Department Average Salary',
 Avg(d.average_incentive_pay) AS 'Department Average Incentive Pay',
 Avg(d.average_benefit_cost) AS 'Department Average Benefit Costs'
 FROM m_employee_review d
 WHERE d.department_id = $DEPT and d.division_id = $DIV
 GROUP BY d.time_period_year
-->
```

The final scorecard system presents users with a hierarchy of Web pages that provide various views of the metrics defined in the human resource administration information page. These pages are presented in Figure 14.7.

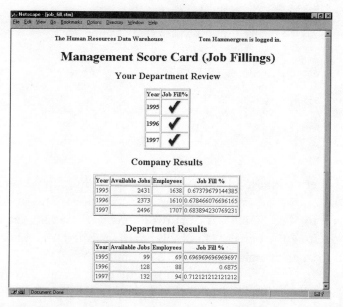

Figure 14.7 *The human resource administration information package application presents managers with their key performance metrics and compares those metrics to a benchmark metric for the entire company.*

Summary

Key metrics that analyze the effective management and satisfaction of employees assists managers in executing business plans or guiding an enterprise through a strategic plan. An employee data mart assist an enterprise in improving loyalty among its most important intellectual asset—its employees. Additionally, an employee data mart assists in areas such as benefits administration, recruitment, and retention of employees.

For example, recent studies show that providing enterprise-wide influenza vaccinations reduces sick time for the flu by 40 percent, Is the cost of such a program worth its cost? Only your management can answer such a question, but providing them with such data will clearly resolve the issue. And a company that provides such benefits to its employees typically is not be viewed as a company trying to curb costs, but as a company compassionate about its employees' health and well-being, which improves the overall loyalty of employees.

Building an employee data mart will assist your company in building a loyal partnership, which will result in a long list of benefits. Happy employees yield greater revenue, recruit other highly skilled employees, and elicit confidence in your customer base. All of these benefits assist in making a company successful. When you look at employee-centric enterprises, several leading employers come to mind, including State Farm Insurance, Southwest Airlines, and IBM. These companies and many others are more cultures than jobs to their employees. And these companies have proven that life-long employment may not yet be dead.

Building a data mart for storage of employee-centric data should focus on the key metrics required to motivate employees and improve their conditions. These metrics should be benchmarked and analyzed in comparison to the enterprise's business and strategic plans to make sure a skills gap is not created between the desires of the company and the realities of the employment force.

We now have covered three of the four knowledge centers of human management: shareholders, who influence the capital behind a company; suppliers, who control the flow of high-quality supplies throughout the supply chain; and employees, who build a positive culture that attracts quality from all of the human centers. This leaves us with one last case study to evaluate, building a customer data mart, which we cover in the next chapter.

15

The Customer Data Mart

Up to this point in the book, we have investigated a wide variety of metrics that cover the shareholders, suppliers, and employees of an enterprise. As defined in the information packaging methodology, all of these human knowledge centers can directly sway your company's ability to be successful. This chapter concentrates on the customer and building data marts to support this very critical human center. In other words, we have left the best for last.

When we analyze our businesses, we begin to see some common trends: product life cycles continue to shrink and competitive advantage in one generation of a product is no guarantee to product leadership in future generations. Companies that compete in rapidly advancing product areas must become masters at anticipating their customers' future needs. The new research and development business cycle has our companies carving out these future product areas; devising new product and service offerings; and rapidly deploying new product technologies into highly efficient delivery processes. Even if your company does not fit this rapidly changing product paradigm, you will find that the need for continuous improvement in processes and product capabilities is critical for your company's long-term success.

Therefore, in building proper support for your users, a customer data mart requires information that delivers:

- Projections of future customers and markets.

- Data on your company's strengths and weaknesses.

- Strategies, strengths, and weaknesses of key competitors.

- Projections about changes in requirements and priorities of existing customers.

- Forecasts that evaluate how new technologies may impact your business.

- Research, testing, and projections of new products and services.

- Information on regulatory trends that may impact your organization.

- Economic and societal trends that may impact your company's business.

All of this information assists your users in building a highly profitable business, one with substantial future growing power. This assists you in becoming a leader in driving future change in your enterprise. As Henry Ford of Ford Motor Company stated: "Business must be run at a profit, else it will die. But when anyone tries to run a business solely for profit, then also the business must die, for it no longer has a reason for existence."

To manage your customers in current and future markets as assets, you must value them as assets. Just as your employees comprise a base of intellectual assets, customers form a base of capital or cash flow assets. This means that you must quantify and predict customer duration and life cycle cash flow.

In the area of shareholder or financial analysis, accountants have developed sophisticated techniques for appraising capital assets and their depreciation; they have learned how to monitor the constantly changing value of work-in-progress; but they have not yet devised a way to track the value of a company's customer inventory. Accounting departments make no distinction between sales revenue generated from new customers and sales revenue from long-term customers. The reality that the accountants do not recognize is that the cost to serve a new customer is far greater than the cost of servicing an existing, loyal customer. Your goal as the architect of a corporate knowledge base is to deliver information with the proper relevance, which includes the data that is currently lacking from internal accounting and order entry systems.

Tools Positioning Overview

In the case study of this chapter, we move into the area of tools that support your users' activities of analyzing the data in a data warehouse. As you work through the tools that support your user base, you will find a required spectrum or suite of products. This type of warehouse tool suite is analogous to the evolution of office automation tools into suites. For example, Microsoft Office contains a word processor, a spreadsheet, a personal database, and a presentation package, with each of these products focusing on a specialty of an office worker's tasks.

In the data warehouse environment, you must deliver applications as well as ad hoc access to data warehouse data stores. The case studies presented in this book have focused on applications that you may develop to deliver information to a wide variety of users. In the customer analysis environment, managers must engage in an intense dialog to review market conditions. The analytical activities review value propositions that the company is delivering to targeted customers and how these propositions relate to future markets and prospective customers. Results of users' analytical activities may be used to reaffirm the fundamental beliefs of the company or to adjust plans.

The requirements for users to interact with this information are difficult to obtain, so delivering fixed applications may be an incorrect strategy to evaluate the customer information. Tools are widely available in the client/server, Microsoft Windows environment and are just now maturing and becoming available for effective deployment in widely distributed environments such as the Internet. In our customer data mart case study, we evaluate Cognos' PowerPlay OLAP.

The OLAP tools market has grown over the years to become quite confusing. The OLAP market is segmenting into various markets, including M-OLAP (*multidimensional OLAP*), R-OLAP (*relational OLAP*), and D-OLAP (*desktop OLAP*). To simplify your understanding of how this market is evolving, we focus on the important aspects of *cube creation*. OLAP tools fundamentally view the world in a multidimensional space, which is in contrast to relational tools, which view data in a two dimensional space (rows and columns). The market has basically evolved based on fundamental beliefs that vendors have built around where their tools should properly locate the cube. As shown in Figure 15.1, the placement of the cube is what distinguishes a tool as M-OLAP, R-OLAP, or D-OLAP. The distinguishing characteristics behind the cube placement is further discussed in Table 15.1.

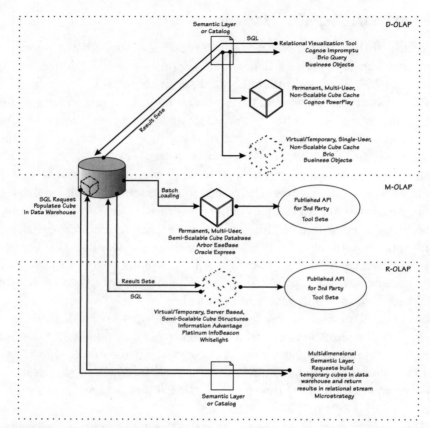

Figure 15.1 *The OLAP marketplace is maturing into separate segments. These segments are defined based on the placement of the multidimensional cube in relation to the tool's deployment.*

Table 15.1 *Distinguishing OLAP market segment characteristics.*

OLAP Market Segment	Characteristics	Sample Vendor
Desktop OLAP (D-OLAP)	Cube is created for a small number of users; the cube is built on nonrobust DBMS structures. The pure focus of these tools is in the area of usability, not high-volume data scalability.	Brio, Business Objects, Cognos

Continued

Table 15.1 Continued

OLAP Market Segment	Characteristics	Sample Vendor
Multidimensional OLAP *M-OLAP*	Cube is created for a larger number of users and is typically deployed on a more robust, server-oriented DBMS structure. The focus of these tools is on structured management of data, and the products tend to offer an API to allow other OLAP tools easy access to their data.	Arbor EssBase, Oracle Express
Relational OLAP *(R-OLAP)*	A virtual cube is created based on users' requests for data from a relational database through an OLAP tool. Each of these products varies in its cube creation, from a virtual cube that is shared among users to a virtual cube that is created for personal use. Most of these tools create their cube in a proprietary structure, which they manage from a server.	Information Advantage, Platinum InfoBeacon, Whitelight, Microstrategy

Defining a Customer Information Package

Various information packages are required to fulfill the broad need for information by your user base. In the case study in this chapter, we build an information package to assist users in analyzing product penetration in customer accounts. This data is segmented over time along dimensions that include products, locations, channels (customers), and margin bands. The specific metrics include purchasing information, including product quantity, product revenue, product cost, and product margin. Figure 15.2 presents a information package diagram for delivering this data.

For the current case study, we build an information package for an original manufacturer that sells its products through various channels; these channels are therefore the end customer. Our customer sales information package contains the following information:

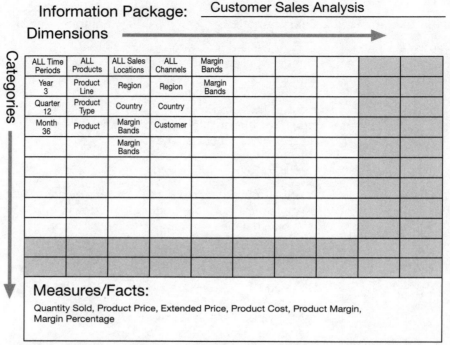

Figure 15.2 *Our customer sales information package assists managers in evaluating current and historic trends of product sales in a customer base.*

- **Time periods:** Information is made available to users for the last three years. This information includes a fully configured time dimension that allows analysis by month, quarter, year, and otherwise. (For detailed information on the time period dimension, see the "The Time Dimension" section in Chapter 12, "The Shareholder Data Mart.")

- **Products:** The product dimension categorizes products offered by the enterprise by product line and product type.

- **Sales locations:** The sales location dimension segments product distribution organization along regional boundaries. The categories of sales location include regions (Europe and North America), country (USA, Canada, and Mexico), branches, and sales representatives.

- **Customer locations (channels):** The channels in which the enterprise's products are delivered include all customers categorized through two separate access paths.

The first access path is based on a customer's physical location, which includes region and country boundaries. The second access path includes the type of customer, which includes independent companies, mass marketers, and various other target marketing customers.

- **Margin ranges:** The margin ranges provide users with access to relevant information related to product profitability. This banding of underlying data allows users of the data mart to see trends and sales activity based on the profitability of a product or product line.

- **Measures:** The measures are the key performance indicators to assist users in better analyzing the data. These measures include quantity, prices, extended price, cost, margin, and margin percentage.

Each dimension in this information package assists users of the customer sales analysis information package in answering ad hoc requests for data. The user can segment the data in the data mart in a large number of ways that refine the level of granularity of data returned from the information package. This granularity also assists in supporting a larger number of users throughout the company from one specific information package. The differing views, facilitated by one common information package, are advantageous to those who are conscious of the long-term maintenance costs associated with building data marts to support a ubiquitous user base. We take a closer look at these data warehouse components in the following sections to gain a better understanding of their purpose and content.

Customer Sales Measures

The measures in the customers sales information package include data to assist users in better characterizing the customers who are purchasing products from the enterprise. The measures describe purchasing activities, including which channels are selling what products and the focus of margin activity occurring throughout the available products. The metrics include:

- **Quantity:** The quantity metric indicates the units of a product that have been purchased. Through analyzing the quantity, users can determine whether orders are increasing or decreasing in size. This analysis can occur by sales territory to determine if one sales branch or sale representative is more effective than others at selling larger quantities of a product while evaluating the channels that consume the largest volume of product.

- **Price:** The price metric is used fundamentally to calculate the extended price. However, the product price also provides relevant information for trending product distribution. Analysis of price sensitivity for distribution metrics such as quantity can occur, answering questions such as: How will a price increase impact quantities purchased?

- **Extended price:** The extended price metric is a calculation for each order. The calculation is frequently accessed, so we store the data in the data mart rather than have users request the calculation. The extended price calculation is: *extended price = quantity * price*.

- **Cost:** The product cost metric is used to calculate the margins returned to the business from a sale. Additionally, placing the product cost in the information package allows those analyzing data to further understand why product price might be increasing. All too often, we separate revenue metrics from cost metrics, and people do not have enough information to fully understand the profitability equation. Inclusion of cost in this information package allows users to fully evaluate the factors that impact profitability of a product.

- **Margin:** The margin metric allows users to see how much money is returned to the enterprise as a result of a product sale. When analyzing products, it may be more important to track sales based on margin rather than the revenue generated. Some products, which are high in revenues, may in fact not return high dollars to the corporation, so the margin metric allows users of the data mart to understand the true bottom line impact a product has on the overall company and which high-margin products versus low-margin products attract customers.

- **Margin percentage:** The margin percentage metric allows users to see the margin metric in percentage terms versus a raw number. This metric also is used as a category to group sales and allow users of the data mart to better visualize the products that attract customers. Differing management and enterprise structures are required to support a customer base purchasing low-margin products versus high-margin products.

Product Dimension

The product dimension provides a detail categorization of the products delivered to an enterprise's customers. These products are divided by product lines, which include items such as an outdoor line, an environmental line, and a go-sports line. The product lines have been defined to assist users of the data mart in understanding patterns in the customer base.

Is the world becoming more conscious about the environment? If so, users will see spikes in the sales of the environmental line. Are the customers becoming more athletic? If the customers are more athletic, are they attracted more to outdoor sports or indoor sports? Again, the segmenting of product lines allows users of the data mart to understand customer preferences.

In the product lines, products are further segmented by product type. Examples of product types in the outdoor product line include backpacks and tents. This categorization of products allows a further detailed understanding of customer activity in a product line. Finally, users can see individual product brands in product lines and types. This data provides additional detail to better understand how to deliver what the customer wants.

Sales Location Dimension

The customer sales information package provides two separate location dimensions, sales and customer. These dimensions allow analysis that closely relates to how the enterprise supports its customers. Because sales offices should be strategically located to support customers, cross-correlations can be made between the location of a sales office and actual sales to customers.

As users of the data mart evaluate this data, they will see geographically sensitive information pertinent to the running of the enterprise, such as: Are certain regions increasing while others are fading? Are additional sales offices required to support growing customer demand in a region?

The sales location dimension groups sales representatives of the company by region (Europe and North America), country in a region (USA and Canada), and branch in a country in a region (New York and San Francisco).

Customer Location (Channel) Dimension

The customers of the enterprise we are modeling are resellers of products they purchase. These resale companies sell these products of the enterprise to their customers and therefore are referred to as *sales channels*. The customer location dimension is therefore co-named the channels dimension.

The channels that are modeled in our data mart have multiple access paths that are critical for the analysis of the underlying data. Figure 15.3 presents these multiple access paths. The first access path is customer type. Each reseller channel is characterized based on its affiliation, and therefore analysis can occur based on the channel type to determine if trends are isolated to type versus the entire customer base. Examples of channel types are independent reseller and mass marketer.

The second access path is by geographical location. As we discussed in the preceding section of this chapter, the customer channels is segmented by geographical boundaries. The categories in the geographical locations of customer include region (Europe and North America) and country (USA and Canada).

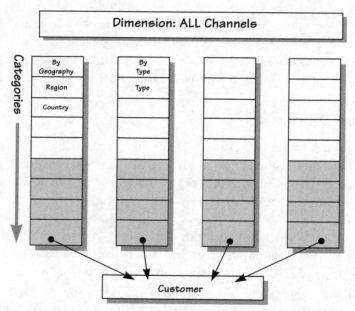

Figure 15.3 *This multiple-access diagram demonstrates the alternative paths with which users can access customer information.*

Building a Conceptual Star Schema Model

Now that we have investigated the dimensions and measures required for our information package, it is time to build the logical model. As discussed in Chapter 3, "Information Package Modeling," the information package and associated details are translated into a star schema as follows:

- Each column of the information package diagram is translated into dimension entities.

- The dimension is formulated with fields from each category, or level, in the column of the information package diagram. You also account for any additional categories that are captured on individual alternate path diagrams created for the given dimension.

- Each of the lowest-level categories are placed in the measure entity.

- Each of the measures are placed in the measure entity.

- If any category is highlighted to include more detail information, a category detail entity is created.

The translation of our current information package diagram to a star schema using information packaging notation is shown in Figure 15.4.

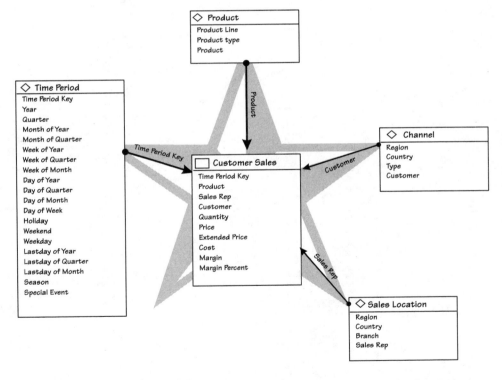

Figure 15.4 *This star schema diagram uses information packaging method notation to assist designers and developers in better translating user requirements into a logical and physical data model for our multidimensional customer sales model.*

Implementing Our Data Mart with PowerDesigner

After the user requirements are gathered in an information package diagram and the conceptual data models are generated with a star schema; we are ready to proceed with the physical implementation of the specification. As we have shown in the previous case studies of this book, PowerDesigner is the tool we use to implement the physical database models. One additional benefit to PowerDesigner is its ability to interface with leading OLAP tools such as PowerPlay for delivering ad hoc multidimensional analysis to your users. The tables that are used to build our physical data mart are shown in Figure 15.5.

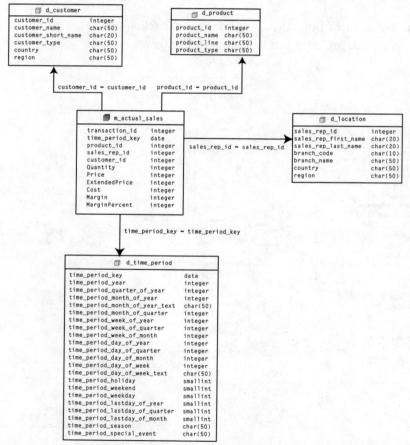

Figure 15.5 *The customer sales analysis information package generates a physical schema like the one shown here. The fact tables, or measure entities are marked with the first two letters of m_, while the dimension entities are marked with the first two letters of d_.*

Building a Multidimensional Model

OLAP and managed query environment tools, such as Cognos' PowerPlay and Cognos Impromptu, have introduced semantic layers that must be managed outside a database to properly support users of these tools. In the semantic layer, most tools provide performance, security, and usability outside the database. Semantic layers allow you to control what a user sees in a database and how data is retrieved from the database.

However, a semantic layer often requires an additional tier of support personnel to implement, because of a lack of comprehensive tools that cover the roles of a database administrator and query tool administrator. PowerDesigner uniquely offers support for both physical database design and tool semantic layer construction.

In PowerDesigner Warehouse Architect, semantic layers can be designed simultaneously with your data models. This functionality assists you in avoiding the complexities of using multiple tools and multiple interfaces to accomplish this data warehouse-specific need.

The multidimensional model is managed through the PowerDesigner Warehouse Architect multidimensional hierarchy. In PowerDesigner, you can define several unique multidimensional structures, including:

- **Dimension:** The axis or index that is used by users of a data model to access a fact.

- **Dimension hierarchy:** A hierarchy of detailed categorizations used to aggregate and filter facts in a data model. Each level in a dimension hierarchy is known as a *dimension* in PowerDesigner.

- **Attribute:** Typically a database column that is used to qualify a dimension.

- **Fact:** A set of variables or measures that correspond to a logical grouping required by users to perform decision-support investigations.

- **Fact hierarchy:** A variable or measure that splits into more detailed variables or measures, usually as a result of an aggregation or partitioning operation in PowerDesigner.

- **Metric:** An individual variable or measure that corresponds to the focus of decision-support investigation in an information package.

The multidimensional hierarchy for our customer sales analysis information package is shown in Figure 15.6.

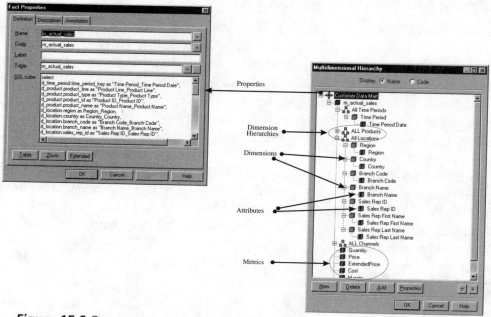

Figure 15.6 *Our customer sales analysis information package multidimensional hierarchy is modeled in Cognos' PowerPlay.*

Much of what you learned for the information package directly transforms into relevant knowledge to deliver a PowerDesigner multidimensional hierarchy. Our specific information package transposes into a PowerDesigner multidimensional hierarchy as follows:

- The entire data mart is modeled in a PowerDesigner Warehouse Architect Model.

- The entire set of information represented by the information package diagram is defined by a *fact*.

- Each column of the information package diagram becomes a *dimensional hierarchy* in the multidimensional hierarchy.

- Each cell in a dimension's column of the information package diagram or multiple access path diagram becomes a *dimension* in the multidimensional hierarchy, and the physical data representing this dimension becomes an *attribute* in the multidimensional hierarchy that details the associated dimension.

- Each measure of the information package diagram becomes a *metric* in the multi-dimensional hierarchy.

After you have defined a multidimensional hierarchy, PowerDesigner generates a comma-delimited representation of the data in the information package through a *select* statement. Our customer sales analysis information package is captured by the following query:

```
select
    d_time_period.time_period_key as "Time Period Date",
    d_product.product_line as "Product Line",
    d_product.product_type as "Product Type",
    d_product.product_id as "Product ID",
    d_product.product_name as "Product Name",
    d_location.region as "Region",
    d_location.country as "Country",
    d_location.branch_code as "Branch Code",
    d_location.branch_name as "Branch Name",
    d_location.sales_rep_id as "Sales Rep ID",
    d_location.sales_rep_first_name as "Sales Rep First Name",
    d_location.sales_rep_last_name as "Sales Rep Last Name",
    d_customer.region as "Customer Region",
    d_customer.country as "Customer Country",
    d_customer.customer_type as "Customer Type",
    d_customer.customer_id as "Customer Number",
    d_customer.customer_name as "Customer Name",
    m_actual_sales.Quantity as "Quantity",
    m_actual_sales.Price as "Price",
    m_actual_sales.ExtendedPrice as "Extended Price",
    m_actual_sales.Cost as "Cost",
    m_actual_sales.Margin as "Margin",
    m_actual_sales.MarginPercent as "Margin Percent"
from
    d_time_period,
    m_actual_sales,
    d_product,
    d_location,
    d_customer
where
    d_time_period.time_period_key =
        m_actual_sales.time_period_key
    AND
    d_product.product_id = m_actual_sales.product_id
    AND
    d_location.sales_rep_id = m_actual_sales.sales_rep_id
    AND
    d_customer.customer_id = m_actual_sales.customer_id
```

Delivering Our Model to PowerPlay's Transformer Module

PowerDesigner can generate the first prototype of your PowerPlay multidimensional cube. This is done in a similar fashion to the generation of the database definition language. In PowerDesigner, you select the targeted OLAP DSS (decision support system) environment, such as PowerPlay, EssBase, or Express. Based on your selection, PowerDesigner determines the proper way to transform the model definition to your targeted environment. After you complete your definition of the physical data model and its associated multidimensional hierarchy, you are prepared to generate the PowerPlay cube, as shown in Figure 15.7.

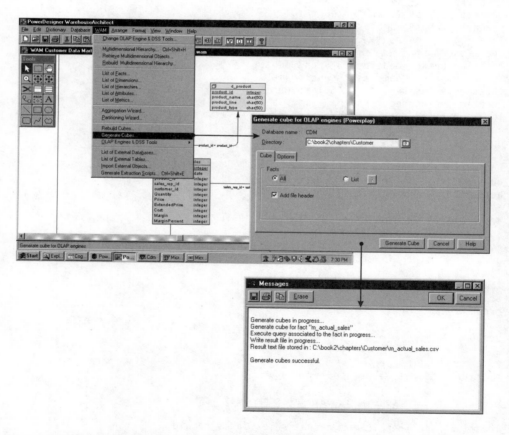

Figure 15.7 *After completion of your physical data model design and multidimensional hierarchy definition, PowerDesigner generates your PowerPlay cube definition.*

As you can see by this small example, the information packaging methodology becomes a critical component to assist you in fulfilling the requirement of your enterprise's data warehouse. To review the steps in defining the complete architecture required to deliver data to your users:

1. Gather user requirements in an information package diagram. This diagram is refined with multiple access path diagrams as required by each dimension.

2. Transform the information package diagram into a refined conceptual star schema diagram with information packaging method notation. This model is synchronized with additional information packages that have been defined either by your project team or others in your enterprise and placed in the overall data warehouse architecture.

3. Refine your star schema design into a physical data model utilizing Sybase's PowerDesigner. This step typically is done in the Warehouse Architect Module, which supports key functionality required by data warehouses, such as aggregations, partitions, query-optimized data store definitions, and multi-dimensional hierarchy definitions.

4. Clearly define users' access patterns for the targeted OLAP or decision-support environment in PowerDesigner's multidimensional hierarchy.

5. Allow PowerDesigner to automatically generate the required physical implementation products, such as the relational database definition language and OLAP product semantic layers.

Using PowerPlay Transformer to Deliver a PowerPlay Cube

The PowerPlay Transformer module helps you transform data from a standard database, such as your data warehouse, into a multidimensional PowerPlay application. After created, the PowerPlay application can be visualized through Cognos' PowerPlay to allow your users to gain immediate insight into the forces that drive your business. With the Transformer, you can package your data in the way that best meets your business needs or you can deliver critical business information to targeted users, presenting the information that is important to them.

The Transformer can refine the model, which specifies the location of your source data and the way that you want to structure the available data. The Transformer then takes your instructions and creates a PowerCube that serves your users' requests to visualize the information package content. The data and definition produced by PowerDesigner are the basis of the Transformer work, as shown in Figure 15.8.

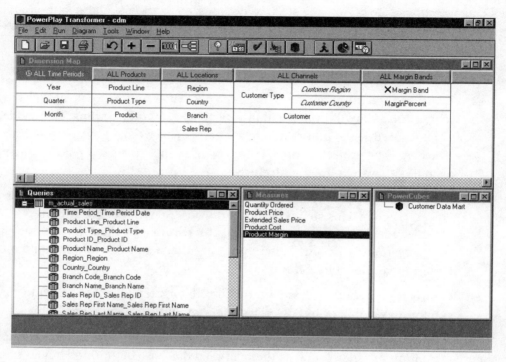

Figure 15.8 *The Cognos' PowerPlay Transformer allows you to refine a physical PowerPlay application produced in PowerDesigner Warehouse Architect.*

The steps required to finish a PowerPlay application include:

1. Make the selections in the New Model dialog box. This includes a model description, the type of source data, the data file, and whether you want the Transformer to automatically create an initial design.

2. Work through query columns, placing them in the desired locations of the dimension map to finalize the multidimensional model. This step may include interjecting data that does not exist in the current data source. An example is the margin range band in our customer sales analysis information package. The margin percent is physically grouped into bands of common percentages to improve users' ability to analyze data, such as *25% and Under*, *26% to 50%*, *51% to 75%*, and *Greater than 75%*.

3. Generate categories to fill out the dimensions for further physical design modifications.

4. Save the model.

5. Create one or many PowerCubes.

6. Explore the PowerCube from in the desktop or the Web version of PowerPlay.

The PowerDesigner Data Warehouse Information Flow

It may be beneficial in completing our discussion of developing multidimensional analysis applications of a data warehouse architecture to summarize the flow of designs and information among all of the tools that we have discussed. We do so in this section.

You first want to design your data warehouse or data mart model. This model is the driving source of data provided to PowerPlay. Often, this model contains far greater amounts of detail data than the PowerPlay application and may well feed several PowerPlay applications.

After you have designed this master model in PowerDesigner Warehouse Architect, you can use PowerDesigner to build an initial multidimensional hierarchy. As with most generation facilities, this only provides a simple framework from to refine your model. The multidimensional hierarchy editor in PowerDesigner allows you to define a series of cubes that you can feed to OLAP and decision-support systems such as Cognos' PowerPlay and Cognos Impromptu.

In this editor, you define series of dimensional hierarchies and fact hierarchies. The dimensional hierarchies are used to access and index the key performance measures. This categorization of your data becomes the foundation of your corporate knowledge base as users come to depend on these common business terms for accessing their data. The fact hierarchies contain a combination of detailed fact tables along with associated aggregation and partitioned fact tables, which allows users to navigate the data in a data warehouse with high performance.

After completing your multidimensional definition, you request PowerDesigner to deliver the data and multidimensional definition to the targeted OLAP or decision-support system—in our example, Cognos' PowerPlay. At this point, you further refine the physical PowerPlay application with Cognos' PowerPlay Transformer. The PowerDesigner query used to populate the first PowerPlay application can be extracted from PowerDesigner and scheduled for continual execution based on your required application refresh rates. Cognos' PowerPlay Transformer then simply takes the results of this extraction query either to incrementally update the in-place PowerPlay application or to fully refresh the PowerPlay application.

This entire process flow is depicted in Figure 15.9.

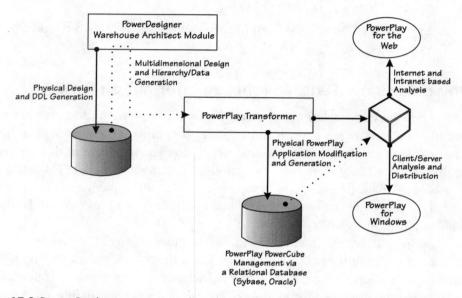

Figure 15.9 *PowerDesigner can centralize the designs for your data warehouse or data mart and your PowerPlay multidimensional cubes.*

Navigating PowerPlay's User Interface

Cognos' PowerPlay Web reports allow users to explore Web-based PowerCubes from a Web browser. Users can drill down on dimensions, filter dimensions, and use various business charts to further analyze the data in your information packages. Users can easily examine key performance metrics, which are used to further evaluate your business.

In the PowerPlay user interface, all Web browser benefits are exploited, including hyperlinking and server optimization. PowerPlay reports are dynamically generated by the PowerPlay Web Server as HTML documents with embedded JavaScript and *.gif* images to improve document usability.

The PowerPlay Web Server produces PowerPlay Web Reports when users:

- Request a specific view of data through their standard Web browser services.

- Change an existing report through drilling down on a dimension.

- Change an existing report by slicing and dicing the dimensions placed on the reporting coordinates.

- Request filtering of the data content of an existing report through the PowerPlay dimension line.

The PowerPlay Web Server uses the standard Cognos PowerCubes as the information sources to fulfill these user requests. These are the same cubes utilized by the legacy client/server PowerPlay product that runs under Microsoft Windows, which allows you to easily support multiple platforms in your data warehouse architecture—namely the Web and Windows platforms. The PowerPlay Web Server is a multiprocessing and multi-threading CGI program that interfaces with your Web's HTTP Server in a similar fashion to Sybase's PowerDynamo.

Following the Direct Manipulation Paradigm

No single system has all of the admirable attributes or design features desired by a user community. Building a system with all of the desired features may be impossible, but the concept of direct manipulation is a feature that gains the enthusiastic support of users and provides the guidelines for building a proper user interface framework. Your data warehouse user interface will benefit through the implementation of several key features, including:

- **Consistency:** Strive for consistency by providing sequences and actions that are similar in comparable situations. This consistency should extend to the standards that you follow for terminology in dialogs, prompts, error messages, menus, and help screens.

- **Error handling:** Your system should provide comprehensive error handling. As much as possible, design your system so users cannot make serious errors. But if an error is made, try to have the system detect the error and offer simple, concise mechanisms for handling it, including the ability to undo what caused the error.

- **Feedback:** Offer informative feedback for every operation. For frequent and minor actions, the response can be modest, such as a line of text on a message line or even a delayed message like the ToolTips found in Microsoft Windows applications. However, infrequent activities should provide substantial feedback and guiding mechanisms that lead users through the process and make it easy, much like Wizards in many Windows applications.

- **Shortcuts:** You should enable shortcuts for the more technically knowledgeable and frequent users of your system. As users become more aware of the capabilities in the tools to which they have access, they want to reduce the number of interactions with the framework and increase interaction with the live tools. Quicker paths to the tools and the data should be built into a framework, and users should be encouraged to investigate and utilize these shortcuts. These characteristics reduce the amount of application code that a data warehouse project team must write and—better yet—maintain.

People talk of data warehouse access and data manipulation in various ways: wading through data, mining data, and data discovery. Whatever term you use, this access and manipulation basically allows users to focus on the content of a data warehouse, rather than on how to operate a data warehouse application. Remember, we want users to focus on business aspects, not on technology. PowerPlay closely aligns itself with these direct manipulation guidelines.

Ad Hoc Multidimensional Analysis with PowerPlay

PowerPlay provides multidimensional capabilities that allow users to analyze and report on the data in a data warehouse. This environment launches users into a data cube and allows them to directly manipulate the presentation of data along any provided dimension in a variety of different display formats. Because these dimensions have been defined to PowerPlay, the product aggregates and presents data in different summarized levels of a business, allowing users to twist and turn the data cube until they have thoroughly analyzed the content.

The heart and soul of PowerPlay is direct manipulation. Users literally are presented with a data cube and asked to manipulate it instead of the traditional reporting schemes in which users must explain how to present, navigate, access, and filter the data—all before they get any results. Figure 15.10 presents the initial exploratory view of our customer sales analysis PowerPlay PowerCube. Notice that PowerPlay immediately graphs a measure, such as revenue, against the first two dimensions of the cube—time and product. Users can refine the presentation of the data by manipulating the dimensions, including time periods, products, sales locations, channels, and margin ranges.

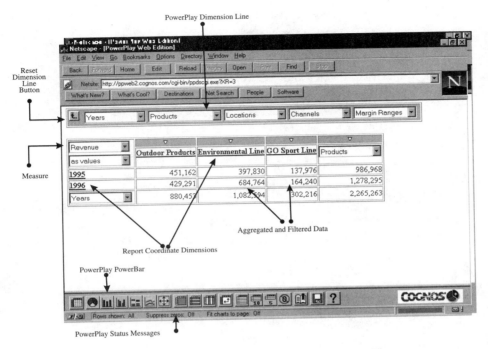

Figure 15.10 *The initial PowerPlay exploratory view of our customer sales analysis information package.*

Drilling Down to Discover Additional Detail

Our first direct manipulation example in PowerPlay involves drilling down, a relatively easy concept to understand. Users want to get more detailed information for data that already is present. They therefore want to drill down to the next detail category in a dimensional hierarchy. In PowerPlay, users are guided to where they can drill through subtle changes in the cursor. PowerPlay presents users with an appropriate cursor when the mouse moves over data containing additional details, while HTML hyperlinks in the data indicate additional areas for drill-down analysis. In continuing to investigate our information package, we can drill down on the Environmental Line of products either by changing the dimension line at the top of the report or selecting the hyperlink in the appropriate column heading. The results of this drill-down activity are shown in Figure 15.11.

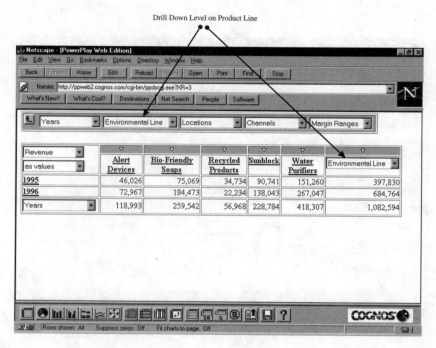

Figure 15.11 *Drilling down on a dimension instructs PowerPlay to refine the level of detail presented from our customer sales analysis information package. Here, we now view only the Environmental Line of products.*

We could also isolate on the data from a specific year by selecting the appropriate hyperlink or dimension line filter. Changes like this one to the PowerPlay view are handled dynamically and provide an analogy to a Rubiks Cube. As users changes or twists the cube, additional views of data allow trends and information to jump off the page.

Slicing and Dicing to Isolate Information

The ability to isolate a dimension and further investigate the data in other dimensions is what provides the true multidimensional analysis required to analyze business data. Figure 15.12 shows PowerPlay isolating on the time period of 1996 and then slicing in the channels dimension. This will change the display to present revenue by channel for the Environmental Line of products. The new display will also be filtered to only include data for 1996.

This activity was accomplished by drilling down on the time period and product line dimensions from the initial view and then selecting the channels dimension in the presentation dialog box at the bottom of the displayed rows.

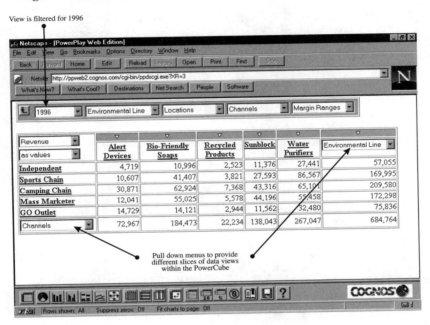

Figure 15.12 *Isolating on data and slicing in different dimensions instructs PowerPlay to refine the presentation of the data. Here, we view a slice of information bound by the Environmental Line of products intersected by the channels dimension and filtered to include only data for 1996.*

Graphical Display and Manipulation

PowerPlay provides both textual presentation and the manipulation of a PowerCube and graphical display. All of the manipulation techniques presented in this chapter are also available while presenting the data graphically. Utilizing the PowerPlay toolbar at the bottom of a Web presentation, users can select the clustered bar button. PowerPlay responds by presenting the current information from the cube in a clustered bar graph, as shown in Figure 15.13. Additional graphical presentation styles include pie charts, bar graphs, clustered bar graphs, stacked bar graphs, and line graphs.

The PowerPlay toolbar provides additional functionality to assist when direct manipulation is inappropriate for modifying report content. The toolbar provides buttons that perform the following functions (from the toolbar's left to right).

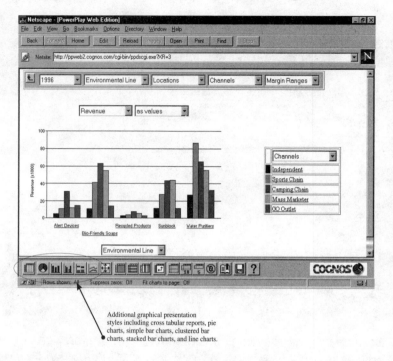

Additional graphical presentation styles including cross tabular reports, pie charts, simple bar charts, clustered bar charts, stacked bar charts, and line charts.

Figure 15.13 *PowerPlay for the Web as well as the desktop version of PowerPlay give users the flexibility of working directly with PowerCubes in various graphical formats. Here, we see a PowerCube presented as a clustered bar graph.*

- **Cross-tabular presentation:** Present the report using cross tabular presentation style.

- **Pie chart presentation:** Present the report using pie chart presentation style.

- **Simple bar chart presentation:** Present the report using simple bar chart presentation style.

- **Clustered bar chart presentation:** Present the report using clustered bar chart presentation style.

- **Stacked bar chart presentation:** Present the report using stacked bar chart presentation style.

- **Line chart presentation:** Present the report using line chart presentation style.

- **Fit chart to page:** Enlarge the chart to maximize its visualization and reduce white space.

- **change measures:** Prompt the user for measures that should be presented.

- **Change rows:** Prompt the user for the reporting coordinates that should be presented in the rows.

- **Change columns:** Prompt the user for the reporting coordinates that should be presented in the columns.

- **Swap rows and columns:** Exchange the presentation coordinates; what is currently a row should be placed in a column and what is currently a column should be presented in a row.

- **Show all rows in cross tab:** Show all rows that match the filters for the current dimension line.

- **Show 10 rows in cross tab:** Reduce the number of rows presented to 10.

- **Show 5 rows in cross tab:** Reduce the number of rows presented to five.

- **Suppress zeros:** Filter any results that present all zeros.

- **Prepare bookmark:** Place a bookmark for the current view of the information cube, allowing the user to easily return to the current point in the analysis.

- **Save to CSV file:** Save the information from the current view in an industry-standard comma-separated file.

- **Help:** Present PowerPlay's help to assist the user in better understanding how to perform specific operations.

- **About:** Present PowerPlay's product information to document critical items about the product and cube that is being investigated.

Measurable Factors for Usability

The slicing of additional dimensions and filtering of dimensions is done through direct manipulation. The following list will help you gauge how usably your application framework presents the data in your data warehouse. These items should be tested with your user community to understand the impact that the overall solution you provide on the entire user base. You should develop a set of benchmark tests that are associated with the requirements defined by your users and have the users use your data warehouse access tool suite to solve the problems contained in that benchmark. Such a usability test will greatly assist your team in delivering a proper solution to your user community.

- **Time to learn:** How long does it take typical users in the target user community to learn the application, the reports, and their applicability to solving information requirements? How long does it take users to access and use your data warehouse with a relevant set of data to solve a relevant information task or decision problem?

- **User error rate:** Errors are a critical component of system usage and therefore deserve extensive study. How many and what kind of errors are made by the users of your data warehouse in benchmark tasks?

- **Speed of performance:** How long does it take to carry out benchmark tasks? How long does it take for users to have enough knowledge to make a decision? Does the application framework respond quickly to users' rapid-fire questioning?

- **Retention over time:** How well do users maintain their knowledge of the system after an hour? A day? A week? Retention may be closely linked to time to learn and is also based on frequency of use. Perform these tests with a cross-section of your user community.

- **Subjective satisfaction:** How much do users like the system? This can be ascertained by interview, written survey, or videotaping testing sessions. Determine overall satisfaction and let users provide free-form comments and feedback on how to improve the system.

Tip: Users' interest is in the information contained in and managed by a data warehouse. Therefore, choose or build a deployment environment that is composed of tools and applications that support the business first—techie stuff much later, if at all.

Producing Static Reports

Besides the PowerPlay Web module, you can easily publish query results from a PowerPlay PowerCube in HTML format. This feature of both PowerPlay and Impromptu allows you to publish multidimensional and relational reports to users who do not have access to the data warehouse tool suite. Additionally, with these features you can take advantage of the

Impromptu and PowerPlay HTML publishing capabilities to immediately or on a scheduled basis produce results of an Impromptu or PowerPlay task and publish them in HTML or email format.

This feature enables you to distribute new information and updates immediately to a wider base of users. To distribute information immediately, you use the Send command in a macro or directly from the interactive environment. The Publish tab for publishing to HTML is only available when you schedule an Impromptu or PowerPlay task. These results can be sent via email through Cognos Scheduler, which distributes your results automatically using macros or sends the results via email to targeted users.

A Layered Approach

The coordinator faces an immense job when deploying a data warehouse. This individual must provide access and customized reports to a large, growing user community with vastly differing reporting needs. These differences include the volume of reporting, the diversity of reporting, and the access strategies involved with both. The challenges of providing adequate facilities and resources to support users and giving them timely solutions to their information needs are demanding.

The key to successful deployment is a good architecture that provides flexibility while reducing the requirement for fixed and standardized reports. If you can build your data warehouse in an easy-to-understand manner and provide your users with the proper tools to access your data, you will achieve a high user satisfaction rating.

Delivering such solutions raises internal Information System issues of performance, security, and ongoing support of a user community. The key to delivering such solutions is insulation. If you insulate users from having to understand technology such as data structures, join strategies, networks, and other highly technical matters, you can solve their problems. To some database administrators, this means creating a lot of security schemes on top of views in their relational database. To those who have successfully deployed data warehouses, the abstraction is even higher than that.

Creating an environment that is safe for corporation and user alike can be done with several modern tools that target the decision-support, OLAP, and data-mining marketplaces. These tools address the security and access issues with semantic layers, or catalogs, that are managed outside a native database.

At a minimum, the application framework provided to users must eliminate the presentation of technology-oriented concepts, such as the technical concept of joining two or more tables. This type of technology concept increases the learning curve for deployment of a data warehouse and potentially introduces the risk of users not accepting the delivered solution. These concepts also prove to be technically risky.

Most data access and query tools that allow users to perform joins have no intelligence in optimizing the join. Therefore, users can easily make mistakes and create meaningless queries with simple point-and-click tools. We often say that the tools of today can assist the knowledgeable in creating fabulous systems quickly, but they can also assist the unknowledgeable in creating the biggest nightmares just as quickly. Exposing concepts like data navigation and join strategies to users introduces danger into a peaceful query environment.

Your final delivery mechanism should allow complete access to your enterprise's data warehouse environment. This system should be built around an architecture that consists of data, technology, and application components. Your data warehouse tool suite is the foundation from which your application framework is delivered to access your various data stores, such as a data warehouse, local data marts, and multidimensional data analysis data stores. A detailed data warehouse application framework is illustrated in Figure 15.14.

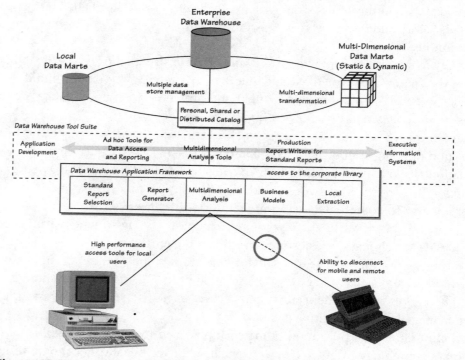

Figure 15.14 *Your data warehouse application framework should contain various components, each meant to address the specialized needs of a diverse user base.*

Summary

The data warehousing tools that support users allow a large population to navigate your corporate data stores. Access can include ad hoc, interactive, repetitive querying. All of this functionality must be provided without impacting mission-critical operational systems. In a given session, users may issue query after query in an iterative manner to explore trends, pinpoint or discover problems, and evaluate business opportunities. This information allows users to make better business decisions in a more rapid fashion, allowing an enterprise to become more competitive.

To make your organization succeed, create an informed environment for widespread knowledge. To make your organization more intelligent, share the business intelligence from the corporate knowledge base with everyone. This freedom of information begins to allow everyone to unite around a common vision of responsibility and accountability. Put the intelligence of every employee to work through maximum use of the information in your data warehouse. Every person can, and will, make a difference in the future. The sooner you get started, the further you will be ahead of your competition and the faster your enterprise can be viewed as a truly intelligent enterprise.

Intensive reviews of customer information assists your users in reaffirming current strategies or revealing the requirements for an entirely new strategy. Your job in delivering a customer data mart is to deliver this new knowledge about the market, market conditions, and internal capabilities to address customer needs. The process of data gathering is the basis of your activities. After you deliver the data in the data mart, users develop business intelligence through a series of activities that involve the creation of hypotheses, testing theorems, reflecting on previous business activities, building strategic learning, and adapting the enterprise to implement new business strategies.

You will find a need for various tools to deliver such capabilities in your data warehousing system. The tools you offer will include a set of applications that offer fixed views of data and a series of tools for confirmation or refuting hypotheses (relational), for testing hypothesis (OLAP), and for discovering system-generated patterns (data mining). Just as office automation products have migrated to tool suites, so shall data warehousing tools. As we have seen in this chapter, Cognos, one of the leading vendors in the data warehouse tools market, has already begun offering their products in such packaging.

The Cognos Business Intelligence Suite includes an ad hoc query tool (Impromptu), an OLAP tool (PowerPlay), a data mining tool (Scenario), and a forecasting tool (4 Thought). This chapter has shown how PowerPlay can be used to support a wide set of users who require access to a data warehouse. This access can occur over the Web or through a client/server Microsoft Windows interface. Either way, your task of delivering the fundamental data architecture and base application architecture can be done with the Cognos' tools and the development tools that are highly integrated with Cognos products, such as Sybase's PowerDesigner.

PowerDesigner allows you to develop your data models and OLAP models in one central architecture. Generating applications in this environment is nearly a point-and-shoot task, which provides your development staff with productivity that matches the productivity users achieve with business intelligence tools.

All of the tools that we have discussed in this book lead your organization to a support infrastructure that enables the strategic learning and feedback process required to build a competitive, market dominating corporate knowledge base. Your users can take the data you provide, turn it into business intelligence, and fulfill the required strategic learning process to feed the next vision and strategy process required by your business for sustainable growth.

When building a technical solution to spread knowledge throughout your organization, it is important for you to understand the distinction between the applications framework provided by a data warehouse and the tool set that delivers the framework. The framework delivers a set of required capabilities to the users of a warehouse. The capabilities that the users derive from the framework are delivered by individual tools, or by tools working together as well as with administrative resources provided by warehouse administrators.

The tools that support a data warehouse application framework may—and more than likely will—change over time. However, these changes should not change the applications framework, except to enhance it.

You should use great care to provide the users of your data warehouse with a complete solution that covers the spectrum of their data access and reporting needs. However, you must realize that users have little to no desire to learn technical nuances of database management systems. Therefore, selection of tools should focus on those tools that totally insulate users from constructs such as table joins. Giving your users power from a tool does not mean that they should learn how to code; it means that they will have power to explore data without learning technology.

In this book, we have discussed the concept and the compelling case for developing a data warehouse that is accessible to the largest possible population of users in your company. The Internet provides an excellent framework for delivery; but without a methodology, you will certainly fail. Fortunately, proceeding in a methodical fashion through all of the essential steps of implementing a successful data warehouse project is what the information packaging methodology is all about. Following such a process makes the interfacing of tools such as the Cognos Business Intelligence Tool Suite and the Sybase design, database management, and development tools a snap.

Appendix A

Information Packaging Methodology Reference Guide

The following appendix captures the key points of a quick reference guide to the information packaging methodology provided in this book. After reading this book, this appendix provides you with a project planning guide, highlighting the important tips of the overall work breakdown structure of your project plan.

Critical Success Factors

Prior to committing to a data warehouse project, it is critical that you address, scrutinize, and follow the following steps. Our experience is that the a of focus behind each of these items assists in the demise of a data warehouse project. Following these items will not guarantee success, but it will certainly place you on the path toward success.

- Obtain management commitment.

- Begin with a manageable project.

- Clearly communicate realistic expectations.

- Assign a user-oriented manager.

- Use proven methods.

- Design based on queries rather than on transactions.

- Load only data that is needed.

- Define the proper system of record.

- Clearly define unique subjects.

- Force the use of, and reference to, a data warehouse.

Work Breakdown and Tips

A project plan defines the work and how it will be done. It provides a definition of each major task, an estimate of the time and resources required to complete the task, and a review process for management control. When properly documented, a project plan becomes an excellent learning vehicle—another data mart or knowledge base to assist future project managers. The benchmarking of actual execution of a plan will assist your organization in better managing and estimating tasks in the future, improving your overall accuracy. It is difficult to boilerplate a data warehouse project plan, but we include some of the major tasks that assist you in formulating your own plan. This should not be viewed as a complete project work breakdown structure, just as a framework to assist you in defining the specific tasks that you will require.

As with other projects, the work breakdown structure is only one element of an overall planning process. You need to define the initial requirements first. From these requirements, you can build the work breakdown structure, each item of which can then be estimated to allow you to project the required resources and formalize the schedule.

Step 0: The Architecture

To deliver all that is required by a data warehouse, you must establish a solid foundation of technology infrastructure—an architecture. The architecture is critical to the overall success of a data warehouse. Without a proper architecture, the connectivity among the required components and underlying technologies of a data warehouse will not occur. After the architecture is completed, you can easily assess the benefit and impact of new data marts and expansions to a data warehouse.

Phase I: Plan the Architecture

Here are the consolidated steps to perform during this phase of the information packaging methodology.

1. Create a vision.

2. Adopt a methodology.

3. Assemble an architecture team.

4. Define the architecture project scope.

5. Define the business goals and objectives.

6. Prepare the architecture plan and work breakdown structure.

7. Obtain management commitment.

8. Evaluate the current architecture.

9. Model the existing enterprise.

10. Phase review.

Phase II: Build the Architecture Blueprint

Here are the consolidated steps to perform during this phase of the information packaging methodology.

1. Define the architecture requirements.

2. Define the data architecture.

3. Define the application architecture.

4. Define the technology architecture.

5. Establish the data warehouse tool suite.

6. Document the data warehouse architecture in a standard document—a blueprint.

7. Phase review.

Here is a consolidation of Architecture Tips that are relevant to this phase of the information packaging methodology.

Architecture Tip 1: You should establish a replication technology that provides an unintrusive data warehouse agent—such as a Log Transfer Manager—to assist in the data warehouse loading and transformation processing. This type of technology minimizes the impact and interruptions that may occur on operational systems.

Architecture Tip 2: The architectural phase and architectural review are outside the development scope. However, they should not be forgotten, because they are the foundation of a proper enterprise data warehousing strategy. Would you build your house without a foundation or blueprint? Data warehouses should avoid the same philosophy.

Architecture Tip 3: Quality obviously is important; the guaranteed pursuit of quality should be too. Therefore, be sure to design an automated quality system in your architecture so that you can automate the testing process and more efficiently perform your integration testing.

Architecture Tip 4: Standards should be defined for each of the components of a data warehouse, including those that follow.

columns	constraints	databases	devices
datatypes	defaults	security groups	indexes
logins	rules	segments	servers
stored procedures	tables	triggers	information packages
views	standard reports	users	catalogs
domains	relationships		

Architecture Tip 5: Your data warehouse standards should be developed prior to tool selection. Try to find the tool that most matches your standards and continually monitor available tools to find the one that is best for your standards. Do not build your standards based on tools. Over time, the tools will change and your standards will be left in the dark ages, or at least at the previous generation of tools.

Architecture Tip 6: A data modeling tool should at a minimum support the following: logical data modeling; physical database modeling; automatic generation of the native, physical data definition language for your chosen database management system; domain management; reverse engineering of legacy data models; native database management system support; and complete reporting capabilities for impact analysis and documentation. Don't settle for less.

Architecture Tip 7: When choosing components of your architecture, choose products and tools that provide building blocks and expansion, or scalability options in the future. The components you select also should involve little to no disruption to your users when scaling or expanding. You should not be required to purchase all of your architectural components and tools in the beginning.

Architecture Tip 8: Look for impossible things in your vendor community, things you think can't be done—then have your vendor prove that they can be done. However, make sure to pay for the proof with something like a money-back guarantee. If you pay for a service, the vendor will realize you are serious and may assign more talented resources to your account than if you want a freebie proof.

Note: Remember, an architecture consists of subarchitectures—namely data, application, and technology—and should also focus on the resources and organization required to support the target architecture.

An Information Packaging Methodology Road Map

After the architectural work has been completed for overall enterprise, you begin to deliver subject-oriented data warehouses. To perform these tasks, you will want to follow the information packaging methodology covered in this book. This is a spiral methodology and should be utilized to build up to an enterprise data warehouse through implementation of several smaller subject-oriented data warehouses. This methodology is depicted in Figure A.1, and a step-by-step summary of its steps is provided in the sections that follow.

Step 1: Project Planning

Failing to plan is planning to fail. The planning phase of your project allows the proper scope to be set and assists your project team in clearly sizing the time and effort required to deliver a data warehouse solution. Here is a consolidation of Planning Tips that are relevant to this phase of the information packaging methodology.

Planning Tip 1: The planning process is one in which you must remember that the most important single factor in determining the final delivery date is the date on which a project begins.

Planning Tip 2: Remember that the initial plan is a starting point from which you will determine the size of a project. Managing this effectively means not over-committing resources by negotiating major time or cost cuts within tasks. Until you reach final agreement on time, resources, and cost, the project plan will not be solidified.

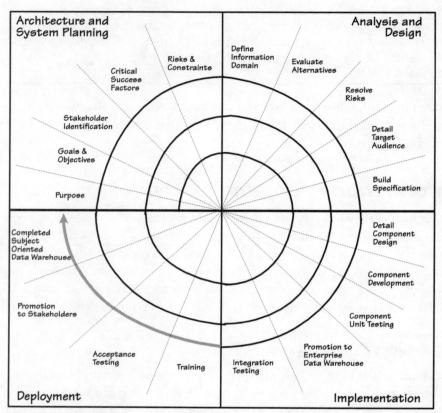

Figure A.1 *A project manager's road map to the information packaging methodology*

Here is a consolidation of the steps to perform during this phase of the information packaging methodology.

1. Define the project purpose.

2. Define the project goals and objectives.

3. Define the stakeholders who have an interest in the project's outcome.

4. Define the project's management team.

5. Define the project's critical success factors.

6. Define the project's risks and constraints.

7. Define the project team.

8. Establish and enforce the project work flow.

9. Phase review.

Planning Tip 3: It is nearly impossible to build a "dream team" with any sort of staying power. Make sure to define a longer-term strategy that supports the needs of your initial team. Satisfying your goals and your people's goals will enhance your ability to succeed.

Planning Tip 4: Hourly rate should not be a decision criterion for selecting resources from the world of consulting. Experience and ability to stand behind a project far outweigh the hourly cost. Your consultants should be held accountable. Make sure their company can guarantee their work.

Step 2: Analysis and Design

The analysis and design phase assists your project team in defining what data is required by users as well as other relevant processing and background information required to successfully deliver a data warehouse. The analysis and design phase is greatly influenced by the knowledge of what is possible within a data warehouse. The final deliverables in this phase are specifications, in the form of dimension maps that define the subject areas and performance measures important to a business. Here is a consolidation of the steps to perform during this phase of the information packaging methodology.

1. Define the information domain.

2. Evaluate alternate solutions.

3. Resolve, or build plans to resolve, defined project risks.

4. Develop detailed knowledge of the target audience.

5. Assemble the specification.

6. Map the requirements and specifications to the standard architecture.

7. Map the information domain with information package diagramming techniques (user requirements).

8. Phase review.

Here is a consolidation of the Analysis and Design Tips that are relevant to this phase of the information packaging methodology.

Analysis and Design Tip 1: All project objectives and requirements for a data warehouse and associated data marts should be mapped to one or more components in the standard architecture. If the mapping cannot occur, the architecture or the requirements are incomplete.

Analysis and Design Tip 2: Preparation for user interviews is important. You will require input from the key personnel in the user community. You will do yourself and your team a large favor by being well prepared and optimizing your visits with users. Remember, their time is valuable to the enterprise. After all, they are making strategic and tactical decisions that are worth millions of dollars to the company.

Analysis and Design Tip 3: The data granularity required by users is typically one detail level lower than the decision point. For example, if a sales manager is only interested in quarterly variance of forecasted revenue to actual revenue because the selling cycle is 90 days and all decisions are based on the selling cycle, you want to deliver monthly variance figures in the data warehouse. By delivering this next layer of detail, you support the process of investigation that is required by the manager, his or her analysts, or the personnel within his or her organization who are typically asked for the reasons behind a change in trends. Though the ultimate business change might be made based on quarterly statistics, the monthly trends information provides insight when variances occur.

Analysis and Design Tip 4: Users will tag key information with common, user-oriented keywords such as by and over. These keywords give additional meaning to data requirements and allow you to easily package the information required by users into the proper structure. For example, a manager may desire to see product sales information by month, by geography, and by product during the last five years. The tags of by assist in defining the dimensions of month, geography, and product. The tag of over assists in defining the content of the time dimension, or how many months are required to fill the information request.

Analysis and Design Tip 5: Data warehouses contain data that is fundamentally dimension and measure oriented. Begin to listen and dissect your users' comments into dimensions (subjects) and measures (facts).

Analysis and Design Tip 6: When working with an information package diagram, try to minimize your access paths, or dimensions. This helps users by simplifying the manner in which the data is obtained. Keep the number of dimensions within a reasonable number, such as under 10. This is not a fixed limit, and many information models require a larger number of dimensions. However, usability is hampered when you exceed this number. Usability should be the number one focus of your warehouse project. The shaded areas on an information package diagram remind you of this usability tip.

Analysis and Design Tip 7: The relationship between category levels and a dimension should be under a 1:10 ratio. This assists users in navigating and understanding the data. This is not a fixed limit, and many information models require a larger ratio between dimensions and categories. However, usability is hampered when you exceed this number. Usability should be the top focus of your warehouse project. The shaded areas on an information package diagram remind you of this usability tip.

Analysis and Design Tip 8: If you get in a situation in which you exceed a reasonable ratio between category levels, you can place an artificial category in your information package that logically organizes the category level into a manageable ratio. A ratio between category levels that exceeds 1:150 should be further analyzed for applying this tip. This is not a fixed limit, and many information models require a larger ratio between category levels. However, usability is hampered when you exceed this number. Usability should be the number one focus of your warehouse project.

Analysis and Design Tip 9: Try to insert the numbers that represent the unique occurrences of a category value within your category cells. These numbers assist you in understanding the volume of potential data and the relationships on types of data that could greatly impact the size of your warehouse. This data assists you if you need to split an information package in the future.

Analysis and Design Tip 10: When analyzing information to design your data warehouse, use multiple information package diagrams. Don't try to cover all of the possible information requests with one information package diagram. Creating several information package diagrams, each tailored to suit a particular information request or information package, allows you to build a data warehouse that performs better and provides a higher degree of user satisfaction.

Step 3: Implementation

Throughout the development process, the data warehouse team will gain a better understanding of the data warehousing process and user requirements. There are practical issues involved in the implementation of a data warehouse, such as how the user accesses the information, from which the development team gains a sense of judgment and experience, allowing it to begin delivering the ultimate data warehouse. A successful data warehouse implementation requires an interlocking of the development processes that guarantees that all elements work together in concert and harmony to provide users with the proper system. The implementation process focuses on the best way to physically implement the designs built in the analysis and design phase. Here is a consolidation of the steps to perform during this phase of the information packaging methodology.

1. Clearly define unique data warehouse entities.

2. Build the logical data model by translating information package diagrams into star schemas.

3. Build the physical data model by translating your star schema logical models.

4. Develop the data import or loading components.

5. Develop the data access components.

6. Unit test all developed components.

7. Perform integration testing of completed information packages, including data quality testing.

8. Phase review.

Here is a consolidation of the Implementation Tips that are relevant to this phase of the information packaging methodology.

Implementation Tip 1: To give a more descriptive meaning to your star schema models, use graphics that communicate a clear meaning for each entity in the model. Recommended graphics are rectangles for measure entities, diamonds for dimension entities, and stop signs for category detail entities.

Implementation Tip 2: Measure entities are composed of the keys to the detail, or lowest level, categories in each dimension of an information package diagram. Each column must relate to all measures of the information package diagram. At this point, determine whether you will store calculated measurements. It is wise to estimate the overhead of users calculating the measurement data each time they access an information package versus the additional storage space and processing time required to precalculate the measurement data.

Implementation Tip 3: Dimension entities are placed on the points of a star schema and have a relationship that projects inward to the center of the star. The relationships among any dimension and measure entities is one to many; one dimension entity instance relates to many measure entity instances. Dimension entities are logical in nature and are the most denormalized of the three major data warehouse entities structures.

Implementation Tip 4: Category detail entity definitions contain information that enhances and adds qualitative data to the measurement, or quantitative, data. The category details transform your star schema diagram into a snowflake schema because of the branching effect that the category details deliver to the star schema. (Note: Some industry gurus have different meanings for snowflake schemas. The type we discuss is controlled and will not be a detriment to your implementation.)

Implementation Tip 5: It is important that you uniquely and clearly define all entities in your data warehouse: What is a Customer? Product? Region? You also need to realize that it is okay for different measure entities to require the same dimension entity to provide relationships at differing levels of category detail: A Time Period relates to Measure Entity 1 at the month level, while Measure Entity 2 relates at a day level. Remember, a relational database, which you typically utilize to implement your data warehouse, allows you to join tables with various entity columns. Therefore, you can take the Month column and join it from the Time Period Dimension Entity to the Month column within Measure Entity 1. You can also join the Date column from the Time Period Dimension Entity to the Date column within Measure Entity 2. Month and Date are both time periods and will be contained within the same entity even though theY provide different levels of detail.

Implementation Tip 6: Be sure to follow the complete refinement process when modeling your data; that is, from information package diagram through star schema to physical data model. This is a key part of the process that should be strictly followed to assist in the overall quality of a data warehouse and its components.

Implementation Tip 7: Data warehouse entities should be driven by the users' query behavior. To this end, dimension entities assist users in navigating and filtering measure entities, and proceed to allowing users to focus on data in category detail entities.

Implementation Tip 8: Become the leader in your company in driving an auditing standard for all operational systems, and data stores in general. This eases the process of extracting data from operational data stores and of loading the cleansed data into data warehouse data stores.

Implementation Tip 9: Just because SQL is a set-oriented language does not mean that everything can be easily and most efficiently done in one pass of data. Remember the policy of keeping things simple; simplicity often, but not always, equates to efficiency. Many cleansing and loading processes require more than one pass of the data. Design your load modules with your eye on the future and your mind in the past. That is, don't forget things such as checkpoint restart logic, which optimized batch jobs of old. These techniques can bridge to the future and optimize your loading process.

Implementation Tip 10: Replication technologies can be extremely useful for the data warehouse loading process. Search for the least intrusive method of trapping data modifications in operational systems. These systems can ill afford an increase in the transaction window, or code revisions. A good replication technology that monitors a data store's log file delivers this least intrusive solution.

Implementation Tip 11: Application packages should not be hard to integrate into your overall data warehouse strategy. However, often they are difficult to integrate due to your company's low technical knowledge in data management for the application. Guarantee that your development team receives adequate documentation and training on any in-house applications that will provide data to a data warehouse.

Step 4: Deployment

After a data warehouse is built, you must guarantee success by formally defining a deployment strategy. This includes the concepts of training users, obtaining their acceptance and feedback, and in general promoting what is available in your data warehouse throughout the enterprise. Here is a consolidation of the steps to perform during this phase of the information packaging methodology.

1. Support staff training.

2. User training.

3. User acceptance—sign off.

4. Promotion.

5. Formal project review.

Here is a consolidation of the Deployment Tips that are relevant to this phase of the information packaging methodology.

Deployment Tip 1: A system is not complete until it is fully accepted by the user community. Only the users can say, "Done."

Deployment Tip 2: The users' interest is in the information contained in and managed by a data warehouse. Therefore, make sure to choose or build a deployment environment that is composed of tools and applications that support the business first—techie stuff way later, if at all.

Deployment Tip 3: In the area of tools, it is unfortunate but true that you get what your pay for. Don't be penny wise and pound foolish when deploying tools to your user community. The more sophisticated a tool is, the more productive users will be and the less burden will be placed on your development team.

Summary

This appendix has provided you with a synopsis of the information packaging methodology covered in this book as well as this book's predecessor, *Data Warehousing: Building the Corporate Knowledge Base*, ISBN#1-85032-856-0. By following these steps and concentrating on the tips outlined in each phase, you and your data warehouse project team can quickly become information packaging experts, fully delivering a corporate knowledge base to your enterprise.

Glossary

action A description of the state or process of acting or doing, typically described by a verb noting that something is being done.

ad hoc An act such as a query against a data store that is not premeditated or that is without preparation, impromptu, and off the top of the head. This word often characterizes a set of query tools that support this behavior.

aggregate Generically, to gather into a mass, sum, or whole; to amount to; total. With regard to a data warehouse, aggregates or aggregation refers to the concept of rolling up data within its dimensional hierarchy. Each dimension contains many levels that, in turn, can present the user with a rolled-up version of data. Example: In a locations dimension, all districts add up to a region. Aggregates and aggregation provide a valuable type of computation within a decision support system or data warehouse. Most users want to see aggregations not only in one dimension, but across dimensional boundaries. Because dimensions are indexes into numerical business measures, this is possible. Example: A regional sales manager wants to see all sales figures, forecast and actual, for each district by product line. For this aggregation, sales figures must be summarized for each city within the district by product line and presented to the user. With regard to standard SQL statements, an aggregate refers to data returned in a result set with the average, summation, count, minimize, and maximize functions typically used with a group by clause.

alternate key An alternate key, or index, is a column or columns designated as a preferred or common means of accessing the instances of a given entity. Example: The primary key to a customer table might be CustomerNumber and the alternate key might be CustomerName. CustomerName does not guarantee uniqueness of the instance of a customer; therefore, a number that is typically generated by the operational system is used to uniquely represent the customer. However, users of the system are more likely to remember the name of the customer, so we provide them that way to access the data.

ANSI American National Standards Institute.

answer set See result set.

application architecture An application architecture defines and supports the software process for implementation of the required business functionality.

architecture A style and method of design and construction; an orderly arrangement of parts.

atomic process A process that has a single action and a single outcome, such as the turning on of a light switch.

audit trail Data that links a sequence of events used to track transactions that have affected the contents of a record. This data allows tracing of the history on things such as accounts and product inventory.

back end process The area of a data warehouse system that utilizes the operational system's data stores to populate the staging area within a data warehouse. This process typically includes data collection and data gathering. The back end process prepares data into a transaction base that updates and feeds a data warehouse system.

batch A program, often referred to as a job, that performs a predefined series of actions with little or no interaction between the user and the system.

bitmap index An index in which a list of bits (either 1 or 0) represents the presence of a given value for a field. The bit represents true if 1 and false if 0. This technique is utilized in many modern data management tools that assist in optimizing data warehouse systems, such as Adaptive Server IQ.

b-tree index An indexing technique that has been utilized in traditional relational database management systems and indexed flat file systems to assist applications in rapidly locating data rows. This technique of indexing involves storing a representation of the index in a tree structure, typically balanced. The processing system works through the branches of the tree in an optimized fashion to find the actual physical page within a data store where data resides.

business cycle A period of elapsed time that begins during the initial identification of an input, or stimulus, into the cycle, such as a customer's need, and concludes with the completion of the task, such as receipt of payment for the product shipped or service delivered to the customer, fulfilling their need.

cardinality A term used in modeling data relationships; the definition of a relationship between two entities. Cardinality is normally stated in ratio terms such as one to many, or 1:M. Example: A customer has a one-to-many cardinality with orders. This example states that each customer places many orders—or 1 Customer:M orders.

Cartesian product A set of all pairs of elements (x, y) that can be constructed from given sets X and Y, such that x belongs to X and y to Y; every result from all tables contained within the join intersect.

category A specifically defined division in a dimension that provides a detailed classification system. This discrete member of a dimension is used to identify and isolate specific data within that dimension. Example: Cincinnati and Central Region are categories within a location dimension.

category detail entity An entity contained within a data warehouse to provide more detail information, often textual or qualitative, to the answer sets derived from measurement data. Examples of this data include legal contract information, warranty information, and contact information.

CGI Common Gateway Interface is the Internet standard interface for invoking server based scripts or compiled programs at the request of clients.

checkpoint A technique for monitoring the process of a long-running batch program. This technique records the status of execution points to speed recovery in the event of a failure. Upon recovering a failed program, the checkpoint logic allows skipping previously completed tasks and continuing with the items that were not successfully completed.

compound document A single document that contains components from multiple sources. Examples: dialogue from a word processor, graphics from a presentation package, and data from a spreadsheet.

conceptual design A preliminary design that captures the concepts behind a user's requirement; this design typically contains minimal information about data relationships and physical implementation. Within this book, a conceptual design is represented by a dimension map.

cookies Are tokens that are temporarily stored and managed by a Web browser or server application to allow information about the Web client to be exposed to server-based applications.

data architecture The organization of the sources and stores of business information throughout an enterprise.

data cleansing The process of taking operational data and applying quality, in essence removing dirty data through data transformation.

data collection A portion of back end processing in a data warehouse system. The data collection process involves intercepting and collecting data that has changed within operational data stores. This assists in the processing of data for a data warehouse's input feeds.

data control language The syntax provided within a data store's query language that allows control-oriented processing. Within Transact-SQL, this refers to syntax such as beginÉend, goto, and ifÉelse.

data cube A storage structure often utilized by products supporting a multidimensional data structure. Synonyms include cube and hypercube. A data cube typically comprises an information package defined by dimensions such as time, product, and geography; and their associated facts, such as revenue.

data definition language The syntax provided within a data store's query language that allows for the definition of the physical objects managed by a data store. Within SQL, this refers to syntax such as create table and create database.

data distribution The process of migrating data from a centralized location to remote locations that require copies of the data.

data extract The process of accessing a data store, retrieving a specified set of data, and populating another data store; typically a local file, such as a comma-delimited text file for importing into a user's spreadsheet application.

data gathering A portion of back end processing that occurs in a data warehouse system. Data gathering involves the pulling of operational data that is associated and related, then placing those transactions into a data warehouse or data warehouse's staging area.

data manipulation language The syntax provided within a data store's query language that allows data to be manipulated. Within SQL, this refers to the select, insert, update, and delete statements.

data mart A component of a data warehouse that is typically focused on a specific information package or business process. A data mart follows the same principles as an overall data warehouse; however, its content is not as comprehensive.

data placement The process of transferring data from either operational data stores or a data warehouse staging area into a data warehouse.

data scrubbing The process of massaging data to give it proper, uniform format and definition prior to placement in a data warehouse.

data store Where data is stored and managed by an application, such as a database.

data transformation The act of interpreting data and modifying its content to conform to a set of requirements and standards, typically involved in taking operational data and placing it into a data warehouse. Transformations include unifying transaction data along identifiers such as common customer numbers, or on populating additional information based on embedded data such as a vehicle identification number, which can identify the year, make, model, and other information about a vehicle.

data warehouse A place in which factual information, especially information organized for analysis or used to reason or make decisions, is stored; a corporate knowledge base.

database administrator A person responsible for a database system, including its design, development, operation, security, maintenance, and use.

database management system A software system that controls the creation, organization, access, and modification of data.

DBA See database administrator.

DBMS See database management system.

DCL See data control language.

DDL See data definition language.

decision support system A system that assists in providing users with relevant information that aids them in making informed decisions. The systems and tools used to build such systems are typically targeted toward knowledge workers and allow them to browse data stores in a free flowing, analytical style.

demographic Data that characterizes people and things, and that is typically the result of a study of their characteristics, such as size, growth, density, distribution, and vital statistics.

denormalize A data modeling technique that is typically utilized in decision support systems and data warehouse design. This technique allows for repetition of data within an entity and its key to data relationships, formulating a data column to key cardinality of one to many. Traditional transaction systems focus strongly on maintaining a normalized data structure in which the data within an individual entity maps in a one-to-one relationship to its key.

detail category A detail category is the lowest level of detail available within a dimension. Example: If a time dimension contains information about time periods that includes year, month, and day, day is a detail category, with the value 1996/11/19 considered an instance of the detail category.

dense data Density is often used with multidimensional databases to refer to the percentage of possible combinations for data compared to actual data. If a relatively high percentage of data combinations exists, the data is referred to as dense.

dimension A dimension is a physical property, such as time, location, or product, regarded as a fundamental way of accessing and presenting business information. A dimension typically acts as an index for identifying data. It is common to think of standard reports that present rows and columns as two dimensional. A manager who evaluates budgets may look at a two-dimensional spreadsheet containing accounts in the rows and cost centers in the columns. The intersecting point between the rows and columns, a cell, contains relevant numerical information about the specific cost center and account, such as product development's salary budget.

dimension entity A derived data structure managed by a data warehouse that assists users in navigating through measurement entities. These structures typically manage only the dimensional hierarchy data (keys and descriptions) and are optimized for user interface operations, filtering operations, and aggregation functions.

direct manipulation A user interface technique that allows an application object to be manipulated directly through items such as drill down, drill up, and drag and drop as distinguished from a more complicated technique such as a command line or syntax-oriented interface.

DML See data manipulation language.

domain The common attributes, including type, size, and possible values, that should be applied to a physical data item. A domain in essence provides a common and consistent data definition across data items that are related to the domain. Example: A money domain can define the presentation and storage attributes of payroll items, such as gross pay and deductions, providing commonality among these related items and avoiding conflict in areas such as calculations into which different storage types may require the data to be converted. In the strictest sense, domains define the columns that participate in a primary-to-foreign-key relationship, allowing data to be joined in a similar consistency as the calculation.

drill down and drill up Drilling down or drilling up is a navigational technique for users to further analyze detail information (down) or aggregate the data to another summary level (up) within a dimension. If you view the categories within a dimension, they for-mulate a hierarchy of valid data points. Example: When viewing information based on a location dimension, users may start by viewing the data organized by country. They could then drill down on a Western Region and further drill down to the state of California. Drilling up works in the opposite manner. Users viewing information organized by state could drill up to region and drill up again to a country view.

DSS See decision support system.

DynaScript Sybases' server side scripting language which is JavaScript compatible.

EIS See executive information system.

entity relationship diagram A data modeling technique typically used with relational data-base management systems that presents entities, or logical groupings of data columns, as tables and their relationships in terms of cardinality. The tables are typically presented using rectangular objects, which surround the columns of data. The relationships are typ-ically presented utilizing lines and end connectors such as multiple arrows, or "chicken feet," to represent the relationship cardinality among the entities. These cardinalities are one to one, one to many, or many to many, and may involve either required or optional relationships.

ERD See entity relationship diagram.

events A well document application programming interface which notifies a program that the user has performed an operation which requires further action.

executive information system A system that is highly focused on providing standard reports to executives that present specific information, often in line with an enterprise's overall goals. These systems comprise an easy-to-use front end application that presents a logical hierarchy of preplanned standard reports. These systems are characterized as easy to use yet expensive to maintain, because each executive typically requires a support staff to build a customized version.

fact See measure.

filter To remove data by passing through a condition, such as only reporting on people with the sex of male. See where clause.

firewall A combination of hosts, routers, and associated software that partitions your company's internal network (Intranet) from the public network (Internet).

foreign key Any column or group of columns within an entity whose values exist as primary key values in a parent entity. When verifying an entity instance's relationships at the key level, the value of the primary key must be present in the instance of the foreign key and vice versa. Example: In an order entry system, the order is typically represented by OrderHeader and OrderLine entities. OrderHeader is typically referred to as the parent entity and OrderLine as the child entity. OrderNumber is a primary key within OrderHeader because it defines a unique occurrence of an order. OrderNumber is considered a foreign key within the OrderLine entity because it defines the relationship between OrderLine and OrderHeader. Each OrderLine must contain an OrderNumber, because without an OrderHeader instance, an OrderLine instance will never exist.

from clause Specifies the tables or queries that contain the fields listed in a SQL select statement.

front end process The front end process of a data warehouse system involves granting proper access to users for the information contained within a data warehouse as well as repopulating any catalog or metadata information required by the user's tools.

FTP File Transfer Protocol is the Internet protocol for transferring files from one computer to another.

GB Abbreviation for gigabyte.

gigabyte Unit of information equal to one billion (10^9) bytes.

Gopher is an information system designed at the University of Minnesota that provides an efficient way to organize information and provide it for other people to browse on the Internet. Many of the current services available within Web browsers on the Internet have made Gopher obsolete, or at least seldom utilized.

graphical user interface A style of computer interface that presents users with pictorial representations of programs and associated application objects, and that allows users to interact with the system utilizing tools such as a mouse. The pictorial representation of application objects includes windows, icons, and menus. Examples: Microsoft Windows, MOTIF, X Windows, and Macintosh user interfaces.

group by clause Combines records with identical values in a specified select list into a single record. A summary value, or aggregate, is created for each record within the result set if you include an SQL aggregate function, such as sum or count, in a select statement.

GUI See graphical user interface.

HTML HyperText Markup Language is the standard language for creating richly formatted documents on the World Wide Web. HTML is a descriptive language that assists developers in creating hypertext documents. It is an international standard whose specification is maintained by the Internet Engineering Task Force.

HTTP HyperText Transport Protocol is the standard language that is utilized by Web servers to communicate with Web clients (browsers).

incremental load The process of only loading data that has changed since the preceding loading process.

index A physical object managed by a data store that provides an optimized data access path. An index can be a single column, such as CompanyName, or multiple columns concatenated to create a single object, such as OrderNumber + OrderLine.

information Knowledge derived from the study of the data relating to a specific event or situation; a collection of facts or data; statistical information.

integrity The protection of data from inadvertent or malicious destruction or alteration.

ISAPI Internet Server API is Microsoft's proprietary API that enables user requested service communication between Microsoft's Web server and server based scripts or compiled programs.

iterative development A process of developing systems within shorter cycles that delivers portions of logically grouped and complete functions required by an overall system in more than one development cycle.

Java An object oriented programming language created by Sun Microsystems that enables the creation of network-centric applications which feature a near-zero deployment cost.

JavaScript A scripting language, originally developed by Netscape, for the creation of simple applications that can be entirely embedded in HTML documents. Like other scripting languages that extend the capabilities of applications with which they work, JavaScript extends the standard Web page to support more interaction between the Web browser and the user.

join A where clause operation that brings data from more than one table or query together in a query result set.

latency A term, often used in replication technology, that refers to the time period of a delay, such as a latency period of two seconds between transactions committing on two distributed data stores is acceptable.

leading indicator A data artifact that apprises someone of the need for an action.

legacy system A term in information management that refers to any application not developed using the applications development approach currently promoted as the standard. For data warehouses, a legacy application is a source of operational data.

location dimension A physical property, such as time or product, regarded as a fundamental way of accessing and presenting business information; typically the location dimension is composed of all cities in which a company has offices, the districts that contain the cities, the regions that contain the districts, and the countries that contain the regions.

logical design A data design that captures relevant data items derived from a conceptual design and from system and user requirements; this design typically defines data item groups or entities as well as relationships among these groups. Within this book, a conceptual design is represented by a star schema, which in turn is used to transform into traditional data modeling tools and their associated logical data models.

many to many A descriptive adjective to describe the cardinality or relationship between two entities. Example: A consultant participates in many projects and a project utilizes many consultants, sometimes expressed as M Projects:M Consultants. This relationship is typically viewed as a poor physical design, but it is quite common in logical designs. The resolution is to create a derived entity that manages the relationship between the tables in a one-to-many fashion. In this example, an entity such as Project_Participant would be created to resolve the many-to-many relationship, such that the project has many project participants and a consultant participates in many projects.

mass loading The process of totally refreshing the contents of a data warehouse. This process typically only occurs when new entities are added to the data warehouse or a component of the data warehouse is being recovered after a failure. However, depending on an operational data store's ability to monitor changes within its data, mass loads may be the only way to transform operational data to a data warehouse.

measure A measure—also referred to as a key performance measure, a fact, or a key business measure—is a device to measure business information along dimensions. Measures are typically quantities, capacities, or money that will be ascertained by comparison with a standard. These data points can then be used for the quantitative comparison of business performance.

measurement entity An entity that is managed by a data warehouse. This entity typically contains quantitative data, which is the primary focus of a data warehouse. The physical structure for a measurement entity is typically the lowest-level detail category key for each dimension mapped to the measurement, and the measurement data itself.

metadata Data about data. Metadata describes the structure, content, and source of the data within a data warehouse. Metadata must be as easily available through the data warehouse as the traditional data values maintained in an organization's databases.

metadata repository Refers to a dictionary providing details about data. This information includes an inventory of data sources and their associated standards. The data inventory describes the data that is available in both data capture and data access environments. The inventory information should also describe when the data was last updated and when future updates are planned—basically, the schedule of data maintenance. Data inventory also describes the physical attributes of the data; that is, how it is stored. This inventory is then utilized by data consumers to determine what data is available and where.

methodology A body of practices, procedures, and rules used by those who work in a discipline or engage in an inquiry; a set of working methods.

metric See measure.

mid-tier process The mid-tier process of a data warehouse system utilizes the staging area of the data warehouse to process and finalize the data that will be made available to users. This process typically incorporates data scrubbing, data placement, data distribution, and standard report compilation and indexing. The goal of a mid-tier process is to make the data more digestible by the user while minimizing the downtime of the data warehouse for any repopulation of data.

MIME Multipurpose Internet Mail Extensions tell computers what kind of program to use to view a file which is transmitted over the Internet.

multidimensional Multidimensional refers to information that is defined or accessed by having several dimensions. In a geometric world, the easiest description of a multidimensional entity is a cube. The cube has three specified dimensions: width, height, and depth. Surprisingly, most business models are represented in a multidimensional view. The budgetary example described in the definition of dimension describes two dimensionsÑcost center and accounts. In reality, this is missing an important dimension, time. Most financial analysts evaluate their data with a minimum of three dimensions. A dimension map provides a technique for modeling a user's information in a multidimensional space. This design provides a visual representation of the business analyst's mental model of the information.

NNTP Network News Transport Protocol is the standard protocol for newsgroup distribution, such as Usenet, the most common newsgroups.

normalize A data modeling technique that is typically utilized in OLTP systems. The focus of this design technique is to maintain a data structure in which the data within an individual entity maps in a one-to-one relationship to its parent key.

NSAPI Netscape's Server API is a proprietary Web server API to interface between server based scripts and compiled programs and Netscape's Web servers.

null Refers to an entity's column that has no value.

OLAP See online analytical processing.

OLTP See online transaction processing.

one-to-many A descriptive adjective used to describe the cardinality or relationship between two entities. Example: An order has many line items describing what was ordered. This can be represented as 1 Order contains many Order Line Items, or 1:M.

one-to-one An adjective that describes the cardinality or relationship between two entities. Example: a US citizen has a social security number. This can be represented as 1 Citizen: 1 Social Security Number.

online Describes the user-to-program interaction that typically occurs through an interactive session with an input device such as a terminal and a program running on a computer.

online analytical processing A term used to describe the environment required to support business decision-making as opposed to online transaction processing. An OLAP environment supports analytical queries against data representing an organization's state at a specific time.

online transaction processing A term used to describe the environment required to support business operations, as opposed to OLAP. An OLTP environment is transactional in nature, requiring access to current data.

operational data store The database associated with an operational system. These databases are typically required to support a large number of transactions on a daily basis with minimal latency for processing the transactions.

operational system An operational system is one that assists a company in its day-to-day business. These systems provide immediate focus on business functions and are typically run in an OLTP computing environment.

order by clause Sorts a query's result set on a specified field or fields in ascending or descending order.

parallel processing A query optimization technique in which a request is decomposed into a series of queries that is initiated simultaneously and distributed across multiple processors.

parent-child relationship In data modeling, this term refers to the relationship between two entities, one that is a controlling entity (parent) and the other that is the dependent entity (child).

physical design A data design that captures the relevant characteristics of data items (tables, columns, indexes, keys, and so forth) that are derived from a logical design; that is, from system and user requirements. This design is optimized to a physical database management system that will manage the data within the system being defined.

POP Post Office Protocol is the standard for managing server side mailboxes for users as well as passing messages addressed to a particular user to the appropriate POP client.

primary key Refers to a column or set of columns whose values can be used to uniquely identify instances of an entity. A means of access, control, or possession; a vital, crucial element. Example: The key to an order is typically an OrderNumber, which uniquely defines all associated data managed by that order.

prototype An early, typical example, form, or instance of a system that serves as a model on which later stages are based or judged. In iterative development, a prototype typically is produced as the first phase or development cycle to prove the concept and validate it with users.

query A request for information from a data store by a user or application. Example: A user issues a query requesting all year-to-date sales of widgets for the Northeast region.

query tool A component, a product, or an application that issues queries against information sources such as relational database management systems. These queries are often in the form of standard SQL select statements, which return result sets to the users. The tools automate the building of such statements as well as the execution of the process to retrieve and display the results produced from the statements.

RDBMS See relational database management system.

relational database management system A database management system that is organized and accessed according to relationships among items. The data is organized into normalized table structures that consist of rows and columns. The relationships among tables are defined among data values rather than pointers or location. Most relational database management systems adhere to such standards as SQL, which provide a common access syntax for users to retrieve and manipulate data managed within the systems.

replication The process of creating and maintaining associated replicas of original data at distributed sites. Within a replication architecture are typically a publisher of data and a subscriber of data. The publisher is the original, or controlling, source. If we utilize a CRUD diagram to represent the publisher, it would be characterized as the source that creates and deletes the data—or more easily stated, controls the capturing and purging of data from a corporation. A subscriber, on the other hand, is a system that needs access to the data, but only from a referential perspective; in other words it is a reader within the CRUD diagram of the specified entities.

result set The information returned from a database as a result of a query operation. With regard to an SQL select statement, this typically represents a set of records.

RPC Remote Procedure Call is a formal protocol used within distributed systems for executing a procedure on a remote server.

S-HTTP Secure HTTP is a security enhanced version of HTTP proposed by Enterprise Integration Technologies and commercially implemented by Terisa Systems.

select list The names of the fields, columns, or calculations to retrieve data from within an SQL select statement. If you include more than one field, they are retrieved in the order listed.

select statement Instructs a database that utilizes the SQL standard to return information as a set of records.

SET Secure Electronic Transactions is an electronic commerce standard originally developed by VISA and MasterCard, among others, to make the Internet a viable platform for electronic commerce. The SET standard is specifically for safeguarding credit card transactions across the Internet.

SLIP/PPP Serial Line Internet Protocol/Point-to-Point Protocol is used as a communications protocol across telephone lines with modems to allow computers to dial into a network and establish a network connection.

SMTP Simple Mail Transfer Protocol is the standard for transferring mail to and from various mail servers.

snowflake schema Refers to an extended star schema. While a star schema typically creates a two-tier structure, one with dimensions and measures, a snowflake schema creates additional tiers. In the techniques discussed in this book, this is typically extended only to three tiers: dimensions (dimension entities), measures (measurement entities), and related, descriptive data (category detail entities). Snowflake schemas beyond a three-tier model should be avoided in data warehouse systems, because they begin to resemble normalized structures more prone to supporting OLTP applications versus the denormalized structures that are optimal for data warehouses and OLAP applications.

sparse data Often used with multidimensional databases to refer to the percentage of possible combinations for the data compared to the actual data. If a relatively low percentage of data combinations exist, the data is referred to as sparse.

SQL See Structured Query Language.

SSL Secure Sockets Layer is an open and widely endorsed channel security protocol standard. SSL was originally defined by Netscape but is in the process of being signed over to the Internet Engineering Task Force. SSL provides message encryption, client and server authentication, and message integrity services to many applications protocols such as HTTP, FTP, and NNTP.

staging area A temporary storage location for organizing and cleansing data—where the data is assembled and processed prior to placing it into a production data warehouse.

standard report A report that is automatically created by a data warehouse. It typically has a fixed format and distribution, which makes it highly inflexible; however, it dictates how users should view the data. This is sometimes a desirable attribute.

star schema The optimal design model for data warehouse applications; named due to its physical appearance as a center entity, typically containing measurement data, and radiating data, typically dimensions assisting in navigating and aggregating the measurement data. The results of star schema modeling often are query-aware data structures that provide data structures optimized for rapidly responding to users' query requests. Star schemas frequently produce a two-tier model that contains dimensional data and measurement data.

Structured Query Language The standard language for accessing relational database management systems. SQL is defined and standardized through joint ANSI committees.

system of record The system from which data was obtained. Typically, this refers to a system that manages the creation and overall management of a data item. However, many operational systems have conflicting sources, each thinking it is the system of record. Example: An order entry system thinks it owns the customers and therefore uniquely provides customer numbers and other system-generated data items. Meanwhile, a sales management system also thinks it owns the customers and performs similar yet inconsistent data item maintenance.

TB Abbreviation for terabyte.

TCP/IP Transmission Control Protocol/Internet Protocol has become the standard protocol to enable Internet services such as telnet, FTP, and Email. TCP/IP allows computers to easily communicate even if they do not belong to the same network.

technology architecture A computing infrastructure that enables data and applications to successfully interact seamlessly throughout an enterprise.

telnet A protocol to enable a user to log into a remote host computer. After the user logs into the remote computer, they can interact with the software running the session similar to using a keyboard directly connected to the remote computer.

terabyte A unit of information equal to one trillion(10^{12}) bytes.

time dimension A physical property, similar to location or product, that is regarded as a fundamental way to access and present business information. Often, a time dimension is composed of all days of the year, weeks of the year, months of the year, and possibly multiple years.

time stamping A data auditing technique that allows a user or application to determine when an activity occurred, such as when data was added or when it was last updated. A timestamp typically includes the date and time to the lowest possible level, such as hundredths of a second (11/19/1995 11:15:01.24).

tool suite A set of tools packaged together to assist in solving a spectrum of tasks. Example: Office automation tool suites typically include a word processor, spreadsheet, presentation package, and personal data manager. Within a data warehouse, a tool suite should be delivered that covers the user-requirement spectrum, including EIS, DSS, ad hoc reporting, standard reporting, and production reporting components, to name a few. Additional tool suites should also be defined for data warehouse administrators and for individual processes that comprise an entire data warehouse system, including front-end, mid-tier, and back-end processes.

trailing indicator A data artifact that is the result of actions performed within any business process.

transaction A logical unit of work that constitutes a business action.

trend analysis A method of proof in which a series of data samples are reviewed to determine sequences or series concerned with limits and convergence, or the general direction in which something tends to move.

URL Uniform Resource Locator provides the addressing system of the Internet and World Wide Web and is the standard for locating and accessing an object on the Internet, for example OBJX Inc's home page can be found at the URL "http://www.objx.com."

VBScript A scripting language created by Microsoft that enables the creation of simple applications that may be entirely embedded in HTML documents, much like JavaScript. VBScript is a subset of Microsoft's popular Visual Basic for Applications.

VRML Virtual Reality Modeling Language is the standard modeling language for creating three-dimensional worlds on the Internet, through which users can interact and navigate.

where clause Specifies which records from the tables listed in a from clause are affected by a select, update, or delete statement in standard SQL.

WAIS Wide Area Information Services is an information retrieval service and protocol that was designed to create a distributed network publishing system that can help people find information simply by asking questions. Most of the available search engines available on the Web belong to this family of services.

Index

conceptual data model (CDM), 400, 408
denormalization of demographic data, 408–10
domain management, 401–02
physical data model (PDM), 408
relationships in star schema model, 405
sales analysis information package entities, 403–04
Data authentication, 37
Database administrators (DBAs), 391, 399
Database architectures, 177–81
Database management systems (DBMS), 168, 180
data access, 152–53
Database optimizer, 205
Databases, 181
Database triggers, 31
Data cardinality, 378–79, 405
Data cleansing
buried data, 44
data integrity, 45
Legacy standard, 43–45, 398
noncentralized key data, 45
Data collection, 34, 37, 47, 176–77
partitioning, 37, 482–84
Data compression, 372–74
Data control language (DCL), 182, 385–86, 398
Data definition language, (DDL), 182, 385–86, 385, 398,452
native database syntax, 411
Data distribution systems, 33, 124–25
Data driven security table, 524
Data element sources, 31
Data explosion, 373–74, 393
Data gathering techniques, 21, 34
Data integrity, 45
Data manipulation language (DML), 182–84

select statements, 183–84
project statements, 183–84
equijoin statements, 183–85
Data marts, 173–74, 363–66
customer, 547–78
data mining processing, 176–77
definition of, 24
employee, 515–46
relational, 33
shareholder, 439–68
supplier, 469–513
Data mining, 34, 37, 47, 176–77
Data normalization, 181
Data quality loops, 128–29
Data replication, 44
Data staging process, 33–35
placement and distribution, 34–35
scrubbing, 33–34, 39
standard report compilation and indexing, 35
Data standards
character case, 91
complete words, 91
consolidation and duplicates, 129–30
domains, 91
format patterns, 129
synonyms, 130
underscores versus hyphens, 91
Data stores, 33, 171–72
permanent staged source entity, 112
Data synchronization
batch file transfer, 43
data replication, 44
gateway batch processing, 43–44
Data transformation, 42–43
Data volumetrics, 95–97
Date warehouse
complex analysis, 29
definition of, 16
dynamic business environment, 29